IDENTITY AND DIALECT PERFORMANCE

Identity and Dialect Performance discusses the relationship between identity and dialects. It starts from the assumption that the use of dialects is not just a product of social and demographic factors, but can also be an intentional performance of identity. Dialect performance is related to identity construction and in a highly globalised world, the linguistic repertoire has increased rapidly, thereby changing our conventional assumptions about dialects and their usage.

The key outstanding feature of this particular book is that it spans an extensive range of communities and dialects; Canada, Colombia, Egypt, French Guiana, Germany, Italy, Japan, Libya, Morocco, Nigeria, Scotland, Senegal, Spain, Syria, The Netherlands, The Sudan, and the UK and US.

Reem Bassiouney is Professor of Linguistics at The American University of Cairo Her recent book publications include *Functions of Code-Switching in Egypt* (2006), *Arabic Sociolinguistics* (2008), *Arabic and the Media* (2010, editor), *Arabic Language and Linguistics* (2012, co-editor), *Language and Identity in Modern Egypt* (2014), and *The Routledge Handbook of Arabic Linguistics* (forthcoming, co-editor).

Routledge Studies in Language and Identity
Series Editor: Reem Bassiouney

The Routledge Studies in Language and Identity (RSLI) series aims to examine the intricate relation between language and identity from different perspectives. The series straddles fields such as sociolinguistics, discourse analysis, applied linguistics, historical linguistics and linguistic anthropology. It aims to study identity and language by utilizing novel methods of analysis as well as ground breaking theoretical approaches.

Titles in series:

Arabic in Israel: Language, Identity and Conflict
Muhammad Amara

Identity and Dialect Performance: A Study of Communities and Dialects
Reem Bassiouney

For more titles, please visit www.routledge.com/languages/series/RSLI

IDENTITY AND DIALECT PERFORMANCE

A Study of Communities and Dialects

Edited by Reem Bassiouney

LONDON AND NEW YORK

First published 2018
by Routledge
2 Park Square, Milton Park, Abingdon, Oxon OX14 4RN

and by Routledge
711 Third Avenue, New York, NY 10017

Routledge is an imprint of the Taylor & Francis Group, an informa business

© 2018 selection and editorial matter, Reem Bassiouney; individual chapters, the contributors

The right of Reem Bassiouney to be identified as the author of the editorial material, and of the authors for their individual chapters, has been asserted in accordance with sections 77 and 78 of the Copyright, Designs and Patents Act 1988.

All rights reserved. No part of this book may be reprinted or reproduced or utilised in any form or by any electronic, mechanical, or other means, now known or hereafter invented, including photocopying and recording, or in any information storage or retrieval system, without permission in writing from the publishers.

Trademark notice: Product or corporate names may be trademarks or registered trademarks, and are used only for identification and explanation without intent to infringe.

British Library Cataloguing-in-Publication Data
A catalogue record for this book is available from the British Library

Library of Congress Cataloging-in-Publication Data
Names: Bassiouney, Reem, 1973– editor.
Title: Identity and dialect performance : a study of communities and dialects / edited by Reem Bassiouney.
Description: Milton Park, Abingdon, Oxon ; New York, NY: Routledge, 2017. | Includes index.
Identifiers: LCCN 2017018132 (print) | LCCN 2017027081 (ebook) | ISBN 9781315279732 (eBook) | ISBN 9781315279725 (pdf) | ISBN 9781315279718 (ePub) | ISBN 9781315279701 (Mobipocket) | ISBN 9781138241756 (hardback : alk. paper) | ISBN 9781138241787 (pbk. : alk. paper)
Subjects: LCSH: Dialectology. | Languages in contact. | Group identity.
Classification: LCC P367 (ebook) | LCC P367 .I33 2017 (print) | DDC 417/.2—dc23
LC record available at https://lccn.loc.gov/2017018132

ISBN: 978-1-138-24175-6 (hbk)
ISBN: 978-1-138-24178-7 (pbk)
ISBN: 978-1-315-27973-2 (ebk)

Typeset in Bembo
by Apex CoVantage, LLC

CONTENTS

List of figures viii
List of tables x
List of contributors xi
Acknowledgements xvii

   Introduction 1

PART I
Dialects in localised and delocalised contexts **15**

1 Nonstandard dialect and identity 17
 John Edwards

2 The elusive dialect border 35
 Dick Smakman and Marten van der Meulen

3 Dialect performances in superdiverse communities:
 The case for ethnographic approaches to language
 variation 49
 Anna De Fina

PART II
Nation-states and identity construction in relation to a standard and a dialect   69

4   The construction of linguistic borders and the rise of national identity in South Sudan: Some insights into Juba Arabic (Árabi Júba)   71
Stefano Manfredi

5   From language to dialect and back: The case of Piedmontese   86
Mauro Tosco

6   Darija and the construction of "Moroccanness"   99
Dominique Caubet

7   "Sloppy speech is like sloppy dress": Folk attitudes towards nonstandard British English   125
Carmen Ebner

PART III
Contact, variation, performance and metalinguistic discourse   141

8   From varieties in contact to the selection of linguistic resources in multilingual settings   143
Isabelle Léglise and Santiago Sánchez Moreano

9   "You live in the United States, you speak English," decían las maestras: How New Mexican Spanish speakers enact, ascribe, and reject ethnic identities   160
Katherine O'Donnell Christoffersen and Naomi L. Shin

10   The social meanings of Wolof and French: Contact dialects, language ideology, and competing modernities in Senegal   179
Fiona Mc Laughlin

11   The social value of linguistic practices in Tetouan and Ghomara (Northwestern Morocco)   192
Ángeles Vicente and Amina Naciri-Azzouz

12 New presentations of self in everyday life: Linguistic
transgressions in England, Germany, and Japan 210
Patrick Heinrich

13 Language and identity in Siwa Oasis: Indexing belonging,
localness, and authenticity in a small minority community 226
Valentina Serreli

PART IV
The media, dialect performance, and language variation 243

14 YouTube Yinzers: Stancetaking and the performance of
'Pittsburghese' 245
Scott F. Kiesling

15 Performing identity on screen: Language, identity, and
humour in Scottish television comedy 265
Natalie Braber

16 Identity, repertoire, and performance: The case of
an Egyptian poet 286
Reem Bassiouney

17 Ruination and amusement – dialect, youth, and revolution
in Naija 303
Anne Storch

18 Dialectal variation and identity in post-revolutionary
Libyan media: The case of Dragunov (2014) 321
Luca D'Anna

19 The effect of TV and internal vs. external contact on
variation in Syrian rural child language 340
Rania Habib

Index 357

FIGURES

3.1	Percentage of turns with Sicilian by day.	55
3.2	Marked vs. neutral speech acts in Sicilian.	60
3.3	Distribution of marked speech acts (boys and girls).	61
6.1	*Telquel* magazine, June 2002 © Dominique Caubet.	109
6.2	*Le Journal Hebdomadaire*; drawing by Beyoud. © Dominique Caubet.	112
8.1	Imbabura and Chimborazo.	149
14.1	Pitch track of an example of the L*+H L% falling question intonation.	255
14.2	Frame of Donny from the 'Idlewild' episode. Approximately line 51 in the transcript.	256
14.3	Frame grab of Kreutzer from the 'Idlewild' episode. Approximately line 50 in the transcript.	256
14.4	Frame grab of Greg from the 'Idlewild' episode. Approximately line 50 in the transcript.	257
15.1	Glasgow mug design, used with permission, Sprint Design, Glasgow.	272
15.2	Drinks coaster with local phrase (this is a catch phrase from *Chewin' the Fat*), used with permission, Sprint Design, Glasgow.	272
15.3	Ned (this is not from *Chewin' the Fat* as no images were available, but of a Glaswegian comedian, Neil Bratchpiece, dressed as a *ned*). Used with permission, Creative Commons Attribution Licence.	275
15.4	Banter Boy: Gary, used with copyright permission BBC.	276
17.1	About Naija lingo (Ofunne & Nwokogba 2007: http://www.naijalingo.com/about).	311
17.2	Revolutionary collections of 'campus slang' (Chigozie 2015).	312
17.3	Musings of a Crazy Nigerian (Farouk 2012).	313

17.4	Blasted English (http://www.nairaland.com/2132954/girl-failed-english-exam).	316
19.1	Main effects of the fixed effects TV, internal and external contacts. Fixed Effects Target: [?] / (q)	350
19.2	The effect of internal contact with friends and relatives who use [?] predominantly on the use of [q] vs. [?].	350
19.3	Coefficients indicating the significant categories within each fixed factor. Fixed coefficients target: [?] / (q)	351

TABLES

3.1	Class composition.	53
3.2	Children of foreign origins born in Italy.	54
3.3	Children born abroad.	54
3.4	Distribution of turns by participants.	56
4.1	Paradigm types.	75
6.1	Figures of online audiences in Morocco, courtesy of *internetworldstats*.	119
9.1	Participants of the New Mexico and Colorado Spanish Survey.	163
13.1	Interviewees' information.	230
15.1	Variables for the Neds.	278
15.2	Variables for the Banter Boys.	281
16.1	Stance and linguistic repertoire of the poet in the four poems analysed.	293
18.1	Demonstratives for near deixis in TA, MA, and BA.	326
18.2	Near-deixis demonstratives in the speech of the five characters under analysis.	326
18.3	Distribution of the hādv and hēdv variables in pro- and anti-Ghaddafi characters.	327
19.1	General Distribution of [q] and [ʔ] in the speech of the 50 children and boys and girls.	348
19.2	Gender and age group differences in the use of [q] and [ʔ].	348
19.3	Social and linguistic distribution of [q] and [ʔ] in the speech of individual participants.	348

CONTRIBUTORS

Reem Bassiouney (DPhil, Oxon) is Professor of Linguistics at The American University of Cairo. Her recent book publications include *Functions of code-switching in Egypt* (2006), *Arabic sociolinguistics* (2008), *Arabic and the media* (2010 editor), *Arabic language and linguistics* (2012 co-editor), *Language and identity in modern Egypt* (2014) and *The Routledge handbook of Arabic linguistics* (2018 co-editor; forthcoming). Her research focuses on topics in sociolinguistics, including; identity, code-switching, language and gender, levelling, register and language policy and ideology. She is also an award-winning novelist.

Dr Natalie Braber is Reader in Linguistics at Nottingham Trent University. Her current research interests include sociolinguistics and language variation. In particular, her research examines language variation in the East Midlands in the UK. She is author of *Nottinghamshire dialect* (Bradwell Books, 2015), co-author of *Pit talk of the East Midlands* (Bradwell Books, 2017); *East Midlands English*, in the *Dialects of English Series* (De Gruyter, forthcoming) and co-editor of *Sociolinguistics in England* (Palgrave Macmillan, forthcoming); *Exploring language and linguistics* (Cambridge University Press, 2015). She has published research articles in *English Today*, *Oral History*, *Journal of Pragmatics* and *Identity*.

Dominique Caubet is Professor Emeritus of Maghribi Arabic at the Institute of Oriental Languages (INALCO), Paris, and Associate Researcher at the Centre Jacques Berque, Rabat. Her research interests include general linguistics (aspect, tense, modality, nominal determination, negation and enunciative particles), sociolinguistics, from code-switching to youth languages, and the social status of minority languages in the Maghreb and the European diaspora (France and The Netherlands). She has published several books and numerous articles, including *Corpus-based studies of lesser described languages, the CorpAfroAs corpus of spoken Afro-Asiatic languages* (2015), *Arabic in the city, issues in dialect contact and language variation*

(2007), and 'Arabic Sociolinguistics in the Middle East and North Africa (MENA)' (2009).

Luca D'Anna received his PhD in Arabic Linguistics and Dialectology from the University of Naples 'L'Orientale' in 2014. He currently holds the position of Assistant Professor of Arabic at the University of Mississippi (Oxford, MS). His fields of interest include Arabic linguistics and dialectology, Libyan Arabic, Sulaymite dialects, Arabic sociolinguistics, and teaching Arabic as a second language.

Anna De Fina is Professor of Italian Language and Linguistics in the Italian Department and Affiliated Faculty with the Linguistics Department at Georgetown University. Her research interests and publications focus on identity, narrative, discourse, and migration, as well as diversity. Her books include *Identity in narrative: a study of immigrant discourse* (2003), *Analyzing narratives* (2012), and the *Handbook of narrative analysis* (2015).

Carmen Ebner was a Doctoral Researcher in the project 'Bridging the unbridgeable: linguists, prescriptivists and the general public' at the University of Leiden. For her PhD thesis, Carmen conducted a sociolinguistic investigation into attitudes towards usage problems in British English. Her research interests also include language ideologies and the field of language and identity. Her publications include 'Blaming the media? Folk attitudes towards the state of the English language and its "wrongdoers"' (2016), 'Language guardian BBC? Investigating the BBC's language advice in its 2003 News Styleguide' (2015), and 'The dangling participle – a language myth?' (2014).

John Edwards received his PhD from McGill University in 1974. After working as a Research Fellow at the Educational Research Centre in Dublin (now part of Dublin City University), he moved to St Francis Xavier University in Nova Scotia. He is now Senior Research Professor there, and also Adjunct Professor (Graduate Studies) at Dalhousie University. He is a member of several psychological and linguistic societies, as well as scholarly organisations for the study of ethnicity and nationalism. He is a fellow of the British Psychological Society, the Canadian Psychological Association, and the Royal Society of Canada. His main research interest is the maintenance and continuity of group identity, with particular reference to language in both its communicative and symbolic aspects. He has lectured and presented papers on this topic in thirty countries, and his work has been translated into half a dozen languages. Edwards is on the editorial boards of a dozen international language journals and is the editor of the *Journal of Multilingual and Multicultural Development*. He is also the editor of the *Multilingual Matters* book series. Edwards' books include *Multilingualism* (1995), *Language in Canada* (1998), *Language and identity* (2009), *Multilingualism: understanding linguistic diversity* (2012) and *Sociolinguistics: a very short introduction* (2013). He is also the author of many articles, chapters, and reviews.

Contributors **xiii**

Rania Habib is Associate Professor of Linguistics and Arabic and Coordinator of Arabic Program at Syracuse University. Dr. Habib specializes in sociolinguistics, particularly language variation and change with interests in bilingualism, cross-cultural communication, child and adolescent language and second language/dialect acquisition, phonology, pragmatics, and syntax. Her research is interdisciplinary and has applied diverse qualitative and quantitative methods of analyses to sociolinguistic variation and change, including Optimality Theory and the Gradual Learning Algorithm. Her present research deals with dialectal variation in the colloquial Syrian Arabic of rural migrant and non-migrant speakers to urban centers and the change that their speech undergoes due to linguistic, social, and psychological factors, such as prestige, age, gender, residential area, contact, identity, ideology, social meanings, social practices, etc. For the past few years, she has been investigating the spread of urban linguistic features in the speech of rural children, adolescents, and adults in Syrian Arabic, comparing the speech of children to that of their parents to inform linguistic theory about whether children's acquisition of variation is a mere statistical learning of their parents' input or is developmental in nature. Her work has appeared in prestigious journals such as *Journal of Pragmatics, Language Variation and Change*, and *Journal of Child Language*.

Patrick Heinrich is an Associate Professor in the Department of Asian and Mediterranean African Studies at Ca' Foscari University of Venice. Before joining Ca' Foscari, he taught at universities in Germany, France, and Japan. His present research interests focus on globalising sociolinguistics, language shift dynamics, language policy, and ideology. His recently edited books include *Globalising sociolinguistics* (2017), *Handbook of the Ryukyuan languages* (2015), *Language crisis in the Ryukyus* (2014), and *Language life in Japan* (2011). His latest monograph is *The making of monolingual Japan* (2012).

Scott F. Kiesling is Professor in the Linguistics Department at the University of Pittsburgh. He received his PhD from Georgetown University. His research interests include stance, language and masculinity, and Pittsburgh speech and society. His publications include *The handbook of intercultural discourse and communication* (2012), *Linguistic variation and change* (2011), and *Intercultural discourse and communication: the essential readings* (2005).

Isabelle Léglise is a Senior Researcher in Linguistics at the French National Centre for Scientific Research (CNRS, Paris), where she heads programmes on multilingualism, language variation, and contact at the SeDyL-CNRS (*Structure et Dynamique des Langues*). Since 2000, she has been engaged in research projects in French Guiana, Suriname, and Brazil, with a special focus on multilingualism related to migration and educational issues. She has published widely on language variation and contact-induced changes, languaging and heterogeneous corpora, as well as discourse analysis and language policy related to education and health. Her most recent publications include *Exploring language in a multilingual context: variation, interaction and ideology in language documentation* (2013; with B. Migge), *The interplay* *of variation and change in contact settings* (2013), and *In and out of Suriname: language, mobility and identity* (2015).

Stefano Manfredi is a Junior CNRS Researcher at SeDyL (*Structure et Dynamique des Langues*). His main areas of interest are Arabic-based pidgins and creoles, Arabic dialectology, the linguistic and sociolinguistic effects of language contact, and language policy and planning in Sudan and South Sudan. He has published numerous articles and chapters on Juba Arabic, as well as on western Sudanic Arabic dialects. He recently edited, in collaboration with Mauro Tosco (University of Turin), a special issue of the *Journal of Pidgin and Creole Languages* dedicated to linguistic and sociolinguistic aspects of Arabic-based pidgins and creoles. He is a member of several international projects, such as the *Atlas of pidgin and creole structures* (Max Planck Institute, Germany), *Pidgins et créoles en contact* (TUL, France) and *Linguistic and cultural areas of transition in Africa* (FRB, Italy). Notably, he has constructed a corpus of spoken Juba Arabic for the project *CorpAfroAs* (ANR, France).

Fiona Mc Laughlin is a Professor of Linguistics and African Languages at the University of Florida. She has worked extensively on the phonology and morphology of Pulaar, Wolof, and Seereer, and her current research is on language contact and multilingualism in urban Africa, with a focus on Dakar. She has published widely in these fields. Her translation of Boubacar Boris Diop's novel, *Murambi, le livre des ossements*, was published by Indiana University Press in 2006, and her edited volume, *The languages of urban Africa*, appeared in 2008 with Continuum Press. Fiona's work has been supported by fellowships from the National Endowment for the Humanities, the American Council of Learned Societies, the Camargo Foundation, and Fulbright. She has taught at the Université Abdou Moumouni in Niamey, Niger and the Université Gaston Berger in Saint-Louis, Senegal and is a former director of the West Africa Research Center in Dakar.

Amina Naciri-Azzouz is a PhD candidate at the University of Zaragoza (Spain). She obtained her Bachelor's degree in Arabic Philology (2006-2011) from the Complutense University (Madrid, Spain). Her research focuses on the description of the Ghomara Arabic varieties (Northwestern Morocco) in a context of linguistic change in progress. Thus, her research interests include Arabic dialectogy and socio-linguistics, ethnolinguistics, and language contact.

Katherine O'Donnell Christoffersen is an Assistant Professor of Applied Linguistics at the University of Texas Rio Grande Valley. She holds a PhD in Second Language Acquisition & Teaching from the University of Arizona. Her research analyzes the social contexts of bilingualism, code-switching, and identity construction through the use of ethnographic and conversation/discourse analytic methodologies. She has published articles in publications such as the *Portuguese Language Journal, Working Papers on Educational Linguistics, Arizona Working Papers*, and *GiST Education and Learning Research Journal*.

Santiago Sánchez Moreano is a postdoctoral fellow at the SeDyL research center (Structure et Dynamique des Langues, CNRS, INALCO, IRD) and lecturer in Spanish Linguistics at the Université Sorbonne Nouvelle in Paris. His main research interests are Spanish varieties in contact with Amerindian languages in Colombia in relation to identity construction and language variation and change. He is currently studying the linguistic and identity consequences of the transnational immigration of Ecuadorian Quichuas in Cali (Colombia) from a Sociolinguistic, Contact Linguistics, and Sociocultural Linguistics perspective within the Research Program LABEX EFL Axe 3 LC1, 'Multifactorial analysis of language changes'.

Valentina Serreli is Junior Professor of Arabic Studies at the University of Bayreuth, Germany. She graduated in Middle Eastern Studies at Ca' Foscari University of Venice and she completed a jointly supervised PhD at the University of Sassari, Italy, and the University of Aix-Marseille (IREMAM), France. She conducted her doctoral research, falling within the framework of Linguistic Anthropology, in the Amazigh-speaking oasis of Siwa, Egypt, to observe the community's language practices and ideologies in context. She is currently working on the Arabic spoken in Siwa, within a Interactional Sociolinguistic framework. Her domains of research are Arabic sociolinguistics, linguistic anthropology, and language attitudes and ideologies.

Naomi L. Shin is an Assistant Professor of Linguistics and Spanish at the University of New Mexico. Her primary interests include bilingualism and child language acquisition. Her research focuses on patterns of morphosyntactic variation, examining how these patterns are acquired during childhood and how they change in situations of language contact. Her articles have appeared in journals such as *Language Variation and Change*, *Language in Society*, *Journal of Child Language*, the *International Journal of the Sociology of Language*, *Language Acquisition,* and *Spanish in Context*.

Dick Smakman is a Lecturer at Leiden University. His interests include intra- and inter-speaker pronunciation variation, the effects of attitudes on language choices, and the sociolinguistics of second-language acquisition. He has taught courses in linguistics (sociolinguistics, phonetics), applied linguistics (second-language acquisition, language teaching didactics), as well as language acquisition courses (English and Dutch) at universities in the Netherlands, England, Poland, and Japan. His recently edited books include *Globalising sociolinguistics* (with Patrick Heinrich; 2015). He is currently writing *Discovering sociolinguistics for Macmillan* (2017), a practical introduction to sociolinguistic theory and methodology for undergraduates.

Anne Storch is Professor of African Linguistics at the University of Cologne. Her principal research has been on various languages of Nigeria, the Atlantic language region, and on Western Nilotic. Her work combines contributions on cultural and social contexts of languages, the semiotics of linguistic practices, epistemes and ontologies of colonial linguistics, as well as linguistic description. She has contributed to the analysis of registers and choices, language as social practice, ways of speaking and complex repertoires. Presently, she is interested in epistemic language, metalinguistics, noise and silence, as well as language use in complex settings such as tourism. Her publications include *Secret manipulations* (2011), *A grammar of Luwo* (2014), and besides several other volumes, *Consensus and dissent* (2017). In 2017, she received the prestigious Leibniz Prize for her work in Critical Africanistics.

Mauro Tosco is Professor of African Linguistics at the University of Turin. His main area of research is the Horn of Africa, where he has been working on the analysis and description of underdescribed Cushitic languages from an areal and typological perspective. His publications include *The Gawwada language* (forthcoming), *The Dhaasanac language* (2001), *Af Tunni. Grammar, texts and vocabulary of a Southern Somali Dialect* (1997), and *A grammatical sketch of Dahalo, including texts and a glossary* (1991). A native speaker of Piedmontese, an endangered language, he works on the expansion and revitalisation of minority languages, language policy, and ideology. The fields of pidgins, creoles, and language contact (*Pidgin and creole languages: a basic introduction*; with Alan S. Kaye; 2001) are his third main domain of research.

Marten van der Meulen is a PhD student at the Radboud University Nijmegen. In his project, he investigates the interplay between language use and prescriptivism in Dutch, working on effects, argumentation and development. Before this, he worked at the Meertens Institute (Amsterdam), first on the evolution of folk tales, and later on language choice in different domains of Dutch. Marten has (co-) authored several popular scientific books on language, and was one of the creators of the Massive Open Online Course Miracles of Human Language. An Introduction to Linguistics (with Marc van Oostendorp and Inge Otto) on Coursera.

Ángeles Vicente is a tenured Lecturer of Arabic and Islamic Studies at the Universidad de Zaragoza, Spain. Her works focus on Arabic dialectology and sociolinguistics, with particular attention to Moroccan Arabic. She has published several books and articles on these issues, including 'Glossing in Semitic languages: a comparison of Moroccan Arabic and Modern Hebrew' (with Il Malibert and Alexandrine Barontini; 2015), "The Past and Present of a Conservative Arabic Dialect: Tetouan (Morocco)" (2017) and *La région du Nord-Ouest marocain: Parlers et pratiques sociales et culturelles* (editor with Dominique Caubet and Amina Naciri-Azzouz; 2017).

ACKNOWLEDGEMENTS

I would like to thank the dynamo of this work, my assistant, colleague, and former student, Nourhan Sorour, whose efficiency, diligence, and vast knowledge of linguistics is exemplary. She is as always a pleasure to work with.

I would also like to thank the anonymous reviewers of the proposal of this book for their useful suggestions. The anonymous reviewers of individual articles also did a thorough and detailed job. Thanks for your time and effort.

Andrea Hartill, senior publisher at Routledge, is the ideal publisher to deal with on all levels. Thanks for working with me on this and other projects. I would also like to thank the Routledge editorial team, including editorial assistants Camille Burns and Zoe Meyer.

There are two scholars of linguistics who were not directly involved in preparing this volume, but with whom I worked closely on other projects while writing and editing this book. I would like to dedicate this work to both of them.

Keith Walters remains one of the most knowledgeable and integral scholars I know and his support throughout my career is a blessing.

Amira Agameya is also one of the most knowledgeable and integral scholars of linguistics. Her integrity, courage, hard work, and grace are exemplary.

This book is dedicated to you both for showing me that it is indeed through an individual's performance, linguistic and other, that true identity is revealed.

INTRODUCTION

Identity and dialect performance

This book discusses the relation between identity and dialects. It starts from the assumption that the use of dialects is not just a product of social and demographic factors, but can also be an intentional performance of identity. The book provides case studies of performance and metalinguistic discourse in diverse communities and contexts. By focusing on different linguistic processes involved in identity construction, it opens up new trajectories in the study of identity in relation to linguistic choices.

The argument that dialect performance is related to identity construction forms the backbone of this work. In a highly globalised and mobile world, the linguistic repertoire of individuals has increased rapidly, changing in the process our conventional assumptions about dialects and their usage.

Rationale and themes

This volume takes as its departure point the position that linguistic variation and code choice are not just the result of a correlation between linguistic and sociolinguistic variables, but the product of an ideological process in which talk *about* language is at times as significant as linguistic choices, and in which an individual's linguistic choices are not just natural but performed and at times a result or reflection of a wider conflict with a specific government or ideology. Over the next couple of paragraphs, I will provide a brief introduction to the concepts of identity, performance, and metalinguistic discourse and their roles in linguistic variation, all of which are examined in detail throughout the book.

One of the main aims of sociolinguistics is to study language variation within or across communities. Variationist research was first concerned with collecting data from different social communities, in order to 'correlate a linguistic variable with a sociolinguistic one such as gender, social class, age or education' (Hazen, 2014, p. 10). Since then, as Hazen argues, the methods and questions that utilise variationist research have developed in complexity and reach '[f]rom broader levels of society to social networks, with different density and multiplexity to communities of practice to the individual who "(re)create[s] sociolinguistic styles in the ebb and flow of social meaning and personal identity"' (Hazen, 2014, p. 14). To give an example, in the 1970s, a researcher would ask: 'How do women speak differently from men?' Whereas, in 2010, the question would be modified; instead, the researcher would ask: 'How does this speaker in this local context construct gender through language?' (Hazen, 2014, p. 17). The difference between first wave (cf. Labov, 1972) and third wave (cf. Eckert, 2008) variationist research is the focus on the means by which individuals construct identity and meaning (cf. Hazen, 2014). To tease this out further, according to Eckert, researchers should be concerned with 'the social value of variation' (2008, p. 473).

Coupland's seminal work on style argues that variation is 'multidimensional' (2001, pp. 198–99) – that is, a quantitative approach to variation does not fully explain why people use dialects, nor does it fully account for stylistic differences. Coupland (2001, p. 202) argues that:

> Dialect style should be treated, analytically, as a repository of cultural indices, mediated by individual performance. Its salience will be located not within any aggregated 'level' or 'range' of dialect variants, but in the placement of individual or specifically grouped dialect features relative to other culturally signifying linguistic and discursive forms – dialect styles operating within ways of speaking.

In his discussion of style and sociolinguistic variation, Coupland (2001) contends that language variation does not necessarily entail a binary relation between a standard and a dialect and that variation on the level of the individual is more intricate and multidimensional. Style is related to identity relations, context and discourse – in other words, variation cannot be confined to natural ways of speaking in relation to group membership (2001, p. 187). In fact, linguistic variation itself cannot be limited to dialect variation, but involves other discourse resources, including politeness resources, terms of address, self-presentation and so on (2001, p. 190). Coupland's approach to style places emphasis on the role of performance as an essential component in linguistic variation research. Performance could refer to both written and spoken variation. To explain, linguistic variation should be contextualised in relation to identification processes and identity construction. As defined by Bauman, identity is 'an emergent construction, the situated outcome of a rhetorical and interpretive process in which interactants make situationally motivated selections from socially constituted repertoires of identificational and affiliational resources and craft these semiotic resources into identity claims for presentation to others' (2001, p. 1). That is, the agency of individuals in manipulating linguistic choices is essential to gaining a better understanding of identity as related to linguistic diversity. This brings us to the significance of performance in identification processes and recognising dialect patterns and salient features.

Schilling-Estes defines performance as the 'register' speakers use to 'display' to others a linguistic code/variety, whether this code is their own or that of another 'speech community' (1998, p. 53). Thus, when a linguistic code or dialect is objectified and displayed in relation to forms of speaking, then it is 'performed'. Unlike natural speech, performance speech is 'highly self-conscious' (Schilling-Estes, 1998, p. 54) and speakers focus on forms/ways of speaking, rather than content. Bauman contends that performance as 'an act of expression' is displayed, objectified by the performer and then scrutinised and evaluated by an audience (Bauman, 2000, p. 1).

The importance of performed speech or performed written texts in research on language variation lies in the fact that it illuminates speakers' 'perceptions' of linguistic variables. For example, when speakers or writers perform a dialect, they emphasise variables that they consider salient and stereotypical in this dialect (Schilling-Estes, 1998, p. 54). Performance lends insight into the process of identity construction and the shared cultural associations the performer aims to convey by using salient features of a given code (Bauman, 2000, p. 4).

According to this approach, the role of the individual in a speech community is proactive rather than reactive (Schilling-Estes, 1998, p. 53). As Coupland (2001) argues, style switching is a means by which an individual can project an identity (Coupland, 2007, p. 190). Similarly, Lacoste et al. (2014, p. 8) note that people search for resources to 'construct' and 'deconstruct' their identities during an act of communication, as well as 'stage' their identity. To draw this out, individuals perform an authentic identity, for example, by drawing on salient linguistic resources associated with a known local identity. However, this performance will depend on the perceptions of the speaker or author regarding what constitutes a specific code or dialect. Dialect features in this instance encompass 'stylistic resources' (Lacoste et al., 2014, p. 8). Moll (2014, p. 211) also emphasises the active role of the speaker as an 'agent' who utilises linguistic resources to manipulate or highlight facets of his or her identity.

In addition, performance is reflexive in nature and may include both the display of language features as well as talk *about* language features (Preston, 1996; Schilling-Estes, 1998, p. 64). Thus, talk *about* a language, as well as the conscious use of a language, are essential in better understanding the use of dialects and code choice more generally.

Johnstone (2010, p. 30) argues that:

> [S]ociolinguists have, in fact, talked about "social meaning" for some time [. . .] since then, new ways of thinking about identity and new reasons for talking about it have deepened our understanding of what language can accomplish in addition to denotation and pragmatic illocution.

This suggests that there is a need to examine the meta-linguistic and dialogical associations of codes and the manner in which language is correlated with different facets of identity, including national identity. Bassiouney (2014) argues that identity is performed, as well as being both habitual and ideological. Sometimes individuals, depending on the context, perform identity through the accumulation of stance over a period of time. Linguists have already established that linguistic variation is not just the correlation between social variables and linguistic variants, but, in fact, has ideological and communal indexes. As Gill contends, individuals 'fashion authentic identity from the semiotic resources at their disposal and position themselves in relation to normative associations between linguistic forms and social meaning' (2014, p. 326).

Before delving into the topics covered by this book, I would like to make clear my rationale behind the use of the term 'dialect' throughout the book. First, I understand that as a term it is not as precise as that of the term 'code'. A 'dialect' is usually defined in relation to another dialect, language, or standard code and shows distinct characteristics in terms of its syntax, morphology, and semantic and phonological features (see Cameron, 2011; Crystal, 2008; Hudson, 2014). This rough definition of a 'dialect' is, admittedly, limited and prone to valid claims of vagueness. The difference between a dialect and a language or a standard language is mostly in the perceptions of speakers of different codes. A language usually has an orthography, geo-political boundaries, a heritage, and a history, but becomes a language due to the power and resources available to its speakers or perceived speakers (Lippi-Green, 2012, p. 46). For non-linguist native speakers of languages, the differences between a dialect and an accent are never clear. For linguists, the difference is at the level of variation. Accents refer to ways of speaking, in which variation is at the level of phonological features and not morphological, syntactic, or semantic ones. However, as Lippi-Green argues, an 'accent' is also a 'loose' term and is mainly based on a listener's judgement (Derwing & Monro, 2009, p. 478, cited in Lippi-Green, 2012, p. 45).

For the sake of precision, some linguists have employed the neutral term 'code' to refer to dialects, varieties, accents, and languages (Bassiouney, 2009; Myers-Scotton, 1998). However, given the importance of perceptions, ideologies, and attitudes in discussions about dialects, accents, and languages, and since this book is concerned with the conscious performance of codes as well as talk *about* them, it is essential to use the term utilised predominantly by speakers, which is 'dialect'. In making this editorial decision, it is important to recognise that the usage of the term dialect is loose and not necessarily precise. Discussions throughout the book will further demonstrate this. So, in sum, for the reasons set out above, the use of the terms 'dialects', 'varieties', and 'codes' will be used interchangeably.

The book will cover the following topics, though this is not an exhaustive list:

1. Dialects in localised and delocalised contexts
2. Dialects and identity construction
3. Dialect, standardisation, and national identity
4. Dialects, contact, and variation in relation to identification
5. Crossing, passing, code choice, and identity construction
6. The ideological indexes of dialects in metalinguistic discourse
7. Performance of dialects in the media more generally

The key outstanding feature of this particular book is that it spans an extensive range of communities and dialects, many of which have been neglected and most of which are severely under-researched. For an example of the breadth of coverage, there are chapters that focus on: Italy, Morocco, Egypt, Syria, Japan, Germany, The Sudan, The Netherlands, Nigeria, Spain, US, UK, Scotland, French Guiana, Colombia, Senegal, Canada, and Libya.

This book is significant in that it will move beyond research that focuses on the field of sociolinguistics from a purely Anglo-American perspective, providing new perspectives on dialects and innovative methods of analysis. The book uncovers general patterns and tendencies in the use of dialects in relation to identity construction and performance. In addition to this, the book does not adopt a binary approach to research on performance, but instead adopts an eclectic and holistic approach, in which quantitative and qualitative methods can, and are, combined to give a thorough and systematic account of the process of performance in the context of identity manifestations.

Detailed discussion of the issues explored in Parts I–IV

Part I: dialects in localised and delocalised contexts

Conventionally, dialects are associated with a local area and/or a particular social group (Hudson, 2014). As was mentioned earlier, variationist research and dialectology were concerned with exploring the relation between independent variables, such as locality, social class or political context, and linguistic variables (see Labov, 1972). However, given the highly globalised and politically troubled environment we now live in, mobility has become a common luxury for some and a necessity for others. As Heller (2011, pp. 7–10) argues, with mobility and diversity comes inequality. Consequently, linguistic features become resources that are distributed unequally between members of different communities. Today, for a growing number of migrants, identity is not taken for granted and is rarely connected to the local area they inhabit. Coupland (2014, p. 33) contends that, given the insecurity that has resulted from losing traditional social structure and local area, individuals have become more 'more reflexive and less confident'. To tease this out, they have become more reflexive, both about their identity and linguistic features, and less confident regarding how to maintain their linguistic features and perceived identity (Lacoste et al., 2014).

The book opens with Part I, 'Dialects in localized and delocalised contexts'. In this section, each author challenges the conventional definition of dialect boundaries and the correlation between dialects and locality. As a whole, it moves towards the argument that dialect features which form resources are deeply embedded in the process of identity construction and can be intentionally used by speakers in different contexts in relation to different social variables. In the contemporary moment, with the increase in linguistic resources, dialects cannot simply be studied in relation to social variables such as ethnicity, locality, and religion, but they must be engaged with in relation to concepts of identity, ideologies, and perceptions. A speaker in a delocalised context provides rich material for the study of dialects. In such a context, where there are no tangible borders for speakers, the relationship between identity, ideologies, perceptions, and political contexts is salient. Metalinguistic discourse reflects more than just linguistic practices and language attitudes; it may also reflect political affiliations, identity construction processes, and ideologies. This part has three chapters.

In chapter one, Edwards sets the scene for the coming chapters by emphasising the relation between dialects and identities. He demonstrates that it is not only dialects with powerful social status that reflect and construct identity, but also stigmatised ones. This may explain the maintenance of such dialects in different communities.

In chapter two, Smakman and van der Meulen challenge the conventional ways of drawing dialect borders. In this chapter the authors review the methods used to demarcate dialect borders and delineate the flaws in such methods given the high degree of mobility and contact in our times.

De Fina, in chapter three, also challenges the conventional definitions of dialect borders. Drawing on data from a fifth-grade classroom in Palermo in which the linguistic repertoire of students does not just include the local varieties of Italian and the local dialects but also Arabic, Tamil, and Bangla. De Fina posits that what is needed in research about dialects is an ethnography-based approach that acknowledges the entrenched context-dependent identity claims.

Part II: nation-states and identity construction in relation to a standard and a dialect

After the essential roles of ideology, agency and linguistic resources have been thoroughly established in Part I, Part II builds upon these concepts by providing an extensive range of examples and data, in which ideology plays a crucial role in dialect use and identity construction. Dialects that survive in spite of stigmatisation have previously been touched upon in the works of both Trudgill (1974) and Milroy (1987). However, in contrast to these two perspectives, Part II offers a complex picture of the ambivalent attitude towards stigmatised dialects and talk about these dialects, as well as the different contexts in which they are used to mark identity. With the increasing pressure of a standard and the rise of nation-states, survival of stigmatised dialects is related not simply to identity, but also to recurring talk and indexes of this identity in relation to dialects and the unique political conflicts that are at times dormant and at others clear.

In Part II, the reader is provided with numerous examples of different political contexts in which talk about dialects is prevalent. For example, in contexts wherein a nation imposes a monolingual identity on individuals whose communities are pluralistic in nature, how do individuals oppose this monolingual policy? Here, positive talk about dialects and performance of dialects are a means of resistance. In addition, how does the rise of a nation-state lead to dialect death? Ideologies, combined with a different style of living, economic factors, urbanisation, and industrialisation, could increase the chances of dialect death. In this context, talk about dialects and efforts to revive or use them may reflect a state of nostalgia, rather than a linguistic reality. Another significant issue that is rarely explored is the context in which a state is still 'in the making' and has to choose a dialect that reflects its new identity. Metalinguistic presentation of a dialect in a new nation-state forging a different identity for itself is essential. In such a case, official discourse, ideologies, and attitudes attempt to forge an identity, rather than impose an already established one. This section has four articles.

In chapter four, Manfredi explores the intricate relation between the construction of linguistic borders and the rise of national identity in post-independence South Sudan. Dialect contact and metalinguistic discourse are explored in relation to the ideologies of the state.

Tosco, in chapter five, provides a different pattern of the relation between language and the state. In this chapter the author discusses the current situation of Piedmontese, a western Romance language and a dialect of Northwest Italy. The conflict between language activists who want to revive and establish this dialect and the reduction of linguistic diversity attempted by the state are outlined in this article.

Caubet, in chapter six, looks at the role of dialect Darija in Morocco as the defining factor of a new Moroccan identity. In Morocco, Caubet argues, there is also a conflict, though of a different nature, a conflict between nationalists, conservatives and the people, Darija users. By examining new forms of writing online, she examines the informal establishment of the dialect as an identity marker.

Ebner, in chapter 7, explores, through analysis of perceptions and attitudes, the conflict between British Standard English and stigmatized dialect variables. Ebner argues that the manner in which these variables are perceived may limit access of its speakers to a number of domains and resources and reflect negatively on their identity.

Part III: contact, variation, performance, and metalinguistic discourse

Reflexivity refers to 'the way language inevitably refers to itself' (Johnstone, 2015). In other words, it refers to the way in which language users reflect on their linguistic performance and that of others. As a process, reflexivity is reflected in studies of linguists themselves and not just in interactions between speakers (Cameron, 2012; Johnstone, 2015). Johnstone argues that when individuals engage in metalinguistic discourse – that is, reflect on language and emphasise the indexes and associations, whether social or political, of different varieties – they may be supporting a process that could lead to language change. She cites an example given by Schilling-Estes (1998), in which individuals 'momentarily' use an 'exaggerated accent' (Johnstone, 2015). In Part III, language variation will be explored in relation to reflexivity, including metalinguistic discourse, language ideologies, and attitudes. This part argues that the classification of dialects in metalinguistic discourse is not just the result of local practice but also of ideologies, reflecting attitudes towards the self, as opposed to the Other (Pennycook, 2010). Crossing and passing (Rampton, 1995) reflect the ways in which individuals master and/or perform a dialect. Crossing and passing are the product of identification; importantly, ethnicity can also be performed through crossing, code choice, or even rejection of a dialect. Several of the chapters in this part also approach identity construction as an action, as 'something individuals "do"' (Widdicombe, 1998). Dialects can also be stigmatised through reflexivity, either by its speakers and/or by outsiders. Issues of agency are also discussed throughout this part, including exploring how much freedom individuals actually have in performance. As Part III concludes, identity performance is related to stance-taking and indexicality and is not always context-free. This part has six chapters that deal with linguistic contact, and variation in relation to identity.

In chapter eight, Léglise and Sánchez Moreano focus on methods used to study dialect variation among multilingual speakers. The role of language ideologies and linguistic practices are highlighted. They argue that choice of dialectal features is in fact an act of stance-taking and identity construction. The study provides examples from language practices among Maroons in French Guiana, Suriname, and with Kichwas in Cali, Colombia.

In chapter nine, O'Donnell Christoffersen and Shin examine how New Mexican Spanish speakers negotiate ethnic identity by using 'bilingual talk-in-interaction'. The study adopts an ethnomethodological approach to identity.

Mc Laughlin, in chapter ten, examines the social meanings of Wolof and French in Senegal. She argues that people's beliefs and ideologies about these two codes affect the performance of identity. These performances in Senegal occur as a result of language contact and offer 'alternative views of a postcolonial modernity' that is reflected through language ideologies.

In chapter eleven, Vicente and Naciri-Azzouz examine the linguistic attitudes and social values of two communities in two locations in Morocco, Tetouan and Ghomara. They aim to show how linguistic variables can index social meaning and how linguistic practices and attitudes can lead to language shift.

In chapter twelve, Heinrich re-examines presentations of self in three countries: England, Germany, and Japan. Through analysis of data from these locations, he challenges the role of legitimate codes/varieties and argues that language crossing is nowadays a common means of identity construction.

Serreli, in chapter thirteen, explores the role of Siwi, which is a minority language in Egypt, and how it has become a symbol of authenticity in a highly commodified context. She uses the concept of orders of indexicality to refer to the social value of Siwi as dialect.

Part IV: the media, dialect performance, and language variation

The media, as a 'wider-reaching cultural vehicle', circulates and calcifies ideologies about language, both through discussions about language and also performance or representation of codes (Bucholtz, 2009, p. 158). As Cotter (2015, p. 796) argues, today, the term 'the media' does not just refer to television, radio, and publicly printed resources, but also refers to myriad other public resources in which the audience's proactive role is apparent and visible, including YouTube, Facebook, Twitter, and so on. Androutsopoulos (2014, p. 247) also postulates that 'the media' as an inclusive term does not simply refer to the mass media, but also refers to practices of mediation, 'institutions', and 'technologies'.

Both Cotter (2015) and Androutsopoulos (2014) enunciate the agency of the audience in media discourse. Androutsopoulos (2014, p. 246) distinguishes between two concepts: mediation and mediatisation. According to him, 'mediatisation' is an abstract term that references the role of 'mediated communication' in 'processes of socio-cultural change'. Cotter (2015, p. 801) adds to this definition, stating that the term 'mediatisation' also refers to processes of political thought. The term 'mediation', on the other hand, refers to the communicative function of media discourse (Androutsopoulos, 2014, p. 246). While the concept of 'media discourse' has been neglected for some time in sociolinguistics, the importance of the media lies in the interaction between audience and media discourse (Bell, 1984; 2001), as well as the layered relation that has been built up between the media, repertoires, attitudes, ideologies, and shared beliefs of individuals and communities (see Androutsopoulos, 2014, p. 247).

Androutsopoulos (2014, p. 242) argues that one of the pitfalls of research that focuses on the media and linguistic change and variation is that it regards the media as a static factor that influences speakers or reflects their beliefs, when, in fact, in order to better study the media, one has to examine the dynamic relation between media makers and audiences. According to Androutsopoulos (2014, p. 242) and Stuart-Smith (2011, p. 243), it is the proactive and involved role of the audience, who hold shared belief systems and shared narratives more generally, that is worth investigating. This is precisely what this part aims to achieve.

In Part IV, issues are raised relating to the use of phonological features of a local dialect and the influence of the media on variation, as well as the processes of stereotyping and stigmatising of dialects that also take place in the media. In the media, individuals can utilise the positive indexes of a stigmatised dialect to highlight different aspects of their identity and take a different stance from others in their nation-state. Across Part IV, it is argued that in a socio-political context, through media performance, dialects can be a means of resistance. Media performance of dialects is identifiable across a wide range of mediums, such as TV shows, soap-operas, films, songs, poetry, rap music, and interviews – as will be clear in the six chapters of Part IV.

In chapter fourteen, Kiesling discusses performance indexicality and enregisterment in relation to specific Pittsburghese linguistic features that are used in a series of videos posted on YouTube to create personae for the characters through stance taking. Kiesling also attempts to develop and modify the definition of stance.

In chapter fifteen, Braber examines stylized language in performance of Scottish identity. She looks at television comedy sketches about Glasgow. The article argues that linguistic choices are used to highlight social class, which is an essential part of Scottish comedy and construction of 'Scottishness'.

Bassiouney, in chapter sixteen, examines the linguistic repertoire of a poet from the south of Egypt who performs in more than one code, and whose original dialect is highly stigmatized in Egyptian public discourse. Drawing on the second-order indexes of his own dialect as well as standard Arabic, the poet analysed attempts to situate his own dialect in a more powerful and influential position.

Storch, in chapter seventeen, explores the multiple roles of Naija (Nigerian Pidgin English) in urban youth identity construction in different mediums of the media including music, social media, and images. It is argued that the diverse metalinguistic discourse on Naija emphasise the 'messy space' which in itself is a result of 'colonial experiences of ruination'.

In chapter eighteen, D'Anna shows how media can use dialect variation to politically characterise characters in Libya during and after the 17th of February revolution. The study is based on a Libyan TV show, arguing that in this show, dialect variation is based on political views rather than geographical origin.

Habib, in chapter nineteen, examines the influence of TV in the dialectal variation of children in a village called Oyoun Al-Wadi in Syria. She argues that the use of rural and urban is not related to social networks of kids, nor to the amount of TV watched in which urban dialectal features are used; rather, it is related to identity construction in the case of the kids analysed.

This work is the first of its kind to deal with such a varied amount of data and dialects and to focus solely on linguistic performance as reflected in metalinguistic discourse and the utilisation of dialects. This new contribution sits within a growing field of research on identity, including, notably, the work of John Edwards (2009). However, within this growing body of research, there are few works that specifically deal with identity as a performance.

In addition to this, there are seminal articles on stance-taking, indexicality, and metalinguistic discourse, including the work of Johnstone (2015) and Jaffe (2009). However, this work is distinguishable and affords a significant contribution to the field at large, as it takes as its focal point identity and dialect across widely diverse communities and countries, illuminating general patterns and tendencies, as well as deducing relations between reflexivity as manifested in metalinguistic discourse and dialect use and stance-taking as a step towards dialect construction. This book does not merely concentrate on stance, nor does it solely focus on indexes of dialects; it also alights upon different contexts to provide insightful grounds for constructing a theoretical framework for studying performance in general, as well as dialects and identity in particular.

Collectively, what all chapters in this edited volume have in common is the assertion that dialects are not merely reflections of demographic or social factors, but, significantly, they are reflections of diverse factors in our changing world, including language contact, globalisation, mobility, wider access to the media, multilingualism, and political changes affecting nation-states, with some disappearing and some becoming increasingly influential.

The intended readers of this edited volume will straddle many fields of research, including, but not limited to, sociolinguistics, linguistic anthropology, anthropology, dialectology, sociology, political science, and mass communication.

The book is clear enough to be read by individuals who are new to the field of sociolinguistics, while also being exhaustive and theoretically grounded to a level that will satisfy an expert scholar in sociolinguistics, discourse analysis, or anthropological linguistics.

General bibliography

Adefarakan, T. E. (2015). *The souls of Yoruba folk*. New York, NY: Peter Lang.
Agha, A. (2007). *Language and social relations*. Cambridge: Cambridge University Press.
Albirini, A. (2015). *Modern Arabic sociolinguistics: Diglossia, variation, codeswitching, attitudes and identity*. London and New York, NY: Routledge.
Androutsopoulos, J. (2014). Beyond "media influence". *Journal of Sociolinguistics*, *18*(2), 242–249.
Bassiouney, R. (2009). *Arabic sociolinguistics: Topics in diglossia, gender, identity, and politics*. Washington, DC: Georgetown University Press.
Bassiouney, R. (2014). *Language and identity in modern Egypt*. Edinburgh: Edinburgh University Press.
Bauman, R. (2000). Language, identity, performance. *Pragmatics*, *10*(1), 1–5.
Bourdieu, P. (1991). *Language and symbolic power*. Cambridge, MA: Harvard University Press.
Bucholtz, M. (2009). From stance to style: gender, interaction, and indexicality in Mexican immigrant youth slang. In A. Jaffe (Ed.), *Stance: Sociolinguistic perspectives* (pp. 146–170). Oxford: Oxford University Press.
Bucholtz, M. and Hall, K. (2010). Locating identity in language. In C. Llamas & D. Watt (Eds.), *Language and identities* (pp. 18–28). Edinburgh: Edinburgh University Press.
Chambers, J. K. (2009). *Sociolinguistic theory: linguistic variation and its social significance* (Rev. ed.). Chichester: Wiley-Blackwell.
Coupland, N. (2001). Language, situation, and the relational self: theorizing dialect-style in sociolinguistics. In P. Eckert & J. R. Rickford (Eds.), *Style and sociolinguistic variation* (pp. 185–210). Cambridge: Cambridge University Press.
Coupland, N. (2014). Language, society and authenticity: Themes and perspectives. In V. Lacoste, J. Leimgruber & T. Breyer (Eds.) *Indexing authenticity: Sociolinguistic perspectives* (pp. 14–39). Berlin: Mouton de Gruyter.
Damari, R. R. (2010). Intertextual stancetaking and the local negotiation of cultural identities by a binational couple. *Journal of Sociolinguistics*, *14*, 609–629.
Dragojevic, M., Giles, H., & Watson, B. (2013). Language ideologies and language attitudes: A foundational framework. In H. Giles & B. M. Watson (Eds.), *The social meanings of language, dialect and accent: International perspectives on speech styles* (pp. 1–25). New York, NY: Peter Lang.
Du Bois, J. W. (2007). The stance triangle. In R. Englebretson (Ed.), *Stancetaking in discourse: Subjectivity, evaluation, interaction* (pp. 139–182). Amsterdam: John Benjamins.
Fishman, J. A. (1988). Language spread and language policy for endangered languages. In P. H. Lowenberg (Ed.), *Language spread and language policy: Issues, implications, and case studies. Proceedings of the Georgetown University round table on languages and linguistics 1987* (pp. 1–15). Washington, DC: Georgetown University Press.
Fishman, J. A. (1991). *Reversing language shift*. Clevedon: Multilingual Matters.

Fought, C. (2010). Language as a representation of Mexican American identity. *English Today*, *26*(3), 44–48.
Gill, M. (2014). "Real communities", rhetorical borders: authenticating British identity in political discourse and on-line debate. In V. Lacoste, J. Leimgruber, & T. Breyer (Eds.), *Indexing authenticity: Sociolinguistic perspectives* (pp. 324–342). Berlin: De Gruyter.
González, M. D. (2005). Todavía decimos "Nosotros [los] mexicanos": Construction of identity labels among nuevo mexicanos. *Southwest Journal of Linguistics*, *24*(1–2), 65–77.
Heller, M. (2007). *Bilingualism: A social approach*. Basingstoke: Palgrave Macmillan.
Heller, M. (2011). *Paths to postnationalism: A critical ethnography of language and identity*. Oxford: Oxford University Press.
Hunter, L., & Chaibou, E. O. (1998). Towards a Hausa verbal aesthetic: Aspects of language about using language. *Journal of African Cultural Studies*, *11*(2), 157–70.
Irvine, J. T. (2009). Stance in a colonial encounter: How Mr. Taylor lost his footing. In A. Jaffe (Ed.), *Stance: Sociolinguistic perspectives* (pp. 53–72). Oxford: Oxford University Press.
Jaffe, A. (2007). Codeswitching and stance: Issues in interpretation. *Journal of Language, Identity & Education*, *6*, 53–77.
Jaffe, A. (2009). The sociolinguistics of stance. In A. Jaffe (Ed.), *Stance: Sociolinguistic perspectives* (pp. 3–28). Oxford: Oxford University Press.
Jaworski, A., & Thurlow, C. (2009). Taking an elitist stance: Ideology and the discursive production of social distinction. In A. Jaffe (Ed.), *Stance: Sociolinguistic perspectives* (pp. 195–226). Oxford: Oxford University Press.
Johnstone, B. (2005). Reflexivity in sociolinguistics. In K. Brown, A.H. Anderson, L. Bauer, M. Berns, G. Hirst, & J. Miller (Eds.), *Encyclopedia of language & linguistics* (Vol. 10, 2nd ed., pp. 463–464). Amsterdam: Elsevier.
Johnstone, B. (2009). Stance, style and the linguistic individual. In A. Jaffe (Ed.), *Stance: Sociolinguistic perspectives* (pp. 29–53). Oxford: Oxford University Press.
Johnstone, B. (2010). Locating language in identity. In C. Llamas & D. Watt (Eds.), *Language and identities* (pp. 29–36). Edinburgh: Edinburgh University Press.
Johnstone, B. (2015). *Speaking Pittsburghese: The story of a dialect*. Oxford: Oxford University Press.
Kloss, H. (1967). "Abstand languages" and "Ausbau languages". *Anthropological Linguistics*, *9*(7), 29–41.
Labov, W. (1972). *Sociolinguistic patterns*. Philadelphia, PA: University of Pennsylvania Press.
Lacoste, V., Leimgruber, J., and Breyer, T. (Eds.) (2014). *Indexing authenticity: Sociolinguistic perspectives*. Berlin: De Gruyter.
Mazraani, N. (1997). *Aspects of language variation in Arabic political speech-making*. Surrey: Curzon Press.
Mendoza-Denton, N., & Osborne, D. (2009). Two languages, two identities? In D. Watt & C. Llamas (Eds.), *Sociolinguistics: Language and identities* (pp. 113–122). Edinburgh: Edinburgh University Press.
Migge, B., & Léglise, I. (2012). *Exploring language in a multilingual context: variation, interaction and ideology in language documentation*. Cambridge: Cambridge University Press.
Milroy, J., & Milroy, L. (2002). *Authority in language*. London: Routledge.
Milroy, L. (1987). *Language and social networks*. Oxford: Blackwell.
Myers-Scotton, C. (1998). *Codes and consequences: Choosing linguistic varieties*. Oxford: Oxford University Press.
Ochs, E. (1992). Indexing gender. In A. Duranti & C. Goodwin (Eds.), *Rethinking context: Language as an interactive phenomenon* (pp. 335–358). Cambridge: Cambridge University Press.
Pennycook, A. (2010). *Language as local practice*. London: Routledge.

Preston, D. R. (1996). Variationist linguistics and second language acquisition. In W. C. Ritchie & T. K. Bhatia (Eds.), *Handbook of second language acquisition* (pp. 229–265). San Diego, CA: Academic Press.
Rampton, B. (1995). *Crossing: Language and ethnicity among adolescents*. London: Longman.
Storch, A. (2013). *Secret manipulations*. New York, NY: Oxford University Press.
Suleiman, Y. (2002). *The Arabic language and national identity: A study in ideology*. Washington, DC: Georgetown University Press.
Suleiman, Y. (2013). *Arabic in the fray: Language ideology and cultural politics*. Oxford: Oxford University Press.
Tieken-Boon van Ostde, I. (2008). The codifiers and the history of multiple negation in English, or, why were 18th-century grammarians so obsessed with double negation? In J. C. Beal, C. Nocera, & M. Sturiale (Eds.), *Perspectives on prescriptivism* (pp. 197–214). Bern: Peter Lang.
Tosco, M. (2011a). The nation-state and language diversity. In P. Valore (Ed.), *Multilingualism: Language, power, and knowledge* (pp. 87–101). Pisa: Edistudio.
Tosco, M. (2011b). Between endangerment and Ausbau. In E. Miola & P. Ramat (Eds.), *Language contact and language decay: Socio-political and linguistic perspectives* (pp. 227–246). Pavia: IUSS Press.
Tosco, M. (2012). Swinging back the pendulum: French morphology and de-Italianization in Piedmontese. In M. Vanhove, T. Stolz, A. Urdze, & H. Otsuka (Eds.), *Morphologies in contact* (pp. 247–262). Berlin: Akademie Verlag.
Trudgill, P. (1974). *The social differentiation of English in Norwich*. Cambridge: Cambridge University Press.
Vigil, N., & Bills, G. (2000). El español de Nuevo México: hablamos mexicano. In M. Morúa & G. López Cruz (Eds.), *Memorias del V encuentro internacional de lingüística en el noroeste, 1998: sociolingüística y lexografía* (pp. 197–217). Hermosillo: Universidad de Sonora.
Widdicombe, S. (1998). Identity as an analysts' and participants' resource. In C. Antaki & S. Widdicombe (Eds.), *Identities in talk* (pp. 191–206). London: Sage Publications.
Wodak, R. (1999). *The discursive construction of national identity*. Edinburgh: Edinburgh University Press.
Woolard, K. A. (1998). Introduction: Language ideology as a field of inquiry. In B. Schieffelin, K. A. Woolard, & P. V. Kroskrity (Eds.), *Language ideologies: Practice and theory* (pp. 3–50). Oxford: Oxford University Press.

PART I
Dialects in localised and delocalised contexts

1
NONSTANDARD DIALECT AND IDENTITY

John Edwards

Introduction[1]

It is hardly necessary, here, to provide a definition of dialect – but, for what follows, it *is* important to point out how difficult definitions and distinctions can be. A common distinction between language and dialect, for instance, hinges on the idea of mutual intelligibility, or the lack of it. No one expects speakers of French and English to understand one another, but English speakers from Perth and Pittsburgh are theoretically able to. In practice, however, there may be very considerable impediments to cross-dialect communication. The point is made clearer, perhaps, when we think of dialect continua. Considering hypothetical dialects A to D, Petyt (1980: 14) suggested: 'if A can just understand C, but cannot really be said to understand D, does [a] language division come between C and D? But C and D may understand each other quite well'. On the other hand, the exigencies of politics mean that Norwegian and Danish are to be seen as separate languages, even though their speakers – like those of the adjacent dialects C and D – understand each other very well.

A recent discussion by Xu (2016: 8–9) deals with a perennially interesting and instructive example here, posing the question: 'are the different idioms of northern and southern China dialects or languages?' He cites the views of several scholars. Karlgren (1962: 18) points out, for instance, that these varieties have diverged widely in terms of pronunciation and sounds, but 'in other grammatical respects they agree so closely that they cannot be called different languages'. Kratochvil (1968: 15) suggests that the major Chinese dialects are like the Romance languages, going on to argue that they are linked by 'a common cultural heritage. . . which makes them different from speakers of Tibetan, Burmese, Thai and other languages' (see also Ramsey, 1987). Chao (1943: 66) makes the less familiar point that levels of intelligibility may differ with levels of education. Through social and personal contact, educated non-Mandarin speakers would 'speak Mandarin of sorts... dialect differences are quite negligible.' For the illiterate, however, a limited vocabulary and lack of mobility makes it impossible to cross group boundaries without losing mutual intelligibility. And Xu himself notes that language-dialect distinctiveness can vary with the provenance of descriptions: a 'purely linguistic classification tends to be narrower than the classification invoking attitudinal, cultural and political factors, resulting in a larger number of languages than [does] the sociolinguistic approach' (2016: 8).[2]

In all this, one is reminded of the observation attributed to Max Weinreich (1945): 'a language is a dialect that has an army and a navy.'[3]

The longstanding (and still widely held) idea that some varieties – standard dialects – have achieved their prominence through some inherent qualities is now thoroughly discredited. The work of linguists over the past two generations or so has shown that *all* dialects are valid and 'logical' expressive systems. Labov's investigations of urban African American English (AAE) were of great importance here; see Labov (1969, 1976). The variety was an excellent 'test case' precisely because it was so poorly regarded, so likely to be branded as some sloppy and inaccurate approximation to 'proper' English, so 'sub-standard'. Labov's quite simple investigations supported a very important correction: nonstandard dialects, like all others, have regular and regularly-observed grammatical structures, and, while these differ in some regards from standard forms (and from other nonstandard ones), no system, operating in its own time and circumstance, can be seen as inherently better or worse than another. All scholarly opinion thus agrees with Trudgill (1975: 26; see also Edwards, 1989):

> just as there is no linguistic reason for arguing that Gaelic is superior to Chinese, so no English dialect can be claimed to be linguistically superior or inferior to any other.... There is no linguistic evidence whatsoever for suggesting that one dialect is more 'expressive' or 'logical' than any other, or for postulating that there are any 'primitive', 'inadequate' or 'debased' English dialects.

It is a commonly-held observation among linguists, anthropologists and others that language varieties are always sufficient for the needs of their speakers. This is not to say, of course, that languages and dialects are equal in their expressive power, in the range of their vocabularies, and so on. Why would we expect this, in any case? On the one hand, it would be 'uneconomical' of speakers to develop fluencies and capacities beyond their immediate needs; on the other, and relatedly, it is logically impossible for words to outstrip concepts. If we find that small groups living in the Amazon basin have no terms to describe things like lasers, or abstract concepts like Einsteinian relativity, we should not be surprised. We *would* be surprised, on the other hand, if – once acquainted with new things and new ideas – we found that their language could not expand appropriately.

If a group begins to take an interest in simple arithmetic and, five hundred years later, develops a theory of quantum mechanics, it is surely reasonable to expect that words will grow with increasing sophistication. This is, in fact, what happens. There is, as well, no need to look at 'primitive' societies (in whatever sense 'primitive' might be construed) here: consider our own intellectual and linguistic development. It is the lack of the prerequisite conceptual understanding that prevents a group from possessing modern medical procedures (to cite another instance). Words themselves are only indicators. Thus, the real meaning of a statement like 'language is adequate for its speakers' needs' refers to the fact that language keeps pace with conceptual advancement, which in turn determines the very needs of which speakers can even be aware.

Quite apart from scholarly enlightenment on the matter, the notion that any regularly-used language variety could be inherently deficient in meeting the needs of its users — clearly and without ambiguity — has never been intellectually sustainable. It simply defies common sense. As with other similarly dismissive assessments — the 'cultural deprivation' allegedly endured by some unfortunate communities, for instance (see also below) — the conception of a 'sub-standard' dialect tells us more about those applying the labels than it does about those being described. More specifically, it reveals the underlying flawed idea that there is, in fact, a correct 'standard' from which all others deviate, a variety which is inherently superior.

There *are*, of course, dialect varieties that are accurately labelled as 'standards'. To deny this would be to deny the historical reality in virtually all socially stratified communities. But standards are simply varieties that are used and endorsed by those in positions of social dominance, those segments of society that — more or less literally — set the standards. As linguistic systems they may differ — sometimes greatly, sometimes minimally — from others, but they are not *intrinsically* better. One implication, as already implied, is that there can be no 'sub-standard' forms (where 'sub' connotes basic logical or linguistic inferiority). Another, however, is that a non-pejorative application of the term 'nonstandard' makes perfect sense — if a standard dialect exists in a region, then all others are necessarily 'not standard'.

Nonstandard dialects, in a word, are those that have not received the social imprimatur given to standard forms. The latter rise to the top, as it were, with the fortunes of their speakers; the process typically reflects historical vicissitudes. Standards are the dialects most often used by educated members of society, and are therefore the most likely to appear in official pronouncements, public records, writing and (often) the broadcast media. But, to repeat, there is nothing of a linguistic nature which confers special or superior status here. It is solely because of widespread acceptance and convention that a standard is *primus inter pares*. If York instead of London had become the centre for the royal court, then BBC newsreaders would sound different and school teachers would long have promoted another form of 'correct' English in England.

An interesting – if more minor – case has occasionally been made for the intrinsic superiority of certain dialects, on aesthetic grounds. Thus, for example, a prominent English linguist wrote the following:

> If it were possible to compare systematically every vowel sound in RS [Received Standard English – i.e., what we now more usually call RP, Received Pronunciation] with the corresponding sound in a number of provincial and other dialects, assuming that the comparison could be made, as is only fair, between speakers who possessed equal qualities of voice, and the knowledge how to use it, I believe no unbiased listener would hesitate in preferring RS as the most pleasing and sonorous form, and the best suited to be the medium of poetry and oratory.
>
> *(Wyld, 1934: 4)*

(I need hardly say that such sentiments were not – and are not – restricted to those speaking in and for English.)

In fact, just as the work of Labov decisively revealed the internal 'logic' – that is, the grammatical regularity – of AAE (and, by extension, of all dialects), so work by Howard Giles and his colleagues (Giles *et al.*, 1974, 1979) showed the absence of any aesthetic quality inherent in a dialect. Judgements here, too, derive from social convention, expectation, and stereotype. In one representative study, British students who knew no Greek were asked to evaluate the aesthetic quality – simply the pleasantness – of two Greek dialects, the Athenian and the Cretan. As one might reasonably surmise, the variety of the capital is seen, within the Greek-speaking community, as the high-status standard form – the most 'logical' and the most mellifluous; the island dialect is rough, and its speakers less competent. The student judges, however, did not make those distinctions: if anything, there was a slight tendency for the Cretan dialect to be assessed more favourably.

The implication is that, if one removes (experimentally) the social stereotypes usually associated with given varieties, aesthetic judgements will not be made which favour the high-status standards. Anyone who watches a film or a play in which accents and dialects figure, in which (for example) a woman dressed as a duchess speaks with a Cockney accent, will appreciate the effects achieved. Equally, we can see that someone in the audience who had an understanding of English, but not of the subtle intra-linguistic variations and conventions, would miss a great deal. The norms are 'imposed' by those in the know; the stereotypes which link beauty, or harshness, or comedy to a set of sounds are unavailable to others. None of this, of course, rules out purely individual preferences; I may think Italian sounds the most attractive, you may believe that Gaelic is unrivalled, but we should agree to differ on a matter of subjectivity.

A final introductory note: there are interesting status differences *within* the ranks of nonstandard dialects. Urban varieties, for example, are often viewed as less pleasant than rural ones. Trudgill (1975) demonstrated that, in Britain, the speech patterns found in cities like Birmingham, Glasgow, and Liverpool were judged less pleasant than those in country settings (Devon, for one). The explanation again lies with social connotations, with the ability that social judgements have to turn differences into (perceived) deficits. For many, bucolic areas have charms denied to busy, densely populated, and industrialised centres. There are, as well, a great many studies showing that – while standard-dialect speakers are typically seen to possess greater competence than others – nonstandard varieties are associated with greater integrity, helpfulness, and social attractiveness. One only has to think of the sense of 'down-to-earthiness' that at least some nonstandard dialects evoke.

Relatedly, there is a 'covert prestige' attached to working-class and broadly *non*-prestigious dialects by speakers of more standard varieties, an attractiveness that rests upon the perceived directness or, indeed, tough-mindedness of these forms. This sort of inverted status is of course more likely to recommend itself to males. I was given a fine example of its force some years ago, in the office of a middle-aged, upper-middle-class male American university professor. As the head of his department, he was being pressed by two or three colleagues (also male) on a current academic matter. He was clearly unable or unwilling to go along with their request. After a few minutes of polite and 'educated' give-and-take, my friend turned to the others, smiled broadly and exclaimed, 'Listen boys, you *know* they ain't no way I can do it' (Edwards, 2010: 154). His departmental colleagues immediately ceded the point. Falling into this nonstandard pattern was a signal of directness and firmness, of an egalitarian informality – of the truth. The essence here lies in the perceived contrast between no-nonsense usage, on the one hand, and inflated, evasive, or overly nuanced (academic) language, on the other: straight shooting versus humbug.

Bragg and Ellis (1976) reported the Cockney opinion that if a child were to speak 'posh', friends would label him (or her, of course) as 'a queer'. This is reminiscent of Orwell's famous observation that 'nearly every Englishman of working-class origin considers it effeminate to pronounce a foreign word correctly' (1970a: 85). The class distinction was important for Orwell, who pointed out that the 'upper classes learn foreign languages as a regular part of their education', a fact which only feeds lower-class hostility: 'travelling abroad, speaking foreign tongues, enjoying foreign food, are vaguely felt to be upper-class habits, a species of snobbery, so that xenophobia is reinforced by class jealousy' (1970b: 18). The distinction is important in the present chapter, too, since working-class people generally speak nonstandard dialect. Incidentally, Orwell's further focus – on the English*man* – is borne out by more formal and more recent observation; thus, Carr and Pauwels (2006) have suggested that discomfort in speaking foreign languages 'properly' remains an issue, particularly for males and, more particularly still, for boys at school; see also Kissau (2006) and Edwards (2010) for further discussion of this 'gender issue'. All of this, of course, implies a combination of unease, awareness of class hierarchies, and covert prestige.

Nonstandard language: attitudes and identity[4]

Dialect evaluations along the lines of broad dimensions like competence, integrity, and attractiveness have been formally studied since the 1970s, and more recent attempts have been made at fuller codification; see Edwards (1995). For example, an 'organisational framework' has been suggested involving two broad determinants of language perceptions: *standardisation* and *vitality*. While a standard variety is typically associated with dominant social groups, 'vitality' refers to the number and importance of the functions served by any given variety. It is obviously bolstered by the status that standards possess, but it can also be a feature of nonstandard varieties, given sufficient numbers of speakers and community support. The framework also suggests two main evaluative dimensions, *social status* and *solidarity*, the latter including aspects of 'integrity' and 'attractiveness' that I touched upon in the previous section.[5] Refinements in measurement techniques have been suggested, too, involving direct and indirect assessment, as well as content analysis. The first usually means questionnaire or interview methods, the 'matched-guise' approach is a good example of the second, and the third implies historical and sociological observation, together with ethnographic study.[6] This hardly exhausts the recent developments in the area but it is abundantly clear that, for almost half a century, researchers have continued to find important language judgements involving speakers' competence, prestige, and status, on the one hand, and their warmth, integrity, and attractiveness, on the other – and to map these on to the standard-nonstandard framework.

The relevant literature here confirms what has long been well understood at a popular level. The speech patterns of regional speakers, of ethnic-minority-group members, of lower- or working-class populations – categories that frequently overlap, of course – elicit negative evaluations in terms of perceived status, prestige, and levels of skill and education. The stereotypic patterns seem to hold whether or not listeners are themselves standard-dialect speakers. Some of the earliest studies, undertaken before the more recent emergence of black or Hispanic 'pride', do reveal hints of linguistic and psychological developments to come. Flores and Hopper (1975), for instance, found slight preferences on the part of Mexican-American judges for the speech styles of *compañeros* who referred to themselves as 'Chicano'. But it would be naïve to assume that negative language stereotypes are generally on the wane. Indeed, there is every reason to think that undesirably prejudicial evaluations are still very much with us. Many recent overviews and surveys reinforce the point: see, for example, the work of Bradac *et al.* (2001), Garrett (2010), Garrett *et al.* (2003), Giles and Billings (2004), Giles *et al.* (2006), and Giles and Edwards (2010). All of these suggest that the general pattern of results I have been discussing here is a robust one.

Dragojevic *et al.* (2016) give us a very recent sense of things here. They considered television characters who appeared in prime time broadcasts – well over 1,000 portrayals, across nine networks – putting each of them into one of four accent groups. These were so-called Standard American (SA), Nonstandard American (NSA), Foreign-Anglo (FA), and Foreign-Other (FO). These are far from monolithic categories, and it is to the authors' credit that this point is acknowledged.[7] The study must therefore be seen as rather crude, at least in terms of anything like fine-grained analysis of linguistic stereotyping. Nonetheless, the results are instructive, largely because they reinforce our sense that such stereotyping is alive and well, and that it continues to operate in familiar ways. Television characters in the SA and FA groups were greatly over-represented (about 84% and 5% of all the 1,252 speakers identified, respectively) and – the authors claim – those in the other two groups were 'effectively *silenced* by virtue of their sheer absence and gross under-representation' (59). Where NSA and FO speakers did appear, they were less likely to take main roles, to be seen as high in status. . . or even to be as physically attractive. All in all, the findings reveal an 'accent-based status hierarchy on American television' (75). Speakers with either Standard American or non-American 'Anglo' accents are viewed most favourably, followed by American characters with nonstandard speech and, finally, those with 'foreign' accents *tout court*.

Studies of AAE in California provide another relevant demonstration of the continuation of prejudicial linguistic views, their pervasiveness, and their consequences. Ogbu (1999: 180) has described how black people still consider that 'proper' English is 'white' English, and that AAE is poor slang or, less pejoratively, 'just plain talkin''. On further investigation, it is clear that AAE is seen as the ordinary vernacular, the 'low' variant in a diglossic situation. And Ogbu also reports that, although his respondents did not articulate the notion, they feel caught: the AAE that represents home, familiarity, and group identity is threatened by the mastery of 'proper' English, a mastery that is seen as necessary for school and work success. They believe, in other words, in a sort of 'subtractive bidialectalism'. The 'dialect dilemma', the belief that the necessary acquisition of standard English will tend to erode the vernacular, is sometimes reinforced by a feeling (both within and without academia) that this process is part of the assimilatory intent of 'mainstream' school and society. Ogbu notes that, on the one hand, black professionals, advocates, educators, and communities endorse the learning of standard English, but then turn around and condemn its acquisition on the grounds that it threatens 'Black English identity and racial solidarity' (1999: 80). These are matters with which speakers of more standard dialects do not have to contend, problems that they do not have to face and, indeed, are generally unlikely even to be aware of.

Ogbu goes on to point out, however, that the belief in a predatory and asymmetrical bidialectalism may be unfounded, and unreflective of actual practice. After all, a more or less stable coexistence of dialects is the norm in many contexts, and it is certainly part of the repertoire of large numbers of black Americans. Is there, then, any real dilemma here? Well, it is possible, just as 'subtractive bilingualism' is possible – where the acquisition of a new language gradually ousts an existing one – but, in both cases, any 'subtraction' that occurs is a symptom of larger social forces that make resistance unlikely to succeed. In the case of black American culture and its current pervasiveness – well beyond the boundaries of the black community itself – I should think that a diglossic relationship between AAE and more standard forms is likely to endure for the foreseeable future. But if a 'dilemma' is perceived, it has at least a psychological existence. Ogbu's informants clearly feel that, when a black person 'is talking proper, he or she is *puttin' on* [italics added] or pretending to be white or to talk like white people' (171–172). They told him that it is 'insane to pretend to be white', that speaking standard English is a pretence, a fake. They don't actually speak of betrayal of the group here but the implication is plain, and quite similar to the *vendido/vendu* phenomenon (discussed below).

Ogbu's 'dialect dilemma' is the same phenomenon that Smitherman (2006) has discussed under the rubric of 'linguistic push-pull', a linguistic contradiction whereby black speakers simultaneously embrace AAE and dislike it. 'On the one hand', she says, 'Blacks have believed that the price of the ticket for Black education and survival and success in White America is eradication of Black Talk. On the other hand, Blacks also recognize that language is bound up with Black identity and culture' (129). This 'push-pull' situation obviously affects many speakers of nonstandard dialects, in many settings. The solution, a theoretically plausible bidialectalism by which you can eat your linguistic cake while still having it, is not always easy to maintain; see below.

There is yet further evidence that enlightened opinion about the intrinsic validity of nonstandard dialects has not penetrated as far as might be wished. A discussion by Siegel (2007: 76) shows how little ground has often been gained. Describing creoles and nonstandard dialects in education, he points out that, despite several decades of sociolinguistic insight, accurate depictions of such varieties 'have not filtered down to many educators and administrators'. Zéphir's work (1997, 1999) is also important here, as she draws explicit and telling parallels between the educational reception of creole and that of AAE. In a review of a book on AAE, Kautzsch (2006) points to the necessity for more open-minded and well-informed teachers, and for educational systems committed to 'difference' rather than 'deficit' stances on cultural and dialect variations. Godley *et al.* (2007: 124) provide another classroom demonstration of the continuing assessments that equate 'standard' with 'correct', and Black English with 'incorrect, ungrammatical English'.

I don't want to multiply examples unnecessarily, but an interesting longitudinal perspective can be found in the reports published by the American Dialect Society at twenty-year intervals (1943, 1964, 1984; and Preston, 2003), reports outlining 'needed research' in dialect studies. In the latest of these, several authors write about the important linguistic demonstrations of the validity of AAE and other non-standard dialects, about the useful developments in language-attitude research, as well as progress in 'perceptual dialectology' and 'folk linguistics' mentioned above. While virtually all scholarly writing about AAE has argued for the greater sensitivity to black culture and lifestyles that should logically accompany demonstrations of the validity of black dialects – with the work of Smitherman (1981a, 1981b, 2006) being noteworthy here – it is sad to find that unenlightened stereotypes continue their baleful course. Relatedly, Wolfram and Christian (1989) note that, while researchers and those who teach teachers agree on the importance of information about dialect variation in the classroom, they have been hindered by the lack of appropriate texts. It is interesting, to say the least, that during the years following Labov's (1969) classic demonstration of the 'logic of nonstandard English', little suitable teacher-training material was apparently developed.

As implied already, one of the most poignant aspects in the topic under discussion here is the widely-reported tendency (within and without academia) for nonstandard-dialect speakers to accept and agree with unfavourable stereotypes of their speech styles. Labov (1976) found, for instance, that those whose speech includes nonstandard or stigmatised forms are typically their own harshest critics, a linguistic manifestation of social dominance/subordination and, some would argue, of more blatant social control.

Self-criticism of one's own (nonstandard) speech is often accompanied by an awareness of the difficulty of change, the operation of covert prestige, and a sense that any efforts made to speak in more standard ways will be seen as affectations, and probably met with scorn Added together, these lead to self-assessments like that cited by Bragg and Ellis (1976): 'You won't end up on the Board of Directors with a voice like that'. Thirty years on, Marlow and Giles (2010), in a Hawaiian study embedded in the 'language-criticism' literature, made exactly the same point: the title of their article is 'We won't get ahead speaking like that!'

It is hardly surprising that speakers of less prestigious nonstandard varieties come to feel the power of social convention, attitude, and prejudice – and, more than that, come to believe that it must in fact rest upon what is right and proper. Sociolinguists have thus described a 'minority-group reaction' (see Lambert *et al.*, 1960) in which the codes, postures and practices of the dominant become accepted and normative among the less dominant, even where such acceptance may be grudging, and may coexist with class or group resentment. Still, we might reasonably ask why low-status varieties continue to exist. Might we not expect that – if not within a generation, then at least over one or two – they would gradually be abandoned in favour of less stigmatising forms? Why wouldn't shifting away from nonstandard dialect be a more popular option? Why is it that the levelling of local speech styles and, more pointedly, the gradual disappearance of low-status variants – predicted in some quarters as an inevitable consequence of the growth of literacy, the greater impact of formal and usually compulsory education, and the spread of the broadcast media – seem not to have occurred? So, as Ryan (1979) put it in the title of her article, 'why do low-prestige varieties persist?'; see also Abd-el-Jawad (2006).

Where – as is generally the case – nonstandard varieties *do* in fact persist, some expansion of the linguistic repertoire, some development of bidialectal capacity, might seem to recommend itself to speakers of non-prestigious variants. We know that this is not, in principle, a difficult accomplishment. It is very common among actors, for example; and, at the more mundane levels with which we are all familiar, the process of selecting from a linguistic pool of possibilities according to perceptions of the setting is even more common – well-nigh universal, in fact. Consider the different ways in which one speaks to one's spouse, students, children, the vicar, the policeman who stops one's car, the doctor, friends in the pub, the bank manager, and so on. (Indeed, we would find it immediately odd if there were no such variation across people and places – just as we would be taken aback if our doctor spoke to us the way our mechanic did, or vice versa.) In short, we select from a repertoire which, for most of us, is quite broad, according to our perceptions of situational constraints and demands. The examples just given are not all *dialectal*, of course – some reflect register or style choices – but they all serve to make the point of a very general capacity for linguistic flexibility.[8]

It can hardly be argued, either, that speakers of nonstandard dialects are without adequate models for repertoire expansion. Teachers once comprised the traditional pool here, and today their still-powerful influence has been magnified and enhanced by the pervasive intrusions of the public media into all corners of society. The result is that virtually all nonstandard-dialect speakers have at least passive access to standard forms.

Some *do*, of course, expand their repertoires and, just as bilingualism can be of use in situations of language contact, so bidialectalism can serve within language communities. In some circumstances, in fact – particularly in settings where people have remained for a long time, either voluntarily or because mobility was not possible for them – bidialectalism can have a much longer existence than bilingualism. While bilingualism is often a transitional stage on the way to full language shift, bidialectalism can be quite stable. Two dialects, for instance – one reflecting group solidarity, let us say, and the other elicited by practical or instrumental needs brought about by desired group contact and social mobility – can be maintained at much less cost and with much less energy than can two languages. Dialects often imply mutual intelligibility, after all, and share many common features: 'the gears and axles of English grammatical machinery are available to speakers of all dialects' (Labov, 1976: 64). Relatedly, while speakers of different dialects may customarily inhabit different subcultures, they are by definition all united under one broader language and cultural banner. Dialect variation can thus remain where language variation may not.

It is the continuation of stigmatised nonstandard dialects alone – without, that is to say, a non-subtractive bidialectalism involving more socially approved varieties – that is of central interest here.[9] The most general explanations involve conceptions of group identity, and of its individual reflections. The simple point – one to which I shall return shortly – has to do with the identity-bearing quality possessed by all language varieties. But there are practical impediments to altering speech styles, too, and these at once lessen the likelihood of either outright shift or repertoire expansion. It is no light matter to attempt changes that will set you apart from members of your group. Some severing or impairment of important ties may occur, and you may be seen as a sort of pariah or linguistic quisling, resented or ostracised. You must also hope that transitions come off successfully: falling between linguistic or cultural stools means risking social marginalisation. Even relative success is tricky, particularly if you want to go home again: Mexican Americans who have 'migrated' to English have been labelled *vendidos* ('sell-outs'); the same epithet has applied to French Canadians, too (*vendus*). So, there are practical difficulties here, and this is even assuming that no other group markers (skin colour, for instance) exist to hamper mobility; see Edwards (1995).

There is another very obvious factor that deters some nonstandard-dialect speakers from attempting to 'improve' their speech styles. If we consider, for instance, that negative speech evaluations typically reflect broader social or racial attitudes, then it follows that – particularly for members of 'visible minority' groups – learning and using a standard dialect may not necessarily alter things very much. Indeed, there is some suggestion in the literature that black speakers who sound 'white' may elicit *more* negative attitudes. Some early studies by Giles and Bourhis (1975, 1976) demonstrated this among West Indians in Cardiff, and similar observations have been made in Canada and the United States (see Edwards, 1989). The essential point here is that unfavourable evaluations may increase when their recipients are seen to attempt to 'pass' – even though any accusation is completely undercut when, say, Canadian-born or Welsh-born children of Caribbean parents simply and naturally speak like their white school-mates in Toronto or Tiger Bay.

Beyond such hindrances to change or expansion – some clearly more powerful than others – we are to bear in mind the group-solidarity function possessed by any and all language varieties. They are all able to carry important group meanings, reflect and reinforce social bonds, and act as community boundary markers.[10] A language variety of low social status may be a hindrance – a particularly unfair hindrance, given the fact that there is nothing inherently deficient about it – but it is not yours alone. It is also the variety of your most immediate group. The language of home and hearth, of first expression, of intimacy, is not abandoned or altered on a whim. Standard or nonstandard, all varieties are capable of sustaining connections of the greatest significance. We are dealing here, then, with personal and group identity, and it is clear that language is a potent pillar. It is true that psycho-social identity can survive language or dialect shift – for supporting argument here, see Edwards, 1985, 2009) – but it seems undeniable that, where some 'first' medium does continue to exist, its buttressing function is likely to be strong. Indeed, even those varieties that have lost their ordinary vernacular functions can remain as important, if now unspoken, symbolic quantities. Their very intangibility helps maintain their longevity in the face of communicative shift and the adoption of a new conversational variety.

It should be noted here – and quite pointedly – that lower-class speakers do not always consider their own language patterns to be inferior variants. I have already implied that altered social circumstances can lead to a reawakening or revitalisation of group 'pride' or 'consciousness', and this has linguistic consequences. This process is underlined by the increasingly common tendency to exaggerate or heighten, whether consciously or not, speech styles that were previously disapproved of. What was once an 'inferior' variety goes beyond mere equivalence with erstwhile 'better' forms, and comes to be seen as superior to them: more direct, more pithy, more animated. In a study of black secondary-school students, Fordham reports (1999: 272) that AAE is now the 'norm against which all other speech practices are evaluated'; standard English is no longer privileged; indeed, 'it is "dissed" (disrespected) and is only "leased" by the students on a daily basis from nine to three'. There are attractions here, too, for middle-class and more or less standard-dialect-speaking adolescents – a global phenomenon, given the ever more pervasive and penetrative presence of American pop culture. (And, if we recall once more the concept of 'covert prestige', we realise that attractiveness of nonstandard dialect is not restricted to teenagers and young adults.)

Although, here, I can only refer readers to the notable discussions surrounding the so-called 'deficit' and 'difference' theories of nonstandard dialects (and of the allegedly 'culturally-deprived' environments from which they were thought to emerge), it is quite clear that most people continue to believe in the former – that is, in the idea that certain ways of speaking are incorrect and thus, by logical implication, that others (or, indeed, *one* other) are correct, precise, accurate... logical (Edwards, 1989, 2010). The man or woman in the street may not be able to articulate any sort of theory, may indeed be quite unaware that he or she *has* a theory, but it is the easiest thing in the world to demonstrate the continuing influence of a 'deficit' point of view: just ask people about 'correct' and 'incorrect' language (see, for instance, Trudgill, 1975 or, more recently, Lippi-Green, 1997). And, more to the purpose of this part of the discussion, we are not to imagine that this influence is absent inside the educational cloisters. Of course, I do not mean to single out teachers as the primary villains here, nor do I imagine that their attitudes and actions are anything but well-meaning. Besides the obvious fact, however, that they are members of society first, they are also on the front lines, so to speak, and their roles and their actions are incredibly strong in the lives of young children.

Lippi-Green (1997, p. 111) writes about teachers whose views seem to have 'effectively summarized all of the conclusions drawn from Bernstein's theories of restricted and elaborated codes'; on Bernstein's work and influence, see Edwards (1989), and note 9. Walsh (1991, p. 107) found teachers of Puerto Rican children who felt that their pupils

> come to school speaking a hodge podge. They are all mixed up and don't know any language well. As a result, they can't even think clearly. That's why they don't learn. It's our job to teach them language – to make up for their deficiency. And, since their parents don't really know any language either, why should we waste time on Spanish? It is 'good' English which has to be the focus.

In a study conducted in Nova Scotia, a research student and I found many teachers with similar views – in this case, relating to black and French Acadian children. One representative comment included the following:

> [Disadvantaged children have] lack of experiences, poor language development... cannot articulate their thoughts and feelings... Blacks have a slang language all their own. They will not use proper English when opportunity arises
> *(Edwards, 1995, p. 91).*

Could we ask for clearer or more succinct statements of belief in some intrinsic environmental deficit that undermines the skills of nonstandard-speaking children?[11]

Conclusion

While nonstandard-dialect speakers do not inevitably think badly of their own variety, and while there are times and contexts in which its use is a matter of pride, is celebrated, and is sometimes admired and even adopted by those outside the group, few are unaware that, in more 'dominant' eyes, nonstandard usage is often disdained. This awareness may not incorporate the realisation that social disparagement – and its ramifications – says nothing about any intrinsic speech quality. On the contrary, it is quite understandable that nonstandard-dialect speakers should come to believe that there *is* some inherent flaw in the way they speak and perhaps, by extension, in other aspects of their lives and their community cultures. And they are, in a sense, quite right – because the power of social convention has always been able to transform differences into deficits. The sustained influences and pressures here, given the social, economic and cultural disparities and differences that characterise all stratified communities, and which are quite clear to all, are almost impossible to escape and unlikely to disappear.

This does not mean, of course, that we should neglect any opportunity to correct linguistic misperceptions. Consider, for example, that the intrinsic unfairness of prejudicial evaluations of nonstandard dialects is heightened when set against the very real and often quite tangible difficulties with which their speakers have to deal. As Halliday (1968: 165) once observed: 'A speaker who is made ashamed of his own language habits suffers a basic injury as a human being; to make anyone, especially a child, feel so ashamed is as indefensible as to make him feel ashamed of the colour of his skin'. Some have debated the depth of the injury here; no enlightened opinion, however, doubts the indefensibility, the unfairness, of the process.

Consider, too, that while there is a great deal of evidence that the nature of the difference-into-deficit transformation – the process by which nonstandard dialects are deemed inferior approximations to something better – is poorly grasped by its recipients and insufficiently understood by others, it is also a process that can be quite readily understood by those willing to be instructed. Hoping for rapid and widespread social enlightenment may be overly optimistic, but it is not unreasonable to argue for attitude change in some specific quarters. Schools and classrooms immediately suggest themselves here, simply because the teachers within them are, or have become, standard-language users, because they are virtually all well-meaning when it comes to the education and future prospects of their pupils, because they usually stand at the first important point of contact between nonstandard and standard dialects, and because their influence is a strong and sustained one. Andersson and Trudgill (1990: 179) write that 'teachers who are prepared to take an open-minded, unprejudiced attitude towards the varieties of language spoken by their pupils will be the ones who also succeed best in fostering and developing children's linguistic interests and abilities'. We should expand upon this, and say that such teachers are likely to succeed best in developing *all* of their pupils' potentials.[12]

Unfavourable stereotypes of nonstandard dialect are predictably pervasive in stratified societies: they are the linguistic components of the larger 'packet' of differences which constitutes, in fact, the stratification itself. Notwithstanding the existing and – one hopes – increased future efforts to lessen prejudicial perceptions and to bring more effectively to bear the scholarly insights that make quite clear the different-but-not-deficient status of nonstandard dialect, the continuing social reality involves stigmatisation and disparagement. Nonetheless, the identity-bearing quality of language does not falter where nonstandard dialects are concerned. Given what has been discussed in this chapter, it is clear that a powerful array of constraints and desires helps to maintain such dialects. The former are surely clear enough, essentially involving the difficulties and dangers in trying to 'pass' linguistically and, more generally, the fact that dialect differences are often intertwined with other group markers. The latter are perhaps more subtle and, for that reason, more interesting. A dialect may help to create social barriers and to impede mobility, but – within its community of use, within the context in which its use is entirely natural and unselfconscious, within the nexus of the earliest and usually most intimate interpersonal relations – it has the same deep claims upon its users as any other variety. Whatever may or may not transpire throughout the lives of its speakers, it remains, after all, the maternal variety.

Notes

1 I do not provide here the argumentation behind the points made in this section: for fuller details, consult Edwards (1985, 1995).
2 In a somewhat related paper, Yingmei (2016) points out that speakers may not always be clear, themselves, about the variety they speak. Putonghua and Beijing pronunciations are very similar, but not identical; consequently, the two are 'confused by a substantial number of our respondents' (53). While many Beijing residents 'claimed to speak Putonghua... it was clear... that they were speaking Beijing dialect' (51). Some others were confused in the opposite direction, as it were.
3 In his paper for the journal of the Institute for Jewish Research, Weinreich pointed out that he was not the author of this now-famous phrase – it was, rather, a member of the audience listening to a talk of his in early 1944. And perhaps this audience member was not, himself, the originator of the apothegm: the linguist Antoine Meillet and the French colonial administrator Louis-Hubert Lyautey have also been suggested as its coiners.
4 This section draws largely upon Edwards (2009; 2010; 2011; 2013; 2017).
5 See Dragojevic et al. (2016) for some very recent attention to these matters.
6 The 'matched-guise' technique, introduced by Lambert et al. (1960), investigates reactions to speech variants. Speakers who are able to successfully assume different language or dialect 'guises' are recorded reading the same passage in each of two or more varieties. Listeners (the assessors) are then asked to rate the speakers on various personality scales. It is assumed that the speech samples serve as triggers to evoke stereotypic reactions to the different varieties heard. Any potentially confounding individual variables will of course be constant across the 'guises'.
7 These categories are not beyond criticism. Standard American 'was defined as a generalized, Midwestern accent, often described as "accentless" due to its lack of stigmatized regional or ethnic features' (Dragojevic et al., 2016: 71). This category may of course be far from internally seamless, an observation that applies even more emphatically to the others. Thus, Nonstandard American comprises 'any accent that has distinctive regional, ethnic, or foreign features' (71); Foreign-Anglo includes 'all non-American, Anglo accents (e.g., British, Australian) (65); Foreign-Other means, well, all the rest.
8 Along the continua of formality, jargon, register and so on, within-dialect selection is ubiquitous. One is reminded of the delightful treatment of the theme by Joos (1967). In an informal but not inaccurate treatment of stylistic variation, he outlines a continuum of linguistic formality/informality – the five points on his scale being frozen, formal, consultative, casual and intimate. For a fuller discussion, see Edwards (1995).
9 I do not mean to suggest, of course, that nonstandard-dialect speakers *never* make any alterations in the direction of more standard usage. Fordham's (1999) point (below)

about black students using at least some standard patterns in the classroom is a widely observed one (see also Trudgill, 1975). Even when Bernstein's descriptions of 'elaborated' and 'restricted' speech codes lent so much weight to a 'deficit' view of nonstandard language (see Edwards, 1989, for a comprehensive discussion), researchers were able to point out nonstandard-dialect-speaking children's use of standard forms in classroom settings; see, for example, Robinson (1965) and Rushton and Young (1975). It is, however, the lack of what we might term 'general' bidialectalism – not simply changes adopted (often without much good grace) in very specific and very obviously standard-usage contexts, but also broader employment, in many settings, with the clear hope of improving or expediting social mobility – that remains of particular interest here.

10 I write 'are able' here simply because there are cases – not always few in number in some circumstances – in which early, original, or maternal varieties are firmly repudiated, where they are freighted with unwanted connotations and memories, where their associations are distinctly unsavoury, and so on.

11 I write 'environmental deficit' here because the other traditional, but obviously incorrect, assumption about linguistic and cultural deficit – that it arises because of underlying genetic or 'racial' differences – has become almost completely discredited. . . at least in those segments of society that include most teachers. Again, further and fuller details may be consulted in Edwards (1989; 2010).

12 It is beyond my purpose here to discuss the ways in which the linguistic awareness of teachers (and others) might best be improved, but it seems obvious that any approach must be based upon the appropriate presentation of up-to-date evidence bearing upon linguistic and cultural issues of both general and local importance. For some specific perspectives, see Beykont (2002), Gaine (2005) and Pearce (2005). For more general discussion, see Edwards (1989; 2010).

References

Abd-el-Jawad, H. (2006). Why do minority languages persist? The case of Circassian in Jordan. *International Journal of Bilingual Education and Bilingualism*, 9, 51–74.

American Dialect Society. (1943). *Needed research in American English*. Chicago: A.D.S.

American Dialect Society. (1964). *Needed research in American English (1963)*. Tuscaloosa: University of Alabama Press.

American Dialect Society. (1984). *Needed research in American English (1983)*. Tuscaloosa: University of Alabama Press.

Andersson, L., & Trudgill, P. (1990). *Bad language*. Oxford: Blackwell.

Beykont, Z. (Ed.) (2002). *The power of culture: Teaching across language difference*. Cambridge, MA: Harvard Educational Publishing.

Bradac, J., Cargile, A., & Hallett, J. (2001). Language attitudes: Retrospect, conspect and prospect. In W. P. Robinson & H. Giles (Eds.), *The new handbook of language and social psychology* (pp. 137–158). Chichester: Wiley.

Bragg, M., & Ellis, S. (1976). *Word of mouth*. London: BBC Television.

Carr, J., & Pauwels, A. (2006). *Boys and foreign language learning: Real boys don't do languages*. Basingstoke: Palgrave Macmillan.

Chao, Y. R. (1943). Languages and dialects in China. *The Geographical Journal*, 102, 63–66.

Dragojevic, M., Mastro, D., Giles, H., & Sink, A. (2016). Silencing nonstandard speakers: A content analysis of accent portrayals on American primetime television. *Language in Society*, 45, 59–85.

Edwards, J. (1985). *Language, society and identity*. Oxford: Blackwell.

Edwards, J. (1989). *Language and disadvantage* (2nd ed.). London: Cole & Whurr.

Edwards, J. (1995). *Multilingualism*. London: Penguin.

Edwards, J. (2009). *Language and identity.* Cambridge: Cambridge University Press.
Edwards, J. (2010). *Language diversity in the classroom.* Bristol: Multilingual Matters.
Edwards, J. (2011). *Challenges in the social life of language.* Basingstoke: Palgrave Macmillan.
Edwards, J. (2013). *Sociolinguistics: A very brief introduction.* Oxford and New York: Oxford University Press.
Edwards, J. (2017). The sociology of language teaching and learning. In E. Hinkel (Ed.), *Handbook of research in second language teaching and learning: Volume 3,* 3–14. Oxford and New York: Routledge.
Edwards, J., & McKinnon, M. (1987). The continuing appeal of disadvantage as deficit. *Canadian Journal of Education, 12,* 330–349.
Flores, N. de la Z., & Hopper, R. (1975). Mexican Americans' evaluations of spoken Spanish and English. *Speech Monographs, 42,* 91–98.
Fordham, S. (1999). Dissin' "the standard": Ebonics as guerrilla warfare at Capital High. *Anthropology & Education Quarterly, 30,* 272–293.
Gaine, C. (2005). *We're all white, thanks: The persisting myth about 'White' schools.* Stoke-on-Trent: Trentham.
Garrett, P. (2010). *Attitudes to language.* Cambridge: Cambridge University Press.
Garrett, P., Coupland, N., & Williams, A. (2003). *Investigating language attitudes.* Cardiff: University of Wales Press.
Giles, H., & Billings, A. (2004). Assessing language attitudes: Speaker evaluation studies. In A. Davies & C. Elder (Eds.), *The handbook of applied linguistics* (pp. 187–209). Oxford: Blackwell.
Giles, H., & Bourhis, R. (1975). Linguistic assimilation: West Indians in Cardiff. *Language Sciences, 38,* 9–12.
Giles, H., and Bourhis, R. (1976). Black speakers with white speech: A real problem? In G. Nickel (Ed.), *Proceedings of the fourth international congress on applied linguistics: Volume 1* (pp. 575–584). Stuttgart: Hochschul Verlag.
Giles, H., Bourhis, R., & Davies, A. (1979). Prestige speech styles: The imposed norm and inherent value hypotheses. In W. McCormack & S. Wurm (Eds.), *Language and society* (pp. 589–596). The Hague: Mouton.
Giles, H., Bourhis, R., Trudgill, P., & Lewis, A. (1974). The imposed norm hypothesis: A validation. *Quarterly Journal of Speech, 60,* 405–410.
Giles, H., & Edwards, J. (2010). Attitudes to language: Past, present and future. In K. Malmkjær (Ed.) *Linguistics encyclopedia* (3rd ed., pp. 35–40). Oxford: Routledge.
Giles, H., Katz, V., & Myers, P. (2006). Language attitudes and the role of community infrastructure. *Moderna Språk, 100,* 38–54.
Godley, A., Carpenter, B., & Werner, C. (2007). "I'll speak in proper slang": Language ideologies in a daily editing activity. *Reading Research Quarterly, 42,* 100–131.
Halliday, M. (1968). The users and uses of language. In J. Fishman (Ed.), *Readings in the sociology of language* (pp. 139–169). The Hague: Mouton.
Joos, M. (1967). *The five clocks.* New York: Harcourt, Brace & World.
Karlgren, B. (1962). *Sound and symbol in Chinese.* Hong Kong: Hong Kong University Press. [first published in London: Oxford University Press, 1923.]
Kautzsch, A. (2006). Review of *African American English* (Lisa Green). *Language in Society, 35,* 149–152.
Kissau, S. (2006). Gender differences in motivation to learn French. *Canadian Modern Language Review, 62,* 401–422.
Kratochvil, P. (1968). *The Chinese language today.* London: Hutchinson.
Labov, W. (1969). The logic of nonstandard English. *Georgetown Monographs on Language and Linguistics, 22,* 1–31.

Labov, W. (1976). *Language in the inner city*. Philadelphia: University of Pennsylvania Press.

Lambert, W., Hodgson, R., Gardner, R., & Fillenbaum, S. (1960). Evaluational reactions to spoken languages. *Journal of Abnormal and Social Psychology, 60*, 44–51.

Lippi-Green, R. (1997). *English with an accent: Language, ideology and discrimination in the United States*. London: Routledge.

Marlow, M., & Giles, H. (2010). "We won't get ahead speaking like that!" Expressing and managing language criticism in Hawai'i. *Journal of Multilingual and Multicultural Development, 31*, 237–251.

Ogbu, J. (1999). Beyond language: Ebonics, proper English and identity in a Black-American speech community. *American Educational Research Journal, 36*, 147–184.

Orwell, G. (1970a). The lion and the unicorn: Socialism and the English genius. In S. Orwell & I. Angus (Eds.), *The collected essays, journalism and letters of George Orwell, volume II* (pp. 74–134). Harmondsworth: Penguin. [This essay was first published by Secker and Warburg in 1941.]

Orwell, G. (1970b). The English people. In S. Orwell & I. Angus (Eds.), *The collected essays, journalism and letters of George Orwell, volume III* (pp. 15–56). Harmondsworth: Penguin. [Written in 1944, this essay first appeared in 1947, as part of the *Britain in Pictures* series published by Collins.]

Pearce, S. (2005). *You wouldn't understand: White teachers in multiethnic classrooms*. Stoke-on-Trent: Trentham.

Petyt, K. (1980). *The study of dialect*. London: André Deutsch.

Preston, D. (Ed.). (2003). *Needed research in American dialects*. Durham, NC: Duke University Press.

Ramsey, S.R. (1987). *The languages of China*. Princeton: Princeton University Press.

Robinson, P. (1965). The elaborated code in working-class language. *Language and Speech, 8*, 243–252.

Rushton, J., & Young, G. (1975). Context and complexity in working-class language. *Language and Speech, 8*, 366–387.

Ryan, E. (1979). Why do low-prestige varieties persist? In H. Giles & R. St Clair (Eds.), *Language and social psychology* (pp. 145–157). Oxford: Blackwell.

Siegel, J. (2007). Creoles and minority dialects in education: An update. *Language and Education, 21*, 66–86.

Smitherman, G. (Ed.). (1981a). *Black English and the education of Black children and youth: Proceedings of the national invitational symposium on the King decision*. Detroit: Center for Black Studies, Wayne State University.

Smitherman, G. (1981b). "What go round come round": King in perspective. *Harvard Educational Review, 51*, 40–56.

Smitherman, G. (2006). *Word from the mother: Language and African Americans*. London: Routledge.

Trudgill, P. (1975). *Accent, dialect and the school*. London: Edward Arnold.

Walsh, C. (1991). *Pedagogy and the struggle for voice*. New York: Bergin & Garvey.

Weinreich, M. (1945). Der YIVO un di problemen fun undzer tsayt. *Yivo-Bleter, 25*(1), 3–18.

Wolfram, W., & Christian, D. (1989). *Dialects and education: Issues and answers*. Englewood Cliffs, NJ: Prentice-Hall.

Wyld, H. (1934). The best English: A claim for the superiority of received standard English. *Society for Pure English*, 4(39), 603–621.

Xu, D. (2016). Speech community theory and the language/dialect debate. *Journal of Asian Pacific Communication, 26*, 8–31.

Yingmei, J. S. Z. (2016). Attitude, maintenance, and use of Beijing dialect and Putonghua among younger generation Beijing-born residents. *Journal of Asian Pacific Communication, 26*, 32–55.

Zéphir, F. (1997). Haitian Creole language and bilingual education in the United States: Problem, right or resource? *Journal of Multilingual and Multicultural Development, 18,* 223–237.

Zéphir, F. (1999). Challenges for multicultural education: Sociolinguistic parallels between African American English and Haitian Creole. *Journal of Multilingual and Multicultural Development, 20,* 134–154.

2
THE ELUSIVE DIALECT BORDER

Dick Smakman and Marten van der Meulen

Introduction

The outlines of national languages are relatively uncontested, as they often coincide with generally agreed-upon political borders. However, drawing boundaries between language varieties that are not national languages is often more challenging. For example, language varieties do not always stop at political borders, such as is the case for Spanish in South America and for Russian in Europe. Smaller varieties also cross national borders, as is the case for the dialects that are part of the South Slavic dialect continuum, which runs through Bosnia, Serbia, and Croatia. Moreover, such dialect continua may be interrupted in unexpected ways. For instance, speakers of the language varieties Rakhaing, Intha, and Tavoyan, which are classified as dialects of Burman, all view their own dialects as being separate and non-Burman. Indeed another issue is the views of speakers themselves. As an illustration, speakers of Palaung varieties, as spoken in Burma, China, and Thailand, often claim that they speak one and the same language, yet they are not usually mutually intelligible (Müller & Weymouth, 2016). All of these factors present challenges for those wishing to draw boundaries between language varieties.

The most obvious and common criterion to separate one language variety from another is linguistic. This is how traditional dialectology has operated since the 19th century, as exemplified by the establishment of geographical boundaries for the Linguistic Atlas of France (Guilliéron & Edmont, 1902–1910). While drawing dialect boundaries has always been challenging, in today's highly mobile and linguistically versatile world new challenges have presented themselves.

Chapter overview

This chapter discusses the dividing lines between dialects. It firstly describes what we generally know about dialects. The distinction between 'dialect' and 'language' is explored, as is the geographical and social distribution of dialects and the differences between rural and urban dialects. After that, ten ways to delineate dialects are discussed, particularly the distinction between linguistic and perceived boundaries.

Dialect

Definition

Various definitions of dialect exist. The European Charter for Regional or Minority Languages (CoE, 1992) referred to 'regional or minority languages' as languages that 'are traditionally used within a given territory of a State by nationals of that State who form a group numerically smaller than the rest of the State's population; and [which are] different from the official language(s) of that State' (1–2). This agrees with the general definition of dialect. For Ethnologue (Lewis, Simons, & Fennig, 2014), dialects are the result of the interplay between linguistic characteristics, shared history, and ethnic identity. Dictionary definitions often refer to geographical and linguistic features (deviation from the language norm) to define and distinguish dialects, as is the case for Italian (Gabrielli, 2015) and, for instance, Albanian (Cipo, Çabej, Domi, Krajni, & Myderrizi, 2005).

Whether a language variety should be referred to as 'language' or 'dialect' is not always straightforward. For example, while Abruzzese is often considered to be a dialect of Italian, from a historical perspective it stems from a different branch of the Romance family, making it a sister language of Italian rather than a dialect. Cantonese is another language variety that is officially a dialect, but its codification as well as its broad usage and functions would make it seem to be a language.

The definition of 'dialect' adhered to in this chapter is that a dialect is a language variety that is in some way distinct from the standard language and that has developed relatively freely from prescriptive codification. This definition is in accordance with definitions found in dictionaries. Examples of such varieties are the dialect of Hokkaido (Northern Japan), the Geordie dialect (North East England), and dialects such as Appalachian, Minnesotan, or Texan English (United States of America). Although laymen generally associate dialects with rural areas, urban dialects, such as the Cologne dialect (Germany) and the Beijing dialect (China), are also considered parts of the dialect landscape.

Linguistic characteristics

Dialects constitute fully fledged linguistic systems. The reason to use the word 'dialect' rather than 'language' is to distinguish it from the codified language norm (which might be called the 'standard', 'official' or 'national' language). Unlike the language norm, dialects are less likely to receive official acceptance and support. Also, they are less likely to be codified and used in formal and official settings. This indirectly affects the actual linguistic features of dialects. For example, the intonation patterns of dialects and norm languages may be different, because these two varieties are associated with different registers and different communicative contexts. Also, the norm language often has a larger lexicon, because it covers a broader range of functions and registers. Dialects are more often used in less formal situations (i.e., at home or between friends), and they are associated mostly with spoken communication, which means that they are not usually constrained in their development and usage by a written norm.

Another linguistic observation is that the linguistic distance between different types of dialects and the broader language norm can differ: in general, urban dialects tend to be closer to a broader language norm than rural dialects are. For example, the distinctive Beijing dialect is close to Standard Mandarin Chinese (Xu, 1992). Similarly, the urban dialect of Tokyo is linguistically close to Standard Japanese (Inoue, 1991). Finally, the Palestinian city dialects are known to resemble the city dialects of nearby Lebanon and Western Syria without being direct neighbours (Al-Wer, 2002). This linguistic sameness among urban dialects and their closeness to the language norm are due to trade and political relations and to communication among cities.

Determining dialect borders

Border types

Borders between dialects can be drawn on the basis of several criteria. These criteria often overlap and none of them is ever the only factor in establishing dividing lines. Nevertheless, an effort is made here to discuss them separately. The most obvious border is a linguistic one. Besides linguistic borders, there are perceptual borders that exist in the minds or lay speakers, including the speakers of the dialects themselves. Furthermore, there are socio-historical factors that may have played a role in the emergence of these borders. Factors we discuss in this sense are geography, politics, and religion. Finally, there are dialect borders that depend on factors emerging in changing societies and are related to communication and identity. These are ethnic borders, identity borders, social connotations borders, and communication-based borders.

1. Linguistic borders

Dialects are most often distinguished on the basis of linguistic characteristics. Dialect speakers have linguistic traits in common and these can be used to identify them as a group and to distinguish them from other groups. As Chambers and Trudgill (1998) stated, the traditional method of linguistically separating language varieties is by drawing isoglosses, lines 'marking the boundaries between two regions which differ with respect to some linguistic feature' (89). These linguistic features are mostly lexical and phonetic. Usually, dialects are separated by bundles of such isoglosses, where a number of isoglosses fall more or less together. In the 19th century, research was done in several European countries to establish dialect boundaries by closely investigating the ways local speakers pronounced words or made lexical choices. The best known example is the research that was done in France (Guilliéron & Edmont, 1902–1910), which established French dialect borders. From this and similar research arose the boundary in France between the dialects of the north (*langue d'oc*) and those of the south (*langue d'oil*) (Jochnowitz, 1973).

Modern-day efforts are being made to calculate the linguistic distance between dialects by Chiswick and Miller (2005), among others, who applied so-called Levenshtein distances to linguistics. This measure calculates the distance between two items based on the minimum number of single-character edits (insertions, deletions, or substitutions) that are required to change one item (lexical or phonemic, for instance) into the other. This method was used by, among others, Valls et al. (2012) for Catalan dialects, by Osenova, Heeringa, and Nerbonne (2009) for Bulgarian dialects, and by Heeringa, Johnson, and Gooskens (2009) for Norwegian dialects.

Nevertheless, no uniform approach exists for quantifying the linguistic distance between dialects. Lexical relatedness, and particularly the sharing of cognates, is an important predictor of linguistic distance, and it deserves more attention in determining linguistic distance and boundaries; the more cognate words dialects share, the lower the linguistic distance. Dividing lines are even thinner if these etymologically related words mean the same or similar things. German *sterben* ('to die') and English 'to starve' share an etymological source but do not mean the same thing, while German *sterben* and (neighbouring) Dutch *sterven* mean the same thing. Cognates may even have opposite meanings, like Polish *biały* ('white') and English *black*. So, besides the percentage of cognates, the percentage of semantically similar or identical cognates should be counted. Besides cognates, other aspects that are often measured are similarities of syntax and written forms.

Increased linguistic, methodological, and historical awareness may lead to the reconsideration of firmly established dialect borders, and it could in fact lead to the acknowledgement of new dialects or languages. A recent example is Kashubian, as spoken in the Pomorze region in North West Poland. Long considered a dialect of Polish, it is now increasingly treated as a separate language on linguistic grounds (Szul, 2015). This language contains a number of features that do not exist in Polish dialects, such as nine distinct vowels (standard Polish has only five), and some of its subdialects have phonemic word stress, unlike Polish. This recent acceptance is partly of a political nature, but it could not have taken place without developments in the field of linguistics.

2. Perceived borders

Researchers may try to employ objective criteria to draw lines between dialects, but dialect speakers may (partly) disagree with these borders, based on their perception of and attitudes towards dialects and their boundaries. Such views are relevant because they have been shown to be a factor in the maintenance or shaping of dialect borders (Britain, 2014). Several methods have so far been tried out to measure perceived language borders.

The Dutch dialectologist Weijnen (1946, 1947) developed the so-called *pijltjes-methode* ('Arrows Method'). After asking informants to name places in their own region where people spoke either the same or differently, Weijnen drew arrows between places that were marked as similar, while drawing borders between places that were never marked as such. In this way, perceived micro-dialectal areas could be identified. Weijnen's method received criticism on several points. For instance, he failed to demarcate what he meant by one's 'own' region/surroundings, i.e., the point of view of participants. Furthermore, he only focussed on similarities and did not deal with contradictory results (Goeman, 1989; Preston, 1999), although these are equally relevant. Perhaps because of the criticism, but also probably because of the complications regarding aggregating results, the Arrows Method remains little used.

In Japan, the so-called Degree-of-Difference method (Grootaers, 2000 [1959]; Mase, 1999 [1964]) was developed. Informants were asked to grade the similarity of the language in surrounding areas on a scale from one to four. Based on these results, dialect areas could be defined. A third method uses the map-drawing technique by Preston (1982), who built on practices developed in perceptual geography. Preston asked informants to draw dialect areas on maps and give (linguistic) characteristics of speakers in the drawn areas. By aggregating results of individual participants, estimates could be made as to where perceptual dialect boundaries lay. The map-drawing task has received quite a following, like Pearce (2011) and Montgomery (2012), especially since computational methods for calculating and plotting aggregates have become easier. It has now been used in a variety of other countries, including Turkey (Demirci & Kleiner, 1999), Germany (Dailey-O'Cain, 1999), Canada (McKinnie & Dailey-O'Cain, 2002), and New Zealand (Nielsen & Hay, 2006). A general problem with perceived borders is that they may be strongly influenced by political or geographical boundaries, and, more importantly, may vary widely between speakers. However, this may be solved by the increasingly robust statistical methods that are used to aggregate perceptions.

In most cases, perceptual borders in these investigations agreed with traditional borders, but in some cases, dialect borders that dialectologists considered to exist were not distinguished by participants or were located differently. In such cases, researchers have tried to combine linguistic and perceptual results. Daan and Blok (1969) did this for Dutch and Benson (2003) worked on data for Ohio in the United States.

3. Geographical borders

Natural landmarks, such as mountain ranges, rivers, or impenetrable forests, can hinder communication or even prevent it, resulting in linguistic differences and ultimately different dialects. The Fens, an area in East England, are an example of a region where this happened. Here, the marshes between towns and villages were a natural obstacle, both real and perceived, that hindered travel. This geographical characteristic created a sense of distance and this negatively affected the intensity of communication (Britain, 2014; Britain & Trudgill, 2005), and, as a result, it affected dialect formation and dialect boundaries. Research by Calabrese et al. (2011) in the United

States of America showed that even perceptions of natural boundaries (especially distance) affect communication, which was in line with the findings on the Fens area.

It may even be that geographical features that are no longer relevant are still an indication of historically evolved boundaries. Britain (2014) demonstrated how, despite the disappearance of certain obstacles in the landscape in the English Fens (the marshes were largely drained in the 17th century), the effects of old geographically motivated dialect boundaries remain relatively persistent today. Conversely, geographical features do not always affect dialect formation. As Beswick (2014) explained, landscape obstacles may be of limited importance if cross-border communication is still lively. Beswick took the Minho River as an example, which separates Portugal and Galicia, but which has had little dialectological impact.

4. Political borders

Political and local government borders affect mobility and can thus shape dialect areas. The existence of political borders may induce people to adjust their language and may affect dialect formation. In the Kleverland dialect continuum, the Dutch and German dialects diverged under the influence of the state border (Giesbers, 2008) between the Netherlands and Germany. Other examples are the differences in pronunciation in the two parts of the Dutch language area (the Netherlands and northern Belgium), which are increasing although the political dividing line is weak (Van de Velde, 1996). At the Scottish/English border, too, the national border affects dialect use on either side (Watt, Llamas, Docherty, Hall, & Nycz, 2014).

The natural, language contact-induced shaping of dialects may in fact be overruled by politics. Some dialects are even separated from neighbouring ones through political or ideological lines. For example, Chinese children are generally taught that Cantonese is a dialect of Chinese, which is not true from a linguistic or sociolinguistic point of view.

5. Economic borders

Economic motivations are an important impetus for linguistic contact. The ensuing language contact is known to create linguistic similarities and have a levelling effect. Comparing results of a late 19th century German dialect survey with current data, Falck, Heblich, Lameli, and Südekum (2010) combined economic, linguistic, cultural, and historical information to discover whether 21st century economic exchanges are still affected by cultural borders laid in the past. Their research confirmed that many such borders are indeed time-persistent and continue to determine modern-day economic exchange, thereby still affecting dialects.

6. Religious borders

The distribution of religion may divide or connect speakers of dialects, as people often have more contact with likeminded people. Fox (2010), Baker and Bowie (2009), Hamburger (2005), and Di Paolo (1993) investigated religion as a means of identifying groups of speakers and all concluded that religion can impact one's speech and, as a result, dialect borders.

Religion may in fact lead to a reshuffling of language and dialect borders. For instance, after the fall of Yugoslavia in the 1990s, the population in Croatia spoke three main dialects. The new Croatian government wanted their own distinctive language, as did the neighbouring new country of Serbia. In the existing dialect continuum, lines could not be drawn on the basis of linguistic differences, and instead, religious affiliation became the criterion. Most inhabitants of the Serbian part of the dialect were Orthodox and most of the dialect speakers on the Croatian side were Catholic. The difference between the two languages was emphasised by the promotion on the Catholic side of the Roman script and on the Orthodox side of the Cyrillic script, thus creating an even deeper schism within the area through orthography.

7. Ethnic borders

Ethnicity is strongly associated with borders between language varieties of all kinds. The South African situation is a good example of this. Ethnicity is an inherited quality that groups of people share and often identify with. It is a combination of shared cultural heritage, ancestry, history, religion, mythology and ritual, cuisine, dressing style, art, physical appearance, and, for instance, homeland. The more of these features people have in common, the stronger their shared ethnicity. This joint identification is rooted in a set of shared social, cultural, and ancestral experiences, an important one of which is language. If a shared language is seen as being the distinctive feature of an ethnic group, then this group has an ethnolinguistic identity. This means that other features of the group are less visible than language. The Gaels are an example of an ethnolinguistic group. This group is indigenous to northwestern Europe and is most strongly associated with a certain language, namely Gaelic, which comprises several branches that are not necessarily mutually intelligible, such as Irish, Manx, and Scottish Gaelic. Language is the only real way in which this group is distinct from their English-speaking neighbours.

While often associated with rural living, ethnic dialect formation also takes place in urban settings. Wardhaugh and Fuller (2014) emphasised that ethnic dialects in such settings are not the same as foreign accents of a majority language. Their speakers, as they pointed out, are native speakers of the majority language. Ethnic dialects act as in-group ways of speaking the majority language. An example of such an urban ethnolinguistic group are speakers of African American Vernacular English, which is often unambiguously referred to as African American English, because it is spoken primarily by Americans of African descent. Denham and Lobeck (2010) felt that this type of English should be defined as an ethnic rather than a regional dialect, although it is associated with certain neighbourhoods.

8. Identity borders

It should be clear that ethnicity and identity strongly interact. In societies based on migration, such as Australia and the United States, speakers from different ethnic backgrounds are nowadays often in continuous and close contact with other ethnic groups. Ethnolinguistic identity then starts to function as a strong identity marker (Wolfram & Ward, 2006). The British sociologist Maher (2005) proposed the phenomenon of 'metro-ethnicity', defining it as 'a hybridized "street" ethnicity deployed by a cross-section of people with ethnic or mainstream backgrounds who are oriented towards cultural hybridity, cultural/ethnic tolerance and a multicultural lifestyle in friendships, music, the arts, eating and dress' (83). In this view, individuals play with ethnicities, both from their own background and those from others, for aesthetic effect, without being sentimental about ethnic markers such as language. This goes against the essentialist view of a fixed set of basic attributes belonging to individuals that determine their identity, with these speakers living in a certain place and sharing dialect features.

Cornips and De Rooij (2013) and Cornips, Jaspers, and De Rooij (2015) revealed the possible mechanisms of identity assertion in large cities. They demonstrated how ethnically mixed groups may highlight mutual differences in communication with other such groups by giving different meanings and connotations to existing language items. Certain connotations of words were associated with certain neighbourhoods in Amsterdam, the Netherlands. Dyer (2001) also demonstrated identity mechanisms when she found that younger speakers in the English town of Corby seemingly consciously used a pronunciation characteristic that was not part of their village's dialect, but rather a feature of their ancestors' Scottish heritage. Watt et al. (2014), furthermore, showed how a national border can function as an identity border by referring to the break in the dialect continuum that occurs at the Scottish/English border, while on both sides non-standard English is the daily language of communication. Aitken (1992) even considered the bundle of isoglosses at this border to be excessively high. In view of separatist sentiments in Scotland, it can be assumed that the Scottish differentiation from England-based dialect styles is particularly active. As Boberg (2014) showed, the border between Canada and the United States has a similar identity function.

9. Social connotations borders

Traditionally, dialects have a strong association with certain speakers and a particular way of living. As Chambers and Trudgill (1998) stated: 'In common usage, [...] dialect is a substandard, low-status, often rustic form of language, generally associated with the peasantry' (3). Two images of dialects tend to emerge in lay circles. First, there is the dialect as a linguistic deviation from the norm, which is spoken by speakers of questionable repute and with little social success. The more romantic interpretation is that of a language variety full of character, as used in a certain region by kind and helpful people, who are typically farmers. This language represents local customs and folklore. Chambers and Trudgill (1998) famously describe the biases even early dialectologists had in selecting informants: the typical dialect speakers were Non-mobile, Older, Rural Males (NORMs), selected because of the stability of the linguistic influences that they have been exposed to during their lives. With less mobility comes less adjustment to a broader norm. A low educational level is also associated with dialects. While in lay circles, dialects are associated with rural regions, cities also hold dialects. Speakers of these dialects are also associated with less mobility and a low educational level. Urban speakers might typically have a blue-collar profession, like factory worker.

Evaluation research – as described, for instance, by Fasold (1987) – in which dialect speakers were contrasted with speakers of the norm language and speakers of city dialects, has provided a more nuanced picture of the way dialect speakers are viewed. A study by Šimičić and Sujoldžić (2004) illustrates this well. This investigation focussed on the evaluation of characteristics of speakers of Standard Croatian and of Croatian dialects. They showed that a rural dialect speaker was evaluated very positively for social attractiveness but very low for status. Conversely, in the same study the speaker of Standard Croatian was evaluated as high in competence but low in social attractiveness. The study also showed that an urban dialect may be evaluated on the basis of its closeness to the standard, with stereotypical speakers of urban dialects that are closer to the norm being evaluated similarly to speakers of that norm language.

Modern-day situations are often at odds with the stereotypical images described above. As for rural dialects, it is common for educated speakers to speak (or choose to speak) a dialect. In the Dutch province of Limburg, for instance, this is very common. A local GP, who is university educated and who may or may not be originally from the area, will function as bilingual in his/her local practice and speak the dialect in many cases.

It is common for a city dialect to carry a certain prestige, even outside its own geographical area. Consequently, the prototypical urban dialect speaker is nowadays defined as a progressive and ambitious dialect speaker. Cairene Arabic is a prestigious city dialect in Egypt, for instance, and other dialects from the capitals of countries in this region have a similar type of status; for instance, the dialect from Casablanca in Morocco (Hachimi, 2007) and that of Tripoli in Libya (Bassiouney, 2015; Pereira, 2007). Ambitious people, including ambitious newcomers to the city, seem drawn to these urban dialects. Goeman (2000) put forward the urban equivalent of NORMs, the 'MYSFs' ('Mobile Younger Suburban Females'). This group will typically be likely to speak a more urban dialect or a dialect that is between that of the local city dialect and a broader language norm. This reinforces the mixed association of dialects with social ambition.

10. Communication-based borders

Before the twentieth century, language contact necessarily took place through face-to-face contact among individuals. With the steady growth of non-face-to-face contact, old geographical dividing lines are increasingly being challenged. Modern-day speakers spend growing amounts of time communicating from a distance, either talking on the phone or online or through texting (Barasa, 2015). In the post-modern age, digital communities are emerging, which are not restricted by geographical boundaries but defined partially by digital interactions. This seriously challenges the concept of map-drawn dialect boundaries.

Research done at IBM Research, MIT Senseable City Lab, and AT&T Labs (Calabrese et al., 2011) revealed data on digital communication among people in the United States of America that put regional boundaries in a different perspective. The researchers used information on social connectedness through telephone and SMS interactions among inhabitants. The maps and other data arising from this investigation into anonymised and aggregated mobile phone data, which was not collected for any sociolinguistic purpose, proved highly insightful regarding the formation of new speech communities and the nature of the dividing lines between them.

On the basis of phone connectedness, some adjacent states became separated, while other states merged. The researchers found the age of communicators to be the determining factor; young people text more eagerly and intensively and they do so with their age counterparts rather than with other generations. SMS communications, in addition, turned out to cover shorter distances than phone calls and were thus less likely to affect connectedness beyond the state level. More, and smaller, communities emerged this way. Similar research was done in Great Britain, by Ratti et al. (2010), and communities emerging from phone contact there turned out to be more cohesive than communities existing on the basis of geographical and administrative boundaries. It should be noted that Ratti et al. (2010) looked at landline phone communication, which may have affected older rather than younger people.

Rural and urban dialects are developing differently, so the above investigations suggest. Contact among nearby cities is leading to mutual similarities between cities that traditional language contact cannot account for. This approach provides a means to delineate geographical areas on the basis of relationships between people. As it turned out, the named connectedness sometimes follows traditional demarcations such as state lines.

Conclusion

Traditionally, 'dialect' referred to a language that deviates from the norm language and is identifiable on a combination of linguistic grounds and associated with a specific (limited) geographical spread and a certain type of speaker. It is passed on naturally and subconsciously from generation to generation, often in a monolingual situation, and gradually changes intergenerationally under little outside pressure as part of a dialect continuum. While this type of dialect is still quite common, it has been superseded by new settings of dialect usage. Mostly, new situations arise because of a higher number of competing languages and the changed mobility of speakers. Urban dialects are increasingly considered to be part of the dialect landscape.

The number of languages that dialects compete with is growing. Multilingual and semi-speakers of various varieties, including dialects, are growing in number in areas that were originally reserved for dialects and perhaps one more language, namely the norm language. This change is disrupting the general view of dialects, which was that they are default communication systems for monolinguals that were sometimes under pressure only from the language norm of the larger area.

Newer generations are nowadays often born and raised in a situation where they are exposed to a range of languages of which their dialect is just one. As a result, they do not automatically pick up only the dialect during their critical period. Instead, they acquire a dominant language (possibly the dialect) and are faced with a choice as to what to do with the other languages on offer. While dialects are still being passed on as a default communication tool, increasing numbers of dialect speakers nowadays have the choice to speak the dialect, reject it, speak it in a 'mild' form, or simply adopt some identifying features of the dialect. They can use the dialect for certain symbolic reasons besides communicative ones, and they may use the dialect or selected stylised features outside the original area of origin of the dialect.

The high degree of fluidity in the individual use of dialects nowadays by many multilingual speakers is a challenge to those wanting to draw dialect boundaries. Traditional dialect speakers, whose lives are in line with the above-named traditional stereotypes, are still high in number, and the geographical areas associated with dialects are often still largely in place, but the notion of a linguistically and geographically static dialect can now increasingly be called into question. All types of mobilities as well as individual choices and identity negotiation call for new ways to approach the outlines of these language varieties.

References

Aitken, A. J. (1992). Scots. In T. McArthur (Ed.), *The Oxford companion to the English language* (pp. 893–899). Oxford: Oxford University Press.

Al-Wer, E. (2002). Jordanian and Palestinian dialects in contact: Vowel raising in Amman. In A. Jones & E. Esch (Eds.), *Language change: The interplay of internal, external and extra-linguistic factors* (pp. 63–79). Berlin: Mouton de Gruyter.

Baker, W., & Bowie, D. (2009). Religious affiliation as a correlate of linguistic behaviour. *University of Pennsylvania Working Papers in Linguistics*, 15(2), 1–10.

Barasa, S. N. (2015). Ala! Kumbe? "Oh my! Is it so?" Multilingualism controversies in East Africa. In D. Smakman & P. Heinrich (Eds.), *Globalising sociolinguistics: Challenging and expanding theories* (pp. 39–53). London: Routledge.

Bassiouney, R. (2015). *Language and identity in modern Egypt*. Edinburgh: Edinburgh University Press.

Benson, E. J. (2003). Folk linguistic perceptions and the mapping of dialect boundaries. *American Speech*, 78(3), 307–330.

Beswick, J. (2014). Borders within borders: Contexts of language use and local identity configuration in Southern Galicia. In D. Watt & C. Llamas (Eds.), *Language, borders and identity* (pp. 105–117). Edinburgh: Edinburgh University Press.

Boberg, C. (2014). Borders in North American English. In D. Watt & C. Llamas (Eds.), *Language, borders and identity* (pp. 44–54). Edinburgh: Edinburgh University Press.

Britain, D. (2014). Where North meets South? Contact, divergence and the routinisation of the Fenland dialect boundary. In D. Watt & C. Llamas (Eds.), *Language, borders and identity* (pp. 27–43). Edinburgh: Edinburgh University Press.

Britain, D., & Trudgill, P. (2005). New dialect formation and contact-induced reallocation: Three case studies from the English Fens. *International Journal of English Studies*, 5(1), 183–209.

Calabrese, F., Dahlem, D., Gerber, A., Paul, D., Chen, X., Rowland, J., Rath, C., & Ratti, C. (2011). *The Connected States of America: Quantifying social radii of influence*. Paper presented at The Third IEEE International Conference on Social Computing (SocialCom 2011), Boston.

Chambers, J. K., & Trudgill, P. (1998). *Dialectology* (2nd ed.). Cambridge: Cambridge University Press.

Chiswick, B. R., & Miller, P. W. (2005). Linguistic distance: A quantitative measure of the distance between English and other languages. *Journal of Multilingual and Multicultural Development*, 26(1), 1–11.

Cipo, K., Çabej, E., Domi, M., Krajni, A., & Myderrizi, O. (Eds.). (2005). *Fjalor i Gjuhës Shqipe [Dictionary of the Albanian Language]*. Tirana: Botime Çabej.

CoE. (1992). *European charter for regional or minority languages*. European Treaty Series. 148. Retrieved July 20, 2016 from http://humanrights.maltepe.edu.tr/sites/default/files/files/euroepan_charter_for_regional_or_minority_languages-5XI1992.pdf.

Cornips, L., & De Rooij, V. A. (2013). Selfing and othering through categories of race, place, and language among minority youths in Rotterdam, The Netherlands. In P. Siemund, I. Gogolin, M. E. Schulz, & J. Davydova (Eds.), *Multilingualism and language diversity in urban areas: Acquisition, identities, space, education* (pp. 129–164). Amsterdam: John Benjamins.

Cornips, L., Jaspers, J., & De Rooij, V. A. (2015). The politics of labelling youth vernaculars in the Netherlands and Belgium. In J. Nortier & B. A. Svendsen (Eds.), *Language, youth and identity in the 21st century: Linguistic practices across urban spaces* (pp. 45–68). Cambridge: Cambridge University Press.

Daan, J., & Blok, D. (1969). *Van Randstad tot landrand*. Paper presented at the Bijdragen en Mededelingen der Dialectcommissie van de KNAW XXXVI, Amsterdam.

Dailey-O'Cain, J. (1999). The perception of post-unification German regional speech. In D. R. Preston (Ed.), *Handbook of perceptual dialectology* (Vol. 1, pp. 227–242). Amsterdam/Philadelphia: John Benjamins.

Demirci, M., & Kleiner, B. (1999). The perception of Turkish dialects. In D.R. Preston (Ed.), *Handbook of perceptual dialectology* (Vol. 1, pp. 263–282). Amsterdam/Philadelphia: John Benjamins.

Denham, K., & Lobeck, A. (2010). *Linguistics for everyone: An introduction* (2nd ed.). Boston: Wadsworth.

Di Paolo, M. (1993). Propredicate do in the English of the Intermountain West. *American Speech*, 86, 339–356.

Dyer, J. (2001). Changing dialects and identities in a Scottish-English community. *University of Pennsylvania Working Papers in Linguistics*, 7(3), 43–57.

Falck, O., Heblich, S., Lameli, A., & Südekum, J. (2010). *Dialects, cultural identity, and economic exchange*. Bonn: Institute for the Study of Labor.

Fasold, R. W. (1987). *The sociolinguistics of society*. Oxford: Blackwell.

Fox, S. (2010). Ethnicity, religion, and practices: Adolescents in the east end of London. In C. Llamas & D. Watt (Eds.), *Language and identities* (pp. 144–156). Edinburgh: Edinburgh University Press.

Gabrielli, A. (Ed.) (2015). *Grande dizionario Hoepli italiano [Hoepli's great dictionary of Italian]*. Milan: Hoepli.

Giesbers, C. (2008). *Dialecten op de grens van twee talen: Een dialectologisch en sociolinguïstisch onderzoek in het Kleverlands dialectgebied*. Utrecht: LOT.

Goeman, T. (1989). Dialectes et jugements subjectifs des locuteurs. Quelques remarques de méthode a propos d'une controverse [Dialects and the subjective judgments of speakers: Remarks on controversial methods]. In D. Preston (Ed.), *Handbook of perceptual dialectology* (Vol. 1, pp. 135–144). Amsterdam: John Benjamins.

Goeman, T. (2000). Naast NORMs ook MYSFs in het veranderende dialectlandschap en het regiolect [Besides NORMs also MYSFs in the changing dialect landscape and the regiolect]. *Taal en Tongval, 52*(1), 87–100.

Grootaers, W. A. (2000 [1959]). Origin and nature of the subjective boundaries of dialects. *The Japanese Journal of Language in Society, 2*(2), 58–77.

Guilliéron, J., & Edmont, E. (1902–1910). *Atlas Linguistique de la France*. Paris: H. Champion.

Hachimi, A. (2007). Becoming Casablancan: Fessis in Casablanca as a case study. In C. Miller (Ed.), *Arabic in the city: Issues in dialect contact and language variation* (Vol. 5, pp. 97–122). London: Routledge.

Hamburger, L. (2005). The main motivating factors dictating language choices in three Jewish women. *Leeds Working papers in Linguistics and Phonetics, 10*.

Heeringa, W., Johnson, K., & Gooskens, C. (2009). Measuring Norwegian dialect distances using acoustic features. In J.-L. Gauvain, M. G. J. Swerts, & K. Paliwal (Eds.), *Speech communication* (Vol. 51 (2), pp. 167–183). Amsterdam: Elsevier.

Inoue, F. (1991). New dialect and standard language: Style shift in Tokyo. *Area and Culture Studies, 42*, 49–68.

Jochnowitz, G. (1973). *Dialect boundaries and the question of Franco-Provençal*. The Hague/Paris: Mouton.

Lewis, P., Simons, G. F., & Fennig, C. D. (2014). *Ethnologue: Languages of the world 17*. Retrieved November 24, 2015, from www.ethnologue.com

Maher, J. C. (2005). Metroethnicity, language, and the principle of cool. *International Journal of Sociology of Language, 2005*(175/176), 83–102.

Mase, Y. (1964 [1999]). Hôgen ishiki to hôgen kukaku [Dialect consciousness and dialect divisions]. In D. Preston (Ed.), *Handbook of perceptual dialectology* (Vol. 1, pp. 71–99). Amsterdam: John Benjamins.

McKinnie, M., & Dailey-O'Cain, J. (2002). A perceptual dialectology of anglophone Canada from the perspective of young Albertans and Ontarians. In D. Long & D. R. Preston (Eds.), *Handbook of perceptual dialectology* (Vol. 2, pp. 277–294). Amsterdam/Philadelphia: John Benjamins.

Montgomery, C. (2012). The effect of proximity in perceptual dialectology. *Journal of Sociolinguistics, 16*(5), 638–668.

Müller, A., & Weymouth, R. (2016). *Constructing and deconstructing Kachin and Palaung linguistic identities*. Paper presented at the Language, Power and Identity in Asia. Creating and Crossing Language Boundaries, March 14–16, 2016.

Nielsen, D., & Hay, J. (2006). Perceptions of regional dialects in New Zealand. *TeReo, 48*, 95–110.

Osenova, P., Heeringa, W., & Nerbonne, J. (2009). A quantitative analysis of Bulgarian dialect pronunciation. *Zeitschrift für Slavische Philologie, 66*(2), 425–458.

Pearce, M. (2011). Exploring a perceptual dialect boundary in North East England. *Dialectologia et Geolinguistica, 19*, 3–22.

Pereira, C. (2007). Urbanization and dialect change: The Arabic dialect of Tripoli (Libya). In C. Miller & E. Al-Wer (Eds.), *Arabic in the city: Issues in dialect contact and language variation*. London/New York: Routledge.

Preston, D. R. (1982). Perceptual dialectology: Mental maps of the United States dialects from a Hawaiian perspective. *Working Papers in Linguistics (University of Hawaii), 14*, 5–49.

Preston, D. R. (1999). *Perceptual dialectology*. East Lansing: Michigan State University.
Ratti, C., Sobolevsky, S., Calabrese, F., Andris, C., Reades, J., Martino, M., . . . Strogatz, S. H. (2010). Redrawing the map of Great Britain from a network of human interactions. *PLoS ONE*, *5*(12), 1–6.
Šimičić, L., & Sujoldžić, A. (2004). Cultural implications of attitude and evaluative reactions toward dialect variation in Croatian youth. *Collegium antropologicum*, *28*(1), 97–107.
Szul, R. (2015). Poland's language regime governing Kashubian and Silesian. In L. Cardina & S. K. Sonntag (Eds.), *State traditions and language regimes* (pp. 79–96). Montreal/Kingston/London/Ithaca: McGill-Queen's Press.
Valls, E., Nerbonne, J., Prokic, J., Wieling, M., Clua, E., & Lloret, M.-R. (2012). Applying the Levenshtein distance to Catalan dialects: A brief comparison of two dialectometric approaches. *Verba: Anuario Galego de Filoloxia*, *39*, 35–61.
Van de Velde, H. (1996). *Variatie en Verandering in het Standaard-Nederlands (1935–1993) [Variation and change in Standard Dutch (1935–1993)]*. Utrecht: Landelijke Onderzoeksschool Taalwetenschap (LOT).
Wardhaugh, R., & Fuller, J. M. (2014). *An introduction to sociolinguistics* (7th ed.). Malden/Oxford: Wiley-Blackwell.
Watt, D., Llamas, C., Docherty, G., Hall, D., & Nycz, J. (2014). Language and identity on the Scottish/English border. In D. Watt & C. Llamas (Eds.), *Language, borders and identity* (pp. 8–27). Edinburgh: Edinburgh University Press.
Weijnen, A. A. (1946). De grenzen tussen de oost-Noord-Brabantse dialecten onderling. In A. A. Weijnen, J. M. Renders, & J. Van Ginneken (Eds.), *Oost-Noordbrabantse dialectproblemen: Bijdragen en Mededelingen der Dialectencommissie van de Koninklijke Nederlandwe Akademie van Wetenschappen* (Vol. 8, pp. 1–15). Amsterdam: KNAW.
Weijnen, A. A. (1947). *De onderscheiding van dialectgroepen in Noord-Brabant en Limburg [The dividing lines between dialect groups in Noord Brabant and Limburg]*. Paper presented at the Akademiedagen, Amsterdam.
Wolfram, W., & Ward, B. (Eds.). (2006). *American voices: How dialects differ from coast to coast*. Malden/Oxford: Blackwell.
Xu, D. (1992). *A sociolinguistic study of Mandarin nasal variation*. (Ph.D.), University of Ottawa, Ottawa.

3
DIALECT PERFORMANCES IN SUPERDIVERSE COMMUNITIES

The case for ethnographic approaches to language variation

Anna De Fina

Introduction

In this paper I examine the use of Sicilian dialect in identity performances by children of a superdiverse fifth-grade classroom. I use ethnographic observation to analyze how identities are indexed through the deployment of linguistic resources and to investigate the significance attributed to language varieties in different contexts of interaction. I will argue that attention to the details of interaction and to local meaning construction are particularly important in the context of the study of relatively recent sociolinguistic phenomena such as the use of language repertoires in superdiverse communities like the one studied here, as such environments force us to abandon well-trodden paths of sociolinguistic analysis.

I will start with some general considerations on sociolinguistic approaches to language varieties and on how shifts in sociolinguistics have affected the way researchers analyze language varieties and their uses. I will then provide some background on the differences between the standard and dialects in Italy. In the following sections I will introduce the study and present the analysis of the data. I will conclude with a discussion and implications.

Language varieties, dialects, and style

Sociolinguistics has gone through a series of seismic shifts since the 1960s, when William Labov (1966) established the pillars of classical variationism. As noted by Bassiouney in the introduction to this volume, first wave variationism posited a one-to-one relation between social categories such as class, age, territorial origins and the use of specific linguistic variables. Such one-to-one correspondence has been contested and problematized over the years through different waves of sociolinguistic variationism.

According to Eckert:

> The first wave of variation studies established broad correlations between linguistic variables and the macro-sociological categories of socioeconomic class, sex class, ethnicity and age. The second wave employed ethnographic methods to explore the local categories and configurations that inhabit, or constitute, these broader categories.
>
> *(2012, p. 41)*

However, both waves focused on structure and did not pay sufficient attention to agency and to the local construction of meaning through indexical processes. These processes were at the center of the third wave, represented by Eckert's own work on the use of linguistic variables by different groups of students in a Californian high school (see Eckert, 1989).

In the following years sociolinguists continued to problematize some of the most fundamental tenets of variationism: on the one hand, the notion that variation could be studied by isolating sounds or specific syntactic/morphologic phenomena, and on the other, the idea that linguistic varieties could easily be distinguished from each other.

Seminal work on style (see Coupland, 2001) showed for example that style variation is related to bundles of features and that they operate together with "other culturally signifying linguistic and discursive forms" (p. 202) within very specific contexts of interaction. On the other hand, work on conversational code-switching (Auer, 2007) profoundly problematized the possibility of clearly distinguishing codes independently of their context of usage and introduced notions of hybridity and ambiguity such as Woolard's concept of "bivalency" (1999). Finally, work on social media (Androutsopoulos, 2013) superdiversity (see Blommaert & Rampton, 2011) and complexity (De Fina, 2015) has highlighted the need for new theoretical-methodological tools to analyze sociolinguistic situations characterized by the coexistence of people with very different linguistic and cultural backgrounds and by the impact of displacement and mobility. In particular, scholars in this field have highlighted the complexity of migrants' trajectories and their internal diversity, the inadequacy of the notion of "speech community" to capture ways in which indexicalities are managed and understood, and the existence of hybrid linguistic phenomena that go well beyond classic language mixing and code-switching, since they often involve the use of multiple semiotic resources within multiple modalities.

These trends led towards the recent shift in sociolinguistic studies towards ethnography-based and practice-oriented studies of dialect which focus on the concrete processes through which indexicalities are created and interpreted, on the simultaneous use of linguistic and other semiotic resources, and on the convergence of different scales in the production and interpretation of meanings. As I have argued elsewhere, one way of looking at the way indexicalities are managed and interpreted is, for example, through the lens of the "chronotope" (see Blommert & De Fina, 2017) as a construct that allows for the analysis of ways in which performances and their interpretation of those performances is closely contextualized and tied to subtle shifts in time/space configurations. As we will see below, linguistic resources do indeed work in different ways according to different time-space configurations in the classroom.

Dialects and the standard in Italy

Let me first introduce the notion of "dialect" as used in the Italian context, since it reflects the particularities of language development in that country. Italian "dialects" are vernacular languages that mostly developed from Latin in interaction with local varieties. These vernaculars are extremely different from each other given the particular history of each of the Italian regions in which they are spoken: some vernaculars are mutually intelligible with Standard Italian (which developed from the Tuscan vernacular), some are not intelligible, some have a rich written tradition, and some don't. These difference notwithstanding, most Italian regional languages have been lumped under the category of "dialects" (see De Mauro, 1963). Sicilian belongs to the group of so called "extreme southern" varieties and it is not intelligible to Italian speakers from most other regions. Although the grammatical structure of Sicilian is similar to that of Italian, its pronunciation and vocabulary are very different from those of the standard, due to the influence of the many languages spoken by the different foreign invaders and settlers who inhabited the island. Sicily is also one of the regions in which dialect is spoken the most not only among older people but also among the youth (Assenza, 2006; D'Agostino, 2007; D'Agostino & Scarpella, 2008).

The status of dialect among language varieties spoken in Italy has been a focus of discussion and conjecture among linguists (see Sobrero, 2002). Indeed, while the steady increase in the use of Italian throughout the years made some linguists hypothesize that dialect would disappear (see Berruto, 1994), recent trends demonstrate that dialect is not on its way to extinction just yet. Statistics released by the Italian Institute for National Statistics (see ISTAT, 2014) about the year 2012 on the use of Italian and dialect reveal that 53% of Italians use mostly the national language within the family. The percentage increases in more informal contexts and with age, in the sense that the younger the individual, the lesser the use of dialect. However, combined use of Italian and dialect in family contexts is still common considering that 32.2% of the population report using both in the family and 30.1% report using it with friends. It is also important to note that the use of dialect increases in the south of Italy. While in the northwest 58.8% of the population speaks mostly or exclusively Italian, in the south the percentage falls to 27.9%. Thus, about 1/3 of Italians speak both the national language and their dialect in all contexts examined by ISTAT.

The significance of such data has been the focus of a variety of interpretations from sociolinguists (see for example Berruto, 2002; 2006), but what is uncontroversial is that dialects are still part of the language repertoire of many Italians and people of different origins living in Italy. This is particularly true for Sicilian, as this language variety still has a significant role in the life of the inhabitants of the island.

If we look at statistics by region for 2006 (ISTAT, 2007), we find that Sicily is among the regions where Sicilian is spoken the most and where use of both dialect and Italian is at its highest levels (48%). Previous research on Sicilian investigated everyday contexts of interaction and pointed to the significant role that code-switching between Sicilian and Italian plays there (Alfonzetti, 1992; Paternostro, 2012). Yet, we still need a great deal of research on the concrete uses of dialects in everyday domains of communication and in new contexts. In this paper, I focus on the use of dialect in an elementary school by the children of a fifth-grade superdiverse classroom and their teachers, and my focus will be on ways in which dialect is used to perform identities by boys and girls.

The study

The data on which this chapter is based come from an ethnographic study conducted in spring 2011, in one fifth-grade elementary school in an inner city area in Palermo. The study consisted of intensive (two or three hours per observation) participant observations of classroom activities and breaks, video and audiotaping, and interviews with children and teachers (for further details see De Fina, 2017). Observations were carried out between January and March 2011, but tape recording continued until June 2011 with the teacher self-recording some lessons in April and May of the same year. The focus of the study was the insertion of immigrant children in Italian schools. In particular, I was interested in observing classroom interaction among the children and with the teacher to understand how immigrant children or children of immigrant origins fitted in Italian schools both linguistically and socially. The school site was chosen as a research site because it is an institution with a high presence of immigrant children. Migration of foreign workers in Palermo has been increasing dramatically in the last 20 years and there are now about 15,000 foreign students in the city schools. In the school that constituted my research site about one-third (28.57%) of the students are immigrant or immigrant origin children. Countries from which students originate in the school, according to a 2010 report, were Tunisia, Morocco, Bangladesh, Mauritius, Pakistan, Sri Lanka, Ghana, China, Costa Ivory Coast, Philippines, Ecuador, Cameroon, India, Romania, and the former Yugoslavia.

As is the case in many other schools in Palermo, teachers and administrators struggle to accommodate for the needs of such diverse population, but they also deal with the very complex social reality of inner city areas. The classroom that I observed was composed of 18 students all between 10 and 11 years old: 10 boys and eight girls. Of these, 11 (seven boys and four girls) were born in Sicily of Italian parents, five (four girls and one boy) were born abroad of foreign parents, and two were born in Sicily of Tunisian parents. Among the foreign-born children, three girls were from Bangladesh, one was from Sri Lanka, and one boy was from Morocco. Among the Sicilian children, one girl was a special-needs student.

The classroom teachers were two females. One taught science and math, while the other one taught Italian, history, and foreign language. There was also one teacher

TABLE 3.1 Class composition.

Italian parents	Foreign-born	Born in Italy of Italian parents
7 boys	1 boy (Morocco)	2 boys (Tunisia)
4 girls	4 girls (3 Bangladesh, 1 Sri Lanka)	
Total boys = 10		
Total girls = 8 (including special-needs student)		

devoted to the special-needs student. As mentioned, data for this paper come from recordings of classroom interaction among children and among children and teachers, and interviews with teachers and children. The total number of hours recorded was 36, but the present paper is based on transcripts that cover about 12 hours distributed in six days of observation. My role in the classroom was that of a participant observer in the sense that for the most part I sat next to the children or the teacher and took notes, but sometimes I participated in classroom activities supporting the teachers. Since I recorded both fronted classroom interaction and peer-to-peer conversation I was able to capture what was going on in different communicative events. As mentioned, I complemented the recordings with interview data.

Students and language varieties

Given the classroom composition, students' linguistic ability in Italian varied. Tables 3.2 and 3.3 present information on children who are of foreign origins or born abroad and their competence in Italian and their home languages. Note that all names used here are pseudonyms.

As seen in the tables, while all the boys were perfectly fluent in Italian, two of the girls were not. One girl from Sri Lanka, Sena, had recently arrived to Italy and was in the process of acquiring Italian. She had a teacher who worked with her individually. Sena didn't speak much in the interactions with teachers, but she did speak Italian with her classmates. She was able to carry on a conversation in Italian and to do her homework with the help of the other girls. The second girl, Parveen, was born in Bangladesh and had been in Italy for three years but she had a preference for speaking Bangla and I never heard her speaking Italian. She almost exclusively spoke with her girlfriends from Bangladesh and did not interact with the rest of the class. The other two Bangladeshi girls, Bani and Nandita, were perfectly fluent in Italian.

The three boys of foreign origins were all fluent in Italian. Indeed, the two boys from Tunisia, Rym and Motaz, were born in Palermo, while their parents were born in Tunisia. The Moroccan boy, Mehdi (Mohammed), had been in Sicily for three years. All the children of immigrant origins were fluent in their L1 or in the L1 of their parents.

54 Anna De Fina

TABLE 3.2 Children of foreign origins born in Italy.

Gender	Born in Italy	Origin	Italian language competence	Language at home
Male (Rym)	Palermo	Tunisia	Native	Tunisian Arabic
Male (Motaz)	Palermo	Tunisia	Native	Tunisian Arabic

TABLE 3.3 Children born abroad.

Gender	Born abroad	Italian language competence	Language at home
Male (Medhi)	Morocco	Native-like	Moroccan Arabic
Female (Bani)	Bangladesh	Native-like	Bangla
Female (Nandita)	Bangladesh	Native-like	Bangla
Female (Parveen)	Bangladesh	Little competence (no Italian spoken)	Bangla
Female (Sena)	Sri Lanka	In the process of learning (spoke Italian with peers)	Tamil

Although, as I mentioned, Bangla was spoken at certain moments by the girls, the language of interaction at school was Italian. Teachers implemented the rule that foreign languages should not be spoken during class time by explicitly inviting the girls to switch to Italian whenever they heard them speaking Bangla. I never heard the boys speak Moroccan or Tunisian Arabic among themselves, except for moments of conflict with the girls when they would use their own language to exchange insults with them.

During my observations I became aware, however, that Sicilian was spoken in class even though it was almost excluded from formal interactions between students and teachers. Most turns in or with Sicilian were spoken in peer-to-peer interaction during class time or breaks, and mostly by boys. Space constraints prevent me from discussing the complex question of the distinction between Italian and Sicilian. Here it will suffice to say that between the two languages there are a great deal of grey areas, phenomena of bivalency (Woolard, 1999), and mixing. For this reason I have characterized turns where Sicilian was spoken as turns "with Sicilian," rather than "in Sicilian."

Figure 3.1 shows the percentage of turns with Sicilian for each day of transcribed data (in the case of 2-17, data was transcribed from two different recorders). As shown in the figure, turns in Sicilian averaged 8% of the total. However, I also noted that it was much more common for boys (independently of their origin) to speak dialect than for girls. Table 3.4 shows the distribution of turns by participant considering the children's gender.

The table shows that while boys averaged 18% of turns with Sicilian, girls only averaged 2%. As expected, given the fact that dialect is a dispreferred choice in official interactions, the teachers were the ones who used Sicilian the least

Dialect performances **55**

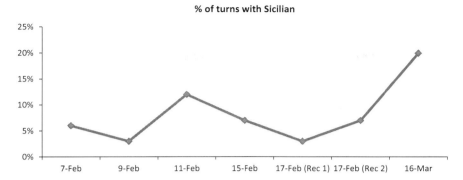

FIGURE 3.1 Percentage of turns with Sicilian by day.

(for a discussion see De Fina 2017). These results seem to confirm some well-documented trends in sociolinguistics which point to significant differences in language use and behavior between girls and boys (see among others Kyratzis, 1999; Marcato, 2007; Sheldon, 1990; Talbot, 2006; Thompson & Moore, 2000). Specifically, girls are shown to prefer more standard and less aggressive language. However, this big picture does not tell the whole story and it is through a detailed analysis of interactional data that we can get to a more in-depth understanding of indexicalities related to dialect usage and also of differences among groups and individuals.

Indeed, while boys used a great deal of dialect, they did not necessarily treat it as a separate language variety and did not seem to always attach particular indexical associations to utterances in Sicilian dialect. Often, talk exchanges among the boys involved the use of a hybrid variety in which Sicilian and Italian elements were blended, and breaks into unmixed utterances were not marked in any way. See the following example, where the children are playing with the tape recorder. The children involved are Carlo, Antonio, Medhi, and Rym. The first two are Sicilian born while Mehdi and Rym were born in Morocco and Tunisia, respectively. Utterances and words in dialect are in italics and glosses of utterances are in square brackets.

Example (1)

1. Carlo: Antonio lo metti da capo?
2. Antonio: See::::!
3. Mehdi: Così la maestra *nni fa i* complimenti
4. Rym: Se::::! Se::::! i cretini *ca siemo*!
5. Medhi: Siamo molto cretini e molto scemi (...)
6. Antonio: (...) *'ca chi state dicienno viero che l'â fermari?*

TABLE 3.4 Distribution of turns by participants.

Day	Turns by unidentified speaker, researcher, and other visitors	Turns by teachers	Turns with Sicilian by teachers	% with Sicilian	Turns by boys	Turns by boys in dialect	% with Sicilian	Turns by girls	Turns by girls with Sicilian	% with Sicilian
2-7	20	99	0	0	82	12	15%	2	0	0
2-9	147	255	9	0.3%	210	10	5%	148	0	0
2-11	134	160	6	0.4%	267	81	30%	276	11	4%
2-15	131	264	3	0.1%	533	68	13%	131	0	0
2-17 rec. 1	194	434	5	0.2%	512	41	8%	107	3	3%
2-17 rec. 2	43	54	0	0	82	16	19%	111		4%
3-16	78	99	0	0	305	132	43%	168	0	0
Total	747	1,365	23	1.6%	1991	360	18%	943	19	2%

Translation

1. Carlo: Antonio can you start it again?
2. Antonio: Wha:::t!
3. Medhi: So the teacher *gives us* compliments! [praises us]
4. Rym: Wha:::t! Wha:::t! Stupid *that we are*! [we are so stupid!]
5. Medhi: We are very stupid and very silly.(...)
6. Antonio: (...) *what are you talking about? Isn't it true that he has to stop it?*

Feb. 11, rec. 1, file 0026

In this example children are producing utterances in Italian (1, 2, 5), mixed with elements of Italian and Sicilian (3 and 4) or entirely in Sicilian (6). I will not examine bivalent elements here for the sake of brevity, as there are words that could be attributed to Italian or Sicilian such as the noun phrase "i cretini" (line 4). It would be extremely artificial to try and attribute specific meanings to each switch between "codes," first of all because no marked frame change is occurring here, and secondly because these types of patterns recur throughout the recordings. Thus, it can be said that the children (at least the boys, and I will come back to that) in normal conversation use elements associated with Sicilian and Italian as part of their repertoire of resources. However, the use of Sicilian seems to become more marked in exchanges that involve fights and verbal aggressions of various kinds within peer interaction. Let us look at the following example, taken from the recording of March 16, a day in which a number of fights erupted among the children. The protagonists here are Marco and Nino, two Sicilian children.

Example (2)

1. Nino: Eh Marco finiscila! *TINNI VAI*!
2. Marco: *Suca*
3. (...)
4. Marco: *A cu ci rici suca?*
5. Nino: *Suca ci u rici a* (...)
6. (...)
7. Nino: *Puo' ammuttari quantu voi tanto* (...)
8. Marco: *Nino e' na munnizza!*

Translation

1. Nino: Ehi Marco stop it! *GO AWAY*!
2. Marco: *Fuck off*
3. (...)
4. Marco: *Who are you telling to fuck off?*
5. Nino: *You tell fuck off to* (...)
6. (...)

7. Nino: *You can push as much as you want since* (...)
8. Marco: *Nino is trash!*

The fragment reproduced above represents one of the many violent exchanges among boys. Nino is telling Marco to stop bothering him. He starts in Italian but then shouts an order to go away in Sicilian. Marco also responds with an insult in Sicilian. As the exchange turns more aggressive with both children becoming more confrontational only Sicilian is spoken. And indeed, switches into Sicilian are extremely common during mocking, insulting, and fighting sequences in peer-to-peer interaction. See the following examples in which boys are often extremely violent and crude in their language.

Example (3)

1. Rym: Aho! senza trucchetti ora!
2. Gino: (...) *Ma chi bbuòi*! Io posso fare i trucchetti se voglio.
    ((silence))
3. Rym: Mica *po' fare r'accussì tu*!

Translation

1. Rym: Ehi! Without tricks now!
2. Gino: (...) *What do you want*! I can do tricks if I want to.
    ((silence))
3. Rym: *But you can't do it like this*!

Example (4)

9. Nino: *T' â llevari!*
10. Marco: *un mi lìevo!*

Translation

1. Nino: *You have to move away!*
2. Marco: *I'm not going to!*

Example (5)

1. Boy1: Ora chi la tocca e chi parla,
2. Boy2: *È un figghi' i buttana* da ora

Translation

1. Boy1: Now anobody who touches it and talks,
2. Boy2: *Is a son of a bitch* from now

Example (6)

1. Marco: ((singing)) Carlo è una *negghia*!
2. GIni: Ahò *si manciò i cugghiuna*! Diglielo alla maestro! Diglielo!
3. Nino: (. . .) *comu a ttia*!
4. Gino: ((singing)) Nino e' una *negghia*
5. Marco: ((in a girl's voice)) Nino è nâ *munnizza*

Translation

1. Marco: ((singing)) Carlo is *useless*!
2. Gino: Ehi *he ate his own balls!* Tell the teacher! Tell her!
3. Nino: (. . .) *just like you*!
4. Gino: ((singing)) Nino is *useless*!
5. Marco: ((in a girl's voice)) Nino is *trash!*

All the examples above represent moments of conflict between children, usually in peer-to-peer exchanges while playing as in Examples (3)–(5), or during peer-to-peer conversations as in Example (6).

Thus, dialect use in aggressive acts is much more common and pervasive than in more neutral acts such as asking, calling attention, making suggestions, etc., and dialect is present in a positive act (a compliment) only once, in the following utterance where Nino is complimenting another boy over his use of color:

Example (7)

1. Nino: Bello *colorasti u giallo è bellissimo stu giallo!*
   Beautiful *you colored the yellow it's very nice this yellow*!

Indeed, in the March 16th lesson in which a fight broke out among the boys, the number of turns with dialect was much higher and most of those turns were used for aggressive acts such as insulting, mocking, and fighting. In order to corroborate this observation I coded utterances in Sicilian as representing neutral or marked speech acts. I classified neutral speech acts as acts that are not aggressive, such as describing, asking a question, or calling attention, and marked speech acts as those that represent a departure from normal communication in the classroom and encode strong negative positionings such as challenging, insulting, or fighting. The category of fighting is not very easy to define in theory as it may overlap with challenges, orders, etc., but I have tried to distinguish individual challenges and orders from utterances that were either embedded in disputes or that were pronounced to initiate confrontations. Insults, on the other hand, can be embedded in fights but are easier to label as such. The following shows that marked speech acts were much more often expressed in Sicilian than unmarked ones.

The examples discussed and the chart show that while the use of dialect per se was not necessarily indexical of particular meanings, it assumed an indexical power

60 Anna De Fina

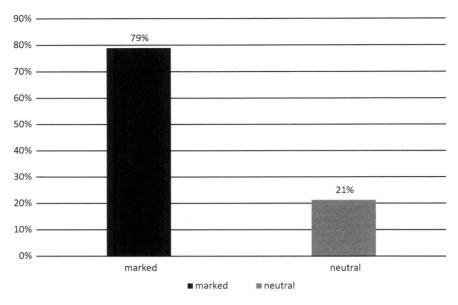

FIGURE 3.2 Marked vs. neutral speech acts in Sicilian.

in relation to specific situations. In official interactions switches into Sicilian always seemed to signal frame switches. On the other hand, its consistent association with aggressive and verbally violent acts suggests that boys associated dialect with manliness when it came to confronting each other. This is confirmed by the fact that they also used dialect with girls in situations of tension. See the following examples:

Example (8)

1. Marina: La penna l'avevo presa io!
2. Gianni: *Sì, tu ti pigghi tutt' i cose tu!*
3. Rym: @@@

Translation

1. Marina: That pen I had taken it!
2. Gianni: *Yes, you always take everything!*
3. Rym: @@@

Example (9)

1. Rym: *un mi batte iḍḍu m'à battere tu?*
2. Bani: io ha la forza!
3. Ra: *un mi batte iḍḍu m'à battere tu?*

Translation

1. Rym: if *he can't beat me how can you beat me?*
2. Bani: I have the strength!
3. Ra: if *he can't beat me how can you beat me?*

In Example (8) Gianni is fighting Marina because, according to him, she has taken his pen. In (9) Bani and Rym are engaged in arm wrestling and Rym is trying to put Bani down by comparing her to another boy who, according to him, has not been able to beat him. In both cases the boys were using dialect in connection with aggressive utterances, thus it seems that dialect is used as an index of a more "macho" persona in the case of fights and confrontations.

Comparison between boys and girls

The examples above present an interesting phenomenon: while the boys speak in dialect to mock the girls, the girls (a Sicilian girl in Example (1) and a Bangladeshi who is fluent in Italian in Example (2)) do not respond in dialect but prefer Italian. We have noted that the percentage of turns with dialect by the girls is much lower than that of the boys, and we concluded that this difference responds to general trends towards correction found in previous research on gender and discourse. We see these differences also in the types of speech acts that were carried out in the dialect or partly in the dialect. I grouped data for all the days excluding March 16, given the particularities of that day's interactions. Figure 3.3 shows a comparison between boys and girls in terms of the types of speech acts that they carried out within the marked category, which is the only one that they share.

As seen in Figure 3.3, boys and girls only share five categories of speech acts. Girls prevalently used dialect in fights, while the other instances in which they used

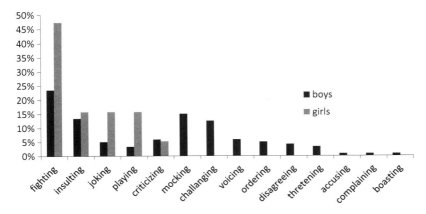

FIGURE 3.3 Distribution of marked speech acts (boys and girls).

it were in insults, jokes, play and criticizing. Let us remember that the total of these utterances was only 19.

As I mentioned at the beginning of the chapter, the big picture does not tell the whole story and does not give us enough insight into the use of language varieties in this particular community of practice. Let us look more closely at the data. Indeed, a very interesting fact here is that there is differentiation among the girls in terms of the use of dialect. The only girls who uttered talk in dialect were two of the foreign-born girls, and indeed, neither Sicilian girls nor the other two foreign-born girls ever used it. At least I never found any example of them using dialect in my recordings. The reasons for this differentiation are not easy to find. One possible explanation lies in the fact that dialect is commonly used in families and households of lower income and therefore it is associated with low education and other negative connotations. It could be that Sicilian girls avoided the use of dialect precisely to escape those kinds of negative associations and thus to differentiate themselves from boys in terms of behavior. On the other hand, the fact that neither Parveen or Sena used dialect is probably due to their lower competence in Italian in general. In light of this, Bani's and Nandita's experimentation with dialect merits a closer scrutiny. As mentioned, they used Sicilian sometimes in joking interactions and sometimes in aggressive ones. Let us look at a few examples. Example (10) exemplifies the use of dialect in fights:

Example (10)

1. Bani: Bella Sena! Sena!
2. Nandita: Tu non sei bella!
3. Bani: Se tu non-
4. Nandita: (. . .) non sei bella
5. Bani: @@@@@
6. Nandita: AH! *scimunnita tu si' scimunnita*! tu m'hai fatto questo! ((pointing to scratch on her arm))

Translation

1. Bani: Beautiful Sena! Sena!
2. Nandita: You are not beautiful!
3. Bani: If you don't-
4. Nandita: (. . .) You are not beautiful
5. Bani: @@@@@
6. Nandita: AH! *Stupid! you are studpid!* You did this to me! ((pointing to scratch on her arm))

In Example (10) Bani was paying a compliment to Sena, the Sri Lankan girl that both she and Nandita had befriended. Nandita starts a confrontation with Bani saying that she is not beautiful, to which Bani reacts and Nandita repeats the same utterance.

At this point Bani laughs but hits her on her arm. In line 6 Nandita responds with an utterance in Sicilian. Thus, because Sicilian spoken by girls is so rare in this corpus, it seems to emphasize the confrontational nature of the exchange and therefore by using Sicilian Nandita seems to be indexing a "strong girl" persona. On the other hand, Sicilian dialect also seems to be an object of secret desire for these girls as it is so strongly associated with male behavior but also with unruly behavior in general. Indeed, in most of the interviews that I conducted with children, use of Sicilian was connected with ignorance and lack of discipline. In addition, children reported that their parents encouraged them not to speak in Sicilian or even prohibited them from using it. These attitudes seem to underlie the absence of utterances in dialect among Sicilian girls. All the girls in the classroom came from impoverished homes and environments in which dialect was very likely the most common language variety. The fact that they did not speak it seems to indicate their wish to adhere to a model of education and good behavior that would distinguish them from boys and also elevate them in the eyes of the teachers who were clearly against the use of Sicilian in class.

However, as mentioned before, Nandita and Bani were the only ones to utter some exchanges in Sicilian. The following example is particularly illuminating:

Example (11)

1. Bani: *Pari mia!*
2. Nandita: *Pari mia!*
3. Bani: *Pari mia!* uhh
4. Nandita: Loro giocano!

Translation

1. Bani: *Even for me!*
2. Nandita: *Even for me!*
3. Bani: *Even for me!* uhh
4. Nandita: They play!

In this exchange Bani and Nandita are pronouncing the utterance *pari mia* (even for me) which accompanies a game that only the boys play in class. The game involves displaying cards with images of soccer players whose jerseys carry even or odd numbers and calling even or odd as the choice to win before displaying the card. The utterances that accompany the game are always in Sicilian. In the game the player bids that the player number will be even or odd and then throws the card. Notice that Nandita and Bani do not have the cards in their hands and that Nandita says at the end of the exchange: "They play," where "they" clearly refers to boys. Thus here Sicilian indexes an object of desire: a game that the girls would like to, but cannot, play because of implicit gender norms. In this way the behavior and attitudes of Nandita and Bani towards Sicilian differs from that of their peers.

We may define their choice of language here as experimentation into crossing (Rampton, 1995). Rampton defines crossing as the use of a variety that belongs to an outgroup, and indeed, Nandita and Bani do not seem to know Sicilian since they never speak more than a few words in it and do so in an emphatic way and in marked exchanges. This pleasure with experimenting corresponds to their more general profile in the class. Both Bani and Nandita were quite active in the classroom and very often assumed the role of leaders. They were followed by the other girls who tried to break into their very closed inner circle and they were always the first to raise their hand in class. More importantly, they showed no fear of the boys who often mocked them and fought with them, but who also sought their help when it came to doing work in class. As we have seen above, Bani even ventured into arm wrestling and challenging one of the boys in the game which was usually the exclusive domain of the males. Another interesting aspect of Bani's and Nandita's behavior was their interest in teaching Italian to the other girls, in learning Tamil, the language of their friend Sena, and in acting as cultural mediators: see the following exchange with the art teacher, Sara, who had asked the girls to copy a drawing in which some people were represented:

Example (12)

1. Sara: No? perché no?
2. Nandita: No perché:::
3. Bani: Ci sono le persone e non le può fare
4. Nandita: Ci sono le persone che e suo padre e sua madre non vogliono
5. che disegna persone.
6. Sara: E se fai solo il paesaggio senza le persone?
7. (. . .)
8. Sara: Quindi fai solo le rocce il cielo il mare. La bandiera la puoi
9. fare?
10. ((Bani talks to Parveen)) (. . .)
11. Bani: Si

Translation

1. Sara: No? why not?
2. Nandita: No becau:::se
3. Bani: There are people and she can't draw them
4. Nandita: There are people and her father and mother don't
5. want her to draw people.
6. Sara: And if you just draw the environment without the people?
7. (. . .)
8. Sara: So you only draw the rocks the sky and the sea. The flag can
9. you do it?
10. ((Bani talks to Parveen)) (. . .)
11. Bani: Yes

This interaction was recorded during a time when children were asked to copy images related to the period of the Italian Independence for a celebration in which they had been invited to participate. Sara was asking Parveen why she did not want to draw, and at this point Nandita starts an explanation that is co-constructed with Bani over three turns (2,3,4) in which they clarify to the teacher that Parveen's parents do not allow her to draw people. They don't say that this is because she is a Muslim, but we see that the teacher changes the proposed task for her, allowing her to change the drawing. This is one of many instances in which the two girls took the initiative to act as mediators. On other occasions, which I cannot discuss here for lack of space (but see De Fina, 2017), Bani and Nandita also experimented with translanguaging and language teaching and learning.

Conclusions

The analysis of the use of dialect in this fifth-grade classroom has demonstrated how an ethnographic, practice, and interactionally oriented approach is the most productive to account for people's communicative practices and for the role of languages within them. We have seen that big social categories such as those of migrant, native, non-native, female, or male do not correlate with language use in any simple way. Indeed, the analysis showed that boys of both immigrant and non-immigrant origins have a preference for dialect in peer-to-peer interaction, but also that dialect may be connected to the performance of masculinities only within certain interactional events and not always. Conversely, we saw that although in quantitative terms all females tend to use preferably Italian, within this group there are differences and those differences involve foreign-born girls but not all of them. For Bani and Nandita, use and experimentation with dialect turned out to be a way of performing aggressive or joking personae at one level, but was also part of their curiosity and ability to express their skills and desires that made them leaders in the classroom even if they came to the school as second language learners and had little knowledge about the local culture at the beginning.

The analysis then confirms the need to pursue a shift towards a sociolinguistics grounded in ethnography and qualitative methodologies in order to capture the complex articulations of linguistic and social processes in superdiverse communities.

References

Alfonzetti, G. (1992). *Il discorso bilingue. Italiano e dialetto a Catania*. Milano: FrancoAngeli.
Androutsopoulos, J. (2013). Participatory culture and metalinguistic discourse: Performing and negotiating German dialects on YouTube. In D. Tannen & A. Trester (Eds.), *Language and new media* (pp. 47–71). Washington, DC: Georgetown University Press.
Assenza, E. (2006). Parlar giovane tra Scilla e Cariddi. In C. Marcato (Ed.) *Giovani, lingue e dialetti* (pp. 151–156). Padova: Unipress.
Auer, P. (Ed.). (2007). *Style and social identities: Alternative approaches to linguistic heterogeneity*. Berlin: Mouton De Gruyter.

Berruto, G. (1994). Scenari sociolinguistici per l'Italia del Duemila. In G. Holtus & E. Radtke (Eds.), *Sprachprognostik und das 'italiano di domani'* (pp. 23–45). Tübingen: Narr.

Berruto, G. (2002), Parlare dialetto alle soglie del 2000. In G. L Beccaria & C. Marello (Eds.), *Dalla parola al testo. Scritti per Bice Mortara Garavelli* (pp. 33–49). Alessandria: dell'Orso.

Berruto, G. (2006), Quale dialetto per l'Italia del Duemila? In A. A. Sobrero & A. Miglietta (Eds.), *Lingua e dialetto nell'Italia del duemila* (pp. 101–123). Galatina: Congedo Editore.

Blommaert, J., & De Fina, A. (2017). Chronotopic identities: On the timespace organization of who we are. In A. De Fina, D. Ikizoglu, & J. Wegner (Eds.), *Diversity and super diversity: Sociocultural linguistic perspectives* (pp. 1–15). Washington, DC: Georgetown University Press.

Blommaert, J., & Rampton, B. (2011). Language and superdiversity. *Diversities 13*(3). Retrieved from www.unesco.org/shs/diversities/vol13/issue2/art1

Coupland, N. (2001) Language, situation, and the relational self: Theorizing dialect-style in sociolinguistics. In P. Eckert & J. R. Rickford (Eds.), *Style and sociolinguistic variation* (pp. 185–210). Cambridge: Cambridge University Press.

D'Agostino, M. (2007). *Sociolinguistica dell'Italia contemporanea*. Bologna: Il Mulino.

D'Agostino, M., & Scarpella, I. (2008) Lo spazio del dialetto ieri e oggi in un quartiere di Palermo. Ma quale dialetto? In G. Marcato (Ed.), *L'Italia dei dialetti* (pp. 325–334). Padova: Unipress.

De Fina, A. (2015). Ethnography as complexifying lenses for sociolinguistic analysis. *Tlburg Papers in Culture Studies*, 146.

De Fina, A. (2017). Diversity in school: Monolingual ideologies versus multilingual practices. In A. De Fina, D. Ikizoglu, & J. Wegner (Eds.), *Diversity and super diversity: Sociocultural linguistic perspectives* (pp. 191–208). Washington, DC: Georgetown University Press.

De Mauro, T. (1963). *Storia linguistica dell'Italia unita*. Bari: Laterza.

Eckert, P. (1989). *Jocks and burnouts: Social categories and identity in the high school*. New York: Teachers College Press.

Eckert, P. (2012). Three waves of variation study: The emergence of meaning in the study of variation. *Annual Review of Anthropology, 41*, 87–100.

Istat. (2007). *Indagine multiscopo. La lingua italiana, i dialetti e le lingue straniere*. Retrieved from http://www3.istat.it/salastampa/comunicati/non_calendario/20070420_00/

Istat. (2014). Anno 2012. L'uso della lingua italiana, dei dialetti e di altre lingue in Italia, 27 ottobre 2014. Retrieved from www.istat.it/it/files/2014/10/Lingua- italiana edialetti_PC.pdf?title=Lingua+italiana%2C+dialetti+e+altre+lingue+-+27%2Fott%2F2014+-+Testo+integrale.pdf

Kyratzis, A. (1999). Narrative identity: Preschoolers' self-construction through narrative in same-sex friendship group dramatic play. *Narrative Inquiry, 9*(2), 427–455.

Labov, W. (1966). *The social stratification of English in New York City*. Washington, DC: Center for Applied Linguistics.

Marcato, C. (2007). *Dialetto, dialetti e italiano*. Bologna: Il Mulino.

Marcato, C. (Ed.). (2008). *L'Italia dei dialetti*. Padova: Unipress.

Matranga, V. (2007). *Trascrivere. La rappresentazione del parlato nell'esperienza dell'Atlante Linguistico di Sicilia*. Palermo: Centro Studi Linguistici e Siciliani

Paternostro, G. (2012), Argomentare oralmente e in dialetto. Analisi dei dati dell'Atlante Linguistico della Sicilia (ALS). In G. Marcato (Ed.), *Scrittura, dialetto e oralità* (pp. 217–224). Padova: Cleup.

Rampton, B. (1995). *Crossings: Language and ethnicity among adolescents*. London: Longman.

Sheldon, A. (1990). Pickle fights: Gendered talk in pre-school disputes. *Discours Processes, 13*(1), 5–31.

Sobrero, A. (2002). Il dialetto c'è ancora? *Italiano & Oltre, XIII*, 19.

Talbot, M. (2006). Gender stereotypes: Reproduction and challenge. In J. Holmes & M. Meyerhoff (Eds.), *The handbook of language and gender* (pp. 468–486). London: Blackwell Publishing.

Thompson, R., & Moore, K. (2000). Collaborative speech in dyadic problem solving. *Journal of Language and Social Psychology, 19*(2), 248–255.

Woolard, K. (1999). Simultaneity and bivalency as strategies in bilingualism. *Journal of Linguistic Anthropology, 8*(1), 3–29.

PART II

Nation-states and identity construction in relation to a standard and a dialect

4
THE CONSTRUCTION OF LINGUISTIC BORDERS AND THE RISE OF NATIONAL IDENTITY IN SOUTH SUDAN

Some insights into Juba Arabic (Árabi Júba)

Stefano Manfredi

Introduction

Until nowadays, two theoretical paradigms have dominated the description of creole-lexifier language contact (Goury & Léglise, 2005). The first one is the Fergussonian paradigm of diglossia, which describes creole-lexifier contacts as stable sociolinguistic situations involving two linguistic varieties with specific functional assignments (Ferguson, 1959; Carayol & Chaudenson, 1978). The second one is decreolization, which postulates an asymmetric contact producing the gradual replacement of creole features by those of its lexifier along the lines of a unidirectional continuum running from two poles, the basilect and the acrolect, through a series of mesolectal varieties (De Camp, 1971; Bickerton, 1973). Different from diglossia, which focuses on functional variation and societal norms, the notion of decreolization refers back to the structural effects of a process of attrition leading to language shift.

Despite its relative success, the decreolization paradigm has been repeatedly criticized during the past decades. Above all, it has been argued that decreolization does not tell anything about variation induced by internal factors (Aceto, 1999; Mufwene, 1994). Furthermore, being essentially descriptive, decreolization is unable to reflect language attitudes and ideologies lying behind creole-lexifier language contacts (Migge & Léglise, 2011). Lastly, the fact that decreolization is often analyzed in the light of a (post-)creole continuum represents a vexing problem for linguists since it is extremely difficult to draw implicational scales reflecting the gradual shift towards the lexifier language. This is because each speaker tends to have his or her own way of mixing creole and lexifier features, some converging more on phonological features, others on morphology and/or lexicon (Miller, 2007). Irrespective of this epistemological problem, (post-)creole continua are generally assumed to be different from dialect continua in that the basilectal and acrolectal poles are typologically dissimilar to such an extent that they are considered to be distinct languages (Siegel, 2010).

In this last regard, a common assumption of post-modern sociolinguistics is that linguistic differentiation always involves ideologically embedded and socially constructed processes (Irvine & Gal, 2000). This is the core point of view of globalization studies which postulate that named languages are ideological constructions tied to the emergence of nation-states and that there are not truly distinct linguistic systems bounded by grammars, as habitually argued by descriptive linguists (Blommaert & Rampton, 2011; Jørgensen et al., 2011). In this framework, language borders in contact situations are conceived as means of social categorization, which are only relevant when the speakers deliberately construct them (García & Li Wei, 2014). It is not surprising, then, that most studies relativize the outcomes of the semiotic process of language differentiation by putting emphasis on the lack of coincidence between the linguistic borders constructed by speakers and those drawn by linguists (Bert & Costa, 2014; Cornips, 2014).

It is against this background that the present study addresses the issue of the social construction of linguistic borders in a creole-lexifier contact situation. It focuses on Juba Arabic, an Arabic-based pidgincreole spoken in South Sudan (Manfredi, 2017). Before the independence of South Sudan in 2011, Juba Arabic has been extensively exposed to contact with Sudanese Arabic, the dominant language of the former unified Sudan. Thereafter, new contact situations between the pidgincreole and its lexifier emerged due to returnees entering South Sudan from Arabic-dominant regions. This prolonged contact eventually led to different degrees of linguistic interference. The first to analyze Juba Arabic in terms of the (post-)creole continuum was Mahmoud (1979). Miller (1989; 2007), on her part, insists on the fact that, although affected by its lexifier, the evolution of the South Sudanese pidgincreole is far from being a linear continuum towards Sudanese Arabic. In the light of the above, the present study faces the question of whether Juba Arabic speakers argue for a differentiation between their language and Sudanese Arabic and, if it is the case, to what extent the construction of this linguistic border depends on local ideological factors or on the identification of relevant linguistic features.

As a matter of fact, due to their atypical conditions of emergence, pidgins and creoles are particularly relevant for the discussion of the ideological link between language and identity (Edwards, 2009). Being spoken as vehicular languages, pidgins do not function as identity markers. In contrast, nativized creoles may develop identity functions in relation to ethnic groups (e.g., the Arabic-based Ki-Nubi creole in Kenya and Uganda) or nation-states (e.g., the French-based Haitian Creole). As far as Juba Arabic is concerned, it is a pidgincreole (Tosco & Manfredi, 2013), that is, an intermediary category defined by the fact that an earlier pidgin has become the first language only for a part of its speakers (Bakker, 2008). This means that, although Juba Arabic is largely used as vehicular language, it shares some sociolinguistic properties with creoles. Miller has already stressed that Juba Arabic functions as marker of a super-ethnic South Sudanese identity since the early 1970s (Miller, 1991; 2002). More recently, the South Sudanese independence further straightened the identity functions of Juba Arabic. Accordingly, this study is also concerned with the question of which effects the rise of a South Sudanese national identity have on language categorization and on the construction of language borders.

The paper is organized as follows. Section 2 provides a background to language policies and language categorization in post-independence South Sudan. Section 3 deals with the definition of Juba Arabic from a descriptive perspective, and presents the main features used by linguists for distinguishing between Juba Arabic and its lexifier. Section 4 then analyzes the linguistic borders constructed by speakers in relation to both prominent grammatical features of Juba Arabic and local ideological factors. Section 5 finally investigates the nexus between speakers' attitudes towards Juba Arabic and the rise of a South Sudanese national identity.

1. Background: language policies and language categorization

South Sudan presents a high degree of linguistic diversity, with about 70 languages belonging to three out of the four language families attested in Africa (i.e., Nilo-Saharan, Niger-Congo, and Afro-Asiatic). In this complex linguistic landscape, the Arabic-based pidgincreole called *árabi juba* (Juba Arabic) represents the first means of interethnic communication of the country, while being nativized by the largest part of the urban population of Juba, the capital city of South Sudan (Manfredi & Tosco, forthcoming).

Following the Sudan's comprehensive peace agreement in 2005, South Sudan moved from a strict Arabic monolingualism to a policy of multilingualism. In 2011, English has been recognized as the official language, whereas all the "indigenous" languages of the country were accorded the status of national languages. What really counts as "indigenous language" is obviously difficult to say, since this category can only be defined in opposition to an "alien language," in most cases represented by a colonial language. The fact remains that Juba Arabic is officially considered to be a variety of Arabic, and therefore it is not recognized as an "indigenous language" of South Sudan (Manfredi & Tosco, forthcoming). Most importantly, being a vehicular language, Juba Arabic does not fit within the ethnic understanding of "indigenous languages" inherited from the colonial language policy and renewed by the independence of South Sudan (Abdelhay, 2007; Abdelhay et al., 2011). Despite this, I will show that the institutionalization of "indigenous language" as a sociolinguistic category has a significant impact on the social categorization of Juba Arabic.

As a further matter, Arabic-centric folk linguistic ideologies are still at work in post-independence South Sudan, and these also affect language categorization. The enduring semiotic opposition between the labels *luġa* and *ruṭāna* is a case in point. The Arabic term *luġa* (*lúga* in Juba Arabic) means "language" and has a normative value in Sudan. It refers to a high-prestige linguistic variety, with an established written tradition and wide community of speakers. *Luġa/lúga* is primarily used in relation to Arabic, but it can also be applied to European languages and other languages of wider communication. In contrast, the Sudanese Arabic term *ruṭāna* (*rután* in Juba Arabic) can be broadly translated as "incomprehensible (ethnic) language; patois" and it conveys a marked (depreciative) value. It refers to low-prestige languages, with no written tradition and spoken by small ethnic groups. Sudanese Arabs usually adopt the term *ruṭāna* for labeling all the non-Arabic linguistic entities present in the region.[1]

The analysis of the interviews in Sections 4 and 5 shows that Juba Arabic occupies an ambiguous position within the traditional *luġa*/*ruṭāna* semiotic dichotomy. However, since discursive phenomena are always hierarchically ranked (Blommaert, 2007), I will illustrate the different intertextual meanings of the terms *luġa*/*lúga*, *ruṭāna*/*rután*, and *indigenous language* when used for categorizing Juba Arabic and/or Sudanese Arabic. These considerations will turn out to be useful when analyzing the construction of a linguistic border between the South Sudanese pidgincreole and its lexifier.

2. Is Juba Arabic different from Arabic? the linguists' perspective

This section aims to illustrate the main features used by linguists for establishing a border between Juba Arabic and its lexifier. These will furnish a comparative basis for the analysis of the metalinguistic representations expressed by ordinary speakers of Juba Arabic in Section 4.

Creole languages are considered to be different from other spoken languages in that they came into existence as a consequence of the disruption of the intergenerational transmission of the lexifier language from parent to child (Comrie, 2011). These uncommon conditions of language emergence entail different processes of language change linked to second language acquisition, substratum interference, and internal developments. Having emerged in a situation of second language acquisition with limited access to the target language, Juba Arabic presents typical features of creole languages (Tosco & Manfredi, 2013).

First of all, Juba Arabic draws about 80% of its lexicon from its Arabic lexifier (Manfredi, 2017). The remaining 20% is composed of an increasing number of loanwords from Nilotic languages whose integration mostly affects the non-basic (i.e., culturally marked) lexicon of the pidgincreole. Most loanwords are from Bari, the main substrate/adstrate language of Juba Arabic; these are either nouns (e.g., *lógoro* "heron") or verbs (e.g., *kúruju* "cultivate," Nakao, 2012). We also find a number of borrowed nouns from European languages (mainly from English, e.g., *síster* "nun;" *nígas* "street boy") as well as from other languages of wider communication like Swahili (e.g., *wéwe* "East African migrant"). All things considered, lexicon is certainly not the most relevant domain for establishing a linguistic border between Juba Arabic and Sudanese Arabic.

The phonology of Juba Arabic, on its part, has been forged by a process of second language acquisition in combination with an important substrate interference. On the one side, Juba Arabic is characterized by the loss of Arabic complex realizations which are absent in the Nilotic substrate (i.e., velar fricatives *x* and *ġ*; pharyngeal fricatives *ḥ* and '; all the pharyngealized consonants *ṭ, ḍ, ṣ*, etc.). On the other side, it presents non-Arabic complex realizations which have entered the language from substrate/adstrate languages via lexical borrowing (e.g., the voiced bilabial implosive in *bʼondó* "village" and the voiced alveolar implosive in *dʼéŋele* "bile"). Furthermore, Arabic stress has been reinterpreted as pitch accent in Juba Arabic. Phonology thus provides good linguistic evidence for distinguishing between Juba Arabic and Sudanese Arabic. Nevertheless, other vehicular varieties of Arabic spoken by minority groups in the Arabic-dominant regions of Sudan and South Sudan display similar phonological features (Manfredi, 2014), and these are not the product of a process of pidginization/creolization as in the case of Juba Arabic.

Turning to morphosyntax, Juba Arabic is characterized by an important reduction of the inflectional and derivational categories of Sudanese Arabic. More generally, an important typological difference between Juba Arabic and Sudanese Arabic resides in the isolating morphology of the pidgincreole as compared to the fusional morphology of its Arabic lexifier. In this regard, Versteegh (1993, p. 73) affirmed that "agreement markers in the verbal system of Juba Arabic is of the utmost importance for the comparison between creole and "normal" (Arabic) dialects." The following table corroborates this view.

As we can see, the Sudanese lexifier, here exemplified by the Baggara dialect of Kordofan, presents a typical Arabic imperfective paradigm with personal affixes indexing aspect, number, and gender, and a proclitic marking the indicative mood on the verb. In contrast, in Juba Arabic, the subject is indexed by an independent pronoun preceding an invariable verbal form marked for irrealis. In this respect, Juba Arabic is also different from other vehicular varieties of Arabic that, though affected by some degree of morphological simplification (as showed by the conflation of 1st singular and plural persons), do not display the same degree of restructuring of the South Sudanese pidgincreole.

It is important to remember that Versteegh, basing his argument on the variationist study of Mahmoud (1979), has argued that Juba Arabic is increasingly integrating personal affixes from Sudanese Arabic and, consequently, "we can envisage a future in which the linguistic varieties spoken in Juba become more and more similar to Khartoum Arabic. [. . .] In the end, this scenario might lead to a situation where Juba Arabic would be nothing more than a regional variety of Sudanese Arabic." (Versteegh, 1993, p. 75). Almost twenty years after this prediction of the

TABLE 4.1 Paradigm types.

Baggara Arabic (Kadugli, Sudan) (Manfredi, 2010, p. 129)	*bi=na-mš-u* IND=1-go-PL "We (will) go"
Vehicular Arabic (Kadugli, Sudan) (Manfredi, 2014, p. 30)	*na-mši* 1-go "I (will) go, we (will) go"
Juba Arabic (Juba, South Sudan) (Manfredi, 2017, p. 83)	*ánna bi=rówa* 1PL IRR=go "We (will) go"

direction of change, we can affirm that it did not come true, since the bulk of Juba Arabic speakers still present typical creolized verbal paradigms (Manfredi, 2017). This fact may find a reason in the ideological resilience to integration of highly identifiable linguistic items from Sudanese Arabic. The analysis of interviews in Section 4 indeed shows that verbal morphosyntax is a cognitively relevant linguistic feature for the construction of a border between Juba Arabic and Sudanese Arabic.

3. Is Juba Arabic different from Arabic? the speakers' perspective

In this section, I shall investigate the metalinguistic representations that Juba Arabic speakers express about their language based on the analysis of qualitative interviews recorded in Juba in July–August 2013.[2] The aim of the analysis is to individuate the linguistic features used by speakers for indexing Juba Arabic *vis-à-vis* its lexifier and to compare them with those features that are meaningful to linguists (*cf.* Section 2).

When asked whether there is any linguistic difference between the South Sudanese pidgincreole and its lexifier, Juba Arabic speakers who do not speak Sudanese Arabic broadly recognize the existence of a linguistic border without referring to any particular features, as we can see in the following interview excerpt.[3]

Excerpt 1. Speaker 1[4]

fi férig kebír // mar-át ána ma gi=fáhim // kan bíga/úmon bi=dákal fi árabi ta kartúm   de/ána ma bi=fáhim kúlu kúlu // úmon kamán ma gi=fáhim árabi tái // úmon bi=kélim gal/hája de rután //

"There is a huge difference. Sometimes I do not understand. If they start speaking Khartoum Arabic, I do not understand at all. They also do not understand my Arabic. They would say: this is a *rután*."

The view articulated by this young speaker is that Juba Arabic and Sudanese Arabic are distinct languages. His empirical assumption is based exclusively on the low degree of mutual intelligibility experienced by the speakers of the two languages. This factual reality is also acknowledged by linguists (Manfredi, 2017). More interestingly, in order to stress the perceived linguistic distance, the interviewee evokes the depreciative term *rután* as used by Sudanese Arabic speakers when referring to Juba Arabic. Thus, in this case, *rután* does not give evidence of the speaker's semiotic processing of sociolinguistic categories. It rather reproduces the downscaling of Juba Arabic operated in conformity with the Sudanese Arabic-centric layered system, opposing a high-prestige variety (i.e., Sudanese Arabic) labeled as *luġa* "language" to a number of low-prestige "incomprehensible (ethnic) languages" (*cf.* Section 1).

In contrast, Juba Arabic speakers who also speak Sudanese Arabic tend to construct linguistic borders constrained by specific linguistic features, as we can see in the following interview excerpt.

Excerpt 2. Speaker 2[5] (Manfredi & Bizri, forthcoming)

*úo ma árabi // [. . .] zey hása fi šamál bi=nadí gal/**luġa 'arabiyya** // árabi júba kamán/gi=nadí gal lúga // zey ána bi=kélim gal/ána kélim le íta // lakín úmon henák/úmon bi=kélim gal/**b=a-gūl lē=k** //*

"(Juba Arabic) is not (Sudanese) Arabic. Like, for example, in the north it is called *luġa 'arabiyya* ("Arabic language"). Juba Arabic too is called *lúga*. Like, I say: *ána bi=kélim le íta* ("I say to you"). But, over there, they say: *b=a-gūl lē=k* ("I say to you")."

This trilingual speaker uses the normative term *luġa/lúga* for referring to both Sudanese Arabic and Juba Arabic.[6] He thus operates an upscaling in the local system of sociolinguistic categories. This means that he accords Juba Arabic the same linguistic prestige as its lexifier language and considers it a full-fledged "language." Besides, the speaker constructs a linguistic border between Juba Arabic and Sudanese Arabic by opposing two verbal clauses; these are *ána bi=kélim le íta*, 1SG IRR=say to 2SG, "I say to you" in Juba Arabic, and *b=a-gūl lē=k*, IND=1SG-say to=2SG.M, "I say to you" in Sudanese Arabic. Regardless of the different lexical verbs conveying the meaning of "(to) say," we can note that, in the Juba Arabic example, the verb lacks personal affixes and both the subject and the indirect object are encoded by independent pronouns. Conversely, in the Sudanese Arabic example, the subject and the indirect object of the verbal clause are respectively encoded by a person affix on the verb and a clitic pronoun attached to the preposition *lē* "to." What makes this excerpt particularly interesting is that the factual-descriptive border constructed by the speaker clearly corresponds to the linguists' representation of Juba Arabic as an isolating language (*cf.* Section 2).

The third interview excerpt also confirms that verbal morphosyntax is a cognitively prominent feature for the identification of Juba Arabic.

Excerpt 3. Speaker 3[7]

*másalan/<u>for example</u> // ána kan gi=wónus kílma // másalan/ána gi=rówa // aw ánna gi=fútu // de árabi juba // <u>for example</u>/kan zol min kartúm gal // **mašē-na** // aw/**mašē-t** // ána tawáli b=ágder árif kalám de <u>took rise</u> min zol al ja min kartúm // aw kan gi=géni fi kartúm ketír // <u>so on and so forth</u> //*

"For example, if I say, for example: *ána gi-rówa* ("I am going"), or *ánna gi=fútu* ("we are passing"). This is Juba Arabic. For example, if someone from Khartoum says: *mašē-na* ("we went"), or *mašē-t* ("I went"), I can immediately know that this discourse took rise from someone who came from Khartoum, or who spent a long time in Khartoum, so on and so forth."

This interviewee also gives a factual representation of Juba Arabic based on the opposition between different verbal paradigms. These are *ána gi=rówa* ("I am going") and *ánna gi=fútu* ("we are passing"), corresponding to the perceived morphological norm of Juba Arabic, and *mašē-na* ("we went") and *mašē-t* ("I went"), representing the deviated Arabic-like verbal paradigms. In this particular case, the speaker operates a process of iconization (Irvine & Gal, 2000) when considering the occurrence of person affixes on the verb as formally congruent with returnees "who spent a long time in Khartoum." In so doing, the interviewee constructs a community-internal linguistic border between South Sudanese returnees, who have evidently been much exposed to Sudanese Arabic, and South Sudanese long-term residents, who are perceived to be the norm holders.

Juba Arabic speakers may also focus on lexical features for distinguishing between the pidgincreole and Sudanese Arabic, as exemplified by the following interview excerpt.

Excerpt 4. Speaker 4[8]

úo ma árabi // [. . .] *de rután adíl* // *de rután baráu* // *úo* / *of course* / *ána árif úo ja min árabi* // *wo borrowed kalim-át min rutan-át* / *local* // *rutan-át/bári/rután šunú šunú* / *wo biga mulágbat* / *le dérija* / *árabi* / *árabi ma gi=fáhim* // *you know* // *árabi ma gi=fáhim* //

"(Juba Arabic) is not (Sudanese) Arabic. This is a *rután*, a *rután* on its own. It, of course, I know that it derived from Arabic and that it borrowed words from *rutan-át*, local, *rutan-át* such as Bari, whatever *rután*, and it became mixed to such extent that Arabs do not understand. You know, they do not understand."

The view articulated by this speaker is that, even if Juba Arabic clearly derives from (Sudanese) Arabic, it is a distinct language to such an extent that "Arabs do not understand it." He then refers to the South Sudanese creole with the term *rután*. Different from Excerpt 1, here *rután* does not convey a depreciative value, but rather points out the centrality of the category "local" in the discourse regarding Juba Arabic. Not surprisingly, the term *rután* is coupled with a metalinguistic representation concentrating on the lexical contribution of "local" languages to Juba Arabic. This view is further strengthened by the following interview excerpt.

Excerpt 5. Speaker 5[9]

Juba Arabic is different // *it has been indigenized in some way* // *some tribal words of the indigenous languages* / *in the south* / *have gone inside* // [. . .] *such as Bari* / *b'ángiri* / *kúrju* // *So you can see* / *be taríga de* / *árabi júba šílu* / *yáni* / *šikil* / *šikil* / *afrígi* // [. . .] *laánu kalim-át al=maḥalliyya* / *dákalu fógo ketír* //

"Juba Arabic is different. It has been indigenized somehow. Some tribal words from South Sudanese indigenous languages have been integrated. Such as Bari, *b'ángiri* ("cheek"), *kúruju* ("cultivate"). So you can see, in this way, Arabic took an African shape. Because many *maḥalliyya* ("indigenous") words have gone inside."

This highly-educated interviewee overtly argues that the linguistic difference between Juba Arabic and Sudanese Arabic resides in the "indigenized" nature of the pidgincreole. In his perspective, Juba Arabic is a language with an "African" shape presenting "tribal" words borrowed from South Sudanese "indigenous languages." This view confirms that, though rare (*cf.* Section 2), substrate/adstrate loanwords in Juba Arabic have a strong iconic function in relation to the official notion of "indigenousness." When the speaker portrays Juba Arabic as an "indigenous language" (using also the Arabic term *maḥalliyya* "indigenous"), he operates an upscaling in relation to the State's prescriptions of the sociolinguistic regime. In other words, he attempts to legitimize Juba Arabic within the sociolinguistic space of post-independence South Sudan while accepting without any criticism the notion of "indigenous language."

4. Language attitudes and the rise of a South Sudanese national identity

While the previous section dealt with metalinguistic representations and the construction of linguistic borders, the last part of this study analyzes language attitudes, here defined as beliefs and values that people have about their language (Garret, 2010), in relation to the rise of a South Sudanese national identity.

Most Juba Arabic speakers have a positive attitude towards the South Sudanese pidgincreole. This general opinion goes hand in hand with the appreciation of the vehicular function of Juba Arabic in the multilingual landscape of South Sudan.

Excerpt 6. Speaker 6[10]

árabi júba lúga / ašán bi=límu jenúb kúlu // <u>for example</u> / kan íta rówa fi kénya / lúga tómon wáhid / yawú swahíli // swahíli bi=límu kúlu // nína fi jenúb sudán / hája al bi=límu nína kúlu/árabi júba // yála rután de bíga ta gebíla táki // kan íta abukáya / íta bi=wónusu abukáya // lakín árabi júba de ma gi=derisú // bes fi bét / árabi júba gi=wonusú/zey rután // lakín úo hása bíga lúga //

"Juba Arabic is a *lúga*, because it bonds the whole South (Sudan). For example, if you go to Kenya, they have one language, that is Swahili. Swahili bonds everyone. As far as we are concerned in South Sudan, the thing that bonds us is Juba Arabic. The *rután* is something that belongs to your tribe. If you are Abukaya, you speak Abukaya. But Juba Arabic is not taught. It is spoken only at home, like a *rután*. However, it became a *lúga*."

In the previous excerpt, a young trilingual girl labels Juba Arabic as *lúga*. This upscaling in the local categorization of languages finds a reason in the emphasis put on the unifying role of Juba Arabic in South Sudan. This view is reinforced by comparing the vehicular function of Juba Arabic with that of Swahili, and by contrasting it to the category *rután*, which is perceived as inevitably linked to single tribal entities. Furthermore, when the speaker states that, even if Juba Arabic became a *lúga*, it is acquired at home like a *rután*, she gives evidence of the perception of the ongoing nativization process of Juba Arabic.

The following interview excerpt also confirms that the vehicular function of Juba Arabic is perceived as an important element of the achievement of South Sudanese national unity.

Excerpt 7. Speaker 5

Juba Arabic as a lingua franca / is the language that has a future in this country // it is a uniting bond that can bring South Sudanese together // because no one can claim dominating the other through this language // no Dinka would say / it is ours // [. . .] so it encompasses the whole South (Sudan) / as an important language that can equally go to primary schools / to / to basic level schools //

Here, the speaker who previously emphasized the "indigenous" nature of the South Sudanese pidgincreole in Excerpt 5, rather stresses that Juba Arabic is the only unifying *lingua franca* of South Sudan, and because of this, it cannot be instrumentalized in light of the official ethnic-oriented understanding of language diversity. In the speaker's view, a non-ethnic language like Juba Arabic can also be "indigenous," and as such, it should be recognized as a national language and taught in primary schools.

In this context, it should be remarked that the glottonym *árabi júba* still hinders the adoption of Juba Arabic as a marker of the new South Sudanese national identity. First, the term *árabi* establishes an evident link with the former dominant language. Secondly, the toponym Juba can be interpreted as an exclusive geographic label by outsider groups, and in particular by the Dinka political elite. In the following excerpt, the interviewee spontaneously brings out the question of the glottonym in relation to the non-recognition of Juba Arabic as an official language.

Excerpt 8. Speaker 7[11]

jenub-īn / fi eyy maḥall / gi=wónusu árabi juba // lakín / I think / hukúma / I don't know // **dayr-īn i-duss-u** árabi / lakín nas lísa gi=wónusu árabi // wa nas ma gi=wónusu bes árabi sákit // **law mašē-t fi šári/hum** gi=wónusu árabi juba // **ána šāyif al=muškila al=kabīr //** **hum** ma ligó ísim le árabi de // šenú **hum ma dayr-īn i-nad-ú árabi juba** ↑ wa ma éndu ísim le úo // le lúga de // so / úmon bi=jérib ámulu ignore lúga de // lakín you can't ignore al hája ey zol gi=híbu de // árabi juba is growing everywhere // de reality lázim hukúma bitána árif // **law hum ma dayr-īn i-samm-ú árabi juba / i-fattiš-u isim táni / árabi jenúbi / wála hája //** [. . .] **law šuf-ta kiswahili /** éndu a lot of Arabic words // lakín geyrú ísim to / it developed now / it is a new language / [. . .] so / the same thing / lázim **i-fattiš-u ísim /** yála árabi juba bi=kún kamán official language //

"South Sudanese people, in every place, speak Juba Arabic. I think, the government, I don't know, want to hide Arabic, but people still speak Arabic, and they don't speak whatever kind of Arabic. If you go into the streets, they speak Juba Arabic. I think that the main problem is that they did not find a name for this Arabic. Why don't they want to call it Juba Arabic and they don't have a name for it, for this *lúga*? So, they just try to ignore this *lúga*, but you cannot ignore something that is appreciated by everyone. Juba Arabic is growing everywhere. This is a reality that our government should know. If they don't want to call it Juba Arabic, let us look for another name, like *árabi jenúbi* ("Southern Sudanese Arabic") or something else. If you look at Kiswahili, it has many Arabic words, but they changed its name, it has evolved and it became a new language. So, the same thing, let us look for another name so that Juba Arabic can eventually be a national language."

This young returnee is a heritage speaker of Juba. He shows many instances of morphological integration from Sudanese Arabic and he switches frequently to English. Despite his limited proficiency in Juba Arabic, the interviewee puts emphasis on the linguistic distinctiveness of the pidgincreole and calls for the official recognition of this *lúga*. In his view, the status of national language necessarily occurs through the adoption of a new and more inclusive glottonym such as, for example, *árabi jenúbi* "Southern Sudanese Arabic." Similar to speaker 6 in Excerpt 6, the interviewee further strengthens his position with an explicit reference to Swahili, which is supposed to have evolved as an independent official language because the adoption of a new glottonym.

An opposite position concerning the glottonym *árabi júba* is the one expressed in this last interview excerpt.

Excerpt 9. Speaker 5

Juba / was where the word separation was first pronounced // There was no alternative for the future of South Sudan / except to go in the independence // Juba here // So you could see / this was a starting point / for nationalism / and patriotism // and if Juba Arabic is called Juba Arabic / I would wonder it could offend any liberally minded person // Any person who is not ignorant / actually //

As we can see, speaker 5 argues for an overt association between the toponym Juba and the rise of national South Sudanese identity. Consequently, he takes a position against the adoption of a new glottonym for Juba Arabic. This means that the "indigenous" border constructed by the interviewee in Excerpt 5 is not perceived as necessarily in contrast with the appreciation of the vehicular nature of Juba Arabic nor with the recognition of its local glottonym, which is considered symbolically associated with South Sudanese nationalism.

Conclusions

In this paper, I have tried to illustrate how the construction of linguistic borders in South Sudan interacts with locally available language ideologies. Evidence shows that the indexicalities of Juba Arabic, when compared to Sudanese Arabic, are interwoven with complex social discourses. First and foremost, in contrast to the State's decision to consider Juba Arabic a variety of the former dominant language, speakers of the pidgincreole overtly construct linguistic borders between Juba Arabic and its lexifier.

The most significant border marker for Juba Arabic speakers who do not speak Sudanese Arabic is still represented by the low degree of mutual intelligibility between the two languages (Excerpt 1). Juba Arabic-Sudanese Arabic bilingual speakers, for their part, make use of different features for constructing linguistic borders. The question could be then raised as to why certain linguistic features are only meaningful for some speakers and not for others. A reasonable answer is that metalinguistic representations of Juba Arabic are increasingly driven by the ideological hegemony enacted by the State through its discourse on "indigenous languages." In truth, metalinguistic representations focusing on linguistically relevant features like verbal morphosyntax (Excerpt 2) are gradually giving way to more politically emblematic representations which emphasize symbolic linguistic features such as the presence of "indigenous" loanwords in Juba Arabic (Excerpts 4 and 5). The tendency towards the "indigenization" of language is also reflected in the politically emblematic use of verbal morphosyntax for the construction of community-internal borders between South Sudanese long-term residents and returnees from north Sudan (Excerpt 3). It is also worth noting that speakers do not usually refer to phonological features for the construction of linguistic borders between Juba Arabic and Sudanese Arabic. The erasure (Irvine & Gal, 2000) of this relevant linguistic domain may be due to the fact that Juba Arabic shares some of its phonological features with other vehicular varieties of Arabic (*cf.* Section 2). Thus, speakers tend to eliminate details that are inconsistent with an exclusive linguistic identification of Juba Arabic.

As a further matter, the social construction of linguistic borders in South Sudan is evidently related to the emergence of a national identity. In contrast to the fact that Juba Arabic is not (and probably will never be) recognized as a national language, speakers consider it the only interethnic means of communication that can guarantee a national unity against the rampant tribalism enacted by the State by means of its language policies (Excerpts 6, 7). This view, which is also reinforced by the gradual upscaling of Juba Arabic in the local system of language classification (Excerpts 2, 6, 8), is not antithetical to the representation of the pidgincreole as an "indigenous language." This shows that the emerging national identity of South Sudan is inexorably linked with the notion of "indigenousness" inherited from colonial policies.

This paper inevitably simplifies a sociolinguistic reality that is much more complex. However, it reveals that linguistic borders constructed by speakers are not ideologically driven *per se*, since they can also be constrained by cognitively prominent features which are meaningful for descriptive linguists. Nevertheless, linguistic borders inevitably interact with local linguistic ideologies which move metalinguistic representations away from a factual linguistic reality. This state of affairs eventually brings to the fore the need for a more nuanced and multifaceted approach to language borders than those founded exclusively on ideological premises.

List of abbreviations

1, 2	first, second person
IND	indicative
IRR	irrealis
PL	plural
M	masculine
SG	singular

Notes

1 In this regard, it is interesting to note that, in the Arabic-based Ki-Nubi creole of Uganda and Kenya, the term *rután* simply means "language" (see Luffin, 2003).
2 Fieldwork in Juba (South Sudan) was carried out by Stefano Manfredi and Mauro Tosco (University of Turin) and it was made possible by a grant from the Italian Ministry of Education, University and Research (MIUR) within the project "Areas of Linguistic and Cultural Transition in Africa" (ATrA).
3 The interviews used for this study mainly focused on the metalinguistic representations and language attitudes towards Juba Arabic (see also Manfredi and Tosco, forthcoming). The interviews were conducted in Juba Arabic, English, and Sudanese Arabic. The following interview excerpts are coupled with metadata relating to each speaker. These include sociolinguistic information such as gender, age, place of birth, degree of formal education, patterns of bi/multilingualism and, when relevant, migration trajectories. Speech chunks in Juba Arabic, Sudanese Arabic, and Modern Standard Arabic are phonologically transcribed, whereas English is orthographically transcribed. Juba Arabic is reproduced in *italic*; Sudanese Arabic and Modern Standard Arabic are reproduced in **bold**, and English is underlined. All the excerpts display both morphological and prosodic segmentation (= and - respectively mark clitic and affix boundaries, // and / mark major and minor prosodic boundaries, ↑ indicates a rising intonation).
4 Male, 25 years old, born in Yei, primary education, L1 Juba Arabic, L2 Pojulu, moved to Juba in 1995.
5 Male, 38 years old, born in Juba, secondary education, L1 Juba Arabic, L2 Sudanese Arabic, L3 Bari.
6 In the first occurrence of the term, we can observe a code-mixed sentence corresponding to a prosodically isolated instance of direct speech including the two adjacent elements *luġa 'arabiyya* "Arabic language" which are both drawn from Arabic, as testified by the presence of the voiced velar fricative /ġ/ and the voiced pharyngeal fricative /'/. In the second occurrence, the realization of the term *lúga* conforms to the phonological rules of Juba Arabic (i.e., absence of the voiced velar fricative /ġ/) and it is not prosodically marked.
7 Male, 31 years old, born in Juba, secondary education, L1 Juba Arabic, L2 English, L3 Sudanese Arabic.
8 Male, 31 years old, born in Juba, higher education, L1 Juba Arabic, L2 Kuku, L3 English, moved to Maseru from 1990 until 2005.
9 Male, 59 years old, born in Juba, secondary education, L1 Mundari, L2 Juba Arabic, L3, Sudanese Arabic, L4 English, moved to Kampala from 1972 until 1979.
10 Female, 25 years old, born in Juba, secondary education, L1 Juba Arabic, L2 Arabic, L3 Abukaya.
11 Male, 27 years old, born in Khartoum, secondary education, L1 Sudanese Arabic, L2 Juba Arabic, L3 English, L4 Swahili, moved to Nairobi from 1995 until 2011.

References

Abdelhay, A. (2007). *The politics of language planning in the Sudan: The case of the Navaisha language policy* (Doctoral dissertation). University of Edinburgh, UK.

Abdelhay, A., Makoni, B., & Makoni, S. (2011). The Naivasha language policy: The language of politics and the politics of language in the Sudan. *Language Policy*, *10*, 1–18.

Aceto, M. (1999). Looking beyond decreolization as an explanatory model of language change in creole-speaking communities. *Journal of Pidgin and Creole Languages*, *14*(1), 93–119.

Bakker, P. (2008). Pidgins versus creoles and pidgincreoles. In S. Kouwenberg & J. V. Siegler (Eds.), *The handbook of pidgin and creole studies* (pp. 130–157). Oxford: Blackwell.

Bert, M., & Costa, J. (2014). What counts as a linguistic border, for whom and with what implications? Exploring Occitan and Francoprovençal in Rhône-Alpes, France. In D. Watt & C. Llamas (Eds.), *Language, borders and identity* (pp. 186–205). Edinburgh: Edinburgh University Press.

Bickerton, D. (1973). On the nature of a creole continuum. *Language*, *49*, 640–669.

Blommaert, J. (2007). Sociolinguistic scales. *Intercultural Pragmatics*, *4*(1), 1–19.

Blommaert, J., & Rampton, B. (2011). Language and superdiversity. *Diversities*, *13*(2), 1–22.

Carayol, M., & Chaudenson, R. (1978). Diglossie et continuum linguistique à la Réunion. In N. Gueunier, E. Genouvrier, & A. Khomsi (Eds.), *Les français devant la norme* (pp. 175–190). Paris: Champion.

Comrie, B. (2011). Creoles and language typology. In C. Lefebvre (Ed.), *Creoles, their substrates, and language typology* (pp. 599–611). Amsterdam: John Benjamins.

Cornips, L. (2014). Language contact, linguistic variability and the construction of local identities. In A. Ajarli & B. Maehium (Eds.), *The sociolinguistics of grammar* (pp. 67–90). Amsterdam: John Benjamins.

DeCamp, D. (1971). Toward a generative analysis of a post-creole speech continuum. In D. Hymes (Ed.), *Pidginization and creolization of languages* (pp. 349–370). Cambridge: Cambridge University Press.

Edwards, J. (2009). *Language and identity*. Cambridge: Cambridge University Press.

Ferguson, C. (1959). Diglossia. *Word*, *15*, 325–340.

García, O., & Li, W. (2014). *Translanguaging: Language, bilingualism and education*. Basingstoke: Palgrave Macmillan.

Garret, P. (2010). *Attitudes to language*. Cambridge: Cambridge University Press.

Goury, L., & Léglise, I. (2005). Contacts de créoles, créoles en contact. Présentation. In L. Goury & I. Léglise (Eds.), *Contacts de créoles, créoles en contact: Etudes Créoles, XXVIII* (pp. 9–22). Paris: L'Harmattan.

Irvine, J. T., & Gal, S. (2000). Language ideology and linguistic differentiation. In P. V. Kroskrity (Ed.), *Regimes of language: Ideologies, polities, and identities* (pp. 35–84). Santa Fe: School of American Research Press.

Jørgensen, N., Karrebæk, M. S., Madsen, L. M., & Møller, J. S. (2011). Polylanguaging in superdiversity. *Diversities*, *13*(2), 23–38.

Luffin, X. (2003). L'évolution sémantique du terme "riṭāna" dans les parlers arabes soudano-tchadiens. *Annales Aequatoria*, *24*, 159–177.

Mahmoud, U. (1979). *Variation in the aspectual system of Juba Arabic*. Washington, DC: Georgetown University.

Manfredi, S. (2010). *A grammatical description of Kordofanian Baggara Arabic* (Doctoral dissertation). Università degli Studi di Napoli "L'Orientale", Italy.

Manfredi, S. (2014). Native and non-native varieties of Arabic in an emerging urban centre of Western Sudan: Evidence from Kadugli. In M. Lafkioui (Ed.), *African Arabic: Approaches to dialectology* (pp. 13–51). Berlin: De Gruyter.

Manfredi, S. (2017). *Arabi Juba: un pidgin-créole du Soudan du Sud*. Louvain-la-Neuve: Peeters.
Manfredi, S., & Bizri, F. (Forthcoming). The sociolinguistics of Arabic-based pidgins and creoles. In E. Alwer & U. Horesh (Eds.), *The Routledge handbook of Arabic sociolinguistics*. New York: Routledge.
Manfredi, S., & Tosco, M. (2014). Language uses vs. language policy: South Sudan and Juba Arabic in the post-independence era. In E. Dansero, F. De Filippi, E. Fantini, & I. Marocco (Eds.), *Proceedings of the III CUCS Congress, Turin 19–21 September 2013, Journal of Universities and international development Cooperation 1*, 798–802. Turin: University of Turin.
Manfredi, S., & Tosco, M. (Forthcoming). A new state, an old language policy and a pidgin-creole: Juba Arabic in South Sudan. *Sociolinguistic Studies*.
Migge, B., & Léglise, I. (2011). On the emergence of new language varieties: The case of the Eastern Maroon Creole in French Guiana. In L. Hinrichs & J. Farquharson (Eds.), *Variation in the Caribbean: From creole continua to individual agency* (pp. 207–229). Amsterdam: John Benjamins.
Miller, C. (1989). Kelem kalam bitak: langues et tribunaux urbains en Equatoria. *Materiaux Arabes et Sudarabiques, 2*, 23–58.
Miller, C. (1991). Le changement linguistique à Juba et à Khartoum. In H. Bleuchot, C. Delmet, & D. Hopwood (Eds.), *Sudan-history, identity, ideology/histoire, identités, ideologies* (pp. 153–180). Ithaca: Ithaca Press.
Miller, C. (2002). Juba Arabic as a way for expressing a Southern Sudanese identity in Khartoum. In A. Youssi, F. Benjelloun, M. Dahbi, & Z. Iraqui-Sinaceur (Eds.), *Aspects of the dialects of Arabic today: Proceedings of the 4th conference of the AIDA* (pp. 114–122). Rabat: Amaaptril.
Miller, C. (2007). Do they speak the same language? Language use in Juba local courts. In E. Ditters & H. Motzki (Eds.), *Approaches to Arabic linguistics presented to Kees Versteegh on the occasion of his sixtieth birthday* (pp. 607–638). Leiden: Brill.
Mufwene, S. (1994). On decreolization: The case of Gullah. In M. Marcyliena (Ed.), *Language and the social construction of identity in creole situations* (pp. 63–99). Los Angeles: Center for Afro-American Studies.
Nakao, S. (2012). Revising the substratal/adstratal influence on Arabic creoles. In H. Osamu (Ed.), *Challanges in Nilotic linguistics and more, phonology, morphology and syntax: Studies in Nilotic linguistics* (pp. 127–149). Tokyo: ILCAA.
Siegel, J. (2010). Decreolization: A critical review. In J. C. Clements, M. E. Solon, J. F. Siegel, & B. D. Steiner (Eds.), *IUWPL9* (pp. 83–98). Bloomington: IULC Publications.
Tosco, M., & Manfredi, S. (2013). Pidgins and creoles. In J. Owens (Ed.), *The Oxford handbook of Arabic linguistics* (pp. 495–519). Oxford: Oxford University Press.
Versteegh, K. (1993). Levelling in the Southern Sudan: From Arabic creole to Arabic dialects. *International Journal of the Sociology of Language, 99*, 65–97.

5
FROM LANGUAGE TO DIALECT AND BACK

The case of Piedmontese

Mauro Tosco

A traditionally variegated linguistic landscape

Like so many Romance varieties, Piedmont, nowadays a region in northwestern Italy, saw the first written attestations of local varieties early in the Middle Ages. After a few words engraved in churches and dating from the 11th century, the bulk of the early documentation comes from the 12th to the 14th centuries and consists of various legal documents, often translated from Latin, coming from the medieval communes. One of the oldest is probably the "Oath of the Saint George's Company," itself a part of the Statute (written in Latin) of this mutual help society. The Oath is dated around 1321 and comes from the town of Chieri (Chér in Piedmontese). From a linguistic point of view, Clivio (2002, pp. 45–47) notes how a few graphic choices point to features of the local variety still found nowadays in the same area.[1] In other words, koineization and the creation of an Ausbau language (following Kloss, 1967), or ausbauization (Tosco, 2008), had not yet been attempted.

Much later, in 1563 Piedmont's capital, Turin, became the seat of the Duchy of Savoy under Duke Emmanuel Philibert. Since then, Italian has been the official language of the Duchy south and east of the Alps, while French was used in Savoy itself and in Alpine areas. As usual, the actual language situation was much more complicated and can be described as a typical diglossic or multiglossic situation: Italian never played much of an active role as a spoken language, and Italian was accompanied by French as the "high" variety and literary language (as well as of course by Latin as the language of the Church and partially of higher education). Although Italian was taught at school, French was the language mostly spoken at court and was widely known or at least understood by the growing bourgeoisie well into the 19th century. It was also, of course, the international language par excellence. The continuous and widespread use of more than one high variety – a "high bilingualism" ante litteram, both in written and oral domains – is by itself a striking difference from most cases of traditional diglossia.

The lexical, phraseological, and, to a lesser extent, morphosyntactic influence of French on the local languages is very strong. Thus, while Piedmontese shares with neighboring varieties a great number of isoglosses, its greatest originality[2] – and the reason of its general unintelligibility to speakers of neighboring local languages (not to mention speakers of Italian)[3] – lies perhaps in its lexical stock, which is rife with items borrowed from French at different historical periods and other words not found in the Italian cultural area at large.[4] All this is obviously a reflex of the peripheral position of Piedmont, in both geographical and political terms, throughout much of Italian history.

Historically, across most of the area different Piedmontese varieties were spoken, as well as, in the higher parts of the Alps, Occitan (ISO 639-3 code: oci) and Franco-Provençal (frp) varieties, and isolated Walser (Alemannic German; wae) pockets. To the East and South, Piedmontese gave way to Lombard (lmo) and Ligurian (lij) varieties.

Differing from the usual pattern of sociolinguistic dialects and from a simple diglossic situation, Piedmontese evolved over the centuries a koiné, essentially based upon the variety of the capital, Turin, which was extensively used by speakers of different varieties in the army, the markets, and wherever speakers of different varieties and languages (as with Occitan and Franco-Provençal speakers) met. As a written medium, Piedmontese was used mostly in belletristic literature (poetry, theater) and, to a limited extent, "high prose," and rose to its apex in the 18th and 19th centuries. Literature in the local varieties was always very scanty, and it is actually more common today than in the past (Regis, 2012).

The traditional language repertoire in Piedmont, as was probably common at the periphery of many cultural areas, was therefore variegated. It included at least:

- a local variety;
- the koiné, generally referred to simply as "Piedmontese" and used as a common medium in the marketplace, in the army, and wherever speakers of different varieties came into contact; it was also used, to a limited extent, as a written medium, but never as the "neutral" or more common one;
- a certain knowledge (depending, among other things, on schooling) of Italian as an official and "high" variety and as a written medium (and, therefore, a frequent source of loans);
- a varying amount of exposure to French, spread horizontally from across the Alps and reinforced vertically from above (and another much-used source of loans).[5]

The road to language uniformity

As expounded upon in preceding publications (Tosco, 2011a; 2011b; 2012; 2014; 2016), I think that contemporary language homogenization finds its main historical and ideological causes in the philosophical foundations of the modern state, especially since the rise of the nation-state. That modern states have a problem with multilingualism is probably a truism. As remarked by Kuehnelt-Leddihn (1952, pp. 100–101):

> a society consciously and collectively safeguarding a common *political* ideology is automatically pledged to common *cultural* values resulting in a rigorous homogeneity as to its "way of life."

Kuehnelt-Leddihn's requirement of "homogeneity" is further detailed in Smith's (1986, p. 136) words on the "solidarity of citinzenship" and the "common religion" required in modern societies:

> territorial nations must also be cultural communities. The solidarity of citizenship required a common "civil religion" formed out of shared myths and memories and symbols, and communicated in a standard language through educational institutions. So the territorial nation becomes a mass educational enterprise. It *[sic]* aim is cultural homogeneity. Men and women must be socialized into a uniform and shared way of life and belief-system, one that differs from those round about, which marks them off from outsiders who lack empathy with the national symbols and myths, and for whom the national values and memories hold no meaning.

Smith argues at length against the role of language as the main or sole differentiating mark of ethnicity, and notes that other cultural features may supersede language altogether:

> language is one of the most malleable and dependant cultural categories; apart from the great language fissures (for example, between Romance, Slavonic, and Germanic language groups in Europe), particular linguistic formations[6] are largely the product of the interplay of religion and political organization in a given area.
>
> *(Smith, 1986, p. 27)*

One might argue that "homogeneity" is too strong a word, especially in the light of the modern democratic state and the current profusion of language and minority rights in many multilingual countries. Still, it seems hard to prove Laponce (1984, pp. 192–193) wrong:

> [L]'État moderne, celui surtout qui recherche la mobilité géographique et sociale de ses citoyens, s'accomode mal du multilinguisme. À moins qu'il n'établisse des obstacles institutionnels dont le plus puissant est la frontière linguistique, il suit une pente naturelle qui le mène à l'unilinguisme, qui le mène vers cette situation où la langue cessant d'être un clivage interne, on peut parler vraiment d'État sans langue, au sens où Marx parlait d'État sans classe.

Laponce is clearly addressing here a modern, democratic state, which "strives for the geographic and social mobility of the citizens." It is this higher goal which provides a moral justification to language uniformization and which gives it its progressive character.

In this light, the repression of language diversity is part and parcel of the modern state's ideological foundations and a necessary step in nation-building. In a nutshell, Abbé Grégoire's *anéantissement des patois* was not the paradox that Phillipson (1992, p. 19) thought it to be (the fact that "[E]ven the influence of more democratic social ideas resulting from the French Revolution was filtered through monolingualism"). Monolingualism was not an accident of history nor a tragic aberration of the French Revolution and its noble goals; it was, on the contrary, pivotal to the attainment of those same goals. It is with an eye to the drive for language uniformity in modern states that we come back in the next section to the fate of language in Piedmont.

Becoming a dialect

In the case of Piedmont, as elsewhere in Europe, language loss has involved the shift from a multilingual and multidialectal competence to basically Italian monolingualism. Linguistic homogenization was certainly bolstered by the advent of the Italian national state (1861), but Italianization was given a decisive boost only later in the 20th century when it was coupled with massive industrialization, urbanization, and immigration from other parts of Italy, as well as universal literacy in Italian. The net result may be summarized as follows:[7]

- Italian became the only high variety;
- knowledge of "Piedmontese" (in the sense sketched above, i.e., the koiné) became less and less useful and therefore common, and the koiné itself is more and more perceived as "the dialect of Turin;"
- knowledge of the local variety persisted and, to a certain extent, continues today;
- French, which in the first half of the 19th century was still the most common medium in print, simply became a foreign language (nowadays much less taught in schools than English – which has become a compulsory subject in Italian schools).

It may be argued that Italian monolingualism is valid only at the societal level,[8] being supplemented by a rising knowledge of a foreign language at the individual level. As remarked by Blommaert and Verschueren (1998, p. 207) for European countries in general:

> Individual multilingualism may be encouraged – and it is effectively encouraged in almost every European state – as a key to European citizenship and to socioeconomic prosperity. Intrasocietal institutionalized multilingualism, by contrast, is actively discouraged by the same states (for instance, by means of

new and restrictive language legislation), while multilingualism at the level of international (European) institutions is again encouraged and even strongly defended whenever tendencies to reduce the number of the "working languages" in these institutions emerge.

To the authors, this is simply a consequence of a dogma of homogeneity. This is "a view of society in which differences are seen as dangerous and centrifugal and in which the 'best' society is suggested to be one without intergroup differences," while "[p]luriethnic and plurilingual societies" are seen as "problem-prone" (Blommaert & Verschueren, 1998, p. 195). But a point is missed here – one which may additionally help explain why individual multilingualism is favored, aside from the ideological goal of European citizenship and the unlikely wish on the part of governments to raise general socioeconomic prosperity. Traditional languages are territorial; they run against language uniformity at the institutional level and are potentially disruptive of societal cohesion and – what is more – state unity. Foreign languages (insofar of course as they remain foreign) are none of this: Their knowledge and use pertain to the individual and there they remain. It is not by chance that whenever foreign languages creep into the linguistic habits of the community through codeswitching and massive borrowing, their presence is officially resented.

What were the linguistic correlates of "becoming a dialect" in the case of Piedmontese? As anticipated earlier, literature in Piedmontese, though never massive, was especially abundant in the 18th and 19th centuries. As long as it was spoken in a situation of diglossia, sharing its roles with one (or, in this case, two) literary languages, there was no need for a policy of border keeping. The domains prescribed to each variety within the community may be tightly compartmentalized, but the varieties themselves, being shared by the whole community and, in principle, each and every speaker, are fully permeable to reciprocal contact and influence. There is little room for puristic attitudes; they will operate for the high varieties only, if ever; and will operate both horizontally (in order to reduce foreign influence and keep different high varieties apart) and vertically (to reduce the influence of low varieties and keep class distinctions). The influence will mainly proceed from the top and penetrate the lower varieties with borrowings, but the varieties are still kept separate in their roles. The written production in the lower varieties will tend to fill distinct niches of belletristic literature. In no case will it encroach upon the domains of higher varieties – therefore, no need for corpus planning will have to be met.

Late in the 19th century, increased urbanization and the rise of a literate lower middle class were met by literature in Piedmontese with a first bold attempt at stepping beyond its time-honored limits with the development of popular novels, first published often as separate installments in periodicals. Piedmontese popular prose of the period mimics its Italian contemporary counterparts, and its language is heavily Italianized. While in Tosco (2012, p. 256), where a few lexical cases of Italianization are reported, I traced the result to the ongoing Italianization of the language in towns, I rather suspect now that Italian words, but also affixes, syntax, and phraseology were simply grafted onto Piedmontese raw material. The result was a "Mischsprache" which did not reflect any real language, but nicely epitomized the upcoming end of diglossia: just as the traditional division of roles among varieties were coming to an end, so the low language was made to look as much as possible as the high one. Waiting for language uniformity in the society, the distance between languages was compressed, both in the linguistic material and in society. It is the "near-dialectization of a sister language – brought about, of course, by its sister" (Kloss, 1967, p. 34), and it is, in a way, language planning – although of a very peculiar nature. It is language planning designed to reduce language diversity, both in corpus and status. It is also, of course, exactly the contrary of what you are expected to do when you plan for reversing language shift and for language maintenance and development.

Resisting dialectization, courting folklorization

Breakdown in language transmission and use occurred still much later, especially after the Second World War. Never in its long history an official language, Piedmontese is nowadays for all purposes a sociolinguistic endangered dialect; its koine has been replaced in its former roles by Italian and the local varieties relegated mainly to older generations and in-group conversation.[9]

To measure the extent of such an abrupt decay in language transmission and use is not an easy task. Estimates about the current number of speakers of Piedmontese vary wildly; the *UNESCO Atlas of the World's Languages in Danger* suggests 2,000,000, adding "compromise figure based on various sources, possibly inflated," and classifies Piedmontese as "definitely endangered." The same is contended by Salminen (2007, p. 223), who judiciously writes that "it seems impossible to say anything about the numbers of speakers" of Piedmontese and other minority languages of Italy. *Ethnologue* suggests 1,600,000 speakers in Italy,[10] and, surprisingly, gives it a Language Status of "5 (Developing)".[11]

Against the backdrop of a shrinking number of speakers, one witnesses a growing interest in Piedmontese and an outburst of activism, publications, and political lobbying (so far, largely ineffectual) in order to have Piedmontese recognized.

Here as elsewhere, language activism operates in a situation in which culture is mostly a public good, freely provided for or at least subsidized by government agencies. Recognition implies subsidization, and the "language rights" often amount to little more than reserving language minorities (or their agents) a cut from the cake of public expenditures. As any funding reduces the marginal interest of unfunded activities, private, grassroots work soon runs the risk of being driven out of the market. The efficacy of the language preservation activities will also decrease, because their existence and survival will no longer be decided by market forces (i.e., by the members of the minority language themselves as consumers of cultural products), but by the favor of the politicians, and on political grounds.

Secondly and even more importantly, the "consumers" (i.e., the members of the language community) will soon lose interest and realize that, just as for much political activity, language preservation has little connection with real life. Minority language preservation will become a matter of interest for government-subsidized intellectuals and will lose any appeal for active people ready to risk their money in using the language in the modern fields of life (in marketing, advertisement, or public relations) and young people who could pass on the language to the next generation of speakers. Left to intellectuals and politicians, language preservation will soon become a matter of academic debate, folkloristic research, and political flimflam. The futility of much of the resulting cultural activities in support of language protection has been described, with examples ranging from Frisian to Australian languages and from Basque to Irish, by Fishman (1991, p. 91):

> The road to societal death is paved by language activity that is not focused on intergenerational continuity, i.e. that is diverted into efforts that do not involve and influence the socialization behaviors of families of child-bearing age [. . .] Song concerts, theatrical performances, poetry readings, lectures, publications and prizes are RLS[Reversing language shift; MT]-means, not RLS-ends in themselves. As RLS-means they are not intergenerationally continuous. Families are not formed, the daily and intergenerational societal channels of Xish communication are not re-established and the oralcy or literacy of the young are not substantially fashioned by such activities or by the institutions that maintain and conduct them.

Attention is often concentrated on literary uses, rather than on the necessity to create a modern, full *Ausbausprache*. Unable to speak to younger generations and cater to their needs, the paradoxical result of much revitalization is thus what Fishman (1988) aptly called the "folklorization" of language – its use for irrelevant domains. Again, this move is perfectly consonant to the language policies of the nation-state, and was conceived and carried on for the first time during the French Revolution. Having accomplished the task of eradicating difference, one can proceed to transform it in folklore. It is illuminating that, even while still fighting his war against language diversity, Abbé Grégoire enquired about the possibility of collecting data on the *patois* and regretted the loss of the lexicographic material of those same local languages at whose destruction he was busy: languages are reduced to vestiges or tombstones, and their preservation becomes a public duty (de Certeau, Julia, & Revel, 1975, p. 75). Diversity is not eliminated, but neutered and made politically and ideologically inoffensive. Having lost any societal and economic value, languages also lose their communicative value.

Often, the difference between the welfare-based support of a minority language and its folklorization is thin: as Fishman (1991, p. 161) notes, the securing of intergenerational transmission

> is difficult to manipulate and, therefore, tends to be either overlooked or given a lower priority than it deserves, while other more eye-catching but ephemeral efforts receive the lion's share of attention.

At the folklorization stage, a national language fulfills the whole range of the communicative needs of the community, while the historical language will no longer be a medium and becomes what Laponce (1984, p. 162) calls "une langue de boutonnière:"

> La langue-identité, souvent réduite à n'être guère plus qu'une langue de boutonnière, se suffit de peu : des crèches ou des jardins d'enfants dans la langue de l'ethnie d'origine, des chèques bilingues, des formulaires administratifs ou des étiquettes bilingues, des sermons ou des discours dans la langue minoritaire. [. . .] Ces marques de politesse envers une langue minoritaire réduisent, on l'espère, les effets négatifs d'un bilinguisme soustracteur. Le minoritaire acceptera plus volontiers d'utiliser la langue du groupe dominant si, de ci de là, on met en valeur, on donne un coup de chapeau à la langue de ses origines. Cette langue des origines, qui appartient à ce que nous avons appelé la langue-identité, se prête mieux que la langue-instrument aux solutions de type personnel [. . .] c'est un langue symbole qui, à la limite, n'a presque pas besoin d'être parlée.

In the case of Piedmontese, which lacks official recognition, even this role as an "identity language" is precluded. As elsewhere, the revitalization efforts have so far failed in bringing about the only thing which really matters in language diversity: a reversal in language transmission, attitudes, and language use.

A new language?

In spite of all this, the use of Piedmontese remains quite vigorous on the net and to a lesser degree in printing. The Wikipedia in Piedmontese boasts at the time of writing these lines 63,989 articles[12] – ranking #71 among Wikipedias by number of articles, and well above many national and official languages, from Albanian (#72), to Icelandic (#87), Irish (#88), and Swahili (#92), but also hosts of better-off or at least better-studied and recognized minority languages, from Breton (#73) to Low Saxon (#100), or, in Italy, Sardinian (#164) and Friulian (#191).[13]

Modern printed literature in Piedmontese comes to grips with previously unexplored genres, from crime novels to science fiction. In the – sparse and ephemeral – periodicals one may come up today not only with traditional poetry but also with articles on local and international politics, economics, and social affairs. Of course, the use of a sociolinguistic dialect in scientific or journalistic prose is born out of a will to prove that "you can say whatever you want in language X" – i.e., to reject diglossia. Conversely, it is no coincidence that such a move is not shared by literature in the local varieties, which, as anticipated earlier in the chapter, has actually been on the rise in recent times (Regis, 2012). Such a literature is a direct result of the weakening of the koiné, but does not share with it the desire to build a new *Ausbausprache*.

In Tosco (2012) I pointed to the use of Frenchization as a tool for enhancing the language diversity of Piedmontese vis-à-vis Italian, giving various examples of the use of French lexical and morphological material rediscovered (and sometimes simply newly introduced) with an eye to increase its distance from the dominating language and follow what in Tosco (2008) I called the "Ausbau golden rule:" "to maximize external difference and minimize internal variation."

Apart from neologisms, there is something else, and potentially of much greater importance, in such expressions as *sgav archeològich* "archaeological excavation(s),"[14] *tampa gravitassionala* "gravitational pit," or *calcul spantià* "distributed computing." Corpus planning operates here in a peculiar way: afterall, *sgav* "dig(ging), excavation" is a common word in Piedmontese, as is the related verb *sgavé* "to dig." *Archeològich*, although maybe not so common, is just as evident to the reader, if nothing else for its obvious affinity to similar words in other languages. *Tampa* is a common word meaning "hole, pit," and *spantià* is a participle and adjective meaning "scattered, spread out." The operation of language planning results here simply in the use of, e.g., *sgav* in a context (and a domain) which is usually barred from the language. Moreover, for their very meanings, *sgav* and *tampa* are more likely to be heard in a rural context rather than in science – the disorientation effect upon the reader thus becoming all the greater.

We touch here one of the great lessons of Kloss's (1967) seminal paper on Ausbau:

> in our age it is not so much by means of poetry and fiction that a language is reshaped (and perhaps salvaged) but by means of non-narrative prose.
> *(Kloss, 1967, p. 33).*

Kloss did not take into account the economics of *Ausbau*: non-narrative prose is, in general, less marketable than fiction. Kloss (1967, pp. 33–34) himself mentioned three levels of non-narrative prose: "popular" ("primers, community development, devotional and/or political booklets"), "sophisticated" ("literary criticism, summaries of essential findings of science"), and "learned" ("intricate presentations of research problems, procedures, results, original research on group-oriented problems, other original research work"). It is easy to see that at least the first of them is often the work of governmental agencies or is dictated by their policies (as when primers for minority languages are written and published following government-mandated curricula). Kloss's "learned" category, being the least marketable of all, is likewise subject to governmental subsidization – as well as by the need to reach a very limited and widely dispersed audience through a common medium. It is perhaps no coincidence that many publications on the net target the second ("sophisticated") category: politics and popular science belong here, as well as encyclopedias.

The downside, of course, is that reliable figures on the effects of such efforts are not easy to come by, and much publishing (physical or on the net) in minor languages runs the risk of becoming a game played by the authors and few others. As always (cf. Ó Riagáin & Stolz (2004) for many cases where an Ausbauized language becomes barely understandable to the "common" speaker), the results of the neological enterprise may pose a heavy burden to the reader. In the case of Piedmontese, the lexicon resorts as usual to the revitalization of inherited but long-forgotten or local words and expressions, but also to French or French-like borrowings and to outright creation (again, often on the model of French, never of Italian). *Età ëd Mes* ("Age-of-Middle") for "Middle Ages" would be transparent to a speaker of English or French, much less so to a Piedmontese literate in Italian, which uses the less transparent *medioevo*. *Arnassensa* "Renaissance" is obviously built on the model of French but using the corresponding native roots and derivational affixes. Although the raw material is of course common to Romance languages, the result is quite different from Italian *Rinascimento*. Examples can be multiplied (cf. Tosco, 2012, for a selection). If the fact that a tiny minority only of speakers is literate in Piedmontese, and that at first sight the Piedmontese orthography may appear daunting[15] were not enough, one must add the biggest stumbling block of all (often forgotten by language activists): the simple fact that no speaker of Piedmontese really "needs" to read and learn in this language, being already literate in another (Italian), in which more abundant, variegated, and cheaper information is available. The same applies, of course, to many, maybe most, minority languages all over the world. The only real need, if any, is linked to the quest for an identity (even a reinvented or created one) to be played against the majority. Which brings us back to issues of diversity and separateness – and, at least potentially, to the great taboo of the nation-state: political separation, i.e., secession.

Conclusion

The purposeful rejection of a traditional (but by now largely abandoned) diglossia is the hallmark of sociolinguistic dialects on the verge of becoming *Ausbau* languages. Already Fishman (1988, p. 4) noticed that,

> the diglossic solution to the problem of endangered languages is a very difficult one to arrive at under any circumstances, whether philosophically or empirically, all the more so under typically modern circumstances.

The rejection of diglossia goes hand in hand with the will, and need, to keep the "roof language" at bay. A national language is not, as per Hentschel's (2003) pious wish, the common roof under which new regional, minority languages are recognized and developed: where changed social conditions have ousted diglossia, the whole vertical dimension of language variation within a community has collapsed.

Quite the contrary; if regional languages are to survive through linguistic modernization and functional expansion, they will do it *against* such a roof – trying to topple it from below, as it were. The only alternative, to repeat Kloss's and Fishman's lesson, is dialectization and the loss of language diversity.

Sources

Wikipedia in Piedmontese: https://pms.wikipedia.org
é! (bimonthly in Piedmontese, 2004–2006)[16]

Notes

1 In particular, the rhotacism of *l* to *r*, and the palatalization of a final *n* in the plural, as in *agn* /aɲ/ "years" vs. singular *ann* /an/).
2 Still, the greatest isogloss separating Piedmontese from other Romance varieties is syntactic in nature and lies in the postverbal position of the object clitics in the Past; e.g.,

Present *i lo pijo*
i=lu= ˈpi-u
SBJ.1=OBJ.3M=take-PRES.MAIN.1SG
"I take it"
vs.
Past *i l'hai pijalo*
i=ˈlaj ˈpj-a=lu
SBJ.1=have-PRES.MAIN.1SG take-PART=OBJ.3M
"I took it"
and
i l'hai pijajlo
i=ˈlaj ˈpja=j=lu
SBJ.1=have-PRES.MAIN.1SG take-PART=IND.OBJ.3=OBJ.3M
"I took it from him"

All other Romance languages have preverbal object clitics (Romanian has postverbal object clitics with limitation to the Feminine Singular; Joseph, 1999). Cf. Tosco (2002) for the presence of *l* in front of the tensed forms of the verb "have" (as in *i l'hai* in the examples above). *l* may etymologically be either the object clitic or part of the subject clitic but synchronically it is just an element in the conjugation of 'to have.' Crucially, when used alone *i l'hai* means "I have," not "I have it," and **i hai* is impossible.
3 Cf. Tamburelli (2014) for a case study of intelligibility between a Northern Italian minority language (Lombard) and standard Italian. The results also apply, probably with even higher scores, to Piedmontese.
4 The recent *Repertorio Etimologico Piemontese* (Cornagliotti, 2015) provides ample (but far from complete) evidence of the role of French in the Piedmontese lexicon. The "Frenchization" of contemporary Ausbauized Piedmontese as a means to stress its diversity is analyzed in Tosco (2012); cf. also below.
5 A map of historical language use in Piedmont and a graphical representation of the varieties in diglossia is provided in Tosco (2011b, pp. 284–285) and Tosco (2012, pp. 250–251).
6 Smith's "particular language formations" obviously remind the linguist of Kloss's (1967) Ausbau languages which will be discussed at length further below.
7 Coluzzi (2008) provides an overview of the linguistic situation in Italy, many details on orthographies and language planning, and the legal provisions for language minorities.
8 New local varieties of Italian are of course developing, with the Italian spoken in Piedmont being characterized, as elsewhere, by a number of features at all levels (phonetics, phonology, morphosyntax, and, maybe prominently, the lexicon and phraseology). While their peculiarities largely go unnoticed to the speakers themselves, these are authentic dialects in the strictly linguistic sense of the word, being fully comprehensible (though at times "odd") to speakers of other varieties. As a result of this relatively "new entry" in the linguistic landscape, the label "dialect" usually bestowed upon both the local languages and the new varieties of Italian is particularly misleading.
9 A caveat may be in order here: data are missing on the frequent case of "newborn" speakers, who start actively and often massively using the language at a mature age as part and parcel of an in-group identity. Impressionistically, the phenomenon is widespread.
10 An active Piedmontese minority is found abroad, most notably in Argentina.
11 As Piedmontese is not recognized as a separate language, Italian censuses do not take into account knowledge and use of Piedmontese (and hosts of other minority languages) and bilingualism rates.

12. https://pms.wikipedia.org/wiki/Intrada, accessed on Dec. 26, 2016.
13. Both Sardinian and Friulian are recognized as minority languages (as per Italian Law no. 482, Dec. 15, 1999).
14. Consonant-ending nouns are not morphologically marked for number. Plurality may be expressed through the use of articles or quantifiers or through co-reference on the verbal form.
15. Together with a literary koiné, Piedmontese has a somewhat established orthography. Still, much spontaneous writing mimics the frequent codeswitching with Italian, and uses an Italianized orthography with few if any rules. On spontaneous writings in Piedmontese, cf. Miola (forth.).
16. An (almost) complete collection of *é!* can be downloaded as pdf at my webpage: www.maurotosco.net/an-piemonteis.html

References

Blommaert, J., & Verschueren, J. (1998). The role of language in European nationalist ideologies. In: B. B. Schieffelin, K. A. Woolard, & P. V. Kroskrity (Eds.), *Language ideologies: Practice and theory* (pp. 189–210). New York: Oxford University Press.

Clivio, G. P. (2002). *Profilo di storia della letteratura in piemontese.* Torino: Centro Studi Piemontesi/Ca dë Studi Piemontèis.

Coluzzi, P. (2008). Language planning for Italian regional languages ("dialects"). *Language Problems and Language Planning*, *32*(3), 215–236.

Cornagliotti, A. (Ed.). (2015). *Repertorio etimologico Piemontese.* Torino: Centro Studi Piemontesi/Ca dë Studi Piemontèis.

de Certeau, M., Julia, D., & Revel, J. (2002 [1975]). *Une politique de la langue: La révolution française et les patois: l'enquête Grégoire.* Paris: Gallimard.

Fishman, J. A. (1988). Language spread and language policy for endangered languages. In P. H. Lowenberg (Ed.), *Language spread and language policy: Issues, implications, and case studies: Proceedings of the Georgetown University Round Table on Languages and Linguistics 1987* (pp. 1–15). Washinton, DC: Georgetown University Press.

Fishman, J. A. (1991). *Reversing language shift.* Clevedon: Multilingual Matters.

Hentschel, G. (2003). New minor "Abstandsprachen" under the roof of a genetically close literary language? The case of Polish vs. Kashubian, Silesian and Podhalean. In J. Sherzer & T. Stolz (Eds.), *Minor languages: Approaches, definitions, controversies* (pp. 59–74). Bochum: Brockmeyer.

Joseph, B. D. (1999). Romanian and the Balkans: Some comparative perspectives. In S. M. Embleton, J. E. Joseph, & H.-J. Niederehe (Eds.), *The emergence of the modern language sciences: Studies on the transition from historical-comparative to structural linguistics in honour of E. F. K. Koerner* (pp. 217–234). Philadelphia/Amsterdam: John Benjamins.

Kloss, H. (1967). Abstand languages and Ausbau languages. *Anthropological Linguistics*, *9*(7), 29–41.

Laponce, J. A. (1984). *Langue et territoire.* Québec: Presses de l'Université Laval (English translation: *Languages and their territories.* Toronto: University of Toronto Press, 1987).

Miola, E. (forthcoming). Contested orthographies: Taking a closer look at spontaneous writing in Piedmontese. In M. Tosco & M. Tamburelli (Eds.), *Contested languages: The hidden multilingualism of Europe.* Amsterdam: John Benjamins.

Ó Riagáin, D., & Stolz, T. (Eds.). (2004). *Purism: Second helping.* Bochum: Brockmeyer.

Phillipson, R. (1992). *Linguistic imperialism.* Oxford: Oxford University Press.

Regis, R. (2012). Centro/periferia, Torino/Mondovì. In N. Duberti & E. Miola (Eds.), *Alpi del mare tra lingue e letterature* (pp. 97–118). Alessandria: dell'Orso.

Salminen, T. (2007). Endangered languages in Europe. In M. Brenzinger (Ed.), *Language diversity endangered* (pp. 205–232). Berlin: Mouton de Gruyter.

Smith, A. D. (1986). *The ethnic origins of nations*. Oxford: Basil Blackwell.

Tamburelli, M. (2014). Uncovering the "hidden" multilingualism of Europe: An Italian case study. *Journal of Multilingual and Multicultural Development*, 35(3), 252–270.

Tosco, M. (2002). When clitics collide: On 'to have' in Piedmontese. *Diachronica*, 19(2), 367–400.

Tosco, M. (2008). Introduction: Ausbau is everywhere! In M. Tosco (Ed.), *Ausbau and Abstand languages: Traditional and new approaches* (pp. 1–16). Berlin/New York: Mouton de Gruyter.

Tosco, M. (2011a). The nation-state and language diversity. In P. Valore (Ed.), *Multilingualism: Language, power, and knowledge* (pp. 87–101). Pisa: Edistudio.

Tosco, M. (2011b). Between endangerment and Ausbau. In E. Miola & P. Ramat (Eds.), *Language contact and language decay: Socio-political and linguistic perspectives* (pp. 227–246). Pavia: IUSS Press.

Tosco, M. (2012). Swinging back the pendulum: French morphology and de-Italianization in Piedmontese. In M. Vanhove, T. Stolz, A. Urdze, & H. Otsuka (Eds.), *Morphologies in contact* (pp. 247–262). Berlin: Akademie Verlag.

Tosco, M. (2014). The tension between language diversity and state building in Africa. *Incontri Linguistici*, 37, 169–180.

Tosco, M. (2016). Language diversity, development, and the state. In F. Gobbo (Ed.), *Lingua, politica, cultura: Serta gratulatoria in honorem Renato Corsetti* (pp. 40–46). New York: Mondial Books.

von Kuehnelt-Leddihn, E. (1952). *Liberty or equality: The challenge of our time*. London: Hollis & Carter.

6

DARIJA AND THE CONSTRUCTION OF "MOROCCANNESS"

Dominique Caubet

Darija (Moroccan Arabic) has undergone drastic changes in practices in the emerging Moroccan civil society from the beginning of the century. Its status was influenced by the place it had taken in the Moroccan landscape. Voices claimed that Darija was a key element for the definition of a new Moroccan identity, "Moroccanness."

Long before the Arab Spring, language representations had evolved in the wake of a cultural movement comparable to the Spanish *Movida Madrileña* – the *Nayda*[1] – which emerged around 2005. There have also been public debates around the defense of Amazigh (Berber) and of Darija (Moroccan Arabic), and around the plural nature of the Moroccan identity. One can observe a growing de facto "Moroccanisation" of the linguistic landscape which can be heard and read in the civic realm.[2]

A name for a language

Some languages bear different names, depending on the periods and the status given to them. Morocco has two mother tongues or home languages, namely Moroccan Arabic/Darija and Berber/Amazigh, while some families from the elite use French, English, or Spanish[3] as one of their home languages.

In French, Arabic vernaculars are often referred to as "arabe dialectal," "dialecte," or "arabe marocain/algérien, etc." In Algeria, the writer Kateb Yacine used to call it "arabe populaire" in the 1970s. Similarly, in English, one would use "colloquial/Moroccan Arabic" or "dialect." The identity relies on the adjective.

Darija

In today's Morocco "Darija" is the common name. According to G. S. Colin, the root *d-r-j* has the meaning "to progress slowly, step by step; to walk with little steps (like a pigeon); to walk fast with little steps (like a donkey)" (Iraqui-Sinaceur, 1993, vol. 3, pp. 514–516). *D-dārīja/l-lōġa d-dārīja* is "la langue courante, l'arabe dialectal." The general idea is that of "progressing step by step," of "pervasiveness," very different from the Eastern idea behind *'āmmiyya* conveying the idea of "common, vulgar, plebeian."

Scholars do not know exactly when the term was first used to name the language.[4] They do agree, however, that the adjective *dārij/dārija* qualifies *luġa* (language), *lahja* (dialect), or *'arabiyya* (Arabic). Some written uses in Classical Arabic are found in dictionaries: Kazimirski (1860, p. 686) has it as one of its meaning, used as an adjective and nominalized: "*dārij* (...) 5. *al-'arabiyya al-dārijah*: Vulgaire, usuel, parlé (arabe). (...) *fī al-dārij*: Dans l'arabe usuel." ("Vulgar, common, spoken (Arabic)").

Dozy (1927, p. 432) refers to Egypt in 1822: "*dārij*. Espèce de poème = *muwashshaḥāt*. Descr. de l'Eg. XIV, 209." ("Poem of the *muwashshaḥ* type.") Beaussier (1958, p. 329), who deals with North African Arabic only, has it as an adjective not associated with a language name: "*dārij* adj. Qui a cours, qui est à la mode. *hādhā dārij al-yawm*. C'est ce qui est à la mode aujourd'hui." ("Prevailing, fashionable; this is fashionable today.")

The general impression is that this use of Darija as a language name is fairly recent, but we haven't been able to trace it exactly. In the old days, people used to refer to *l-'arbiya dyal-na* ("our Arabic"), or just *l-'arbiya*, when opposed to Berber or French; or *l-lehja* ("speech, parlance"), when opposed to *l-foṣḥa* ("Classical Arabic").

This reference to Darija has developed tremendously since the beginning of the century, together with a form of public recognition. Nowadays, it is used massively in Arabic – and in French as "*la darija*."

The denominative verb *derrej* has even been reoriented from its original meaning of "moving forward step by step, distributing one by one, to organize harmoniously etc." (see Colin's dictionary, Iraqui-Sinaceur, 1993), to "speak/express yourself in Darija."

The term was used publicly in an editorial in the weekly *Telquel* (230, June 2006), by the director and founder Ahmed Benchemsi, "*Wa derrej a khouya!*" ("Come on brother, speak Darija"). To emphasise its "Moroccanness," he tried to give Darija a new name, "*L'Maghribiya*" (Moroccan):

> We must at all costs get out of this linguistic-identity issue. We must decide, and make it simple: our only common language is Darija. Some translate Darija by "Moroccan Arabic". I do not agree with this translation. It's Moroccan, that's all (...) It is unbelievable that we still ask ourselves about our true identity, when we have it every day on the tip of the tongue![5]:

Amazigh

The name "Berber" has been considered degrading or inappropriate by some, who associated it with its etymology ("Non-Greek, foreigner, incomprehensible" in Greek). In Darija, the generic term used in everyday talk (particularly when opposed to Arabic or French) was "*š-šelḥa*"[6]; again, this term was considered improper.

When it received official recognition – and during the preceding process – the language actually changed its name to "*l'amazigh(e),*" a masculine, in French, to "*l-luġa l-amaziġiya/l-amaziġiya*" in Arabic, and "*tamaziɣt*" in Amazigh.

Amazigh and the "legitimation paradox"

Darija suffers from its internalized dependency from its umbrella language, Classical Arabic. It was long considered a dialect, a distorted derivation from an idealized "mother language," Classical Arabic.[7] Amazigh also suffered from the same kind of subordinate status, but it was always considered different from Arabic, and thus had a form of independence.

The "legitimation paradox"

By "legitimation paradox" I mean a situation created when official recognition comes too late, at a time when the language's vitality is already declining.[8] Recognition, although decisive in terms of symbols, is accompanied by constraints imposed by institutions, and their weight can also lead to curtailing the development of the language.

In Morocco the Berber militancy, which had started in the 1960s among student movements, was long muzzled or diverted into folklorisation. Aït Mous and Wazif (2008, p. 282) sum up post-independence cultural policy in Morocco:

> The cultural policy of the early years of independence was marked by the exploitation of culture in a nationalist perspective. The newly independent state mainly focused on the consolidation of the national constants, i.e., Islam, the monarchy, Arabism and territorial unity.

Aomar Boum (2012) stresses the folkloric developments and the construction of "colorful subculture:"

> The Arab-identified state would recognize difference, but only in non-political terms: Berbers, for instance, were seen not as people with historical grievances against the state, but as people with striking dance steps, attractive clothes and jewelry, and beautiful casbahs. (. . .) The Marrakesh festival[9] provided an occasion for the state to construct Berberness as a colorful subculture that could lure tourists to the country. At the same time, the staged dances and exhibits were moments for the state to highlight its message of tolerance of all groups in Morocco – a message aimed at both Moroccans and foreign guests. (. . .) For the Moroccan state, however, the festivalization of arts and culture has been a key method of managing dissent, blunting the force of social movements.

Feliu (2006) shows how 1994 was to become an important step in a passage called "the official appropriation of the problem," with the decisive speech by Hassan II.

The official appropriation of Amazigh

A few dates: Hassan II's speech in 1994; the National Charter for Education in 1999; the creation of IRCAM in 2001; the Constitution adoption in 2011; and the Organic Laws in 2016.

Hassan II in 1994: a plural, l-lahajat (the dialects)

Berber's existence was first officially considered in a speech given by Hassan II (August 20 1994),[10] where he mentions the introduction of *"lahajatina"* (a plural: "our dialects") in education:

> As we undertake a national reflection on teaching and the curricula, we should consider introducing in the programs, the learning of our dialects (*lahajatina*), knowing that these dialects have contributed, alongside with Arabic, the mother language, the one that carried the word of God (…) in shaping our history and our glories.

Why avoid naming the languages? Should one read between the lines to guess if a language is recognized? Some linguists saw, behind the plural term *"lahajat,"* the possibility to include Darija, but nothing followed. Berber was not introduced at school in 1994, but was introduced on television, in the form of a short news bulletin in the three dialects around lunch time.

Paradoxically, the process was slowed down with the nomination of Abderrahmane Youssoufi's government of change in 1998, comprising a coalition of parties linked to the National Movement and its Arabo-Bassist ideology. Feliu (2006, p. 280) writes:

> But times have changed and though they (the parties) do not refer to the Amazigh question in their programs, A. Youssoufi said in his first speech to Parliament, that he would take into account "the Berber dimension" within Arab-Islamism. A key test for the new government is the development in 1999 of a National Charter for Education and Training.

The charter for education in 1999

The idea of introducing Berber at school was revived by the "Commission Spéciale Education Formation" (COSEF), which handed in a report in October 1999, la "Charte Nationale d'Education et de Formation," recommending the introduction of "the Amazigh language" as "a transition language supporting the learning of the official language." This was engaged just before the death of King Hassan II in July 1999 by Youssoufi's government.

Verbatim

In "Espace 3" of the Charter, "Levier 9"[11] is entitled: "Perfectionner l'enseignement et l'utilisation de la langue arabe et maîtriser les langues étrangères et s'ouvrir sur le

Tamazight" ("Improve the teaching and use of the Arabic language, master foreign languages, and open up to Tamazight"). In this document, two names are used, "Tamazight" (which would disappear in 2001 with the creation of IRCAM), and "the Amazighe/Amazigh Language" which was to become the official name. In the Charter, both terms were used, in association with an enigmatic expression "tout dialecte local" ("any local dialect"), which might be an allusion to Darija, if one reads between the lines.

The Charter allows a timid opening since Tamazight was not to be taught for itself but optionally, in order to facilitate the learning of Classical Arabic, the official language:[12]

> *115. Les autorités pédagogiques régionales pourront (. . .) choisir l'utilisation de la langue Amazigh ou tout dialecte local dans le but de faciliter l'apprentissage de la langue officielle au préscolaire et au premier cycle de l'école primaire.*
>
> "115. Regional educational authorities will be able (. . .) to choose to use the Amazigh language or any local dialect, in order to facilitate the learning of the official language at the preschool level and during the first cycle of primary school."

The creation of IRCAM: 2001: a first legitimation for Amazigh and standardisation

On the occasion of the second anniversary of his enthronement, in his "Discours du Trône" (30 July 2001),[13] Mohammed VI announced the creation of an Institute dedicated to Amazigh and gave his vision of an already plural Moroccan identity:

> (. . .) A plural identity, because it is built around various confluences: Amazigh, Arabic, Sub-Saharan, African, and Andalusian, many soils which by their openness to varied cultures and civilizations, and interacting with them, helped to refine and enrich our identity.

This statement prefigures what was to be introduced in the new post-Arab Spring constitution of July 2011, but Mohammed VI left no ambiguity as to the lack of status for Darija; even when quoting the 1999 Charter, he only mentioned "Amazigh," without reference to the "local dialects:"

> This charter has drawn the outlines of a clear language policy which gives the Arabic Language, as the official language and the language of the Holy Qur'an, the main language of instruction in all levels of education; which advocates the openness to foreign languages and introduces, for the first time in our country, Amazigh in the national education system.

The Institut Royal de la Culture Amazighe (IRCAM) was inaugurated by the Ajdir Speech, 17 October 2001. The language received its legitimation under the name "Amazigh:"

> Since Amazigh is a key element of the national culture, and a cultural heritage whose presence is reflected in all the expressions of the Moroccan history and

civilization, we pay particular attention to its promotion in the frame of the implementation of our project for a democratic and modern society, based on the consolidation and enhancement of the Moroccan personality and of its linguistic, cultural and civilizational symbols.

The promotion of Amazigh is a national responsibility, because no national culture can deny its historical roots.[14]

On 14 January 2002, the King appointed Mohamed Chafiq as "Recteur" of IRCAM, while the council and the administrative structures of the Institute were established during 2002.

Standardisation in a few months

The introduction of Amazigh at school was decided for September 2003, which means that standardization had to be organized in nine months' time, including the choice of an alphabet! The choice was between the Arabic script (not very adapted symbolically), and the Latin one (associated with the Algerian choice for Kabyle and with colonialism). In the end, Morocco chose *tifinagh*, which had been devised by the Kabyle "Académie Berbère" in Paris at the end of the 1960s, as a compromise. A new *recteur* for IRCAM, Ahmed Boukous, was appointed on 23 November 2003.

Legitimation = constraints and control: a Jacobin model

The three main Moroccan dialects (Rif, Middle Atlas, and Souss) are *not mutually intelligible* and the choice was made to create a standard variety, a very Jacobinic decision. Pouessel (2013:21) notes that "the re-development of the Amazigh language borrows the model of a single language" (*langue unique*).

In an interview to the site yabiladi.com in November 2011,[15] Ahmed Boukous, in response to the question "How much progress has been made towards the reunification of the Amazigh languages?", answers as follows:

> *Mais le choix qui est fait consiste à aménager ces dialectes de manière à en faire une langue amazighe commune qui est en train d'être codifiée, standardisée à l'IRCAM.*
>
> "But the choice made promotes the development of the dialects in order to transform them into a common Amazigh language which is in the process of being codified, standardized at IRCAM."

The risk incurred by the *"langue unique"* approach is that of creating a new artificial diglossia between the real dialects spoken and the new language developed at IRCAM, and all the problems this entails.

Pouessel (2013, p. 20) shows how this recognition was done via a "nationalization of Amazighity in the sense that it is proclaimed and deployed by the state as a culture belonging to all Moroccans and not restricted to a 'minority.'" This may seem a noble idea, but some observers argue this was done for fear of separatism.

Post-Arab spring: the constitutionalisation of Amazigh: an official language – 2011

Aït Mous (2011, p. 128) argues that the long-awaited constitutionalisation of Amazigh was made possible after the Arab Spring and the 20 February Movement in 2011:

> This claim for constitutionalisation remained unanswered by the State until the demonstrations initiated by the February 20 movement. In his speech of March 9, 2011, King Mohammed VI addresses the issue of Amazighity in the frame of the constitutional revision. Some saw in these words pure political expediency and a kind of diversion from the Amazigh activists' negative assessment of the management of Amazighity (the failure of the teaching of Amazigh, the banning of Amazigh names, the creation of an undersized Amazigh TV channel, etc.).

To everyone's surprise the Amazigh language became an official – and not national (as was claimed) – language. The initial version of Article 5, suggested by the Advisory Board for the revision of the Constitution, was (Aït Mouss, 2011): "The Arabic language and the Amazigh language are the two official languages of Morocco." But this was modified during the final consultations led by M. Mouatassim, the King's counsellor, in June of 2011, with the consent of the political parties. In order to please the conservative and pan-Arab parties (Istiqlal and PJD), the formulation became uneven, which considerably reduced the scope of the legitimation:

> *L'arabe demeure la langue officielle de l'Etat.*
> *L'Etat œuvre à la protection et au développement de la langue arabe, ainsi qu'à la promotion de son utilisation.*
> *De même, l'amazighe constitue une langue officielle de l'Etat, en tant que patrimoine commun à tous les Marocains sans exception.*
> *Une loi organique définit le processus de mise en œuvre du caractère officiel de cette langue, ainsi que les modalités de son intégration dans l'enseignement et aux domaines prioritaires de la vie publique, et ce afin de lui permettre de remplir à terme sa fonction de langue officielle.*
> "Arabic remains the official language of the State.
> The State works for the protection and development of the Arabic language and the promotion of its use.
> Likewise, Amazigh constitutes an official language of the State, being common patrimony of all Moroccans without any exception.
> An organic law defines the process of implementation of the official character of this language, as well as the modalities of its integration into teaching and into the priority areas of public life, in order to enable it to fulfill its function as an official language."[16]

The last paragraphs of Article 5 concern the "other" (non-official) languages and a new Council (my emphasis):

> *L'Etat œuvre à la préservation du Hassani, en tant que partie intégrante de l'identité culturelle marocaine unie, ainsi qu'à la protection des expressions culturelles et des parlers pratiqués au Maroc. De même, il veille à la cohérence de la politique linguistique et culturelle nationale et à l'apprentissage et la maîtrise des langues étrangères les plus utilisées dans le monde, en tant qu'outils de communication, d'intégration et d'interaction avec la société du savoir, et d'ouverture sur les différentes cultures et sur les civilisations contemporaines.*
>
> *Il est créé un Conseil national des langues et de la culture marocaine, chargé notamment de la protection et du développement des langues arabe et amazighe et des diverses expressions culturelles marocaines, qui constituent un patrimoine authentique et une source d'inspiration contemporaine. Il regroupe l'ensemble des institutions concernées par ces domaines. Une loi organique en détermine les attributions, la composition et les modalités de fonctionnement.*

"The State works for the preservation of *Hassani*, as an integral component of the Moroccan cultural united identity, as well as for the protection *of the cultural expressions and the dialects spoken in Morocco* [Note: "*parlers pratiqués*"]. Likewise, it sees to the coherence of the linguistic and cultural national policy and to the learning and mastering of the foreign languages of greatest use in the world, as tools of communication, of integration and of interaction with the knowledge society, and as a gateway to different cultures and to contemporary civilisations.

A National Council of the Moroccan Languages and Culture is created, in charge – inter alia – of the protection and the development of the Arabic and Amazigh languages and of *the various Moroccan cultural expressions*, which constitute one authentic patrimony and a contemporary source of inspiration. It brings together the institutions concerned in these domains. An organic law determines its attributions, its composition, and its operating procedures."

The future organic laws: changes expected

It took over five years to implement the organic laws concerning Amazigh and the Council. The project was presented during the summer of 2016, and after consultation, it was adopted during the cabinet meeting on 27 September 2016 and approved by the King, only days before the legislative elections. However, the law will have to be discussed and voted on by the newly elected parliament. A year later, in August 2017, nothing has been done in that sense.

The definition of Amazigh present in the bill is very different from the "*langue unique*" developed by IRCAM during the last fifteen years; according to article 1,[17] Amazigh consists of "all the dialects spoken in the different regions of the Kingdom," as well as "the Amazigh linguistic and lexical output issued by the competent institutions." Note that IRCAM is not mentioned here.

New developments are to be expected, especially with the organic law concerning the future "Conseil national des langues et de la culture marocaine" (CNLCM).[18] This body is to absorb all pre-existing institutions, such as "L'Académie Mohammed VI pour la langue arabe" and IRCAM. Other structures are to be created for the non-official languages ("Hassani and the other dialects and Moroccan cultural expressions"), and for the development of foreign languages. Thus, IRCAM is set to lose its independence. *HuffPost Maroc* wonders whether it will disappear,[19] since the organic law on Amazigh only mentions the competence of the CNLCM.

Comparing the statuses of Amazigh and Darija, Catherine Miller (2015, p. 106) shows how, in both cases, the authorities met popular expectations:

> The modalities of the political recovery are very different from that of Amazigh, since, in the case of Darija, there has not been a formal institutionalisation process like the creation of the IRCAM and the constitutionalisation of Amazigh. But in both cases, one will note the intelligence of the political power that seems to go in the direction of social demands and to meet the most immediate requirements: "save" Amazigh by ordering its codification and its teaching; "democratise" the public space by letting Darija sneak into the interstices of modernity.

Darija as an element of "Moroccanness"

Darija played a central part in the artistic productions of the urban scene, partly because the artists of the *Nayda* mostly come from a popular background where Darija is the only language used daily. Unexpectedly, after the heavy Arabicization of the schooling system in the mid-1970s and the pan-Arabic ideology spread by the political class since Independence, youngsters claimed that their language, as Moroccans, was Darija, and that they could take pride in it – a feeling completely new in North Africa, where vernaculars had been systematically stigmatised.[20]

This music scene was followed and accompanied by young journalists, managers, architects, and designers who admired their creativity, and who, although they were trained in French or in MSA, also started using Darija in all kinds of new domains for them, like the press, advertising, dubbing foreign series, etc.

However, one must remember that this movement is also set in a new socioeconomic context, with the opening of markets, the rise of advertising, the development of mobile phones, the social media, and the arrival of young people as potential clients, which accelerated the evolution of practices and the need for economic operators to adapt to this market law using a language closer to people's practices (see Miller, 2015, p. 105): "certain economic spheres recycle this dynamic making Darija coexist with modernity and patriotism."

The language situation in North Africa has been mainly described in terms of conflicts, opposing languages: MSA vs. French, MSA vs. Darija, Darija vs. Amazigh, etc. The civic movement examined here tried to rehabilitate Darija, to make it regain dignity in the eyes of its millions of daily users, after decades of stigmatisation, but it did not use violent terms against the other languages. Darija only makes sense as part of a plurality, in the context of coexistence of several languages, and a plural identity.

Darija unchained

Darija is not a minority language, since it is spoken and used by an enormous proportion of the population; it is not endangered either, but it has no legal status. The last 2004 census showed that:

> A very large majority (nearly all) of the population speaks first the Arabic dialect "Darija", with 89.8% (96% in urban areas and 80.2% in rural areas).[21]

Being "illegitimate" involves some positive aspects, such as freedom and lack of control, especially when legitimation comes from the civil society. During the massive spontaneous passage to writing, writing and reading in Darija on keyboards became natural and has even recently led to a novel form of literacy in a non-codified language, due to informal language planning.[22] In over eight years of exchanges on the social networks, I have never seen any form of reproach on how a word or an expression was spelt or in which script (Arabic or Latin).

We will examine the various stages of this process over the last fifteen years. The first signs of a change in mentalities for Darija came as early as 2002, when the weekly *Telquel* published a long article on "Darija, National Language," linking it explicitly to a new Moroccan identity. From then on, it became a recurrent subject of social debate.

2002–2010: Darija becomes visible

After the first pioneer *Telquel* headline in 2002, the subject was to grow after the tragic events of 2003, when Moroccan society started to open up on a number of taboo subjects.

The interest in Darija goes beyond the language itself; it is a means to claim a new definition of the Moroccan identity, to convey things in a more Moroccan way, and to use a language accessible to all.

Telquel 2002: Darija langue nationale

The first headline appeared in *Telquel* weekly in June 2002, claiming Darija as "Langue Nationale:" "Moroccan Arabic, our everyday speech/parlance, is not taken seriously. Yet it is the only language that unites us all."[23] The press in French is not read massively, and the taboo lines are much more flexible than in Arabic, which means that the impact was limited at the time and it went unnoticed by a vast audience. But it remains historical.

FIGURE 6.1 *Telquel* magazine, June 2002 © Dominique Caubet.

2003: A traumatic year with unexpected developments

2003 was a very traumatic year for Morocco, with two events that helped Moroccan society speak out after years of silence since *les années de plomb* ("the years of lead") imposed by the former king's rule (1970–1990). In February, there was the arrest and trial of 14 young metal musicians accused of satanic rites, which resulted in an unexpected mobilisation that finally led to their release in March.

It was soon followed by seven simultaneous kamikaze bombings on 16 May, by 14 young men in Casablanca, causing the death of 33 people and many injuries. Both events, occurring in such a short period of time – linked to a loosening of political control (and/or a wish for the power to fight fundamentalism?) and the first successful mobilisation – led to a very novel public questioning by the Moroccan society, especially of the educational system, that had produced these fundamentalist kamikazes, and on the identity of Morocco (see Caubet, 2008; 2009).

Darija as a language of modernity, of democracy: Noureddine Ayouch – 2003

In December 2003, the businessman Noureddine Ayouch[24] announced his project to apply for the creation of a TV channel in Darija, *Moufida*, during the process of liberalisation of the audio-visual media (which ended the state monopoly)[25]; in an interview to the weekly *Maroc Hebdo International*, he explained the general attitude that led him to this idea, linking Darija to cultural identity, to certain moral values, and to democracy:

> (...) We believe that in Morocco, we have a cultural identity issue.
>
> (...) Through this project, we want to tackle the problems of obscurantism, violence and intolerance that are harmful to the development of our country. For these reasons, we believe that this project is essential for our country. *Moufida* will also take part in building democratic Morocco, relying on its strong traditional values, such as solidarity, respect for others and the entrepreneurial spirit.
>
> (...) Our goal is to show the other face of Morocco, the Morocco that moves forward, undertakes, and is successful, and that is neither fatalistic nor obscurantist. This is the spirit of the channel *Moufida*.

N. Ayouch was one of the first to openly link Darija and progress, Darija and modernity, and to discard the stance associating it with tradition, backwardness, and obsolescence. In an interview recorded in 2004 (Caubet, 2005, p. 139) he adds: "I told myself that we had to launch *a civic channel*, that would raise cultural and social issues; and for that channel, without any hesitation, we chose Colloquial Arabic."

His ideas put in practice, or how the Moufida project influenced public television

Although his channel was not created officially, it had great influence on the Moroccan audiovisual landscape; from the beginning of 2004, he had started shooting pilot episodes for future programs. He decided to produce and circulate *Moufida* on DVDs, showing them in the local offices of his foundation Zakoura.

Some of the presenters and producers who worked on the project later proposed pilots to the public TV channels such as Al-Aoula or 2M, the most striking being

Oussar wa Houloul,[26] a talk-show where interviews and discussions are led in Darija. It is one of the most popular family-oriented programs that has been going on for ten years.

2005–2007 Darija as a component of a new Moroccan identity

The journalist and singer Reda Allali, in *Telquel* 231 (June 2006) – in a column called "Who are we?" – revisits the Moroccan identity, defining Darija as its "common denominator:"

> For very long, public speech was monopolized: one TV, one radio, the press under control (. . .) A single voice to remind us *ad nauseam*, that we are Arabs, that our popular music is unworthy, that salvation lies necessarily in an imitation of the East. But the state-subsidized culture is dead. There are numerous voices nowadays. Rappers or Amazigh singers or Amazigh rappers (yes, there are!), can be heard shamelessly. They cannot even protect their work to the Moroccan Office of copyright since they have no confidence in the system. To silence them, some explain that they are not Moroccan. A question: What should their nationality be, then? Suddenly, diversity comes to light, it imposes itself despite years of silence. And the old lie about culturally monolithic Morocco standing at attention and watching the "Sahra Fennia kobra" on TV, is shattered. This is an opportunity to finally look ourselves right in the eye, and see that we are Arabs, but also Amazighs, Africans (. . .) Fans of Oum Kalthoum, but also of Bob Marley. This is an opportunity to seek our common denominator – eg Darija.

Another important weekly, *Le Journal Hebdomadaire* (which started in 2001 and was shut down in January 2010 – like *Nichane* a few months later, using advertising boycott) also had a special issue on Darija (5–11 May 2007)[27]:

> Is the biggest visibility of Darija in the urban and media landscape an indication of *a reconciliation of Moroccans with themselves*? Is this a claim for an identity with multiple components? (. . .) Isn't this language, which has evolved tremendously during the twentieth century, the main vehicle of our cultural heritage?

Darija, a language for reconciliation with themselves, after years of self-hatred, a language that makes you accept who you really are, leading to a "claim of a plural identity." Beyoud's drawing on the cover illustrates this plurality (see Figure 6.2):

> What is happening today is that languages in presence coexist more peacefully than before. (. . .) But what emerges is the refusal of a Jacobin model, that of an arabisation that would impose a language over others.

112 Dominique Caubet

FIGURE 6.2   *Le Journal Hebdomadaire*; drawing by Beyoud. © Dominique Caubet.

Darija in the press: the Nichane experience (2006–2010)

In September 2006, A. Benchemsi (director) and *TelQuel*'s editor in chief, Driss Ksikes, launched an Arabic weekly called *Nichane* ("direct/straightforward") in Darija. It was written in a mix of MSA and Darija, using *l'Maghribiya* mostly for the transcription of interviews and for headlines (see Miller, 2012b). Benchemsi's weekly column was always in Darija (the same as that of *Telquel* translated into Darija). The journal was extremely popular among young people, because Darija on the cover was really appealing, and the reading in mixed Arabic went smoothly for non-intellectuals.

Its easy access by a popular audience, and the impact of its insolent front-pages in Darija, made it much more potent than the French version of *Telquel* whose readership was a social elite. Each copy was read by at least five people and it sold over twenty thousand copies, which made it the first weekly in Arabic. It soon became a victim of its own success, with several trials against the journalists and its banning for several months. All this ended with the advertising boycott which slowly but surely smothered the journal, which published its last issue in October 2010, only months before the Arab Spring.

Ahmed Benchemsi explained the reasons for its closure linking it to its editorial line[28] – "a different view of society. In the early 2000s, the concepts of secularism, of individual freedom, of cultural upsurge, were not yet part of the public debate."

The issue of language is essential to understand the scope of this weekly. Even though the magazine was mostly written in MSA, the presence of Darija in some key places (name, cheeky headlines and titles, editorial, interviews), associated the journal with Darija. A. Cohen (2011:259) sees its use as "an act of transgression:"

> *Nichane* gives popular classes the opportunity to question, in their language, taboo issues – such as Islam and politics – which constitute the foundation of the power of the elites who seek to ensure control over them.

Nichane has shown where the limits – "the red lines" – for the public use of Darija stand, and even more so, under its written form. The several trials of *Nichane* were mostly linked to its use of Darija: "mocking Islam" (n. 14, December 2006, three and a half years of jail suspended for two journalists and three months' ban), for an article with Moroccan jokes in Darija; and "lack of respect for the person of the King" for addressing him in Darija (July 2007).[29] But as C. Miller (2012b:424) writes, its role was decisive: "the *Nichane* experience has helped free 'journalistic' Darija from its purely humorous register and touch a wider readership."

Is Darija suitable for dubbing TV series? 2009

This was to be another episode of public debate regarding the use of Darija in public and the type of Darija chosen: which Darija? Which variety? Is Casablanca (the economic capital and a metropolis counting over 4 million inhabitants) Darija too "vulgar" or associated with "street language" to be used on television? This was all very much linked to sensitive identity questions, showing how intricately the bonds were felt between the variety used and the representation of a collective Moroccan personality.

In 2008–2009, Salim Cheikh, the Director of 2M TV Channel (based in Casablanca), decided to try something completely new: the dubbing of Spanish-speaking Mexican *telenovelas* into Darija, similar to what was done in Syria. They started out with the Mexican series. After two months of intensive work of dubbing by the firm Plug-in (Casablanca), for whom it was a premiere, the first episode was broadcasted on 4 May 2009. It soon became extremely popular, starting with 38% of audience shares and reaching up to 59% in 2010.

But paradoxically, it received attacks from all sides (Miller, 2012):

> A "conservative" wing/discourse criticizing westernization, consumerism, low moral value of these TV novelas and considering that the use of Darija was the tool of French-speaking groups in order to marginalize the place of al-'arabiya (MSA).

And a debate about the inadequacy of the Darija chosen among progressives:

> the "progressive wing" was rather divided concerning this first TV novela in Darija, and critics around the dubbing cut across political and ideological stand. A recurrent argument was that the translation sounds hilarious or ridiculous for Moroccan ears; it was impossible to imagine Moroccans engaged in such type of love interactions; the vocabulary was inadequate; it sounded like advertising; stylistic choices were not pertinent with the characters, too vulgar, based on the street language of Casablanca only, without reflecting the geographic and social diversity of Moroccan Arabic.

Reda Allali, in his chronicle Zakaria Boualem, imagined the first reaction of his character: laughter due to surprise and embarrassment:

> He bursts out laughing. Not an ironic chuckle, no, a real burst that leaves the spinal cord and reaches the mouth, bypassing the brain. On the screen, the object of ridicule, (. . .) Ignacio declares his love to the beautiful Isabella in these terms: *Chetti ya Isabella, ana kan mout 3alik, oullah. . . ma kantkhiyilch bla bik. . . rani 3iit* (you see Isabella, I'm crazy about you, I swear. . . I can't imagine myself without you. . . I can't stand it anymore). Isabella replied threateningly: *Ana machi dial tfelia, ila kounti baghi chi haja dial bessah, 3ayet lwalid ou chouf m3ah chi hal* (I am not the kind of girl you play with, if you want something serious, call my father and arrange a solution with him).[30]

Moroccans felt embarrassed to see Ignacio declare his love to Isabella on television in Darija, a situation hardly plausible in Morocco, where even in private, they might use French euphemistically (see Ziamari & Barontini, 2013).

There is a gap between the immediate identification with their language and the situations presented on the screen. But after the first shock, people have become used to it; other series were dubbed in Darija, including an excellent season of CSI New York (in 2010), which was not repeated. But after seven years of practice, the

Minister of Communication, a member of the majority conservative party PJD, proposed to prohibit this dubbing in July 2016 during a debate in the Parliament about the reform of the HACA (High Authority for Audiovisual Communication).[31] Whether this amendment was adopted or not in the final version of the law, the mere fact that the PJD group should fight against dubbing in Darija in 2016 is significant.

Should Darija be considered a street language or a language for all Moroccans? The question is recurrent in the public debates. Its entry into politics and its use by the different actors have shown how it has been used.

Darija after 2011: entry into politics

Darija has been used in two radically different ways: one with the aim of being accessible to all, the other with a cruder approach.

A new way of doing politics: the 20 February movement: Darija for the people

In 2011, the 20 February Movement (#feb20) was created as a Facebook group called "Mouvement de liberté et démocratie maintenant;"[32] it imposed a new way of doing politics – in connection with the social medias – where Darija played an important part.

Up to February 2011, the Moroccan Facebook was a peaceful, carefree community, but the announcement of this demonstration, linked to the Tunisian and Egyptian contexts, caused nervousness from the authorities and soon resulted in a major split between pro- and anti-#feb20. Violent and sustained cyber-attacks were launched against the pro-#feb20 side, trying to intimidate the future demonstrators. Web users who had so far shared cultural tastes suddenly realized that they were in complete disagreement politically. Several articles on the web reported on this situation:

> A comment posted repeatedly "explained" that these young people aimed at "destroying a country created in 780" and the author "doubted they were Moroccan". According to that same person, their aliases indicated that they were homosexual, atheist, secular, failed journalists, Jews (...) Ending with a threat: "We know who you are ...".[33]

Nevertheless, they persisted, and on 13 February published a video on YouTube[34] with young people explaining in Darija and Amazigh why they were going to go out and protest and saying: "*Ana maghribi, ghadi nkhrej 20 Feb.*" ("I am Moroccan, I will go out on 20 February"), followed by a reason. It was very brave for them to appear with their faces uncovered in this violent context; some of them were attacked personally and considered as "traitors to the country" and as "non-Moroccans," as "agents of the Polisario" and as "converted Christians."

During the weekly demonstrations and sit-ins that followed every Sunday from 20 February to the end of June, the slogans chanted were mostly in Darija, written in a style close to poetry or quatrains (see Caubet & Miller, 2016). H. Maghraoui

(2013, p. 170) stresses that "once the political discourse has incorporated Moroccan Arabic, most people are more and more interested in political life."

Darija and vulgarity

From the other side of the political spectrum, A. Benkirane, the Prime Minister (from the conservative PJD Party) – who was nominated in November 2011 and who has just been asked to form a new government after winning the elections again in October 2016 – has gained a reputation for his use of Darija. Finally, he had to resign in February 2017 after failing to form a government.

His first appearance on television (3 December 2011) in the program *Liqa'* ("Encouter") left an impression. He conversed very naturally with the journalist for over an hour, impressing the audience, who were used to the usual "*langue de bois*" ("political cant") in MSA. The Prime Minister became famous for his expression: *fhemtini wella la?* ("Did you understand me or not?"), which was also used to mock him on the web.

Populism and street language

Benkirane uses Darija skillfully, exploring all the facets of the language, including the most vulgar; this led to numerous comments, showing the impact Darija can have in politics.

Before the last elections, the writer and journalist Driss Jaydane wrote a column entitled "Why should Benkirane leave;"[35] one of the reasons was the way he uses "our Darija," opposing two possible attitudes:

> And if we decided to use *our Darija* to be closer to the people – which is a good thing – the Prime Minister will have allowed proximity and vulgarity to merge. Turning political speech – henceforth audible by ordinary citizens – into street language. *Mine is bigger than yours. . .!*

The latter expression is a quotation of the Prime Minister addressing a woman MP from the opposition in Parliament on 3 February 2015,[36] and comparing their political parties.

It is no wonder he should take a stance against the presence of Darija in education (see below), if he can only use it in such vulgar way.

Darija goes a step forward: a national debate on its use in education and a Moroccan passage to literacy

The recent developments (2013–2016) of Darija can be described as *a qualitative step forward*, changing the nature of its public scope. These phenomena have been described at some length in very recent publications and I will just sum up the issues at stake. Novel things are happening so fast that scholars actually do research on on-going processes and debates, with the flow of the trend.[37]

Darija as a language for teaching: another failure (2013–2015)

In the song "60%,"[38] the group *Hoba Hoba Spirit* (whose author is Reda Allali), use the same affectionate expression as Driss Jaydane "ddarija dyalna," to regret the shamefulness associated to it:

> L'9raya ça marche pas, o l'hedra 7ta hiya,
> 7it ddarija dyalna semmitoha loghat zzen9a
> W gelto 7choma t3ebbar biha.
> Education does not work, neither does the language,
> Since you called our Darija a street language,
> And you said it was shameful to use it to express ourselves.

C. Miller (2015, p. 108) sums up the issues: "However, the area where the tensions and obstacles are stronger, is that of education and the possible use of Darija as a teaching language," showing the difference with Amazigh, which "has been taught as a 'subject' since 2003, and not used as a teaching medium. Thus, it does not challenge the present teaching in MSA."

The failure of the education system has been flagrant for years and the question of the languages of teaching is one of the issues (see Caubet & Miller, 2016). Following a royal speech asking for change in education,[39] Noureddine Ayouch's Zakoura Foundation organized a conference "The Pathways to Success" on 4–5 October 2013, to reconsider the education policy. They proposed recommendations[40] very close to the 1999 Charter, and designed to ensure "the continuity of a royal policy that goes beyond the contingencies of government changes" (Miller, 2015, p. 109). Two royal counsellors were present, as well as Rachid Belmokhtar, who was nominated Minister of Education five days later through a government reshuffle. All this would have passed unnoticed – except from the usual articles in the press – if Ayouch had not given an interview to the daily in Arabic, Akhbar Al yom (13 October, 2013) where in answer to "Which languages?", he said:

> We believe that the first language of learning must be Darija, the Arabic dialect, and then afterward, the other languages would be introduced gradually.
> *(Miller, 2015, p. 113).*

This triggered violent reactions and sparked off a national debate that went on for two years. Darija was considered by its opponents as the Trojan Horse of Francophonie. The "Conseil supérieur de l'éducation, de la formation et de la recherche scientifique" was set to work.

Two sides of the same coin

In a column in *Telquel*,[41] Souleiman Bencheikh stresses the ambiguity of the debate that took place between Ayouch and historian A. Laroui on 27 November 2013: "But they represent the two sides of the same coin, that of the Makhzen." Very lucidly he continues: "the two faces of the same hesitant Janus clashed: the debate we witnessed was a reflection of the ambiguity that prevails at the top of the state, hammering the urgency of reform, without telling us which one." Morocco is a country where "two competing identities coexist, unable to imagine a common destiny" alluding to "arabophones," "francophones," and "berberophones," and pleading for Darija, which should enhance unity:

> Which is the language, dialect, idiom — call it as you want — where the souls of Moroccans nest? What is the link that allows a Riffian to be understood by a Soussi or a Fassi? Call it what you will, but you will agree that it would be logical if in Morocco one would speak and teach Moroccan; logical too that this language should be a reflection of our diversity.

On 4 February 2015, the Prime Minister warned that "The integration of Darija in textbooks is a red line not to be crossed;"[42] and for this purpose — contrary to other habits — he chose to conscientiously speak in MSA for sixteen minutes!

During its session of May 2015 the Council was considering adopting the presence of Darija, but under last-minute pressure, decided against it — even as support language — and only mentioned the official languages.[43]

Darija expresses Moroccanness through creative writing[44]

If Darija cannot manage to get any institutional recognition, it has evolved on the *informal* front. This was done for pragmatic reasons, since Darija is the language that is understood by all; but also for more ideological reasons linked to Moroccanness.

Reading and writing in Darija on keyboards is standard practice nowadays and in both scripts (Latin and Arabic, although Latin is still a majority). The writing practices have changed completely. Smartphones have become tools which can be used by artists to write and where one can stock texts (like computers). Nowadays rappers and slammers can often be seen reading out freestyles from their smartphones, not from paper.

Figures

When a text is published on social media, it can get a very large audience, if one looks at the evolution of the figures for Morocco since the beginning of the millennium, according to the site *internetworldstats*[45]:

TABLE 6.1 Figures of online audiences in Morocco, courtesy of *internetworldstats*.

Year	Users	Population	% Penetration
2000	100,000	29,890,700	0.3 %
2005	1,000,000	31,003,311	3.2 %
2007	4,600,000	30,534,870	15.1 %
2009	10,442,500	31,285,174	33.4 %
2011	15,656,192	31,968,361	49.0 %
2016	20,207,154	33,655,786	60.0 %

20 million users, and the number of Facebook pages has grown from 1 million at the end of 2009 to 2.6 million in January 2011, reaching 4 million in December 2011, 7 million in 2014, and 12 million in June 2016.[46]

Moroccanisation and conventionalisation

"Elaborate" texts are mostly published in Arabic script: both because their authors are more familiar with it, and also because it probably eases the reading of Darija. One has to remember that normally you have to learn to read and write a language; in the case of Darija, practice has led people to teach themselves. Over the years, they have gained fluency collectively, through "conventionalisation,"[47] i.e., collective behaviour and repeated usage, so that separate actions have an impact on the community. If authors choose to publish long literary texts in Darija on blogs or on Facebook, it is because it addresses Moroccans' collective imagination directly.

I am referring to the blogger Harabich who has published since 2013, or to the blogger Mohamed Sokrate and rapper Mouad Belghouate, also known as l7a9d, who had both been sentenced to prison on false accusations (2011–2014).[48] Sokrate started publishing in Darija in 2014 when he came out of jail. L7a9d had never written prose and his series of twenty texts is a premiere. Both authors published on the press site goud.ma, which is an heir of *Nichane*, "*goud*" being a synonym of "*nichane*," meaning "direct, straightforward;" the site was created by journalists coming from *Nichane*. All three authors post links on their Facebook pages.

Conclusion: Moroccanness revisited

We have seen how Darija regained dignity among the civil society although it repeatedly failed to be recognized by all types of institutions. The contradictions inside the elite have also appeared clearly and Darija has always lost the battle against the conservative parties.

For years the term "*marocanité*" was only used in politics to claim the Moroccanness of the Sahara. It is now being used to define a Moroccan way of doing things. Darija has become a means of expressing Moroccanness publicly through creativity, and not just through nationalism. Artists and citizens have often chosen to change writing habits – or to simply start writing – in Darija.

Darija and its advocates – or just its users – have had to cope on a daily basis and just "go ahead and do it," in a civic effort that collectively has given unforeseen results. Far from the noisy campaigns that have regularly punctuated the public debate, they have taken over and managed empowerment through conventionalisation: a spontaneous passage to writing and then to literacy, the mastering of two alphabets, a collective informal language planning. They have ensured the diffusion of their ideas and their texts via the Internet, online or through events advertised on Facebook.

Parallel development, real freedom of expression, diffusion via – very! – social networks, and everyday use: the new Moroccanness is underway!

Notes

1 The *Nayda* was the name given to a cultural movement that took place during the years 2005–2008, when young creators invested in the field of the urban arts. See Caubet, 2008 and 2010 and the film *Casanayda!* ("It's moving in Casablanca"), Caubet, Benlyazid & Mettour, 2007.
2 For an experience of "Tunisification" see Achour-Kallel 2015.
3 Northern Morocco was a Spanish protectorate during the colonial period and Spanish is still very present.
4 I had some discussions on the matter with Federico Corriente, Jérôme Lentin, and Ángeles Vicente, let them be thanked here.
5 Unfortunately, the archives of *Telquel* are no longer accessible online.
6 In Darija, names of languages are always feminine: *l-franṣawiya, š-šelḥa, r-rusiya* (French, Berber, Russian).
7 Idealised both by the Pan-Muslim and the Pan-Arabic ideologies.
8 At the international level, this qualified Berber as an "endangered language." Another paradox: how can a language remain endangered when it has become official?
9 The Marrakech *National Festival of Popular Arts* was held for the first time in 1960; it is the oldest festival in Morocco.
10 The extracts concerning languages can be heard at www.youtube.com/watch?v=5n4p TUEVJ9c (accessed 4 October 2016).
11 See www.men.gov.ma/Fr/Pages/CNEF_espace3-3.aspx (accessed 4 October 2016).
12 www.men.gov.ma/Fr/Pages/CNEF_espace3-3.aspx (accessed 4 October 2016).
13 Discours du Trône, 30 July 2001: www.maroc.ma/fr/discours-royaux/discours-%C3%A0-loccasion-du-deuxi%C3%A8me-anniversaire-de-lintronisation-de-sa-majest%C3%A9-le-roi (accessed 4 October 2016).
14 Ajdir speech: www.maroc.ma/fr/discours-royaux/discours-de-sm-le-roi-mohammed-vi-lors-de-la-c%C3%A9r%C3%A9monie-dapposition-du-sceau (accessed 17 October 2016).
15 www.yabiladi.com/articles/details/3624/ahmed-boukous-notre-objectif-d-introduire.html (accessed 7 October 2016).
16 See www.amb-maroc.fr/constitution/Nouvelle_Constitution_%20Maroc2011.pdf (accessed 6 Octtober 2016).
17 See www.huffpostmaghreb.com/2016/07/27/amazigh-projet-de-loi_n_11221686.html?1469644042 (accessed 6 October 2016)
18 See www.medias24.com/MAROC/DROIT/165949-Les-details-sur-le-Conseil-des-langues-et-de-la-culture-marocaine.html (accessed 6 October 2016)
19 See www.huffpostmaghreb.com/2016/07/29/ircam-amazighe-disparition_n_1125272.html (accessed 12 October 2016).

20 See Caubet, Benlyazid & Mettour, 2007, Caubet, 2008.
21 See www.hcp.ma/Presentation-des-premiers-resultats-du-RGPH-2014_a1605.html (accessed 6 October 2016).
22 See Caubet, 2013, 2017a and 2017b.
23 *Telquel* n. 34, 15–21 June 2002. "L'arabe marocain, notre parler de tous les jours, n'est pas pris au sérieux. Pourtant, c'est la seule langue qui nous unit."
24 N. Ayouch is known for his proximity with the Palace. He is the founder of *Zakoura* Foundation which started by doing microcredit in 1995. As early as 1997, the education branch was created, experiencing teaching in Darija in their remedial classes. See www.maghress.com/fr/marochebdo/58327 (accessed 9 October 2016) *Maroc Hebdo International* n. 583, 5 December 2003. In 2013, he was at the center of a fierce national debate on the introduction of Darija as a language for teaching (See Miller, 2015), a debate still in progress.
25 For a history of the Moroccan media and their recent developments, see Miller, 2013. Announced by a royal speech (30 July 2002), the process started in 2003 and led in 2006 to the creation of numerous private radio stations, but no TV channel, probably because of Ayouch's daring proposal.
26 Produced by Yasmine Chami (Gaia Production) who started at Zakoura Foundation and *Moufida* in 2004. See an interview dating back to 2005 http://lematin.ma/journal/2005/Yasmine-Chami—a-euro%EF%BF%BDa-euro%EF%BF%BDOussar-wa-houloul − c-est-un-miroir-qu-on-tend-vers-la-famille/54671.html and an article on its immediate impact: www.bladi.net/oussar-wa-houloul.html. Also see www.libe.ma/Yasmine-Chami-Une-battante-qui-se-consacre-au-bien-etre-de-la-societe_a7715.html (all links accessed 14 October 2016).
27 The article is still online: www.bladi.net/darija-maroc.html (accessed 9 October 2016)
28 The editorial « *Nichane une belle aventure* » (*Telquel* n. 442, 9–15 October 2010), can still be found at http://fr.ossin.org/maroc/663-une-belle-aventure (accessed 7 October 2016).
29 On the various episodes of trials and bans, see Aguadé, 2012, Miller, 2012b, Cohen, 2011 and Caubet, 2012.
30 In *Telquel*, 13 June 2009. Not accessible anymore.
31 See http://aujourdhui.ma/culture/series-etrangeres-en-darija-cest-fini (accessed 18 October 2016). The PJD MP's asked for the High Authority, HACA to "monitor the use of oral formulations of colloquial Arabic and prohibit their use in foreign productions."
32 See Caubet, 2013 and Caubet & Miller, 2016. The following article was published on 8 February 2011, before the first demonstration: www.yabiladi.com/articles/details/4507/manifestations-fevrier-maroc-bulle-facebook.html (accessed 18 October 2016).
33 www.yabiladi.com/articles/details/4477/manifestations-fevrier-maroc-facebook-s-embrase.html (accessed 18 October 2016).
34 www.youtube.com/watch?v=A_LF0JqnMzw and www.youtube.com/watch?v=mZm750joM0U (accessed 18 October 2016).
35 www.lesiteinfo.com/pourquoi-abdelilah-benkirane-doit-partir/; published and accessed 4 October 2016.
36 see http://telquel.ma/2015/02/04/benkirane-mien-mon-parti-grand-tien_1433038 with the video (accessed 18 October 2016).
37 C. Miller wrote on the debate about the use of Darija as a language for teaching; whereas I studied the passage to literacy via DIY (Do It Yourself: an attitude developed by the punk subculture in the 1970s, and now associated with anti-consumerism) informal language planning leading to new elaborate written forms; see Miller, 2015, Caubet & Miller, 2016, Caubet, 2016, 2017a, and 2017b.
38 In the album *El Gouddam* ("Forward"), 2008.
39 20 August 2013 www.maroc.ma/fr/discours-royaux/texte-integral-du-discours-royal-la-nation-loccasion-du-60eme-anniversaire-de-la (accessed 18 October 2016).
40 There are 30 pages of recommendations: www.fondationzakoura.org/wp-content/uploads/2015/06/Actes-du-Colloque-International-Le-chemin-de-la-russite.pdf

41 http://telquel.ma/2013/12/15/decalages-les-identites-concurrentes_10099 (accessed 18 October 2016).
42 www.bladi.net/darija-ecole-maroc,41271.html. See www.youtube.com/watch?v=FLwbj6-qiy0
43 www.h24info.ma/maroc/enseignement-le-cse-pour-la-gratuite-contre-la-darija/32921; www.csefrs.ma/pdf/Vision_VF_Fr.pdf (p. 46). The council is chaired by a royal counsellor, Omar Azziman. In the following, an interview with our colleague A. Youssi: www.jeuneafrique.com/229813/societe/maroc-la-pol-mique-darija-divise-le-royaume/. For a summary of the question also see www.middle-east-online.com/english/?id=71904 (all sites accessed 18 October 2016).
44 See Caubet, 2017a and 2017b.
45 www.internetworldstats.com/af/ma.htm
46 See Caubet, 2013 and for the 2016 figures www.internetworldstats.com/stats1.htm
47 Gunvor Mejdell suggested the use of the sociological concept, see Caubet, 2017b.
48 Harabich, https://harabich.wordpress.com/;
l7a9d, www.goud.ma/%D9%85%D8%B0%D9%83%D8%B1%D8%A7%D8%AA-%D9%85%D8%B9%D8%A7%D8%B0-%D9%84%D8%AD%D8%A7%D9%82%D8%AF-%D9%85%D9%86-%D8%B9%D9%83%D8%A7%D8%B4%D8%A9-%D9%84%D9%85%D9%88%D9%84%D9%86%D8%A8%D9%8A%D9%83-1-201284/
Sokrate, www.goud.ma/%D9%85%D8%AD%D9%85%D8%AF-%D8%B3%D9%82%D8%B1%D8%A7%D8%B7%D9%88%D8%A3%D8%AE%D9%8A%D8%B1%D8%A7-%D9%82%D8%B1%D8%B1%D8%AA-%D9%86%D8%AA%D8%B2%D9%88%D8%AC-80201/

References

Achour-Kallel, M. (2015). Ici on parle tunisien: Ecriture du politique et politique de l'écriture ou qui ne peut pas être passeur? In M. Achour-Kallel (Ed.), *Le social par le langage: La parole au quotidien* (pp. 94–117). Paris: Khartala.

Aguadé, J. (2012). Monarquía, dialecto e insolencia en Marruecos: en caso *Nichane*. In M. Meouak, P. Sánchez, & Á. Vicente (Eds.), *De los manuscritos medievales a internet : la presencia del árabe vernáculo en las fuentes escritas* (pp. 441–464). Estudios de dialectología árabe n. 6 Zaragoza: Universidad de Zaragoza.

Aït Mous, F. (2011). Les enjeux de l'amazighité au Maroc. *Confluences Méditerranée* 3/2011 (N° 78), 121–131.

Aït Mous, F., & Wazif, M. (2008). Summer festivals in Morocco: International influence and a factor of Social Cohesion. *Mediterranean Yearbook, Med.2008, IEMED*, 295–299.

Babassi, O. (2004). Peut-on parler d'une communauté 'virtuelle' bilingue franco-arabe 'algéroise' sur l'Internet Relay Chat ? In T. Bulot, I. Léglise, C. Miller, D. Caubet, & J. Billiez (Eds.), *Parlers jeunes, ici et là-bas, pratiques et représentations* (pp. 271–286). Paris: L'Harmattan.

Beaussier, M. (1958). *Dictionnaire pratique Arabe-Français: Nouvelle édition, revue, corrigée et augmentée par M. Ben Cheneb*. Alger: La Maison des Livres.

Bouhjar, A. (2012). De la langue du terroir à une langue au pouvoir: Officialisation de la langue amazighe (berbère) au Maroc. *Lengas, 71*, 29–40.

Boum, A. (2012). Festivalizing dissent in Morocco. *Middle-East Report* n. 263, *The Art and Culture of the Arab Revolts*, 22–25.

Caubet D. (2004). L'intrusion des téléphones portables et des 'SMS' dans l'arabe marocain en 2002-2003. 'Algéroise' sur l'Internet Relay Chat? In D. Caubet, J. Billiez, Th. Bulot, I. Léglise, & C. Miller (Eds.), *Parlers jeunes ici et là-bas, Pratiques et Représentations, Espaces Discursifs* (pp. 247–270). Paris: L'Harmattan.

Caubet, D. (2005). Darija, langue de la modernité: Entretien avec Noureddine Ayouch. *EDNA, Estudios de Dialectología Norteafricana y Andalusí, 7*, 135–141.

Caubet, D. (2007). Génération *Darija! EDNA: Estudios de Dialectología Norteafricana y Andalusí, 9*, 233–243.

Caubet, D. (2008). From "Movida" to "Nayda" in Morocco: The use of darija (Moroccan Arabic), in artistic creation at the beginning of the 3rd millennium. In S. Procházka & V. Ritt-Benmimoun (Eds.), *Between the Atlantic and Indian Oceans: Studies in contemporary Arabic Dialects* (pp. 113–124). Vienna: LIT.

Caubet, D. (2009). Nouveau mouvement culturel et social, nouveau rôle pour la darija (marocain): le Maroc d'après 2003. *Revue d'études berbères 001*. Retrieved from http://reb.centrederechercheberbere.fr/nouveau-mouvement-culturel-et-social-nouveau-role-pour-la-darija-marocain-le-maroc-dapres-2003.html?revue=1

Caubet, D. (2010). *"Nayda" or how a pseudo-verb became a much disputed substantive*. . . . Retrieved from www.academia.edu/8810799/_Nayda_or_how_a_pseudo-verb_became_a_much_disputed_substantive

Caubet, D. (2012). Apparition massive de la darija à l'écrit à partir de 2008–2009 : sur le papier ou sur la toile : quelle graphie? Quelles régularités? In M. Meouak, P. Sánchez, & Á. Vicente (Eds.), *De los manuscritos medievales a internet : la presencia del árabe vernáculo en las fuentes escritas* (pp. 377–402). Estudios de dialectología árabe n. 6 Zaragoza: Universidad de Zaragoza.

Caubet, D. (2013). Maroc 2011 – Messagerie instantanée sur l'internet marocain : *facebook, darija* et parlers jeunes. In M. Benitez, C. Miller, J. J. de Ruiter, & Y. Tamer, (Eds.), *Evolution des pratiques et des représentations langagières dans le Maroc du 21ème siècle* (Vol. 1, pp. 63–88). L'Harmattan: Collection Espaces Discursifs.

Caubet, D. (2016). "D.I.Y. in Morocco from the mid 90's to 2015: back to the roots?" In P. Guerra & T. Moreira (Eds.), *Keep it simple, Make it fast! 2016, KISMIF, Volume 2: An approach to Underground Music Scenes* (pp. 249–256). Facultade de Letras, Universidade do Porto.

Caubet, D. (2017a). New elaborate written forms in Darija: blogging, posting and slamming in 2015 Morocco. In A. Benmamoun & R. Bassiouney (Eds.), *Routledge handbook on Arabic linguistics*. London: Routledge.

Caubet, D. (2017b). Morocco: An informal passage to literacy in Darija (Moroccan Arabic). In J. Høigilt & G. Mejdell (Eds.), *Writing change: The politics of written language in the Arab world*. Leiden: Brill.

Caubet, D., & Miller, C. (2016). Quels enjeux sociopolitiques autour de la darija au Maroc? In C. Sini & F. Laroussi (Eds.), *Langues et mutations sociopolitiques au Maghreb* (pp. 123–138). Rouen: PURH (Publications des universités de Rouen et du Havre).

Caubet, D., Benlyazid, F. & Mettour, A. (2007). *Casanayda!*, a documentary film written by D. Caubet, directed by F. Benlyazid & A. Mettour, produced by Sigma Technlogies, Casablanca Accessible on youtube in 6 parts, see https://www.youtube.com/watch?v=aRrT1zRzmFQ.

Cohen, A. (2011). La langue du silence dans le Maroc urbain contemporain. *Revue de l'Histoire des Religions, 2*, 245–263.

Dozy, R. (1927). *Supplément aux Dictionnaires Arabes, Tome I* (2ème éd.). Leiden/Paris: Brill & Maisonneuve. Quoting *Description de l'Egypt*e, 2è édition, Paris, 1822, Etat Moderne, t. XI–XVIII.

Elinson, A. E. (2013). Darija and changing writing practices in Morocco. *International Journal of Middle East Studies, 45*, 715–730.

Feliu, L. (2006). Le mouvement culturel amazigh (MCA) au Maroc. *L'Année du Maghreb, 1*, 274–285.

Kazimirski, A. de B. (1860). *Dictionnaire Arabe-Français*. Paris: Maisonneuve. (Réédition Librairie du Liban, Beyrouth. Tome I).

Maghraoui, H. (2013). La darija: quel statut dans le discours politique? In M. Benitez, C. Miller, J. J. de Ruiter, & Y. Tamer (Eds.), *Evolution des pratiques et des représentations langagières dans le Maroc du 21ème siècle* (Vol. 1, pp. 157–174). Paris: L'Harmattan.

Miller, C. (2012a). Mexicans speaking in Darija (Moroccan Arabic): Media, urbanization and language changes in Morocco. In R. Bassiouney & E. G. Katz (Eds.), *Arabic language and Linguistics* (pp. 169–188). Washington, DC: Georgetown University Press.

Miller, C. (2012b). Observations concernant la présence de l'arabe marocain dans la presse marocaine arabophone des années 2009–2010. In M. Meouak, P. Sanchez, & A. Vicente (Eds.), *De los manuscritos medievales a internet: la presencia de l'arabe vernaculo en las fuentes escritas* (pp. 419–440). Zaragoza: University of Zaragoza.

Miller, C. (2013). Evolution des usages linguistiques dans les nouvelles radios marocaines. In M. Benitez, C. Miller, J. J. de Ruiter, & Y. Tamer (Eds.), *Evolution des pratiques et des représentations langagières dans le Maroc du 21ème siècle* (Vol. 1, pp. 89–118). Paris: L'Harmattan.

Miller, C. (2015). Evolution des pratiques, évolutions des représentations? Petit retour sur le débat autour de la valorisation de la darija au Maroc. In *Revue des Etudes berbères, Volume 10, Berbère et Arabe Maghrébin: Études de linguistique et de sociolinguistique* (pp. 101–120). Paris: INALCO.

Pouessel, S. (2013). Des dialectes du bled à la langue du Roi: éléments d'une 'ascencion' linguistique amazighe et miroir de l'arabe dialectal. In M. Benitez, C. Miller, J. J. de Ruiter, & Y. Tamer (Eds.), *Evolution des pratiques et des représentations langagières dans le Maroc du 21ème siècle* (Vol. 2, pp. 17–34). Paris: L'Harmattan.

Ziamari, K., & Barontini, A. (2013). Ana: Parlez-vous arabe marocain? Quand les séries réconcilient avec la darija. In M. Benitez, C. Miller, J. J. de Ruiter, & Y. Tamer (Eds.), *Evolution des pratiques et des représentations langagières dans le Maroc du 21ème siècle* (Vol. 1, pp. 119–144). Paris: L'Harmattan.

7

"SLOPPY SPEECH IS LIKE SLOPPY DRESS"

Folk attitudes towards nonstandard British English[1]

Carmen Ebner

> To me, sloppy speech is like sloppy dress: it's alright to wear an old t-shirt with [h]oles in [it] and a pair of baggy pants at home, but make yourself presentable out of doors if you want me to approach you in a friendly manner. You wouldn't wear a [sic] pyjamas to a cocktail party with your local MP, so don't use double negatives if you expect them to carry your case in Parliament.
>
> —(Student, 18–25 years old, male)

Introduction

In this chapter, the construction of linguistic identities is discussed on the basis of the so-called usage debate revolving around disputed and stigmatised language features, such as the split infinitive or *literally* as an intensifier. Linguistic features such as these fall into somewhat of a grey area between standard and nonstandard language. It is, however, known that the use of nonstandard as well as standard forms and constructions has become "ideologized as distinctive and as implicating a distinctive kind of people" (Woolard, 1998, pp. 18–19). That the knowledge of and compliance with the standard norms of correctness and legitimacy are used to pass judgements on speakers, as is illustrated in the example of a young student quoted above, is an established fact. Nevertheless, how non-compliance is used to exclude speakers from certain domains of life will be illustrated in this chapter by conducting a qualitative analysis of comments gathered through an online questionnaire. While the usage debate has traditionally been dominated by prescriptivists and descriptivists, the opinions of the general public have often been overlooked. In this chapter, I will not only provide insight into the study of usage attitudes in general, but also highlight how such studies bring to light vital social conventions and norms held by speakers within a speech community by focussing on the attitudes of the general public. The notion of "Standard English" is essential for this study and hence needs to be understood not only as "the most important dialect in the English-speaking world", but also as a geographically non-restricted variety of English in Great Britain (Trudgill, 1999, pp. 123–127). The qualitative data discussed here comprise 176 responses of members of the general public of England to an open-ended question included in an online questionnaire.

Before describing the methodological background of my study, I will provide essential background information on the usage debate. Furthermore, I will discuss the role of prescription in the standardisation process and outline how studies on usage problems have evolved. Next, I will report the findings of a direct elicitation test, in the form of an open-ended question concerning the state of the English language, which was included in an online questionnaire. The qualitative analysis of answers to this question has brought to light lay people's tendencies to distance themselves from usages which they have deemed unacceptable. This distancing not only establishes the notion of an in-group and an out-group and a distinction between "us" and "them" (Joseph, 2006, p. 262), but it also provides insight into how speakers using stigmatised language features are perceived. The indexing function of usage problems, as well as the awareness and experience of the interlocutor with regard to such stigmatised features, are important factors in this discussion, as they shape the perceived linguistic identity of a speaker (Joseph, 2013, p. 144). Lay people's attitudes towards stigmatised nonstandard language and their users will be discussed in detail in the third section, which will highlight the gatekeeping function of the standard variety in England.

Prescriptions and standard English

An intriguing phenomenon, which Nash (1986, p. 1) described as being part of human nature, is our inclination "to judge others by their language". Such a judgement is found in the telling comment of a young student above which also provides an example of how linguistic identities are constructed: sloppiness in language use is equated with a sloppy appearance. Whether a speaker is perceived as careless, educated, or belonging to a particular social class depends, however, not only on actual language use. Perceptions are also heavily influenced by the experience of the interlocutor at the perceiving end, as well as the situational contexts in which the encounter takes place. The complexity of such attitudes increases even more with disputed language issues. Language usage, or what should be considered "proper" language usage, has often been described as a battlefield (cf. Mittins et al., 1970, p. 1) in which the lines have been drawn between prescriptivists on the one side and descriptivists on the other.

Aiming at fixing and ascertaining the standard variety once and for all, prescriptivists have not eschewed voicing – boisterously and publically – their opinions on what is part of this standard variety and what is not. This is much to the dismay of descriptivists whose aim of describing actual language use is reflected in the scientific study of language. Bearing in mind the mantra of "linguistics is descriptive, not prescriptive" (Cameron, 1995, p. 5), linguists have, unsurprisingly, avoided active participation in this debate which revolves around so-called usage problems (Ilson, 1985, p. 167). Usage problems have been defined by Ilson (1985, p. 167) as actually occurring, fairly widespread language features which can be discussed publically without causing offence. While Ilson's definition partly circumscribes usage problems, such stigmatised and disputed language features can be found in syntax (e.g., dangling participles), phonology (e.g., the pronunciation of *nuclear*), lexis (e.g., the meaning of the verb *decimate*), and morphology (e.g., the distinction between *disinterested* and *uninterested*).

While prescriptivists tend to have clear ideas about what is "correct" and "proper", and descriptivists are often accused of the "anything goes" approach (Cameron, 1995, p. 230), the general public as language users is left to navigate through the minefield that is language usage, risking being judged negatively by others upon any misstep. Linguistically insecure speakers are, however, not left unguided as a plethora of usage advice is being made available to them. Usage guides, such as Henry Watson Fowler's (1926) *A Dictionary of Modern English Usage* and journalist-cum-usage guide author Simon Heffer's (2010) *Strictly English*, have offered prescriptivists the chance to disseminate their ideas about Standard English and to instruct an eager audience of socially mobile yet insecure speakers on what to use and what to avoid (cf. Peters, 2006, p. 775; Tieken-Boon van Ostade, 2008, p. 208). Starting in the late eighteenth century, the so-called usage guide tradition now spans almost 250 years in which an ever-increasing number of usage guides have been published. Today, the debate and usage guide tradition has also gone online in the form of blogs and podcasts offering language advice such as Mignon Fogarty's *Grammar Girl: Quick and Dirty Tips*.[2] That the divide between standard and nonstandard language use is strengthened through the usage debate does not need to be stressed. The notion of Standard English is often tied to standard language ideology and what Milroy (1999, p. 18) has described as "standard language culture", which describes an awareness of the "superordinate" status of the standard variety. This awareness is enforced through the use of the standard variety in different institutions, such as the media and education (Milroy, 1999, p. 18). Milroy's standard language culture further entails the equation of the standard variety with correctness and legitimacy, which Curzan (2014, p. 30) highlights by stating that "[i]t is not just standard: it is 'English'".

The process of standardising a language variety includes a vital stage: prescription. This stage aims at keeping variation and change within the variety to a minimum, if not to eradicate variation in usage all together by suppressing so-called "optional variability" (Milroy & Milroy, 2012, p. 22). From this "optional variability" stems a great number of usage problems, as one variant was chosen to be part of the standard, while others were deemed "improper", "vulgar", or "barbarous" (cf. Sundby et al., 1991). For instance, splitting an infinitive by the insertion of an adverb between *to* and the infinitive, as in the famous line from Star Trek, ***to boldly go*** *where no man has gone before*, was deemed incorrect based on a Latinate rule which was used to project the ideal of Latin infinitives as one-word structures onto English infinitives (Aarts, 2014). Aesthetic, historical, and logical arguments have been used to distinguish and delineate standard from nonstandard variants (cf. Ilson, 1985, p. 165). Using Latin as a role model for English and arguing for the logic behind two negatives making a positive are just two examples of such arguments, which often seem arbitrary and resemble etiquette rules and dress codes (cf. Milroy & Milroy, 2012, p. 1). In order to enforce the selection of variants to be included in the standard, prescriptions and proscriptions were formulated which, according to Milroy and Milroy (2012, p. 22), form the basis of the last stage of the language standardisation process. How successful such prescriptive efforts have been, however, is debatable, as stigmatised nonstandard variants have continued to be used. An example of this is the above-mentioned double negative, as in *he **didn't** do **nothing***, a construction found in most English varieties spoken on the British Isles and whose development was described by Hughes et al. (2005, p. 24) as follows: "it is in fact the standard dialect which has diverged from the other varieties, not the other way round".

In spite of the somewhat conspicuous absence of linguists' involvement in the usage debate, scientific studies have investigated attitudes towards usage problems, albeit to different extents in American and British English. While a comparatively large number of usage attitude studies has been conducted in the United States of America (cf. Leonard, 1932; Bryant, 1962; Hairston, 1981; Gilsdorf & Leonard, 2001; Grey & Heuser, 2003; Queen & Robin, 2015; Kostadinova, in progress), only one usage attitude study dealing with Standard English, namely Mittins et al.'s (1970) *Attitudes to English Usage*, could be identified in the British context. A comparison of previous usage attitude studies reveals not only a focus on the language of educated speakers in early investigations such as Leonard's study, but also a clear move towards including sociolinguistic theory. Focusing on the language use of educated speakers was seen as the solution to settling disputes about usage problems and as a way to revise outdated teaching material (cf. Leonard, 1932, p. xiii; Mittins et al., 1970, p. 3). As mentioned above, standard varieties are used in and enforced by institutions such as the schooling system. That usage attitude studies have gradually incorporated sociolinguistic theory is noteworthy, as such attitudes have been shown to vary among speakers. Mittins et al.'s (1970) study highlighted the increased linguistic intolerance found in older speakers. In order to illustrate this sociolinguistic variation and the connection to the education system, I will briefly discuss Mittins et al.'s (1970) *Attitudes to English Usage* in more detail.

As part of a wider research initiative of the Schools Council for Curriculum and Education in 1966, W.H. Mittins and his colleagues at the University of Newcastle upon Tyne investigated attitudes towards 55 usage problems such as the split infinitive and *literally* as an intensifier (Burgess, 1996, pp. 55–56). Given the study's context, the sample consisted mainly of educationalists, such as teachers, lecturers, examiners, and students training to become teachers. Sixty non-educationalists completed their sample of 457 informants who were asked to identify the contexts in which a stimulus sentence including a stigmatised nonstandard language feature was considered acceptable (Mittins et al., 1970, p. 18). There were four contextual choices: formal writing, formal speech, informal writing, and informal speech.

However, these choices were restricted for five of the investigated usage problems, as the researchers believed the occurrence of the stimuli in these contexts to be impossible (Mittins et al., 1970, pp. 20–21). What needs to be mentioned is the elicitation method the researchers applied in their study, as this method was characterised by its directness. The 55 stigmatised nonstandard language features were underlined by the researchers and included in a questionnaire. Highlighting parts of the stimuli sentences could have potentially biased the questionnaire respondents in that they were led to believe something to be wrong with the underlined parts of the stimuli sentences. Thus, respondents could provide so-called socially desirable answers and accordingly express something other than their true unbiased attitudes towards the stimulus sentence (Garrett, 2010, p. 44). Distinguishing between elicitation methods is vital, as the directness of a test can greatly influence the elicited attitudes. It is therefore possible to obtain consciously offered attitudes, which can show traces of the social desirability bias for instance, as well as subconsciously offered attitudes. The latter are considered to be true, unbiased attitudes towards a stimulus (Kristiansen, 2015). Yet, it has to be stressed that consciously offered attitudes should not be discarded, as they can provide insights into social norms and conventions which speakers do not consider controversial, but rather find acceptable or have agreed upon within a community.

The Mittins study was conducted in a crucial period in Great Britain in which the education system, especially the teaching of English grammar, had been in a state of flux. The traditional and "rigid" approach to teaching grammar in schools was abandoned "in the 1960s and 1970s [producing] a language-vacuum" which was eventually filled by linguistics (Hudson, 2010, p. 35). As a consequence of these developments, the "first grammarless generation" of students was said to have left the British education system (Keith, 1990, p. 83). Pressure from the government as well as teachers resulted in a reform of English teaching, and ultimately in the creation of the first National Curriculum for English. What needs to be mentioned, however, is the government's influence on the creation of this curriculum. Both the Kingman (1988) and Cox (1989) reports came under criticism from the government, who did not approve of the conclusions reached by these two committees (Cameron, 1995, p. 88). While conservative politicians would have liked to have seen the implementation of a traditional approach towards grammar teaching aiming "to ensure that pupils would learn to use standard English correctly", both reports suggested a more contemporary approach influenced by linguistics (Cameron, 1995, p. 89). Despite the open criticism from the government, the National Curriculum for English was introduced in 1989 and was characterised by a lack of prescriptive tendencies as described by Hudson (2010, p. 41):

> One of the main changes in our schools which is at least partly due to the influence of linguistics is a remarkable reduction in prescriptivism both among teachers and among those who draft official documents. Indeed, prescriptivism came to such a complete end that many English teachers were reluctant even to teach standard English.

The government's reaction to the committee reports caused a public debate which was incited by the media (Cameron, 1995, p. 84). Causing a moral panic in British society, the changes in English grammar teaching were not only perceived as signs of the decay of the English language, but they were extended to be synonymous with a decline of the English society in general (Cameron, 1995, p. 86). Cameron (1995, p. 82) describes moral panic as the sudden foregrounding and discussion of a "social phenomenon or problem... in public discourse... in an obsessive, moralistic and alarmist manner".

As part of the standardisation process, prescriptions and proscriptions have been used to delineate the standard variety from nonstandard language features. Using negative labels to stigmatise nonstandard language features further helped to distinguish between the "correct" and "incorrect", "proper" and "improper". That the usage debate is linked to the education system has been shown in the historical development of usage attitude studies which have not only aimed at providing updated teaching material, but also at settling the debate by focussing on the language use of the educated. It is intriguing to find a greater number of usage attitude studies in the United States than in Great Britain, where the subject seems to be widely neglected. Nevertheless, the topicality of the usage debate and the necessity for current studies dealing with disputed and stigmatised language features become apparent in the moral panic which seems to have subliminally endured in British society. Having provided the necessary background information, I will now turn to a brief description of the data discussed in this chapter before turning to its analysis.

Linguistic identities and usage attitudes

An online questionnaire including 11 usage problems, such as the split infinitive and *literally* as an intensifier, was completed by 230 respondents from England only. Part of this questionnaire was also an open-ended question dealing with the current state of the English language which was, however, not compulsory, and was hence completed by 176 respondents, 51 men and 125 women. The focus of the present study is a qualitative analysis of the questionnaire respondents' answers in reply to this open-ended question.[3] With 9,580 words, the collection of obtained answers was analysed for recurring topics which offered insights into the current state of English as perceived by the questionnaire respondents. Through a discussion of this investigation, the validity of the moral panic revolving around the alleged decay of English – and by extension, of British society – is also addressed.

Despite their gradual incorporation of sociolinguistic theory, usage attitude studies have yet to be investigated with regard to linguistic identity constructions. Differences in language use, be they regional or social dialectal, are essential in that they serve as the signals through which "social belonging" is established (Joseph, 2013, p. 140). The indexicality of language plays a vital role in the construction of linguistic identities as a link "between linguistic forms and social meanings" (Bucholtz & Hall, 2010, p. 21). How distancing and differentiating have been used to construct and strengthen national or group linguistic identities has been shown by Thomas (1991, p. 54). Block (2014, p. 5) furthermore draws on the notion of self-presentation and defines a speaker's identity not only through affiliation, but also through disaffiliation, by quoting Sayer (2005, p. 54) who describes this concept as a frequently used "practice of defining one's identity through a contrast with a stigmatised other". Fish's (1980) concept of "interpretative community" fits neatly into the discussion of usage attitudes, as it describes a community in which "its members may never come into direct physical contact with one another, yet share norms spread by the education system, books or the media" (Joseph, 2010, p. 14). In the following discussion, I present qualitative data collected through my questionnaire in support of how stigmatised nonstandard language use is perceived by lay people and used to establish an in-group and out-group of speakers.

176 questionnaire respondents provided an answer to the following question: *What do you think about the state of the English language?* The aim of this somewhat broadly phrased question was to elicit attitudes from respondents in a rather direct manner and, in doing so, to obtain consciously held attitudes. That such attitudes could be subject to the social desirability bias needs to be borne in mind (Garrett, 2010, p. 44). Five main recurring topics can be identified in the 9,580-word collection of the respondents' answers: evaluative comments on the changing state of English (n=107), the link between education and standard language (n=58), the influence of media and new technology on language use (n=49), the gatekeeping function of standard language (n=21), and the interplay between clear communication and grammatical knowledge (n=21). Apart from providing brief insight into the validity of the moral panic, the focus of this chapter lies on standard language and its application in education, as well as its gatekeeping function. The examples discussed in this chapter are representative of the topics identified in the qualitative analysis.

It does not come as a surprise to find traces of the moral panic revolving around the decay of the English language and the decline of British society in the respondents' answers. Examples (1) and (2) illustrate lay people's perceptions of this ongoing moral panic. While a nurse in (1) comments on the moral panic in that the perceived "decline is greatly exaggerated", she hints at the persistence of this phenomenon by stating that falling "standards have been getting worse for centuries". The respondent aligns herself with what she calls the "'language evolves' camp" and so positions herself clearly on one side of the debate. Comment (1) also shows how communication is prioritised over conforming to standards, one of the five main recurring topics identified in the analysis.

(1) Its decline is greatly exaggerated! People have been saying standards have been getting worse for centuries. I am very much in the "language evolves" camp. As long as you can understand what someone is trying to communicate, I don't think it matters that [m]uch.

(Nurse, 26–30 years old, female)

The second answer discussed here describes a slightly more negative outlook on the state of English. Despite acknowledging a frequently found descriptive argument according to which language is a living entity which "changes as society changes", the specialist tutor in (2) admits a reluctance to accept changes. The reason for this is her upbringing, which she describes as being "trained in strict rules". How this reluctance affects her attitudes and perceptions of the state of English becomes clear when she goes on not only to describe the state of English as "sloppy", but also the language use of her grandchildren as "limited".

(2) It is a living language and so changes as society changes. This can be difficult to accept if you are older and were trained in strict rules. But – sometimes it seems too "sloppy" and my grandchildren can seem limited in their use of language.
(Specialist tutor for adult dyslexic students, over 60 years old, female)

Examples (1) and (2) provide insight into facets of the moral panic. The recurring character of the moral panic around falling standards has been highlighted in (1) in which the respondent clearly aligns herself with the "'language evolves' camp". This needs to be seen in contrast to (2), which represents a more negative outlook on the development of English. The respondent's strict upbringing in terms of rule compliance poses a hindrance to her ability to accept changes. The age difference between these two respondents is in line with findings that suggest a stricter, more prescriptive attitude among older speakers, as exhibited by the specialist tutor in (2) (cf. Mittins et al., 1970). Having provided brief insights into the moral panic by presenting examples dealing with its validity and persistence, I now turn to the two main topics: education and standard language use, and the gatekeeping function of standard language.

Education and standard language use

The historical link between educational institutions and the standard variety has been encapsulated in Curzan's (2014, p. 16) definition of institutional prescriptivism, which she describes as being backed by "the cultural and social power" of authoritative institutions. The adoption of standard language in schools fall within the realm of institutional prescriptivism. As mentioned above, the English educational system has undergone a number of considerable changes affecting the way English grammar has been taught in schools. In response to the open-ended question included in the questionnaire, numerous respondents reported on the effects and consequences of such changes. Below, I discuss a few of these answers.

The retired school teacher in (3) provides valuable insight into a teacher's perspective on the changes affecting the approach towards English language teaching. Interestingly, the respondent highlights how technological changes, such as texting and Twitter, have caused contextual appropriateness to become a central theme in the teaching of English. That technological advances such as texting or the Internet have had a negative influence on English is an often-cited popular belief (Kamm, 2015, pp. 88–89). Yet Crystal (2008, pp. 162–163) has shown that the effects of what he calls Txt-speak are widely exaggerated, as children and young adults are very well aware of the contextual differences between these different language media. Regardless of this, the retired teacher in (3) concludes that it is the teacher's responsibility to teach students the standard variety, and furthermore to instruct them on the correct use of a number of usage problems such as the difference between *less* and *fewer* and the personal pronouns *I* and *me*. According to him, teachers failing "to take this duty seriously are disadvantaging their students". Although the respondent in (3) exhibits a tolerant attitude towards the new online uses of English, he insists on teaching prescriptive rules to maintain "correct Standard English". Why the retired school teacher believes that a failure to do so would disadvantage students is not mentioned.

(3) The types of English used in texting, Twitter, etc. are absolutely fine, so long as people know that, in other contexts, they would be unacceptable or inappropriate. Furthermore, it's the duty of educationalists to help learners use all types of communica[t]ion effectively; people should be able to move effortlessly from one mode of discourse to another and be confident in all of them. People should know about "less/fewer"; "me/I"; "was/were" and so on, and be able to speak and write in correct Standard Eng[l]ish when the occasion requires it. Teachers who fail to take this duty seriously are disadvantaging their students.
(Retired school teacher, over 60 years old, male)

This answer needs to be viewed in contrast to a primary school teacher trainee's answer in (4). What needs to be highlighted in the answer of this teacher trainee in (4) is an apparent conflict between dialects. While she acknowledges the importance of the standard variety, the respondent criticises how other dialect speakers are being treated insofar as they are being discouraged "from engaging in a classroom discussion if they are going to be harassed constantly about their dialect". In a similar manner to the retired school teacher in (3), the respondent in (4) argues for the teaching of grammar rules, yet she offers an explanation in that the ability to "write adhering to grammar rules" seems to be an acceptance criterion for advancing both educationally and professionally.

(4) Spelling can be difficult for a lot of children but this does not mean they are unable to use "form[a]l" English in their writing when they are required to. It would be completely inappropriate to demonise and discourage children from engaging in a classroom discussion if they are going to be harassed constantly about their dialect. Children need to know [h]ow to write adhering to grammar rules so that they can successfully apply for jobs and universities places.
(Primary school trainee teacher, 18–25 years old, female)

While both examples (3) and (4) offer a professional's point of view on the link between education and standard language, the answer of a digital market consultant in (5) adds a lay person's perspective to the discussion. The phenomenon of judging others by their language use, which has been described at the beginning of this chapter, is mentioned by the digital marketing consultant who not only considers "bad language use" a sign of "poor education and intelligence", but also argues for "bad language use" to be "a good indicator of" who she would like to be friends with. This shows how language is not only used to judge a speaker in terms of level of education, but also to judge a speaker's personality. Hence, "bad language use" is not only associated with a lack of education and intelligence, but it also is used by the respondent to determine whether someone could be friend-material or not.

(5) [I] [t]ink bad language use shows poor education and intelligence and yes I do judge people on their use of English. However, I also think it's a good indicator of people I do or do not want to be friends with, so I don't want it taught for the sake [o]f it, if [y]ou see what I mean!
(Digital marketing consultant, 31–40 years old, female)

These three examples highlight the link between education and the standard language variety in the perspectives of professionals as well as of lay people. What has to be mentioned here is a crucial component of usage attitudes, namely, awareness. Being a language professional does not necessarily entail being aware of stigmatised or nonstandard language features, as the shift from prescriptivism and explicit grammar teaching to a more descriptive approach has also affected teacher training (cf. *The Grammar Papers*, 1998, p. 26). The changes in the teaching approach towards English grammar have also resulted in shifting attention to contextual appropriateness, which has been shown in (3) and (4). Nevertheless, the two educationalists emphasised the importance of Standard English and grammar rule teaching. A reason for this emphasis has been provided by the young teacher trainee in (4) who argued that knowing how to write according to grammatical rules was essential for successful job and university applications. In contrast, the answer of the digital marketing consultant in (5) brought to light how "bad language use" is not only associated with a lack of education and intelligence, but how it can also be used to construct a speaker's linguistic identity with regard to personality traits. Example (5) shows how "bad language use" was used as a friend-material indicator by the digital marketing consultant, who would dismiss people as possible friends based on their language use.

The gatekeeping function of standard language

As indicated in examples (4) and (5) already, compliance with a shared set of Standard English norms performs a gatekeeping function which distinguishes an in-group from an out-group of speakers. As illustrated above, this out-group is not only defined by its association with incorrect or "bad language use", hence showing non-compliance with the accepted and expected norms of the in-group, but it is also defined by its insufficient education and intelligence, and unfavourable personality traits. That this non-compliance with Standard English norms can have far-reaching consequences is illustrated in the examples below.

A writer and journalist provided an intriguing answer to the open-ended question which is shown in (6). In previous examples, a phenomenon has come to light in which language changes are accepted and considered "natural" yet, at the same time, importance is attributed to Standard English. What is striking about this respondent's answer, however, is the mentioning of Standard English, in particular "standard rules of grammar and orthogra[p]hy of English" and its function as a gatekeeper. Mockingly, the writer and journalist replicates nonstandard writing in (6) below which, according to him, would prevent a speaker from getting a job. This is in line with the comment of a university lecturer in (7) who argues that job applicants who provide "Facebook-style comments" in job interviews will fail to secure the position.

(6) I think there are many people who try to fossilise English and are not accepting of natural changes in the language. Nevertheless, if u rite lyk dis den u iz neva gona get a job, so it is important to be aware of the standard rules of grammar and orthogra[p]hy of English.

(Writer and journalist, 26–30 years old, male)

(7) Individuals need to be made aware that everyone makes judgements on people's use of language and different context[s] [sic] demand different patterns of use – answering job interview questions for most jobs with Facebook-style comments are unlikely to secure you the position.

(University lecturer, 41–60 years old, male)

That non-compliance with Standard English grammar can act as a glass ceiling preventing speakers from entering certain domains is further stressed by a retired arts consultant in (8) who states that she has "never employed anybody who wrote a cv/application letter with spelling mistakes". Despite distinguishing between different varieties in formal and informal contexts, the respondent in (9) extends the notion of a glass ceiling to spoken language. She goes on to argue that not only does non-compliance add a stigma to those unable to "speak reasonably grammatical English", but it also prevents them from obtaining well-paid jobs.

(8) Grammar and spelling are certainly in decline. Personally I never employed anybody who wrote a cv/application letter with spelling mistakes...

(Retired arts consultant, over 60 years old, female)

(9) I think the inability to speak reasonably grammatical English stigmatises people and makes it harder for them to get decently paid jobs. However, it doesn't matter what variety you use with your friends.

(Retired, over 60 years old, female)

Acknowledgement of Standard English as a glass ceiling can also be found in the answer of a floating support worker in (10a). Providing examples, this respondent states how specific professions such as that of a local councillor or general practitioner come with expectations towards "correct English usage". Only if such expectations are met are speakers able to progress in these professions.

(10a) You wouldn't want your local councillor starting a conversation with "Awright, luv?", nor your GP writing a medical report full of grammatical mistakes. I suppo[s]e from this point of view that correct English usage (whatever that means at the present time, as I'm sure it is fluid and changes over the decades) is essential to progress in certain professions.
(Floating support worker, 31–40 years old, female)

That the glass ceiling of "Standard English" can, however, also pose an obstacle for speakers of the in-group is illustrated by the floating support worker in (10b). Her middle class accent and correct language use widen the divide between her and her "less well-educated clients". In order for her to be successful, the floating support worker feels the need to "adjust" her language use to her interlocutors. In the case of her "less well-educated clients", she reports to speak with "a notably stron[g]er 'Southampton accent'" and to use different "word usage".

(10b) I work in mental health, and in my job my middle-c[l]ass accent (or to me, lack of accent!) and reasonably correct language can actually create a barrier between me and some of my less well-educated clients. I've learnt to adjust my accent and usage depending on who I'm speaking to, and have a notably stron[g]er "Southampton accent", along with differing word usage, when interacting with certain people or groups.
(Floating support worker, 31–40 years old, female)

Nonstandard language use, i.e., incorrect usage or even simple spelling mistakes, seems to form an exclusion criterion based on which speakers are prevented from progressing into certain domains of life. This phenomenon has been illustrated with the aid of examples (6)–(10). Functioning as a gatekeeper, a shared set of Standard English norms is used to distinguish between an in-group, who are capable of using this shared set of norms, and an out-group, who are defined by their lack of sufficient knowledge of this set. That is why Standard English acts as a glass ceiling for speakers of the out-group, while attentive speakers of the in-group appear to be able to transgress this "barrier" as described by the respondent in (10b).

Concluding remarks

The aim of this chapter was to highlight how linguistic identities can be constructed on the basis of stigmatised nonstandard language features in the usage debate. Such linguistic features serve as indicators which signal a speaker's belonging to a specific group. By conducting a qualitative analysis of respondents' answers to the open-ended question *What do you think about the state of the English language?*,

I was able to get insight into how the current state of English is perceived. Furthermore, it also brought to light how incorrect or "bad language use" is equated with a lack of education, intelligence, and unfavourable personality traits, such as the sloppiness mentioned in a student's answer quoted at the beginning of this chapter.

Changes in the approach to English language teaching occurring in the second half of the 20th century and an ensuing moral panic revolving around the decay of the English language and British society seem to have left a mark on some of the respondents. While language is frequently seen as a living entity which is thought to change with the needs of society, Standard English norms are maintained by respondents such as (3) and (4) quoted above, who, despite emphasising the need to teach the contextual appropriateness of different uses of English, argue for teaching standard language norms. That the compliance with, and knowledge of, these norms are used as exclusion criteria according to which an in-group and out-group is established, is essential in this discussion. Standard English acts as a glass ceiling hindering speakers from the out-group from participating in specific domains of life. This has been illustrated in examples (6)–(10a) above, which showed that stigmatised nonstandard language use or spelling will restrict a speaker's access to jobs, for example. Similar tendencies have been found in Hairston's (1981) and Grey and Heuser's (2003) studies which investigated American professionals' attitudes towards errors such as spelling mistakes and sentence fragments.

What needs to be stressed here, though, is that compliance with the agreed set of standard language norms is not always a matter of choice, as speakers need to be aware of the stigmatised status of usage features such as the split infinitive or double negative. As mentioned earlier in Curzan's (2014, p. 16) definition of institutional prescriptivism, the education system is the main actor through which an awareness of stigmatised language features can be achieved. With a shifting focus from traditional grammar teaching to a teaching approach devoid of prescriptivism (cf. Hudson, 2010, p. 41), awareness of such usage problems has become secondary. It is, however, intriguing and worrying to see that prescriptive norms are still used as a yardstick to measure speakers' abilities on issues they may not even be aware of, and consequently restrict their access to certain professions. This chapter has shown that studying conscious usage attitudes enables a better understanding of the workings of the usage debate. Furthermore, qualitative analyses such as the one conducted here may bring to light agreed-upon social conventions and norms of language use and, more importantly, the effects and consequences of non-compliance with such conventions and norms.

Notes

1 This chapter was written in the context of the research project *Bridging the Unbridgeable: Linguists, Prescriptivists and the General Public*, financed by the Netherlands Organisation for Scientific Research.
2 www.quickanddirtytips.com/grammar-girl.
3 The results of the other elicitation tests mentioned here will be discussed elsewhere (Ebner, to appear).

References

Aarts, B. (2014). Split infinitive. In *The Oxford dictionary of English grammar*. Oxford: Oxford University Press. Retrieved from www.oxford reference.com/view/10.1093/acref/9780199658237.001.0001/acref-97801996582 37-e-1403

Block, D. (2014). *Social class in applied linguistics*. London: Routledge.

Bryant, M. (1962). *Current American usage: How Americans say it and write it*. New York: Funk & Wagnalls.

Bucholtz, M., & Hall, K. (2010). Locating identity in language. In C. Llamas & D. Watt (Eds.), *Language and identities* (pp. 18–28). Edinburgh: Edinburgh University Press.

Burgess, T. (1996). English. In P. Gordon (Ed.), *A guide to educational research* (pp. 53–81). Oxon: The Woburn Press.

Cameron, D. (1995). *Verbal hygiene*. London: Routledge.

Crystal, D. (2008). *Txting: The Gr8 Db8*. Oxford: Oxford University Press.

Curzan, A. (2014). *Fixing English: Prescriptivism and language history*. Cambridge: Cambridge University Press.

Ebner, C. (to appear). *Proper English usage: A sociolinguistic investigation of attitudes towards usage problems in British English*. LOT dissertation series no. 468. Utrecht: LOT.

Fish, S. (1980). *Is there a text in this class?*. Cambridge, MA: Harvard University Press.

Fowler, H. W. (1926). *A dictionary of modern English usage*. Oxford: Oxford University Press.

Garrett, P. (2010). *Attitudes to language*. Cambridge: Cambridge University Press.

Gilsdorf, J., & Leonard, D. (2001). Big stuff, little stuff: A decennial measurement of executives' and academics' reactions to questionable usage elements. *The Journal of Business Communication, 38*(4), 439–471.

Qualifications and Curriculum Authority. (1998). *The grammar papers: Perspectives on the teaching of grammar in the national curriculum*. London: Qualifications and Curriculum Authority.

Grey, L. S., & Heuser, P. (2003). Nonacademic professionals' perception of usage errors. *Journal of Basic Writing, 22*(1), 50–70.

Hairston, M. (1981). Not all errors are created equal: Nonacademic readers in the professions respond to lapses in usage. *College English, 43*(8), 794–806.

Heffer, S. (2010). *Strictly English: The correct way to write. . . and why it matters*. London: Random House.

Hudson, R. (2010). How linguistics has influenced schools in England. In K. Denham & A. Lobeck (Eds.), *Linguistics at school: Language awareness in primary and secondary education* (pp. 35–48). Cambridge: Cambridge University Press.

Hughes, A., Trudgill, P., & Watt, D. (2005). *English accents and dialects: An introduction to social and regional varieties of English in the British Isles* (4th ed.). London: Hodder Education.

Ilson, R. (1985). Usage problems in British and American English. In S. Greenbaum (Ed.), *The English language today* (pp. 166–182). Oxford: Pergamon Press.

Joseph, J. E. (2006). Linguistic identities: Double-edged swords. *Language Problems and Language Planning, 30*(3), 261–267.

Joseph, J. E. (2010). Identity. In C. Llamas & D. Watt (Eds.), *Language and identities* (pp. 9–17). Edinburgh: Edinburgh University Press.

Joseph, J. E. (2013). Indexing and interpreting language, identities and face. In V. Vihman & K. Praakli (Eds.), *Negotiating linguistic identity: Language and belonging in Europe*. Bern: Peter Lang.

Kamm, O. (2015). *Accidence will happen: The non-pedantic guide to English usage*. London: Weidenfeld & Nicolson.

Keith, G. (1990). Language study at key stage 3. In R. Carter (Ed.), *Knowledge about language and the curriculum: The LINC reader* (pp. 69–103). London: Hodder Arnold.

Kostadinova, V. (in progress). *Attitudes to usage in American English* (Doctoral dissertation). University of Leiden, The Netherlands.

Kristiansen, T. (2015). The primary relevance of subconsciously offered attitudes. In A. Prikhodkine & D. R. Preston (Eds.), *Responses to language varieties: Variability, processes and outcomes* (pp. 87–116). Amsterdam: John Benjamins.

Leonard, S. A. (1932). *Current English usage*. Chicago: The Inland Press.

Milroy, J. (1999). The consequences of standardisation in descriptive linguistics. In T. Bex & R. J. Watts (Eds.), *Standard English: The widening debate* (pp. 16–39). London: Routledge.

Milroy, J., & Milroy, L. (2012). *Authority in language*. London: Routledge.

Mittins, W. H., Salu, M., Edminson, M., & Coyne, S. (1970). *Attitudes to English usage: An enquiry by the university of Newcastle upon Tyne Institute of Education English Research Group*. London: Oxford University Press.

Nash, W. (1986). *English usage: A guide to first principles*. London: Routledge.

Peters, P. (2006). English usage: Prescription and description. In B. Aarts & A. MacMahon (Eds.), *The handbook of English linguistics* (pp. 759–780). Oxford: Oxford University Press.

Queen, R., & Boland, J. (2015). I think your going to like me: Exploring the role of errors in Email messages on assessments of potential housemates. *Linguistic Vanguard, 1* (1), 283–293.

Sayer, A. (2005). *The moral significance of class*. Cambridge: Cambridge University Press.

Sundby, B., Bjørge A.K., & Haugland, K.E. (1991). *Dictionary of English normative grammar, 1700–1800*. Amsterdam: John Benjamins.

Thomas, G. (1991). *Linguistic purism*. Harlow: Longman.

Tieken-Boon van Ostade, I. (2008). The codifiers and the history of multiple negation in English, or, why were 18th-century grammarians so obsessed with double negation? In J. C. Beal, C. Nocera, & M. Sturiale (Eds.), *Perspectives on prescriptivism* (pp. 197–214). Bern: Peter Lang.

Trudgill, P. (1999). Standard English: What it isn't. In T. Bex & R. J. Watts (Eds.), *Standard English: The widening debate* (pp. 117–128). London: Routledge.

Woolard, K. A. (1998). Introduction: Language ideology as a field of inquiry. In B. B. Schieffelin, K. A. Woolard, & P.V. Kroskrity (Eds.), *Language ideologies: Practice and theory* (pp. 3–50). Oxford: Oxford University Press.

PART III
Contact, variation, performance and metalinguistic discourse

8
FROM VARIETIES IN CONTACT TO THE SELECTION OF LINGUISTIC RESOURCES IN MULTILINGUAL SETTINGS

Isabelle Léglise and Santiago Sánchez Moreano

This chapter focusses on various methodologies we can rely on to study heterogeneity and dialectal variation among multilingual speakers. We first focus on linguistic variation in contact settings, and present a methodology to describe heterogeneous and multilingual corpora and show how languages sometimes overlap. A second part focusses on (dialectal) language boundaries and how speakers may sometimes use unmarked elements showing fuzziness or reorganization of language boundaries. The role of ideology is highlighted in discourse but also at play in language practices and in doing-being 'multilingual', 'urban and modern', or performing authenticity. The third part focusses on how speakers use dialectal and linguistic resources from their linguistic repertoire in their everyday life interactions as stances and acts of identity.

1) Variation in multilingual settings

Although we know societal multilingualism is the norm and monolingualism is the exception, a special case, linguistic description, from the 16th century onwards, focussed on languages or dialects (in fact a language or a dialect at a time) by forgetting the multilingual environment of the speakers. The 'persistent use of language as a synecdoche for community' (Gal & Irvine, 1995, 968) relies on a pervasive ideology: to consider languages as spoken within monolingual and monocultural communities. This ideological construct is still very lively, although it was criticized 50 years ago, because it leaves on the side questions of variation, multilingualism, and social construction of language (Hymes, 1967). So we should conceptualize communities as imagined entities, or imagined communities (Anderson, 2006).

Sociolinguistic research on variation has also mostly focused on monolingual populations, even if variationists knew the speech communities under consideration were heterogeneous and socially and linguistically diverse. The pioneering studies on social stratification in New York (Labov, 1966, 1972) or social differentiation of English in Norwich (Trudgill, 1974) excluded, for example, non-native speakers and focused on intra-varietal change (Labov, 1994: 20). But communication ordinarily takes place not in monolingual linguistic communities perceived as homogeneous, but in a multilingual 'contact zone' (Pratt, 1991). Research on multilingualism and code-switching (Fishman, 1967; Gumperz, 1982; Myers-Scotton, 1993; Auer, 1998; Muysken, 2000 among others) took this multilingual contact zone seriously. But it has been difficult to integrate the results of these different lines of research, perhaps because it is widely assumed that the 'variability found in bi- and multilingual speech communities is more extensive than that found in monolingual and majority-language communities' (Sankoff, 2002, p. 640). There is still a relative lack of published research on variation in multilingual settings (but see for example Meyerhoff & Nagy, 2008 or Léglise & Chamoreau, 2013), except in the sub-field of dialects in contact (Gumperz, 1958; Trudgill, 1986; Siegel, 1987; Mesthrie, 1993; Kerswill & Williams, 2000; Auer, Hinskens, & Kerswill, 2005, etc.).

Most studies in contact linguistics and code-switching nevertheless also assumed languages as discrete and bounded systems in contact, and terms such as 'matrix language' or 'code-alternation' are good examples of this hypothesis (Léglise, in press). A shift in focus can be noticed within the last decade, from how bounded communities come into contact and with what kind of linguistic outcomes, to how social actors produce and negotiate social meanings, social positions, and relations through their language practices. Within the scope of multilingualism, lots of terms were coined the last 10 years to give a voice to this heterogeneity, such as crossing (Rampton, 2005), trans-idiomatic practices (Jacquemet, 2005), translanguaging (Garcia, 2009, Garcia & Li, 2013, Creese & Blackledge, 2010), or (poly)languaging (Jørgensen et al., 2011). Hall & Nilep (2015), in their review of 40 years of research on codeswitching, show very clearly how contemporary research, much centered on linguistic repertoires, wonderfully illustrates the disruption of presumed connections between language, community, identity, and spaces. This of course has an impact on how to deal with linguistic variation in multilingual settings. The three sociolinguistic waves (Eckert, 2012) also took the same path in monolingual environments, from the analysis of varieties of global communities to communities of practices and to individuals' practices.

In this paper we will address language variation as a linguistic resource in multilingual, heterogeneous language practices and look at what kind of methodology we can rely on. In the first part, we will focus on language tagging in plurilingual heterogeneous corpora before getting to two case studies: language practices among Maroons in French Guiana, and with Kichwas in Cali, Colombia. We will consider how social actors make use of their linguistic repertoire to communicate – to what purpose and with what kind of construction of social meaning – instead of looking at the consequences of their 'dialects in contact'.[1]

2) Methods for analyzing variation in heterogeneous corpora

Following the French tradition in sociology of language and sociolinguistics, we consider language practices as social practices. *Pratiques langagières* is a term coined 40 years ago to insist on the fact that language practices are determined and constrained by social order, and at the same time they construct social meaning, produce social effects, and contribute to changing these (Boutet, Fiala & Simonin, 1976). Social practices, social formations, and symbolic power are to be understood here through a theory of practice such as that of Bourdieu (1977). In a multilingual environment, these language practices are heterogeneous (Léglise, 2013) in the sense that they are made of linguistic resources attributable to various sources and due to the diverse linguistic repertoires of the languagers. *Languaging* may constitute a good translation. As Jørgensen (2011) puts it: '[a languaging perspective] emphasises that people do not primarily use "a language", or "some languages", but use language, linguistic resources."

To describe precisely the linguistic make-up of these language practices, a methodology has been developed through various research programs.[2] We use the term 'plurilingual corpora' to designate the heterogeneous corpora we created based on heterogeneous language practices (i.e., made of resources from multiple languages within the same recordings). They illustrate not only instances of codeswitching and codemixing but also *languaging* through the use of linguistic bricolage. They are performed by plurilingual speakers with varied skills, competence, and diverse repertoires (Blommaert & Backus, 2011). They also exhibit variation and non-standard forms, often neglected by monolingual corpora, or controlled for by general parameters (such as the types of speech). These plurilingual corpora are still few in number, not readily available to the linguistic community, and rarely 'processed' by the available computer software. They pose formidable problems, not only in the identification of forms, but also in their transcription and annotation.

In corpus linguistics, the Text Encoding Initiative (TEI) proposes a set of standards for annotating corpora. We refer the reader to Vaillant and Léglise (2014) for technical details on the annotation system established, but would like to mention a major adaptation for heterogeneous corpora. The TEI recommends identifying the basic language of each sentence, and noting in angle brackets when an item from another language is introduced, for instance as <foreign item belonging to language x>. A first problem, when faced with heterogeneous practices, is that the systematic allocation of one basic language for each speech turn is not possible (see Léglise & Alby (2016) for a discussion). In most cases, we observe several linguistic resources in the same speech turn produced by the same speaker. For example, in (1), a client is addressing an employee of the national electricity company, in Cayenne, French Guiana; the first line can be attributed to Créole guyanais (a French-based creole), and the second line seems to begin in Creole and end in French, whereas the third line seems to begin in French and end in Creole. Here, bold stands for Créole guyanais, Roman for French, and italics+bold are for Antillean Creole insertions.

(1) Corpus EDF Clapoty – Nelson/Léglise[3]

a. **Yèr** mo té pasé la
Yesterday 1SG PST went here
Yesterday I was here

b. i **té** **gen** *an ::* madame un peu costaud
3SG TE.PST have ART.INDF misses a little. ADV sturdy
There was a:: woman a little bit sturdy just here

à côté là
next to. ADV here. ADV
just here

c. i m' a donné [...] comme **té** *ni*
3SG 1SG have given as if. CONJ TE.PST have
(s)he gave me [...] *as if there was*

problem
problem.N
a problem

Rather than selecting – often arbitrarily – one language as the matrix language (Myers-Scotton, 1993, see Nunez & Léglise, 2017 for a discussion), we propose to consider that the utterance is multilingual and we represent this visually here by a frame. We then identify elements assignable to a particular language within each multilingual turn.

A second problem, when faced with heterogeneous practices, is that many elements can be attributed to various languages. For example, in (1), *i* at the beginning of the third line can be both interpreted as third person singular pronoun in spoken French (classical pronunciation of *i* for *il*) or in Creole (being Créole guyanais or Créole antillais). These homophonous diamorphs or bivalent elements have been long identified in the literature on code-switching (Muysken, 1990, Woolard, 1998) but never treated as such in corpus linguistics. We follow here the proposition of Ledegen (2012) to adopt a double or floating transcription in order to show the various possible interpretations, so the third line would offer the following possibilities:

(2) Corpus EDF Clapoty – Nelson/Léglise

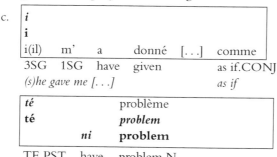

c. *i*
i
i(il) m' a donné [...] comme
3SG 1SG have given as if.CONJ
(s)he gave me [...] *as if*

té	problème
té	***problem***
ni	**problem**

TE.PST have problem.N
there was a problem

We see clearly here how languages sometimes overlap and imagine what it could imply for the study of linguistic variation.

3) (Un)marking dialectal language boundaries

As a first case study, we will focus now on the Maroon people in French Guiana who speak three related English-lexified creoles that originally emerged on the plantations of Suriname, namely Aluku, Ndyuka, and Pamaka. These languages are associated with three independent Maroon communities bearing the same names and residing in French Guiana, especially along the Maroni River, for more than two centuries, or who are recent migrants from the interior of Suriname. Based on sociohistorical and comparative linguistic data, linguists argue that they are dialects of a common language called *Nenge(e)*, *Businengetongo,* or *Eastern Maroon Creole* (Migge, 2003, Goury & Migge, 2003).

They may also speak Sranan Tongo, the mother tongue of the descendants of slaves who did not flee the plantations of Suriname. Sranan Tongo also serves as a lingua franca in multiethnic Suriname and is the language of the urban population (Carlin et al., 2015). Although all these four English-based Creoles descend from the same plantation varieties, they differ somewhat linguistically, and are not fully mutually intelligible due to partially different linguistic developments. For example, urban varieties of Sranan Tongo have been subject to relatively strong influence from Dutch.

Over the last 20 years, mobility to urban contexts has led to an expansion of the linguistic repertoires of the population, which are now more diverse or heterogeneous. Maroons had to acquire some competence in the regional lingua franca Sranan Tongo, or in Créole guyanais and French, the official language, to interact with the members of the other local populations. The expansion of the linguistic repertoire has also led to changes in individual and community language practices, so we find a greater use of Sranan Tongo in in-group encounters. On the coast, where the members of the different Maroon groups are now in regular contact with each other and with members from other local social groups (e.g., Haitians, Amerindians, Créole guyanais, metropolitan French), Maroons have developed a different sense of ethnic belonging. Unlike previous generations of Maroons, who generally emphasized inter-Maroon differences, they now emphasize the similarities that exist between the different Maroon groups. This is linked to a new pan-Maroon identity that transcends the traditional ethnic divisions.

While interested in the emergence of language varieties (Migge & Léglise, 2011), we showed that this process of identity formation was giving rise to processes associated with koineization (i.e., involving mixing of features from different related regional dialects, levelling of such features, formal reduction, and finally focussing of a new 'mixed' variety (Siegel, 1985). Dialect mixing involving Sranan Tongo and the Maroon varieties is now widespread even in in-group encounters. We also found processes of leveling in progress. For example, ethnically marked morphosyntactic features such as the verbal negation marker (*á* (Ndyuka), *án* (Pamaka/Aluku)) and the negative potential marker (*man* (Pamaka, Aluku), *poi* (Ndyuka)) were replaced with more ethnically neutral equivalents that usually come from Sranan Tongo, namely *no* and *kan*.

Using the method we developed has made it possible to show that in some corpora, almost all the turns can be attributed to one or the other variety, to one or the other language, as in Example (3) where the discussion between three men in a bar could be viewed as either Nenge(e) or Sranan Tongo (nine elements could be both, and four from Sranan).

(3) Discussion between men in a bar in Saint-Laurent (corpus CLAPOTY_Migge)

B	a	fu	den	man	dati	ya
	a	**fu**	**den**	**man**		
	FOC	for	the	man	DEM	yes

It's because of these men, yes

C	i	wani	go	na	dape	a	didon
	i	**wani**	**go**		**dape**	**a**	**didon**
	2SG	want	go	at	there	3SG	lie.down

Do you want to go where he is lying?

Our deliberate choice to present all the possibilities in the transcriptions transforms the way we look at the corpora. Rather than viewing Extract (3) as spoken in Nenge(e) with some inserted items of Sranan Tongo (Migge & Léglise, 2011), we can conclude that the speakers prefer to use items common to both languages to express themselves. In doing so, they use bivalent, unmarked elements showing fuzziness or a form of reorganization of language boundaries (Léglise, in press). They may also signal the fuzziness expressed by the name applied to it, *takitaki*, a useful label (Migge & Léglise, 2013) which avoids reference to ethnic identification (Pamaka, Ndyuka, Aluku), language names, and boundaries such as Nenge(e) vs. Sranan Tongo. Because language denominations and categorizations are always situated, *takitaki* offers a useful fuzziness to express homogeneity or differentiate ways of speaking when necessary ('this is all the same language' vs. 'there are different kinds of *takitaki*').

But, at times, people meaningfully select a particular and iconic feature from their linguistic repertoire to signal differences. For example, in urban settings, young people generally employ a form of code-switching with Sranan Tongo to construct themselves as sophisticated and urbanized Maroons, and code-mixing to assert membership in the social group of young men whose salient properties are modern urban sophistication (Migge, 2007, Migge & Léglise, 2013). They may also include linguistic resources from other languages (such as Dutch, English, or French) as a way of doing-being multilingual, urban, and modern to differentiate from more traditional ways of speaking linked to rural areas.

4) Linguistic resources as stances and acts of identity

Our second case study focusses on how speakers use dialectal and linguistic resources from their linguistic repertoire in their everyday life interactions as stances and acts of identity. Examples here are taken from features from several varieties of Spanish spoken by Kichwas in Cali, Colombia. Cali is the third-largest city in Colombia, with more than two million people including indigenous (0.55%) and afrocolombian

(26.95%) minorities. 71.56% of people are self-recognized as non-ethnic, i.e., metis and white people. Although this seems to be a clear and steady image for the Colombian Administrative Department for Statistics (DANE, 2005),[4] the heterogeneity of Cali's populations seems to be more complex and dynamic if we look at it from an ethnographic perspective. Indigenous populations, for example, in most cases, have been forced by social, economic, and security factors to leave their original territories to look for better life conditions in the cities. In the cities, they are socially organized and recognized by local and national authorities. They constitute *Cabildos urbanos*, a sort of institutional and administrative form of organization for indigenous populations in urban settings. One of these groups is the Ecuadorian Kichwas, who come from two different regions in Ecuador: Imbabura and Chimborazo (Map 1).

They have lived in Cali since the 1960s, and today, at least two generations have been born in the city. Most of them work in the downtown streets selling hand-made products and traditional clothes, as well as other manufactured products. Their informal labor activities lead them to interact constantly with the local retailers and with the other indigenous groups. The estimated number of Kichwas in Cali is 376 people, gathered in 90 families (Anacona, Cardona, & Tunubala, 2012). The asymmetrical contact of populations in Cali results in a multi-ethnic and multicultural environment shaped by different dynamic social variables such as ethnicity, mobility, transnational migration, integration to the economic and social life, and language practices. This complex social

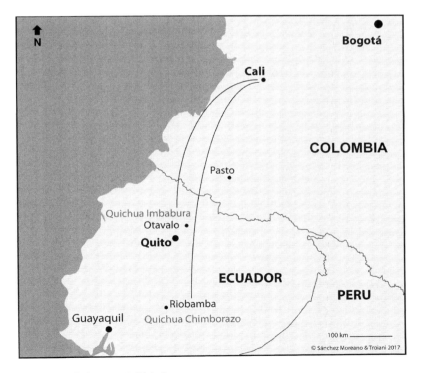

FIGURE 8.1 Imbabura and Chimborazo.

situation has important sociolinguistic consequences which entail, for example, the use of specific linguistic forms drawn from speakers' linguistic repertoires.

Kichwas in Cali speak the Ecuadorian varieties of Andean Spanish (AS), a broader Spanish variety largely described in the literature as being influenced by Quichua and Aymara languages (Haboud, 1998; Merma Molina, 2008; Palacios Alcaine, 2005; 2013; Adelaar and Muysken, 2004; Muntendam, 2013; Pfänder, 2009). AS has its own characteristics which make it different from other Spanish varieties. One of these features is the high frequency of OV syntactic constructions, the vocalic system reduction, the simplification of the pronoun system, and the particular use of gerunds, among others. Kichwas also adopt and use linguistic forms of Caleño Spanish (CS), the local Spanish variety, less known in the literature[5] but forming part of the Colombian Spanish described by some studies in dialectology (Montes, 1992; Flórez, 1961; Patiño, 2000; Mora, 1996). CS's most salient feature is probably the well-described phonetic reduction of /s/ (Brown and Brown, 2012; Ramírez Espinoza and Almira Vazquez (2016).[6]

They also speak Imbabura Quichwa (IQ) and Chimborazo Quichua (CHQ), two varieties of Andean Highlands Quichua.[7] However, a language shift situation (Thomason and Kaufman, 1988), favored by the local Spanish hegemony, is observed in this context. These Quichua varieties are relatively well-known in the literature, although they may be considered non-standard varieties.[8] Interestingly, these two varieties may serve as a means for indicating difference between Kichwas from Imbabura and Chimborazo.

The fact that AS and CS but also IQ and CHQ have come into contact due to the Kichwas' transnational migration to Cali has at least two consequences: 1) their linguistic repertoires have become heterogeneous; and 2) their language practices are heterogeneous and show evidence of phenomena that can be describe as codeswitching, dialect-switching, languaging, and other (contact-induced) linguistic variations at various (phonetic, morphosyntactic, interactional) levels. We believe that the choice of one specific linguistic marked form within conversations is socially meaningful, as we will show below. As for the annotation, we decided to annotate as unmarked Spanish the forms with no particular specificity. For example, in (4) the speaker uses *buenas*, a form of unmarked Spanish (A). Then he uses a linguistic form attributable both to Caleño Spanish (B) or to Andean Spanish (C). In fact, it may belong to C (Andean Spanish), as we observe the lengthening of the vowel /a/ and the Ecuadorian phonetic variant [ɹ]. These two elements are phonetic characteristics of Ecuadorian Andean Spanish. This element may also belong to B (Caleño Spanish) since we can observe the reduction of phoneme /s/. On the other hand, *si* in (5) is the only element unequivocally marked as Caleño Spanish [B] because of its pronunciation.

(4)

AB
  C   ['ta::deh]

      buenas **['ta::ɹde]**
      good   afternoon
      ADJ   N
      Good afternoon

(5)

ABC[B]	si	va	quedar	conmigo		
	si	**va**	**quedar**	**conmigo**		
	si	va	quedar	conmigo	si [ʰi]	*(laughing)*
	yes	go.3SG	stay.INF	with.PREP;1SG DAT	yes	
	ADV	V	V	ADP;PRN	ADV	

yes *she will stay with me, yes*

For the purpose of the exposition, in the case of ABC, in (5), we may indicate below only A as unmarked. And finally, we may label a whole turn as an instance of a particular variety, as in (6), where the word order (OV) and the use of the discursive maker *nomás*[9] are criteria to label the turn as Andean Spanish.

(6)

C	puro	Español	nomás	habla
	pure	Spanish	only	speak.3SG
	DET	N	ADV	V

Pure Spanish only she speaks

Example (7) shows how a speaker, as a social actor, makes linguistic choices to express brief affiliation. M is an elderly Kichwa lady working downtown. She spends her work time with other colleagues who may be indigenous, afrocolombian, or non-ethnic. C is a non-ethnic *Caleño* who asks M, in the first turn, to keep an eye on his stuff (001). He uses what are undeniably forms of Caleño Spanish. Interestingly, M answers affirmatively to his request using a Quichuan affirmative adverb *ari* in the second turn (002). C recognizes this element as Quichua and replies, introducing in the third turn (003) a linguistic form of Quichua: *shuhuas* (thieves). Then M replies again using Quichua (004).

(7)

001. C	B2	M	echámele un ojito	a ↗ hí	voy
		M.PROPR	watch.IMP	there.DEM.LOC	to.go.1SG.SBJ.PRS
		N	V	PRN	V

M, can you watch my stuff, I go

		a	la	↗ otra	↗ cuadra
		to.PREP.LOC	ART.DEF.SG.F	other	block
		ADP	DET	ADJ	N

to the other block

	B2	me	hace ['ahe]	el	favor
		1SG.DAT	do.3SG.SBJ.PRS	ART.DEF.SG.M	favor
		PRN	V	DET	N

please

	B2	vo	a	sacar [ha'kar]	unas [unah]
		to.go.1SG.SBJ.PRS	to.PREP.LOC	take.out.INF	ART.INDEF.F.PL

fotocopias
photocopy.PL
I am going to make some photocopies

002. M   D1   (toux) ↗ ari   ↗ ari   ↗ ari   ↗ ari
              (cough), yes, yes, yes, yes

003. C   BDC2   **ojo**   **con**   **los ['loh]**   chugua-s ['ʧuwah]
                                                                              shuhua-s ['ʧuwah]
                eye   with.PREP.ASSOC   ART.DEF.M.PL   thief-PL
                N   ADP   DET   N

                ahí
                there.DEM.LOC
                PR.N
                watch out for the thieves!

004. M   D1   *a ↗ ri*
              Yes

Following Auer's (1995) interactional annotation,[10] we observe the pattern B2 D1 BCD2 D1: it means C starts using Caleño Spanish, while M follows in Quichua. In 003, C uses not only forms of Caleño Spanish, but selects a specific form which may be construed as Quichua (D) or Andean Spanish (C), two language varieties spoken by M. He shows he is able to understand the forms of Quichua introduced by M, and to use a term that was not supposed to belong to his linguistic repertoire (he is supposed to only speak Caleño Spanish).

This sequence also shows the interesting use of the term ['ʧuwah], *shuhua* in Quichua. First, ['ʧuwah] shows evidence of phonetic variation as a consequence of the appropriation C makes of it. In fact, C produces the original Quichua word ['ʃuwah] as a voiceless palato-alveolar affricate [ʧ], the common realization of the written letters <ch> in Spanish. Moreover, he produces a final /s/ reduction, i.e., /s/ aspiration. ['ʧuwah] means 'thief' or 'thieves' and it is usually used among Kichwas to alert others to the presence of a thief nearby, without the thief himself realizing it. The fact that C uses it shows evidence of his strategy for convincing M to keep an eye on his stuff while he goes away momentarily. It may also be considered a way of expressing a social position of brief affiliation to the Kichwas group in order to support his request, which can be considered as a search for solidarity among retail traders.

Example (8) also shows the use of a specific linguistic feature from one of the Spanish varieties in contact in Cali. M is an elderly Kichwan lady speaking Andean Spanish and Quichua. T is a Caleño Spanish speaker who is talking to L, her niece, a 10-year-old girl. She says to L that she should stay with M to learn Quichua. But, before L answers, M replies for her using an affirmative adverb clearly realized as Caleño Spanish. The phonetic transcription shows the reduction of /s/, a well-known feature of Caleño Spanish.

(8)

003. T: B3	**usted**	**se**	**va**	**a**	**quedar**	**aquí**
	2SG.SBJ	3SG.REFL	go.3SG.SBJ.PRS	à.PREP	stay.INF	here
	PRN	PRN	V	ADP	V	ADV
	You are going to stay here					

	pa	**aprender**
	to	learn.INF
	ADP	V
	to learn	

004. M: B1	**sí ['hi]**
	yes
	ADV
	Yes

This choice is socially meaningful. T uses first Caleño Spanish and is followed by M who uses a specific form of Caleño Spanish. By using it, M expresses an affiliation to the majority group to which T belongs. This affiliation is the consequence of the asymmetrical contact situation in which Kichwas evolve in Cali. Due to the linguistic ideology which says that Caleño Spanish (as a language spoken by the majority group) benefits from a positive view rather than the Andean Spanish variety spoken by a minority indigenous group, Kichwas tend to align with their interlocutors to express this affiliation.

However, the linguistic choice of an element may also express differentiation or exclusion. For example, in Excerpt (9), the use of Andean Spanish shows that M switches from A to C after the evaluation that she makes of an element represented in the discourse situation. S asks M if L is her daughter. M answers negatively. Then S asks M if L speaks Quichua, but M does not answer this question directly. Rather, she uses a SOV syntactic structure and a restrictive adverb (*nomás*), both highly frequent in Andean Spanish (004).

(9)

001. S:	A2	¿y	ella	es	su	hij-it-a? ↗ /
		and.CO	3SG.SBJ	to.be.3SG.SBJ.PRS	3SG.POSS	daughter-DIM-F
		CONJ	PRN	V	DET	N
		And she is your little daughter?				

	A2	¿su /	su	niet-a?
		3SG.POSS	3SG.POSS	granddaughter
		DET	DET	N
		your granddaughter?		

002. M:	A2	no
		No

003. S:	A2	¿ella	habla	quichua?
		3SG.SBJ	speak.3SG.SBJ.PRS	quichua
		PRN	V	N

Does she speak Quichua?

004. M:	C1	ella	amig-a ↗ nomás	es ↘
		3SG.SBJ	friend-F only	to.be.3SG.SBJ.PRS
		PRN	N ADV	V

Lit. she friend only is / She is only a friend

By using these forms, M positions herself as a speaker of Andean Spanish, therefore as belonging to the group of Kichwas from Cali, a group to which L does not belong to. By doing this, M excludes L from the groups of Kichwas.

As we may see, the selection of linguistic features is socially meaningful in these interactions, as it entails social implications for speakers within conversation. These choices may construct social positioning expressing brief affiliation and differentiation. However, if we look in depth at the interactional sequences, these social positionings are framed within a broad act of stance. Social identities are linguistically indexed through different related indexical processes that contribute directly or indirectly to the construction of social identities. According to Bucholtz and Hall (2005)'s model for analyzing identity as it emerges in social interaction, these processes may include, among others, displayed evaluative and epistemic orientations to ongoing talk, as well as interactional footings and participant roles. The selection of specific linguistic forms from heterogeneous linguistic repertoires in Cali contributes to the expression of evaluative and epistemic orientations. That is what Ochs (1992) calls 'stance', a concept developed by Du Bois (2007) and Kiesling (2011). Stance is an act of social positioning implying an evaluation of an element (stance focus) existing in the discursive context by a social actor (stancetaker). It implies also his positioning *vis-à-vis* the stance focus and his/her alignment or dis-alignment *vis-à-vis* another social actor.

The examples discussed above show how a speaker may align or dis-align with his/her interlocutor within conversation through the choice of a specific linguistic form belonging to his/her linguistic repertoire. These (dis-)alignments form part of a single act of stance which includes an evaluation of some element in the communicative environment. This element will determine a positioning by the speaker and then an alignment or dis-alignment shaped on the selection of a linguistic form. For example, in (7), the stance focus is the utterance in 002 produced in Quichua by speaker 1. Speaker 2 evaluates this focus and then positions himself as someone able to use Quichua words to support his requests. This positioning is followed by an alignment with his interlocutor. The whole act is a stance of brief affiliation by the speaker 2 to the group of Kichwas to accomplish his request.

In (8), the stance focus is the fact that T speaks the prestigious local variety of Spanish. M evaluates this focus and positions herself as belonging to the majority group by aligning herself with T. By doing so, she leaves behind, momentarily, her own ethnicity to accomplish an act of stance of brief affiliation.

On the contrary, we observed in (9) that the selection of specific linguistic features may also express differentiation and exclusion. In this interaction, the stance focus is the question asked by S in 003 about whether L speaks Quichua or not (speaking Quichua meaning that she may belong to the group of Kichwas). M evaluates this question and dis-aligns with S. This dis-alignment means that neither S nor L belong to the group of Kichwas from Cali.

Conclusion

Language variation is a linguistic resource in multilingual, heterogeneous language practices. The annotation method we followed reveals the heterogeneity of language practices, and at the same time shows how languages or varieties sometimes overlap, making it irrelevant to draw arbitrary lines and boundaries between linguistic resources. This has a great impact on the way we – as linguists – consider the attribution of language (or variety) labels to linguistic forms.

Language practices among Maroons in French Guiana showed the strong tendency for languagers to use unmarked or bivalent elements that could belong to two or more languages (or language varieties). As language denominations and categorizations are always situated, it makes no sense to ask people what they think about a form's belonging to a language (or language variety): their response may vary as often as the context changes, and in relation to the local or more global necessity of affiliation or differentiation. These language practices tell us that using bivalent elements as linguistic resources is a way of showing fuzziness and challenging language boundaries. In this case, it may be a way to assert a pan-Maroon identity (by challenging the boundaries of varieties) or a way to perform urbanity and masculinity (by challenging language boundaries).

Language practices with Kichwas in Cali showed that the selection of linguistic features is socially meaningful, as it constructs social positioning expressing brief affiliation and differentiation. However, if we look in depth at the interactional sequences, these social positionings are framed within a broad act of stance. These stances observed in social interactions may reveal larger mechanisms of identity construction towards the majority society, and as Kichwas in Cali. At a local level, they confirm that languagers sometimes affiliate with imagined communities (Kichwas or Caleños for example) at their convenience through the selection of specific linguistic forms within their heterogeneous linguistic repertoires, or sometimes show, on purpose, dis-affiliation as means of differentiation or exclusion. All are illustrations of social meanings and positionings constructed by language practices.

Notes

1 For such an analysis, we refer the reader to Léglise (2013) for the consequences of contact between French and Creole, Migge & Léglise (2013) for varieties of English-based Creoles in contact, and Sánchez Moreano (2015) for the consequences of contact of Quichua on Spanish.

2 The methodology was developed within the CLAPOTY project, funded from 2009 to 2014 by the ANR under the number 09-JCJC-0121–01 and further tested within the Language Contact program funded by the French Investissements d'Avenir – Labex EFL program (ANR-10-LABX-0083) whose PI was I. Léglise.
3 The recording and first transcript comes from Nelson (2008). Annotation was done through the Clapoty project.
4 *Departamento Administrativo Nacional de Estadística*, 2005.
5 Varieties of Spanish spoken in Bogotá, Medellín, Barranquilla, and Valledupar, for example, are being studied within variationist projects such as the *Proyecto para el estudio sociolingüístico del español de España y de América* (http://preseea.linguas.net/).
6 Phoneme /s/ reduction is a characteristic feature of several varieties of spoken Spanish in America and Spain (Brown and Brown, 2012, 89). It is a widespread and well-known phonological phenomenon in Spanish linguistics (Lipski, 1984).
7 From the northern branch of the Quechua family.
8 For there are no studies of these varieties in contact with Spanish in urban settings in Colombia.
9 *Nomás* in Andean Spanish would be influenced by the enclitic prefix – *lla* from Quichua (Cerrón-Palomino, 2003, 193).
10 Where (varieties of) languages are coded with letters and interlocutors with numbers.

References

Adelaar, W., and Muysken, P. (2004). *The languages of the Andes*. Cambridge/New York/Madrid: Cambridge University Press.

Anacona, A., Cardona, M. I., & Tunubala, M. (2012). " *Estudio de Caracterización de Pueblos Indígenas: Kofán, Misak -Guámbianos, Quichuas, Ingas, Yanaconas, Nasas habitantes de Santiago de Cali* ". *Informe de proyecto:* " *Asistencia Técnica para la Implementación de la Política Pública Indígena en Santiago de Cali* ". Cali: Alcaldia de Santiago de Cali.

Anderson, B. (2006). *Imagined communities: Reflections on the origin and spread of nationalism* (Revised). New York: Verso Books.

Auer, P. (Ed.). (1998). *Code-switching in conversation: Language, interaction and identity*. London/New York: Routledge.

Auer, P., Hinskens, F., & Kerswill, P. (2005). *Dialect change: Converge and divergence in European languages*. Cambridge: Cambridge University Press.

Auer, Peter. (1995). The pragmatics of code-switching: a sequential approach. In L. Milroy & P. Muysken (Eds.), *One speaker, two languages: Cross-disciplinary perspectives on code-switching* (pp. 115–135). Cambridge: Cambridge University Press.

Beukema, R. W. (1975). *A Grammatical Sketch of Chimborazo Quichua* (Thèse de doctorat). Ann Arbor: Yale University Press.

Blommaert, J., & Backus, A. (2011). Repertoires Revisited: "Knowing Language" in Superdiversity. *Working Papers in Urban Language and Literacies*, 67, 1–26.

Bourdieu, P. (1977). *Outline of a theory of practice*. Cambridge: Cambridge University Press.

Boutet J., Fiala P. et Simonin-Grumbach J., (1976) Sociolinguistique ou sociologie du langage? Critique, 344, 68–85.

Brown, E. K., & Brown, E. (2012). Syllabe-final and Syllabe-initial /s/ Reduction in Cali, Colombia: One variable or two? In R. File-Muriel & R. Orozco (Eds.), *Colombian varieties of Spanish* (pp. 89–106). Madrid/Frankfurt: Iberoamericana/Vervuert.

Bucholtz, M., & Hall, K. (2005). Identity and interaction: A sociocultural linguistic approach. *Discourse Studies*, 7(4–5), 585–614.

Carlin, E. B., Léglise, I., Migge, B., & Tjon Sie Fat, P. B. (Eds.). (2015). *In and out of suriname: Language, mobility and identigy*. Amsterdam: Brill.

Cerrón-Palomino, R. (2003). *Castellano andino: aspectos sociolingüísticos, pedagógicos y gramaticales*. Lima: Pontificia Universidad Católica del Perú, Fondo Editorial/Cooperación Técnica Alemana.

Creese, A., & Blackledge, A. (2010). Translanguaging in the bilingual classroom: A pedagogy for learning and teaching? *The Modern Language Journal, 94*(1), 103–15.

DANE (Ed.). (2008). *Censo general 2005: nivel nacional*. Colombia: República de Colombia, Departamento Administrativo Nacional de Estadística.

Du Bois, J. W. (2007). The stance triangle. In R. Englebretson (Ed.), *Stancetaking in discours, subjectivity, evaluation, interaction* (pp. 139–182). Amsterdam/Philadelphia: John Benjamins Publishing Company.

Eckert, P. (2012). Three waves of variation study: The emergence of meaning in the study of linguistic variation. *Annual Review of Anthropology, 41*, 87–100.

Fishman, J. A. (1968). Sociolinguistic perspective on the study of bilingualism. *Linguistics, 39*, 21–49.

Flórez, L. (1961). El Atlas lingüístico-etnografico de Colombia (ALEC): nota informativa. *Thesaurus: boletín del Instituto Caro y Cuervo*, XVI(1), 77–125.

Gal, S., & Irvine, J. T. (1995). The boundaries of languages and disciplines: How ideologies construct difference. *Social Research, 82*(4), 967–1001.

Garcia, O., & Wei, L. (2013). *Translanguaging: Language, bilingualism and education* (2014 ed.). Hampshire: Palgrave Pivot.

Gumperz, J. J. (1958). Dialect differences and social tratification in a North Indian village. *American Anthropologist, 60*(4), 668–682.

Gumperz, J. J. (1982). *Language and social identity*. Studies in Interactional Sociolinguistics 2. Cambridge: Cambridge University Press.

Haboud, M. (1998). *Quichua y Castellano en los Andes Ecuatorianos. Los efectos de un contacto prolongado*. Quito: Ediciones Abya-Yala.

Hall, K., & Nilep, C. (2015). Code-switching, identity, and globalization. In D. Tannen, H. E. Hamilton, & D. Schiffrin (Eds.), *The handbook of discourse analysis* (pp. 597–619). Hoboken, NJ: John Wiley & Sons, Inc.

Hermon, G. (2001). Non-canonically marked A/S in Imbabura Quechua. In A. Y. Aikhenvald, R. M. W. Dixon, & O. Masayuki (Eds.), *Non-canonical marking of subjects and objects* (Vol. 46, pp. 149–179). Typological Studies in Language. Amsterdam/Philadelphia: John Benjamins Publishing.

Hurley, J. K. (1995). The impact of Quichua on verb forms used in Spanish requests in Otavalo, Ecuador. In C. Silva-Corvalán (Eds.), *Spanish in four continents: Studies in language contact and bilingualism* (pp. 39–51). Washington DC: Georgetown University Press.

Hymes, D. (1967). Why linguistics needs the sociologist. *Social Research, 34*(4), 632–647.

Jacquemet, M. (2005). Transidiomatic practices: Language and power in the age of globalization. *Language & Communication, 25*(3), 257–277.

Jake, J. L. (1983). *Grammatical relations in Imbabura Quechua (Ecuador)* (Ph.D.). University of Illinois at Urbana-Champaign.

Jørgensen, J. N., Karrebaek, M. S., Madsen, L. M., & Moller, J. S. (2011). Polylanguaging in superdiversity. *Diversities*, 13(2). Retrieved from www.unesco.org/shs/diversities/vol13/issue2/art2

Kerswill, P., & Williams, A. (2000). Creating a New Town Koine. *Language in Society, 29*, 65–115.

Kiesling, S. F. (2009). Style as a stance: Stance as the explanation for patterns of sociolinguistic variation. In A. Jaffe (Ed.), *Stance: Sociolinguistic perspectives* (pp. 171–194). Oxford: Oxford University Press.

Kiesling, S. F. (2011). *Stance in context: Affect, alignment and investment in the analysis of stancetaking*. Paper. Mean Conference, The University of the West of England, Bristol, UK., avril 15.

Labov, W. (1966). *The social stratification of English in New York City*. Washington, DC: Center for Applied Linguistics.

Labov, W. (1972). *Language in the Inner City*. Philadelphia, PA: University of Pennsylvania Press.

Labov, W. (1994). *Principles of linguistic change, vol 1: Social factors*. Oxford: Blackwell.

Ledegen, G. (2012). Prédicats "flottants" entre le créole acrolectal et le français à La Réunion : exploration d'une zone ambiguë. In C. Chamoreau & L. Goury (Eds.), *Changement linguistique et langues en contact : approches plurielles du domaine prédicatif* (pp. 251–270). Paris: CNRS Éditions.

Léglise, I. (2013) Multilinguisme, variation, contact. Des pratiques langagières sur le terrain à l'analyse de corpus hétérogènes. Habilitation, Paris: INALCO. Retrieved from https://tel.archives-ouvertes.fr/tel-00880500

Léglise, I. (In press). Pratiques langagières plurilingues et frontières de langues. In L. Greco & M. Auzanneau (Eds.), *Dessiner les frontières*. Lyon: ENS Editions.

Léglise, I., & Alby, S. (2016). Plurilingual corpora and polylanguaging, when corpus linguistics meets contact linguistics. *Sociolinguistic studies*, *10*(3), 357–381.

Léglise, I., & Chamoreau, C. (Eds.). (2013). *The interplay of variation and change in contact settings*. Amsterdam: John Benjamins.

Lipski, J. M. (1984). On the weakening of /s/ in Latin American Spanish. *Zeitschrift für Dialektologie und Linguistik*, *51*(1), 31–43.

Merma Molina, G. (2008). *El contacto lingüístico en el español andino peruano: Estudios pragmático-cognitivos*. Alicante: Publicaciones Universidad de Alicante.

Mesthrie, R. (1993). Koinéization in the Bhojpuri-Hindi Diaspora, with Special Reference to South Africa. *International Journal of the Sociology of Language*, *99*, 25–44.

Meyerhoff, M., & Nagy, N. (Eds.). (2008). *Social lives in language. Sociolinguistics and multilingual speech communities*. Amsterdam: John Benjamins.

Migge, B. (2003). *Creole formation as language contact: The case of the Surinamese Creoles*. Amsterdam: John Benjamins.

Migge, B. (2007). Codeswitching and social identities in the eastern maroon community of suriname and French Guiana. *Journal of Sociolinguistics*, *11*(1), 53–72.

Migge, B., & Léglise, I. (2011). On the emergence of new language varieties: The case of the Eastern Maroon Creole in French Guiana. In L. Hinrichs & J. Farquharson (Eds.), *Variation in the Caribbean: From Creole Continua to individual agency* (pp. 181–199). Amsterdam: John Benjamins.

Migge, B., & Léglise, I. (2013). *Exploring language in a multilingual context: Variation, interaction and ideology in language documentation*. Cambridge: Cambridge University Press.

Montes Giraldo, J. (1992). El español hablado en Colombia. In C. Alonso Hernández, Pabecal [Spain] (Ed.), *Historia y presente del español de América* (pp. 519–142). Madrid: Junta de Castilla y León.

Mora Monroy, S. (1996). Dialectos del español de Colombia. Caracterización léxica de los sub dialectos andino-sureño y caucano-valluno. *Thesaurus: boletín del Instituto Caro y Cuervo*, *51*(1), 1–26.

Muntendam, A. (2013). On the nature of cross-linguistic transfer: A case study of Andean Spanish. *Bilingualism: Language and Cognition*, *16*(1), 111–131.

Muysken, P. (1990). Concepts, methodology and data in language contact research. *Papers for the Workshop on Concept, Methodology and Data. Network on Code-Switching and Language Contact*. Strasbourg: European Science Foundatation, 15–30.

Muysken, P. (2000). *Bilingual speech: A typology of code-mixing*. Cambridge: Cambridge University Press.

Myers-Scotton, C. (1993). *Social motivations for codeswitching: Evidence from Africa*. Oxford, UK: Clarendon Press.

Nelson, L. (2008). *Le contact de langues au travail: l'étude de l'alternance codique entre les langues français-créole dans les situations de service à l'accueil direct d'EDF Guyane*. Mémoire de master 2, Université Lyon 2.

Nunez, J. J. F., & Léglise, I. (2017). Ce que les pratiques langagières plurilingues au Sénégal disent à la linguistique de contact. In M. Auzanneau, M. Bento, & M. Leclere (Eds.), *Espaces, mobilités et éducation plurilingues: éclairages d'Afrique ou d'ailleurs*(pp. 99–119). Editions des archives contemporaines.

Ochs, E. (1992). Indexing Gender. In A. Duranti & C. Goodwin (Eds.), *Rethinking context: Language as an interactive phenomenon* (pp. 335–358). Cambridge: Cambridge University Press.

Palacios Alcaine, A.. (2005). La influencia del quichua en el español andino ecuatoriano. In C. Ferrero & N. Lasso-von Lang (Eds.), *Variedades lingüísticas y lenguas en contacto en el mundo de habla hispana* (pp. 44–52). España: Bloomington-AuthorHouse.

Palacios Alcaine, A. (2013). Contact-induced change and internal evolution: Spanish in contact with Amerindien languages. In I. Léglise & C. Chamoreau (Eds.), *The interplay of variation and change in contact settings* (pp. 165–198). Studies in Language Variation. Amsterdam/Philadelphia: John Benjamins.

Paris, J. (1961). *Gramática de la lengua quichua*. Quito: Ed. Santo Domingo.

Patiño, C. (2000). Español, lenguas indígenas y lenguas criollas en Colombia. In Carlos Patiño, Instituto Caro y Cuervo (Eds.), *Sobre Etnolingüística y Otros Temas* (pp. 57–99). Bogotá: Imprenta Patriótica.

Pratt, M. L. (1991). Arts of the contact zone. *Profession, 91*, 33–40.

Ramírez Espinoza, A., & Vazquez, A. A. (2016). Variación del fonema /s/ en contextos de juntura de palabra en el español caleño: una mirada sociolingüística1. *Lenguaje*, 1(44), 11–33.

Rampton, B. (1998). Language crossing and the redefinition of reality. In P. Auer (Ed.), *Code-switching in conversation* (pp. 290–317). London/New York: Routledge.

Rampton, B. (2005). *Crossing: Language and ethnicity among adolescents* (2nd éd.). Manchester, UK/Northampton, MA: St. Jerome Publishing.

Reyburn, W. D. (1954). Quechua I: Phonemics. *International Journal of American Linguistics, 20*(3), 210–214.

Sánchez Moreano, S. (2015). *Conséquences linguistiques e identitaires du contact linguistique et dialectal à Cali (Colombie): le cas de l'ordre des constituants* (PhD diss.). Paris: Université Paris Diderot/Sorbonne Paris Cité. Retrieved from https://hal.archives-ouvertes.fr/tel-01314442

Sánchez Moreano, S. (2017). Enoncés de type OV et positionnements sociaux dans l'espagnol parlé par les Quichuas équatoriens à Cali, Colombie. *Sociolinguistics Studies. Equinox*, 11(1), 65–105.

Sankoff, G. (2002). Linguistic outcomes of language contact. In J.-K. Chambers, P. Trudgill, & N. Schilling-Estes (Eds.), *The handbook of language variation and change* (pp. 638–668). Oxford: Blackwell Publishing.

Siegel, J. (1985). Koines and koineization. *Language in Society, 14*, 357–378.

Siegel, J. (1987). *Language contact in a plantation environment*. Cambridge: Cambridge University Press.

Trudgill, P. (1974). *The social differentiation of English in Norwich*. Cambridge: Cambridge University Press.

Trudgill, P. (1986). *Dialects in contact*. Oxford: Blackwell.

Vaillant, P., & Léglise, I. (2014). A la croisée des langues: Annotation et fouille de corpus plurilingues. *Revue des Nouvelles Technologies de l'Information*, RNTI-SHS-2, 81–100.

Vertovec, S. (2007). New directions in the anthropology of migration and multiculturalism. *Ethnic and Racial Studies, 30*(6), 961–978.

Vertovec, S. (2010). Towards post-multiculturalism? Changing communities, conditions and contexts of diversity. *ISSJ International Social Science Journal, 61*(199), 83–95.

Wurm, S. A. (1996). *Atlas des langues en péril dans le monde*. Paris: UNESCO.

9

"YOU LIVE IN THE UNITED STATES, YOU SPEAK ENGLISH," DECÍAN LAS MAESTRAS

How New Mexican Spanish speakers enact, ascribe, and reject ethnic identities

Katherine O'Donnell Christoffersen and Naomi L. Shin

1. Introduction

The New Mexican Spanish variety has a unique linguistic history. It has been referred to as the oldest surviving Spanish dialect (Lipski, 2010) and the oldest variety of European language in the U.S. (Bills, 1997). Spanish has been spoken in New Mexico since 1598. In their overview of language policy in New Mexico, Travis & Villa (2011) review three influential periods. During the Colonial Period, New Mexico gained independence from Spain in 1821, and the official language was Spanish. In 1850, with the Treaty of Guadalupe Hidalgo, New Mexico entered the Territorial Period. During this time there was no official language policy, although the "de facto" official language was English, and Spanish was subordinated. In 1912, New Mexico became a state, and although the state never had any legal bilingual status, there were certain protections for non-English speakers, such as providing translators for jurors.

Travis & Villa (2011) posit that the introduction of public school during this time played a major role in the loss of Spanish in New Mexico. In 1912, universal English education was instated. Before and after the First World War, public education policy was to eradicate Spanish, and there are many reports of how children were punished for speaking Spanish in school (Espinosa, 1975, p. 101; Gonzales, 1999, p. 2). Narratives reporting these incidents are a recurring theme throughout the New Mexico Colorado Spanish Survey corpus, the data for the present study (Bills & Vigil, 2007, 2008). In the southwest, Spanish-speaking students were routinely segregated in different schools. After the ruling of Brown v. Board of Education in 1954, Spanish-speaking students were integrated into schools. However, many schools continued to stress the acquisition of English as a "means of assimilation of American values" (MacGregor-Mendoza, p. 356), and "no Spanish rules" in classrooms endured, prohibiting the use of Spanish (Acuña, 1988).

While this is changing with the instatement of the Bilingual Education Act in 1968 and a current resurgence of interest in dual language education, the history of these linguistic policies has left a clear impact on New Mexican Spanish speakers and the New Mexican Spanish variety. Investigations into personal narratives in New Mexican Spanish speaker interviews allow for a deeper insight into these processes and their long-lasting effects, especially given the strict oppression and punishment inflicted upon students in public education. In particular, these narratives reveal the performance of ethnic identities through code-switching, crossing, and passing.

Performance of ethnic identity

Any discussion of the performance of ethnic identities must inevitably address the complicated issue of "what constitutes ethnicity?" Attempts to define ethnicity have not always been complementary; in fact, in some cases, they are competing (Fought, 2006). For example, Barth (1969) states that ethnicity "makes up a field of communication and interaction." However, Zelinksy (2001) purports the exact opposite, suggesting that ethnicity is "an imagined community *too large* for intimate contact among its members" (p. 44). For the present chapter, we will use the working definition of ethnicity as set forth by Fought (2006, p. 13) as a construct "that is highlighted most clearly where ingroup/outgroup boundaries are part of the context," and we will seek to situate the discussion of language and ethnicity within a particular community's ideologies about such boundaries.

In the present chapter, this working definition of ethnicity is rooted in the theorization of identity as performance. The performance of identity is based in the critical theorization that identity is not something we have, but something that we "do," or more specifically "something people do which is embedded in some other social activity, not something that they 'are'" (Widdicombe, 1998, p. 191) Thus, identity is a product, not a source, of linguistic practices. We do not speak a certain way because of any fixed identity; instead, the manner in which we speak creates multiple and shifting identities. In this respect, our identities are "talking into being." Language plays an important role in the performance of identity, and the concept of performance is significant, as it implies an audience. The audience interprets the performance of linguistic features, such as gestures, tone, and pitch. The performance of identity is perhaps especially important in the context of interviews, since it recognizes the role of the interviewer and the co-construction of the dialogue. For this reason, the present chapter analyzes the language of both the interviewee and the interviewer, in order to clearly identify the performance aspects of narrative and the interview as a communicative context (Atkinson & Delamont, 2006; see also Wortham, 2001).

The performance of ethnic identity through code-switching, crossing, and passing

Several studies have investigated the performance of ethnic identity through code-switching, the alternation between two or more languages within the same utterance or conversation (Gumperz, 1982). For example, Myers-Scotton (1993, p. 104–5) demonstrates how speakers in Kenya use Kikuyu to index ethnic pride, Swahili to index urban identity, and English to index education. In a later study, Myers-Scotton (2000) finds evidence that mother tongue indexes African ethnic identity while the "official" language indexes a "multi-ethnic elite" (p. 146). Bailey (2000b) cites examples of how Dominican American teenagers alternate between Spanish, AAVE, and code-switching depending on context, such as whether they are talking with family or friends. In a study on African American drag queens, Barrett (1999) finds the use of stereotyped "women's language" in a display of femininity and low pitch and taboo words for heightened masculinity. Thus, this body of research demonstrates that code-switching constitutes an important tool that speakers employ in order to perform their identities. This point is particularly well articulated by Jamila Lyiscott's (2014) "Three ways to speak English," in which she performs her identities using three dialects: Standard English, Caribbean English, and African American English.

Crossing, also called "language crossing" or "code-crossing," is defined as "the use of language varieties associated with social or ethnic groups that the speaker does not normally 'belong' to" (Rampton, 1999). Crossing arises because people generally speak like those they want to be like (Hewitt, 1982, 1986). Among adolescents in South London in the 1980s, Hewitt (1986) finds evidence of "crossing" by white Anglo-descent adolescents who use creole or "patois." Similarly, Rampton (1995, 1999) finds instances of "crossing" by Anglo adolescents performing creole identities in Britain. In addition, he finds speakers of Asian origin crossing by adopting the creole variety of English, and Afro-Caribbean speakers crossing by adopting stylized Asian English and Panjabi in the South Midlands of England.

Passing is a similar albeit distinct phenomenon, as it requires validation from the outside. Bucholtz (1995) defines passing as "the ability to be taken for a member of a social category other than one's own." Based on this definition, other factors such as gender and skin tone play a role in passing. Research on passing has analyzed negative views of individuals' attempts to pass as a member of the dominant "white" group (McCormick, 2002a), which is often criticized as "pretending to be white" (Urciuoli, 1996). However, Bucholtz (1995) argues that social motivations and meanings for passing are more complex than has been assumed, and that passing serves a number of functions, not necessarily signaling a rejection of one's "real" identity.

The present study stands to make a significant contribution to the literature as a first analysis of the construction of ethnic identity through code-switching, crossing, and passing among New Mexican Spanish speakers. Specifically, this analysis addresses how New Mexican Spanish speakers enact, ascribe, and reject ethnic identities through code-switching.

2. Data and approach

The New Mexico and Colorado Spanish Survey (NMCOSS) project, initiated in 1991, documents the Spanish language spoken throughout the state of New

Mexico and 16 counties of southern Colorado (Bills & Vigil, 2007, 2008). The NMCOSS corpus was collected by trained field workers, who tape-recorded interviews with 350 speakers employing both controlled elicitation and free conversation (Vigil, 1989). Each NMCOSS interview averaged three and a half hours in length, beginning with compilation of personal information regarding the consultant and followed by specific linguistic elicitation and free conversation. Currently, about ten percent of the interviews have been orthographically transcribed.

The dataset for this study was created from the free conversation portions of the interviews. A subset of 20 interviews were selected at random from the NMCOSS study corpus. After inspecting all 20 interviews, ten were chosen for close analysis based on their relevance to the performance of ethnic identity through code-switching, crossing, and passing. These interviews included six female and four male interviewees with an average age of 61.5, and were conducted between January 1992 and June 1993. The following table depicts the specific participants, the regional location of their homes, sex and age.

TABLE 9.1 Participants of the New Mexico and Colorado Spanish Survey.

Participant	Alias	Date	Location	Sex	Age
1	Alejandra	1/9/1992	Española, NM	F	88
2	Eva	4/25/1992	Questa, NM	F	82
3	Juan	1992	Albuquerque, NM	M	48
4	Margarita	2/24/1993	Albuquerque, NM	F	65
5	Ricardo	6/28/1993	Albuquerque, NM	M	56
6	María	6/3/1992	Mountainair, NM	F	47
7	Laura	6/17/1992	Roy, NM	F	74
8	Tomás	6/15/1992	Albuquerque, NM	M	45
9	Antonio	7/14/1992	Chamisal, NM	M	48
10	Ana	1992	Bernalillo, NM	F	62

Interviews are unique social encounters (Briggs, 1986; Cicourel, 1964), which should not be analyzed as spontaneous conversation. It is imperative that we recognize the context-embeddedness of narratives in interviews as discourse that is co-constructed between interviewer and interviewee. Without considering context, we run the risk of neglecting the performance aspects of narrative and the interview as a communicative context (Atkinson & Delamont, 2006; see also Wortham, 2001). Perhaps the most important limitation to consider is that one interview cannot accurately describe the entirety of experiences of that individual. As Rampton (2005) writes, people "express their group identification in inexplicit, non-propositional ways, for example through style, activity and accent, and so some of the most important ethnic processes can be missed in studies that rely on the answers given in questionnaires and interviews" (p. 20). Yet, interviews constitute situations in which individuals make sense of their experiences, specifically through the re-elaboration of ideologies and common sense understandings (Wortham et al., 2011). In particular, narratives within interviews are powerful sites for the performance of identity (Baynham, 2003; Bucholtz, 1999; De Fina, 2003; Georgakopoulou, 2007; Schiffrin, 1996). Narratives within interviews reflect and shape social realities and relationships (Baynham, 2003; De Fina et al., 2006; Maryns & Blommaert, 2001; Wortham, 2001). We follow De Fina & King (2011) in positing that a close analysis of how these participants negotiate identities through narratives in these interviews can "yield deeper understandings of people's sense-making about social issues" (p. 167).

From the close analysis of the narratives within these interviews, three themes related to the performance of ethnic identities emerged: 1) the voice of the oppressors, 2) the changing linguistic realities of younger generations, and 3) instances of crossing and passing. "The voice of the oppressor" is defined as any instance in which the participant distinguishes the voice of another as an individual of oppression. In many instances, these situations coincided with code-switches. The participant would switch into another language to describe or quote the language of the other/the oppressor. "Changing linguistic realities of younger generations" was the second common theme throughout these narratives of ethnic identity performance. Within this theme, the participants described how older generations spoke Spanish while many younger generations, often in their own families, did not speak Spanish. Finally, narratives of "crossing" and "passing" (defined above) were ripe with references to the performance of ethnic identity, often depicting how individuals were taken as members of another group such as "monolingual English speakers."

Our examination of the narratives pays close attention to *positioning*, which explores how narrators manage the interaction of identities in storytelling (Bamberg, 1997; Davies & Harré, 1990; Wortham, 2001). Three domains are typically explored in analyses of positioning: a) communicative event, b) storytelling world, which is the world in which the interlocutors are communicating at the time of narration, and c) storyworld, which is the world described by the narrative (Young, 1987). Bamberg and Georgakopoulou (2008) describe positioning as existing in the interplay of three levels: the first analyses how the narrators manage the interaction of characters identities in the storyworld; the second analyzes how narrators position themselves with interlocutors in the story-telling world; and the third explores how the storyteller "positions a sense of self/identity with regards to dominant discourses or master narratives" (p. 385) and how he/she makes them relevant to the interaction.

3. New Mexican Spanish narratives and analysis

Here we will analyze three narratives that demonstrate aspects of the performance of ethnic identity. The analysis will include one excerpt for each of the aforementioned recurring themes: the voice of the oppressors, the changing linguistic realities of younger generations, and crossing/passing.

The voice of the oppressors

The first dominant theme in the interviews was that of the voice of the oppressors. In the following excerpt, Juan, a 48-year-old from Albuquerque, discusses the language policy enforced in school. The interviewer begins by asking how Juan learned English. Juan responds that he learned in school and expounds upon that experience following the promptings of the interviewer.

(1) "You live in the United States, you speak English.": Juan (J) and interviewer (I)

1 I: ¿Y cuándo aprendiste inglés?
2 J: Pues en las escuelas públicas de a la edad de seis años. El, el primer día que yo fui a la escuela no
3 sabía ni una palabra de inglés. Fue una:, un viaje, cómo se dice aquí.
4 I: "*A real trip*". Y qué hiciste o que pasó? Cómo fue?
5 J: Pues allí había una fuerza uh día por día, año tras de año se fue aprendiendo lo básico del inglés
6 para entender, que se estaba de que se trataba la escuela.
7 I: ¿Cómo te pareció éso?
8 J: Pues fue algo, algo, algo nuevo, algo estran uh estranjero. Algo de que fue necesario. Importante.
9 Es creo que lo que hace uno uh bilingüe.
10 I: Pero tú crees que la forma en que te, en que aprendiste era, fue necesario?
11 J: No, no, no, no uh, fue me fue uh fue el asunt uh, un en, un enseño a ver forzado. Abajo de
12 amenazen de castigo. "*You live in the United States, you speak English,*" decían las maestras.

Translation

1 I: And when did you learn English?
2 J: Well in the public schools at the age of six years old. The, the first day that I went to school I didn't
3 know a word of English. It was a, a trip, as you say here.
4 I: "*A real trip*". And what did you do or what happened? How did it go?
5 J: Well there there was a push day after day, year after year, one learned the basics of English to
6 understand, what it was what school was all about.
7 I: How did that seem to you?
8 J: Well it was something, something something new, something strang- something uh strange.
9 Something that was necessary. Important. It's that I think that it's what makes one bilingual.

10   I: But do you think that the way in which you learned was necessary?
11   J: No, no, no, no uh, it was, it was, it was the thing- a forced teaching. Under the threat of
12   punishment. "*You live in the United States, you speak English*," said the teachers.

Our analysis begins by examining first two levels of positioning, focusing on how Juan manages the interaction of characters' identities in the storyworld and how he positions himself with interlocutors in the story-telling world. In Line 1, the interviewer asks when Juan learned English, a question that prompts the following narrative sequence. In lines 2–3, Juan responds that he learned English in public school, which he began at 6 years of age. He elaborates that he "didn't know a word of English" on that first day of school and comments that it was "un viaje" [a trip]. At this point, in line 4 we note the interviewer's role in the co-construction of the narrative, and as a bilingual Spanish-English speaker: the interviewer translates "un viaje" [a trip] with the phrase "a real trip," positing that this is the expression Juan was seeking to reference with "como dicen aquí" [as you say here]. Juan does not correct the interviewer's rendering of this phrase in English, and thus it becomes reified as a part of the storyworld. The interviewer then prompts Juan to further expand on his experiences, and in this way the interviewer is actively engaged in prompting the storytelling and the elaboration of the characters in the narrative. In lines 5–6, Juan describes learning English as a "fuerza," which literally translates to "strength," but here means something closer to "effort" or "push." In doing so, he ascribes agency to the main character, 6-year-old Juan, who makes a deliberate effort to learn English and understand school. Notably, he does not recognize anyone else as teaching him, but rather emphasizes his own effort. When prompted to elaborate again in line 7, Juan describes the experience with three adjectives, which construct a situation in the storyworld that is "strange," "necessary," and "important" (lines 8–9). Finally, he justifies the "necessary" and "important" nature of the experience by finishing the argument sequence with an exemplum that "it's what makes one bilingual" (line 9). In doing so, Juan reasons that the experiences he went through to learn English were important, perhaps because it shaped his bilingual identity. In line 10, the interviewer poses his interrogative statement in such a way that it questions Juan's previous exemplum. It is here that we note the crucial and distinct aspects of the interactional relationships in narratives in interviews. The question "But do you think that the way in which you were taught was necessary?" has a very specific effect, as it calls into questions Juan's own description of the event, in which he described his experience as "necessary." The interviewer's prompting yields Juan's response (lines 11–12): he replies "no" several times, thereby negating his previous remarks. Only then does Juan introduce the teachers as characters in the storytelling world who employ "forced teaching" and "threat of punishment." Juan not only narrates the teachers' teaching styles, but he also directly quotes the teachers. The last line, "'*You live in the United States, you speak English,*' said the teachers" is powerful, and it is significant that Juan quotes the teachers as a collective group, which suggests that this was a pervasive discourse or school language policy followed by the teachers. He constructs this statement as one that the teachers would often say, through the use of the imperfective past tense "decían."

Now we delve into the third level of positioning to consider the position of Juan's sense of self in relation to dominant discourses and master narratives. In line 12, Juan switches into English for the voice of the teachers: "You live in the United States, you speak English." In this code-switch, Juan ascribes an identity of arbiter of proper language use and oppressor of language choice to the teachers. In this switch, Juan also constructs his own ethnic identity as tied to the Spanish language. By code-switching, he depicts a social distance between himself and the teachers, as well as a distance from the ideology invoked (Mendoza-Denton & Osborne, 2009). Also, by code-switching into English, Juan uses the oppressor's discourse for his/her own purpose, with new intention. This is an example of "double-voicing" (Bakhtin, 1984) in the sense that Juan repeats the teachers' words "You live in the United States, you speak English," but the repetition is in order to demonstrate their attitudes, actions, and ideologies. The words he is speaking do not reflect his own language ideology.

By aligning himself with Spanish and aligning the teachers with English, Juan's narrative exemplifies the Herderian ideology of "one nation, one people, one language" (Hobsbawn, 1990; Bourdieu, 1991; Woolard, 1998). Since speaking English is tied to American nationalism, the act of speaking Spanish constitutes a type of "sovereign betrayal" and "a symbolic threat to the social order" (Santa Ana, 2002, 237). Consequentially, the quoted language policy requiring people to speak English in the United States illustrates how "dehumanizing and marginalizing discursive practices. . . devalue immigrant and ethnolinguistic miniority languages, denaturalize nonethnic identity claims, and in general limit the types of identities available to ethnolinguistic minority subjects" (Carter, 2014, p. 236). Through the teachers' quoted speech, Juan depicts "English Only" as the school policy, which is constructed as reflecting the nation's linguistic policy, "You live in the United States. . .". Santa Ana (2002) has argued that "English Only" is a linguacism, "an ideology and a set of institutional operations used to legitimate and reproduce an unequal division of power and resources among groups. . . on the basis of language" (p. 237). Unfortunately, the reproduction of this power dynamic has actual far-reaching effects, including the intergenerational loss of Spanish in the U.S. (Zentella, 1997, p. 148).

The changing linguistic realities of younger generations

The second recurring theme in the corpus is the "the changing linguistic realities of younger generations." In the following narrative the interviewer asks Margarita about her children and whether they understand or speak Spanish. Margarita replies with a narrative about Johnny who learned the "pledge of legiance" in mexicano [New Mexican Spanish].

(2): "Pledge of Legiance": Margarita (M) and interviewer (I)

1   I: Y este, tiene.. hijos?
2   M: Oh yeah.
3   I: hijos que entiendan el.. español. que hablen español.
4   M: El – uno de ellos es – entiende poquitito. no muncho. el Lucas. . . Él le – él le – sabe dijir
5   la.. pledge of legience to the flag in mexicano. . . . En la escuela le enseñaron and he learned it... 6   and he knows it.
7   I: It's too bad that all they – that's all they teach them.
8   M: That's all. Mhm.
9   I: Nada – nada más de – de su lengua, de su cultura.
10   M: De su lengua. Ojalá que les enseñaran más.

Translation

1   I: And um, do you have children?
2   M: Oh yeah.
3   I: Children that understand.. Spanish. That speak Spanish?
4   M: He – one of them is – understands a little bit. Not a lot. Lucas. He – he – knows how to
5   say the –.. pledge of legience to the flag in Spanish. . . . In the school they taught him and he
6   learned it... and he knows it.
7   I: It's too bad that all they – that's all they teach them.
8   M: That's all. Mhm.
9   I: Nothing – nothing more of – of their language, of their culture.
10   M: Of their language. I wish they would teach them more.

In this excerpt, the storytelling world and storyworld are framed by the prompting of the interviewer in lines 1 and 3, asking a question about whether Margarita has children, and then the follow up question of whether those children understand or speak Spanish. Margarita responds in line 4–6, narrating a storyworld that includes Lucas as a character. Lucas is described as knowing a little bit of Spanish, not a lot. Specifically, Margarita states that Lucas knows how to say the "pledge of legiance [sic]." The school is introduced as having taught this to Lucas, but Lucas is depicted as having an active role in learning and retaining this knowledge: "and he learned it. . . and he knows it." The interviewer responds to the narrative in line 7 with a negative evaluation, suggesting that the school should teach more Spanish. Here again we note the role of the interviewer in co-constructing the narrative. Without the interviewer's thoughts and opinions here, it is likely that the ending exemplum of the story could have been a positive note, pride in Lucas' understanding. The interviewer's expressed negative opinion of this learning as limited impacts Margarita's subsequent turns of talk. In line 8, Margarita confirms that was all the school taught, echoing the interviewer's words "That's all." The repetition of the interviewer's exact words is an element of cooperative dialogue and suggests that Margarita's style of speech prefers high engagement and interaction, and it may also signal a willingness to be influenced by her interlocutor. In line 9, the interviewer reiterates the negative evaluation of the school teaching of Spanish. In stating that they teach nothing more of their language, of their culture, perhaps the interviewer is checking that it is true that the school taught nothing beyond the pledge to Lucas. In line 10, Margarita again confirms that is the case by echoing the words of the interviewer "of their language." Then, Margarita espouses a final exemplum to end the narrative, a wish that the school would teach more. Though phrased in an elided sequence here, it is likely that Margarita means she wishes the school would teach more "of their language," meaning Spanish or perhaps a combination of language and culture.

Throughout the interviews, families frequently referred to language shift, the use of less Spanish by younger generations. Often, the individuals would code-switch when quoting speech of younger family members. For example, Margarita notes that despite limited Spanish, Lucas "*knows how to say the* pledge of legiance to the flag in *'mexicano'*. *In school they taught him.* And he learned it... and he knows it." (Italics denote Spanish.) First, we note that it is common for New Mexican Spanish speakers to refer to the language they speak as "mexicano," which they often distinguish from Spanish that is spoken in the border areas or in Mexico (Dowling, 2005; Dolores González, 2005). Margarita's switching to English to refer to the Pledge of Allegiance may reflect the association of the Pledge with English-speaking American culture and the English language itself.[1] Even though Lucas learned to say the Pledge in Spanish, the Spanish version is a translation from English. Moreover, due to the child's limited Spanish language proficiency, it is possible that Lucas did not understand the individual Spanish words he was taught, but was solely memorizing and repeating sounds.

Margarita's narrative and the recitation of the Pledge in Spanish offers a particularly striking example of Bourdieu's (1991) symbolic capitol, as Spanish gains capitol only when it is learned through school and for the purpose of the majority language and culture's Pledge of Allegiance. At the same time, an analysis of the 2006 "Nuestro Himno" controversy may offer an alternative perspective. 13 years after Margarita's interview took place, Spanish became a national controversy when a Spanish version of the Star Spangled Banner gained popularity. At that time, President George W. Bush stated, "people who want to be citizens of the United States should learn English and 'ought to learn to sing the national anthem in English'" (Vandehei, 2006). Carter (2014) aligns the "Nuestro Himno" controversy with the Latino Threat Narrative (Chavez, 2008), depicting "U.S. Latinos as disinterested or unable to sing the national anthem in English" (p. 213). In one case, New Mexican teachers instruct Hispanic heritage speakers to memorize a translated Spanish version of the Pledge of Allegiance, which is still common practice in New Mexico, and in the other, then-President of the United States George W. Bush condemned a Spanish translation of the Star Spangled

Banner. In both cases, though, it is clearly a top-down mandate of linguistic policies. Although the United States does not now and has never had an official national language or language policy, symbolic domination of English (Zentella, 1997) and "pressure against Spanish is a ubiquitous fact of American life" (Hill, 2008). Since Spanish is iconic for Latino ethnicity (Urciuoli, 1996; Barrett, 2006), statements that link speaking Spanish to lack of respect, suspicious behavior, or other negative traits concomitantly link those traits to Latinos.

This narrative speaks to the fact that knowing Spanish is culturally valuable for non-Latinos, although it is often associated with costs for Latinos. In fact, linguists have long noted that schools in the United States undermine immigrant languages, although they also simultaneously struggle to teach these languages to non-native speakers (Fishman, 2004). Spanish in particular figures as a productive resource for Anglos and as cultural baggage for Latinos (Urciuoli, 1996; Zentella, 1997; Hill, 2008). In this excerpt we see this troubling reality play out among both Margarita and Lucas in the storyworld and the story-telling world. In the story-telling world, Margarita describes Lucas as understanding "a little," "not much." Based on the surrounding societal values for Latinos, this boosts Lucas' status. It limits his "cultural baggage;" after all, we assume if he doesn't know much Spanish, he must be quite fluent in English. Yet it is immensely unfortunate that in order to gain higher status, Latinos must lose a valuable and productive resource. As Zentella (1997) writes: "Why is the bilingualism of the well-to-do a source of linguistic security and a sought after advantage while the bilingualism of the poor is a source of insecurity and a disadvantage? How do we explain the fact that bilingual education is looked down upon as remedial program while many mainstream adults pursue second language studies?"

Crossing/passing

The final repeated theme in this subset of interviews was crossing and passing. These related yet distinct concepts are again defined as follows. Crossing is defined as "the use of language varieties associated with social or ethnic groups that the speaker does not normally 'belong' to" (Rampton, 1999), while passing is "the ability to be taken for a member of a social category other than one's own" (Bucholtz, 1995). Excerpt (3) is a narrative by Ricardo, a 56-year-old from Albuquerque, relating his experiences with crossing and passing.

(3) "Ya casi no sabía qué era mi idioma": Ricardo (R)

1 R: So me, yo orgullos ya comencé, ah, a trabajar pero cuando llegaba a Kansas allí por eso
2 rumbos uh tuve- Me [sic] contaba que todos mis amigos eran gringos? Pues no, siempre andaban el
3 camino con los gringos y ya aprendía su acento y aprendía hablar co- como ellos. Y ya despe-

4   después uh, entraba ya un restaurante allí, ahi a la gente pues, uh, ya ya casi ya ya no sabía qué qué
5   era, qué era mi idioma mía. Y luego era diogüero y muy blanco en ese tiempo pues también en
6   esa aspecta pues también me los se equivocaban y no no sabía ni lo que era yo. Cuando llegué ir a
7   México también allí querían hablarme en inglés los mexicanos poquito a poquito. No no crea pues
8   está que me están hablando eh, en inglés. Pues yo soy mexicano. Pues, como es tan güero y como
9   está tan blanco él, pero. . . .
10 I: No, no cara de gringo o algo. Y este allí, su español pues.

Translation

1   R: So I I was proud I had begun, ah, to work but when I arrived to Kansas there in those parts uh I
2   had- Did I tell [you] that all my friends were gringos? I always was going out with the gringos
3   and I learned their accent and I learned to speak li-like them. And then aft-after uh I entered a
4   restaurant there, there the people, well, uh they almost they they didn't know what what I was,
5   what was my language. And then I was half- "light-skinned" and very white at that time well
6   also in that aspect well also I they made a mistake and they didn't know what I was. When I
7   got to go to Mexico also there they wanted to speak to me in English the Mexicans little by little.
8   Don't don't believe, well, this that is speaking to me eh in English. Well, I am Mexican. As he is
9   so "light-skinned" and as he's so white, but. . .
10 I: No, no face of a gringo or something. And that, your Spanish, so.

Narrative (3) is distinct from several of the others with regards to the involvement of the interviewer. Ricardo does most of the speaking; however, we must acknowledge that even without talking much, the interviewer plays a role in the construction of this narrative. As mentioned previously, all narratives are performed, especially in the context of an interview. The attitudes that the interviewer expressed earlier in the interview, facial expressions and gestures, and many more contextual features may influence Ricardo's story-telling world. For example, earlier in the interview, the interviewer mentioned the fact that discrimination may exist in a different way today. This may impact the willingness of the narrator to approach the topic of race and skin color in this narrative.

The narrative quoted above is preceded by a story in which Ricardo recounts how he was given his job driving a truck up north, entrusted by a friend who had hurt his hand. For this reason he starts the story "yo orgullos" [I was proud] (line 1). His truck driving took him up to Kansas, which is the setting for the storyworld in the narrative quote above. In this storyworld, he situates not only himself but also "all" his friends who he describes as gringos (line 2). In lines 2–3, Ricardo accounts that he learned "their" accent and how to speak like "them," which can be interpreted as crossing: Ricardo learned to use a language variety that he himself describes as belonging to the gringos. By designating the accent as "theirs" and the ways of speaking to "them," Ricardo distances himself and sets himself apart from his gringo friends' ethnic/linguistic identity. He constructs contact and proximity, always "hanging around" or "going along" with his gringo friends, as a reason for his successful crossing (lines 2–3). In line 3, Ricardo describes having learned "aprendía" this accent and way of speaking (line 3). It is a skill which storyworld Ricardo purposefully enacts, rather than an accent that he has picked up. This demonstrates another key aspect of crossing as "the use of" a certain language variety. It is not a site of language change or accommodation but a purposeful adaptation by an agentive speaker.

In lines 4–5, Ricardo switches to an account of passing. The setting is a restaurant. Ricardo mentions that the people didn't know "what I was, what was my language." In line 5, he constructs an explanation for their inability to judge his ethnicity, that he was half-light skinned and very white in the storyworld. In line 6 Ricardo describes the people in the restaurant as making "a mistake," which is the moment of the narrative that provides confirmation that Ricardo indeed passed as a monolingual English speaker.

In line 7, Ricardo provides another example of passing. This time the storyworld is Mexico, and he recounts that the people in Mexico wanted to speak to him in English (line 7). Here Ricardo insists on his own identity, "Well, I am Mexican" (line 8). Then Ricardo changes stance and adopts the voices of the people in Mexico as they describe him and explain their confusion: "As he is so light-skinned and as he's so white." This explanation echoes Ricardo's own justification for his ability to pass as a monolingual English speaker. In line 10, the interviewer responds by reaffirming Ricardo, stating that he doesn't have the face of a gringo and he speaks Spanish. With these reasons, the interviewer suggests that others should know he is Mexican. The reasons provided are also significant as they point to language and phenotype, the exact same characteristics which Ricardo references in his story as enabling his incidents of passing.

In this quote, we see examples of both crossing and passing. First, the participant describes crossing, "learning how to speak like them," followed by the instances of passing in which native English speakers mistook the participant's identity, and the participant passed for a native speaker of English. The participant constructs a reason for this, stating that he was half-güero (referring to a person with light complexion or blond hair) and very white. However, he does not change his ethnic alignment but still maintains that these groups were mistaken; this suggests that despite several instances of passing, the participant continues to retain his identity as a Spanish-speaking member of the New Mexican community. This narrative, then, corroborates the importance of the Spanish language to Mexican American identity (Fought, 2010).

Ricardo's experiences illustrate what is referred to in mixed-race studies as the "incident" (Wallace, 2002): "a situation in which a mixed individual is challenged to defend or perform one of their affiliations or is confronted with an attempt to erase one of them" (Potowski, 2016, p. 153). Ricardo does not refer to himself as mixed race, but as he describes Ricardo from the storyworld, he highlights his light skin and whiteness. Whether or not Ricardo is a mixed individual, Ricardo in the storyworld is presented as having potentially mixed-race characteristics, which bring about the "incident." In these two cases, Ricardo is confronted with an attempt at erasure, and he defends his ethnic identity.

Ricardo explicitly refers to an ideological link between language and ethnicity in order to justify his ethnic identity. Many scholars have examined this powerful association and how individuals may pass as group members solely based on their linguistic practices (Bucholtz, 1995; Bailey, 2000a; Fought, 2006; Potowski, 2016). In these "incidents," language can be used as "a tool that can either reinscribe or subvert the ethnic identities assigned by outsiders" (Potowski, 2016, p. 357). In fact, Ricardo in the storyworld setting of the restaurant uses this very notion to explain why he passed as a monolingual English speaker in that context. The interviewer also uses language to defend Ricardo's status and subvert the ethnic identity of a non-Mexican ascribed by Mexicans in the Mexico storyworld setting: "And that, your Spanish, so" (line 10).

Another important aspect of this excerpt is how Ricardo describes his physical features as a reason for his ability to pass. In these stories, we see examples of "lookism," the act of an individual being defined by others' perceptions about one's physical features. The people in the restaurant who "didn't know what [he] was" and the Mexicans who "tr[ied] to speak to [him] in English" are practicing "lookism." In fact, the Mexicans espouse disbelief when Ricardo defends his ethnic identity: "I am Mexican." This attempt at erasure is reminiscent of previous descriptions of "the incident" in which people challenge an individual's own assessment of his or her ethnic identity (Potowski, 2016, p. 174). Similar situations are especially common among Dominican Americans based on their phenotype and linguistic practices. Bailey (2000a) explains that the "everyday enactment of a Dominican American identity involve[s] negotiating disparities between self-ascription and other-ascription of identity, and resisting phenotype-racial categorization, a fundamental form of social organization in the U.S." (p. 556). As Bailey (2000a) notes, phenotype racial categorization is so fundamental to the social structures of the United States that "incidents" such as those described by Ricardo are very common, especially in cases where an individual has a phenotype which does not match mainstream society's association with a certain linguistic or ethnic identity. These individuals are faced with frequent "lookism," and in the face of these situations, they may choose to accept other-ascriptions of identities and the potential conflict site this creates with their own perceived ethnic-linguistic identity, or they may actively resist the others' phenotype-based ascription, as Ricardo does when he states "I am Mexican" (line 10).

4. Conclusions

The close analysis of the performance of ethnic identity in New Mexican Spanish speaker narratives demonstrates how New Mexican Spanish speakers enact, ascribe, and reject ethnic identities through code-switching, crossing, and passing. Recurring and dominant themes related to the performance of ethnic identity in these narratives included a) the language of the oppressors, b) the changing linguistic realities of younger generations, and c) crossing and passing. The positioning framework from narrative studies (Davies & Harré, 1990; Bamberg, 1997; Wortham, 2001; Bamberg & Georgokopoulou, 2008) enabled the analysis of the multiple embedded contexts of the narratives: how narrators negotiate the identities of the characters in the storyworld; how the narrators position themselves with interviewers in the story-telling world; and how the storyteller positions the identity with regard to dominant discourses and national narratives in the broader societal context.

While similar in demonstrating the performance of ethnic identities, these three narratives are distinct. For instance, the narrators co-construct understandings with the interviewers to different extents. In (1), we see the interviewer as encouraging elaboration of the story and possibly influencing the final coda or exemplum. In (2), the interviewer and narrator are highly participatory in their dialogue with a quick succession of turns and repetition of the interlocutor's phrasing. In (3), however, the interviewer responds at the end of the story only, while the narrator holds the floor for two narratives in succession. The narratives also differ with respect to the ethnic identities represented. In (1), Juan distances himself from the discourse of the oppressor through code-switching, self-ascribing an ethnic identity as separate from the teachers and the espoused ideology: "You live in the United States, you speak English." In (2), Margarita portrays her grandchild Lucas as knowing a little Spanish, suggesting a loss of a language that is very closely linked to ethnic identity among Hispanics in the U.S. In (3), Ricardo describes instances of crossing and passing, which he attributes to his "light-skinned" and "very white" phenotype. Yet here, Ricardo rejects the identity of an English monolingual speaker which is ascribed to him through "lookism" by others.

The ethnic identities narrated in the storyworlds are also contextualized within national narratives and dominant discourses in society. In (1), Juan quotes the teachers as perpetuating the classic one-nation, one-language ideology, commonly referred to as "English Only" within the United States (Hobsbawn, 1990; Bourdieu, 1991; Woolard, 1998). In (2), Margarita references the symbolic domination of English, the pressure against Spanish, and the contradictory state of Spanish as "cultural baggage" for Latinos but a resource for non-native speakers (Urciuoli, 1996; Zentella, 1997; Hill, 2008). Lastly, Ricardo's narrative in (3) amplifies the strong link between ethnicity and linguistic practices which allow for passing, as well as how individuals with a phenotype that does not stereotypically match their ethnic identity confront "lookism," or an imposed ascription of a different ethnic identity by others.

These interviews demonstrate the longstanding impact of ethnically and linguistically charged conflict sites, especially since some of these narratives are remembered events from the past. Yet, in confronting these conflict sites, New Mexican Spanish speakers are figured as empowered to reject identities that are ascribed to them by others and to enact ethnic identities on their own terms, often through the use of language. In doing so, the New Mexican Spanish speakers represent the characters in the storyworlds and themselves as active agents in the performance of their own ethnic identities. In these narratives, code-switching, crossing, and passing are seen to be especially powerful resources for the performance of ethnic identities.

Note

1 Currently, many elementary schools in New Mexico continue this practice of reciting the Pledge in both English and Spanish. Thus, even children who do not speak any Spanish are familiar with both versions. This suggests that there may be an ongoing shift in how New Mexicans perceive the Pledge and the associations formed surrounding this ritual. Perhaps, whereas it was previously associated solely with the English-speaking American culture, younger New Mexicans will associate it with a bilingual ritual.

References

Acuña, R. (1988). *Occupied America: A history of chicanos*. New York: Harper Collins.

Atkinson, P., & Delamont, S. (2006). Rescuing narrative from qualitative research. *Narrative Inquiry, 16*(1), 173–181.

Bailey, B. (2000b). Language and negotiation of ethnic/racial identity among Dominican Americans. *Language in Society, 29*, 555–582.

Bakhtin, M. (1984). *The problems of Dostoyevsky's poetics* (C. Emerson, Trans.). Minneapolis, MN: University of Minnesota Press.

Bamberg, M. (1997). Positioning between tructure and performance. *Journal of Narrative and Life History, 7*, 335–342.

Bamberg, M., & Georgakopoulou, A. (2008). Small stories as a new perspective in narrative and identity analysis. *Text & Talk, 28*(3), 377–396.

Barrett, R. (1999). Indexing polyphonous identity in the speech of African American drag queens. In M. Bucholtz, A. C. Liang, & L.A. Sutton (Eds.), *Reinventing identities: The gendered self in discourse* (pp. 313–331). New York: Oxford University Press.

Barrett, R. (2006). Language ideology and racial inequality: Competing functions of Spanish in an Anglo-owned Mexican restaurant. *Language in Society, 35*(2), 163–204.

Barth, F. (Ed.). (1969). *Ethnic groups and boundaries: The social organization of culture difference*. Boston: Little, Brown.

Baynham, M. (2003). Narrative in space and time: Beyond "Backdrop" accounts of narrative orientation. *Narrative Inquiry, 13*(2), 347–366.

Bills, G. & Vigil, N. (2007). *New Mexico and Colorado Spanish survey*. Albuquerque: University of New Mexico. http://hdl.handle.net/ 1928/20424

Bills, G. & Vigil, N. (2008*). The Spanish language of New Mexico and Southern Colorado: A linguistic atlas*. Albuquerque: University of New Mexico Press.

Bourdieu, P. (1991). *Language and symbolic power*. Cambridge, MA: Harvard University Press.

Briggs, C. (1986). *Learning how to ask: A sociolinguistic appraisal of the role of the interview in social science research*. Cambridge: Cambridge University Press.

Bucholtz, M. (1995). From Mulatta to Mestiza: Language and the reshaping of ethnic identity. In Hall & Bucholtz (Eds.), *Gender articulated: Language and the socially constructed self* (pp. 351–374). New York/London: Routeledge.

Bucholtz, M. (1999). You Da Man: Narrating the racial other in the production of white masculinity. *Journal of Sociolinguistics, 3*(4), 461–479.

Carter, P. (2014). National narratives, institutional ideologies, and local talk: The discursive production of Spanish in a "new" US Latino community. *Language in Society, 43,* 209–240.

Chavez, L. (2008). *The Latino threat: Constructing immigrants, citizens, and the nation*. Palo Alto, CA: Stanford University Press.

Cicourel, A. (1964). *Method and measurement in sociology*. New York: Free Press of Glencoe.

Cohen, R. (1978). Ethnicity: Problem and focus in anthropology. *Annual Review of Anthropology, 7,* 379–403.

Davies, B., & Harré, R. (1990). Positioning: The social construction of selves. *Journal for the Theory of Social Behaviour, 20,* 43–63.

De Fina, A. (2003). *Identity in narrative: A study of immigrant discourse*. Amsterdam: John Benjamins.

De Fina, A., & King, K. (2011). Language problem or language conflict? Narratives of immigrant womens' experiences in the US. *Discourse Studies, 13*(2), 163–188.

De Fina, A., Schiffrin, D., & Bamberg, M. (Eds.). (2006) *Discourse and identity*. Cambridge: Cambridge University Press.

Dolores González, M. (2005). Todavía decimos "Nosotros [los] mexicanos": Construction of identity labels among nuevo mexicanos. *Southwest Journal of Linguistics, 24*(1–2), 65–77.

Dowling, J. (2005). "I'm not Mexican... pero soy mexicano": Linguistic context of labelling among Mexican Americans in Texas. *Southwest Journal of Linguistics, 24*(1–2), 53–63.

Espinosa, A. (1975 [1917]). Speech mixture in New Mexico: The influence of the English langauge on New Mexican Spanish. In E. Hernández Chávez, A. Cohen, & A. Beltramo (Eds.), *El Lenguaje de los Chicanos: Regional and social characteristics used by Mexican Americans* (pp. 99–114). Arlington, VA: Center for Applied Linguistics.

Fought, C. (2003). *Chicano English in context*. New York: Palgrave Macmillan.

Fought, C. (2006). *Language and ethnicity*. New York: Cambridge University Press.

Fought, C. (2010). Language as a representation of Mexican American identity. *English Today, 26*(3), 44–48.

Georgakopoulou, A. (2007). *Small stories, interaction and identities*. Amsterdam: John Benjamins.

Gonzales, M. (1999). Crossing social and cultural borders: The road to language hybridity. In L. Galindo & M. Gonzalez (Eds.), *Speaking Chicana: Voice, power and identity* (pp. 13–38). Tucson: University of Arizona Press.

Gumperz, J. J. (1982). *Discourse strategies*. Cambridge: Cambridge University Press.

Hewitt, R. (1982). White adolescent creole users and the politics of friendship. *Journal of Multicultural Development, 3,* 217–232.

Hewitt, R. (1986). *White talk Black talk: Inter-racial friendship and communication amongst adolescents*. Cambridge/New York: Cambridge University Press.

Hill, J. (2008). *The everyday language of white racism*. Malden, MA: Blackwell.

Hobsbawm, E. J. (1990). *Nations and nationalism since 1780*. Cambridge: Cambridge University Press.

Lipski, J. M. (2010). Description and beyond: The Southwest at the center. In S. Rivera-Mills & D. Villa (Eds.), *Spanish in the U.S. Southwest: A language in transition* (pp. 181–188). Madrid: Iberoamericana.

Lyiscott, J. (2014). 3 ways to speak English. *TEDSalon NY2014*. Retrieved October 14, 2016, from www.ted.com/talks/jamila_lyiscott_3_ways_to_speak_english?language=en

MacGregor-Mendoza, P. (2000). Aquí no se habla español: Stories of linguistic repression in Southwest schools. *Bilingual Research Journal, 24*(4), 355–367.

Maryns, K., & Blommaert, J. (2001). Stylistic and thematic shifting as a narrative resource: Assessing asylum seekers repertoires. *Multilingua, 20*, 61–84.

McCormick, K. (2002a). *Language in Cape Town's District Six*. Oxford/New York: Oxford University Press.

Mendoza-Denton, N., & Osborne, D. (2009). Two languages, two identities? In D. Walt & C. Llamas (Eds.), *Sociolinguistics: Language and identities* (pp. 113–122). Edinburgh: Edinburgh University Press.

Myers-Scotton, C. (1993). *Social motivations for code-switching: Evidence from Africa*. Oxford: Clarendon Press.

Myers-Scotton, C. (2000). Code-switching as indexical of social negotiations. In L. Wei (Ed.), *The bilingualism reader* (pp. 137–165). London/New York: Routledge.

Omi, M., & Winat, H. (1994). *Racial formation in the United States: From the 1960s to the 1990s*. New York/London: Routledge.

Potowski, K. (2016). *IntraLatino language and identity: MexiRican Spanish*. Impact Studies in Language and Society. Amsterdam: John Benjamins.

Rampton, B. (1995). *Crossing: Language and ethnicity among adolescents*. New York: Longman.

Rampton, B. (1999). Styling the other: Introduction. *Journal of Sociolinguistics, 1999*, 421–427.

Rampton, B. (2005). *Crossing: Language & ethnicity among adolescents* (2nd ed.). Manchester: St Jerome Press.

Santa Ana, O. (2002). *Brown tide rising: Metaphors of Latinos in contemporary American public discourse*. Austin, TX: University of Texas Press.

Schiffrin, D. (1996). Narrative as self portrait: Sociolinguistic constructions of identity. *Language in Society, 25*, 167–203.

Smelser, N. J., Wilson, W. J., & Mitchells, F. (Eds.). (2001). *America becoming: Racial trends and their consequences* (Vol. 1). Washington, DC: National Academy Press.

Travis, C., & Villa, D. (2011). Language policy and language contact in New Mexico: The case of 1330 Spanish. In C. Norrby & J. Hajek (Eds.), *Uniformity and diversity in language policy: global perspectives* (pp. 126–140). Bristol: Multilingual Matters.

Urciuoli, B. (1996). *Exposing prejudice: Puerto Rican experiences of language, race and class*. Boulder, CO: Westview Press.

Vandehei, J. (2006). President wants anthem sung in English. *The Washington Post*. Washington, DC.

Vigil, N. (1989). Database for a linguistic atlas of the Spanish of New Mexico and southern Colorado: Computer methods in dialectology. *Journal of English Linguistics Special Issue, 22*, 69–75.

Vigil, N., & Bills, G. (2000). El español de Nuevo México: Hablamos mexicano. In M. Morúa & G. López Cruz (Eds.), *Memorias del V Encuentro Internacional de Lingüística en el Noroeste, 1998: Sociolingüística y lexografía* (pp. 197–217). Hermosillo: Universidad de Sonora.

Wallace, M. I. (2002). Losing the self, finding the self: postmodern theology and social constructionism. In C. A. M. Hermans, G. Immink, A. de Jong, & J. Van der Lans (Eds.), *Social constructionism and theology* (pp. 93–111). Leiden: Brill Academic Publishers.

Widdicombe, S. (1998). Identity as an analysts' and participants' resource. In C. Antaki & S. Widdicombe (Eds.), *Identities in talk* (pp. 191–206). London: Sage.

Woolard, K. (1998). Introduction: Language ideology as a field of inquiry. In B. Schieffelin, K. Woolard, & P. Kroskrity (Eds.), *Language ideologies: Practice and theory* (pp. 3–47). New York: Oxford University Press.

Wortham, S. E. F. (2001). *Narratives in action*. New York: Teachers College, Columbia University.

Wortham, S., Mortimer, K., Lee, K., Allard, E., & White, K. D. (2011). Interviews as interactional data. *Language in Society*, 40(1), 39–50.

Young, K. G. (1987). *Taleworlds and storyrealms*. Dodrecht: Martinus Nijhoff.

Zelinsky, W. (2001). *The enigma of ethncity: Another American dilemma*. Iowa City: University of Iowa Press.

Zentella, A. C. (1997). *Growing up bilingual*. Malden, MA: Blackwell.

10
THE SOCIAL MEANINGS OF WOLOF AND FRENCH

Contact dialects, language ideology, and competing modernities in Senegal

Fiona Mc Laughlin

Introduction: contact dialects in Senegal

The West African nation of Senegal is a multilingual country where the former colonial language, French, serves as the official language. French, however, plays a very limited role as a lingua franca in Senegal, especially when compared to other francophone West African countries such as Côte d'Ivoire, due to the robust role of an indigenous language, Wolof. One of more than thirty languages spoken in Senegal, Wolof serves as an urban vernacular and national lingua franca, and has assumed the informal and unofficial role of national language, giving rise to a situation in which French is the *de jure* national language, but Wolof the *de facto* one. Senegalese often refer to Wolof as the national language, although it has no formal status as such above or beyond that of any other recognized Senegalese language. The Wolof ethnic group compose only slightly more than forty percent of the Senegalese population, but at least ninety percent of Senegalese speak Wolof as a first or other language, a figure that is estimated to rise to more than ninety-five percent in urban areas such as the capital, Dakar (Cissé, 2005; Mc Laughlin, 2008a).

Wolof has long served as a lingua franca in northern Senegal, as well as in urban areas and along the Senegalese coast. Although there is a long history of documentation of the language, there are few studies on Wolof dialects.[1] Both Robert (2011) and Irvine (2011, p. 49) comment on a paucity of dialectal variation in the language, but in the absence of a body of research on the issue the question remains open, and future studies may very well reveal more diversity than is currently documented. While regional dialects of Wolof are for the most part mutually intelligible, continued contact with French, the former colonial language, has contributed to a salient divergence in Wolof dialects, linked to extensive lexical borrowing from French, a factor that will become important in one of the case studies described later on in this chapter. In a parallel development, the French spoken in Senegal has developed into a colonial variety that differs in many ways from metropolitan French, given that it is influenced by Senegalese speakers' various L1s. These differences are phonetic, phonological (Boutin, Gess, & Guèye, 2012), morphological, and syntactic, as well as lexical. Most pertinent for this discussion are the phonological differences between Senegalese and metropolitan varieties of French. This chapter investigates these different varieties of Wolof and French, the complex meanings that people ascribe to them, and the ways in which they inform the Senegalese popular imagination. It also investigates how people's beliefs about those varieties affect the ways in which identity is performed through language in the Senegalese context. These performances, I suggest, offer alternative views of a postcolonial modernity reflected most clearly in language ideology.

Language contact and its outcomes on the Senegalese coast

Wolof and French have been in contact on the West African coast for more than three hundred and fifty years. The French first established a *comptoir*, or commercial outpost, in 1638 on the island of Bocos near the mouth of the Senegal River, relocating upstream approximately twenty years later to the uninhabited island of Ndar, which they renamed Saint-Louis du Sénégal. In 1678 a second *comptoir* was established on the island of Gorée, off the Cape Verde peninsula not far form the current capital, Dakar, a city that was founded only in 1857. The establishment and subsequent growth of these *comptoirs* marked a significant rupture away from the old trans-Saharan trade routes and towards a commercial engagement with the Atlantic world. By the middle of the eighteenth century, important African populations had settled on the islands, including a group of influential and economically independent slaveholding Wolof women, known as *signares* (from *senhora*, the Portuguese word for "lady"). Although the origin and role of the signares merits a detailed historical discussion which is beyond the scope of this chapter,[2] suffice it to say that they formed mutually beneficial commercial and personal alliances with French traders and sailors. Beginning with these unions, a complex Afro-European *métis* society emerged in both Saint-Louis and Gorée, many members of which became prominent members of Senegalese society, serving as entrepreneurs and politicians.

The linguistic outcome of urbanization on the Atlantic island cities of the Senegalese littoral was not the emergence of a creole, despite the similarities between the social makeup of Saint-Louis and Gorée and other West African coastal cities such as Freetown where a creole, Krio, came into being within another distinctive *métis* society. Perhaps the relative interdependence of actors (French sailors and African *signares*) at the earlier stages of contact did not contribute to the kinds of social hierarchy that seem always to be involved in creole formation. Instead, as argued in Mc Laughlin 2008b, language contact resulted in the emergence of an urban way of speaking Wolof, which borrowed liberally from French. This way of speaking can be attributed in at least some part to bilingual linguistic "brokers," many no doubt from among *métis* society, and one of whom, Louis Descemet, authored a bilingual phrase book in 1864. The book, originally intended for use in

Senegalese schools, was written when Descemet was secretary to French governor Louis Faidherbe, and it contains two thousand French phrases with their translation into the Wolof of Saint-Louis du Sénégal, a Wolof that is characterized, like today's urban Wolof, by substantial lexical borrowing from French, a practice that must predate the publication of the book. From its origins in eighteenth-century Saint-Louis, urban Wolof has continued to borrow from French, and as Wolof has spread throughout the country to become a national lingua franca, so too has this urban way of speaking been adopted by speakers in cities and towns throughout Senegal. Attitudes towards urban Wolof, as one might imagine, are often contradictory, as the following section reveals.

Metalinguistic discourse and attitudes towards Wolof and French

Metalinguistic discourse or talk about language in Senegal provides an important window into the ways in which speakers think of Wolof and their attitudes on how it is spoken. A term that is used quite widely, not only in Senegal but elsewhere in Africa, involves the concept of "deep" language. "Deep Wolof," or *olof bu xóot*, as it is called in Wolof, captures a way of speaking that is rich in vocabulary, eloquent in its turns of phrase, and clever in the use of proverbs. It also involves a kind of Wolof that is not always readily accessible to the average speaker because it includes lexical items whose meaning is not necessarily known, possibly because they are archaic forms. Those who speak deep Wolof are considered to have an excellent command of the language, and are viewed as repositories of an authentic language. Deep Wolof is a concept that is known to all Wolof speakers, but it will not be central to the discussion of identity performance in this chapter.

A second designation, which comes from contact with French, is the notion of *olof piir*, a phrase meaning "pure Wolof," by which is meant a Wolof free of French borrowings. Ironically, the term itself contains a French borrowing, *piir*, from French *pur* "pure," and the syntax of the noun phrase is also French. The concept of "pure Wolof," from its first documentation by the governor general of French West Africa, Louis Faidherbe, in 1864, has always been invoked to talk about its opposite, namely Wolof that borrows from French and which, by implication, is not "pure" Wolof. In his *Vocabulaire* of fifteen hundred French words translated into three Senegalese languages, including Wolof, Faidherbe, who was an amateur linguist, takes pains to point out that the Wolof words listed therein are from the Wolof of Saint-Louis du Sénégal, the most important city on the Atlantic coast of Senegal at the time.[3] Describing the geographic extent to which Wolof is spoken, he provides the reader with a good sense of the role of the language as a lingua franca, and then provides a value judgment on the kind of Wolof he describes:

> The Wolof language is spoken in Saint-Louis, in Gorée, in Saint Mary's of Gambia, in the Waalo, in Kayoor, in Jolof. It is understood by half of the inhabitants of Bawol, Siin and Saalum. It is the commercial language of all

Senegal; half of the Trarza speak it. It extends along the African coast to Sierra Leone... It is the Wolof of Saint-Louis that we present here; *it is not the purest*, but it is the one that is most useful to know.

(Faidherbe, 1864, p. 4, emphasis added)

Commenting on French borrowings in the Wolof of Saint-Louis and the lack of equivalents in the two other languages of the interior included in his *Vocabulaire*, Faidherbe writes:

Many objects introduced by us, in the country, are designated, in Wolof, by the mangled French name, and naturally have no name in the languages of the interior.

(Faidherbe, 1864, p. 3)

Faidherbe's comments point to the integration of French loanwords into Wolof and the phonological changes that they undergo, changes that to Faidherbe's metropolitan ear sound "mangled" (*estropié(s)* in French). Already in 1864, then, value judgments were being placed on a type of Wolof that incorporated loanwords from French, a practice that was to flourish in Saint-Louis, and which eventually came to index a cosmopolitanism and modernity associated with urban life (Mc Laughlin, 2008b), and which today is more closely associated with Dakar, the current capital.

The idea of *olof piir* continues to reflect both loss of and nostalgia for an imagined African authenticity in which "the African peasantry is regarded as the fundamental expression of indigenous Africa" and in which "the city has long been thought of exclusively in terms of the colonial ethnology of detribalization, rural exodus, and the loss of authentically African traits and values" (Diouf, 1998, p. 227). In contrast to *olof piir*, urban or Dakar Wolof has no name because it is an unmarked variety for urban speakers, so much so that speakers have difficulty describing its characteristics. Witness the words of OD, a professional in his thirties, talking about Dakar Wolof or, as he calls it, *sunu olof* "our Wolof:"

Our Wolof is light like this, Wolof that... you know, Wolof, Wolof... just like that, it's the Wolof we speak, you know, just the Wolof we speak.

(OD, interview May 2010, Dakar)

Urban Wolof is occasionally referred to as *njaxas*, a word meaning patchwork, which draws attention to its mixed nature. More often it is simply referred to as the Wolof of Dakar, thus in the Senegalese popular imagination it is strongly associated with the city, and it is often the negative attributes of urban life in general – the hectic pace, the alienation, the rootlessness – that are projected onto the urban language. But at the same time, it carries a certain covert prestige because of its association with urbanity and modernity that has endured from its eighteenth- or nineteenth-century origins in Saint-Louis up to the present. As in 1864, there is still much metalinguistic discourse about urban Wolof, and it is a frequent topic of conversation among its speakers.

As the cornerstone of France's colonial *mission civilisatrice*, the instrument by which Africans were to "become" French, the French language has been subject to multiple discourses and associations in Senegal. Much has been written about the French colonial project and the role of language in the *mission civilisatrice* (e.g., Conklin, 1997), but contemporary discourses and ideologies about French tend to center on the complex and polarizing figure of the late Léopold Sédar Senghor (1906–2001) who assumed the presidency of the republic at independence in 1960. A French-educated philosopher and poet who was to become the first Black member of the French Academy, Senghor was a great admirer of the French language. He believed in the ideal of a universal civilization to which all cultures would contribute, and did not shy away from elaborating what he thought each culture could or should bring to the table. Senghor thus attributed values to African cultures that distinguished them from other cultures. Many of his statements on language seem outrageous from today's perspective. He exhorted his compatriots to speak French like Parisian bourgeois, and called French the language of reason and clarity as opposed to African languages whose particular genius he considered to be their association with "instinct."

One of Senghor's detractors, the historian, anthropologist, and politician, Cheikh Anta Diop (1923–1986), had a different orientation. Diop was interested in discovering the African origins of civilization and the unity of African cultures. His best-known linguistic work compares Wolof to Ancient Egyptian, and although he did not make the claim himself, his followers have attributed to him the hypothesis that Wolof has an Egyptian origin, a hypothesis that few linguists would agree with. Nevertheless, Cheikh Anta Diop's African orientation stood in stark contrast to Senghor's European orientation, and captured the imagination of many young intellectuals who considered Senghor too French, hence inauthentic. This sentiment continues up to the present, and Cheikh Anta, as he is affectionately known, is a much more popular cultural figure in Senegal, especially among youth, than is Senghor. In 1987 the University of Dakar was renamed Cheikh Anta Diop University. Although the francophone elite in Senegal no longer have an economic or cultural monopoly, France and the French language remain points of reference in the Senegalese popular imagination, but they must now compete with other orientations, both Western and Eastern.

Performing identity between Wolof and French

The notion of dialect continuum has typically been used to refer to the distribution of dialects of a language across a geographic area: the micro-differences between adjacent dialects do not impede mutual comprehension, but speakers of dialects at opposite ends of the continuum or dialect chain may have substantial difficulty understanding each other. The notion of continuum has also been applied to the range of polylects that creole speakers manipulate between the acrolect or standard, metropolitan language and the basilect or "deepest" variety of the creole, most different from the standard language. Building on these prior notions of linguistic continua, and particularly on the latter, I propose a continuum of language contact as a rough diagnostic that helps to conceptualize the ways in which people put their Wolof and French linguistic resources to use in Senegal. The endpoints of this continuum, namely Wolof devoid of French influence (*olof piir*) and French devoid of Wolof influence, are not actual linguistic practices for most Senegalese, but rather idealized constructs to which speakers may orient in their linguistic behavior. Ways of speaking along this continuum are of course modulated by external factors such as the level of speakers' knowledge of French and their exposure to urban forms of Wolof, but they are also modulated by choices that speakers make in deploying their linguistic resources in any given situation. These choices may involve lexical items, but also syntactic and morphological constructions as well as phonological and phonetic features, resulting in significant linguistic variation. The following case studies afford a closer look into how speakers may manipulate some of these variables to perform very different kinds of identities.

Case study 1: the sophisticates

The first case study involves French, and focuses on the tendency of upwardly mobile Senegalese women to use a variant typically associated with metropolitan varieties of French as a marker of sophistication. These women are typically members of the workforce, and range from bank tellers to supermarket cashiers, and from secretaries to teachers or journalists. While their use of the metropolitan variant that is the focus of this case study allows them to assume a sophisticated persona that they believe distinguishes them from other women, they are often considered to be inauthentic, much in the way that women who use skin lighteners are also considered to be inauthentic, namely by turning their backs on African values and embracing Western ones.

The unmarked variety of French in Senegal is the local variety of Senegalese French. The focus here is on the phonological characteristics of Senegalese French, three of which stand out for their salient difference from metropolitan French. First of these is the substitution of the voiced and voiceless palatal stops [c] and [ɟ] for the palatalized alveolar stops [tj] and [dj] in metropolitan French. Examples include the words *tiède* "lukewarm" and *diabète* "diabetes" which are pronounced [cɛd] and [ɟabɛt] respectively in Senegalese French as opposed to the metropolitan forms, [tjɛd] and [djabɛt]. Second is the attribution of the phonological feature [+ATR] (Advanced Tongue Root) to high vowels and the spread of the feature to mid vowels through vowel harmony within the domain of the phonological word. An example here would be the French word *politique* [pɔlitik] "politics," where all vowels acquire the [+ATR] feature. In Wolof, the high vowels /i/ and /u/ always surface as [+ATR] vowels. The mid-vowel /o/ may surface as either [+ATR] or [-ATR]. Within this word, vowel harmony causes the [+ATR] attribution of the high vowels to spread to [o], making all vowels in the word [+ATR], a feature that is simply absent in metropolitan varieties of French. Finally, Senegalese French replaces the metropolitan uvular [ʁ] with the apical tap [r] typical of Wolof and other Senegalese languages.

The differences between metropolitan and Senegalese French open a space of variation to which sociolinguistic meaning can be attached. The variable to be considered here is /r/, whose two variants are the apical Senegalese (r) and the metropolitan uvular (ʁ). Given that the unmarked form of French spoken in Senegal is Senegalese French, (ʁ) is the marked variant, reflected in the preponderant use of (r) amongst the Senegalese population. Beyond the context of this chapter, the variable deserves a thorough quantitative variationist analysis, but several observations can nonetheless be made, illustrated by a small sample of speech forms described below. With regard to gender, men almost always prefer the apical (r), so the vast majority of variation occurs within the speech of female speakers, and in particular, those who are upwardly mobile. To move this observation beyond the anecdotal, I describe and analyze a 6 minute and 44 second long video recording of a news story that aired on Flash Infos (Flash News) on SEN TV, a Senegalese television channel, on October 5, 2016.[4] The topic is introduced by an anchorwoman, after which three journalists, Amina Guèye (female), Fatima Sylla (female), and Pape Bathily (male), interview a number of teachers and school administrators as well as a parent and a child at schools in Dakar and in Kolda, a small regional capital in the southern region of the country. We hear Amina Guèye in Dakar and Pape Bathily in Kolda speaking to their interviewees, but not Fatima Sylla. The topic of the news story is a program entitled *Ubbi tey, jàng tey* ("Open today, learn today") that encourages parents to send their children to school starting from the beginning of the school year. The main language of the program is French, and all participants speak French with the exception of the child who is interviewed briefly (we do not hear his interlocutor) and Khady Ndiaye, the mother of one of the students, both of whom speak Wolof. In addition to the anchorwoman and the journalists, Amina Guèye and Pape Bathily, there are eight interviewees who speak French, five female and three male. There are thus a total of seven female French speakers: the anchorwoman, a journalist, four teachers (two in Dakar and two in Kolda), and a spokeswoman from Ministry of Education. In addition to Pape Bathily, the three male French speakers are a school director in Dakar, and an academic inspector and a teacher in Kolda.

The first finding from the recording is that the four men consistently use the apical (r) across the board, confirming the observation that variation is associated with female speech. Turning now to the female speakers, it becomes necessary to cast the variation in a slightly different way. Rather than looking at whether they actually pronounce (ʁ) or (r), it is more productive to consider their target sound. The variant (r) poses little problem since it is a phoneme in Wolof and other Senegalese languages, so the target and the reality are one and the same. With regard to the (ʁ) variant, however, some speakers, and especially the anchorwoman, sometimes produce a slightly rounded labiovelar sound that on occasion approaches a glide. It is clear, however, that she is not attempting to produce the apical (r). The variation, then, can more clearly be described in binary terms as an apical vs. a non-apical pronunciation, with the French metropolitan /ʁ/ as the target in the latter case.

The female participants can be divided roughly into two categories: first, the journalists (including the anchorwoman), and second, the teachers and spokeswoman from the Ministry of Education. As educators, the teachers are actors within a francophone regime of language that is implemented within the school system, and the spokeswoman from the Ministry is an administrator within the same system. All of these women are professionals and could be considered upwardly mobile, but not all of them exhibit variation. The two journalists, Amina Guèye and the unnamed anchorwoman, show a consistent orientation towards the metropolitan variant (ʁ) with little if any use of (r). The two female teachers from Kolda, on the other hand, show a consistent orientation towards the Senegalese apical variant (r). The first one to speak uses only (r), while the second one produces only one instance of non-apical (ʁ). It is among the Dakar-based teachers and the spokeswoman from the Ministry of Education, however, that we hear the most variation. All three of them move back and forth between (r) and (ʁ), often starting and ending their utterances predominantly with (ʁ), and using predominantly (r) in the middle.

A variationist study, however limited, is not the object of this case study, but the results are quite revealing and lend themselves to a number of interpretations that are pertinent to the notion of identity performance. First, the variation is strongly associated with women, and not men; second, it is associated with professional, upwardly mobile women; and third, it is associated primarily with women in the capital, Dakar. The women who most consistently oriented towards the non-apical metropolitan variant, (ʁ), were the anchorwoman and the reporter. This orientation, as well as other aspects of their speech, points most clearly to an aspirational francophone bourgeois identity that is highly valued in female journalists, and especially anchorwomen, given the general preponderance of this type of speech among that group. The anchorwoman in this study was dressed in western-style clothing and her head was uncovered (the other journalist, Amina Guèye, is only heard, not seen), but even anchorwomen who wear hijab in this predominantly Muslim country orient towards the non-apical variant, so it cannot be seen as playing a central role in religious identity. We might conclude that metropolitan French maintains siginificant prestige for upwardly mobile professional women who seek to project a sophisticated identity by adopting or attempting to adopt some of its characteristics. Whether the majority of Senegalese actually value this way of speaking in the same way is an open question, and one that can only be answered by future research.

As an addendum to the discussion, the (ʁ) variant sometimes turns up in the Wolof of the same demographic, namely upwardly mobile professional women. A case in point is that of Adji, an executive secretary for an international organization in Dakar. Adji asked the husband of her supervisor, who was traveling to Abidjan, to bring back some small plants for her garden to be delivered to him at his hotel by her aunt who lived in Côte d'Ivoire. He returned empty-handed, and told Adji that her aunt had arrived at the hotel carrying some very tall coconut plants that were too large for him to carry on the plane. Adji was chagrined and disappointed, and expressed her surprise by saying "*Allahu akba(ʁ)!*" Although the expression *Allahu akbar* "God is the greatest," is originally an Arabic phrase, it has become integrated into Wolof as an expression of surprise or amazement, and Adji's marked pronunciation correlated with her identity performance as a self-styled sophisticate.

Case study 2: performing a Mouride identity

The second case study in identity performance centers on Wolof, and especially the way in which *olof piir* "pure Wolof" has been attached to a very specific Muslim identity. Such associations have their origins in the history of Senegalese Islam, but the case study I present here is much more recent, and is associated with a reformist Sufi movement founded in 1975 at what was then the University of Dakar (now Cheikh Anta Diop University). There have been Muslims in what is now the country of Senegal since the 11th century CA, but the major conversions of the Wolof populations came about primarily in the nineteenth and early twentieth centuries, during a time of great social and political upheaval associated with European contact and the trans-Atlantic slave trade. Although there is increasing diversity in the ways in which Islam is practiced in Senegal, as well as in Africa in general, Muslim populations have typically followed the Saharan model of adherence to one of a number of Sufi orders such as the Qadiriyya and the Tijaniyya, that emphasize the role of the spiritual leader or shaykh, also known as a *marabout* in French and *sëriñ* in Wolof. In Senegal the Sufi orders constitute vast networks of patron-client relationships, and many social activities are organized around them. They are thus an important element of the social fabric.

Most relevant to the case study presented here is the founding of an indigenous Senegalese Sufi order, the Mourides or Muridiyya. The spiritual leader and founder of the order, Shaykh Amadou Bamba Mbacké (d. 1927 CA), was a Sufi ascetic, renowned for his piety and his extensive corpus of devotional writing, including a set of poems to the glory of God written in Arabic. Bamba was himself a member of the Qadiriyya Sufi order, and as Cruise O'Brien (1971) explains, the order only began to attract a wide following after his death. Much of the popularity of the Mouride order can be attributed to the founder's message in which he told the small minority of his followers who were so disposed to study Islamic texts and lead a life of contemplation, but for the vast majority who could not aspire to such a life he told them that hard work would substitute for prayers, instilling in them a kind of Mouride work ethic. This opened an important space within the Senegalese religious landscape for members of the peasantry to become pious Muslims, and inspired a wave of conversion. Many miracles are attributed to Shaykh Amadou Bamba, and after the French exiled him to Gabon for a number of years he became something of an anti-colonial hero in the popular imagination. The seat of the Mouride order is the holy city of Touba, located in the Wolof heartland, which boasts the largest mosque in sub-Saharan Africa. As with other shaykhs who founded Senegalese branches of Sufi orders such as the Tijaniyya, Bamba is venerated and held up as an exemplar for his followers.

Turning now to the details of the case study, in 1975 a Sufi reform movement emerged at the University of Dakar among an association of Mouride disciples under the leadership of a certain Atou Diagne, himself a student of geography. The movement, known as the Hizbut Tarqiyya, grew quickly and gained the patronage of the Mouride caliph in Touba. The movement's leaders professed a strong attachment to the founder of the order, Shaykh Amadou Bamba, but also grappled with the pressure to "modernize," given the strong reformist critiques that were circulating at the time (Villalón, 2007, p. 182). The growth of the movement came to an abrupt halt in 1994 when Atou Diagne questioned the notion of hereditary leadership within the Mouride caliphate, incurring the wrath of the caliph and his family, whose support was withdrawn. One of the ways in which the Hizbut Tarqiyya attempted to modernize was through an important educational project that has had long-lasting effects. In their nativist vision of education, the Hizbut Tarqiyya focused on teaching in Wolof, something that the Senegalese state has never committed to, and on teaching *ajami* literacy, namely Wolof written in the Arabic script, an old but informal tradition in the country. Because of their original attachment to Shaykh Amadou Bamba, they also taught students to memorize and recite a long and elaborate account of his life in Wolof in much the same manner that Qur'anic students memorize and recite sections of the Qur'an. Most importantly for the purposes of this chapter, however, the Hizbut Tarqiyya taught and encouraged students to imitate the shaykh in all ways, including using a Wolof unadulterated by French borrowings which more closely approximated Bamba's supposed pure rural variety. Ngom (2002) claims that within the Muridiyya as a whole, an impulse to reject colonialism and its legacy leads to the rejection of French and an embrace of Wolof and Arabic borrowings. Citing Babou (1999, p. 6), Ngom (2002, p. 220) says that Shaykh Amadou Bamba was said never to have pronounced a word of French, and that he communicated with his followers in pure Wolof and worked in classical Arabic. What the Hizbut Tarqiyyah contributed to this orientation is a systematic program of instruction and education, resulting in the widespread valorization and enactment of a variety of Wolof that is different from the unmarked urban variety that includes the liberal use of French borrowings.

Competing modernities

In situations of sustained language contact such as the Senegalese one described in this chapter, contact dialects often emerge, and one or more aspects of them may ultimately become imbued with sociolinguistic meaning. As diametrically opposed as they might seem to be, the two case studies of dialect performance presented in this chapter, namely the metropolitan tendencies of upwardly mobile professional women in Dakar and the nativist tendencies of the Hizbut Tarqiyya in their imitation of the speech of their founder, are practices that grow out of a complex postcolonial linguistic legacy that involves both Wolof and French. They both reveal ideologies that result from the circumstances of language contact, the former in the embrace by a certain class of Wolof speakers of a sociolinguistic variant associated with metropolitan French, and the second in its rejection of one of the outcomes of language contact as an anti-colonial (or neocolonial) statement. Both make use of features that set them apart from unmarked ways of speaking: in the first instance, the non-apical (ʁ) is marked in Senegalese French, and in the second, the unmarked form of Wolof is the urban variety that borrows from French and has moved well beyond the confines of Dakar.

Competing visions of modernity are at stake in these different performances of identity in Senegal, but they are only two among myriad visions of modernity within the country. It is important not to embrace binary and mutually exclusive categories of modernity envisioned by different social groups, first and foremost because the performance of identity though language is just that, a performance, and individuals are capable of multiple, different, and even contradictory performances depending on what they want to accomplish with their linguistic resources at any given time. The nativist orientation of the Mouride Sufi order and its rejection of French that Ngom (2002) describes, for example, is not necessarily representative of Senegalese Muslims. The branch of the Tijaniyya Sufi order based in Tivaouane, for example, has a very different attitude towards French, and its leaders are known for enacting a linguistically cosmopolitan vision of modernity by switching between Wolof, French, and classical Arabic in their public addresses, a very different view from that of the Mourides. Likewise, the anchorwomen alluded to above, who appear on television stations such as WALF-TV wearing hijab – a sartorial rather than linguistic performance of identity – conform to the behavior of other women of their class, profession, and aspirations by adopting the non-apical (ʁ). We cannot say, then, that an orientation either towards or away from French can be associated with either an Islamic vision of modernity or a bourgeois vision of modernity in Senegal, and besides, those two visions might turn out to be very compatible with each other, as suggested by the consumerist yet pious vision of Muslim life projected in Ramadan advertising in recent years in Dakar.

The meanings with which dialects of French and Wolof have been imbued in Senegal reflect the dense layering of ideology associated with language, starting with Faidherbe's observations on the Wolof of Saint-Louis and the mangled French loanwords of 1864, in Senghor's differential valuing of what French and African languages can bring to his civilization of the universal, and Cheikh Anta Diop's embrace of his African legacy and his followers' attribution of an Egyptian origin for Wolof to his work. Language ideologies in Senegal are thus grounded in a complex history of colonial contact between African and European speakers and their languages, and are played out and performed in contemporary Senegal in new and constantly evolving ways.

Notes

1 There are some studies on individual dialects, such as Sauvageot's (1965) study of the Jolof dialect. More recently, Mitsch (2016a; 2016b) has investigated dialectal differences between Senegalese and Gambian Wolof on the borderlands between the two countries.
2 Interested readers are referred to Brooks, 1976 and Jones, 2013.

3 A more detailed discussion of Faidherbe's comments, within the context of the emergence of an urban variety of Wolof in Saint-Louis du Sénégal, can be found in Mc Laughlin, 2008b. The translations presented here are my own, and are taken from that article.
4 The broadcast can be viewed at the following site, last accessed on March 3, 2017: www.seneweb.com/news/Video/flash-info-de-la-sentv-du-05-octobre-201_n_194987.html

References

Babou, C. A. (1999). *Cheikh Ahmadou Bamba: Un résistant africain contre la domination coloniale*. Retrieved from www.senbotin.sn/touba/preface/htm (no longer accessible).

Boutin, B. A., Gess, R., & Guèye, G. M. (2012). French in Senegal after three centuries: A phonological study of Wolof speakers' French. In R. Gess, C. Lyche, & T. Meisenburg (Eds.), *Phonological variation in French: Illustrations from three continents* (pp. 45–71). Amsterdam/Philadelphia: John Benjamins.

Brooks, G. E. Jr. (1976). The signares of Saint-Louis and Gorée: Women entrepreneurs in eighteenth-century Senegal. In N. J. Hafkin & E. G. Bay (Eds.), *Women in Africa: Studies in social and economic change* (pp. 19–44). Stanford: Stanford University Press.

Cissé, M. (2005). Les politiques linguistiques du Sénégal: Entre attentisme et interventionnisme. *Kotoba to Shakai* [Language and Society], Special Issue on Post-Empire and Multilingual Societies in Asia and Africa, 266–313.

Conklin, A. J. (1997). *A mission to civilize: The republican idea of empire in France and West Africa, 1895–1930*. Stanford: Stanford University Press.

Cruise O'Brien, D. B. (1971). *The Mourides of Senegal: The political and economic organization of an Islamic brotherhood*. Oxford: Clarendon Press.

Descemet, L. (1864). *Recueil d'environ 1,200 phrases françaises usuelles avec leur traduction en regard en ouolof de Saint-Louis*. Saint-Louis, Senegal: Imprimerie Nationale.

Diouf, M. (1998). The French colonial policy of assimilation and the civility of the *originaires* of the four communes (Senegal): A nineteenth-century globalization project. *Development and Change, 29*, 671–696.

Faidherbe, L. (1864). *Vocabulaire d'environ 1.500 mots français avec leurs correspondants en Ouolof de Saint-Louis, en Poular (Toucouleur) du Fouta, en Soninké (Sarakhollé) de Bakel*. Saint-Louis, Sénégal: Imprimerie du Gouvernement.

Irvine, J. T. (2011). Société et communication chez les Wolof à travers le temps et l'espace. In A. M. Diagne, S. Kesseler, & C. Meyer (Eds.), *Communication wolof et société sénégalaise: Héritage et création* (pp. 37–70). Paris: Harmattan.

Jones, H. (2013). *The Métis of Senegal: Urban life and politics in French West Africa*. Bloomington: Indiana University Press.

Mc Laughlin, F. (2008a). Senegal: The emergence of a national lingua franca. In A. Simpson (Ed.), *Language and national identity in Africa* (pp. 79–97). Oxford: Oxford University Press.

Mc Laughlin, F. (2008b). On the origins of urban Wolof: Evidence from Louis Descemet's 1864 phrase book. *Language in Society, 37*(5), 713–735.

Mitsch, J. (2016a). *Bordering on national language varieties: Political and linguistic borders in the Wolof of Senegal and the Gambia* (Unpublished doctoral dissertation). The Ohio State University, Columbus, OH.

Mitsch, J. (2016b). The use of discourse markers among youth in Senegambia borderland. *Sociolinguistic Studies, 10*(1–2), 67–87.

Ngom, F. (2002). Linguistic resistance in the Murid speech community in Senegal. *Journal of Multilingual and Multicultural Development, 23*(3), 214–226.

Robert, S. (2011). Le wolof. In E. Bonvini, J. Busuttil, & A. Payraube (Eds.), *Dictionnaire des langues* (pp. 23–30). Paris: Dicos Poche.

Sauvageot, S. (1965). Description synchronique d'un dialecte wolof: Le parler du Dyolof (Unpublished doctoral dissertation). University of Dakar, Dakar.

Villalón, L. A. (2007). Sufi modernities in contemporary Senegal: Religious dynamics between the local and the global. In M. van Bruinessen & J. D. Howell (Eds.), *Sufism and the "modern" in Islam* (pp. 172–191). London: I.B. Tauris.

11

THE SOCIAL VALUE OF LINGUISTIC PRACTICES IN TETOUAN AND GHOMARA (NORTHWESTERN MOROCCO)

Ángeles Vicente and Amina Naciri-Azzouz

Introduction

Some studies have shown that the social meanings of different variants have an influence on the linguistic behaviour of speakers, and in order to analyse the variation and linguistic change within an oral community, it is also necessary to consider the sociolinguistic value of the different traits and the speakers' awareness of the different connotations of their linguistic practices (for example, Labov, 1976). This line of research has also been applied to Arabic-speaking societies in recent years (see for instance, Lentin, 2002; Al-Wer & Herin, 2011; Hachimi, 2011, 2012; and Germanos, 2011).

Following these principles, this chapter is an analysis of the diverse linguistic attitudes observed in two Moroccan communities, the meaning of these attitudes, and their impact on the linguistic process of levelling and accommodation. We will focus on a particular context: Northwestern Morocco, and specifically on the city of Tetouan and the adjacent rural region of Ghomara. In these Moroccan societies under study, social and economic changes plus generational gaps have brought about several linguistic transformations, but taking these very different contexts into account, we have found that the linguistic changes occurred at different speeds and have therefore yielded diverse outcomes.

We will first focus on the city of Tetouan, which we consider interesting because it has two varieties competing for social prestige. In this context, the social significance of origin and of local and regional identities, and their influence on the linguistic state of the city, will be analysed. Afterward, we will focus on the rural region of Ghomara, describing different attitudes observed in several Ghomara Arabic speakers towards linguistic variation. Also, the general attitudes towards Ghomara Berber will be analysed and, in a few cases, towards Senhaja Berber as well.

Before starting, the two settings will be briefly described, as well as the fieldwork and methodology carried out in collecting the data based on the speech corpora.

The Moroccan Arabic varieties

We will here briefly describe the linguistic situation in Morocco. The Arabization of Morocco occurred in two different stages. The first stage took place in the seventh century with the arrival of Muslim troops to the North of the Maghreb. The Arabic varieties spoken in part of the territory which we nowadays call Morocco are the sedentary-type of Moroccan varieties (also known as *pre-hilalien* or *non-hilalien* varieties). They are divided into two types of varieties simultaneously: the sedentary dialects spoken in the cities, and the sedentary dialects spoken in rural areas. These types of varieties can be found above all in the North of Morocco (in both rural and urban contexts), in some old cities such as Rabat, Fez, etc., and also the Judaeo-Arabic of Moroccan Jews.

The second stage of the Arabization of Morocco took place several centuries later, in the eleventh century with the arrival of Bedouin tribes (the Banu Hilal among others) who had been expelled from Egypt. The Arabic varieties brought by them are another type of Arabic dialect, known as Bedouin varieties (also called *hilalien* varieties). They are mainly spoken in central and southern regions of the country, for example, principally in the famous cities of Marrakech and Casablanca.

Nowadays, this historical dichotomy, Bedouin vs. sedentary, may hardly represent the Moroccan linguistic reality, taking into account the high rate of urbanisation in past decades; since 1950 it has moved from 25.3% to 53.8% in 2005 (Miller, 2007, p. 24) and is rising considering that this urbanisation has not concurrently concerned all parts of the country.

The emergence of what has been termed *parlers nouveaux urbans* "neo-urban vernaculars spoken by the new urban dwellers" (Miller, 2007, p. 10) is the reality in several large and not-so-large urban centres where different linguistic features have emerged in different processes of levelling. Due also to the different backgrounds of these migrations and the linguistic diversity of the country, it is not clear that these different "neo-urban varieties", such as in the case of Casablanca, Meknes, Fez, etc., display the same patterns, as will be shown below in the case of Tetouan.

The two settings of the study: Tetouan and Ghomara

Tetouan

The geographic and social context where Tetouan is set has played a central role in its evolution. Thus, its position in a mountainous area resulted in its separation from the Rabat-Casablanca axis, an isolation which hampered fluid relationships between the central and southern regions of the country and the northern zone, where Tetouan is located.

In terms of social background, Tetouan is the administrative centre for nearby localities and the location where most of the crafts and industry in the region are concentrated (though in any case nothing compared with Tangier, the biggest and most industrialised city in the north of Morocco). In addition to this, a process of socio-economic change can be noted, linked mainly to the improvement of the infrastructure and the development of tourism which have gained relevance in the past decade.

This situation of extreme polarisation between the urban and rural contexts has resulted in significant migratory movements, particularly from neighbouring rural areas but also from other places in Morocco, which has in turn generated rapid and unmanageable urban growth. Due to this, the city has seen sustained growth, both in terms of size and population.

The distribution of the newly arrived population is an interesting factor when analysing the linguistic geography of Tetouan. This increase in population has occurred particularly in specific districts. Some of these outlying districts were former hamlets and have currently been incorporated into the city. This is the case, for example, of the neighbourhood Torreta.

The constant influx of families coming from several places in Morocco and their settlement within the city has favoured social mixture and linguistic interactions. The main consequence of this has been the development of a new urban variety of Tetouan where the younger generation is the most innovative.

Ghomara

Ghomara is currently a small region in Northwestern Morocco, and its ethnonym refers to the nine tribes which are located between the Laou and Ouringa rivers, stretching to the Rif Mountains. Ghomara is part of the Jbala region which forms a linguistic and cultural continuum. However, Ghomara has its own specific traits. Access to some hamlets and towns is still difficult today despite the improvement in communications between Tetouan and the coast over the past decade. Moreover, there is still a small Berber speaking area within the tribe of Bni Buzṛa and in the faction of Bni ʕrūs in Bni Mənṣūṛ.

Nevertheless, socio-economic changes in northern Morocco are reaching this region as well, although at a slow pace. In addition, migrations to the coast and the neighbouring cities like Tetouan and Tangier favour linguistic phenomena, such as levelling and accommodation, related to interdialectal contact, the spread of education, mass media, etc.

In such a context, Ghomara presents an important variation: first of all, there is an internal dialectal variation that is typical in a rural mountain region of Arabic-speaking communities; and secondly, there is a variation that corresponds to a linguistic change in progress.

The fieldwork

The two areas of fieldwork have been conducted with many types of informants, that is to say, those whose sociolinguistic profiles were different. They are of different ages, both men and women, and with different levels of education.

In the case of the city of Tetouan, the informants live in the area of the city called Medina,[1] as well as in other neighbourhoods of the centre and the periphery.

They come from families of various origins ranging from those living in the city for generations to other newcomers, usually from the nearby rural areas but not always. Data from Tetouan were collected over several stays in the city between 2008 and 2014, this fieldwork was conducted by Ángeles Vicente.

Data from Ghomara were gathered during different trips between March 2014 and June 2015, the longest of which lasted three months, in fieldwork conducted by Amina Naciri-Azzouz. Different villages across Ghomara (province of Chefchaouen) were visited: Qāʕ Asrās (rural commune of Tizgane) and Šmāʕla (rural commune of Bni Bouzra) in the coast, and different villages in inland Ghomara. Some of them have more direct contact with Ghomara Berber or Ketama Berber, such as the region of Bab Berred.

In order to analyse speakers' attitudes towards the different Arabic varieties spoken in Tetouan and Ghomara, or even a different language in the case of the latter, we examined two types of information obtained from our interviews. On the one hand, the speakers' overt attitudes were elicited by asking about the linguistic practices of the two regions, in order to obtain accurate information about the social meaning of these practices; and on the other hand, and only in Tetouan, the linguistic traits linked to these attitudes were described.

The linguistic variation in Tetouan and Ghomara

To analyse the linguistic variation in the two places under study, the most important fact that should be considered is the increasing contact between varieties because of the greater mobility and interaction within the population over the past decade. This is obvious above all for the youth, for whom education and access to social networks and a wider cultural sphere allow for greater contact with other Moroccan varieties. As is logical, this situation is more evident in the urban environment (Tetouan) than in the rural (Ghomara).

Tetouan

The linguistic evolution of the city of Tetouan is peculiar when compared with other varieties spoken in Morocco. Tetouan Arabic is not totally isolated, it also takes part in the process of levelling and linguistic accommodation currently underway within the country, and some influences are consequently received through various media.

As has already been stated, two varieties competing for social prestige are found in this city. Firstly, we find the *mdini* or traditional Tetouan variety, which is spoken by the families considered the older dwellers of Tetouan, the "pure" Tetouan people,[2] regardless of the district in which they live, though this variety usually survives only amongst adults and older generations. These people have been living in the city for generations, although some were immigrants from the rural areas who arrived a few decades ago and probably levelled towards this variety, the prestigious one at the time.

Secondly, we can also find the urban Arabic variety where some of the older features have disappeared; it is formed by a mixture of surviving traits of the traditional Tetouan variety but also by the features brought by the inhabitants of the neighbouring rural varieties, or of other nearby or distant cities due to more recent migrations. This urban variety is used mostly by young people, who are leading the accommodation and levelling process.[3]

Some of the features of traditional Arabic of Tetouan run the risk of disappearing since they are being relegated to speakers of older generations, and because young people are more innovative, as we noted earlier. In any case, it should not be forgotten that Tetouan is also a city marked by conservatism at all levels, even the linguistic one, as has been shown (Vicente, 2017).

In the meantime, most of the traits of the variety spoken in Tetouan are used by a large number of people within the language community and have survived without problems, despite not coinciding with the features of the urban dialect of Rabat-Casablanca,[4] that is to say the Moroccan variety which is, broadly speaking, considered the most prestigious nationally. Even other northern Moroccan varieties share some of these features, which differentiate northern from southern Moroccan dialects. For this reason, *əl-haḍra əš-šāmāliyya* (or "northern variety"), which Tetouan Arabic is part of, continues to identify, and to stigmatize, speakers from northern Morocco throughout the rest of the country.[5]

Ghomara

The Arabic varieties of Ghomara belong to the *Jebli* dialects, whose literal meaning is "from the mountain", a group of dialects spoken in northwestern Morocco.[6] The study of some linguistic features of Ghomara Arabic so far indicates an important variation in which two regions can be distinguished: a western one, closer to *Jebli* dialects such as Chaouen (Moscoso, 2003) and Anjra (Vicente, 2000), and an eastern one in which the convergence or influence of Berber seems to be more important because of their more direct contact and proximity (El Hannouche, 2008, 2010; Lafkioui, 2007; Mourigh, 2016).

As a matter of fact the situation is not that simple: the loss of some of those variants indicates a process of linguistic change, mainly along the coast, that will lead to the loss of traditional dialectal distinction – as in other regions thoroughly studied such as Spanish, but also some Arabic dialects from the Gulf to Morocco (Miller *et al.*, 2007; Holes, 1995, etc.) – but in the case of Ghomara we are not yet at this stage, as it is only evident in the younger generations where the variables of age and education correlate and play an important role.

Attitudes towards *Jebli* dialects are usually negative because of their association with "illiteracy", "rurality", etc., and this attitude could act as a force leading towards language change in Ghomara.

Ghomara Berber is the other language present in the region, along with Senhaja Berber, composed of an independent group from those constituted by the varieties of Tarifit, which belong to the Zenata group (Kossmann, 2017). Ghomara Berber is a nonpareil Berber language due to the large influence of Arabic. Thus, it has resulted in an almost identical phonological system, parallel systems in morphology, an equally similar syntax, and a strong influence of Arabic terms in the lexicon (Mourigh, 2016).

Language attitudes in Tetouan

It is known that the origin of linguistic changes and phenomena like levelling and accommodation is contact among different varieties resulting from geographic mobility and the improvement of education and means of transportation. In the city of Tetouan, contact with other Moroccan varieties has been constant above all over the last 15 years when the northern region of the country has been part of tourist routes for people from the interior regions of Morocco. Geographic mobility also exists and the education of children and young people has become generalized. In this way, above all among this younger generation, there is a certain degree of dialectal levelling with stable and unstable variants.

The analysis of our data leads us to affirm that the idea of linguistic prestige among the informants of this city changes depending on the social value of the linguistic traits. This situation is obvious, on the one hand, when the origins of the inhabitants are considered, and on the other, when the question of local or regional identity comes into play.

The meaning of linguistic attitudes

The dwellers living in the districts in the centre of Tetouan (which they themselves call the Medina) have a very distinguished social prestige, which is connected to a supposed Andalusi origin. It is known that the Andalusi population (the Muslims living in Al-Andalus in the Middle Ages, but also the Moriscos expelled from Spain in the Modern Age) arrived in Morocco and settled in different cities in the country, one of them being Tetouan. This origin may hold true for some of these people, as seen in certain family names.[7] In addition, the families who have lived in these neighbourhoods for a long time but show no signs of having an Andalusi origin also take on this social prestige, as they are considered the "pure" or oldest people of Tetouan.

So, the immigrants who settled in the neighbourhoods of the Medina, many of them during the time of Spanish protectorate in the region (1912–1956), and inhabitants settled in some districts that formed the periphery at that time, such as the districts called the Barrio Malaga and Mulay Hassan, could level towards the *mdini* variety, which might be seen as prestigious, in order to better integrate into the city.

Nowadays, these districts are no longer on the periphery, but are not considered part of the Medina either, and their inhabitants, who arrived decades ago, are included in what is considered the traditional people of Tetouan, given that they speak the *mdini* variety.

This means all of them attach prestige and social standing to this form of traditional speech, and they are aware that their way of speaking demonstrates their origins and they are proud of this.

Example 1 (informant 1: a 64 year-old man, living in old Medina):

> It means your parents' origin is also from Tetouan?
> Informant 1: *iyyəh, ṭəṭwān fhamṭi? liʔanna l-haḍɪa dyāli dʕarrəfni*
> "Yes, from Tetouan, do you understand? Because of this my speech shows my origin".

This informant affirms that he continues to speak this variety in other Moroccan regions, further proof of what it means for him.

Example 2:

> Informant 1: *u mšīṭ n-əd-dāxīliyya, mšīt āna u dxult n wāḥəd d-dāxīli u daymān b-əl-lahža dyāli ma tbəddəlt-š*
> "I went to the interior region, I went and entered in a boarding school, and (I spoke) always in my dialect, I did not change".

It must be remembered that people of the northern region are stigmatised because of their dialect, and because of this they tried to adapt their speech.

Nevertheless, the younger generations do not show the same adherence to these linguistic practices. For them, the *mdini* variety has negative connotations, since they consider people who speak it presumptuous and arrogant. Because of this, they are called *allūka* (a word that is not in dictionaries and whose etymology cannot be ventured). This word means "person who comes from a good family or who has a pure Tetouan origin", but for young people, it has come to mean "you are snobby, posh, arrogant", a way of telling them that they consider themselves superior to others. Also, these younger generations consider the *mdini* variety as feminine, even if the oldest men speak it.

Another aspect to consider is that they are aware of the traits that characterise their speech, and even what characterises that of others, which means the differences between the northern varieties and those spoken in other Moroccan regions are apparent at a phonetic as well as at a lexical level.

Example 3:

> How is the Tetouan variety?
> Informant 1 : *ʔāl li, ʔult lək, hūma ka-yʔūlu gāl li, gult lək, ma nəʕɪaf-š, š-šaɪžəm, hna ka-nʔūlu ṭ-ṭāqa*
> "*ʔāl li, ʔult lək* (he said to me, I said to you), they say *gāl li, gult lək* (he said to me, I said to you), I don't know, *š-šaɪžəm* (window), here we say *ṭ-ṭāqa* (window)".

Example 4:

> Informant 1: *f fās ʕandum fḥālum wālākin l-lahža š-šamāliyya, ka-yʔūlu ʔāl li u ʔult lək, u ha mūlāy ʔdīm, mūlāy drīs, wālākinna l-muṣṭalaḥāt hūma māši dyālna, ṛbāṭiyyīn ʕawəd ka-yhədṛu hayda qāl li, qult lu, wālākin muṣṭalaḥāt dyālum māši dyālna, fhamṭi?*
> "In Fes, they have their way, but in the northern dialect, they say *ʔāl li u ʔult lək* (he said to me and I said to you), and here is *mūlāy ʔdīm* (Mulay the Old one), Mulay Dris, but the vocabulary, his is not like ours. Rabat people also speak like this *qāl li, qult lu* 'he said to me, I said to him' but their vocabulary is not like ours, do you understand?".

Example 5 (informant 2: a 55–60-year-old woman, from the Barrio Malaga district):

> What is different in Tetouan variety?
> Informant 2: *īwa əl ɹ u əl ʔ hād š-ši lli kāyən f ṭətwān ɹ ma ka-nnəṭqu-ši r, ma ka-nhədṛu ši b-əl q ka-nhədṛu b-əl ʔ*
> "Yes, the ɹ and the ʔ, this is what it is, in Tetouan is ɹ, we don't pronounce r, we don't speak with q, we speak with ʔ".
> Even the young people are aware of this situation.

Example 6 (informant 3: man, 23 years old, Jebel Dersa district):

> Informant 3: *ka-yqūlu ġīr f kāza, māši hnāya*
> "This is said only in Casablanca, not here".

The local identity

The overt representation of this social meaning is also seen with the preservation of some significant traits in their speech. These traits are a mark of local identity, and because of this, they benefit from latent prestige (Germanos, 2011, p. 50). The analyses of these variants show that the levelling process is also reached, above all, when informants have lived outside Tetouan.

a) The approximant alveolar [ɹ] pronunciation of the phoneme /r/.[8] This is clearly a trait of the Tetouan *mdini* variety currently relegated to adults and older speakers.

Examples 7–9 (informant 1):

> 7. *ṭəṭwān fīha ḥāḍāɹa l-andālūsiyya u l-ḥāḍāɹa l-maġɹībiyya*
> "There is the Andalusi civilisation and the Maghrebi civilisation".
> 8. *gzāyɹiyyīn bəzzāf žāw n-hna n ṭəṭwān*
> "Many Algerians came here, to Tetouan".
> 9. *žāw mən l-žazāyəɹ məṭɹūdīn*
> "They came from Algeria, driven out".

Examples 10–12 (informant 2):

> 10. *mšīna, kunna f-ḍ-ḍāɹ ʔuddām ṣbīṭāɹ español* (Spanish loanword)
> "We went, we were at the house in front of the Spanish hospital".
> 11. *hnāya dāba l-žīɹān sāknīn mʕāk f-əl-ʕīmāɹa mɑ tʕəɹfum ši*
> "Here now, the neighbours who live with you in the building, you don't know them".
> 12. *ʕandi dikɹāyyāt bəzzāf hnāya f ṭəṭwān*
> "I have many memories here in Tetouan".

The younger generation, regardless of the neighbourhood they live in, and speakers of the urban or modern variety of Tetouan pronounce the trill, alveolar phoneme /r/ as in the rest of Morocco /r/.

Examples 13–15 (informants 4: boys and girls, 15/20 years old, several districts):

> 13. *bārāka mən rōyo*
> "Leave alone".
> 14. *flewrtīt mʕāha*
> "I have flirted with her".
> 15. *āba la čitarra!*
> "What an ugly car!"

b) The other characteristic feature of the *mdini* Tetouan variety is the glottal pronunciation [ʔ] of the unvoiced velar occlusive phoneme /q/. This pronunciation is also found in other cities in the region such as Chefchaouen, and in some Judeo-Arabic dialects in the Maghreb.

Examples 16–19 (informant 1):

> 16. *bḥāl əl-baʔlāwa, əl-baʔlāwa, əl-aṣl dyāla sūri*
> "As the *baqlāwa*,[9] its origin is Syrian".
> 17. *šnu xəṣṣək? ʔūl li*
> "What do you need? Tell me".
> 18. *ʕandna ka-nʔūlu mātāl*
> "Amongst us there is a proverb".
> 19. *k-īʔrāw ṭ-ṭbīb*
> "They study medicine".

Conversely, in the urban Arabic of Tetouan the most common pronunciation is the unvoiced velar /q/.[10]

Examples 20–24 (informants 4):

> 20. *u bqīna ka-nqūlu fīn ġa-nqəṣṣru hād-əl-līla*
> "And we stayed saying where shall we go tonight".
> 21. *ši wərqa d-əl-libro*

"A cigarette paper".
22. *fīya l-qərda*
"I have withdrawal symptoms".
23. *yāllāh nʕaddlu ši qahwa*
"Let's drink coffee".
24. *hūwa mbuwwaq*
"He is on drugs".

For younger speakers and newcomers, the pronunciation of these two traits by some old dwellers of Tetouan is a form of endorsing the ancient background of their families within the city. In other words, on the one hand, these pronunciations involve some form of prestige but, on the other hand, have pejorative connotations especially for young people. However, it is necessary to insist that the actual linguistic practices of the speakers of the *mdini* variety do not always coincide with their overt attitudes in such a way that the levelling process also exists among them and a stable situation is difficult to find, above all concerning the variable /q/.

The regional identity

The two previous features show the importance of local prestige on linguistic practices, now this third example displays the importance of the regional identity on them.

The pharyngealised voiceless dental [ṭ] is the common pronunciation in Tetouan (*mdini* and urban varieties) and in most dialects of northern Morocco. It may be considered one of the features of the northern Moroccan variety or *əl-haḍra š-šāmāliyya*.

Examples 25: *mūṭaʕ* "place", *ṭahri* "my back", *mrīṭa* "sick (F)", *bayṭa* "egg", *ġlīṭ* "fat".
However, in Moroccan varieties spoken in central and southern regions, the pharyngealised voiceless dental /ḍ/ is more common.
Examples 26: *mūḍaʕ* "place", *ḍahri* "my back", *mrīḍa* "sick (F)", *bayḍa* "egg", *ġlīḍ* "fat".

In Tetouan, this voiced pronunciation is perceived as a foreign and non-prestigious form,[11] a quite curious fact if we bear in mind that the voiced phoneme coincides with the pronunciation in classical Arabic, the most prestigious Arabic variety amongst Arab-Muslims. The adherence to regional identity has a social meaning and linguistic consequences, although the permanence of the voiceless pronunciation causes a certain stigmatisation of the northern population throughout the rest of Morocco.

This stigma is reciprocal and answered with several nicknames used by young people referring to *n-nās d əd-dāxəl* "people of inside". This is the neutral form used for people living in central and southern regions of the country. But they also use other disrespectful terms such as *grīḥa* pl. *grāyəḥ* "bumpkin", and *ḥarḍūn* pl. *ḥrāḍən* "lézard".[12]

Ghomara's attitudes towards *Jebli* and "more" *Jebli* varieties

One of the most recurrent topics that has been dealt with by informants during the fieldwork was the linguistic variation in Ghomara; we may confirm an awareness of this variation even though it was difficult to elicit specific linguistic features linked to a specific area or tribe. Therefore, it was possible to observe language attitudes, values, and the behaviour of Ghomarans towards linguistic variation, at least overt ones.

For Ghomara youth, attending boarding schools is a reality that should be taken into consideration as well, considering that it implies making friends from different parts of Ghomara; besides, the majority of the teachers use the northern Moroccan variety of Arabic which may be considered the target variety in Ghomara.

This situation results in a double variation as it has been noted above, an internal variation within Ghomara and a variation due to the linguistic change in progress, which simultaneously implies a levelling process across Ghomara. In this way, a relevant difference between the coast and the interior has been found. Mountainous areas are generally perceived as more conservative, and therefore more *Jebli*, by the coastal people. In the villages of the coast, when the interest in dialects and oral traditions has been explained, the common advice was to visit inland regions because:

Example 1 (a 40-year-old woman, Qāʕ Asrās):

1. *ṭəmma kull čar ʕəndu l-haḍra dyālu, ḥna hna ržaʕna fḫa m-mdina*[13]
   "Each village there has its own speech; here, we have become like the city".

But then the situation is not exactly as it has been described; even though the process of levelling is much more widespread on the western coast, the differences due to levelling and accommodation are mainly found among the youngest speakers who tend to lose the salient *Jebli* features.

In inland and coastal Ghomara, elderly and middle-aged men and women display similar patterns of language use; the differences are mainly due to differences between Ghomara varieties. What might explain this value is the fact that some Western Ghomara varieties seem to be closer to the target variety spoken in the cities than to the eastern one. Nevertheless, the stage of language change surely plays a role as well. But not only could the linguistic features explain this value, in this point the semiotic process of *iconisation* identified by Irvine and Gal (2000, pp. 37–38) may be applied. Due to an accelerating urbanisation of the western coast in the last decade where some icons of *Jebli* life, like traditional customs, are missing, which may be helping in this categorisation of more *Jebli* in the interior, it is not possible to draw a boundary between the social factor and the linguistic feature.[14]

Example 2 (roughly 70-year-old man, Šmāʕla):

2. *lli bāqi ġmāra d-əṣ-ṣaḥḥ hūma d-əǧ-ǧbəl*
   "Who are still real Ghomara are those of the mountain".

Thus, for example, from a phonetic point of view, one of the most salient *Jebli* features still alive in Ghomara is the presence of the following spirantised allophones: [ḇ], [ṯ], [ḏ], [ḏ̣], and [ḵ].[15] This phenomenon is very unstable among the youngest generation of inland Ghomara and rarely found among the educated youth from the coast. Nevertheless, it is a phenomenon still widespread among elderly and middle-aged people across Ghomara. While the spirantized realization [ḏ̣] of /ḍ/ is found in inland Ghomara, its presence on the coast is very rare, even among elderly people, where the voiceless /ḍ/ > [ṭ] is the norm as in the rest of north-western Morocco, as has been noted above.

Another example is the assibilated realisation of /t/, which is the norm in the western varieties of Ghomara whilst its presence is very rare in Eastern Ghomara varieties (see Naciri-Azzouz, in progress).

Then we focused on some statements from young women aged between 16 and 26 from different parts of Ghomara which could shed some light on what has been explained. Through their values and uses of the language, the complexity of linguistic variation and the different categorisation of *Jebli* life are exposed.

Among the youngest women (about 18 years old) who are still studying, accommodation and levelling towards the Tetouan variety are often the norm, which is the loss of the most salient *Jebli* features. During the first visits of Qāʕ ʕasrās, a young woman of 18 years proposed to visit Šmāʕla, where some of her friends at boarding school are from, and the reason was as follows:

Example 3 (18-year-old woman, Qāʕ ʕasrās):

3. ṣḥābāti ṭəmmāk ka-yhəḏru ʕlāyən fḥāli bḥaq yəmmāhum fə-škəl, māši fḥānna hnāya
"my friends there [in Šmāʕla] speak almost as I do, but their mothers do so in a different way, not as we do here".

She was right: this group of young women from Šmāʕla do not use the salient *Jebli* features found among the adults, such as spirantisation. However, this situation is complex because it depends on the context and the interactions, but what is clear is the capacity of these young girls for accommodation at least. This situation raises a difficult question: Is this the tendency across Ghomara?

Access to secondary education is not yet the norm in Ghomara, not even on the coast, especially among girls. These girls are aware of their special status and they highlight the fact of going to Tetouan to continue their studies at the university.

Moreover, they always tried to look for friends of more or less the same age, some of them married, whom they considered more interesting for the research because they better represent what is traditional Ghomara speech, considering themselves not representative of that[16]:

Example 4–6 (roughly 18 year-old women, Šmāʕla):

4. hiyya dʕāwəd lək ḥsən, bāqi ʕanda dik l-haḍra d-əǧ-ǧbəl
"She will tell you better, she still has this *Jebli* speech".

5. *dāba hād əl-žəll dyānna ḥnāya huwwa lli ka-yfūṭ l-bakaluṛya, ka-yqṛa f-əl-kulliyya*
"Now this generation, ours, this is the generation that finishes high school, studies at the university".
6. *ḥnāya ḥnāya bəzzāf bəzzāf, bənt ka-dwəṣṣal s-sādəs, ka-dxṛəž. ḥna məḥsūbīn ḥnāya*
"There are a lot, a lot of girls, a girl that goes to primary school, leaves it. There are only a few of us".

In this process of urbanisation, the variable of education is important in the process of language change in Ghomara, as has been noted for other Arabic-speaking communities, and the loss of *Jebli* markers, especially lexicon, is perceived as a consequence of schooling, as shown by this statement when the kin terms are elicited:

Example 7 (a 40-year-old woman, Akumsām):

7. *lə-ʕyāl a-yləqṭu ku-ši mə-l-mədrasa, hayda yqūlu žəddu, ḥbību*
"Children learn (pick up) all in the school, so they say "my grandfather", "my maternal uncle" [instead of *ḥnīni* and *Xāli* which are the most commonly used forms in Bab Berred].

By contrast, young women from inland Ghomara, who are generally unschooled, present different patterns of language use. Even though there are differences due to age, the presence of salient Jbala features may be very unstable (Eckert, 1996).

To sum up, attitudes and values towards Ghomara varieties are related to "level of rurality", that is, some varieties are perceived as more rural than others, but in general it is due to some shared features between western Arabic varieties of Ghomara and the target variety, or simply the process of indexation where the social factors play an important role, considering that in Ghomara the linguistic variable does not seem to play an identity role. As a matter of fact, the language change due to rapid social changes is still at an early stage where *Jebli* features coexist with incoming features.

Ghomara's attitudes towards Ghomara Berber

A part of Ghomara is still Berber-speaking, and Ghomara Berber[17] is a very unique language because of the large influence of the local Arabic, as has been highlighted above. Across Ghomara only people who have some contact with Ghomara Berber are aware of its existence. For example, in Qāʕ Asrās and Bāb Bərrəd (inland eastern Ghomara), a lot of people do not know that a Berber-speaking area exists a few kilometres away from them. In the case of Bāb Bərrəd, they all know about Senhaja Berber, and even when they have been asked about *š-šəlḥa*[18] "Berber" close to them and the existence of Ghomara Berber is confirmed, they tried to clarify that those are not Ghomarans, and they are more likely Ktāma or Riffians.

Examples 8–10 are parts of a conversation between several women from Akumsān aged between 22 and 60 years old:

8. *š-šəlḥa, mši l-Ktama, n-Isagən, ġi ṛafayna. kāyna ṛafayna r-rīfiyya. a-yhədru b-əš-šəlḥa bḥaqq ma-ši š-šəlḥa r-rīfiyya, tik əš-šəlḥa mruwwna ʕandəm, may a-dgləs, xəṣṣək tšədd ʕla ṛāṣək haytak.*
"Berber, you have to go to Ktama, Isagən, nearby there. Rifiyya is there. They speak in Berber but it is not as Tarifit, this Berber is chaotic, when you sit [with them], you want to pull your hair out".

9. *ma ʕəmmṛi smaʕt bīha. ma ʕəmmərna tīhna mʕa ši-wāḥit ġmāri ihdər b-əš-šəlḥa zaʕma dyanna. ḥna šay ʕanna hnāya xtilāf f-əl-haḍra. l-lahža dyānna*
"I've never heard of it. We've never met someone ġmāri who speak in our Berber. What we have here is different speeches, our dialect".

10. *kāyən baʕḍ ən-nās qdāmīn kānu a-yhədru b-əš-šəlḥa, kānu ʕayšīn mʕa ryāfa fūq*
"There are some elderly people who were speaking in Berber, they were living up with Riffians" [referring to Bni Mensour, a Berber-speaking area up in the mountains].

Around the Ghomara Berber area, while people know about Ghomara Berber and have contact with Berber speakers, the fact of a Berber language spoken inside Ghomara should be clarified, because initially everybody answered in this way: *mə-Mtīwa l-līhən* "beyond Mtīwa", that is, Tarifit. Then, they tried to explain what kind of language it is.[19]

This is an interesting extract where two elderly men of about 70 years old from Bni Səlmān were trying to explain what kind of language Ghomara Berber is and, generally, it shows what has been found among Ghomara Arabic speakers:

Example 11:

11. Ḥ1: *r-rīf, qālu š-šəlḥa žāt ka-tfəṛṛaq, ka-tfəṛṛaq, wəṣlət lə-bni buẓra, təmmək l-fətər qrəb dyāla*

Ḥ1: "Rif, it has been said that Berber was being distributed, distributed, from Rif, and it arrived to Bni Buzra. There it was growing colder (fig.)".
Ḥ2: *təmma xallāwha*
Ḥ2: "There, it was left".

Do they still speak Berber?

Ḥ1: *ma ka-yhədru ġa bīha*
Ḥ1: "They only speak it".
Ḥ2: *wālu dīk əš-šəlḥa, wālu, mayši š-šəlḥa*
Ḥ2: "Nothing this Berber, nothing, it is not Berber".
Ḥ1 *t-tulta b-əš-šəlḥa, u-t-tuluṭ...*
Ḥ1: "One third in Berber, and one third"...

Ḥ2: *quṯ lək, ḥa l-kəlma b-əš-šəlḥa u-tlāṯa w-aṛbʕa b-əl-ʕarbiyya, mxalḷṭa*
Ḥ2: "I said to you, one word in Berber and three and four in Arabic, mixing".

So, do you understand it?

Ḥ1: *la, la, la ... ma nʕəṛfūha-ši, ši kəlma u-kān.*
Ḥ1: "No, no, no, we don't understand it, only a few words we do".

Attitudes towards Ghomara Berber are "negative" in the sense of being perceived as a strange language that they are not able to completely understand. Furthermore, it lacks the prestige or acknowledgement of other Berber languages. Nevertheless, its use seems normal:

Example 12 (woman roughly 60 years old, Darwannu, Bni Grir):

12. *wāxa ka-yzuwwzu ləhna [...]wa-hna ka-yəḇdāw yqūlu š-šəlḥa. nqūlu mṛa buẓṛāṯiyya u-rāžəl grīri. iwa w-hiyya ka-dəḇda ḏqūl š-šəlḥa mʕa n-nas dyāle*
"Even if they get married [...] here they speak in Berber. For example, a woman from Bni Buzra and a husband from Bni Grir. Well, she speaks Berber with her family [when they visit her]".

Example 13 (man roughly 70 years old, Darwannu, Bni Grir):

13. *la, a-wlīḏi, məlli ka-yžīw ʕandək ka-yhəḏṛu b-əl-ʕarbiyya, kimma ka-nhəḏru ḏāḇa. walākin mʕa baʕḍum ka-yhəḏṛu b-əš-šəlḥa*
"Not, my son, when they visit you, they speak in Arabic, as we do now. But among them, they speak in Berber".

Conclusion

Studies of variation in Arabic-speaking areas were mainly focused on cities due to the interesting linguistic situations produced by the contact caused by internal migration and that resulted in new urban varieties. The aim of this chapter is to show the need to analyse different situations in order to have a more complete picture of the influence of speakers' attitudes and their linguistic consciousness of variation, since the rhythm and outcomes are different depending on the context: large and small cities, and the rural environment.

In Tetouan, the two varieties competing for social prestige demonstrate a different behaviour towards the levelling process, but the perception of some features as local or regional identity markers has an influence on variation, since their social prestige prevents a faster levelling process. So, in the *mdini* variety, some traditional features remain despite the arrival of external influences thanks to which they have a social prestige. However, these features cause the stigmatisation of speakers, and this is the reason they are disappearing among the young people. On the other hand, in the new urban variety, even if the levelling process is underway, some features persist because they are part of a prestigious regional variety, defying the stigma that this causes throughout the rest of the country.

In the case of rural contexts in Ghomara, attitudes towards local "traditional" varieties might work as forces driving linguistic change if we consider that *Jebli* dialects are linked to "illiteracy", "rurality", etc. However, change is at a very early stage and so far it only concerns the youngest generations where age and schooling correlate.

Speakers' attitudes towards Ghomara Berber spoken in the region generally depend on their contact with it. Even though general attitudes towards Ghomara Berber are "negative" because it is perceived as a local language, and used only by its native speakers, its use is perceived as normal and I did not gather any specific stereotypes linked to Berber speakers.

To conclude, the two situations under study show the importance of the context and the social value of linguistic practices in the evolution of the leveling process. In Tetouan, the favourable attitudes towards some features, even stigmatised, permit a slow levelling process. In the meantime, unfavourable attitudes and stigmatisation in a rural context (Ghomara) could lead to the disappearance of traditional varieties and the minority language as well.

Notes

1 We refer to the part of the city that is considered the centre by its dwellers; this includes the old medina (intramuros) and the commercial area known as Ensanche.
2 As they themselves say.
3 This is certainly not a new phenomenon, as similar processes have been described in other Moroccan cities such as Casablanca, Tangier, or Marrakech. Nonetheless, we have to say that some differences exist. For instance, Bedouin-type dialects – widespread in other southern regions, such as Casablanca – do not exist in this northern region, which means the factors taking part in the levelling process are not the same.
4 See Vicente, 2017.
5 About the *əl-haḍra əš-šāmāliyya*, see Sánchez & Vicente, 2012.
6 For an overview of the salient linguistic features of Jbala dialects among other Moroccan dialects see Heath, 2002, and Vicente et al., 2017.
7 This question has been studied by two Moroccan scholars: Mohamed Daoud and Mohamed Ben Azzouz Hakim. Both of them have written about the families of Tetouan with an Andalusi origin.
8 The analysis of a greater number of recordings of Tetouan leads us to affirm that this allophone is approximant alveolar and not uvular fricative, as has previously been considered, and like the pronunciation found in Chefchaouen.
9 The *baqlāwa* is an oriental pie, probably of Turkish origin, made with puff pastry, ground walnuts and honey.
10 In southern and central regions of the country, the voiced pronunciation /g/ is found. Thus, speakers of the *mdini* variety say: *ka-nʔūl* "I say", speakers of urban variety pronounce *ka-nqūl*, rather than *ka-ngūl* as in the centre-south of the country.
11 Even as a rural feature, since it is characteristic of the neighbouring and rural variety of Anjra, Vicente, 2000, p. 50.
12 They mean "a fake crocodile", it refers to shirts of the Lacoste brand, and they explain that the reason is because people from these regions of Morocco love to buy fake brands.

13 A broad phonetic transcription is used and only the spirantisation has been marked to remark this rural variety.
14 It is not our aim to delve deeply into this question, but this is an ideal time to study this process of urbanisation of the Jbala region where different linguistic and social phenomena are overlapping.
15 For spirantisation of dentals and the variation of preverbs see Naciri-Azzouz, 2016.
16 It should be noted that all these girls identified themselves are *ġmāriyya* (from Ghomara) even though they didn't always identify the name of the tribe, especially when the name of the tribe didn't coincide with the name of the rural commune.
17 For an overview of the sociolinguistic situation of Ghomara Berber in one of the largest Berber-speaking villages, see Mourigh, 2016, pp. 2–3.
18 In general how Berber languages are known.
19 It should be noted that even though Ghomara Berber speakers have different attitudes towards Berber, "speakers with a good command of Berber can clearly indicate what is Berber and what is Arabic" (Mourigh, 2016, p. 3).

References

Al-wer, E., & Herin, B. (2011). The lifecycle of Qaf in Jordan. In M. Germanos & C. Miller (Eds.), *Langage et société N° 138 : Villes du monde arabe: Variation des pratiques et des représentations* (pp. 59–76). Paris: Maison des Sciences de l'Homme.

Eckert, P. (1996). Age as a sociolinguistic variable. In F. Coulmas (Ed.), *The handbook of sociolinguistics* (pp. 151–167). Oxford: Blackwell.

El Hannouche, J. (2008). *Ghomara Berber: A brief grammatical survey* (Master's thesis). Universiteit Leiden, The Netherlands.

El Hannouche, J. (2010). *Arabic influence in Ghomara Berber* (Master's thesis). Universiteit Leiden, The Netherlands.

Germanos, M. (2011). Représentations linguistiques et contact dialectal : Remarques sur l'évolution de cinq variantes régionales à Beyrouth. In M. Germanos & C. Miller (Eds.), *Langage et société N° 138 : Villes du monde arabe: Variation des pratiques et des représentations* (pp. 43–58). Paris: Maison des Sciences de l'Homme.

Hachimi, A. (2011). Réinterprétation sociale d'un vieux parler citadin maghrébin à Casablanca. In M. Germanos & C. Miller (Eds.), *Langage et société N° 138 : Villes du monde arabe: Variation des pratiques et des représentations* (pp. 21–42). Paris: Maison des Sciences de l'Homme.

Hachimi, A. (2012). The urban and the urbane: Identities, language ideologies, and Arabic dialects in Morocco. *Language in Society, 41*, 321–341.

Heath, J. (2002). *Jewish and Muslim dialects of Moroccan Arabic*. London: Routledge Curzon.

Holes, C. (1995). Community, dialect and urbanization in the Arabic-speaking Middle East. *Bulletin of the School of Oriental and African Studies, 58*, 270–287.

Irvine, J., & Gal, S. (2000). Language ideology and linguistic differentiation. In P.V. Kroskrity (Ed.), *Regimes of language: Ideologies, polities, and identities* (pp. 35–83). Santa Fe, New Mexico: School of American Research Press.

Kossmann, M. (2017). La place du parler des Senhaja de Sraïr dans la dialectologie berbère. In Á. Vicente, D. Caubet & A. Naciri-Azzouz (Eds.), *La région du Nord-Ouest marocain: Parlers et pratiques sociales et culturelles* (pp. 93–105). Zaragoza: Prensas de la Universidad de Zaragoza.

Labov, W. (1976). *Sociolinguistique*. Paris: Les Éditions de Minuit.

Lafkioui, M. (2007). *Atlas linguistique des variétés berbères du Rif*. Köln: Rüdiger Köppe Verlag.

Lentin, J. (2002). Variantes dialectales 'objectives' et 'subjectives': L'écart entre différences de forme et différences de statut sociolinguistique, et ses implications pour l'enquête dialectologique. In A. Youssi, F. Benjelloun, M. Dahbi, & Z. Iraqui-Sinaceur (Eds.), *Aspects of the dialects of Arabic today* (pp. 43–54). Rabat: Amapatril,

Miller, C. (2007). Arabic urban vernaculars: Development and Changes. In C. Miller, E. Al-Wer, D. Caubet, & J. C. E. Watson (Eds.), *Arabic in the city. Issues in dialect contact and language variation* (pp. 1–30). London/New York: Routledge, Taylor.

Miller, C., Al-Wer, E., Caubet, D., & Watson, J. C. E. (Eds.). (2007). *Arabic in the city: Issues in dialect contact and language variation*. London/New York: Routledge, Taylor.

Moscoso, F. (2003). *El dialecto árabe de Chauen (N. de Marruecos)*. Cádiz: Universidad de Cádiz.

Mourigh, K. (2016). *A grammar of Ghomara Berber (North-West Morocco)*. Köln: Rüdiger Köppe Verlag.

Naciri-Azzouz, A. (2016). Les variétés arabes de Ghomara ? s-sāħəl vs. ǧ-ǧbəl (la côte vs. la montagne). In G. Grigore & G. Bițună (Eds.), *The Arabic varieties: Far and wide* (pp. 405–412). Bucharest: Editura Universității din București.

Naciri-Azzouz, A. (in progress). *La(s) variedad(es) árabe(s) de Ghomara (noroeste de Marruecos)*. (Doctoral dissertation). Universidad de Zaragoza, Spain.

Sánchez, P., & Vicente, Á. (2012). Variación dialectal en árabe marroquí: əl-haḍra š-šāmālīya u la-hḍra l-maṛṛākšīya. In A. Barontini, C. Pereira, Á. Vicente, & K. Ziamari (Eds.), *Dynamiques langagières en Arabophonies: Variations, contacts, migrations et créations artistiques. Hommage offert à Dominique Caubet par ses élèves et collègues* (pp. 223–252). Zaragoza: Universidad de Zaragoza.

Vicente, Á. (2000). *El dialecto árabe de Anjra (norte de Marruecos): Estudio lingüístico y textos*. Zaragoza: Universidad de Zaragoza.

Vicente, Á. (2017). The past and present of a conservative Arabic dialect: Tetouan (Morocco). In O. Durand, A.D. Langone & G. Mion (Eds.), *Lisan al-arab: Studies in contemporary Arabic dialects. Proceedings of the 10th International Conference of AIDA* (pp. 295–309). Vienna: LIT Verlag.

Vicente, Á., Dominique, C., & Naciri-Azzouz, A. (Eds.). (2017). *La région du Nord-Ouest marocain: Parlers et pratiques sociales et culturelles*. Zaragoza: Prensas de la Universidad de Zaragoza.

12

NEW PRESENTATIONS OF SELF IN EVERYDAY LIFE

Linguistic transgressions in England, Germany, and Japan

Patrick Heinrich

> When an individual enters the presence of others, they will commonly seek to acquire information about him or to bring into play information about him already possessed. They will be interested in his general socio-economic status, his conception of self, his attitudes towards them, his competence, his trustworthiness, etc. [...] Information about the individual helps to define the situation, enabling others to know in advance what he will expect of them and what they may expect of him.
> —Erving Goffman, *The Presentation of Self in Everyday Life*

Erving Goffman's (1959) seminal book *The Presentation of Self in Everyday Life* was the first book to ever devote its main attention to mundane face-to-face interaction. Goffman's principal idea was that people tried avoiding embarrassment in their interaction with others by performing set roles, very much like actors on a stage. Goffman thus established the idea that individuals are "social actors", taking on specific roles in specific contexts and for specific purposes. According to Goffman, playing an appropriate role for a chosen setting and a chosen end resulted in "coherence". This chapter is about the exact contrary, i.e., purposeful "incoherence" in interaction. It is about anti-roles and anti-language. Let me briefly explain what I mean by this. To speak a language implies knowledge of what passes as appropriate or socially accepted speech. In other words, it is based on and reproduces metapragmatic rules. While speakers can diverge from such rules governing unmarked language use, deviance comes at a price. Deviant use may lead to correction, exclusion, and stigmatization as a way to bring such speakers "back into line". Speaking, as Silverstein (2003) makes clear, not only involves a transmission of propositional content (first order indexicality) but also the creation of an image or a role of the speaker (second order indexicality). However, this only functions if speakers stick to conventions and the unwritten metapragmatic rules linking language use to roles and images. In other words, it only works if speakers are "coherent". However, a growing number of individuals can be found to be purposefully incoherent, thereby undermining the ground on which the self is linguistically represented. The results are new representations of self.

Purposeful incoherencies cannot be ignored in studies on language and identity, given the vast number of publications on "deviant ways" of presenting oneself through language such as, for example, through crossing in England (Rampton, 2005), Verlan in France (Doran, 2004), Kiezdeutsch in Germany (Wiese, 2012), straattal in the Netherlands (Cornips, 2008), Chicano in the US (Eckert, 2008), or dialect guise in Japan (Tanaka, 2011). In this chapter I seek to explore the similarities between the emergence of new social styles and roles. I do so by examining three existing case studies (England, Germany, and Japan). Before doing so, let me briefly elaborate on coherence in language and social roles in the modern world.

Coherence between language and identity

Coherence and incoherence are structured. One needs to identify the right people to study either one or the other. I can vividly remember my failed attempts to interview elderly inhabitants born in the 1920s on their identities in Yonaguni Island in the Ryukyus. For them, there was no room to negotiate "identity". They had difficulties understanding what I was actually after. They were Japanese from Yonaguni, spoke what they said was a "dialect" of Japanese, had specific jobs, a specific gender, a specific age, were married to a specific person, had a specific number of children, and that was all there was. It was all clear to them. I realized that they were utterly modern individuals. Modernity, to recall, is not simply a specific period of time, it is an attitude towards the world that gained prominence at a particular period of time, in particular parts of the world. Bauman (1992) notes that at the heart of modernity is the attitude of ordering the world with the aim of improving it. Modern individuals perceive the world as it is as chaos and hence perceive it as an incentive to act. According to these modernist attitudes, order is paramount with "universality", "homogeneity", "monotony", and "clarity" and ordering the world along these lines constitutes "progress". Homogeneity and clarity were also sought after for language and identity, and these ideas led to the very changes ("progress") that were envisioned (cf. Heinrich & Galan, 2011). What is called "language modernization" did not only result in the development and standardization of the "language system", it also led to shift and loss of "dialects" and "minority languages". "Pre-modern" diversity was reduced in an attempt to render the sociolinguistic situation in modern states "clearer". Note, in passing, that the entire sociolinguistic meta-language (system, dialect, minority, pre-modern, etc.) reflects the modernist agenda of ordering a chaotic world in order to improve it.

This chapter draws on research which has discussed in great detail the specific ways of viewing and assessing language in modernity, and how these modernist language ideologies are affecting language use (e.g., Bauman & Briggs, 2003; Kroskrity, 2000; Schieffelin, Woolard & Kroskrity, 1998). On a macro-level, the events resulting in language shift and dialect decline are firmly anchored in modernist language ideology, which legitimized and mobilized for the creation of national languages represented by standard languages. Quasi as a side effect thereof, the notions of dialect and minority languages were created. The idea of "dialect" makes no sense in the absence of modernist concepts such as "standard language", "national language", or "official language". While I had sought to study "the invention of Japanese as a national language" by interviewing speakers of the endangered minority language of Yonaguni in the extreme south of the Japanese Archipelago, my consultants were reproducing this very invention, and they never considered its artificial and ideological character. It never occurred to them that their grandparents had lived in the Ryukyuan Kingdom and thus had no sense of "being Japanese", that "Japanese identity" as such was a construction of the late nineteenth century, and that Yonaguni had not been considered being part of the Japanese language before it was "modernized" at the end of the nineteenth century (for a full discussion, see Heinrich, 2012, pp. 60–70). The gap and the contradiction between the existing language ecology, on the one hand, and modernist language ideology, on the other hand, was not visible to them. Dominant language ideology constituted the basis for seeing the world as ordered and coherent, and for acting accordingly in ordered and coherent ways. Hence, they called their language, as they had been told in school, by the media, by politicians, etc., a "dialect" (*hōgen*) of Japanese, and treated it accordingly, despite the fact that people on the neighboring island of Iriomote would not understand their "dialect", let alone people from the capital of Tokyo, located 2,200 kilometers north of Yonaguni. Students of language ideology know that such attitudes and behaviors are not "normal" or "natural", and that they are "coherent" only *on the basis* of "modernist ideology".

Purposefully incoherent language use, which is the topic of this chapter, requires such an awareness of "modernity as ideology". It is therefore unsurprising that incoherent use of language requires language that has become "marked" in modernist settings, i.e., accents, switching and mixing, dialects and minority languages, etc. Incoherence is more than lack of coherence. The incoherencies discussed in this chapter are *purposeful deconstructions* of what passes as "coherent" in modern sociolinguistic settings.

Arguably, nobody has summarized expectations on speakers in modern settings better than Pierre Bourdieu. Bourdieu (1977; 1991) emphasized that human behavior is the product of incentives to which individuals are exposed to in their concrete social life. Behaviors that are rewarded are repeated over and over again and thereby become part of an individual "habitus". A habitus results in specific "dispositions", that is to say, inclinations to act in specific ways, and these specific actions feed back again into the habitus of a person. Behavior may be changing over a lifetime, but every change is rooted or anchored in past experiences. The habitus results in a "feel for the game", that is, knowledge also of how to act in new and unexpected situations. Having the "right" feel for the game results in coherence.

With regard to language, every habitus includes the acceptance of what Bourdieu (1991, pp. 43–65) called "legitimate speech". Legitimate speech is a prestigious way of talking – it is the kind of speech "that is accredited, worthy of being believed"

(Bourdieu, 1991, p. 69). It is universally recognized as being legitimate by everyone, thus resulting in various restrictions for all those who have not fully mastered it. Legitimate speech is imbued with high "linguistic capital", that is to say, produces a profit of positive distinction with every social exchange. This renders legitimate speech the best way to getting heard (Bourdieu, 1991, pp. 55–56). Knowledge about one's own position in society, and knowledge about how others evaluate this position, is part of the habitus. This includes seeing legitimate speech as superior to "popular speech", even by those who are not or not fully proficient in legitimate speech. By recognizing legitimate speech as being legitimate, subjects whose language repertoires are considered to be "deviant" thus participate in their own subjugation. This manifests in various ways; linguistic insecurity and hypercorrection is one way, silence another one. In other words, individuals seek to be coherent, and if they know that they are not, seek to hide their incoherence. (By the way, this is the very reason why sociolinguists are at pains to gather authentic speech and have to think of various ways to overcome the observer paradox).

Pierre Bourdieu convincingly underlined that variability in language is *always* linked to inequality. The fact that "linguistic exchanges [. . .] are also relations of symbolic power" (Bourdieu, 1991, p. 37) requires different linguistic capital being ascribed to the different ways of speaking. There exists a linguistic market where such price formation takes place, and the most valuable and authoritative way of speaking a given language is called "legitimate language" by Bourdieu. Let me briefly provide some background of how legitimate speech has been established in England, Germany, and Japan, and to what effect for local dialects and minority languages. In England, the invention of the printing press by William Caxton constituted a significant contribution to the creation and spread of a commonly shared and standardized language. The southeastern dialects, in particular the London dialect, spread through writing and served as a common language by Renaissance scholars from the sixteenth century onwards. Written language became the yardstick by which correctness was to be measured, as well as with regard to spoken language (Milroy, 2001). Prescriptive grammars of English such as those by John Priestly in 1761 or Robert Lowth in 1762 played a crucial role in ascribing positive features to the kind of English they prescribed (and to its speakers), and projecting negative views onto every other use of English (and onto those using such language). In Germany administrative writing in chanceries led to the first steps in standardizing written German (*Kanzleideutsch*), and it was this kind of written language that Martin Luther drew on when he translated the Bible in 1522. Grammar and orthography were subsequently standardized by the work of grammarian Johann Christoph Adelung in the eighteenth century and later by lexicographer Konrad Duden. At the end of the nineteenth century, stage language (*Bühnensprache*) set an example for an audibly clear pronunciation. Such standardized German started to replace dialects in northern Germany quickly, because the distance between the standard and the dialects was much larger there. Also in the south, albeit at a slower pace, local dialects were replaced by larger regional dialects as an effect of language leveling and the growing influence of Standard German on local speech (Besch, 1988). In Japan, finally, language standardization started later than in Europe, partly as an effect of Japan's seclusion from the outside world, and of having writing based on Chinese until spoken and written language were unified at the end of the nineteenth century (Heinrich, 2005). The language of Tokyo's "uptown" neighborhoods of Yamanote served novelists at the time as a model for writing conversations in their works of fiction. This kind of language was then codified by a National Language Research Committee and spread through the Japanese education system as Standard Japanese (*hyōjungo*). Dialects became suppressed, resulting in a shift from local dialect to Standard Japanese (Inoue, 2011).

In England, Germany and Japan – as in all modernized countries – it was no longer sufficient to simply "speak" in an ever-growing number of contexts. One had to now "speak appropriately", in other words, "speak correctly". "Standard language cultures" rather than simply standard languages had been created (Smakman, 2012), and it is for this reason that that standard language was not simply added to the repertoire of dialect speakers, but that "deviant" language use was "corrected" into standard language. The language shifts and dialect leveling we are witnessing across the modern world today are thus the effect of countless acts of preferring – and thereby transmitting and reinforcing – the standard variety of the dominant language. It is the expression of attempts to correspond to ideologically mediated expectations of how to present oneself. In other words, it is an attempt to be coherent in the modern world. But the modern world as we know it (universal, homogenous, monotonous, clear) is coming to end.

Before there was any language "crossing" in England, there were centuries where persons sought to "pass" as speakers of legitimate speech; before there was Kiezdeutsch in urban multicultural neigborhoods in Germany, there were attempts to speak a regionally and socially unmarked German; and before there any was "dialect guise" in Japan, there was a "dialect complex" in what is probably the fastest and most thorough standardization process ever witnessed. These shifts to legitimate language were initiated by speakers who, in view of the negative assessment of their own language use, made efforts to act coherently along the lines of modernist language ideology. They sought to play the roles they were required to in order to participate in their respective modern societies.

Something happened

To many, the period of "seeking coherence" with modernist imaginations of sociolinguistic order is over. For a large number of young and middle-aged people in urban centers in England, Germany, and Japan seeking coherence is no longer a pressing objective. Something happened. Besides a more positive outlook on dialects and minority languages in the twenty-first century (Coulmas, 2005, p. 31), this change is crucially triggered by the fact that an ever-growing number of individuals (in particular young, middle-aged, and urban), are actually recognized as standard language speakers today. They no longer need to "pass", to hide their regional background, nor do they need to have complexes about the way they speak. Many speak unmarked language, and this constitutes a whole new sociolinguistic situation. Language repertoires have changed as a consequence of standard language cultures. The ways in which language repertoires are formed differ, too. Individuals dominant in a minority language or in local dialects are increasingly hard to come by. Legitimate speech (standard language, dominant language) is no longer acquired afterwards or incompletely. It is the first language, the language of the family. This notwithstanding, variation and diversity remains, but it is different than imagined in modernity, and by extension by modern linguistics.

The sociolinguistic situation has become more similar to modernist imaginations, but it has also become more complex to study language and identity. The former standard/dialect or majority language/minority language divide is no longer in place. Blommaert, who has extensively studied "late modern"[1] sociolinguistic settings, stresses that nobody "knows *all* of a language" (Blommaert, 2010, p. 103, emphasis in the original). Individuals have specific language repertoires that come into existence in different ways. That is to say, speakers have "truncated language repertoires" that reflect their personal life trajectories. Furthermore, language repertoires are not made up by a number of languages or dialects, but speakers employ "linguistic items" drawn from the "linguistic pool" that is available to them (cf. Nettle, 1999). Consider some random examples. One does not need to be a speaker of Italian in order to utter *bellisimo*, *spritz*, or *grazie mille*, nor of German in order to use *Gestalt*, *Weltschmerz*, or *Schadenfreude*, or of Japanese in order to have *tsunami*, *miso*, or *emoji* be part of one's language repertoire. Likewise, people can use t-glottalization without being speakers of Cockney, palatalize *ich* as *isch* without being from Germany's south-western regions, or negate verbs by the inflexion *-hen* instead of Standard Japanese *-nai* without being a speaker of western Japanese dialects. Taking this into account is important, because speakers employ all linguistic items available to them as linguistic resources for indexical functions. They don't simply speak "a language" or "a dialect", but use whatever is available to them in order to speak. They often employ "unexpected" elements in their speech. They purposefully and prominently do so when they engage in linguistic transgressions.

Linguistic transgression

While Bourdieu (1991, p. 122) wrote that legitimate language functions in a way "to discourage permanently any attempt to cross the line, to transgress, to desert", we nowadays find an ever-growing number of sociolinguistic studies which, quite on the contrary, describe purposeful crossings, transgressions and desertions. In the following, I briefly review three case studies of such transgressions in order to exemplify some of their main characteristics.

Crossing in England

In *Crossing – Language and Ethnicity among Adolescents,* Rampton (2005) presented his studies on young adolescents with foreign backgrounds, enrolled at schools with a high percentage of children whose parents were born outside England. Initially interested in a study of code switching, Rampton noticed a new form of using language codes by social or ethnic groups that the speakers did not "belong to" (Rampton, 2005, p. 28). That is to say, these adolescents were "crossing" boundaries of social groups by usurping or imitating the language. The basic issue that interested Rampton thus moved from code switching patterns per se towards the social meaning of language crossing. Hence, he shifted attention to the very reasons behind the acts of crossing.

Three languages were involved in this case study, Panjabi, Creole, and Stylized Indian English. Panjabi was used by students of Anglosaxon and Afro-Caribbean descent, Creole was used by students of Anglosaxon descent and by Panjabis, while Stylized Indian English was used by all. At the school which Rampton studied, students were thus employing language that (1) was not part of the language repertoire one would expect from them, and (2) that bore little overt prestige (Panjabi, Creole) and (3) that had been subject to correction (Stylized Indian English).

Asian youths described their own use of Stylized Asian English generally as a ploy to use with substitute teachers, or other people who did not know them, but nevertheless had some authority over them. They feigned minimal competence in English, as one student explicitly explained to Rampton. "If a copper comes up to you right, and you ain't done anything [. . .] or just say you got a supply teacher in, Ben and she asks you a question and Asif or someone will say *'excuse me me no understanding'* [. . .] and she knows very well that you can understand her" (Rampton, 2005, p. 81, emphasis in the original).

Students at this school were crossing into identities, such as immigrants with imperfect English (Stylized Asian English), that were negatively perceived by large parts of Anglosaxon society. In so doing, they were provoking stereotyped perceptions of the non-migrant population towards migrants through their language choice. That is to say, they were deliberately shifting into a role of a negatively perceived part of the population by borrowing from a language or imitating a language that was not part of their "normal" or "expected" language repertoire. They acted incoherently. In doing so, a sense of confrontation was created and existing stereotypes were reproduced. Due to different stereotypes linked to specific linguistic behaviors, students used the languages they were crossing into in different ways. Stylized Asian English was often used to check whether Anglosaxon adults harbored stereotypes and biases towards migrants and their descendants. Stylized Asian English was employed among the students themselves in order to promote solidarity within mixed-race groups of friends, i.e., it was used as a "we-code". These various types of language use led Rampton (2005, p. 14) to conclude that language crossing was "a form of everyday cultural politics".

In particular, four points from Rampton's study are important for our discussion. Firstly, ethnic absolutism is absent. There is no fixed and inseparable link between language and ethnic groups. Stylized Indian English can be used by students of Indian descent, but also by students of any other descent alike. Everyone may potentially draw on everything. Only the absence of a link between language and ethnicity allows for the various types of crossings he encountered. Secondly, the practice of crossing requires awareness about the role of language in the construction of identities. Crossing is an exercise in deconstructing the linkage between language and identity. Thirdly, crossing is not an act of claiming membership to the group one is crossing into. Crossing is an exercise in style that serves to display particular stances in communication. In Rampton's case study, this stance was predominantly protest against racist views. Last but not least, crossing is not connected to language proficiency. A limited pool of words and fixed expressions suffices to engage in crossing. Not language "proficiency" is required, but "awareness" of how language use gives rise to specific ideas about identities, and how these are socially evaluated. If we are all actors, as Goffman convincingly claimed, then crossing is a way of acting which underlines the very fact that we are acting. Ideas about set identities and the associated stereotypes were contested through acts of crossing, which thus served as a means of comment, criticism, or resistance. As an effect, the hegemony of dominant ideologies and practice is broken. Coherence is lost. Anyone navigating on modernist assumptions is either left surprised, and if unable to adapt and to play along, "left behind" or "left outside" in such types of interaction.

Kiezdeutsch in Germany

It has been noted for a number of years that migrant children growing up in Germany spoke "somehow differently". For many years, their use of German was mainly thought to consist of "mistakes". Newspaper editorials condemned such kinds of speech (e.g., Kaube, 2012), while linguists tended to ignore the topic. This changed in the new millennium when researchers like Heike Wiese (2012) but also the Institute for German Language (Hinnekamp & Meng, 2012) started turning attention to such uses of German. Such sociolinguistic research has clarified that the language use of migrant children does not constitute "errors", but that it incorporates systematic innovations on the levels of grammar, vocabulary, and pronunciation. Famous examples are the use of southwestern German dialect *isch* /iʃ/ instead of standard German *ich* /iç/ for the first personal pronoun, and contracted expressions such as *lassma* (Standard German: *lass mal*, "it's ok") or *ischwör* (Standard German: *ich schwöre*, "I swear [it's true]"). This language use also frequently includes loanwords from Turkish or from Arabic. Probably the most famous loanwords are *lan* ("you") from Turkish and Arabic *yalla* ("let's go"), respectively. Researchers studying what are now widely regarded as "ethnic dialects" of German pointed out that the negative perception of such language use was not based on some kind of underlying unsystematic rules ("mistakes"), but on the low social status of the speakers associated with such language.

Wiese (2012) terms this kind of German "Kiezdeutsch". "Kiez" originally referred to Slavic settlements in Germany outside the city walls. Even in the twentieth century, Kiez had a negative connotation, meaning something like "poor and remote neighborhoods with inhabitants of low formal education". In Berlin, however, people began to refer in local speech to one's multiethnic and multicultural neighborhood as "Kiez", and to do so positively. Kiezdeutsch is thus a kind of language use that affirms loyalty to a multiethnic neighborhood in the big city. For the majority of speakers, Kiezdeutsch is simply one part of their linguistic repertoire, that is to say, they speak other varieties of German, too. Other than Kiezdeutsch, young urban speakers may also be proficient in a regional dialect, in regional spoken common language (*Umgangssprache*), and in Standard German. Kiezdeutsch is predominantly spoken among peers. It is a language of familiarity, personal loyalty and informality. For a large number of individuals, the use of Kiezdeutsch is thus a matter of context.[2] In particular, for young urban speakers, Kiezdeutsch is used as an expression of belonging to a multicultural part of German society. It is an avowal to a multiethnic identity via a stylized use of a German ethnolect. Kiezdeutsch is, in a nutshell, a social style. In other words, it is a style available to speakers with a language repertoire that includes also regional common language and Standard German (they can switch it on or off), but it is the sole German available to speakers with language repertoires that consist only of an ethnic variety of German, and hence cannot switch it off.

Three things about Kiezdeutsch are important for our discussion. Firstly, young urban speakers in multiethnic neighborhoods use Kiezdeutsch. Secondly, Kiezdeutsch draws on language that does not "belong" to their language repertoire, for example incompletely acquired German spoken by the first generation of migrants. By and large, young urban residents with multiethnic background are no longer proficient speakers of their "heritage language" such as, for example, Turkish or Arabic. Many of them are simply inserting tokens in what is their dominant language, (Standard) German. Thirdly, Kiezdeutsch is used to draw a boundary between "us" and "them". In this case, "us" are people embracing multiethnicity, and the life style that comes along with it in their neighborhood, while "them" is the old monoethnic German "establishment". While Kiezdeutsch draws on various languages and dialects, it is used among young inhabitants of multiethnic neigborhoods, irrespective of the fact whether their own families have migrated to Germany or not. Kiezdeutsch is not about ethnicity and family background. It is about attitudes towards diversity. Kiezdeutsch is a purposeful positioning in social space through stylized language use. Just like the case of crossing in England, Kiezdeutsch requires first and foremost awareness of how language is involved in the construction and the display of identities. Only such knowledge allows the purposeful employment (or recycling) of negatively perceived linguistic elements in order to take a positive stance towards oneself and one's neighborhood.

Dialect guise in Japan

Language standardization in Japan started only in the twentieth century, but the Japanese standardization process is probably unparalleled in the modern world for its rapidness and thoroughness (cf. NINJAL, 2013). In very broad terms, the sociolinguistic situation of dialect and standard in Japan is as follows. The prevalent number of speakers nowadays speak Standard Japanese in all domains, that is to say, local dialects in Japan are endangered. Dialects are still used by elderly speakers, and middle-aged people understand dialects and are able to use parts of dialects, while the young generation has only a restricted token knowledge of dialect vocabulary but no knowledge of dialect grammar. Hence, older speaker can carry on with informal daily life exclusively in dialect, and middle-aged speakers can step into dialect speaker roles with a number of restrictions, while younger speakers can insert a limited number of dialect features into their Standard Japanese utterances.

The language standardization process in Japan can be seen as an illustrative case in which modernist attitudes of "universality", "homogeneity", "monotony", and "clarity" were realized. Indeed, the sociolinguistic situation in Japan would today be set for an exclusive use of Standard Japanese in the near future had not a process of "language destandardization" (*datsu-hyōjungo-ka*) set in twenty years ago (cf. Inoue, 2011). Language destandardization in Japan is a form of resistance against the idea of language as a "purely referential tool", that is, an opposition to the modernist dream that all nationals speak the same kind of language. Due to its thorough spread, Standard Japanese has come to index only "being Japanese", and that is not much of an index in a country where less than 2% of the population are foreign, and where the vast majority of these foreign nationals are linguistically fully integrated Asians, i.e., an "invisible" minority. If we stick to Goffman's ideas about individuals playing theater, then the Japanese are stuck playing the same role for decades. They are safe from embarrassment but heavily constrained in their use of the language.

"Dialect guise" (*hōgen cosplay*) may be the most typical case to analyze the desire to express distinctions via language in a society that has almost completed the standardization process. Standard Japanese has become the first language of young and middle-aged Japanese, they have been socialized in the standard language, and they have had little exposure to other varieties. Data shows that 70% use almost exclusively Standard Japanese in their life and that 25% have absolutely no knowledge about local dialects of the region where they live and also no longer know whether a local dialect was once spoken there (Tanaka et al., 2016). For such individuals, language variation is no longer linked to a specific locality. The link has been lost. As an effect, language has not simply been standardized in Japan; it has also been largely "emptied" from its identificational functions. Therefore, dialect elements that remain to be known as "linguistic items" are borrowed and used just like costumes during carnival. On the one hand, the almost complete realization of language standardization has "liberated" people from the stigma that had once been associated with dialects (see Sibata, 1977 on "dialect complex" in Japan); on the other hand, young and middle-aged Japanese have a very limited knowledge of Japanese dialects today.

Let us briefly consider how dialect guise works in practice. Two types of knowledge are necessary for engaging in it. The first type of knowledge is about stereotypes of local identities in Japan. Widely spread conceptions include, for example, the idea that men from Kumamoto in the south are "macho" (*otokorashii*), women from the ancient capital of Kyōto are "refined" (*kunren sareteiru*), people from northern Aomori are "simple" (*soboku*), people from subtropical Okinawa in the extreme south are "gentle" (*yasashii*), etc. (Tanaka, 2011: 28). As a second prerequisite, some regional linguistic items of Japanese must be known. This includes most prominently specific sentence-final modal particles such as *-yan* or *-ja* (associated with western Japan), *-dabe* or *-tabesa* (associated with northern Japan), *-ken*, *-tai* (associated with southern Japan) or *-yake*, *-kee* associated with central Japan. Tokyo is located in eastern Japan and hence eastern dialect elements play a subordinate role for engaging in dialect guise because Standard Japanese evolved from Tokyo speech (Tanaka, 2011, p. 18). Employing dialect guise means adding a regional dialect element to a Standard Japanese utterance in order to suggest specific associations, e.g., evoke marked masculinity by using a southern sentence-final particle. In that way, dialect items serve as an "accessory" for utterances. They add a "flavor" to their statement, if you will. Unmarked Standard Japanese, on the other hand, cannot provide for such functions.

Dialect guise is more than simply a new use of language. It reveals a new attitude towards language variation. For young and middle-aged non-dialect speaking Japanese, dialect no longer carries social stigma. After all, they do not speak dialect and are all more or less equally proficient in Standard Japanese. Using elements of dialect carries no risk. Given the existing linguistic uniformity, it is of rather little surprise that the language of Tokyo is the least beloved variety and is frequently declared to be "boring" (*tsumaranai*) or "not pretty" (*kawaikunai*) in language attitude surveys. At the same time, local dialects, no longer spoken by the majority of young and middle-aged Japanese, enjoy much popularity and are assessed to be "cool" (*kakkoii*) or "splendid" (*hokorashii*) (Tanaka, 2011, pp. 67–91). Given such attitudes, it basically suggests itself to borrow some of the "cool stuff" (dialects) in order to pep up one's otherwise "boring language" (Standard Japanese).

The situation of using dialects and Standard Japanese is complex, as "real" local dialects are still used, albeit by a rapidly decreasing part of the predominantly old and rural population. In general, however, dialect vitality is decreasing rapidly and dialect leveling is rampant.[3] The result is, however, not an exclusive use of standard language. New forms of using Japanese have sprung up. These new forms are layered in that Standard Japanese speakers may either (1) employ dialect elements of their hometown, or (2) use dialect items associated with any other Japanese region. In the first case, speakers engage in what is called "homesick dialect" (*jimo hōgen*), and in the latter case in "fake dialect" (*nise hōgen*). Both contrast with the use of real, authentic dialects (*junsui hōgen*) (Kinsui, 2003). Use of homesick dialect and fake dialect share the fact that there no longer exists a fixed and solid connection between language varieties, speakers and their respective identities. Variation in language is simply used in order to render one's utterances more colorful and vivid. Speaking standard only, and on all occasions, results in the perception of a speaker being stiff, cold, and, ultimately, boring. Language guise is practiced in all of Japan, but it is most fervent in Tokyo, where unmarked Standard Japanese is "at home", so to speak. For young Tokyoites in particular, Toyko language has become totally unmarked. It stands for nothing (Heinrich & Yamashita, 2017). If we all play roles, then the roles played by Standard Japanese speakers are no longer playful. This notwithstanding, there remains a craving to take a stance and to play a role in Japan. The result is a "dialect boom" by speakers who no longer speak dialect, and therefore employ dialect items in new ways and with new effects. Using (elements of) dialect is no longer the default and unmarked language spoken in regional settings, but a way of pepping up or decorating Standard Japanese utterances in informal but not necessarily regional settings.

Emic and etic perspectives on linguistic transgressions

Let us consider the theoretical implications of these three case studies next. Theory building focuses on shared features, on the one hand, and difference between various cases, on the other hand. It provides for an account of what is universally constant and what it culturally variable at the same time. The former aspect is called "etic", the second "emic" (adapted from "phonetic" and "phonemic", respectively). Let's start with insights with regard to an etic perspective.

In order to discuss the topic at hand in an etic way, we need, to start, a metalanguage that is not tied to specific cultural (emic) phenomena. In other words, we should not use terms such as "crossing" or "dialect guise" outside their specific settings, because they refer to culturally different ways, functions, and effects of undermining legitimate language through stylized speech. I suggest using "linguistic transgression" as a culturally neutral way to discuss what, for example, is similar in crossing, Kiezdeutsch, or dialect guise.

The three cases all imply "incoherent" behavior. Identities and the language varieties associated with specific groups are employed despite the fact that one "does not belong" to this group of speakers. This is done for two reasons. Firstly, people engage in transgressions in order to display a specific stance. They do so implicitly, that is, stance is not expressed overtly in discourse (e.g., "I suspect that you are racist", "I like living in my multicultural neighborhood", "I'm a fun person"), but such stance is expressed by code choices. In other words, these attitudes are expressed by "implicit meta-pragmatics". Secondly, those engaged in transgressions do not play along with the roles expected from them. They quit playing along, because they do not like the script for a number of very different reasons. Through these acts of transgression, speakers set themselves apart from others. The "other" are all those who stick to the play and the roles, in our case to a script reproducing the dominance of legitimate language and their speakers above anything and everybody else. The act of transgression itself renders the border between legitimate and illegitimate language visible. It unveils that the indexical functions of language on identity has a basis in power inequalities. It reveals the suppressive character which provides for the ideological basis of indexical meaning. All cases of transgression involve a new and reflexive level of awareness about the language and identity nexus. Those engaging in transgressions have mastered the art of "how to do things with words", and they do not like how these things are getting done. Hence, they are now engaged in "showing how things are done with words, by doing unexpected things with words, in order to change how things are done with words". Obviously, this requires some kind of expertise, and also new ways to study this in sociolinguistic research.

Let us consider the three cases from an emic perspective next. The particular stances expressed in the acts of transgression differ from case to case. In the case of England, crossing served to undermine ethnic prejudices. In Germany, Kiezdeutsch is a pledge of allegiance to one's multiethnic neighborhood. In Japan, dialect guise is ludic language use. In light of the fundamental similarities identified above, these differences hint at the fact that transgression must be understood as being part of a deeper, culturally unrelated social change that is under way in late modern societies. In other words, crossing is about more than an antiracist stance, Kiezdeutsch is more than a pledge of local loyalty, and dialect guise is more than cool communication. All of these transgressions are manifestations of a new and higher level of awareness of how language impacts identity. The mechanism through which access to and proficiency in legitimate speech regulates society has lost its ideological function. Language ideology has become visible to all those engaging in transgression. This is why one is now free to either align to this ideology and to use legitimate speech (be coherent), or one may choose to reject this ideology, make it visible, play with it, and confuse the sociolinguistic order it seeks to establish. You are free to be incoherent if it serves you some purpose.

Transgressions highlight, as the term suggests, the existence of borders, and the effects of highlighting these borders results in exposing the function of legitimate speech in creating and reproducing inequalities with a given speech community. If modernity meant to stage a "moral play" and crucially involve language therein, then this play may at times turn into a "comedy" in late modernity. The purpose of the play may be subverted at any time. We can now clearly see that something has happened. The "feel for the game" has changed. The relation between language and identity is no longer fixed and solid. It is fleeting, liquidizing, and subject to change. Plurality, variety, contingency, and ambivalence have taken the place once occupied by universality, homogeneity, monotony, and clarity. Not being able to deal with plurality, variety, contingency, and ambivalence may now lead to embarrassment in presentations of self in everyday life. The task has become more difficult and only those with a heightened awareness of language and identity can participate. New qualities have taken the place which cultural capital and social power had once occupied. Transgressions are manifestations of "Cool", with a capital C. Capitalized Cool is the abstract (etic) mechanism that incessantly creates new cool behaviors, language use, and artifacts. According to Pountain and Robins (2000, pp. 23–24), Cool "is a rebellious attitude, an expression of a belief that the mainstream mores of your society have no legitimacy and do not apply to you. [. . .] Cool was once an attitude fostered by rebels and underdogs – slaves, prisoners, political dissidents – for whom open rebellion invited punishment, so it hid its defiance behind a wall of ironic detachment, distancing itself from the source of authority rather than directly confronting it."

If legitimate language is possessed by (almost) all, as is most clearly the case in Japan, or if the racist and excluding functions of legitimate language become visible as in England and in Germany, then *legitimate languages suffers a loss of legitimacy*. Participating in a moral play that urges you to "speak correctly" has lost its appeal. What counts to late modern individuals is "speaking in cool ways". Cool is thereby the opposite of power. There is no cool way of speaking legitimate language. Cool language is all about how innovative and spontaneous you can be, and about how many (non-legitimate) language resources you can draw on and include in your speech. You know some sign language? Cool! (cf. Maher, 2005). Cool language stylization requires unusual and new materials, and these can only be found in non-legitimate speech, because non-legitimate speech is detached from power, and because it has been suppressed or corrected *by powerful actors or institutions*. Sticking to power is out – detachment from power is cool. New representations of self in everyday life are here to stay.

Sociolinguistics should add Cool to its analytical toolbox. After all, Pountain and Robins (2000, p. 167) predict that "Cool is destined to become the dominant ethic among the younger generation of the whole developed world and billions of 'wannabes' in developed countries." What is more, they are unlikely to drop it once they get older, because cool is not a limited number of artifacts or a specific way of talk, but a deeply rooted, new attitude.

Notes

1 "Late modern" is understood here as "modern" plus an awareness that modernity, too, is simply an ideology which can therefore be challenged and improved. This implies perceiving, naming, and reacting to oppressive aspects of modernity. Late modern individuals know that they are modern, and this gives them the freedom to challenge and change specific aspects of modernity.
2 At the same time, since Kiezdeutsch originates in neighborhoods with a high percentage of immigrants, many individuals living there do not have fully developed language repertoires. In particular, Standard German may be absent, and *Umgangssprache* may be influenced to various extent by their ethnic German dialect. Full proficiency in Standard German and in written German is usually only acquired in middle class families and/or through long exposure to the education system (Löffler, 2010, pp. 99–107). It is therefore important to differentiate between the various speakers employing what is subsumed under the umbrella term "Kiezdeutsch".
3 Note that the Kansai dialects around the former capital of Kyōto are to some extent an exception to this trend.

References

Anderson, B. (1991). *Imagined communities* (2nd ed.). London: Verso.
Bauman, R., & Briggs, C. L. (2003). *Voices of modernity, language ideology and the politics of inequality*. Cambridge: Cambridge University Press.
Bauman, Z. (1992). *Intimations of postmodernity*. London: Routledge.
Besch, W. (1988). Standardisierungprozesse im Deutschen. *Sociolinguistica*, 2, 186–208.
Blommaert, J. (2010). *The sociolinguistics of globalization*. Cambridge: Cambridge University Press.
Bourdieu, P. (1977). *Outline of a theory of practice*. Cambridge: Cambridge University Press.
Bourdieu, P. (1991). *Language and symbolic power*. Cambridge: Polity Press.

Chambers, J. K. (2002). Dynamics of dialect convergence. *Journal of Sociolinguistics*, 6(1), 117–130.
Chun, E. W. (2001). The construction of White, Black, and Korean American identities through African American vernacular English. *Journal of Linguistic Anthropology*, 11(1), 52–64.
Cornips, L. (2008). Loosing grammatical gender in Dutch: The result of bilingual acquisition and/or an act of identity? *International Journal of Bilingualism*, 12(1/2), 105–124.
Coulmas, F. (2005). *Sociolinguistics: The study of speakers' choices*. Cambridge: Cambridge University Press.
Doran, M. (2004). Negotiating between *Bourge* and *Racaille*: "Verlan" as youth identity practice in suburban Paris. In A. Pavlenko & A. Blackledge (Eds.), *Negotiation of identities in multilingual contexts* (pp. 93–124). Clevedon: Multilingual Matters.
Eckert, P. (2008). Where do Ethnolects stop? *International Journal of Bilingualism*, 12(1/2), 25–42.
Goffman, E. (1959). *The presentation of self in everyday life*. London: Penguin Books.
Heinrich, P. (2005). Things you gave to leave behind: The demise of "elegant writing" and the rise of Genbun Itchi style in Meiji-Period Japan. *Journal of Historical Pragmatics*, 6, 113–132.
Heinrich, P. (2012). *The making of monolingual Japan: Language ideology and Japanese modernity*. Bristol: Multilingual Matters.
Heinrich, P., & Galan, C. (Eds.). (2011). *Language life in Japan: Transformations and prospects*. London: Routledge.
Heinrich, P., & Yamashita, R. (2017). Tokyo: Standardization, ludic language use, and nascent superdiversity. In D. Smakman & P. Heinrich (Eds.), *Globalising sociolinguistics in the city: Urban language ecologies across the globe* (pp. 130–147). London: Routledge.
Hinnekamp, V., & Meng, K. (Eds.). (2012). *Sprachgrenzen überspringen: Sprachliche Hybriditat und polykulturelles Selbstverständnis*. Mannheim: Institut für Deutsche Sprache.
Hinskens, F. (1996). *Dialect levelling in Limburg: Structural and sociolinguistic aspects*. Tubingen: Niemeyer.
Inoue, F. (2011). Standardization and de-standardization processes in spoken Japanese. In P. Heinrich & C. Galan (Eds.), *Language life in Japan: Transformations and prospects* (pp. 109–123). London: Routledge.
Kaube, J. (2012, February, 28). Heute geh ich Diktat. *Frankfurter Allgemeine Zeitung*.
Kingston, M. (2000). *Dialects in danger: Rural dialect attrition in the East Angelian County of Suffolk* (Master thesis). Essex University, UK.
Kinsui, S. (2003). *Vācharu nihongo, yakuwarigo no nazo* [Virtual Japanese. The miracle of role language]. Tokyo: Iwanami.
Kroskrity, P. V. (2000). *Regimes of language*. Santa Fe: School of American Research Press.
Löffler, H. (2010). *Germanistische Soziolinguistik*. Berlin: Erich Schmidt Verlag.
Maher, J. C. (2005). Metroethnicity, language and the principle of cool. *International Journal of the Sociology of Language*, 2005(175/176), 83–102.
Milroy, J. (2001). Language ideologies and the consequences of standardization. *Journal of Sociolinguistics*, 5(4), 530–555.
Nettle, D. (1999). *Linguistic diversity*. Oxford: Oxford University Press.
NINJAL, National Institute of Japanese Language and Linguistics. (2013). *Dai-yonkai Tsuruoka-shi ni okeru gengo chōsa, kekka to gaiyō* [Fourth survey in Tsuruoka City: Results and summary]. Tokyo: NINJAL.
Pountain, D., & Robins, D. (2000). *Cool rules: Anatomy of an attitude*. London: Reaktion Books.

Rampton, B. (2005). *Crossings: Language and ethnicity among adolescents*. Manchester: St. Jerome Publishing.
Schieffelin, B. B., Woolard, K. A., & Kroskrity, P. V. (Eds.). (1998). *Language ideologies: Practice and theory*. Oxford: Oxford University Press.
Sibata, T. (1977). Hyōjungo, kyōtsūgo, hōgen [Standard language, common language, dialect]. In Bunkachō [Cultural Agency] (Ed.), *Kotoba shīrizu* (volume 6). *Hyōjungo to hōgen* (pp. 22–32). Tokyo: Bunkachō.
Silverstein, M. (2003). Indexical order and the dialectics of sociolinguistic life. *Language and Communication*, *23*, 193–229.
Smakman, D. (2012). The definition of the standard language: A survey in seven countries. *International Journal of the Sociology of Language*, *218*, 25–58.
Tanaka, Y. (2011). *Hōgen kosupure no jidai* [The age of dialect guise]. Tokyo: Iwanami.
Tanaka, Y., Hayashi, N., Maeda, T., & Aizawa, M. (2016). *Ichiman-nin kara mita saishin no hōgen, kyōtsūgo ishiki* [Latest trends in nationwide language consciousness and standard language of 10,000 People]. Tokyo: NINJAL.
Trudgill, P. (1984). *Sociolinguistics* (2nd ed.). London: Penguin Books.
Wiese, H. (2012). *Kiezdeutsch: Ein neuer Dialekt entsteht*. München: Beck.

13

LANGUAGE AND IDENTITY IN SIWA OASIS

Indexing belonging, localness, and authenticity in a small minority community

Valentina Serreli

Introduction

This chapter discusses the changing meaning indexed by the languages of a community characterised by multilingualism and language contact. It endorses a social constructivist approach to identity (Bucholtz & Hall, 2004; Gumperz, 1982; Ochs, 1992; 1993) and draws on the concepts of indexicality and orders of indexicality (Collins, 2011; Eckert, 2008; Johnstone, 2010; Ochs, 1992; Silverstein, 2003) to explore the values attached to local and superposed languages in Siwa.

The social constructivist approach to identity assumes that social identities do not exist *a priori* as independent variables, but that they are constructed during the communicative process, and that the association between linguistic features and social categories is a sequence of semiotic associations (Gumperz, 1982; Ochs, 1992; 1993). Moreover, language does not reflect one's culture and identity, but it is a fundamental resource for cultural and identity production (Bucholtz & Hall, 2004, p. 382). In fact, linguistic forms can be used to evoke or create social meanings or, in other words, they *index* meanings (Bucholtz & Hall, 2004; Johnstone, 2010; Ochs, 1992; Silverstein, 2003). More specifically, as argued by Silverstein (2003), social meaning is created through the way in which macro-sociological categories are evoked in micro-level interaction, that is, in situated communicative practices (Collins, 2011; Eckert, 2008). In other words, "social meaning is based upon (indexically) understood regularities between language use and social orders" (Collins, 2011, p. 411).

Silverstein's (2003) orders of indexicality follow Labov's distinction between indicators, that is, categories which speakers are not necessarily conscious of; markers, variables that have attracted speakers' attention; and stereotypes, variables characterised by a higher level of consciousness and subject to metapragmatic discussion (Eckert, 2008, p. 463). In Silverstein's terms, indicators are first-order indexes, while markers and stereotypes become second-order indexes, because they are available to the speakers, who can use them to create social meaning.

Johnstone fruitfully uses indexicality to explain how given variables became used and usable by speakers for "self-conscious, performed identity work" (2010, p. 397). Starting from the assumption that renewed attention to the local language is an inevitable result of globalisation, she demonstrates how local speech forms became, firstly, markers of correctness and, secondly, indexes of localness, as they are consciously used to perform the Pittburghese identity (2010, pp. 387–388). Johnstone argues that mobility and contact prompt both dialect levelling and the awareness of dialectal differences, and that such awareness is followed by metapragmatic practices that create new social meanings for the variables, that is, n+1th-order indexicality. The process described by Johnstone (2010) is very pertinent to our discussion, because it can clearly explain the process that leads the local language to become, at first, associated with given social features attributed to the local population (e.g., lack of education, rurality, conservatism) and, secondly, a positive index of (consciously performed) local identity through capitalising on the concepts of peripherality, localness, and authenticity.

A good number of publications have recently been devoted to the study of multilingualism and globalisation in "the peripheries" (e.g., Pietikäinen & Kelly-Holmes, 2013a) and to the language endangerment discourses that flourish within or about linguistic minorities (e.g., Duchêne & Heller, 2007). According to Pietikäinen and Kelly-Holmes (2013b, pp. 2–4), "centre-periphery is a common spatial metaphor used to describe and explain the unequal distribution of power in the economy, society, and polity" and, although a fixed divide has become problematic in the age of globalisation, the ideas of centre and periphery are still powerful. The periphery acquired a new value related to its perceived authenticity and exoticism and, within the new forms of economy that developed in the peripheries in the age of globalisation, "authenticity has become a necessary capital for both political mobilisation and economic development" (Pietikäinen, 2013, p. 77). Moreover, peripheries are also ideally connected with heritage, because both of them are located in the past: as put by Pujolar (2013, p. 56), "the concept of heritage is indexical of peripherality within the framework of modernity" and, therefore, the peripheral communities concerned can easily invest in a conception of identity as heritage through the commodification of cultural representations, among which are included the local languages, that acquire an added value as "enduring relics of state-building, industrialization, and modernization more generally" (Pujolar, 2013, p. 72).

This chapter explains the meaning acquired by languages in the Siwa Oasis with reference to the theoretical framework of indexicality, and accounts for the emergence of processes of commodification of culture and identity proper of the globalising peripheries, similar to those outlined above. Specifically, after outlining the studied area and the research methodology, it discusses how the local Siwi language has come to index Siwanness, which is connoted as a site of authenticity, characterised by a slow(er) and more traditional lifestyle in harmony with the environment.

The Oasis of Siwa: background information

Siwa, together with the smaller oasis of el-Gara situated about 100 km northeast, represents the sole Berber enclave within Egypt. Situated in the Western Desert, about 50 km away from the Libyan border, it is connected to the closest city of Marsa Matruh by a paved road that was completed in the 1980s.

The combined population of Siwa and el-Gara exceeds 28,000 inhabitants, mostly residing in Siwa (personal communication, Governorate of Marsa Matruh, 2015). The oasis dwellers consist of three groups, named Siwans, Bedouins, and Egyptians. Siwans are the Berber portion of the population and the one regarded as "local"; they represent the majority group and are divided into ten tribes, one of which resides in el-Gara. Bedouins constitute a tribe that claims lineage ties with the Awlād ʿAli and settled in Siwa in the early twentieth century (Bliss, 1984, p. 57). Finally, the appellative "maṣriyyīn" is used to refer to nonlocal Egyptians who have moved to Siwa from different regions of the country, mostly for working purposes.[1] This classification subtends lay people's discourses to the extent that it became automatic, but more detailed numbers are not available because the censuses do not report Egyptian citizens' change of residence within the country's borders.

Great distance and the absence of infrastructure kept Siwa and its inhabitants apart from their fellow Egyptians until the last century. In fact, in spite of the oasis' incorporation into the Egyptian political and administrative system through a negotiation between the state and local actors during the nineteenth century (Ellis, 2012), it was not until the second half of the twentieth century that the circulation of people, goods, and knowledge began to end its isolation. Besides the building of the asphalt road mentioned above, Siwa's opening was favoured by a number of other factors, such as the diffusion of radio, television and – at a later time – internet; Siwans' greater mobility (regular recruitment into the Egyptian army after the 1952 Revolution (Cole & Altorky, 1998, p. 72), enrolment in the universities of the major Egyptian cities); and the growing presence of non-locals in the oasis (workers, public employees, tourists) and the consequent growth of intermarriage rates.

Geographical and social isolation preserved a community characterised by dense and multiplex social networks (Milroy, 1980). This network structure favoured the maintenance of cultural elements and traditional practices, including the local Siwi language, and the development of a sense of group and distinctiveness which is still perceptible. The field research (Serreli, 2016) shows, in agreement with other scholars (e.g., Schiattarella, 2015; Souag, 2013), that Siwi remains the major language of communication within the group: both horizontal and vertical use are mostly maintained and still prescribed by the community's normative system. However, the process of change triggered by the factors listed above affected the oasis dwellers' everyday life in many ways, modifying both the economic sector and the quality of social network characterising the community. It also favoured Arabisation. As a result, almost all Siwi speakers, with the exception of some preschool-aged children and elderly women, speak Arabic in addition to Siwi. However, Arabic proficiency varies greatly across the population: Siwans who are young, more highly educated, or likely to speak Arabic more often are fluent, while at the other end of the spectrum there are people who only have a passive knowledge. Moreover, while elderly Siwans are more likely to target a Bedouin Arabic of the kind spoken by the Awlād ʿAli tribe, young and adult Siwans target Egyptian Arabic. In the process of Arabisation, Siwa does not represent an exception in the North African context, where the transitions of other Berber-speaking communities from Berber monolingualism to a Berber/Arabic bilingualism followed similar patterns (Kossmann, 2013). Indeed, Arabisation was a gradual process which is still not completed, and the sociolinguistic situation is ever-changing, as the impact of globalisation, with faster socioeconomic changes, further affects the values and functions of the languages in use (Serreli, forthcoming).

Methodology

The data presented in the chapter was collected in the frame of a doctoral research project aimed at investigating the sociolinguistics of the Siwa Oasis from a double perspective, the insiders' and the researcher's. The research falls into the field of folk linguistics (Niedzielsky & Preston, 2000), a subfield of sociolinguistics emphasising the study of non-specialists' perspective on linguistic facts. A qualitative approach was preferred in order to provide an in-depth understanding of the studied phenomena and to be able to account for individual nuances.

Data was elicited through interviews (direct approach) and obtained through the technique of participant observation, within the so-called "societal treatment approach" (Garret, 2006) or "anthropological-cultural approach" (Preston, 2011, p. 18), between 2013 and 2015. My participation in the community's daily life allowed me to establish a relationship of trust with the informants, to acquire the local contextualisation, and to better observe people's social relationships and linguistic behaviour. The network of contacts is very rich. It reproduces the dense and multiplex structure of the community's network at large, important because informants' interpersonal ties are useful background data for understanding individual behaviour. Interviews and informal conversations sought to elicit speakers' overt comments about their own sociolinguistic identity and the place and values of Siwi and Arabic varieties in the community. 61 recorded interviews were conducted, unstructured or semi-structured and varying greatly in length (five minutes to two hours) according to the interviewee's characteristics. Interviewees are male (3/4) and female (1/4), aged between 9 and 70 years, and they have different educational backgrounds, from uneducated to PhDs. Most of the interviewees are Siwi native speakers (3/4); the remaining interviewees are native speakers of Bedouin or Egyptian Arabic (Serreli, 2016).

The chapter presents data drawn from both interviews and observation. A number of extracts from interviews are reported and commented on. Extracts are numbered progressively and the reported words are preceded by the first letter of the interviewee's name ("V." precedes the interviewer's words). Overall, 21 interviewees are quoted. Table 13.1 provides information about the interviewees' sex, age, first language, degree of education, and profession at the time of the interview; the last column provides the number that identifies the extracts in the text.

TABLE 13.1 Interviewees' information.

	Name	Sex	Age	Family language	Education	Profession	Extract nr.
Int.-1	H.	m	40s	Siwi	low-educated	farmer	(1) (27) (34)
Int.-2	A.	m	40s	Siwi	mid-educated	farmer	(2)
	M.	m	40s	Siwi	mid-educated	farmer	
Int.-3	M.	m	30s	Siwi	high-educated	receptionist	(3)(23)
Int.-4	M.	m	70s	Siwi	low-educated	unemployed	(4) (7)
Int.-5	O.	m	20s	Siwi	low-educated	military service	(5) (9) (17) (20)
Int.-6	A.	m	40s	EgAr	mid-educated	employee/tourist	(6)
Int.-7	K.	m	late teens	Siwi	low-educated	workman	(8)
Int.-8	H.	f	20s	Siwi	low-educated	housewife	(10) (15)
Int.-9	A.	m	20s	Siwi	high-educated	employee/municipal	(11) (30) (32)
Int.-10	S.	m	40s	Siwi	mid-educated	farmer	(12)
Int.-11	S.	m	40s	Siwi	high-educated	teacher	(13) (21)
Int.-12	A.	f	40s	Siwi	low-educated	housewife	(14)(25)
Int.-13	B.	m	40s	Siwi	low-educated	workman	(16)
Int.-14	M.	m	30s	Siwi	high-educated	teacher	(18)
Int.-15	M.	m	40s	Siwi	mid-educated	farmer	(19)
Int.-16	M.	f	20s	EgAr/Siwi	high-educated	employee/cultural	(22) (31)
Int.-17	M.	m	30s	Siwi	high-educated	employee/municipal	(24) (29)
Int.-18	Z.	f	30s	Siwi	low-educated	housewife	(26)
Int.-19	M.	m	30s	BdAr/Siwi	high-educated	employee/education	(28)
Int.-20	I.	m	20s	Siwi	high-educated	employee/cultural	(33)

The major language of the fieldwork was Egyptian Arabic; Siwi was sometimes used in basic everyday conversations with elderly speakers who were not at ease while speaking Arabic, or to signal proximity and familiarity within my network of contacts. The interviews were likewise conducted in Egyptian Arabic, but this seems not to have affected the interviewees' accounts, which are consistent with data collected by other researchers using Siwi (Souag, personal communication, 2016); moreover, the interviews were read and analysed on the basis of the background knowledge of the field and the informants that was acquired during the fieldwork. All the extracts are reported only in English due to space constraints.

Language and identity in Siwa

First-order indexicality: group membership

First-order indexes indicate membership in a group or population based on regional or geographical criteria, and are therefore usually agreed upon by the entire population.

Siwi identifies a speaker as Siwan. The centuries-long correspondence between a people, a land, and a language, helped by the remoteness and partial isolation of the oasis, favoured lay people's perception of a straightforward and automatic connection between the Siwi language and Siwan group. Therefore, Siwi signals membership in the Siwan group and is a criterion of group inclusion and exclusion.

(1) H.: We are from Siwa and we speak the Siwi speech!
(2) M.: If one doesn't speak Siwi he is not Siwan.
[...] A.: Because he doesn't speak our language or wear our clothes.
[...] M.: In order to be Siwan one must speak the Siwi language and, of course, the Siwan customs are not found anywhere else!

Siwi is perceived as a specificity distinguishing Siwans from fellow Egyptians and from any "other" by both Siwans and non-Siwans, as is shown by the correspondence between extracts (3), (4), and (5), drawn from interviews with Siwans, and extract (6), drawn from the interview with a non-Siwan man who has been living in Siwa for more than a decade.

(3) M.: I mean, as nationality we are all Egyptian, of course, but I say "Egyptian" or "Siwan" based on the different language.
(4) M.: This language is only in Siwa, only in the oasis.
(5) O.: We are the only people who speak the Siwi language in the whole Arab Republic of Egypt! And what about Siwa's traditions? They are unique and its speech is unique!
(6) A.: This is something, what can I say. . . it's theirs, [added in English] special for them.

The Siwi language is regarded as the Siwans' prerogative, to the extent that the speakers underline the unlikeliness that a non-Siwan can reach a perfect fluency, even if he acquires Siwi at an early age. The excerpts below show how an elder interviewee referring to old times (excerpt (7)), is echoed by much younger interviewees referring to the present time (excerpts (8) and (9)).

(7) M.: It is unlikely that people speak their [Siwans'] language... Their language is difficult, nobody can speak it, very few speak it.
(8) K.: If [a Siwan] speaks with him a little bit and then he leaves, he might not understand that he is Egyptian, but if he speaks with him more, if the conversation becomes long, he understands very quickly... because for sure he will get a word wrong!
(9) O.: No matter how he tries he won't get the language exactly! ... There are sounds he cannot pronounce!

Siwi is usually referred to as the community's language, rather than the individual's, both by using first person plural verbs and pronouns (e.g., *luġit-na*, "our language") and by explicitly stating it. For instance, in the extracts reported below, the interviewees point out the pervasiveness of Siwi within the geographical and social spaces of the oasis and its natural acquisition by the new generations.

(10) H.: This is our language, something widespread, it is not something limited to one or two as someone special; no, this is something widespread; anyone you see, [with] anyone you see from Siwa you speak this language.
(11) A.: At home and in the society and everywhere here you speak this language.... You live all your life here with the Siwi language – except if you meet, for example, an Arab and speak with him – just in that case.
(12) S.: The child, as he's born, he speaks Siwi straight away... he hears his mother's and his father's speech and he speaks as well! ... He speaks Siwi naturally.
(13) S.: It is a language acquired from the peers and the environment... we acquire the language from each other.

In a situation of widespread monolingualism, speaking Siwi was neither a matter of choice nor something Siwans thought about and were conscious of. The lack of options made Siwi the language of everyday communication for everybody; its use was a customary, unquestioned practice and an unwritten norm. Nowadays, Siwi is the only available means of communication for only a minority of speakers, but despite the availability of Arabic, the automatism underlying the use of Siwi is maintained among a large portion of the population. The two examples reported below show that the automatism of speaking Siwi is almost the same for a 60-year-old monolingual woman, referred to in (14), and a woman in her mid-twenties who can speak Arabic, referred to in (15): the first one had no choice, as she only spoke Siwi, but the second one does not question the use of Siwi despite knowing Arabic.

(14) A.: My mother, for example, she never saw any Egyptian or any foreigner: she was born Siwan and she lived with Siwans, so how would she speak [Arabic]!?
(15) V.: If you have another son or daughter, will you teach them Siwi or both [Siwi and Arabic]?
H.: I don't know. . . I'll speak Siwi; at home, all of us speak Siwi!

Reactions such as the one in (15) are not exceptional among informants and interviewees. These unspoken reactions of astonishment communicate the fact that speaking Siwi is not an issue that anyone discusses. They are important because they reveal the unmarkedness of the language choice. At this level, speaking Siwi is maintained as a customary practice; Siwi indexes local belonging and no added value is advocated. The recurrent idea that speaking Siwi is a habit is expressed with verbs such as 'it'awwid 'ala ("to become accustomed to"), or 'itrabba fi ("to be reared in"), which point to the use of Siwi in in-group interactions as a spontaneous, unintentional, and undeliberate practice, irrespective of the interlocutors' proficiency in Arabic.

(16) B.: That's it, we're used to it, I can't. . . you can't address a Siwan in Arabic.
(17) O.: Because we're used to the fact that this is our language, we're used to it and that's it.
(18) M.: Because this is the language that we practiced; this is the language we were reared in, basically.

The Arabisation process was delayed and slowed down in Siwa because the community's dense and multiplex social network reduced their need for, interest in, and access to outside resources, since most people maintained a traditional lifestyle characterised by interpersonal connections within the group. Moreover, Arabisation was not a homogeneous process. Although nowadays almost all Siwans can speak some form of Arabic, the use of Siwi within the group remains undeliberate and unquestioned for most of them. It is in this sense that, at this level, Siwi is a first-order index of membership in the Siwan group without carrying additional social meanings that people are aware of or discuss.

Second-order indexicality: social status and social relationships

Second-order indexes are variables that have gained speakers' attention; that is, people are conscious of them and may use them to create social meaning. As stated by Bassiouney (2014, p. 108), "second-order indexes are indexes that are the product of ideologies and attitudes, rather than habits." As we are in the attitudinal field here, we do not deal with reality, but instead with the perception of reality. Moreover, languages and linguistic traits are not evaluated according to their intrinsic qualities but are based on the perception of their speakers. Also, ideology underlies people's evaluation of the speakers; this evaluation becomes stereotypical and reflects the perception of the group to which they belong (Edwards, 1999, p. 103). Unlike first-order indexes, second-order indexes are not necessarily agreed upon by the whole population concerned.

Globalisation processes depend on the availability and accessibility of "infrastructures for globalisation" that enable the connection between local events and translocal processes, and whose distribution is not homogeneous (Wang, Spotti, Juffermans, Kroon, Cornips, & Blommaert, 2014, p. 29). In the peripheries, globalisation is favoured by three types of infrastructure: the new media and communication technologies, the emergence of new forms of economic activity, and new (re)productions of local identity formations (2014, p. 30). As new forms of communication and of economic activities spread and developed in Siwa, they produced new situations and contexts in which new sociolinguistic dynamics arose, characterised by specific rules and power relationships between languages.

Specifically, as Arabic becomes dominant in new contexts and activities and Siwi remains dominant in traditional ones, Siwans start establishing semiotic associations between the languages, on one hand, and their (stereotypical) speakers, on the other, based on the contexts the languages are usually spoken in. Second-order indexes arose in the new context of sociolinguistic differentiation, because the availability of more than one language and the division of functions and domains of use between them create semiotic associations that are adopted by the speakers in a productive way. This means that speakers start to consciously and deliberately choose a given language in order to look or sound a given way. Second-order indexicality emerges during the passage from an unconscious to a deliberate language use.

Siwi second-order indexes: group solidarity, conservatism, backwardness

Siwi becomes a second-order index of group solidarity as speakers become aware that speaking Siwi shortens the distance between interlocutors, allows ease in intergenerational relationships, and puts the interlocutors at the same level. They also become aware of Siwi's role as a unique code of in-group interaction and as an instrument of group cohesion, and start assessing their loyalty to the language on the basis of an integrative attitude, that is, a wish to identify with the group. Furthermore, as Siwi is the sole language perfectly mastered by all and only Siwans, it aptly represents a community traditionally and stereotypically characterised by commonality and members' equality, on one hand, and uniqueness, on the other.

(19) M.: It is the language of the exchange of interactions between us. . . . If it wasn't important nowadays anyone who gets married and has children would speak Arabic. . . . They could say, "Ah, Siwi is not important" and start speaking Arabic, but no, among us it is important!

(20) O.: Everybody speaks Siwi basically, because maybe if you speak Egyptian someone doesn't answer you and says, "Why are you speaking Egyptian? Why are you speaking Egyptian? Talk to me in our language directly!" So Siwi is first and foremost a language that we have to speak between ourselves!

(21) S.: Siwi now has become something needed just because one can't [. . .] I mean, as he is Siwan, not to speak Siwi at all will create a distance between him and his relatives and with the elders of the family.

This index is productive, because Siwi is learnt and used by mixed families' offspring and by non-native speakers who wish to be accepted within the group and conform to it, because the "folk notion of 'fitting in' is felt to be a very powerful force in language acquisition" (Niedzielsky & Preston, 2000, p. 257). Non-Siwans who are born in Siwa, live there from the time they are young, or marry a Siwan usually speak their Arabic variety with Siwans, but in some cases they may use Siwi in order not to let Arabic-speaking outsiders and visitors understand. Siwi may also be spoken routinely with Siwan women, because it indexes solidarity in the women's milieu, as exemplified in the two cases below.

1) A., about 50 years old, was born in Siwa to a non-Siwan family but she learnt Siwi, as her mother already had. She is fluent in both Egyptian Arabic and Siwi. Interestingly, she speaks Arabic with her husband and sons, but Siwi with her Siwan daughters-in-law.
2) M. is a bilingual girl in her late twenties, whose mother is Siwan and whose father is not. Despite speaking Siwi daily with her mother and sisters, she speaks Arabic for most of the day in her workplace and she confesses that she needs to force herself to speak a correct Siwi when dealing with Siwan girls from a peripheral village, because speaking Siwi would favour proximity to the girls, while speaking Arabic would give them the impression that she wants to show off:

(22) M.: They are girls and it is difficult for them to get close to me if I speak Arabic [. . .] I mean, there could be someone who would think that I was showing off [. . .] I don't want that [. . .] for me it is a habit [. . .] they already barely tolerate me because my father is Egyptian [. . .] Otherwise they would say "Why?"

Because it remains dominant in traditional activities, Siwi becomes associated with tradition and also acquires the negative indexes of backwardness and provincialism. The negative indexes are not commented on very much by the interviewees, who prefer to express a positive judgement about Arabic rather than a negative one about Siwi, as discussed later. However, I gathered some interesting comments among teenagers with whom I established a rapport of trust during the fieldwork, which reveal their fatigue of continuing to be "that Siwan," that is, to perform the Siwan identity as requested by the community's norms, including the use of Siwi among members. I will provide two examples.

1) A girl about age 10, raised in Egyptian Arabic within a mixed family, was very happy to tell me that her older sister could teach Arabic to her daughter because her husband, despite being from a Siwi-speaking family, was not a "typical Siwan," meaning that "not everything has to be Siwan, Siwan, Siwan!"

2) A teenaged Siwi-speaking girl confessed that she does not like to greet women with the traditional formulaic Siwan greeting in use among women and girls, preferring to it the faster Egyptian Arabic "Hello, how are you?"

These girls belong to families that are quite wealthy and concerned with education. However, the same feelings have begun to circulate among other segments of the young Siwan population, for whom it may be only an unattainable wish so far. In any case, this is not something Siwan people like to stress while talking to outsiders.

Egyptian Arabic second-order indexes: educatedness, urbanness, progress

Arabic is considered a resource that has spread in Siwa because of its instrumentality. It is used in schools, in public and non-traditional working activities, and to communicate with outsiders. It is, therefore, more frequently used and better mastered by some categories of speakers than by others, according to socioeconomic features. As it becomes associated with specific contexts and speakers, Egyptian Arabic becomes a second-order index of educatedness, urbanness, open-mindedness, and progress, because some speakers may deliberately speak Arabic in order to sound educated, urban, open-minded, or modern. These associations may affect the choices, whether actual or only declared, of some speakers who start speaking Arabic in domains where Siwi is the unmarked choice and the one encouraged by the community's tacit norms, such as the domestic domain and in childrearing. These indexes are especially productive among mid-educated parents in their twenties, but also among teenaged Siwans, who in some cases appeared fascinated by the city lifestyle, which in their case is more imagined than actually known.

In many cases, it is disapproving speakers who explicitly point out the existence and productivity of these indexes, distancing themselves from such "deviant" practices and underlining their own criticism.

(23) M.: They look at it in the perspective of progress: a person who speaks the Arabic language is more advanced, I mean, or if I speak a certain language you feel I am at a higher level. So perhaps they look at this fact in this way: when one speaks Arabic he is open-minded, advanced, better. [. . .] Perhaps they consider this to be civilisation and progress and speaking Siwi is backwardness, for example.

(24) M.: Some families imagine – and this is wrong from my personal point of view – they imagine that civilisation and urbanness are represented by the shift from the Siwi language [. . .] especially now, some families teach their children to speak Arabic.

The ideas of educatedness, urbanness, open-mindedness, and progress are represented by the cover idea of Egyptianness, because lifestyle innovation and change are often perceived as an Egyptianization of customs. This is believed to go hand in hand with a loss of the Siwan traditions, customs, and some specific behavioural and personality traits, such as men's trustworthiness and women's modesty. With reference to the Cairene context, Bassiouney (2014: 359) states that "showing off knowledge of English in a context in which speakers do not have the same access to it implies a lack of identification with the community and a less positive stance towards members of this community." Accordingly, a Siwan's use of Egyptian Arabic among Siwans is perceived as a desire on the part of the speaker to praise and distinguish himself within the group and to sound or look like an Egyptian, where "Egyptian" is stereotypically meant as having the properties of educatedness and so on. The following extracts offer a glimpse of the way these ideas were elaborated and expressed by the interviewees.

(25) A.: Everybody was the same, there wasn't one like this and one like that. Now they've developed [...] Now it's over, they've become Egyptians!
V.: What do you mean by "They've become Egyptians"?
A.: Yes that's it, they've forgotten everything [...] they've forgotten customs and traditions now.

(26) Z.: When there is a ceremony and you go any place, it is like, I mean, they say, people say, "Look how she speaks Arabic to her children! [...] Look how they want to act like Egyptians." You know, people...

(27) H.: When I enter my house I speak to my children, I speak with this and this one, we can't speak Arabic! One would say "What is this? Why is he speaking Arabic? Are we Egyptians or what?"

(28) M.: If we speak Arabic or another language, someone says, "What does he think? Does he think he is better than other people?" He [a Siwan] has to speak Siwi.

Borrowing Johnstone's (2010) terminology, Siwi and Egyptian Arabic acquire social meaning, i.e., they become second-order indexes of, respectively, group solidarity/conservatism and Egyptianness, when they are taken up as sociolinguistic resources and become productive. These indexes may not be found across the whole population. They can be insignificant for those on the fringes who are less familiar with Arabic or less actively multilingual and, consequently, they are less conscious of this variation.

Third-order indexicality: identity performance

Third-order indexes are the result of an ideological move. Meanings are deliberately attached to linguistic variables and varieties, which become symbols of a given identity and are consciously used to perform it (Eckert, 2008; Johnstone, 2010).

As new goods and practices became available to most Siwans and speaking Egyptian Arabic became widespread, what was once an innovation or a status indicator became the norm. Against this backdrop, among some fringes of the population, especially educated and wealthy Siwans aged between 20 and 35 years, Egyptian Arabic loses its appeal and Siwi undergoes a reallocation of meaning, as first- and second-order indexes are taken up and elaborated. In fact, based on its indexes of group membership (first-order) and uniqueness and conservatism (second-order), all of which derive from its strong link to the Siwan group, the Siwi language is praised and promoted as a symbol of the group's identity. Since this new association is deliberate, conscious, and subject to metapragmatic discussion, Siwi becomes a third-order index of Siwanness, where Siwanness is meant as a stereotypical Siwan cultural identity.

The interview data reveals the novelty of the circulation of these ideas among a minority of young people. The "rightness" of this new attitude is often emphasized by opposing it to the "misbehaviour" of those who praise Egyptian Arabic, or it is presented as something needed because the Siwan tradition and the Siwi language are being lost as a result of the inevitable lifestyle innovation.

(29) M.: Now some families teach their children to speak Arabic [. . .] and this is wrong, of course, in my opinion, because it is as if I am selling my identity. As for me, I am proud of Siwi and I teach Siwi to my children, and very often it happens that I'm speaking Arabic and a Siwan word comes out of my mouth as a consequence of my feeling of belonging to Siwa [. . .] every human has his own identity and he is supposed to preserve it.
[. . .] There is the idea of preserving the Siwi language now, I mean, it comes up now. There are many young people like this!

(30) A.: The Siwi language is the language of our grandparents and our language and I respect it and I am proud of it [. . .] There are people who tell you "What do we need Siwi for? It's not needed." [. . .] I think that this means lessening the language [. . .] it would mean that I'm not proud of my language [. . .] No, I am proud of it and I am proud of being Siwan.

(31) M.: It's not that they [Siwans] abandon things. Things got lost [. . .] The circumstances of life changed [. . .] You feel that change goes on by itself [. . .] We aren't happy to the extent that young people started going back to the past. They started to talk about how they could work together to see what is in their hands to bring it back and [. . .] there began to be associations with the purpose of bringing Siwa back.

These ideas grow up within a global awakening of interest towards local languages and authenticity (Pietikäinen & Kelly-Holmes, 2013a) and the spread of public discourses of language endangerment that, as argued by Jaffe (2007, pp. 59–61), are associated with language-rights advocacy and emphasise the iconic relationship between language and cultural groups' identity, or between language and culture. Similarly, Cameron (2007, p. 280) points out that the core of the preservationist argument "lies in the perception of a natural bond between a community and the mother tongue that uniquely expresses its culture and worldview," which makes preservation a natural right.

However, discourses of heritage preservation and heritage-making gain ground in Siwa mostly because of their connection to the touristic sector. Tourism has become very important in the economy of the oasis, because "peripherality is mobilized as a resource in tourism, particularly with the marketization of local landscapes and local produce that draw their value from their scarcity in urban centres" (Pujolar, 2013, p. 72). In 1998, some partnerships were established that launched business investment projects with a sustainable-development perspective (Battesti, 2009). So far, a number of projects have been started to preserve Siwa's intangible and material heritage. For example, the *patrimonialisation* of the traditional clay architecture represents the return of tradition in a reinvented form aimed at giving to the oasis's space a visual identity that satisfies tourists' quest for authenticity, despite the fact that the local population's preference has moved towards the use of white limestone gypsum in the past few decades (Battesti, 2009). Another example is the project Siwa & Tangier,[2] carried out with the aim of preserving and enhancing the local cultural heritage, including the Siwi language and the Berber oral tradition. These projects have had an impact on the local population. Some Siwans, mostly those directly involved, have internalised such narratives and reproduce them, as in the examples given below.

(32) A.: It is not possible for me to speak [Siwi] and lose my customs and traditions. This is not good [...] I can't keep up customs and traditions without my language. They are linked together, because each one of them completes the other.

(33) I.: For me Siwa is not only desert, land, and my family. Siwa is customs and traditions, language [...] It is very important, because if the language disappeared, got lost, you would come here and see that all the customs disappeared with it!

Siwa has become the destination of a cultural tourism made up of "backpackers" who are looking for an authentic encounter with the local population and culture (Battesti, 2009). As Siwans became aware of this, echoing global discourses in favour of diversity and authenticity, they start to emphasize the specificity of Siwa as its major strength in the touristic market, and to present Siwi as an added cultural value.

(34) S.: The language gives us distinctiveness, it gives us specificity, it also characterises us a little bit [...] Anyone who comes to Siwa also hears this language, even from Egypt. A tourist who comes from Egypt, from Cairo [...] he feels he is in a place different from Cairo; he hears a different language and sees different customs and traditions [...] it is something good!

Siwa, like other peripheries, acquires an added value as a provider of "authenticity, slow(er) lifestyle, solitude, and living with the challenges and opportunities afforded by the local environment" and is perceived as "different, exotic, and other-worldly" (Pietikäinen & Kelly-Holmes, 2013b, p. 7). The recent global attention to minorities and peripheries has given Siwans the opportunity to capitalise on longstanding feelings of distinctiveness and uniqueness. Since "ethnicity as periphery is often signalled or iconized through the tokenistic use of local languages" (Pujolar, 2013, p. 72), the Siwi language, which was once merely an indicator of group membership, and then a marker of conservatism and backwardness, becomes in the new framework an identity maker and a symbol of Siwanness. In the new discourse, living practices become cultural heritage. The use and maintenance of Siwi is advocated among other practices, but even more strongly than these others. This stance requires an awareness that is not yet widespread, and it is only found among those who are acquainted with revival actors in the touristic and cultural sectors.

Conclusion

The chapter has shown that Siwi, the local language of the Siwa Oasis, which is a minority within the country but widely spoken in its community, has different levels of indexicality.

At first-order indexicality, the language simply indicates membership in the community: speaking Siwi identifies a speaker as member of the group, but it is an undeliberate practice that does not carry any additional social meaning.

At second-order indexicality, languages become social markers. Siwi indexes group solidarity and conservatism, but also backwardness; Egyptian Arabic indexes modernness, educatedness, and open-mindedness. Speakers stereotypically associate to languages the social features attributed to their speakers: these associations are ideological and productive, because on the basis of the indexes, speakers start using languages deliberately to convey social meaning.

At third-order indexicality, Siwi indexes Siwanness, that is, a consciously performed Siwan identity, characterised by the preservation of specific cultural elements among which is the Siwi language. The mechanism underlying this ideological step was explained throughout the chapter: capitalising on peripherality and localness, the Siwi language becomes a site of authenticity as the result of processes of commodification of language and identity for economic purposes.

The indexical orders originated at different moments, but they are not linearly descendant from one another (Eckert, 2008, p. 464). Moreover, nowadays they are found simultaneously within the community, which is not monolithic but shows a degree of social variability. The Siwi language remains strongly and specifically associated with the group at all indexical orders. What varies as the result of the interplay of local and global trends is the type of relationship established between the language and the speakers, which gradually becomes more conscious, negotiated, and ideological. As a consequence, Siwi acquires social meanings among speakers according to their social features and ideological positioning. Creation and reallocation of meaning for languages are processes in constant and accelerating evolution in Siwa, and further study should prove very fruitful.

Notes

** Special thanks to my friends and colleagues Dr. Valentina Schiattarella and Dr. Luca D'Anna for the fruitful exchange of ideas and their comments on the draft of this paper.
1 Hereafter the terms Siwan(s), Bedouin(s), and Egyptian(s) are used in the sense indicated here, because it is in this sense that they were used and understood during fieldwork and data collection and analysis. The population as a whole will be referred to with unambiguous expressions such as "the oasis dwellers", or "the oasis population".
2 Euromed Heritage التراث الوروبي المتوسطي URL: www.euromedheritage.net/intern.cfm?lng=en&menuID=12&submenuID=13&idproject=47. Last accessed on 27 December 2016.

References

Bassiouney, R. (2014). *Language and identity in modern Egypt*. Edinburgh: Edinburgh University Press.
Battesti, V. (2009). De Siwa au Caire, la fabrique du patrimoine se nourrit du désir des autres. In O. Aboukorah & J. G. Leturcq (Eds.), *Égypte/monde arabe 5–6, Troisième série, Pratiques du patrimoine en Egypte et au Sudan* (pp. 69–101). Cairo: CEDEJ.
Bliss, F. (1984). *Kulturwandel in der Oase Siwa* (2nd ed.). Bonn: PAS.
Bucholtz, M., & Hall, K. (2004). Language and identity. In A. Duranti (Ed.), *A companion to linguistic anthropology* (pp. 369–394). Malden, MA: Blackwell.
Cameron, D. (2007). Language endangerment and verbal hygiene: History, morality and politics. In A. Duchêne & M. Heller (Eds.), *Discourses of endangerment: Ideology and interest in the defense of languages* (pp. 268–285). London: Continuum.
Cole, D., & Altorky, S. (1998). *Bedouin, settlers, and holiday-makers: Egypt's changing northwest coast*. Cairo: The American University in Cairo Press.
Collins, J. (2011). Indexicalities of language contact in an era of globalization: Nagging with John Gumperz's legacy. *Text & Talk, 31*(4), 407–428.
Duchêne, A., & Heller, M. (Eds.). (2007). *Discourses of endangerment: Ideology and interest in the defense of languages*. London: Continuum.
Eckert, P. (2008). Variation and indexical field. *Journal of Sociolinguistics, 12*(4), 453–476.
Edwards, J. (1999). Refining our understanding of language attitudes. *Journal of Language and Social Psychology, 18*(1), 101–110.
Ellis, M. H. (2012). *Between empire and nation: The emergence of Egypt's Libyan borderland, 1941–1911*. (Unpublished doctoral dissertation). Princeton University, Princeton, NJ.
Garret, P. (2006). Language attitudes. In C. Llamas, L. Mullany, & P. Stockwell (Eds.), *The Routledge companion to sociolinguistics* (pp. 116–121). London/New York: Routledge.
Gumperz, J. (Ed.). (1982). *Language and social identity*. Cambridge: Cambridge University Press.
Jaffe, A. (2007). Discourses of endangerment: Contexts and consequences of essentializing discourses. In A. Duchêne & M. Heller (Eds.), *Discourses of endangerment: Ideology and interest in the defense of languages* (pp. 57–75). London: Continuum.
Johnstone, B. (2010). Indexing the local. In N. Coupland (Ed.), *The handbook of language and globalization* (pp. 386–405). Malden, MA: Blackwell Publishing.
Kossmann, M. (2013). *The Arabic influence on Northern Berber*. Leiden/Boston: Brill.
Milroy, L. (1980). *Language and social networks*. Oxford: Blackwell.
Niedzielsky, N., & Preston, D. R. (2000). *Folk linguistics*. Berlin: Mouton de Gruyter.
Ochs, E. (1992). Indexing gender. In A. Duranti & C. Goodwin (Eds.), *Rethinking context* (pp. 335–358). New York: Cambridge University Press.

Ochs, E. (1993). Constructing social identity: A language socialization perspective. *Research on Language and Social Interaction, 26*(3), 287–306.

Pietikäinen, S. (2013). Heteroglossic authenticity in Sàmi heritage tourism. In S. Pietikäinen & H. Kelly-Holmes (Eds.), *Multilingualism and the periphery* (pp. 77–94). Oxford: Oxford University Press.

Pietikäinen, S., & Kelly-Holmes, H. (2013b). Multilingualism and the periphery. In S. Pietikäinen & H. Kelly-Holmes (Eds.), *Multilingualism and the periphery* (pp. 1–16). Oxford: Oxford University Press.

Pietikäinen, S., & Kelly-Holmes, H. (Eds.). (2013a). *Multilingualism and the periphery*. Oxford: Oxford University Press.

Preston, D. R. (2011). Methods in (applied) folk linguistics: Getting into the minds of the tolk. *AILA Review, 24*, 15–39.

Pujolar, J. (2013). Tourism and gender in linguistic minority communities. In S. Pietikäinen & H. Kelly-Holmes (Eds.), *Multilingualism and the periphery* (pp. 55–76). Oxford: Oxford University Press.

Schiattarella, V. (2015). *Le berbère de Siwa: documentation, syntaxe et sémantique* (Unpublished doctoral dissertation). École pratique des Hautes Études, Paris.

Serreli, V. (2016). *Society, languages and ideologies in the Oasis of Siwa (Egypt): Listening to people's voices.* (Unpublished doctoral dissertation). University of Sassari and University of Aix-Marseille.

Serreli, V. (forthcoming). Globalization in the periphery: Arabization and the changing status of Siwi Berber in Siwa Oasis. In J. J. De Ruiter & K. Ziamari (Eds.), *Sociolinguistic studies, Special Issue: Arabic between tradition, globalization, and superdiversity*.

Silverstein, M. (2003). Indexical order and the dialectics of sociolinguistic life. *Language and Communication, 23*, 193–229.

Souag, L. (2013). *Berber and Arabic in Siwa (Egypt): A study in linguistic contact.* Colognen: Rüdiger Köppe Verlag.

Wang, X., Spotti, M., Juffermans, K., Kroon, S., Cornips, L., & Blommaert, J. (2014). Globalization in the margins: Towards a re-evaluation of language and mobility. *Applied Linguistics Review, 5*(1), 23–44. [pre-print version 10.1515/applirev-2014–0002]

PART IV
The media, dialect performance, and language variation

14

YOUTUBE YINZERS

Stancetaking and the performance of 'Pittsburghese'

Scott F. Kiesling

Performance, stance, class, gender

In 1966 William Labov produced a work on the pronunciation of /r/ in New York City department stores that was, to some extent, ethnographic: Labov was a participant observer in asking for items on a particular floor of a department store, and he was familiar with the conventions necessary to find a clerk and get their attention. After a productive afternoon of finding shoes, and with the support of recordings of interviews from the Lower East Side, Labov was able to show that working-class folks tend to vocalize their /r/s more than middle-class folks in New York City.

One reason Labov's paper is foundational to the sociolinguistic canon is that it seems clear that Labov was able to 'control' for what was happening: Everyone he talked to was a clerk talking to a customer and was giving directions to shoes, or shirts, or some other item sold by the store. While this equivalency seems on the face of it to be an unassailable fact, the question remains whether every clerk was approaching the task in the same way: How did these clerks relate to the relatively young man in a fairly conservative but firmly middle-class suit and tie? Was he treated with the deference due to the king, as the customer should be? Or was he treated merely as some dude asking a question (perhaps a question that could have been answered by checking a directory)? Or was he an incidental interaction that required little attention? Or did he ask a question the clerk was unsure of? These are all possible variations of stance that a salesclerk could take when answering such a question.

In this chapter I am going to explore the idea that local dialect is performed (in the acting sense of the word, Coupland's 2007 'high performance') when taking particular stances. I begin by asking what it means for performers to create a 'working-class' identity through dialect. As Austin famously noted (although in a somewhat limited sense), language is used by people to do things. One of the main things people do with language (I argue it is *the* main thing) is to create relationships with other people, ideas, and things. That is, they *take stances*. Here I will ask what kinds of stances dialect 'high performers' take when using a particular feature of local speech to create comedy. I suggest that although the feature does not entail the expression of a single stance all the time, it tends to be used to create a stance of simultaneous opposition and alignment. The feature is the falling question intonation (FQI) on interactionally-recognizable questions, and I show that they tend to use this intonation to take an oppositional stance that is framed as 'play.' That is, in many ways there is opposition but not much investment in that alignment, so that the interaction continues in what the speakers might actually call a friendly manner.

These performances are involved in the enregisterment of 'Pittsburghese' (Johnstone, 2013). Enregisterment requires not just the typification of language, but also the typification of a fairly specific characterological figure, as described by Agha (2007). So stylized performances of dialect are not just context-free performances, but require the performer to inhabit a body that, along with language, takes stances. I suspect that these stances are different from those in the middle class, and possibly other places, but because of the unevenness of the data, such a claim is problematic. In general, my argument will take the form that the performers are doing something at once outside the usual middle-class performed norms of video production, and at the same time are creating typical 'chracterological figures' that are recognizable to people who are from a similar place and class. In the end, the important point is that there is a describable, embodied stance associated with the characterological figure, and that these figures are generally recognizable as local (Pittsburgh), working class, and/or masculine. In Pittsburgh especially, a 'working-class' stance is taken for dialect performance. I ask what it means to perform a working-class identity, and show how this performance is accomplished by taking stances that focus on specific forms of negative alignment and negative assessment. These forms are emblematic not only of masculinity, but also working-class feminity, all in distinction with 'elite' forms of masculinity and femininity. This is a logical extension of the argument in Kiesling (2009), in which it is claimed that stance is the basic or primary signified upon which first-order sociolinguistic indexes of higher order (say, of identity) are created.

There is thus a significant class-gender intersectionality in the performance of dialect. Such a view is actually a more qualitative dimension of an argument made by Eckert and McConnell-Ginet (1999). In this argument, working-class women end up being the most likely to use non-middle-class language, while upper-working-class or lower-middle-class women use the least vernacular/local sounding language. This intersectionality is important because dialect performances show both how people think of indexically linked characterological figures, and reinscribe and strengthen them as these figures. In the cases I view, the videos appear on YouTube and are viewed hundreds of thousands of times.

I show how the actors in videos use a prosodic pattern typical of Pittsburgh (and some other Midland) speech – the FQI – for particular stance work. Although Fasold (1980) originally identified this intonation as marking that the speaker already knows the answer to the question, that fact is used more broadly by speakers in these videos to *mock* the proposition that represents the answer. This is a particular kind of stance in which the speaker asks a question that is not really question; in fact, it is often absurd. But it shows the kind of oppositional stance that enregisters a particular working class 'Yinzer' persona.

To summarize, the questions are, 'how does dialect get performed in terms of stance, and how is that performance related to both class and gender?' The two dimensions of identity have intersectional and interactional effects to the point that we can't say this is a product simply of gender or class. I'll attempt this explanation, eventually, through the ways that dialect is performed in several instances. First, I'll lay the groundwork with discussions of identity, stance, and parody.

Performed dialect

One of the most important works on the enregisterment and performance of dialect is Johnstone's (2013) work on 'Pittsburghese,' the term that Pittsburghers use for the the enregistered variety of Pittsburgh speech. 'Pittsbughese' appears in all types of media in Pittsburgh to the point that it is something Pittsburghers and visitors to Pittsburgh can't avoid. Johnstone brilliantly shows not only the sociohostorical forces that produced Pittsburgh Speech, but more importantly the historical, economic, and demographic forces that led to the enregisterment of 'Pittsburghese,' a dialect arguably more discussed by locals than any other dialect in the US. In her book, Johnstone devotes several chapters to the performance, in various senses of the word, of Pittsburghese: She looks at public online discussions; the selling of Pittsburghese on t-shirts and talking dolls; and 'high performance' in media and in interaction. One of Johnstone's most important insights is that 'Pittsburghese' functions as an interactional resource used for different effects in these different situations (see also Johnstone and Kiesling, 2008). Moreover, she shows that even for a single performance, different people may hear different identities and distinctions depending on the hearer's knowledge and experience, and only one of these interpretations relates directly to the interpretation of the speaker as a Pittsburgher with a local identity. She notes (2011:676) that 'The defining feature of linguistic performance is that it calls meta-communicative attention to itself, putting on display not only what the message means but how.' This attention can then 'reinforce existing form-meaning links, call existing links into question, or create new links, and which combination of these possibilities actually occurs depends on who is listening.' (Johnstone 2013:227)

In other words, performances provide reflexive information to hearers about how to listen to later instances of similar combinations of linguistic features. This is the insight I'd like to pursue here: that the stances taken while a particular intonational feature of Pittsburghese is performed in videos point to how to use these features in Pittsburgh speech, while at the same time reflecting the sense of how White working-class Pittsburgh speakers interact. Another way to say this is that the people performing the Pittsburghese are actually enregistering characters who take habitus, which are kinds of stances. In the videos I analyze, the goal is humor, and much of this humor also relies on the fact that viewers will recognize characters they already know of in the videos. There is thus a dialectal relationship for these kinds of performances between 'existing form-meaning links' and the creation of new links as Pittsburghers share and comment on these videos.

Coupland (2007:146–7) makes a distinction between performance in interaction and 'high performance,' as opposed to 'mundane performance' in everyday conversations. Coupland argues that high performance is created through seven types of communicative focusing in a speech event:

- *Form focusing:* The poetic and metalinguistic functions of language [come] to the fore and considerations of 'style' in its most commonplace sense become particularly salient.
- *Meaning focusing:* There is an intensity, a density, and a depth to utterances or actions, or at least this is assumed to be the case by audiences.
- *Situation focusing:* Performers and audiences are not merely co-present but they are 'gathered,' according to particular dispositional norms. People know their roles.
- *Performer focusing:* Performers hold a 'floor' or a 'stage,' literally or at least in participants' normative understandings of speaker rights and sequencing options.
- *Relational focusing:* Performances are for audiences, not just to audiences. Although audiences are often public, performers will often have designed their performances for specific groups.
- *Achievement focusing*: Performances are enacted in relation to more or less specific demands. 'Stakes' (gains, losses, and risks) are involved, with potential for praise or censure for good or bad performance.
- *Repertoire focusing*: Performers and audiences are generally sensitive to what is given and what is new in a performance. Performances may be versions of known pieces, or at least known genres. Innovative interpretation can be commended. Rehearsal is relevant.

The videos I analyze here are clearly instances of this high performance. Most relevant, style or form is central to the videos, the action is often concentrated in 2–3 minutes of video, audiences must seek and click on a play button to watch the videos, they must focus on the performers as they watch, the videos are clearly performances meant to be watched merely by way of posting on YouTube, there is a thumbs up or down button for evaluation (among other ways of evaluating), and the series creates a sense of repertoire.

Bell and Gibson (2011:557) similarly define 'staged performance' as 'the overt, scheduled identification and elevation (usually literally) of one or more people to perform, typically on a stage, or in a stage-like area such as the space in front of a camera or microphone.' They also emphasize Coupland's point that 'Performances tend to be for the audience, rather than simply to the audience – there is a priority to entertain and to interest, not just to communicate a message.' This aspect is important, especially in the videos I am interested in, because in this case the goal is humor. That it is successful can be seen in the comments made and displayed below the videos in YouTube. I do not analyze these comments in depth here, but it is clear from the many comments praising the humor of the videos that humor is both the expected frame and the successful one.

Parody and humor

If the goal of these videos is humor, for the most part this humor works through the recognition of particular routines and types of people in Pittsburgh who use Pittsburghese. In that sense they have the feeling of parody about them as well – a parody of the chracterological figures of 'Pittsburghese' (sometimes referred to in Pittsburgh through the label *Yinzers*, which derives from the use of the term *yinz* for second person plural pronoun). Johnstone's (2013) analysis of a 'Pittsburghese' version of the Pink Floyd song *Mother* deftly shows how this process can work for performance in Pittsburgh. In this radio skit, the performers intersperse the lyrics (which sound 'serious') with statements by a fictional Pittsburgh mother who uses features of 'Pittsburghese.' Crucially, Johnstone shoes that the mother is portrayed not as the soft and caring mother of the song but as a yelling, harsh, threatening mother, who can be read as working class or Pittsburgh or both. Here the inversion is the characteristic of the mother and the character of the enregistered White working-class Pittsburgh mother, whose stances do not match up with the standard middle-class White stances of motherhood. For this to be funny, listeners need to appreciate the clash of stances in the two voices. A listener need not recognize the 'Pittsburghese mother' as working class or Pittsburgh, but if they don't, then once hearing it they will be able to refer to it and its attendant stances. Those who recognize the working-class and Pittsburgh identities will have another layer of humor to enjoy, and if the character is similar to a mother that they know, even another level of humor. So while parody at first temporarily inverts indexical meanings, once these inversions start to circulate, they help change indexical orders more generally. In parody, then, the indexical connection to the persona is created, changed or strengthened – or all three at once – highlighting a more general process.

With respect to the role of performance in circulation and enregisterment, this tells us about some of the ways that indexical connections get made. Indexicality is sometimes thought (especially in quantitative sociolinguistic work) to proceed based on frequency, but parodies show that salience or memorability of a single use is arguably at least as important. Humor is an important tool in bringing features to salience, because one way for it to be successful is when two clashing indices are brought into juxtaposition. This highlights what may have been unnoticed in a community previously. Humor also creates repeatable baptismal essentializations (Silverstein, 2003), which make the circulation of the new or heightened indexical connection more likely. What is clashing in these cases is not just linguistic features (and other multimodal features such as gesture), or styles, but more centrally different kinds of stances. So at the same time that the parody serves to enregister the persona, it strengthens and reshapes cultural ideas of that persona.

Stance

Stance has multiple definitions in the literature (see Jaffe, 2009 and Lempert, 2008 for useful discussions). A classic use of the term is the *epistemic* stance of an utterance or speaker, which generally refers to the way a speaker knows the utterance or how certain they are about it. Another use has to do with speaker relationality or emotion, or both. Speakers can be said to be 'confrontational' or 'condescending' or 'rude' or 'angry.' In general then, stance is about a relationship of the animator (in Goffman's 1981 sense) to the propositions in their talk and their interlocutors. I define stance as the creation of relationships of speaker (animator) to some discursive figure (human or otherwise). The discursive figure is similar to Du Bois' (2007) stance object, but expands it; it can be an interlocutor, a figure represented in the discourse, the animator, ideas represented in the discourse, or other texts. This list of possible stance figures includes almost all real or imagined entities that language can represent. I will refer to it as the stance focus. I propose three simultaneous dimensions of relationship an animator creates:

- a relationship to something represented in the discourse/text,
- a relationship to the talk itself, and
- relationships to interlocutors.

These dimensions I refer to as affect, investment, and alignment, respectively.

This stance triangle rests fundamentally on evaluation. In Du Bois' terminology, two sides of the triangle are in fact the evaluation of some 'stance object' by two different 'subjects' (interactants, animators). The third side of the triangle is the match or mismatch between the two assessments of the first two sides. For example, in the utterance 'That's a nice watch,' *that* deictically picks out a copresent object as the stance object, while *nice watch* does the evaluative work. This utterance creates one relationship that forms one side of a stance triangle. Since the stance triangle is inherently dialogic, we need to know the next move of this statement. Let's say the compliment is accepted in a way that aligns with the compliment, something like, 'Thanks, I saw it at Kaufman's and just had to have it.' In this case, the second subject evaluates the watch in a similar way as the first subject (the second side of the triangle), and thus aligns with that subject (the third side of the triangle).

Du Bois' stance triangle model represented an exciting theoretical move because for once stance is grounded in specific forms and moves in discourse, and there is an algorithm for analysis. However, there are some things it misses. For one, what happens if an utterance does not involve an assessment? What is the basis for the alignment in this situation? The data I will investigate here are all about questions, and in fact the stance is being done at least ostensibly through a syntactic form that fundamentally leaves open the assertion it questions. As I will show, a simple question like 'Did you get a new watch?' is arguably quite different with standard rising intonation and the falling intonation I'm interested in here, in at least the sense that the latter suggests that the questioner is pretty certain that it is a new watch. Second, the stance triangle model cannot distinguish between different levels of investment (or even, arguably, epistemicity). This is because of the primacy of assessment in this model. For example, the utterance, 'That's a nice watch' is the same as 'Nice watch, dude.' At first this difference may not look like a problem, but there is a very different attempt at alignment and investment in these two utterances. In the stance triangle model, they are basically the same. This is not to say that the stance triangle model should be discarded. It contains important insights about stance and grounds the analysis of stance in a system. However, it can be expanded and built upon, perhaps even by not having a triangle at all but noticing all the different possible alignments and disalignments that speakers can make with each other in a conversation.

In order to update the model, I suggest that the thing that people are talking about or doing is the stance *focus*, rather than a stance object, because focus can be anything that is not even remotely object-like; the suggestion of thing-ness by 'object' is unfortunate and misleading. Let's take the example of the new watch. In the model I propose, 'That's a nice watch' has a positive *affect* on the stance focus of the watch, which is roughly the same as the stance triangle model treats it. However, one could also say 'Nice watch' or 'Wow, that's a really swell watch you got there.' These are not equivalent on *investment*, even though they have the same proposition at their core, so this model makes room for this as a separate stance dimension. Finally, in many ways 'That's a nice watch' attempts to *align* to the addressee, in that one assumes that if someone is wearing a watch they also assessed it positively enough to purchase it and be seen wearing it. But the addressee could do work to distance themselves ('Oh, this? It's just a twenty-dollar Timex!') or even ignore the compliment altogether, which is probably the least aligning move one can make. Note here that we could make a distinction in alignments of the discourse management sort (in which case participating in an argument is alignment in the sense that one is cooperating to participate) and the propositional content sort (in which case an argument is non-aligning because there is disagreement on propositions being put forth).

In any case, what this three-dimensional model of stance provides is a way to discuss the different ways stance comes into a text/conversation. I show in the analysis that these dimensions allow for a discussion of the use of the FQI in performance of Pittsburghese to enact particular figures and identities in these conversations. Of course, in humor, there is really another layer of stancetaking in that there is an implicit stance relating to the speaker in terms of investment. That is, in humorous performance, and especially in parody, investment is inherently low because the audience is supposed to 'get' that this is not a veridical representation of real people, but exaggerations and inversions as noted in the discussion on parody. This can be taken as stipulated and not necessarily something created through the situation of high performance (although in mundane performance the signaling of performance is more important).

Class

In Labov's (1966) New York City study, class was measured through a scale of income, occupation, and other factors that were correlated with linguistic variable use. As sociolinguistic work has progressed, other class correlates/explanatory factors have been successfully proposed, such differences in network patterns, the linguistic marketplace, and more local categories such as 'jocks' and 'burnouts' in Eckert (2000; although note that she specifically shows that these categories are not exactly the same thing as other class measures, though there is some correlation with class measures). It seems, however, that class, like the term 'culture,' is ever contested. For my purposes here, the important insight of this dispute around the theoretical object of class is that class manifests not just in consumption, practices, and beliefs, but also *affects* and *desires*. Class is thus experienced and felt, and it is something that seems to inhere deeply into bodies, and not just in the way people talk. One can see class differences in how bodies are held in conversation and even in how people walk – the *hexis of class*.

The idea of a hexis of class points to stances that might be relevant for the differentiation of class by stance in the United States. Hexis is borrowed from Pierre Bourdieu's (1984) book on distinction and taste. Basically (or partially) his argument is that class distinction and taste has to do with bodily hexis, which is

> a basic dimension of the sense of social orientation, is a practical way of experiencing and expressing one's own sense of social value. One's relationship to the social world and to one's proper place in it is never more clearly expressed than in the space and time one feels entitled to take from others; more precisely, in the space one claims with one's body in physical space, through a bearing and gestures that are self-assured or reserved, expansive or constricted. . . and with one's speech in time, through the interaction time one appropriates and the self-assured or aggressive, careless or unconscious way one appropriates it.
>
> (Bourdieu 1984:474)

I suggest that this 'practical way of experiencing one's own sense of social value' encompasses the habitual stances that people take to one another, to strangers, friends, loved ones, colleagues, co-workers, and even department store customers. Indeed, the *habitus* that is Bourdieu's hallmark could be understood as habitual stancetaking. My argument is then that if class (or distinction, or taste) is hexis-based, and stance is not a deliberative activity but habitual and included in hexis, then stance is also implicated in class. Furthermore, if stance is largely, but not completely, achieved through talk, then it stands to reason that stance is fixed at the center of the process of the social stratification of linguistic variation. Finally, we should be able to see this bodily hexis created in performances of (working class) dialect because these performances are not parodies of speech only, but of the characterological figures that encompass all aspects of identity that include comportment – bodily hexis.

So what characterizes the interactional, affective, and hexis-based distinction between working class and middle class among Whites[1] in the US? How is "working-class White" enregistered in Pittsburgh in ways beyond Pittsburghese? Johnstone (2013:192–194) provides an excellent extended discussion of the the interactional and affective dispositions that could characterize class. Her most important insight is the role of opposition in working-class affect. For example, in his ethnography of working-class culture in Thunder Bay, Ontario, Dunk (1991) shows how opposition saturates the interactions he discusses. This opposition takes many forms, but is true both with friends and with those they don't like. At work, 'the boys' see themselves as opposed to management, who are there simply to exploit them. On the other hand, opposition is also a factor in the kinds of stances they take while hanging out with friends, although in this context it is interpreted as alignment (see also Schiffrin's 1984 analysis of Jewish argument as sociability for a more linguistic example of how disalignment can have the effect of alignment). This 'banter' can also be often found in 'masculine' interactions in the US (see Kiesling, 2005). Oppositional stances here can refer to things like insults, making fun of someone, telling someone they are doing something wrong, disapproval, and simply disagreeing with assertions – in other words, ways in which there is some sort of propositional content or speech act disalignment. In general, then, this stancetaking will show up in the alignment dimension in the stance model discussed above; however, in the sense that negative evaluations are also oppositional, it also manifests itself in affect. In terms of investment, I suggest that disalignment is achieved with higher investment (i.e., more 'direct') for the same evaluation, although there is less investment in situations that are not inherently non-aligning.

Of course, no person has one identity, and this is true of performers as well. People come as bundles of possible identity categories and live lives based on all of them simulataneously, or in intersection (Crenshaw, 1991). I am putting aside for the most part a discussion of intersection with race because in the context I'm analyzing, everyone is assumed to be White. This observation of course has implications for an analysis of race, class, and language, but there's no space here to explore this dimension further. I will simply note that the invisibility of Blacks in the videos and in many discussions of class would be the place to start with a race-class analysis in this context.

Class and gender are the complicated intersection I wish to interrogate here. Gender traditionally (and still, for many people) has only two categories. Sometimes these categories are felt as poles on a continuum, but more recently this binary view has been challenged. There is no space here for an extended discussion of the definition of gender (it changes based on the order of analysis, among other things). However, it is clear that gender and class are not (easily) separable, certainly not in the enregistered identities discussed here. Eckert and McConnell-Ginet (1999) suggest that working-class femininity differs from middle-class femininity in ways that the comparable masculine categories do not. She provides data that show this interaction for sociolinguistc variation. One reason this analysis manifests is the clash between ideal femininity and working-class stances, whereas for masculinity there is no such clash. That is, roughly speaking, ideologies – and language behavior – about femininity suggest stances of accommodation and politeness (see Lakoff, 1975 and Holmes, 1995), while more oppositional and dominating stances are shown for masculinity (see Kiesling, 1997, 1998). The stances encoded through working-class speech for women are often seen as emblematic of violating norms of sexual purity through a metaphor of linguistic contamination. In the videos I analyze, gender is in many ways both heightened and erased, especially in the use of FQI.

Falling question intonation (l*+h l%)

The feature I'm exploring in these videos is one that is shared throughout the eastern Midland dialect area of the US. Fasold (1980) is one of the first to describe this intonation, which exhibits a low to quickly rising tone on the phrase accent similar to 'canonical' questions, but instead of a final rise shows a precipitous fall. I refer to this contour as 'Falling Question Intonation' or FQI. The contour is represented in the ToBI notational system (Beckman, Hirschberg, Shattuck-Hufnagel, 2006) as L★+H L%. In this notation, 'L★+H' represents the low rising tone, while 'L%' represents the falling tone at the end (which would be H% in a canonical American English question).[2] To a native speaker of (non-Pennsylvanian) American English, this intonation is quite noticeable and salient. Fasold suggested in his description, based on its use in the English spoken by the Amish of central Pennsylvania, that this intonation tended to be used when the answer was already generally known by the questioner. For example, if Sophie is eating ice cream voraciously and not really taking note of anything going on around her, Bob might ask

'You like that ice cream Sophie?'

L★+ H L%

Based on the evidence of how she is eating the ice cream, Bob already knows she likes the ice cream (and ice cream is usually something people like anyway), but he is asking the question nevertheless. This allows speakers to ask more obvious questions that provide an opportunity to continue the interaction.

Figure 14.1 provides an example from the data labeled using the ToBI conventions on a waveform. (The word here is indeed *hangry* and not *hungry*. The speaker (Donny) is asking the addressee (Greg) is he is in a bad mood because he is hungry; *hangry* is a relatively new American English term that blends *hungry* and *angry*.) This figure provides a clear picture of the fall-rise-fall pattern that typifies this contour. In this example, it begins at the word *hangry*.

Hedberg et al. (2006) provide support more generally for the potential meanings of FQI. They present a corpus-based study of the meaning of different intonation contours of American English questions. They argue that the falling questions in their corpus are all in some way 'non-genuine,' or more precisely one or more of the felicity conditions for the question is violated. Certainly knowing the answer to a question is a violation of a normal requirement for questions that the questioner not know the answer, as is the mocking stance that I find on some of these questions. There may be other stance indexicalities such as condescension which hold; this possibility is explored further in the analysis in the next section.

Greg and Donny

The videos that I analyze are part of a YouTube series called *Greg and Donny* ('Greg and Donny,' 2016, October 25), most of which are under five minutes. The videos present conversations among two to five friends who live in Johnstown, Pennsylvania,

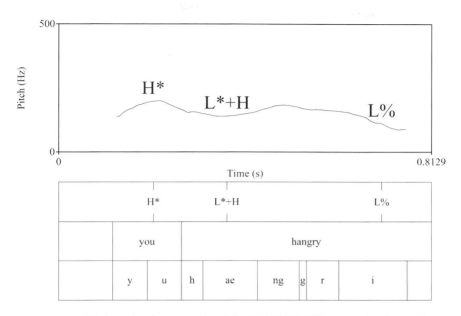

FIGURE 14.1 Pitch track of an example of the L*+H L% falling question intonation.

an industrial town about one hundred kilometers from Pittsburgh (this distance counts as close in the United States). The opening conceit of the videos (first posted in April 2009; 'Greg & Donny Discover Video Chat,' 2016, October 25) is that the friends (and neighbors) Greg and Donny have just discovered video chat. Each video is usually two to four minutes long, although they range from one minute to over seven. The topics are usually mundane or are about Pittsburgh cultural traditions, or holidays (especially Halloween and Christmas/New Year's Eve). The characters expanded to Greg's wife, Gina, and Greg and Donny's friend, Missy Kreutzer (usually only referred to by her last name, the spelling of which is not given and is an educated guess). The episodes are thus composed of conversations among the friends, usually from two vantage points (computers) but sometimes from three, as in the video analyzed below. If there are more than two people in the episode, then there will be more than one person visible on each computer. The focus of the interactions is not explicitly on the way people talk, with the exception of one brilliant episode in which Greg travels to Philadelphia and reports back that people are mocking his accent. However, the episodes are written to be dense with recognizable features of 'Pittsburghese' or 'phono-opportunities' as Coupland (1985) calls them. For example, the episode excerpted below ('Idlewild,' 2016, October 25) in which Kreutzer reports on her visit to the Idlewild amusement park, provides multiple opportunities not only to reference the cultural proactice of visiting this park, but the vocalization of /l/, since /l/ appears twice in the name of the park, both times in coda position where it is likely to be vocalized (it's interesting as well that the Kennywood amusement park is usually taken to be stereotypically Pittsburgh). In short, the videos are comedy skits about working-class people in southwestern Pennsylvania, and language is for the most part performed without metapragmatic comment. The comments sections, however, show many comments that focus both on the use of perceived 'Pittsburghese' and the interactional patterns the characters use.

As representations of working-class culture in Southwestern Pennsylvania, the kinds of interaction presented in the videos is meant to represent and parody the typical people who live there, and their characteristic interaction. In terms of stance, disalignment is the norm, even as the 'banter' creates solidarity. LQI is a resource that some characters, especially Donny, use to help with this playful opposition. As an example, I examine some talk from the *Idlewild* episode. I've provided three frame captures of the three characters for this video in figures two through four. The except begins after a short section in which Donny and Kreutzer criticize Greg for not going to Idlewild the previous summer, and he defends himself. Donny then shifts back to Kreutzer's recent visit to the theme park, asking whether she rode a particular ride.

FIGURE 14.2 Frame of Donny from the 'Idlewild' episode. Approximately line 51 in the transcript.

FIGURE 14.3 Frame grab of Kreutzer from the 'Idlewild' episode. Approximately line 50 in the transcript.

FIGURE 14.4 Frame grab of Greg from the 'Idlewild' episode. Approximately line 50 in the transcript.

Excerpt

30	Donny:	**Yinz ride the Spider Kreutzer?. ((LQI))**
31	Kreutzer:	I don't like that ride
32	Donny:	Ah that's the best ride
33	Kreutzer:	Spiders are creepy
34	Greg:	I like the coaster. Always been a coaster man
35	Donny:	What'd you ride Kreutzer, the uh, choo-choo in Storybook Forest?
36	Kreutzer:	Nice try Smozik
37		Storybook Forest don't got a choo-choo
38	Greg:	Don't go knockin' Storybook Forest
39		You know I had a crush on that Goldilocks
40	PAUSE	
41		Gina don't like me bringin' that up
42	Gina:	((off camera)) Quit talkin' about that Goldilocks or I'm gonna come in there and pop you one Greg
43	Kreutzer:	You wanna see what I won?
44	Greg:	[Alright
45	Donny:	[Alright
46	Kreutzer:	Well do you or don't you?
47	Greg:	A[lright
48	Donny:	[Alright
49	Kreutzer:	((goes off camera to put on a jester hat))
		Ta Da: ((reveal singsong intonation))
50		Isn't it cool?
51	**Donny:**	**Yinz gonna wear that out Kreutzer?. ((LQI))**
52	Greg:	That'd be a sight to see
53	Kreutzer:	No I'm not gonna wear it out

54 Donny: Haha 'cause I'd tell you to take a picture of yourself if you did cause uh:
55   I'd like to see a picture of that
56 Greg: You could send that in to Jay Leno ((host of The Tonight Show at the time))
57 Kreutzer: Oh now it's Laurel and Hardy over there is it?
58   You're a real couple of Abbott and Costellos
59 Greg: Hey Donny who's on first?
60 Kreutzer: [What?
61 Donny: [Huh?
62 Greg: I was just asking Donny who's on first
63 Kreutzer: How's come?
64 Donny: What the hell you talkin' 'bout Greg?
65 PAUSE
66 Greg: Ah never mind I ain't explainin' it
67 Kreutzer: Anyhow
68   I ain't wearin' the hat
69   I'm just gonna keep it on the shelf for the memory

((the video continues))

Donny (who uses LQI the most of all characters) uses LQI on his question in line 30, including using a Pittsburghese feature (*yinz*), although he uses it to address only Kreutzer (*yinz* is usually a plural address form; nevertheless one could imagine he is also referring to the people Kreutzer presumably went to the park with). In any case Donny asks this question with a devilish smile (in figure 2 he is in the midst of this utterance), perhaps because he knows it is a stomach-churning ride. According to the park website, 'riders hold on tightly as they are tossed, dipped, and spun in every direction' ('Adventures, Rides, and Shows at Idlewild', 2016). When Kreutzer says she didn't ride the Spider, Donny disaligns with her by implicitly criticizing her choice (line 32 'Ah that's the best ride'), and Greg goes on on in line 34 to simply say what he likes ('I like the coaster. Always been a coaster man'). None of these moves is particularly aligning except to be on the topic of rides at Idlewild.

Donny asks Kreutzer in a mocking tone in line 35 whether she rode a 'choo-choo' in the Storybook Forest, which is, according to the description from the park ('Adventures, Rides, and Shows at Idlewild', 2016), 'a very special place where little ones can meet their favorite characters from nursery rhymes and children's tales and where parents and grandparents can revisit their youth and reminisce about simpler times.' In other words, it's a section of the park for little kids, so he's making fun of her by saying she stayed in the 'kiddy' part of the park. Note that Kreutzer's response to this is to call Donny out on his knowledge of the park.

When Kreutzer shows her hat and asks if it's cool in line 50, rather than agreeing that it's cool, Donny mocks her with the question he asks about wearing the hat out in line 51. Kreutzer defends herself from the mocking by suggesting it's not funny by ironically calling the two men Laurel and Hardy and Abbott and Costello.

The next section is tangential, in which Greg tries to reference the classic Abbott and Costello routine *Who's on First?* but the other two are apparently unfamiliar with it.

After this excerpt, the three go on to argue about what kind of memory is worthy of 'keeping on a shelf.' Nevertheless, this short section displays the kind of oppositional banter that is typical of the series. The women display some traits ideologically associated with masculinity, including the opposition of Kreutzer and Gina's threat to hit Greg (line 42, 'Quit talkin' about that Goldilocks or I'm gonna come in there and pop you one Greg'). The fact that Kreutzer is referred to by her last name and not *Missy*, her first name, is also a way of making her more 'one of the boys,' as last-name-only address is common among American men and less common for women.

The two uses of LQI by Donny are characteristic of how he uses them throughout the series. The mocking in these uses is not complete and is anticipatory, and sometimes doesn't work out because he might have guessed the answer to the question wrong. In the case of the question about riding the Spider in line 30, it's possible to hear that he wanted to make fun of Kreutzer because of her reaction to riding a ride that spins the riders so much. The question about wearing the hat out in line 51 suggests that he does not think it is cool (which is what Kreutzer asks in the turn before), but rather evaluates it as something one might not want to be seen in public wearing. So both of these uses of LQI evince a mocking tone which disaligns through a negative affect in the sense of belittling what she is doing or has done. However, it does so in a way that shows lower investment in the criticism, in the sense that Donny can claim he is 'only joking.'

Gina is the other characer who uses LQI regularly in the series. She tends to use the contour to express effrontery or outrage. In one episode (*Greg has an accent*) she aligns with Greg against people who find his accent funny by asking 'Are they makin' fun of you?' with the LQI contour. And in another she sees Greg folding her 'snuggie' as if to put it away, and says, enraged, 'Is he foldin' that snuggie?' with LQI. So in a different way that fits her character, Gina uses LQI in opposition as well. Although LQI is not the only contour to be used oppositionally, it tends to be used that way more than other question intonations. Note that Donny asks about the 'choo-choo in Storybook Forest' with a rising intonation. The difference is that in this question the mocking is in the diminutive, childish form of 'choo-choo' and would be hard to imagine if Kreutzer's response is correct.

LQI in this video thus helps to signal that the lower investment of the negative alignment is detected; that is, it signals that the frame is one of banter with the goal of furthering social interaction and friendship even as there is apparent conflict.

Stance, class, and enregisterment

One of the most common markers or responses in these videos is 'Aw Jeez,' an expletive of exasperation derived from the blasphemous 'Ah Jesus.' This response is usually a marker of disapproval and at the same time sympathy for the addressee. Throughout these videos, we see disalignment and even confrontation, apparent glee in another's tribulations, but in the end a kind of camaraderie emerges. This stance of simultaneous local disalignment but overall interactional alignment – they are talking to each other, after all – is represented as typical working-class 'Yinzer' interaction. Viewers in the comments find it to be fairly authentic. In general, only those who mistake the accent (for example, thinking it is supposed to be "southern") criticize the authenticity, and many comment on the authenticity not just of the dialect performances but of the overall interaction as well. LQI is one device to support this authenticity and this stancetaking.

So these videos both serve to enregister these personae and to re-enregister them, and help them circulate. They are typified by an oppositional stance within rather everyday banter that appears 'natural' to viewers familiar with this culture, and rather than responding with outrage, generally comment with recognition and even at times nostalgia. The performed dialect re-enregisters not only the way of speaking, but the way of being in speaking Pittsburghese.

Appendices

Appendix A: Transcription conventions

The transcript is produced in the simplest manner possible, with very little in the way of detail remarks, for legibility. The details that matter for the conversation, such as where LQI is located, are noted. Most of the talk is in 'Pittsburghese' pronunciation, and no attempt is made to specifically transcribe that since it is understood and would be distracting to read. Each speaker is generally shown when they speak, with the head shot frame shown in the figures.

Pauses longer than one second are transcribed on their own line with 'PAUSE.'
LQI and transcriber comments about the transcript are in ((double parentheses)).
Overlaps are marked with square brackets at the point of overlap.

Appendix B: Full transcript of video Idlewild

01	Kreutzer:	((eating cotton candy)) Did I do it right?
02		Guys
03	Donny:	Kreutzer
04	Greg:	How many people are seein' me?
05	Kreutzer:	Huh?
06	Greg:	How many people are on this?
07	Donny:	Just us Greg
08	Greg:	You can talk to one than more person on this?
09	Donny:	Yes, Greg
10	Greg:	Can you talk to a hundred?
11	Donny:	No Greg three
12	Greg:	Didn't know you could talk to more than one person on this. [whisper]

13	Greg:	Where'd you get that cotton candy Kreutzer?
14	Kreutzer:	Just got back from Idelwild
15	Donny:	That's open already?
16	Kreutzer:	Where you been Smozik? ((Donny's last name))
17	Greg:	Gina and me will have to make time to go this year
18	Donny:	You didn't go to Idlewild last year?
19	Kreutzer	That ought to be illegal
20	Donny:	C'mon Greg that's a tradition
21	Kreutzer:	I'd be depressed all year if I didn't get to go to Idlewild
22	Greg:	I just got too much going on.
23	Kreutzer:	Oh that's right Donny, we forgot, teachers are real busy over the summer ((Greg is a teacher))
24		Drinking that lemonade
25		Soaking up them rays
26	Donny:	Eatin' bon bons
27	Greg:	Alright last summer we built them deck chairs, stripped down the fireplace, cut down them shrubs, Gina got book club, babysittin' Bob Nooner's cat, weekends we go down Periwinkle Village in Ligonier go shoppin' for Santas
28	Kreutzer:	God, stop talkin' already
29	Greg:	((sigh))
30	Donny:	Yinz ride the Spider Kreutzer ((LQI))
31	Kreutzer:	I don't like that ride
32	Donny:	Ah that's the best ride
33	Kreutzer:	Spiders are creepy
34	Greg:	I like the coaster. Always been a coaster man
35	Donny:	What'd you ride Kreutzer, the uh, choo-choo in Storybook Forest?
36	Kreutzer:	Nice try Smozik
37		Storybook Forest don't got a choo-choo
38	Greg:	Don't go knockin' Storybook Forest
39		You know I had a crush on that Goldilocks
40	PAUSE	
41		Gina don't like me bringin' that up
42	Gina:	Quit talkin' about that Goldilocks or I'm gonna come in there and pop you one Greg
43	Kreutzer:	You wanna see what I won?
44	Greg:	[Alright
45	Donny:	[Alright
46	Kreutzer:	Wel do you or don't you?
47	Greg:	A[lright
48	Donny:	[Alright
49	Kreutzer:	Ta Da: ((reveal singsong intonation))
50		Isn't it cool?
51	Donny:	Yinz gonna wear that out Kreutzer? ((LQI))

262 Scott F. Kiesling

52	Greg:	That'd be a sight to see
53	Kreutzer:	No I'm not gonna wear it out
54	Donny:	Haha 'Cause I'd tell you to take a picture of yourself if you did cause uh
55		I'd like to see a picture of that
56	Greg:	You could send that in to Jay Leno ((host of The Tonight Show at the time))
57	Kreutzer:	Oh now it's Laurel and Hardy over there is it?
58		You're a real couple of Abbott and Costellos
59	Greg:	Hey Donny who's on first?
60	Kreutzer:	[What?
61	Donny:	[Huh?
62	Greg:	I was just asking Donny
63	Kreutzer:	How's come?
64	Donny:	What the hell you talkin' 'bout Greg?
65	PAUSE	
66	Greg:	Ah never mind I ain't explainin' it
67	Kreutzer:	Anyhow
68		I ain't wearin' the hat
69		I'm just gonna keep it on the shelf for the memory
70	Donny:	What kind of memory is that?
71	Kreutzer:	Any kind of memory I say it is Donny
72	Greg:	Memories are important Donny
73	Kreutzer:	Yeah Donny
74		Butt out
75	Greg:	Like when I was goin' with Goldilocks ((said quietly))
76	Gina:	Dammit Greg
77	Donny:	Stuff you put on the shelf's gotta be a real memory, like a baseball autgraphed by Reggie Jackson
78	Kreutzer:	That ain't a memory Donny
79		You won it at flippin' cards
80	Donny:	Well yeah it's the most I ever won at flippin'
81	Kreutzer:	Well this the most I ever won at knockin' over milk jugs
82	Donny:	Yinz get all three?
83	Kreutzer:	On the floor
84	Greg:	Ahhh them games are rigged
85		They rig them so you can't win
86	Kreutzer:	[I did win
87	Donny:	[She did win
88	Greg:	Yeah they do them to all them games make them seem real simple but you can't win
89		Save your money
90	Long pause	
91	Kreutzer:	[Anyhow
92	Donny:	[Anyhow

93	Donny:	We should get a bunch of people together and go down Idlewild and get trashed
94	Kreutzer:	I'm goin' tomorrow if yinz wanna come
95	Greg:	Ahh nahh Gina and me got movie night with Denny and Georgia
96	Kreutzer:	What are yinz watchin'?
97	Greg:	Watchin' that Wild Hogs
98	Donny:	Aahhh that's a classic
99	Greg:	Yeah everybody's dressin' up
100	Kreutzer:	I don't like movies about grownups
101	Donny:	What the hell yinz goin' back so soon for?
102	Kreutzer:	This ain't gonna last forever ((referring to cotton candy))

Notes

1 It is important to keep in mind that the discussion of Pittsburghese also encodes race, mainly by enregistering Pittsburghese as a White variety. See Eberhardt (2008, 2012) for a discussion of race and language from the Black standpoint. I use the terms White and Black because I believe the euphemistic distinctions attempt to scienize and erase the cultural significance of the categories, and make race less oppositional than it is.
2 Many thanks to Shelome Gooden for help with the ToBI notation of this pitch contour.

References

Adventures, Rides, & Shows at Idlewild. (2016, December 10). Retrieved from www.idlewild.com/things-to-do/attractions

Agha, A. (2007). *Language and social relations*. Cambridge: Cambridge University Press.

Beckman, M. E., Hirschberg, J., & Shattuck-Hufnagel, S. (2006). The original ToBI system and the evolution of the ToBI framework. In J. Sun-Ah (Ed.), *Prosodic typology: The phonology of intonation and phrasing* (pp. 9–54). Oxford and New York: Oxford University Press.

Bell, A., & Gibson, A. (2011). Staging language: An introduction to the sociolinguistics of performance. *Journal of Sociolinguistics*, 15(5), 555–572. https://doi.org/10.1111/j.1467-9841.2011.00517.x

Bourdieu, P. (1984). *Distinction: A social critique of the judgement of taste*. Cambridge, MA: Harvard University Press.

Coupland, N. (1985). "Hark, hark, the lark": Social motivations for phonological style-shifting. *Language and Communication*, 5(3), 153–171. https://doi.org/10.1016/0271-5309(85)90007-2

Coupland, N. (2007). *Style : Language variation and identity*. Cambridge, UK/New York: Cambridge University Press.

Crenshaw, K. (1991). Mapping the margins: Intersectionality, identity politics, and violence against women of color. *Stanford Law Review*, 43(6), 1241–1299. https://doi.org/10.2307/1229039

Du Bois, J. W. (2007). The Stance triangle. In R. Englebretson (Ed.), *Stancetaking in discourse* (pp. 139–182). Philadelphia, PA: John Benjamins Publishing Company.

Du Bois, J. W., & Kärkkäinen, E. (2012). Taking a stance on emotion: Affect, sequence, and intersubjectivity in dialogic interaction. *Text and Talk*, 32(4), 433–451. https://doi.org/10.1515/text-2012-0021

Dunk, T. (1991). *It's a working man's town: Male working-class culture.* Montreal: McGill-Queen's University Press.

Eberhardt, M. (2008). The Low-back merger in the Steel City: African American English. *American Speech, 83*(3), 284–311.

Eberhardt, M. (2012). Enregisterment of Pittsburghese and the local African American community. *Language & Communication, 32*(4), 358–371. https://doi.org/10.1016/j.langcom.2012.08.002

Eckert, P. (2000). *Linguistic variation as social practice.* Malden, MA: Blackwell Publishers.

Eckert, P., & McConnell-Ginet, S. (1999). New generalizations and explanations in language and gender research. *Language in Society, 28*, 185–201.

Fasold, R. W. (1980). The conversational function of Pennsylvania Dutch question intonation. In *New Ways of Analyzing Variation Conference.* Washington, DC.

Goffman, E. (1981). Footing. In *Forms of Talk.* Philadelphia: University of Pennsylvania Press.

Greg and Donny. (2016, October 25). Retrieved from www.youtube.com/user/gregand donny

Greg & Donny Discover Video Chat. (2016, October 25). Retrieved from www.youtube.com/watch?v=kBWnS2RrgxM

Hedberg, N., Sosa, J. M., & Fadden, L. (2006). Tonal constituents and meanings of yes-no questions in American English. In *Proceedings of Speech Prosody.* Retrieved from http://www.isca-speech.org/archive

Holmes, J. (1995). *Women, men and politeness.* London: Longman.

Idlewild. (2016, October 25). Retrieved from www.youtube.com/watch?v=n9UdOnOyRT4

Jaffe, A. M. (2009). Introduction: The sociolinguistics of stance. In A. Jaffe (Ed.), *Stance: Sociolinguistic perspectives* (pp. 3–28). Oxford; New York: Oxford University Press.

Johnstone, B. (2011). Dialect enregisterment in performance. *Journal of Sociolinguistics, 15*(5), 657–679.

Johnstone, B. (2013). *Speaking Pittsburghese: The story of a dialect.* New York/Oxford: Oxford University Press.

Johnstone, B., & Kiesling, S. F. (2008). Indexicality and experience : Exploring the meanings of /aw/-monophthongization in Pittsburgh. *Journal of Sociolinguistics, 12*(1), 5–33. https://doi.org/10.1111/j.1467-9841.2008.00351.x

Kiesling, S. F. (1997). Power and the language of Men. In S. Johnson & U. Meinhof (Eds.), *Language and masculinity* (pp. 65–85). Malden, MA; Oxford: Wiley-Blackwell.

Kiesling, S. F. (1998). Men's identities and sociolinguistic variation: The case of fraternity men. *Journal of Sociolinguistics, 2*(1), 69–99. https://doi.org/10.1111/1467-9481.00031

Kiesling, S. F. (2005). Homosocial desire in men's talk: Balancing and re-creating cultural discourses of masculinity. *Language in Society, 34*(5), 695–726. https://doi.org/10.1017/S0047404505050268

Kiesling, S. F. (2009). Style as stance: Stance as the explanation for patterns of sociolinguistic variation. In A. Jaffe (Ed.), *Stance: Sociolinguistic perspectives* (pp. 171–194). New York: Oxford University Press.

Labov, W. (1966). *The social stratification of English in New York City.* Washington: Center for Applied Linguistics.

Lakoff, R. T. (1975). *Language and woman's place.* New York: Harper & Row.

Lempert, M. (2008). The poetics of stance: Text-metricality, epistemicity, interaction. *Language in Society, 37*(4), 569–592. https://doi.org/10.1017/S0047404508080779

Schiffrin, D. (1984). Jewish argument as sociability. *Language in Society, 13*(3), 311–335. https://doi.org/10.1017/S0047404500010526

Silverstein, M. (2003). Indexical order and the dialectics of sociolinguistic life. *Language & Communication, 23*(3–4), 193–229. https://doi.org/10.1016/S0271-5309(03)00013-2

15
PERFORMING IDENTITY ON SCREEN

Language, identity, and humour in Scottish television comedy

Natalie Braber

Introduction

Coupland (2001, p. 346) has suggested that sociolinguistics over-invested in 'authentic speech' and until relatively recently ignored the extent to which other styles of language can be used at varying levels to construct identity. For example, utterances can be stylized, where speakers are putting on an artificial voice, and analysing such language usage is increasingly common in dialect variation to examine linguistic features (Coupland has argued that performance is an aspect of stylization in Coupland, 2001, p. 350). Such styling considers accent and dialect to be a resource for constructing identity (Coupland, 2009b, p. 312). Schilling-Estes (1998) has also commented that performance speech, where speakers display for others a particular linguistic variety, has received little attention in mainstream variationist literature but can be used for display purposes (either of one's own or another language variety) and that such language use shows patterning in variation which is similar to 'normal' language usage. This chapter follows this lead, by exploring language usage in two comedy sketches which perform Glaswegian identities. It does so by examining language variation in relation to identity as well as the role of identity in the production of comedy. These fields connect through the concept of performance and show how certain identities are performed and portrayed on the small screen.

By examining performance register, we can gain an insight into speaker production and perception of dialectal varieties. We may also gain an understanding of the features speakers are most aware of as we see which features are performed. We know that speakers are more aware of specific forms, which are overtly stigmatised (Trudgill, 1986, p. 11), as well as forms that are radically different from standard varieties. This has effects on processes such as linguistic accommodation, but also on aspects of performance or imitation. It means that linguists can look at the performance of culturally familiar styles to examine language usage. The fact that different varieties of English are associated with different types of speakers and provide clues about these speakers is why writers use them in their work, to provide information about characters (Hodson, 2014, p. 3). Fictional media may not have been seen as being reflective of 'real' language, as unscripted media was (Queen, 2013, p. 218), however, as Schilling-Estes argues (above), performed language offers an important source for examining variation.

Bednarek has written that characterisation in television remains neglected (Bednarek, 2011, p. 3) and this chapter aims to correct this neglect. It will examine two particular characters in the Scottish TV comedy show *Chewin' the Fat* to investigate how different Glaswegian identities are portrayed through the use of performed and stylized speech. In order to do so, it will first consider the concept of identity in Glasgow (and Scotland), language in Glasgow, and previous research on performance, before analysing how these particular characters portray Glaswegian identities through the use of language. Television comedy is a fruitful area for the examination of the ways in which speech is often an important generic element in the production of humour. The use of language to mark out differences in class, geography, and social variability is an important aspect of comic genres and this has particular resonances for Scottish comedy where the cultural specificity of Scottishness is often located in language. Hodson has stated why she thinks that language in film is so rarely analysed, as 'it is simply too easy and too obvious' (Hodson, 2014, p. 15). I would argue that the same goes for television. Therefore, this chapter will consider how language can be used in certain TV comedy programmes to perform particular identities.

Identity and language

Chambers has stated that 'language is not primarily a means of communication; it is, above all, a means of cultural construction in which our very selves are constituted' (Chambers, 1994, p. 22). A wealth of literature exists examining the relationship between identity and linguistic change, from Labov's pioneering investigation in Martha's Vineyard (1963) onwards. It is impossible within the scope of this chapter to discuss this literature in detail, but I will give a summary of identity and how this relates to the case study of Glasgow.

Concepts such as national and local identity may initially appear straightforward, but closer investigation reveals that they are actually difficult to define (Anderson, 1991, p. 3). Despite fluctuations in the political status of Scotland over the past four hundred years, its sense of a distinct identity has always remained strong. Identity studies carried out in Scotland have tended to focus on national, 'Scottish', identity, rather than individual local identities, and unsurprisingly Scots are shown to have a clear sense of their own identity as Scottish, as opposed to British. This sense of 'Scottishness' has been the subject of extensive linguistic research (see Braber and Butterfint, 2008 and Braber, 2009 for a full discussion) and has been shown to be increasing rather than diminishing. Even though national identity is strong in Scotland, it is still a problematic concept. Hagan has commented that historically it would be misleading to talk of a single Scottish identity (Hagan, 2002, p. 72) and this still holds true today. The existence of more local identities within Scotland and issues such as how they are manifested, their underlying psychology, and the role those identities play in language use and change have largely been ignored.

So, there is a Scottish identity, and there may be more Scottish local identities, but how do they relate to language use? Despite the highly complex and ever-changing nature of identity, the hypothesised link between regional or local identity and changes in language has been examined in several varieties of British English (see also Johnstone, 2007 for a study of American English in Pittsburgh). Studies in Middlesborough (Llamas, 1999, 2007) and Berwick (Watt, Llamas, Docherty, Hall, & Nycz, 2014) have as subjects the link between the retention of localised language variants and the speaker's strength of local identity or affiliation. Their results suggest that speakers with a low identification score, and therefore a weaker sense of local identity, tend to use fewer localised language variants (Llamas, 1999).

Tabouret-Keller has stated that individual and social identity are mediated by language – linguistic features bind such identities together and 'language acts are acts of identity' (Tabouret-Keller, 1997, p. 315). This can range from phonetic features, to lexical items and syntactic structures, and language can both create this link as well as express it (Tabouret-Keller, 1997, p. 317; see also Bucholtz and Hall, 2005, p. 586). Language and identity are linked to values, which people share or believe that other groups share (see Omoniyi and White, 2006, p. 1), and Thornborrow has concurred that our use of language is 'one of the most fundamental ways we have of establishing our identity' (Thornborrow, 1999, p. 158). This is a process which has to be built on and re-negotiated throughout our lives, and Johnstone and Bean have added that this is a 'linguistic choice', where speakers choose how to sound (Johnstone and Bean, 1997, p. 222). They have also claimed that this can be influenced strongly by the ways people feel about where they live and that their audiences affect how they speak (see also Jaffe, 2000, p. 40). Ito and Preston (1998, p. 466) have commented that when examining language and identity it may be useful to review the features of language which speakers are not aware of. However, this chapter will examine the features which speakers have chosen to foreground to examine identity, also following Johnstone (1999, p. 514) who has noted that we may have to consider more than just language, including issues such as physical appearance and grooming.

Originally, sociolinguists ascribed identity by social category membership (Dyer, 2007, p. 104), where identity viewed through language was seen as fixed and speakers as agentless, purely products of language. However, speakers can manipulate linguistic resources available to them to create their own identities. This is seen as a form of identity practice where use of language reflects speakers' self-conceptualisation. This allows speakers to express their identification with – or rejection of – particular social groups, as well as their own individuality (Johnstone and Bean, 1997, p. 221). Furthermore, speakers have visions of language and identity which they can draw on, but they also have knowledge about how others use language and can incorporate this information into their own variety (Jaffe, 2000, p. 42), which accounts for features such as phonetic variability (see for example Ito and Preston, 1998, p. 480). In addition to language and identity, Bauman has said we need to add 'performance' (Bauman, 2000, p. 1), which we will discuss later.

Anderson (1991) has coined the phrase 'imagined community' to explain the binding nature of specific identity in a community which exists despite the fact that those within the group do not know their fellow members; this sense of 'collective identity' is important to many (see also Maier, 2007). As the concept of a 'Scottish' identity has been shown to be very important to Scottish people, the existence of a strong sense of community in Glasgow is not altogether surprising. Although heavily stigmatised as a city by outsiders, its inhabitants have retained a strong sense of belonging. The stigmatization has led to Glaswegian being branded as 'slovenly' and 'degenerate' (Andersson and Trudgill, 1990), and previous research (Braber and Butterfint, 2008; Braber, 2009) has shown that Glaswegian is seen as unattractive, even by many of its speakers. This will also be discussed in a later section.

Language in Glasgow

As noted above, Glasgow has long been stigmatised. As an industrial city, Glasgow suffered from the decline of the shipyards and ship-building industry after relying on this source of income and employment for many years. Historically, the city has been plagued with high levels of deprivation. Arguably more than most cities in the UK, Glasgow has acquired a highly stereotyped reputation. The very nature of a stereotype means that such views are unbalanced, often over-emphasising the negative aspects of Glasgow. However, it is through these stereotypes that many see the city and, by extension, its inhabitants.

The linguistic characteristics of Glaswegian have hardly fared better and the stigmatisation of Glasgow as a city has also resulted in negative associations with the linguistic variety (Andersson and Trudgill, 1990; Hagan, 2002, p. 25). As with all speech communities, there is no single linguistic variety in Glasgow, but a continuum which stretches from 'broad' Scots to Standard Scottish English (see for example Wells, 1982; Macafee, 1997), and certain varieties on this continuum are more stigmatised than others (and these can be correlated with social class, e.g., the greatest stigma appears to be attached to the varieties more usually found in the lower socio-economic groups). Speakers can move along the continuum depending on formality and situational context.

A full discussion of the features of varieties used in Glasgow cannot be covered in this chapter, but the references provided in this section can be followed for more information (particularly Hagan, 2002, section 4.1). Many of the linguistic features associated with Glaswegian are not unique to the city, e.g., use of /x/ in words such as *loch*, the distinction between /w/ and /ʍ/, extensive use of the glottal stop in words such as *matter*, and features of the vowel system such as the fronting of /u/ and the length distinctions described by the Scottish Vowel Length Rule (for more information see Aitken, 1981). However, taken together they constitute what, to many people, is clearly a distinctive Glaswegian accent. Many believe that

Glaswegian varieties are hybrid forms, due to the large number of incomers (see Hagan, 2002, p. 87), which may explain some of the changes discussed below.

Anecdotal evidence found during earlier studies (see Braber and Butterfint, 2008 and Braber, 2009) suggests that in spite of this negativity, or perhaps even because of it, many Glaswegians are fiercely proud of Glasgow and use Glaswegian, with its covert prestige to signal solidarity among working-class speakers and the desire to maintain distinctiveness from other social groups (see for example Stuart-Smith, Timmins, & Tweedie, 2007). There are changes in the variety of Glasgow speech features and certain features are undergoing processes of change (for detailed discussion see Macafee, 1997; Stuart-Smith, 1999a; 1999b; Görlach, 2002; Scobbie, Gordeeva, & Matthews, 2006; Stuart-Smith et al., 2007), but it should be noted that the changes appear to be of three different types: those which appear to be 'Scottish-wide'; those which appear to be a move away from traditional Glaswegian and Scottish standards (such as the increasing occurrence of l-vocalisation different to the l-vocalisation which has long appeared in Scots words, such as fitba', where the realisation of coda /l/ as a vowel, seen particularly in working-class adolescents, is not currently noted elsewhere in Scotland); and those that appear to represent the spread of use of more traditional, often negatively viewed, Glaswegian characteristics. Stuart-Smith et al. (2007) have reported that working-class adolescents examined were employing l-vocalisation as a means of signalling their group identity as Glaswegians; l-vocalisation was highly salient to them as a Glaswegian feature and was not viewed as a feature of English-English.

While some of the sound change processes noted in Glasgow appear to represent a move away from the traditional Glaswegian (and Scottish) model (the so-called 'TH' and 'DH' fronting process is a further example), other changes seem to represent the reinforcement of traditional, often highly stigmatised, Glaswegian features. One such process is the apparent increase in the use of the glottal stop in words such as *matter* and *patter*, even among more middle-class population groups (Stuart-Smith, 1999a). Glasgow has been referred to as the 'home of the glottal stop' (Macafee, 1997, p. 528) and t-glottalling is often considered one of the most salient features of the Glaswegian vernacular and is historically a highly stigmatised feature (Stuart-Smith, 1999a). The increase in usage of this feature noted in Glasgow among both working-class and middle-class adolescents (Stuart-Smith, 1999a) appears to suggest a retention and reinforcement of this traditional feature despite the stigma.

There have been studies which examine how language used in Glasgow has been used in literature, for example by Müller (2011), who has also included an analysis of swearing and how this forms a natural part of the language repertoire of Glasgow. Hagan (2002) has examined Urban Scots dialect writing, which includes the varieties used in Glasgow that are frequently seen as corrupt and vulgar forms, both historically and in contemporary usage, even though many novels set in the city use these varieties to different extents.

In short, Glaswegian is a distinct, often stigmatised variety and one which holds many stereotypes both for those in the city and outside its boundaries.

Performed language

In this section, we will look at the concepts of performed and stylized language. With this we mean that speakers can opt to use certain features of language instead of others as they expect that this performance will impact their audience (Coupland, 2009b, p. 315). This type of language usage highlights particular linguistic choices which express self-image and Johnstone and Bean (1997, p. 226) have argued that this type of language is even more revealing in understanding how speakers organize their sociolinguistic resources than vernacular speech. In particular, speakers choose how to sound and how this may affect their relationships with particular groups (Rampton, 1995 has discussed how stylization can be a form of 'subterfuge' when used to undermine other speakers). These linguistic choices express the self-image of such speakers and this is particularly the case with public speech. By examining case studies, we can understand what individuals are doing with language, as we can see the range of a speaker's linguistic resources. Coupland has also added that stylization involves playing personas, including 'in play or parody' (Coupland, 2001, p. 345) and the examination of such language in settings such as TV programmes can be referred to as 'high performance', where the symbolism and antagonism of different varieties can be seen most clearly (Coupland, 2009b, p. 317). It is exactly this type of situation that will be examined in this chapter.

What we are therefore looking at is what Coupland has referred to as 'stylization', which brings into play stereotyped values associated with particular groups; it is tightly linked to specific discourse communities (Coupland, 2001, p. 350). It requires an audience that can understand the values being portrayed and comment on the identities of the speakers. We will be looking at some groups who are relatively easily stylized, because they can be associated with particular socio-cultural and personal associations (to do with social class, trustworthiness, and character). People draw on stereotypical visions of language (Jaffe, 2000, p. 42) and the images associated with these. This can include elements of code-switching and shared identities, both of which will be relevant in our case study. Johnstone and Bean (1997, p. 224) have called this 'multiple models'; communities have different types of speakers with different types of association attached to them.

Although stylized speech may include exaggerated features and stereotypical images, it is also important to look at features that speakers may not be aware of. We need to bear in mind both salient and non-salient features to investigate how people perceive and produce language and we must consider attitudes towards varieties (Ito & Preston, 1998, p. 466). Speakers may be unaware of what their speech reveals about them or about linguistic stereotypes (Johnstone and Bean, 1997, p. 239), but this may not be the case for overt performances such as those examined in this chapter. Without being able to interview the actors involved, it is hard to know which features they are consciously aware of, but by including two different types of performance, it will be possible to see which linguistic features are used differently by them. We can assume, though, that the use of dialect in such sketches allows the actors to give the audience information about the characters without having to 'spell it out' (Hodson, 2014, p. 5). The audience can contribute what it knows about this variety, as well as other extra-linguistic information, to understand the characterisation taking place. We also have to assume that the audience is competent and able to make such decisions (Jaffe, 2000, p. 48). Although research has suggested (for example Ito and Preston, 1998, p. 480) that the unconscious use of language can tell us much about identity, it can be argued that examining which features are consciously used during performance of a variety is equally valid and worth investigation. Baumann has also argued that performances are good sites for the investigation of identity and language, as both performer and audience must construct and negotiate elements of identity and consider how language is used to do so (Bauman, 2000, p. 4). Queen has stated 'fictional media can directly address ideologies of language, mainly as they relate to the indexical associations broadly assumed to hold in a community between types of people and how they speak' (Queen, 2013, pp. 220–221).

Studies discussed by Coupland (2009a, p. 287) have examined different performances of vernaculars, including rap performances and adverts, and how audiences can relate to these. They consider the different local phonological, morphological, and lexical features, as well as local knowledge, required by the audience to relate to the sense of 'local' identity. In this research, Coupland has referred to *indexicality* (Coupland, 2009a, p. 285) where he discusses how a way of speaking is determined by how it is contextualised locally and whether this is *enregistered* as local. For more details on enregisterment, see also Johnstone (2011) who has examined highly self-conscious broadcast performances of language and local identity, where she explores how social identities are being created and how language is used to do so. Coupland has added (2010, p. 100) that 'indexical resources are orderly or structural, in the sense that speakers can draw from a template of known, generalised associations between linguistic styles and social meanings'. Speakers can examine the relationships between language and the relationship with the speaker to make sense of people's performances. Hodson has also emphasised the different orders of indexicality, with the third order being most relevant to the kind of performance discussed within this chapter, where it is possible for people to reference a dialect by using a subset of its features (Hodson, 2014, p. 75). Beal has examined this within song lyrics, where the linguistic features within these lyrics do 'social work' as they are associated with particular social categories (Beal, 2009, p. 224). One of the factors considered alongside indexicality and enregisterment is that of commodification. This has been discussed in some detail by Johnstone (2009), where she describes how local forms become linked with the city due to material artefacts, such as t-shirts with 'local' words and phrases. As well as displaying local speech, a specific value is associated with this type of language and allows people to link local speech with particular social meanings and identities. This type of commodification is certainly rife in Glasgow and a small selection of products available is shown here in Figures 15.1 and 15.2. Although these products signal a sense of pride in the local language variety, they can also provide us with information about cultural stereotypes.

FIGURE 15.1   Glasgow mug design, used with permission, Sprint Design, Glasgow.

FIGURE 15.2   Drinks coaster with local phrase (this is a catch phrase from *Chewin' the Fat*), used with permission, Sprint Design, Glasgow.

Methodology

Before considering the case study of *Chewin' the Fat*, we must first consider some initial research which has influenced the analysis of language used in these two sketches. As part of the research project examining language change and identity in Glasgow (discussed fully in Braber & Butterfint, 2008; Braber, 2009), we have carried out nineteen interviews with Glaswegian speakers (twelve of these speakers were still living in Glasgow and five speakers were now living in England – this was the case as part of the project examined the effect of migration on language change). Each interview consisted of a series of open-ended questions, the aim of which was to encourage participants to talk about their feelings towards Glasgow, Scotland, Britain, and England, their feelings about the Glaswegian accent and speech features, as well as their own speech and language use. We have found the repetition of certain attitudes by the majority of the speakers concerning Glaswegian. Almost all participants commented that certain aspects of Glaswegian were 'ugly' and that they had at times changed the way they spoke for particular purposes. All also commented that Glaswegian was a very distinctive variety and one that could be easily labelled. However, when we asked these participants what made an accent Glaswegian, they found this question very difficult to answer. Some of them commented on the t-glottalling, which is present in Glaswegian, but mostly they gave lexical items (often Scots) as examples of 'Glaswegian' speech. What many did comment on was the concept of a dialect continuum in Glasgow and the particular varieties present in this continuum, and these will be interesting for the data analysis in *Chewin' the Fat*. There were three varieties, which many of our speakers commented on, and these were the names they supplied themselves:

- 'Common' Glaswegian: the variety used by working-class speakers and seen as 'guttural' and 'ugly' (even by those who say they use it themselves).
- 'Normal' Glaswegian: not seen as 'common' as the previous variety, but not prestigious either.
- 'Kelvinside' – this is a highly stigmatised and affected variety used by a particular kind of person. This was sometimes referred to as 'pan loaf'. Traditionally in Scotland there were only two types of bread: 'pan loaf' and 'plain loaf'. Pan loaf was seen as a traditional type of bread, but which was more expensive and fashionable than a plain loaf. Participants in this study commented that to speak with a 'pan loafy voice' is to speak in a posh or affected manner. This is a variety which is more common in older middle-class women, and is treated as a stereotype and caricature by others. 'Kelvinside' is mirrored in Edinburgh, where it is referred to as 'Morningside', which is an affluent area of the city.

The sketches used in this chapter contain the two extreme varieties of Glaswegian: the 'common' Glaswegian and 'Kelvinside'. What we see in these sketches is the performance of two groups of Glaswegians and the stereotypes are very clear (certainly to Glaswegians and other Scots) as belonging to a particular aspect of

Glaswegian identity. Although these are identities with which most probably would not actively associate, they are understood to represent certain groups in the city, and many of the catch-phrases used in the programme have come to be used by large groups of people in Scotland. Jaffe (2000, p. 49) has argued that a large part of humour lies in exaggeration, and this is certainly the case for these sketches. Johnstone (2011, p. 662) has added to this that the quality of the actual performance is important, not just the accuracy of the representations. People do not need to think that this programme represents 'actual' people, but that it plays on cultural stereotypes they stand for (see also Torresi, 2007). Jaffe has commented that these 'voices' must be recognizable to the audience, meaning they that are in some way stereotypical and 'linguistically indexed in conventional ways' (Jaffe, 2000, p. 42).

Chewin' the Fat

The data I consider here are extracts from a Scottish comedy sketches programme broadcast on BBC Scotland. The Scottish division of the BBC was established in 1952. The three BBC Scotland channels (BBC1, BBC2, and BBC Alba) can opt out of national BBC One and Two to broadcast their own programmes in addition to showing networked productions. These channels do continue to produce a high number of local programmes for Scottish audiences, and it was estimated that approximately 75% of those able to receive BBC1 Scotland view the channel. These figures do not take into account that with the increase of freeview digital television, viewers outside the region can also view these stations, but this was not the case when this programme was originally aired.

The show covered in this chapter is called *Chewin' the Fat*, a phrase which means to chat about topics of mutual interest to speakers. It started as a radio show on BBC Radio Scotland and ran as a television programme for four series from 1999 to 2002, and repeats ran until 2009. There have also been six Hogmanay (New Year) specials, which were broadcast and offered as free DVDs to buyers of *The Scottish Sun* newspaper between 2000–2005. The first two series were only shown on BBC Scotland, but series three and four were later broadcast to the rest of the United Kingdom. It is a comedy sketch show, starring Ford Kiernan, Greg Hemphill, and Karen Dunbar, but there are other actors who also appear on the show. The characters examined in this chapter are acted out by Ford Kiernan and Greg Hemphill. The series was mostly filmed in and around Glasgow. There is also an accompanying webpage hosted by the BBC about the programme and containing short downloads as well as personality tests, images, and games.

The sketches involve many different characters from around Scotland, including Gaelic-speaking sock puppets, northern Lighthouse workers, and a spoof Star Trek cast from Tayside. However, many of the sketches involve Glaswegians, for example 'The Big Man', a tough Glasgow gangster; 'Ronald Villiers', the world's worst actor; and 'Tom Gallacher', a Glasgow merchant who sells dodgy merchandise. *Chewin' the Fat* plays on the association of social characteristics mentioned earlier in the chapter and plays on the stigmatised association of Glasgow with crime and violence. The two sets of characters which will be analysed here are acted by the same

Performing identity on screen **275**

individuals (Ford Kiernan and Greg Hemphill), both born in Glasgow. Not all characters appear in every episode and never appear more than once in an individual episode. The two character types which are the focus of this analysis are:

- The Neds (this includes Rab McGlinchy, who appears as an interpreter on the news programme). These are generally working-class adolescent hooligans, also referred to as 'chavs' in England. The word Ned is an acronym for 'non-educated delinquent'. They are typically attired in baseball hats, shell-suits, gold jewellery, and gelled-down hair, while smoking, drinking, and looking angry, and are involved with petty crime and often seen as unemployed.
- The Banter Boys (real names James and Gary). They are two very camp men – pretentious but amused and entertained by the 'Common Glaswegians'. They are keen to belong to the speech community but never quite manage to fit in. They have styled hair and old-fashioned clothing (turtleneck jumpers, waistcoats). They speak in affected pan loaf voices, but frequently talk about 'the banter', the language style used by other Glaswegians. See Figures 15.3 and 15.4 for images of these two characters, dressed as they are for the scene discussed below.

FIGURE 15.3   Ned (this is not from *Chewin' the Fat* as no images were available, but of a Glaswegian comedian, Neil Bratchpiece, dressed as a *ned*). Used with permission, Creative Commons Attribution Licence.

276 Natalie Braber

FIGURE 15.4 Banter Boy: Gary, used with copyright permission BBC.

Coupland (2001, pp. 370–371) has commented that the political situation in Wales, with political devolution and a changed economy, has led to the establishment of new identities. He comments that Wales has a strong sense of national identity and the humour used by comedians is 'laughter WITH rather than AT speakers of Welsh English' (Coupland, 2001, p. 371, emphasis in original). I would argue that this is also the case with the comedy programme reviewed in this chapter. Fictional TV characters frequently stand for attitudes and values (Bednarek, 2011, p. 10) and are used by audience members to identity with (or not) and show affiliation with (or not) and tell us something about the way people think about a city or a group of people. However, as this is a comedy television programme, entertainment remains the most important aspect of the programme (Coupland, 2001, p. 351). There are other studies which consider the use of Scots and other linguistic features, such as Brown and Lenz (1997) who have examined the use of language in the Scottish situation comedy *The High Life*. They have found that characters use local pronunciations and Scots lexis as part of the comedy of the programme.

Analysis

In this section, I will analyse accent and vocabulary and how these are linked with visual aspects, including props, costume, and appearance (as discussed by Hodson, 2014, p. 16) to investigate how these characters perform their linguistic identity. We can see that these characters use particular words with particular pronunciations, they have a way of speaking, and a particular voice. Also, the visual elements are supposed to be representative of the characters, and this includes hair style, clothing, and what they are doing during the sketches. Much of the success of these sketches is based on in-group humour. It is assumed that viewers understand the stereotypes and the references made in the sketches. However, the humour does work on a further level for those who are not aware of these cultural stereotypes and they can appreciate the comic value of the situations without fully understanding the references being made.

The features I will be discussing in connection with these sketches are:

- Word-final and word-medial glottallization of /t/
- Monophthongization of diphthongs
- Fronting of /u/
- Standard vs non-standard pronunciations of specific lexical items
- Scots lexical items, including tags
- Cultural references

The first extract discussed below takes place at a fairground and considers the Neds. As the scene opens, there are rides, flashing lights, and the two characters are walking from one stall to the next. The two 'young men' are unnamed and are dressed in a way that is typical of adolescent youths known as 'Neds' in Scotland (and will therefore be named Ned 1 and Ned 2 below). They are wearing colourful shell-suits, have dark hair that has been gelled right down over their foreheads, and their hands are deep in their pockets. When they start talking, they do so in a heavily nasalized voice, which is a feature of certain urban Glaswegians, specifically young male working-class speakers. Their voices are relatively monotonous and contain little pitch variation. The linguistic features they use show they are from Glasgow. These characters are seen as typical of certain parts of the Glaswegian population and associated with lower working-class individuals.

Extract 1: The Neds

(There is a fairground with flashing lights and rides and the two characters enter screen from the left)

1	Ned 1	I wisnae into that mad ping pong patter by the way
	Ned 2	Nah, your ping pong was pingin' all o'er the shop there. Nae chance o' a goldie, know what I mean
	Ned 1	Fancy a go o' the shootin' but (camera shows the stallholder calling for custom)

5	Ned 2	Aye, man, aye
	Ned 1	Oh eh man, eh, crossbow (both laugh and pick up a crossbow each)
	Ned 2	That's absolutely tops man
	Ned 1	Beautiful (both aim crossbow at the stallholder, stop laughing and look serious)
	Ned 2	Gie us a gonk, ya dobber

This sketch underlines what is known about Neds: they are dishonest and untrustworthy. Although they chat in a very friendly way to each other, when they turn on the stallholder, their attitudes change completely and they stop being friendly and become rather menacing instead. From a linguistic point of view, as mentioned above, both Neds have very nasal voices. They produce many of the features which are typical of this urban variety: glottalling of medial and final /t/, fronting of /u/, and many consonants are elided. See Table 15.1 for more details.

There are other non-standard features which are used by the two speakers. In line 1, the first Ned says he 'wisnae' (for 'wasn't'). This is a typical negative construction used throughout Scotland. There is also the use of the tag 'but', which is not used with its usual means of a conjunction, but used at the end of the sentence to emphasize what the speaker is saying. There are other lexical items, such as 'aye' (for 'yes') and terms such as 'man' when addressing one another, which index this sense of a strong, local identity. There are also taboo words, which are an important part of language in Glasgow. Use of taboo words and swearing are absolutely necessary for the expression of a Glaswegian identity: 'it is crucial for the authentic expression of the everyday experiences of the underprivileged' (see Hagan, 2002, p. 209). The second Ned calls the stallholder 'ya dobber' (a derogatory term which literally means 'penis') when threatening him and asking for the 'gonk' (toy troll). As this is a relatively short extract, there are many other features which appear in other sketches including these characters which are not shown here. These include, for example, fronting of back vowels ('off' produced as /af/ not /ɒf/ and 'want' produced as /want/ where Standard English would use /wɒnt/). There is also frequently retraction of /s/, where /s/ is produced more like /ʃ/.

The second extract consists of the Banter Boys talking about getting a bargain from the Barrows (known locally as the Barras, a very well-known market in Glasgow where there is always a bit of dodgy-dealing going on, but is generally harmless). The word 'banter' itself is interesting. Banter refers to informal, joking chat between friends who may be teasing each other. One of the main threads

TABLE 15.1 Variables for the Neds.

t → ʔ	pa*t*ter, bu*t*, wha*t*, beau*t*iful
u → ʉ	sh*oo*t
əʊ → o	g*o*, crossb*ow*
Consonant elision	o*v*er, o*f*, gi*v*e
ing → in'	shoot*ing*, ping*ing*

running through this TV show is the repetition of stereotypes and catch phrases by particular characters. The audience watching the programme know at the outset of the sketch (if they are regular watchers) what the main point of the sketch will be. For these particular characters, they are always trying to fit in with 'typical' aspects of life in Glasgow, whether that is football, shopping, or chatting to locals. However, their appearance and very camp behaviour immediately show them not belonging to their desired speech community. The normative heterosexuality associated with Glaswegian 'real men' (and indexed by characters such as The Big Man, mentioned previously) ensures that these two characters are clearly outsiders.

Before we look at the linguistic features of these characters, there are other features which are important in setting the scene. They are sitting in a quaint tea room (no alcohol and cigarettes) having 'their tea'; they both have very styled hair, are wearing waistcoats, jumpers and slacks, and one of them is wearing a little gold ring on his pinkie (as opposed to big signet rings that many Neds would wear); there is no other gold jewellery, such as gold chains which are worn by Neds in other sketches; and in this sketch they have bought a silver Rennie Mackintosh tea strainer. Charles Rennie Mackintosh (1868–1928) was a Glaswegian architect, water colourist, and artist. The Mackintosh style, which is typified by strong angles with rose motifs, has had a resurgence in Scotland with furniture, jewellery, crockery, and many other products based on his designs. This particular tea strainer is being held above an anthology of Robert Burns love poetry. Robert (also known as Rabbie) Burns (1759–1796) was a Scottish poet and lyricist of the Romantic period who is known for writing in Scots, and is Scotland's most famous poet. These are both items which would be considered more middle-class by many inhabitants of Glasgow, particularly many of the other characters in *Chewin' the Fat*.

Extract 2: The Banter Boys

(James and Gary are sitting in a very ornate, flowery tea room with an elaborately laid table)

1	Gary	Do you love it, or do you love it, a genuine Rennie Mackintosh tea strainer, if you will
	James	Oh Gary, it's an utter darling, totally tosh
	Gary	Mais oui James and I trust that you will be coming roond for your tea in the Glesgae style?
5	James	Does the pope wear a mitre? Now tell me Gary, where did you pick it up, at some little antique fair?
	Gary	Indeed I did not James, I picked it up doon the Barrows
	James	Ooh, the Barrows
	Gary	Well, it was tagged at £90 but I managed to haggle the stallholder down to £85

10	James	Well, that's the beauty of the Barrows
	Gary	And he threw in an anthology of Rabbie Burns love poetry
	James	Ooh, I love Rabbie Burns
	Gary	I fought murder, policeman, what a bargain, ooh the stallholder, a real Glasgae man
	James	A Glasgae ticket
15	Gary	Absolutely full o' the banter. In fact as he wrapped them, he looked me straight in the eye and said, I saw you comin'
	James	Aah, the Glasgow banter doon the Barrows

The two characters talk about the bargain, one of them states that he managed to haggle the seller from £90 to £85, but does not realise that he has been ripped off (he comments that the salesman even says that he saw him coming, without being aware of the irony that this was not meant in a positive way, and this is one of the important jokes about this sketch, as 'real' Glaswegians would not stand for this). This clearly shows that they do not belong to this community as they do not understand the way of the Barras. Additionally, it also suggests another distinguishing factor: it seems that the money does not matter so much to them, as it suggests they have money for such frivolous items.

The language used by James and Gary is very different to the previous sketch (bearing in mind that the same two actors also performed the Ned scene, so these linguistic features have been specifically chosen to represent these speakers). There is no nasal voice used by either character, instead these two men use voices with considerable pitch movements and excessive intonation (in words such as 'genuine' in Line 1). This manner of speaking is distinctly camp and it can be assumed that these speakers are supposed to be gay. Accompanying the pitch and intonation are also very visible facial expressions, such as eye rolling and eyebrow raising, which are not present in the first sketch.

The linguistic features are also very different to those of the first sketch (see Table 15.2). Some of the features initially look similar, but are used very differently. One of the most obvious differences is the complete lack of t-glottalling, even word finally in words such as 'it' where we would expect glottalling in most speakers. Throughout the second sketch, all instances of /t/ are retained by both speakers. There is very little consonant elision, in fact it only occurs once when Gary says the stallholder is 'full o' the banter'. Some of the other features which look more local are used inconsistently, for example the word 'down' is produced in two different ways by Gary, suggesting that this is not a style he is completely used to, and he gets it wrong. This element of uncertainty is also present in the word 'Glasgow' which is sometimes pronounced in the local form 'Glesgae' but not consistently so. The market they are referring to is locally known as 'The Barras', but is referred to by these two characters as 'The Barrows', which is a standard English variety which does not index local identity. Also, the word 'banter' which is so important to these men is not produced in an accurately local style. It is produced with /æ/,

TABLE 15.2 Variables for the Banter Boys.

t → t	ban*t*er, i*t*, u*tt*er, to*t*ally
a → əʊ	B*a*rr*ow*s
aʊ → u	r*ou*nd, d*ow*n
Consonant elision	o*f*

which is a less fronted and shorter version of what would be expected from Glaswegian speakers. Much of this pronunciation points to an element of hypercorrection where James and Gary are aware of what is required, but cannot produce these consistently enough.

Many features are more similar to Kelvinside than Common Glaswegian, for example the way they say 'and' (sounds more like /ɛnd/): the sound is raised, which is a very salient feature of Kelvinside. They also tend to show a very backed /u/, as opposed to the fronted vowel seen in the Neds.

There are some lexical items which cement the image of the pretentious Kelvinsider, such as 'darling', 'totally tosh', and the French phrase 'mais oui' used by Gary in Line 3, as well as referring to 'some little antique fair' in Line 6, noticeably not 'wee' which would be used by many speakers and is frequently used by other characters in the programme. Not only do James and Gary get the pronunciation 'wrong', this is also the case for some of the other culturally significant items. James in Line 5 responds 'does the Pope wear a mitre' to signal that a question has a very obvious answer, whereas usually it would be 'is the Pope Catholic?' Phrases such as 'I fought murder, policeman, what a bargain' in Line 14 are typical of the pretentious, elaborate speech style of these characters as opposed to the direct vulgarity of the Neds ('ya dobber'). Neither of these two speakers uses local tags such as 'but', or expressions such as 'man', which typify the Neds in other sketches.

From these two different, very short, sketches we can see some of the different linguistic identities which are indexical of Glasgow. This analysis could be elaborated by including more sketches or more characters, to further this evidence. However, we can see two of the most stereotyped identities of Glasgow: on one side, the young, rough adolescents who use obscene language, greater use of localised features and their competence in an 'accurate' Glasgow linguistic identity. On the other hand are the incompetent, middle-class Kelvinsiders who do not really belong, who are trying to fit in, but are not able to accurately and consistently display their linguistic identity.

Conclusion

This chapter has established how different Glaswegian identities are portrayed by two specific characters in a television comedy sketch show. It examined the use of stylized language in performance speech, and as a result it has been able to show that TV comedy is a fruitful area to analyse ways in which speech is an important element in the production of identity. This means that stylized, performed language can be used by sociolinguists to examine issues such as identity and language variation alongside more traditional vernacular forms of language.

In the programme *Chewin' the Fat*, the contrasting characters of the Neds and the Banter Boys were compared. Visually, these characters look and act differently – the Neds dress in shell-suits with gelled-down hair and are linked with petty crime, alcohol, and smoking. The Banter Boys are dressed in a more old-fashioned way with styled hair, and are associated with culture and pretension. Linguistically, these characters also behave differently. The Neds have nasalized voices and produce t-glottalling, consonantal elision, and vowels which are associated with Glasgow speech. Their language contains swearing and references to taboo language. The Banter Boys do not produce t-glottalling or consonantal elision. At times, they appear to try to produce vowels which are associated with the 'common' Glaswegian variety, but their attempts misfire and their variety fits with the 'Kelvinside' variety. Their language does not include swearing or taboo language, but makes reference to art and culture instead.

According to Johnstone, performance speech can be heard in different ways: a linguistic feature can be used to construct a particular persona, whether that be Glaswegian or working-class (or both), or can be seen as a funny sketch because of its content (Johnstone, 2011, p. 675). This mainly depends on the audience. Nardini has added that you have to 'be there' and understand what the comedy is referring to (Nardini, 2000, p. 89), so maybe this is why the programme did not do so well outside Scotland as it did with a local audience who understood the underlying comments. However, what we can see is that language, as well as other features such as clothing, hair, and accessories, are used by speakers to index and enregister their sense of identity. The linguistic features used by the characters reflect what the audience understands about linguistic and cultural associations within Glasgow and what is meant by these.

Coupland has argued that the search for authenticity and the authentic speaker can be seen as 'the elephant in the room' (Coupland, 2010, p. 99), as it is something that sociolinguists may search for but not adequately discuss what this should actually be. This chapter has argued that performed language is an interesting vehicle to examine language variation, as it allows us to further investigate the role of identity in language variation. We can see that such comic roles still follow speech patterns which would be seen in vernacular speech and, as such, reflect reality, even though they can be exaggerated.

As Coupland has argued in his study (2001), the social meanings that are constructed through the radio talk show he examined do not undermine Welshness, and this is similar to the sketches I have examined. The language used in *Chewin' the Fat* is designed to capture a Glaswegianness that people understand and can relate to, if only to identify that they do not belong to either of these two groups, but still to Glasgow. These sketches encapsulate stereotypical Glaswegian ways of speaking and ways of being – these are two cultural groups which Glaswegians are aware of. Speakers share such cultural images and this allows for a feeling of solidarity with one another in their imagined community. Johnstone has commented that 'social stereotypes and collective knowledge are embraced and embroidered: what is being constructed is a representation of a community's sociolinguistic identity' (Johnstone, 2007, p. 181)

The use of language requires speakers to make linguistic choices, and through these choices speakers make claims to social identities. This applies to the audience as well as the characters in these cases. We have seen here that using a 'local' accent becomes linked with a sense of 'localness' (Johnstone, 2007, p. 168), and that can be the case for 'natural' and 'performed' language.

Finally, it is clear that much more work remains to be done, but examination of these sketches enables the provisional conclusion that linguistic features (linked to very important visual features) can be used to portray different social identities, and that in this case, many of the linguistic features reflect those used by speakers (even if many of them have been exaggerated for comic effect). Even if the Glaswegians we questioned found it very hard to pin down the features of Glaswegian English, they would have no problem identifying the different groups that are portrayed in *Chewin' the Fat*. In short, examining stylized or performed speech has been a successful way of examining 'real' language and the features within it, and can tell us much about the way a particular variety is viewed.

References

Aitken, A. J. (1981). The Scottish vowel-length rule. In M. Benskin & M. L. Samuels (Eds.), *So meny peoples longages and tonges: Philological essays in Scots and Mediaeval English presented to Angus McIntosh* (pp. 131–157). Edinburgh: Middle English Dialect Project.

Anderson, B. (1991). *Imagined communities: Reflections on the origin and spread of nationalism* (2nd ed.). London: Verso.

Andersson, L. G., & Trudgill, P. (1990). *Bad language*. London: Penguin Books.

Bauman, R. (2000). Language, identity, performance. *Pragmatics*, *10*(1), 1–5.

Beal, J. (2009). "You're not from New York City, you're from Rotherham": Dialect and identity in British Indie music. *Journal of English Linguistics*, *37*(3), 223–240.

Bednarek, M. (2011). Expressivity and televisual characterization. *Language and Literature*, *20*(1), 3–21.

Braber, N. (2009). "I'm not a fanatic Scot, but I love Glasgow": Concepts of local and national identity in Glasgow. *Identity*, *9*(4), 307–322.

Braber, N., & Butterfint, Z. (2008). Local identity and sound change in Glasgow. *Leeds Working Papers*, *13*, 22–43.

Brown, I., & Lenz, K. (1997). 'Oh dearie me!': Dramatic rhetoric and linguistic subversion in the Scottish situation comedy *The High Life*. In E. W. Schneider (Ed.), *Englishes around the world 1* (pp. 109–123). Amsterdam: John Benjamins.

Bucholtz, M., & Hall, K. (2005). Identity and interaction: A sociocultural linguistic approach. *Discourse Studies*, *7*(4–5), 585–614.

Chambers, I. (1994). *Migrancy, culture, identity*. London: Routledge.

Coupland, N. (2001). Dialect stylization in radio talk. *Language in Society*, *30*, 345–375.

Coupland, N. (2009a). The mediated performance of vernaculars. *Journal of English Linguistics*, *37*(3), 284–300.

Coupland, N. (2009b). Dialect style, social class and metacultural performance: The pantomime Dame. In N. Coupland & A. Jaworski (Eds.), *The new sociolinguistics reader* (pp. 311–325). Basingstoke: Palgrave Macmillan.

Coupland, N. (2010). The authentic speaker and the speech community. In C. Llamas & D. Watt (Eds.), *Language and identities* (pp. 99–112). Edinburgh: Edinburgh University Press.

Dyer, J. (2007). Language and identity. In C. Llamas, L. Mullany, & P. Stockwell (Eds.), *The Routledge companion to sociolinguistics* (pp. 101–108). London: Routledge.

Görlach, M. (2002). *A textual history of Scots*. Heidelberg: Universitätsverlag C. Winter.

Hagan, A. I. (2002). *Urban Scots dialect writing*. Oxford: Peter Lang.

Hodson, J. (2014). *Dialect in film and literature*. Basingstoke: Palgrave Macmillan.

Ito, R., & Preston, D. R. (1998). Identity, discourse, and language variation. *Journal of Language and Social Psychology*, 17(4), 465–483.

Jaffe, A. (2000). Comic performance and the articulation of hybrid identity. *Pragmatics*, 10(1), 39–59.

Johnstone, B. (1999). Uses of Southern-sounding speech by contemporary Texas women. *Journal of Sociolinguistics*, 3(4), 505–522.

Johnstone, B. (2007). Discursive sources of linguistic diversity: Stancetaking and vernacular norm-formation. In Y. Matsumoto, D. Y. Shima, O. W. Robinson, & P. Sells (Eds.), *Diversity in language: Perspectives and implications* (pp. 167–196). Stanford: Center for the Study of Language and Social Interaction.

Johnstone, B. (2009). Pittsburghese shirts: Commodification and the enregisterment of an urban dialect. *American Speech*, 84(2), 157–191.

Johnstone, B. (2011). Dialect enregisterment in performance. *Journal of Sociolinguistics*, 15(5), 657–679.

Johnstone, B., & Bean, J. M. (1997). Self-expression and linguistic variation. *Language in Society*, 26(2), 221–246.

Labov, W. (1963). The social motivation of a sound change. *Word*, 19, 273–309.

Llamas, C. (1999). A new methodology: Data elicitation for social and regional language variation studies. *Leeds Working Papers in Linguistics*, 7, 95–118.

Llamas, C. (2007). "A place between places": Language and identities in a border town. *Language in Society*, 36, 579–604.

Macafee, C. (1997). Ongoing change in Modern Scots: The social dimension. In C. Jones (Ed.), *The Edinburgh history of the Scots language* (pp. 514–548). Edinburgh: Edinburgh University Press.

Maier, C. S. (2007). "Being there": Place, territory and identity. In S. Benhabib, I. Shapiro, & D. Petranović (Eds.), *Identities, affiliations, and allegiances* (pp. 67–84). Cambridge: Cambridge University Press.

Müller, C. (2011). *A Glasgow voice: James Kelman's literary language*. Newcastle: Cambridge Scholars.

Nardini, G. (2000). When husbands die: Joke-telling in an Italian ladies' club in Chicago. *Pragmatics*, 10(1), 87–97.

Omoniyi, T., & White, G. (Eds.). (2006). *The sociolinguistics of identity*. London: Continuum.

Queen, R. (2013). Working with performed language: Movies, television and music. In C. Mallinson, B. Childs, & G. Van Herk (Eds.), *Data collection in sociolinguistics* (pp. 217–227). London: Routledge.

Rampton, B. (1995). *Crossing*. London: Longman.

Schilling-Estes, N. (1998). Investigating "self-conscious" speech: The performance register in Ocracoke English. *Language in Society*, 27, 53–83.

Scobbie, J., Gordeeva, O., & Matthews, B. (2006). Acquisition of Scottish English phonology: An overview. *QMUC Speech Science Research Centre Working Paper* WP-7. Retrieved February 2017, from http://eresearch.qmu.ac.uk/149/1/wp-7.pdf

Stuart-Smith, J. (1999a). Glottals past and present: A study of T-glottalling in Glaswegian. *Leeds Studies in English*, 30, 181–203.

Stuart-Smith, J. (1999b). Glasgow: Accent and voice quality. In P. Foulkes & G. Docherty (Eds.), *Urban voices: Accent studies in the British Isles* (pp. 203–222). London: Arnold.

Stuart-Smith, J., Timmins, C., & Tweedie, F. (2007). "Talkin' Jockney"? Variation and change in Glaswegian accent. *Journal of Sociolinguistics, 11*(2), 221–260.

Tabouret-Keller, A. (1997). Language and identity. In F. Coulmas (Ed.), *The handbook of sociolinguistics* (pp. 315–326). Oxford: Blackwell.

Thornborrow, J. (1999). Language and identity. In I. Singh & J. S. Peccei (Eds.), *Language, society and power* (pp. 158–172). London: Routledge.

Torresi, I. (2007). Quick temper, hot blood: The filmic representation of Italian-American speech and rhetorical strategies. In N. Fairclough, G. Cortese, & P. Ardizzone (Eds.), *Discourse and contemporary social change* (pp. 531–548). Bern: Peter Lang.

Trudgill, P. (1986). *Dialects in contact*. Oxford: Blackwell.

Watt, D., Llamas, C., Docherty, G., Hall, D., & Nycz, J. (2014). Language and identity on the Scottish/English border. In D. Watt & C. Llamas (Eds.), *Language, borders and identity* (pp. 8–26). Edinburgh: Edinburgh University Press.

Wells, J. C. (1982). *Accents of English 2: The British Isles*. Cambridge: Cambridge University Press.

16

IDENTITY, REPERTOIRE, AND PERFORMANCE

The case of an Egyptian poet

Reem Bassiouney

Introduction

This article examines the linguistic repertoire of a poet from the south of Egypt who performs in more than one code, and whose original dialect is stigmatised in Egyptian public discourse as associated with the ignorance and violence of the south. This poet manipulates the linguistic resources at his disposal to create his own local identity, persona, and style through the accumulation of stances in his work. Drawing on the second-order indexes of specific phonological variables in his own dialect as well as Standard Arabic (SA), he differentiates himself from other southern performers, who also have access to different linguistic resources and who, depending on their stance object, resort to Cairene Standard Arabic (CSA) and their own southern dialect Saʿidi Colloquial Arabic (SCA) when performing. He takes advantage of the diglossic situation by sometimes using (SA), a code that is not the native code of any Arab country but that carries positive religious indexes and legitimacy in all the Arab world (see Ferguson, 1959 and Bassiouney, 2009 for details), while attempting to avoid specific phonological variables associated with CSA. The poet analysed in this article uses systematically, in his interviews and performance, salient phonological features from his own local dialect and avoids marked CSA phonological features. In this way he evokes the positive indexes of his dialect and manipulates the stereotype of the south to his advantage. However, when the object of his stance needs to be legitimised, it is SA that he chooses to perform in, not CSA. He thus renegotiates the value of the social resources at his disposal. His choice to avoid marked CSA variables, although CSA is a powerful resource both within and outside Egypt, is a challenge to the existing status quo and an attempt to situate his own dialect in a more powerful and influential position. Not all southern performers in Egypt have access to Cairene media, and those who do try to renegotiate the power of access to their code as opposed to the prevalent Cairene one. This is not just a linguistic process or a styling attempt on the part of the poet; it is in fact a struggle for reassigning value to linguistic resources, a struggle in which access to political and social power has always been in Cairo and not the south.

To elaborate, Coupland (2007, p. 3) argues that 'sociolinguistics can and should move on from the documenting of social styles or dialects themselves. . . . analysing the creative, design-oriented processes through which social styles are activated in talk and, in the process, remade or reshaped'. This is precisely what this article attempts to do. It examines how this poet utilises his linguistic resources and his access to the media to reshape the indexes of different codes in Egypt, as well as indirectly reexamining the social and political distribution of power.

As Rampton (2015, p. 39) argues, speakers of specific dialects 'agentively' rework the 'boundaries' of their own linguistic spaces, trying to 'navigat[e]' from one position to another in search of an identity. Identity, as defined by Bauman (2000, p. 1), is 'an emergent construction, the situated outcome of a rhetorical and interpretive process in which interactants make situationally motivated selections from socially constituted repertoires of identificational and affiliational resources and craft these semiotic resources into identity claims for presentation to others.' In other words, the agency of individuals in manipulating linguistic choices is essential to a better understanding of identity as related to one's linguistic repertoire. In order to construct identity, an individual chooses from his/her linguistic repertoire. To construct a local identity, a local dialect is usually displayed. This display of a local dialect is typically paired with a stance towards one's local identity and overall ideologies.

The poet selected is Hisham Al-Jukh (1978). He is originally from Sohag, a city that lies on the southwest bank of the Nile, approximately 500 kilometers south of Cairo. He currently resides in Cairo and performs throughout the Arab world. He has participated in international competitions within the Arab world and is highly acclaimed in Egypt. Data for this work includes thirty poems by this poet over the span of seven years (from 2010 to 2017). Supporting data include twelve talk shows in which the southern dialects of Egypt are discussed overtly during the period from 2013 to 2017.

Before I delve into the data analysis and theoretical approach of this work, I would like to shed light on the linguistic situation in Egypt.

Egyptian dialects and repertoires

A dialect is a code of language which is associated with a local area and/or a community of speakers that share sociolinguistic variables. Coupland (2007, p. 2) posits that a dialect is usually associated with a social group, a local area, or a specific time. He regards dialects as social styles and a resource for people to forge relations with others (2007, p. 3). A dialect is usually defined in relation to another dialect, language, or standard code, and shows distinct characteristics in terms of its syntax, morphology, semantic features, and phonological features (see Crystal, 2008; Cameron, 2012; Hodson, 2014). Silverstein (2014, p. 183) contends that dialects, accents, or codes no longer simply reflect the local area of their speakers or their social background, but now indicate the position of the speaker in relation to a culture, a belief system, an ideology, and perhaps a location. Lacoste, Leimgruber, and Breyer (2014, p. 183) argue that dialects do not just locate the individual in a particular class or region, but also culturally position an individual by stirring second-order indexes of his/her dialect.

Dialects in Egypt can be divided into urban, rural, and Bedouin types (see Wilmsen, 2011; Behnstedt & Woidich, 1985–1999). Cairo is the largest urban center in Egypt, followed by Alexandria. The dialects/accents of the two cities differ in a small number of lexical items and vowel qualities, but both are urban dialects that are close to one another when compared to rural dialects of the *fellahin* in the Nile Delta or the dialects in Middle and Upper Egypt (Wilmsen, 2011).

Cairene Standard Arabic (CSA) is the variety used in media discourse in Cairo and by Egyptian media producers for both private and public channels that broadcast in Egyptian Arabic both inside and outside Egypt. This variety is different from Standard Arabic (SA), the formal variety of the Arab world, which is not the spoken dialect of any country (see Ferguson, 1959). SA is associated with religion, tradition, and a pan-Arab identity (see Suleiman, 2003 and Bassiouney, 2009). However, in Egypt CSA also carries power and legitimacy.

Milroy and Milroy (2012, p. 172) discuss the process of legitimisation, in which a standard becomes 'identical' with the language and is the only legitimate resource; other resources are not as powerful or legitimate. Chun (2004, p. 353) reaches the same conclusion when she posits that the importance of a linguistic variety comes from its capacity of opening doors to powerful economic and social positions, and that this capacity is directly related to the 'legitimation' of this variety by government institutions. In Egypt there are two legitimate codes. One of these, SA, perhaps carries more prestige with intellectuals and public figures, but, as previously stated, it is not the spoken dialect of any part of the Arab world. However, CSA also carries legitimacy. This is because, since the turn of the twentieth century, Cairo has been the dynamo of the political and cultural renaissance throughout the Arab world. Along with the central role played by Cairo in both the political arena and the sphere of culture came the rise of CSA as the code that indexes power, cultural and political superiority, and authenticity in Egypt. Due to the highly centralised government system, with the seat of the main government offices located in the area around Tahrir Square (the focus of the 25 January 2011 Revolution), CSA holds a commanding position in official life.

In contrast, a group of dialects that are directly and indirectly associated with negative indexes rather than positive ones are those of upper Egypt (SCA). Upper Egypt (Ar. *al-Saiʻd*) is defined as the cultivated Valley of the Nile from Cairo to Aswan in the south – a distance of about 860 kilometers (Hopkins & Saad, 2004, p. 1). The phrase 'Saʻidi dialect' is a general designation used by Egyptians to refer to a group of dialects that are spoken in the area that runs from the south of Cairo to the borders of Sudan. These dialects differ phonologically, morphosyntactically, and semantically from Cairene Arabic (Wilmsen, 2011; Behnstedt & Woidich, 1985–1999).

The most marked phonological variables that differentiate between CSA and SCA are the SA phonological variables /q/ and /dʒ/, which are realised differently in CSA and SCA. In CSA they are realised as [ʔ] and [g] respectively. In SCA they are realised as [g] and [dʒ]. For example, the glottal stop in CSA *yiʔra* ('he reads') becomes a voiced velar /g/ (*yigra*) in Saʿidi dialects, while Cairene voiced velar /g/ in *ge:t* ('I came') is realised as *dʒe:t*, or even *de:t*, depending on the area. These differences are widely known and are commonly regarded as the defining features of Upper Egyptian speech.

However, there are also other, more subtle phonological differences, such as the glottalised pronunciation of /ṭ/ [tˤ] or the shift in stress patterns. For example, in CSA, with words that contain a consonant cluster, the stress falls on the vowel following the cluster, as in *madrasa* ('school'), whereas in most Saʿidi dialects the stress falls on the vowel preceding it, as in *madrasa*. Distinctive lexical variation occurs in the interrogative markers: for CSA *ʔimta, fe:n, izza:y* ('when', 'where', 'how'), Saʿidi dialects have *we:n, me:ta, ke:f*. Lexical variation even extends to commonly used words, such as CSA *hudu:m*/Saʿidi *xalaga:t* ('clothes') or CSA *ʕayyat*/Saʿidi *baka* ('he cried') (Miller, 2005, p. 922). An example of morphosyntactic variation between Cairene and Upper Egyptian dialects can be found in the negation of participles. Whereas in CSA this is formed by the negative particle *miʃ* followed by the participle (e.g., *miʃ ʔa:dir* ['I cannot']), in Upper Egyptian dialects the negative marker is separated as *m-ʃ* and the participle inserted (e.g., *ma-gadir-ʃ* ['I cannot']).

Because of these differences, Upper Egyptian dialects, like that of the poet to be studied here, are readily recognisable. They are also stigmatised and ridiculed because of the indexes associated with the identity of Upper Egyptians. In public discourse, films, songs, and soap operas, Upper Egypt (Saʿidi) is almost always juxtaposed with Cairo, with the former being characterised as a distinct and remote area where people are more conservative, violent, and often narrow-minded and unintelligent (see Miller, 2005; Hopkins & Saad, 2004).

On the basis of observations gathered during field research between 1994 and 1998, Miller (2005, p. 909) examines patterns of linguistic change and accommodation among Upper Egyptian migrants to Greater Cairo, especially those from the governorates of Sohag and Qena living in Giza. She posits that there is pressure to accommodate to CSA and to abandon local features. Miller argues that because of the stigma associated with Upper Egyptian Arabic, which indexes ignorance, narrow-mindedness, and poverty, all migrants acknowledge the inevitability of acquiring CSA and using it in interactions with Cairenes to avoid discrimination (2005, p. 931).

Accommodating to CSA is not an easy, nor always successful, task for many immigrants, and gender, as well as social class, are also factors in this process. However, this is not the focus of this particular article. It is important to note, nevertheless, that migrants' mere belief that CSA is a necessary tool for the success of their children is significant. In fact, the stigma attached to Upper Egyptian Arabic may be the main reason why the announcers of the local radio channel of Aswan in Upper Egypt adhere to CSA in their programs and do not use their own dialects. In doing so, they may be trying to index their sophistication, modernisation, and disassociation from all negative indexes of the local dialect or dialects.

Note that dialects are associated with styles (Coupland, 2007). Style is defined by Eckert (2001, p. 119) as a process in which individuals utilise the total linguistic resources they possess to negotiate and construct meaning. According to Coupland (2007, p. 6), style is a resource for people to transmit social and cultural meaning. Styling, on the other hand, is the 'contextualisation' of dialects or 'social styles' of individuals. Al-Jukh's consistent use of marked SCA phonological variables, except in SA poems, is part of his styling process, which is an essential part of his public persona. The phonological variables that he chooses have established second-order indexes, and have been spoken about in the talk shows analysed here. For example, a Saʻidi dialect coach, Muhammad, in a 2014 interview which he performs in Saʻidi,[1] specifically discusses the salient features mentioned above with the announcer, i.e., the use of /dʒ/ or /d/ in Saʻidi dialects, where CSA has /g/, depending on the location within Saʻid, and the CSA lexical item *baʔa* ('to become') realised as a different lexical item, *ʕa:d*, in Saʻidi dialects. Reflecting about linguistic codes is an essential part of assigning indexes to them.

Agha (2005) and Rampton (2015) argue that reflexivity is inherent in the definition of style, register, variety, or dialect. It is, in fact, through reflexive activities such as crossing, 'tropes', and stylisation that we identify a dialect as such (see Agha, 2005, p. 46; Rampton, 2015, p. 26). As a process, reflexivity is reflected in the studies of linguists themselves and not just in the interaction of speakers (see Cameron, 2012; Johnstone, 2015). Johnstone argues that when individuals engage in metalinguistic discourse – that is, reflect on language and emphasise the indexes and associations, whether social or political, of different varieties – they may be supporting a process that could lead to language change. In another example, actors and actresses who perform in the soap opera *Silsal iddamm* ('Blood Chain') are talking at a press conference (2015):[2] the actress is asked to speak in SCA. She then changes the CSA glottal stop to [g] and by so doing thinks that she is now performing in SCA.

Actress: awil marra atkallim ṣaʕi:di/ wi fil awwil kunt ʔalʔa:na ʔawi
Actor: goli:ha bil ṣaʕi:di
Actress: (in Saʻidi dialect): galga:na gawi
Actress: This is the first time I'm speaking in a Saʻidi dialect. I was so worried at first.
Actor: Say it in Saʻidi!
Actress: I was so worried.

These examples show the display of SCA phonological variables in the media.

Linguistic repertoire is the accumulation of the linguistic resources available to an individual. However, linguistic resources, like all social resources, are distributed unequally and do not carry the same social and political weight. Gal (1989, p. 353) argues that the importance of a dialect or variety lies in its capacity to give power, or economic, political, or social status. Heller (2007) also argues that language is a social practice; speakers are social actors and boundaries are an outcome of social action. Therefore, languages have to be studied in relation to ideology, social practice, and social organisation (Heller, 2007, pp. 1–2). Accordingly, language can be defined as a set of resources that is distributed in unequal ways, depending on the social networks and 'discursive spaces' of individuals. A similar approach to Heller's is adopted by Blommaert (2010, p. 180), who contends that sociolinguists need to start examining language as a resource, within which 'language events and experiences' preside over 'language-as-form-and-meaning.'

Identity, as stated earlier, is 'an emergent construction, the situated outcome of a rhetorical and interpretive process in which interactants make situationally motivated selections from socially constituted repertoires of identificational and affiliational resources and craft these semiotic resources into identity claims for presentation to others' (Bauman, 2000, p. 1). In other words, the agency of individuals in manipulating linguistic choices is essential to a better understanding of identity as related to one's linguistic repertoire. In order to construct identity, an individual chooses from his/her linguistic repertoire. To construct a local identity, a local dialect is usually displayed. This display of a local dialect is usually paired with a stance towards one's local identity and overall ideologies.

Identity performance and stance

Before delving into analysis of the data I would like to shed some light on performance. Schilling-Estes (1998, p. 53) defines performance as the 'register' speakers use to 'display' a linguistic code/variety to others, whether this code is their own or that of another 'speech community'. To elaborate, when a linguistic code or dialect is objectified and displayed in relation to forms of speaking, then it is performed. As one would expect, unlike natural speech, 'performance speech' is, according to Schilling-Estes (1998, p. 54), 'highly self-conscious'; speakers often focus on forms of speaking, rather than content. Bauman contends that performance as 'an act of expression' is displayed, objectified by the performer, and then scrutinised and evaluated by an audience (Bauman, 2000, p. 1). As Coupland (2001) argues, style switching is a means by which an individual can project an identity (see also Coupland, 2007, p. 190). Lacoste et al. (2014, p. 8) argue that people search for resources to 'construct' and 'deconstruct' their identities during an act of communication, as well as 'stage' their identity. That is, people, at times, perform an authentic identity – for example, by drawing on salient linguistic resources associated with a local identity. This performance depends on the perceptions of the speaker or author regarding what constitutes a specific code or dialect, as well as the shared assumptions of both producer and audience. Dialect features in this instance encompass 'stylistic resources' (Lacoste et al., 2014, p. 8). Moll (2014, p. 211) also underpins the active role of the speaker as an 'agent' who utilises linguistic resources to manipulate and highlight facets of his/her identity.

However, the shared assumptions about Saʿidis are, in fact, utilised by those Saʿidis who have access to the media, in order to position themselves as different and unique, in comparison to other Egyptians. The distinction between Saʿidis and Cairenes in particular is conjured up by Saʿidis to delineate their authentic identity as sincere, honest, and strong Egyptians, not sly and sissy like Cairenes. By performing Saʿidi and using the salient phonological Saʿidi variables propagated by the media, they take a stance that reflects a wider identity.

As Gill (2014, p. 326) contends, individuals 'fashion authentic identity from the semiotic resources at their disposal and position themselves in relation to normative associations between linguistic forms and social meaning'. Not all Saʿidis have access to media outlets, but those who do can be examined and analysed with respect to this process of fashioning identity. Saʿidis depend mainly on the use of dialogicality as a resource to express a stance. Bucholtz and Hall (2010, p. 21) posit: '[I]n identity formation, indexicality relies heavily on ideological structures, for associations between language and identity are rooted in cultural beliefs and values'. In other words, dialogicality is an essential dynamic in this process of positioning. Dialogicality is related to access to resources. Some non-Egyptian artists share the indexes of Egyptians towards CSA – regarding it as the code of culture and the key to fame – and are aware of previous dialogues concerning the associations of codes. Dialogicality, according to Du Bois, is apparent when a stance-taker's utterances 'engage with the words of those who have spoken before – whether immediately within the current exchange of stance utterances, or more remotely along the horizons of language and prior text as projected by the community of discourse' (2007, p. 140). That is, during the process of stance-taking of Saʿidi performers (especially poets), they engage with the prevalent dialogue concerning Saʿidis in the media, in order to highlight a distinct identity and, indeed, a more positive one.

Stance is considered by Ochs (1992) as the mediating path between linguistic forms and social identities. Thus, stance is a 'contextualisation cue' that informs interlocutors regarding the nature of the role that the speaker aims to project in relation to the form and content of his or her utterance – for example, choices of aspect, modals, or evidential statements can display a speaker's attitude, together with the claims or content of reported speech (Jaffe, 2007, p. 56). In a single act of stance-taking, three things are achieved: evaluation, positioning, and alignment. 'Evaluation' refers to the process in which a stance-taker 'characterises' an object of stance as having a 'specific quality or value' (Du Bois, 2007, p. 143); 'positioning' is when the stance-taker makes his or her affective stance clear and claims both certainty and knowledge; and 'alignment' is the act of standardising and normalising the relation between different stances (see Du Bois, 2007, p. 144; Damari, 2010, p. 611). Note that Kiesling (this volume) modifies the term 'stance object' to 'stance focus', which is more inclusive: it can be anything, not just a physical object.

This 'positioning' can accumulate to generate a larger entity, which we call an identity. In other words, identity is achieved and not just taken for granted. By studying evaluative expressions, grammar, phonology, and lexis, one can gain a better understanding of the stance of a specific individual (see Bucholtz & Hall, 2010, p. 22).

Al-Jukh's choice of salient phonological variables is part of his stance process, which accumulates into his public persona and identity. The resources that this

TABLE 16.1 Stance and linguistic repertoire of the poet in the four poems analysed.

Name of poem	Direct addressee	Aligns with	Disaligns with	Focus/object	Code choice	Indirect addressee
Mashhad raʾsī min maydān al-taḥrīr ('A birds-eye view from Tahrir Square')	Egypt	Revolutionaries in Tahrir Square	Pro-regime	January revolution	SA	The Egyptians who are wavering about whom to align with, and other Arabs
Al-taʔʃi:ra ('The Visa')	Arab rulers	Arab population	Arab rulers	Pan-Arab unity	SA	The entire Arab-world population
Aywa bagi:ra ('Yes, I am jealous')	His beloved	Saʿidis' character traits	Cairenes	His style of love	SCA	Egyptians
'Goha'	Egypt	Egyptians	Government and corrupt pro-regime cronies	Poverty, corruption, and cruelty of regime	SCA and CSA	Egyptians
The mother	His mother	His mother	Her death	Development of the relation to the other	SA in one part / SCA in three parts	Egyptians

Sa'idi performer utilises are structured through associations/indexes that individuals acquire and resort to. These indexes are directly related to language ideologies, as well as social, political, and demographic variables. That is, these linguistic resources are used in relation to the indexes of different codes and social variables, so that language is part of the social process that individuals engage in. The resources referred to in this article include pronouns, negation, imperatives, and presupposition, among others. Dialogicality and code choice are the dominant concepts examined in this analysis.

By choosing to perform using either SA or SCA linguistic variables rather than CSA ones, the poet is also taking what Jaffe calls a 'sociolinguistic stance' (2009, p. 11). Performance in a dialect is essential, in terms of both identification processes and recognizing dialect patterns and salient features. Jaffe also argues that 'patterns of code choice can also be interpreted as stances in which language ideologies are simultaneously a resource and an object' (2009, p. 17). Al-Jukh renegotiates the second-order indexes of both his SCA-marked variables and those of CSA. He consistently avoids marked/salient CSA variables, a phenomenon worth investigating further.

Data for this work includes thirty poems by the poet Al-Jukh. After examining the linguistic variables in the poems, it was clear that, first, none of the thirty poems include the salient CSA phonological variables, [g] and the glottal stop. The poet consistently uses the SCA equivalents. The poems vary in their degree of mixing between SA, SCA, and CSA. While there are poems that are clearly in SA only, there are others that start with SA and then move to a mixture of SCA and CSA. However, it is significant that none of the poems is only in CSA with no SCA variables.

In Table 16.1, the poet's stance in four poems, and his linguistic choices, are summarised.

Data analysis

Examples of poems performed in SA code

Example 1

Mashhad ra'sī min maydān al-taḥrīr ('A birds-eye view from Tahrir Square')
This SA poem was first performed during the 2011 Egyptian Revolution, in the context of the competition for the best poet in the Arab world. The competition is the well-known Abu Dhabi television competition *Amīr al-shu'arā'* ('The Prince of Poets') – a competition that offers a prize of a million dollars. Al-Jukh could not attend one of the episodes, due to the events in Egypt at the time. However, he appeared unexpectedly in the penultimate episode on February 8, just days before Mubarak abdicated. Before reciting his contribution to the competition, he said – in SCA – that although he only had two minutes, he would like to observe a moment of silence for the martyrs of the revolution. He then began reciting a poem in SA, which contained a clear reply to accusations and attacks on the identity of the people in Tahrir.

Interestingly, he chose to legitimise the identity of the Egyptians in Tahrir Square in SA. By using SA, he reclaimed the possession of 'the real Egyptian'. Through his code choice and discursive resources, he positions himself as the 'real' Egyptian. The second-order indexes of SA are indeed clear in this poem. The prevalent discourse about the participants in the revolution at the time was that they were not Egyptians, they did not speak Arabic (see Bassiouney, 2014), and if they were Egyptians, they were either hired by outsiders to cause chaos or deluded and misled. It is important to mention the impact of this poem on Egyptians during the revolution. The poem started to act as a counterattack by the pro-democracy protestors and sympathisers. One day after Mubarak's abdication, the same recording of the poem was broadcast with images from the revolution on Nile TV.

Xabbiʔ qaṣa:ʔidaka l-qadi:mata kullaha/ wa-ktub li-miṣra l-yawma ʃiʕran miθlaha:
La ṣamta baʕda l-yawmi yafriḍu xawfahu/ fa-ktub sala:ma ni:la miṣra wa ʔahlaha:
ʕayna:ki ʔagmalu ṭiflatayn tuqarrira:n/ bi-ʔanna ha:ða l-xawfa ma:ḍin wa- ntaha:
ka:nat tuda:ʕibuna l-ʃawa:riʕu bil-buru:dati wa-l ṣaqi:ʕi/ wa lam nufassir waqtaha:
kunna nudaffiʔ baʕdana fi: baʔdana/ wa nara:ki tabtasimi:n nansa: bardaha:
wa ʔiða ġaḍibna kaʃʃafat ʕan waghaha:/ wa ḥaya:ʔuna yaʔba: yudannisu waghaha:
la: tatruki:him yuxbiru:ki bi-ʔannani/ mutamarridun xa:na l-ʔama:nati ʔaw saha:
la: tatruki:him yuxbiru:ki bi-ʔannani/ ʔaṣbaḥtu ʃayʔan ta:fihan wa muwadʒaha:
fa ʔana ʔibn baṭnik wa-bnu baṭniki man ʔara:da wa man ʔaqa:la wa man ʔaqarra wa man naha:
ṣamatat fulu:lu l-xa:ʔifi:na bi- dʒubnihim/ wa dʒumu:ʔu man ʕaʃaqu:ki qa:lat qawlaha:

Hide all your old poems, and write to Egypt today poetry that is good enough for her.
There is no silence after today that will impose its fear. So write greetings from the river Nile to Egypt and its people.
Your eyes are like the most beautiful girls that have now decided that this fear is a past that is now over.
Streets were flirting with us with their coldness and frost and we did not mind them.
We used to warm ourselves with each other and when we saw you smile, we forgot our coldness.
And when we did become angry, she showed her face, and then our awe made us stop and not mar her face with our anger.
Do not let them tell you that I am a rebel who betrayed you or forgot you.
Do not let them tell you that I have become something trivial and controlled by foreigners.
I am the son of your womb (your son) and the son of your womb is the one who wants, who deposes, who asserts and forbids.
The crowd of the cowardly is now silent and the masses of those who love you have said their word.

The discursive resources used by the poet in addition to code choice include intertexuality, dialogicality, and recontextualisation, as well as structural resources such as imperatives. The poet uses intertextuality when he says 'greetings from the river Nile'. This phrase is quoted from a poem by poet laureate Aḥmad Shawqī, entitled 'Ghandi' (1931), in which Shawqī welcomes Ghandi to Egypt on his way to India. In the poem, Shawqī hails Ghandi as a peaceful freedom fighter, who shares with Egyptians the same aspirations and demands. It begins:

> Sala:ma n-ni:li ya ġandi:
> Wa ha:ða z-zahru min ʕindi:
> Greetings from the river Nile to you, Ghandi
> And these flowers are from me to you.

By referring to Shawqī, one of the most important SA poets of his time, and the particular poem that deals specifically with Ghandi, Egypt, and the struggle for independence and freedom, the poet relates Egypt's present to its past. Al-Jukh also explains indirectly that the struggle for freedom is not a betrayal of stability, but a noble, continuous process. By referring to Shawqī and quoting from him, he also adds legitimacy and importance to his message. It is as if he says: 'My poetry before that historical event is not good enough. I have to write poetry that is as grand as the event, but I first have to borrow from a great poet who also witnessed a great struggle for freedom'.

Recontextualisation of the events taking place in Tahrir Square from the viewpoint of the revolutionaries is an essential part of the dialogical process in which the poet takes part. Ochs (1992, p. 345) argues that recontextualisation refers to the recreation of past events and takes place through 'verbal practices and forms'. In this poem the poet uses the auxiliary verb *kunna* followed by a verb in the imperfect to denote continuity in the past:

> *kunna nudaffiʔ baʕdana fi: baʔdana/ wa nara:ki tabtasimi:n nansa: bardaha:*
> We used to warm ourselves with each other and when we saw you smile, we forgot our coldness.

This recontextualisation also employs pronouns to refer to this past event. The poet does not just refer to himself but to 'us' as revolutionaries and 'you' (feminine) as Egypt. He assumes that the smile of Egypt is a sign of its satisfaction with their decision to camp in Tahrir Square till the regime falls. Again his emphasis on this interaction between Egypt and the revolutionaries is a dialogic reply to the pro-regime media that casts doubts on the revolutionaries.

The dialogical process continues in the use of the imperatives when the poet orders Egypt, in the legitimate code SA, not to listen to the cowardly pro-regime people.

> *la: tatruki:him yuxbiru:ki bi-ʔannani/ mutamarridun xa:na l-ʔama:nati ʔaw saha:*
> *la: tatruki:him yuxbiru:ki bi-ʔannani/ ʔaṣbaḥtu ʃayʔan ta:fihan wa muwadʒaha:*

Do not let them tell you that I am a rebel who betrayed you or forgot you.
Do not let them tell you that I have become something trivial and controlled by foreigners.

The imperative in this poem would not have indexed power had it been in SCA, nor even in CSA.

Example 2

At-taʔfi:ra ('The Visa')

This poem was also performed in the last round of the *Amīr al-shuʻarāʼ* ('The Prince of Poets') competition. Unlike the first example, this poem is about the Arab world and being an Arab as opposed to possessing a nation-state identity. The poem tackles the frustrations of young people from the Arab world who cannot cross the borders between different Arab countries without obtaining a visa. It also highlights the contradiction between the education system and real life. In the education system, Arab children – and especially, in this poem, Egyptian children – are taught that all the Arab world is one entity and belongs to all. However, once these young people face the real situation they are disillusioned by the differences between Arab rulers and the obstructions to entering other Arab countries. The poet then boldly blames Arab rulers for dividing the Arab world.

Wa qad ʕulimtu fi ṣiġari biʔanna ʕuru:bati ʃarafi wa naaṣiyati wa ʕunwa:ni
Wa kunna fi mada:risna nuraddid baʕḍi alḥa:ni
Bila:du l ʕurbu ʔawṭa:ni wa kullu lʕurbi ixwa:ni
(. . .)
Ana ba:qin
Wa ʃarʕi: fil hawa: baqin
ʔuḥazirukum sa nabqa raġm fitnatakum
(. . .)
Huwa lḥuka:m la ʔantum
Wa la axʃa: lakum aḥada
Huwa al dʒumhu:r la ʔantum
Wa la ʔaxʃa lakum ʔaḥada
Huwa il isla:m la ʔantum
Fakufu: an tidʒaratakum
I was taught when I was young that my Arabness is an honor, an address, and an identity.
In our schools, we used to repeat certain songs:
Arab lands are my country and all Arabs are my brothers
(. . .)
People are the rulers, not you
I am not afraid of you

> People are the audience, not you
> I am not afraid of you
> People are the real Muslims
> So stop commodifying religion

Again, as in the first poem, there is intertextuality and dialogicality. Al-Jukh refers to the poems he used to memorise at school. There is also recontextualisation as well as imperative forms. These two techniques seem to be associated with the use of SA in his poems. SA enables him to use the imperative to order Arab leaders to stop their allegations and assumptions about Islam. He is aware that SCA would not enable him to use these powerful strategies with the same impunity. That is, while the poet may be casting doubt on the legitimacy and positive indexes of marked CSA variables, he does not dare do this to SA. In fact, he employs SA to give himself more power and legitimacy. In that sense his renegotiation of resources does not recognise SA resources as the most powerful ones.

Example 3

Aywa baġi:r ('Yes, I am jealous')

In his poem 'Yes, I am jealous', Al-Jukh addresses his Cairene girlfriend, who, like other Cairenes, believes the dominant stereotype of the anti-feminist, chauvinistic, and narrow-minded Saʿidi. He engages in a dialogue with her in which he flips the prevalent stereotype about Saʿidis to his benefit, emphasizing his morally superior status to Cairenes, as well as his masculinity as opposed to the sissy Cairene men. The fact that the poem is performed in a Saʿidi dialect is, in itself, a significant point. Al-Jukh takes what Jaffe (2009) calls a 'sociolinguistic stance' through his choice of code. Throughout the poem, he plays on the stereotype of the ignorant, narrow-minded, chauvinistic, and naïve Saʿidi.

Ak-Jukh's use of pronouns to refer to himself as a Saʿidi is significant, as he aligns himself with the Saʿidi identity, which is, in effect, distinct from that of other Egyptians, especially Cairenes. The use of pronouns is clear when he says:

> *wi-niswa:n fi bladna: gawa:hir*
> and women in our lands are treasures

In this example, *bladna:* has an attached first-person plural possessive suffix. The word *balad* is a metonymy, which is commonly used in Egypt to refer to one's city or village, not merely one's country. However, the use of *balad* ('land/country') as opposed to *ḥitta* ('area') is significant. It emphasises the difference between Saʿidis and other Egyptians. First- and second-person pronouns are also contrasted to refer to the poet and his girlfriend when he declares (pronouns are in bold):

> Kulli il-farg ma be:**ni** wbe:**nik inni** ṣaʕi:di.
> The only difference between you and me is that I am Saʿidi

The suffix *ni* = first-person pronoun suffix; *ik* = second-person pronoun suffix; *inni* = first-person pronoun.

Negation is also used in conjunction with presupposition, as when Al-Jukh states (negation is in bold):

> *Yibga ana* **lana** *dʒaːhil* **wala** *ġaːfil*
> *Kulli ilfarg ma beːni wbeːnik inni ṣaʕiːdi*
> So I am neither an ignorant nor a naïve man
> The only difference between you and me is that I am a Saʿidi.

The use of negation in *la-na* and *wa-la* is to counter the accusation, presumably made by his girlfriend and other non-Saʿidis, that he is ignorant. It is thus clear that there is a presupposition that there is an accusation, and he feels the urge to reply to this presupposition. According to Benwell and Stokoe (2006, p. 114), presupposition 'refers to the presumed knowledge a recipient needs to make full sense of a text'. It usually uses cultural frames and biased assumptions that are a result of shared cultural beliefs. There is also an epistemic stance in the second line. Epistemic stances are concerned with the truth value of a 'proposition and the speaker's degree of commitment to it' (Irvine, 2009, p. 53). Al-Jukh acknowledges that there is a difference between him and his girlfriend and that it is a difference related to his local identity as a Saʿidi, which entails a difference in perspective towards women, dress code, and expectations, as is clear throughout the poem.

As with all of his poems performed in SCA, Al-Jukh uses two salient phonological variables: the /q/, which is realised as [g] in SCA and as a glottal stop in CSA, and the SA /dʒ/, which is pronounced as [dʒ] or [d] in Saʿidi and [g] in CSA.

> *Willi* **g***aluːlik gert irraːdʒil* **g***illit siga/ aw* **g***illit fahm*
> *Xal***g** *hemiːr*
> Whoever told you that the jealousy of men is lack of trust in women,
> Or lack of understanding, they are just assholes.

Al-Jukh uses /g/ and /dʒ/, as opposed to the SCA glottal stop /ʔ/ and /g/. When the poet positions himself as all sincere Egyptians, or all frustrated Arabs, then his code is SA. When he positions himself as the frustrated individual Egyptian from the south, his code is SCA. While giving voice to his dialect he is aware that it is only SA that can give him enough authority to criticise Arab rulers or authenticate the Egyptian identity of the revolutionaries.

The late poet Abdel Rahman Al-Abnoudi (1938–2015) also came from the south, but unlike Al-Jukh he did not refrain from using CSA variables in his poetry. While still performing masterpieces in a Saʿidi dialect, when his stance object is Egypt it is CSA that he uses. Al-Jukh instead uses SA, a more neutral dialect than CSA in Egypt, and indeed one that certainly has more legitimacy in the Arab world at large.

Discussions and conclusions

This study aims to provide a fresh look at the relationship between language and identity in a diglossic community through the performance of a local poet. In examples 1 and 2, the poet appeals to the legitimacy of SA to position himself first as a frustrated Arab and then as the 'real Egyptian'. When discussing his personal relations and his frustrations with the Egyptian regime, he expresses himself in his own local dialect.

Al-Jukh, as a Saʿidi poet who has access to public space, tries to reassign value to his dialect and renegotiate the Egyptian linguistic hierarchy, in which CSA is the dominant, prestigious, and legitimate dialect and Saʿidi is alien, difficult, and mainly carries negative indexes. Cairo dominates public discourse because of the power the city holds, socially, politically, economically, and demographically. It is in Cairo that salient Saʿidi variables are ridiculed through media outlets; it is also in Cairo that the very same variables, associated with an alien, remote identity, are commercialised as exotic and comic. In recent postcards sold in Cairo, one can find examples such as a Saʿidi man depicted wearing Saʿidi attire with a woman in traditional dress or a woman from an urban center. In the text of the postcard, the Saʿidi uses the salient feature /g/ as opposed to the SCA glottal stop, in addition to English written in Arabic letters to flatter his girlfriend. These postcards are popular in train stations in Cairo and are produced to ridicule the exotic Saʿidi, but also to use the stereotype for financial gain.

As Cameron (2012, p. 215) contends, 'we are constantly intervening in language, whether in support of what we perceive as the status quo or in pursuit of something different'. Intervention in languages includes performers who take a stance and evoke indexes of different codes. As Coupland (2011, p. 598) argues in his study of songs, performance 'opens up diverse new vernacular spaces and allows us to recontextualise our own identities and relationships in relation to them'.

What Al-Jukh did was to try to renegotiate the indexes of CSA specifically. By trying to use consistently either SA or marked SCA phonological variables that are usually ridiculed by Cairenes, he is also trying to impose novel and creative assumptions about the authenticity and social value of these stigmatised variables, and with them the whole dialect. He styles himself as the authentic, sincere, and honest Saʿidi. It is not clear whether this stylisation process on his part will have a general impact on the public discourse in Egypt about Saʿidis or their dialects. It is clear, however, that through the accumulation of stances in different poems, and through his discursive resources and code choice, he manages to create his unique and novel public persona, his identity. However, individuals who do not share the fame and the media access that he enjoys will still feel compelled to get rid of the salient variables associated with the south, as Miller (2004) showed in her study. It is the performers who shake the social and political status quo through their linguistic choices and resources that are worth investigating. The success of these performers may also reflect an underlying revolt against the status quo. This revolt may pit SA and CSA against each other, but does not yet dare to completely challenge SA and its legitimacy.

Notes

1 See https://youtu.be/k-64OMiNQQ0 (accessed 12 June 2016).
2 See https://youtu.be/209vvrTw7Ac (accessed 12 June 2016).

References

Agha, A. (2005). Voice, footing, enregisterment. *Journal of Linguistic Anthropology*, *15*(1), 38–59.
Bassiouney, R. (2009). *Arabic sociolinguistics*. Edinburgh: Edinburgh University Press.
Bassiouney, R. (2014). *Language and identity in modern Egypt*. Edinburgh: Edinburgh University Press.
Bauman, R. (2000). Language, identity, performance. *Pragmatics*, *10*(1), 1–6.
Behnstedt, P., & Woidich, M. (1985–1999). *Die ägyptisch-arabischen Dialekte*. Wiesbaden: Harrassowitz.
Benwell, B., & Stokoe, E. (2006). *Discourse and identity*. Edinburgh: Edinburgh University Press.
Blommaert, J. (2010). *The sociolinguistics of globalization*. Cambridge: Cambridge University Press.
Bucholtz, M., & Hall, K. (2010). Locating identity in language. In C. Llamas & D. Watt (Eds.), *Language and identities* (pp. 18–28). Edinburgh: Edinburgh University Press.
Cameron, D. (2012). *Verbal hygiene*. London: Routledge.
Chambers, J. K. (2009). *Sociolinguistic theory: Linguistic variation and its social significance*. Malden, MA: Wiley-Blackwell.
Chun, E. W. (2004). Ideologies of legitimate mockery: Margaret Cho's revoicings of Mock Asian. *Pragmatics*, *14*(2/3), 263–290.
Coupland, N. (2001). Language, situation, and the relational self: Theorizing dialect-style in sociolinguistics. In P. Eckert & J. R. Rickford (Eds.), *Style and sociolinguistic variation* (pp. 185–210). Cambridge: Cambridge University Press.
Coupland, N. (2007). *Style: Language variation and identity*. Cambridge: Cambridge University Press.
Coupland, N. (2011). Voice, place and genre in popular song performance. *Journal of Sociolinguistics*, *15*(5), 573–602.
Crystal, D. (2008). *A dictionary of linguistics and phonetics*. Oxford: Blackwell.
Damari, R. R. (2010). Intertextual stancetaking and the local negotiation of cultural identities by a binational couple. *Journal of Sociolinguistics*, *14*(5), 609–629.
Du Bois, J. W. (2007). The stance triangle. In R. Englebretson (Ed.), *Stancetaking in discourse: Subjectivity, evaluation, interaction* (pp. 139–182). Amsterdam: John Benjamins.
Eckert, P. (2001) Style and social meaning. In P. Eckert & J. R. Rickford (Eds.), *Style and sociolinguistic variation* (pp. 119–126). Cambridge: Cambridge University Press.
Ferguson, C. (1959). Diglossia. *Word*, *15*, 325–340. Reprinted in Pier Paolo Gligioli (Ed.), *Language and social context* (pp. 232–251). Harmondsworth: Penguin.
Gal, S. (1989). Language and political economy. *Annual Review of Anthropology*, *18*, 345–367.
Gill, M. (2014). 'Real communities', rhetorical borders: Authenticating British identity in political discourse and on-line debate. In V. Lacoste, J. Leimgruber, & T. Breyer (Eds.), *Indexing authenticity: Sociolinguistic perspectives* (pp. 324–342). Berlin: De Gruyter.
Heller, M. (2007). *Bilingualism: A social approach*. Basingstoke: Palgrave Macmillan.
Hodson, J. (2014). *Dialect in film and literature*. Basingstoke: Palgrave Macmillan.
Hopkins, N., & Saad, R. (2004). *Upper Egypt: Identity and change*. Cairo: American University in Cairo Press.
Irvine, J. T. (2009). Stance in a colonial encounter: How Mr. Taylor lost his footing. In A. Jaffe (Ed.), *Stance: Sociolinguistic perspectives* (pp. 53–72). Oxford: Oxford University Press.

Jaffe, A. (2007). Codeswitching and stance: Issues in interpretation. *Journal of Language, Identity and Education*, 6(1), 53–77.

Jaffe, A. (2009). The sociolinguistics of stance. In A. Jaffe (Ed.), *Stance: sociolinguistic perspectives* (pp. 3–28). Oxford: Oxford University Press.

Johnstone, B. (2015). *Speaking Pittsburghese: The story of a dialect*. Oxford: Oxford University Press.

Lacoste, V., Leimgruber, J., & Breyer, T. (2014). Authenticity: A view from inside and outside sociolinguistics. In V. Lacoste, J. Leimgruber, & T. Breyer (Eds.), *Indexing authenticity: Sociolinguistic perspectives* (pp. 1–13). Berlin: De Gruyter.

Miller, C. (2004). Between myth and reality: The construction of a Saîdi identity. In N. Hopkins & R. Saad (Eds.), *Upper Egypt: Identity and change* (pp. 25–54). Cairo: The American University in Cairo Press.

Miller, C. (2005). Between accommodation and resistance: Upper Egyptian migrants in Cairo. *Linguistics*, 43(5), 903–956.

Milroy, J., & Milroy, L. (2012). *Authority in language: Investigating standard English*. London: Routledge.

Moll, A. (2014). Authenticity in dialect performance? A case study of 'Cyber-Jamaican'. In V. Lacoste, J. Leimgruber, & T. Breyer (Eds.), *Indexing authenticity: Sociolinguistic perspectives* (pp. 209–243). Berlin: De Gruyter.

Ochs, E. (1992). Indexing gender. In A. Duranti & C. Goodwin (Eds.), *Rethinking context: Language as an interactive phenomenon* (pp. 335–358). Cambridge: Cambridge University Press.

Rampton, B. (2015). Contemporary urban vernaculars. In J. Nortier & B. A. Svendsen (Eds.), *Language, youth and identity in the 21st century: Linguistic practices across urban spaces* (pp. 24–44). Cambridge: Cambridge University Press.

Schilling-Estes, N. (1998). Investigating "self-conscious" speech: The performance register in Ocracoke English. *Language in Society*, 27(1), 53–83.

Silverstein, M. (2014). The race from place: Dialect eradication vs. the linguistic 'authenticity' of terroir. In V. Lacoste, J. Leimgruber, & T. Breyer (Eds.), *Indexing authenticity: Sociolinguistic perspectives* (pp. 159–187). Berlin: De Gruyter.

Suleiman, Y. (2003). *The Arabic language and national identity: A study in ideology*. Edinburgh: Edinburgh University Press.

Wilmsen, D. (2011). Egypt. In L. Edzard & R. de Jong (Eds.), *Encyclopedia of Arabic language and linguistics*. Brill Online. Retrieved from http://referenceworks.brillonline.com/entries/encyclopedia-of-arabic-language-and-linguistics/egypt-EALL_COM_vol2_0001.

17
RUINATION AND AMUSEMENT – DIALECT, YOUTH, AND REVOLUTION IN NAIJA

Anne Storch

Introduction

A dialect can be different things to different people in different contexts. As emphasized by Reem Bassiouney (this volume), the term remains vague, imprecise, and in need of being filled with social meaning. Defining a dialect, Bassiouney maintains, requires setting it into relation with another dialect, but also with hegemonic norms. 'Dialect' can therefore be a term for different 'codes', but also a term that highlights 'substandard' speech practices in contrast to normed and standardized language. Reflecting upon such and other possible differences between various ways of speaking addresses both the form of linguistic diversity and its meanings. In order to understand how difference is perceived and managed, and how a concept such as a 'dialect' might be constructed in and by a particular society or group, it is essential to consider the social relevance of difference and its cultural treatment.

Such an approach to linguistic diversity has been of importance in Labovian sociolinguistics and beyond, got more pronounced in the framework of Ethnography of Speaking, and gains new relevance in contemporary, third wave sociolinguistics. However, all of these approaches continued to be based on language ideologies and linguistic models that have been developed in the North, and more precisely in European-American academic linguistics. Only now, with an increased awareness of other possibilities of thinking about communication and of the existence of different ideas about language, the perspective changes: linguistic diversity is not in the focus in order to sustain, for example, models of language variation and change, but because it is addressed by the 'speakers', by those who use or own language, referring to alternative language ideologies and metalinguistic discourses. Turning the gaze to the linguistic reflexivity manifest in postcolonial Southern discourse and theory helps to dislodge notions of speakers as 'informants', their metalinguistic knowledge and theories as 'folk linguistics', and diverse language practices as 'dialects' and 'substandard' codes. In this contribution, I intend to make productive use of precisely such alternative perspectives in order to shed more light on how diverse and deviant language practices emerged out of a postcolonial context, and how speakers and Southern theorists (such as local language activists, knowledgeable speakers, artists, and other theoretically interested players) conceptualize the historical experience of colonization and marginalization.

The focus of this chapter thereby is on language practices of Nigeria, a country which, according to commonly used reference sources, hosts some 520 languages (www.ethnologue.com/country/NG). Most of these languages are used by small albeit highly multilingual groups; however, together with more widely spoken languages such as Hausa, Yoruba, Igbo, Bini, Tiv, etc., English serves as a means for transregional communication. The latter language is of particular interest here, as there is a diversity of regional and stylistic varieties of English, which have developed since it gained sociolinguistic importance since the first half of the nineteenth century. As a consequence of the country's colonial history and membership in the Commonwealth, English remains the *de facto* national language, even though new language practices based on English are more used than the previously introduced, standardized form of the same language.

The material presented in this chapter has been collected mostly in the domains where contemporary debates on linguistic correctness, language choice, and standardization take place, namely blogs, social media, and interactive language tools. The analysis of these contributions aims at illustrating how language ideologies concerning variation and, more particularly, the social semiotics of 'dialect' are discussed and evaluated by the players themselves.

Ruins and ruination

Marginalized ways of speaking seem to ask for particular ways of linguistic discussion; studies on alternative communicative practices, such as those of young people, have the potential to be special. They can bear in themselves the notion of departure from traditional ways of doing things and the opportunity to turn to creativity and the liberating, smart, subversive ways of the youth; they can have something about them that Christopher Stroud more recently addressed as 'utopia' (Stroud, 2015), which has a marked beginning and also a ritualized ending. And after having enjoyed a glimpse at the 'what if', there is usually a return to some kind of normality – to daily encounters with discourses on language not as creatively fluid but as fixed and structured, and to a social climate in which the communicative strategies of young people are often framed as being deficient rather than interesting.

Here, I attempt to take a perspective on the linguistics of African youth languages by turning the gaze to what these ways of speaking are actually built on. I will argue that in spite of their structural similarities to various types of manipulated languages in other settings (e.g., initiation, in-law tabooing, etc.), youth languages also have a different basis, being built on colonial ruins and failed linguistic ideologies.

This is not such an original approach, I suspect, as the notion of ruins and destruction has not been all that insignificant in the debates on youth languages led by linguists. Besides the idea that youth languages differ from other languages in so far as they often seem to result in distorted, sub-standard forms of 'real' languages – like some kind of 'broken language' – there has been, at least since the publication of the seminal paper by Roland Kiessling and Maarten Mous (2004), a common understanding that youth languages often also are 'anti-languages'. Michael Halliday (1976, p. 570), from whom this concept has been borrowed, defines anti-languages as codes used by people who belong to social groups who represent non-hegemonic norms, behavior, and practice, such as low-caste groups, street gangs, but also members of queer sub-culture:

> An anti-society is a society that is set-up within another society as a conscious alternative to it. It is a mode of resistance, resistance which may take the form either of passive symbiosis or of active hostility or even destruction. An anti-language is not only parallel to an anti-society; it is in fact generated by it.

Halliday's perspective of anti-ness only makes sense as another utopia; these practices of inclusion and shutting out are decidedly situative, local, and restricted. An anti-language is only 'anti' in the presence of the antagonistic other, and it always is just one out of several ways of speaking available to its users. There is nothing truly unbounded about anti-languages; as in-group codes and ways of speaking that emerge out of social delimitation where they are correlated with agency and emotional investment, they only can be all this because they are conceptualized as a dialectic opposition to a challenged hegemonic norm.

However, framing youth languages as anti-languages seems a bit problematic, for it requires a view on 'youth' as an attack on adulthood, language, society, and so on. But the utopia created and performed in the communicative practices and cultural expressions of young people might be many things, and not necessarily an attempt to destroy its context. The notion of anti-ness in youth languages, therefore, might rather help us to think of them as part of performative expressions of the experience of being constructed as the other, of being placed in marginality, and being objectified and controlled by others.

Even though this is not intended to deny the agency involved in the performative practices of young people, thinking again about anti-ness, in the way I suggest here, requires a change in perspective. Unlike the more established view on youth languages as codes and practices that *emerge*, that come into existence anew, and at an increasing number of urban centers throughout Africa (see Hollington & Nassenstein, 2015, among others), such a perspective reveals that youth languages *result* out of something, of previous practice, events, and experiences.

Working with a concept of ruins and ruination, as I intend to here, permits us to turn our gaze to precisely this: to the durabilities of marginal placement of particular people, namely people who, lacking access to particular economic resources, are considered members of a 'youth'. The construction of street children as witches, of jobless young men as criminal gang members, and of school dropouts as drug dealers, who all share anti-social ways of doing and ways of speaking, can also be seen as the continuation of inequality as a consequence of previous injustice and violence, of whatever kind. My focus here is on the marginalization and deprivation of young people, as well as on the ideological conceptualization of their ways of speaking not as 'proper language' but as 'slang', as instances of ruination.

These ruinations are ongoing processes that more recently have been framed by the anthropologist and historian Ann Laura Stoler as durabilities that imperial formations produce. Stoler points out that there is a 'relationship between colonial past and colonial presents, [and the] residues that abide and are revitalized' (Stoler, 2013, p. 5). The products of ruination thereby are complex and diverse, and while the residues of empire have often been assumed to consist of utterly tangible remains, Stoler argues that there are also other ruins:

> If the insistence is on a set of brutal finite acts in the distant slave-trading past, the process of decay is ongoing, acts of the past blacken the senses, their effects without clear termination. These crimes have been named and indicted across the globe, but the eating away of less visible elements of soil and soul more often has not.
>
> *(Stoler, 2013, p. 1)*

Imperial debris therefore consists not simply of colonial buildings rotting away in the tropics, or, as a more recent phenomenon, in the blasted remains of world heritage sites in the Middle East, but also of ruined lives, of 'persons who become "a human ruin", "leftover" in their unexceptional, patterned subjection' (p. 23) to abandonment and exclusion. In other words, ruination, the production of imperial debris, can result in poisonous environments, such as in Nigeria's Niger Delta, or wastelands, such as the asbestos mine sites in South Africa's North West Province, but also in neoliberal economies that exclude young people from sustainable incomes, and in images of young people as risk factors to social balance and order. Ruin, Stoler says, needs to be framed as a very agentive verb, an action that is powerful and that can be controlled by particular agents. Its duration, however, is out of control of individual actors; she suggests that race is imperial debris, as are resentment, dispossession, and violent environments made by uneven reallocation of access to resources.

The South African artist Jane Alexander found another way of portraying imperial ruination; her sculptural work *Butcher Boys*, currently displayed at the South African National Gallery at Cape Town, consists of three life-sized plaster figures with animal horns and bones, seated on a bench. The figures have no mouths and ears, but feature grotesque forms of excresence instead of lips, and exhibit darkened, sore-looking holes instead of ears; such creatures would be unable to speak and hear anymore. On their back, their spines are exposed, lie open, with nothing there to protect or even sustain the nerves that once were attached to them. Alexander's work is a response to experiences of biopolitical segregation, injustice, and gross social insecurity: racism dehumanizes and creates ruined persons who are not able any longer to really communicate – to talk, listen, and feel.

Ruination as a metaphor, I think, is very clear; focusing on debris as 'the less perceptible effects of imperial interventions and their settling into the social and material ecologies in which people live and survive' (Stoler, 2013, p. 4) helps us to historicize 'emergence', both of the empirical effects of ruination and our models about them. It is not unsurprising that Stoler's thinking is inspired by Walter Benjamin's (1940) essay 'Theses of the Philosophy of History', where a very strong argument for the need to look at debris is presented. And as much as the Angel of History in Benjamin's essay is unable to turn and look at what comes ahead (but looks backwards, at the catastrophe of history instead), we are not able to predict the future. Hence, even though there is always something new that will be made out of ruins, or grow out of the debris, the productivity of ruination is not controlled in the act of ruining itself. The social scientist Niklas Luhmann (1990) argued in a famous paper that the future never begins – it remains ahead and never unfolds. In this sense, youth languages are not so much a phenomenon that helps us to predict what becomes of language itself, but a phenomenon that points back, into some opaque past that continues to hurl debris in front of our feet. This would also mean what my colleague, Nico Nassenstein (personal communication, December 2015), suggests: that the innovations from today are the trash from yesterday. And that could explain why speakers, once a word, lexeme, slang term, or whatever, is uttered, turn away from it, move further, and leave it as debris behind.

Making and unmaking a 'youth language'

But what exactly might this debris be? In 1848, the ship surgeon Hermann Köler published his description of the town and port of Bonny, which includes ethnographical notes and data on the weather, as well as a sketch of the languages spoken there. His short remarks on English used at Bonny are among the earliest written documents available on the sociolinguistics of what now would be termed 'World Englishes'. What really makes this source interesting is that Köler says something about the political economy of English spoken at Bonny:

> Many of the natives of those coastal areas that are visited by the ships of the whites also speak a broken European language. In earlier years, at the zenith of the slave trade, Spanish was best known; now, however, as a result of the complication and limitation of the trade with the so-called black ivory, the interaction with the Spaniards has become rare and brief. While the palm oil trade with England is fast increasing, English ousts all of its rival languages. Hence, almost all people who come aboard the ships in order to trade some goods know the relevant English terms; some of them speak quite fluently, especially those who have made the journey to England. Broken Spanish is spoken only by older people, and only few individuals maintain the names give to them by the Spaniards.
>
> *(Köler, 1848, p. 3; Translation, A.S.)*

Within a generation, Köler suggests, English replaced Bozal, whereby the crucial factor was economical change: palm oil instead of slaves, which, however, did not change any of the complexities in which commodifications of people took place. In Köler's notes, the ruination of an entire trade network translates into a new brokenness of a language, whereas he suggests that brokenness itself has been the experience and practice of the participants in the encounter for a long time.

In Paul Grade's description of West African English, published some 40 years later in 1892 and much more cited than Köler's text, communicative practice is turned into linguistic structure. Grade presents neatly ordered noun morphology and verb forms, discusses differences and similarities with other Black Englishes, and so on. With Hugo Schuchardt's inclusion of Grade's rather brief description into the then newly emerging field of Creole linguistics, West African English became incorporated in a new metanarrative where it was firmly labeled as a Pidgin. But Grade's text also contributed to another fixation of communicative practices. In a comment on Grade's data by Ernst Henrici, an early Africanist and scholar of Ewe, these practices – now turned into a selection of structural features – are also placed within a model of linguistic evolution:

> As for West African Negro English, and for any broken English, there is nothing of relevance but to assign to it its place in linguistic history. [. . .] This is the only reason why I decided to examine this broken English. Here, a basic framework is provided for an explanation of the emergence of a Negro colloquial dialect. A meteor-like occurrence of some two hundred babbled English words otherwise would not be worth a scientific examination, but would simply remain a curiosity.
>
> *(Henrici, 1897, p. 397 ff.; translation, A.S.)*

After a name has been assigned to it, Henrici defines the history of 'West African Negro English'. It is shaped, he says, by the sensuality of its African speakers, in which they differ from the 'Aryans', and its structural features bear in themselves traces of history which only need to be deciphered. Henrici, an expert, is able to do so, he claims, and reconstructs the history of what to Grade had still been 'like music' (1892, p. 362) as a story of violence and ruination. After the forced migrations of people from West Africa across the Atlantic, the first Black Englishes evolved, but then these Englishes went back, into spaces where – like in Liberia – other Black Englishes had come into existence, and traveled on along the West African coast. Kru people, whom Henrici describes as enslaved by their own kings, 'out of whose mouths Negro English sounds still more miserable' (Henrici, 1897, p. 403), are the last in line to further spread its use.

Placed at a stage of primitivism in the models of language evolution of the period, West African English is expected to retain a socially marginal position. Henrici also has someting to say about this:

> West African Negro English is only a means of communication between Negroes and Whites, and sometimes between different nations of coastal

Negroes. It is already on its way into marginalization due to the introduction of various European languages, and will disappear completely in the German, French, and Portuguese colonies; it will, however, endure in the English colonies, where it will, after having undergone modest improvements, turn into a colloquial dialect.

(Henrici, 1897, p. 403; translation, A.S.)

What we know today as Nigerian Pidgin here emerges as a dialect of utter modesty and linguistic misery. However, Henrici was right in assuming that it would be a widespread means of communication among colonized people in the future. In his very comprehensive work on Nigerian Pidgin, Nicolas Faraclas has asked about language policies addressing its sociolinguistic salience:

Despite the fact that Nigerian Pidgin is in most respects the most logical choice for a national language, it has received little recognition from those responsible for language policy in Nigeria. Official attitudes towards Nigerian Pidgin remain negative, perpetuating erroneous notions inherited from the colonial period that Nigerian Pidgin is some form of 'broken English'.

(Faraclas, 1996, p. 2)

By the time Faraclas wrote this, there already existed the notion of a kind of language policy, albeit one that was based on the power of subversion and resistance. While expert discourse largely addressed structural features, aspects of linguistic history, and the probability of some kind of language planning, out there in the real world an entire counter-discourse had evolved. Nigerian intellectuals and artists increasingly identified Nigerian Pidgin as an appropriate medium for the expression of social critique and political opposition, as there seemed to be something utterly powerful and productive in its messiness and noisiness. Whatever Pidgin was, it had never become administered away into some classroom routine, orthography, standardized form, or officially legitimized form. In Lagos, it was spoken by everyone; in Surulere as well as in Victoria Island, and across the country, elites used it as well as small people. In Pidgin, there seemed to exist different, less limiting strategies of expressing social status than in other languages, which allowed people to get along with each other and experience an utterly difficult social reality as still manageable. There had, in other words, been a kind of disorder that suddenly could be turned into something communally sustainable, a strategy shared by subaltern, yet incepiently empowered people.

The Afrobeat artist and intellectual Fela Kuti explained that if music was to be his weapon, this music needed its own language: 'You cannot sing African music in proper English', he said (Barrett, 2016). Even though his own background was a rather privileged one, he performed his songs in a form of Nigerian Pidgin. In *Colomentality* (1977), he explains why:

He be say you be colonial man
You don be slave man before
Dem don release you now

> But you never release yourself
> [...]
> Dem go proud of dem name
> And put dem slave name for head
> No be so?

Proper English could still be, Fela argues, a means of exclusion and mental slavery, and his creation of a very personal voice, an individual style of using the language of the streets, bars, and markets, together with his uncontrollable way of life and very liberating performances, were acts of revolt and revolution. Like Bob Marley's music, the art and life of Fela Kuti on a very wide level 'added a further dimension to the repertoire of youth rebelliousness', as Ibrahim Abdullah and Patrick Muana (1998, p. 173) remark in their work on the African Guerilla.

As a means of expressing critique of imperialism and late capitalism in Afrobeat, a particular form of Nigerian Pidgin had become artifactualized and underwent a quite complex process of enregisterment (Agha, 2005). The conflation of media, sonic environment, a particular way of speaking, and stance made sense to audiences and produced the possibility of conceiving a way of speaking as a register of rebellion. Rotimi Fasan has written more recently about music as a medium that enhances artifactualization of language in Nigeria (2015).

This register is increasingly constructed as a youth language in its form of *Naija*, a name that became especially popular with the spread of social networks in mobile communication, where it is often also written as *9ja*. Even though my attempt at historicizing Naija, albeit in a very brief way, suggests that the notion of the uncontrolled and improper was there very early, independent of age and class, the messiness and unadjustedness of it go well with now-established constructions of 'youth', the rebellious youth, with their brilliant linguistic creativity which they employ in the social media whose digital spaces they inhabit. There is anti-ness readily available here. And even though mobile communication is increasingly shown as a form of communication now shared by people across 'a wide range of social, educational, geographic, and linguistic backgrounds' (Deumert, 2014, p. 1), it is constructed as an emblematic part of youth culture. But turning the gaze to the linguistic metanarratives shared by users of both Naija and social media allows for an understanding that there are other constructions, too.

In many of the websites that offer metalinguistic information on Naija, there is a strong focus on the collection of words rather than making comments on its sociolinguistic role. One of the most professional sites is *Naija lingo* (Ofunne & Nwokogba, 2007), an interactive dictionary where users can enter new lexemes and add – in standard English – explanations on the semantics of Naija words. The site is advertised by the slogan 'Be a part of documenting Nigerian culture! Naija lingo is made by people like you' and contains entries on 1462 Naija lexemes (November 2015). Even though it resembles open wikis and interactive language documentation sites, the 'about' section reveals that it is somehow different: '[...] there has been little done to acknowledge it[s, i.e., Naija's] existence, [and] we need to change that', the hosts say. They take a revolutionary stance: 'The Naija Lingo team knows they cannot make this revolution happen alone so we call on all those far and wide who want to have fun defining a new language, we have given you a space on the internet and have given you the tools to make this happen, incase [sic] you didn't know Nigerian pidgin English is on the verge of becoming a full fledge language of its own, be part of this revolution'. Entering words into an online dictionary here turns into a revolutionary action that assigns considerable agency to each individual, who is at least making a new language. The hosts, two Nigerian web designers, present themselves as free-spirited and original: 'Naija boys that enjoy speaking pidgin and take it a little too seriously'. The metatext of the dictionary directs our gaze to the users and hosts who are equally presented as performers; their actions

FIGURE 17.1 About Naija lingo (Ofunne & Nwokogba 2007: http://www.naijalingo.com/about).

and attitudes are made the objects of attention. Not the Naija terms, in other words, are of interest here, but those who use and collect them – people who claim the agency of creating their own nationalist language ideology, which is the basis of the inversion of any imperial language policy, namely a messy and subversive 'Pidgin'.

This is a recurrent motif of many other Nigerian sites with metalinguistic content. Lists of often rather well-known Naija terms are presented not so much in the sense of an educational effort, but as vehicles of the actual message: subversive patriotism, critique of enduring imperial formations reflected in gross educational inequalities, insufficient language policies based on colonial standards, and unapproachable elites. A post on *BuzzNigeria* on otherwise common Naija 'campus slang' is dominated by the photograph of a raised fist in front of the Nigerian flag (Chigozie, 2015), and the blogger Sir Farouk refers to himself as a 'crazy Nigerian' for his writing about Nigerian daily life practices, such as sex talk in Naija (Farouk, 2012). Again, not the words and meanings presented here challenge hegemonic norms, but the act of presenting them and of stylizing writers and users as sophisticated and empowered.

That Naija is constructed in the media as a strong symbol of liberation and new forms of citizenhood is also visible in the ways global online news about it is circulated on Nigerian social media, such as *Nairaland.com*. An article on the newly established *Radio Wazobia* broadcasting in Naija which was published in 2012 in *The Guardian* was posted as a contribution to *Nairaland*'s 'Language please! Sex and

FIGURE 17.2 Revolutionary collections of 'campus slang' (Chigozie 2015).

FIGURE 17.3 Musings of a Crazy Nigerian (Farouk 2012).

language' thread. It contains a conventional description of polyglossic cacophonia in Lagos and presents 'authentic voices' from Wazobia's audiences:

> In Nigeria's megacity of Lagos, where the country's 500 languages come together in a chaotic medley, the rapid-fire rhythm of pidgin is the symphony of the streets. Africa's largest country is a sometimes fractious mix of 160 million inhabitants divided into 250 ethnicities. But street hustlers and Harvard-educated politicians alike greet each other with: 'How you dey?' or 'How body?' [. . .] As cars swerve through sweaty streets, it can also be heard blaring on Radio Wazobia, a pidgin-only station played in crammed buses, sleek air-conditioned jeeps and roadside food stalls. [. . .] 'The language of Wazobia is clear,' said rubber farmer Sunday Ayodele, alternating Yoruba, his first language, with pidgin. 'Since Wazobia came, we have been enjoying, it's become like a kind of conversation. Before, it was just blowing grammar,' he said, referring to the traditional English of politicians' speeches.
>
> *(Mark, 2012)*

While elites speak *grammar* to their subjects, truth is articulated in Naija, the article suggests. The concept is very successful, and *Wazobia FM* now also is a TV channel that broadcasts very popular shows. Its mission statement is still somewhat subversive:

> Wazobia FM na the pipu's station, na we be the #1 radio station for the whole of Naija and na only we dey bring una the vibrant blend of indigenous artist from naija and all obodo Africa. Wazobia FM musical and jolificate style of entertainment dey blended with national and global tori, top top issues, sport informate, interviews, games plus gbadunment gists wey we all dey sama una for we ogbonge PIDGIN language. Our target audience na the entire masses, those wey tanda for grassroot plus we still get programs wey dey for the highclass.
>
> *(www.wazobiafm.com/lagos/about-us/)*

Wazobia's project is to reswagger Nigeria, but without excluding any social group. Naija is not constructed as the language of the nation, binding different people together and overcoming differences, but as the language of the utopia. It turns into an expression of the 'what if': Köler's trade language and Henrici's folk colloquial remain outside state language policies and official administration; what kind of reality would have been possible if imperial formations had not been lasting? The unruliness of Naija and its subversive yet productive noisiness are powerful resources that have continued to produce personal agency and spaces of resilience.

The fun of it all: more wreckage

Ruination continues. There are other metadiscourses on Naija, and these are not led by bloggers and artists, but by language policy makers, linguists, and mainstream media. The metadiscourses in which they participate have in common, I think, that they frame Naija as something that needs to be homogenized and unified and that should be turned into a part of hegemonic state epistemologies and controlled practice. The powerful ubiquity of Naija is intended to be made useful to a consolidation of imperial formations that had been the reason for its previous marginalization. This quite contradictory effort is mirrored, for example, in the attempt to create a standard for Naija.

Since 2009, the *Naija Languej Akedemi* has been active in creating an orthography, promoting literacy and constructing a corpus that would eventually be the basis for its standardization. This is remarkable because the *Akedemi* is part of the French-Nigerian IFRA project that aims at cutting-edge research in the humanities. However, while current sociolinguistics tends to deconstruct language as bounded structure, and communication is increasingly seen as fluid, multimodal, and semiotically complex practice, the current standardization efforts are based on a concept of Naija as a sequestered thing, defined by structural features and constructed as a separate language. Following approaches like Dagmar Deuber's (2005) study on the *Nigerian Pidgin in Lagos*, where Naija is described as a contact language, the *Akedemi* sets out to undertake a project within a framework of variationist linguistics, which focuses on the features that divide social and geographic groups of speakers, whereas projects such as *Wazobia FM* are not very interested in emphasizing such divisions. After news on the *Akedemi*'s activities and goals were made accessible, many users commented in critical ways, like the following examples from *Nairaland.com* illustrate (www.nairaland.com/518078/pidgin-formal-language):

(1) Sheau: oyibo don tire me, abegi!
(2) usbcable: which of the dialect's will be made standard; 1 waffi, 2 Northerner, 3 yoruba, 4 calabar. to mention a few.
(3) Gamine: Even Jesus sef dey speak pidgin
(4) texazzpete: This logic is laughable. So because we're second users we need varieties of English, abi? We chose English as a national language because we needed a common language to communicate. We couldn't use Hausa or Yoruba or Igbo. That would never have worked. Now after taking that step someone is saying we need even more diversity and variety! No.

The idea of a standard is a bit unswagger. To most users, there was something funny and bewildering in the idea to make Naija 'legal' and 'official'. They express some deep discomfort about the apparent deregisterment of Naija and the removal of its speakers' subversive agency. In her volume on languaging as a postcolonial experience, Rey Chow (2014) wrote about the implementation of colonial language as an epistemic break: 'to adopt and adjust to another group's language for purposes of social regimentation and mobility *without the reverse also occurring*' (Chow, 2014, p. 41) does not create coevalness, but leaves those on whom that other language had been imposed with a tongue that 'exists more or less as an external graft' (ibid.). Hence, Naija, which had existed as a fluid way of speaking and doing, which could be conceptualized as a means of expressing and living diversity, was going to be imposed, in an alienated form, on those who relied on its messiness and uncontrolled form in order to create some anarchical freedom and personal agentivity. Soon, ironic memes and screenshots were circulated, where users illustrated their firm belief in the durée of idiosyncratic usages of the colonial language, and the impossibility of making sense of Naija complexity anyway, Figure 17.4.

While fixing Naija remains a work in progress, assigning it to its proper sociolinguistic environment seems equally difficult. When Nigeria turned 50 in 2010, the BBC launched a short feature on 'What does Naija mean?' (Labaran, 2010). It contained an interview with the Nigerian journalist Peter Okwoche who was quoted saying that 'the word was coined by the country's youth as a way of distancing themselves from the old guard who they blame for Nigeria's woes'. The feature continues as a kind of imitation of blogs by ending with a lengthy section of 'comments', which, however, seem to have been commissioned or selected by the BBC editors themselves. These comments strongly emphasize Naija as owned by the youth, who are portrayed as patriotic and quite conservative (www.bbc.co.uk/news/world-africa-11447252):

Girl failed in english exam

Boy :- I heared you failed in english ?
.
.
Girl :- who telled you ?
it is unpossible ..
i sawed the result yesterday , i passed away"
Boy :- ok bye !!
Girl :- bye bye ..god blast you

FIGURE 17.4 Blasted English (http://www.nairaland.com/2132954/girl-failed-english-exam).

(5) What Naija means to me is: Nai – the old Nigeria with a bad image because of corrupt ex-leaders and Ja – a slang for disappear. So when we say Naija, it means that we, the youth, are determined to cleanse the country and show the world the true colour of this great nation. Naija for real! ***Simon, Enugu, Nigeria***

(6) Naija is a word coined by Nigeria's youth from the local English language spoken mainly in the southern part of the country. You put a lot of stress when pronouncing it to show your love for the country. I love the word Naija. ***Abdulmuminu, Kano, Nigeria***

(7) Naija simply means 'The New Nigeria' – one the average Naija youth is proud to be associated with. The name gives me a sense of belonging. I love Naija. ***Buchy, Nigeria***

This national youth language is a harmless language with no history; slavery and colonialism are deleted from the discourse, and a new Nigeria already seems to be there. This new, dehistoricized Nigeria is the future that has just begun, albeit a fake one, as we can gather from reminding ourselves on Luhmann's work and Benjamin's Angel of History. The celebration of Naija as the language of the future and the youth largely produces exclusion of discourses about violence, disempowerment, and marginalization. It creates a linguistic ambiance of well-being and harmony. Bad things sound better in Naija, as the blogger Uduak Ubak (2015) remarks: 'I love to listen to the News in Nigerian Pidgin English mainly because it makes it less tragic. A good example is when the word "died" is replaced with "delete". When used in a sentence, we have something like, "the man don delete" meaning "the man has died"'.

Youth language here is colonial outfall. Void of history, it is also depersonalized, and its proclaimed owners, the youth, lead an unreal existence. The sociolinguist Crispin Thurlow in his deconstruction of adolescent communication (2005) suggests that this is largely intended everywhere where there is a hegemonic discourse on difference and youth. The patterned generalizations of 'the youth', Thurlow argues, go hand in hand with a compartmentalization and exploitation of young people, whose ways of speaking and being are constructed as an attack on adulthood, and as pathological. Moreover, because 'adolescence' and 'youth' now have a longer durée in peoples' lives, simply because 'being young' is often conceptualized as 'not yet being economically independent', and an increasing number of younger people remain without any access to sustainable jobs, there is a need for rethinking such terminologies and what they describe. If we made a habit out of challenging labels such as 'youth' wherever they appear, such as in the aforementioned BBC feature, Thurlow suggests, we would be able to deconstruct such essentialist concepts of 'youth'. When dealing with young people, difference is constructed on the basis of received stereotypes – of young people as inadequate communicators or as eloquent nation savers. And precisely here an undue ascription of specific communicative strategies to adolescence (Thurlow, 2005, p. 5) produces considerable opacity on identity as a lifelong process, which is now met by people of all ages as being made more complex by an increasing diversity of communicative situations and power formations in a globalized, interconnected world.

In those metanarratives about the Nigerian youth as an unrealistically uniform representation of a 'new generation' that now tackles, once again, the imperialist project of consolidating the nation state, young people are exploited, by being represented in a highly ideologized way, and by being defined by others as a cohesive and therefore controllable group. Thurlow suggests that we, as linguists, can take the role of an advocate by uncovering such disenfranchising constructions. However, there also is considerable writing back. Young social media users post memes and other visual material as comments to 'Naija' as something nationalist attributed exclusively to the youth. These posts are ironic remarks on the state of affairs – portraying Nigeria and Naija ways of doing as leading not to the intended (or officially desired) goal, but just to another implementation of creative southernness.

Wondering where the fun comes from in the communicative practices of young people, I suppose it is not simply that creativity is made so decidedly visible in them, because then one would be equally interested in, let's say, old people's communicative practices (which could be extremely creative). Linguistic creativity alone is a poor explanation for any linguistic practice's outstanding character; it is simply part of languaging and not more pronounced among adolescents than among their middle-aged mothers, for example. Richard Bauman and Charles Briggs have shown in their classic paper on poetics and performance (1990) that within and through processes of decentering and recontextualization, 'individuals gain rights to particular modes of transforming speech' (Bauman & Briggs, 1990, p. 61). The notion of performance as a highly reflexive mode of communication is crucial here:

> Performance puts the act of speaking on display – objectifies it, lifts it to a degree from its interactional setting and opens it to scrutiny by an audience. Performance heightens awareness of the act of speaking and licenses the audience to evaluate the skill and effectiveness of the performer's accomplishment. By its very nature, then, performance potentiates decontextualization'.
>
> *(ibid., p. 73)*

Those mediatized practices of communicative performativity allow for precisely this: evaluation and objectification. But unlike other communicative actions, they allow for a much stronger performativity; they are interesting and meaningful not because of the information on Naija they convey, but because of the multi-layered meta-discourse they transport – this is all about reflexivity, about evaluating the underlying decentering and decontextualization, of meaning, context, power.

Conclusion

In youth languaging and in subversive uses of Naija alike, decentering and decontextualization happen in extreme ways: not much is left intact, and ruination is so profound and so present that it acquires a very prominent place in meta-discourse. While speakers, artists, and bloggers perform their experiences of marginalization and inequality, they hurl ruined order before our feet, leaving us to evaluate the outcome. But as at the same time recontextualization, providing new or different frameworks of evaluation, takes place, meta-discourses here can have iridescent and cacophonic qualities. This might be a reason for frequent perceptions of these reflexive, performative practices as noisy and therefore anti-social: 'Noise does not have to be loud', sound theorist Salomé Voegelin writes, 'but it has to be exclusive: excluding other sounds, creating in sound a bubble against sounds, destroying sonic signifiers and divorcing listening from sense material external to its noise' (Voegelin, 2010, p. 45). This deconstruction of sonic sense into non-sense is often correlated with bad taste and low class: it is a marker of trash aesthetics, but also of 'youth culture' as a culture of disenfranchised people.

And here the notion of fun comes in. There is an element of surprise here, when we realize that reflexivity and metanarratives are not about order and hegemonic structure, but about anarchic messiness and ruination. It seems that we are tempted to think we understand because we know the substance, but then we realize we have to deconstruct things a little before they really make sense. Behind the picture of the veiled woman in the shower there is not only an entire meta-discourse on how Naija stands for things reliably turning out wrong, but also on ruinous sexting, problematic religious differences, Southern subalternity, and so forth. All this is semioticized in a crummy picture with its trash aesthetics. We do not seem to expect complex reflexivity here, and the unexpected as the precise base of irony dissolves in laughter, I suppose. Not creativity and not otherness seem to raise our interest here and make us amused, but some kind of meta-ruination.

Southern and non-hegemonic views on linguistic diversification and the social semiotics of what has often been called a 'dialect', 'jargon', or 'slang' are expressed through and in commentaries such as lyrics in popular music, memes, vocabulary lists provided in social media, comments on websites, and, to a very large extent, pictures. Here, not texts and academic discourse, but a semiotically multi-layered, socially meaningful mélange of text, image, sound, placement, and circulation appears to be the medium for transmission of knowledge and evaluation of language ideologies and metalinguistic expertise outside Northern academia. In order to take the perspectives, voices, and agencies of Southern players seriously, sociolinguists therefore might need to turn to such sources as part of expert debates.

Acknowledgements

I am very grateful to Reem Bassiouney for her helpful comments on an earlier version of this chapter. I also wish to thank Andrea Hollington, Nico Nassenstein, Fridah Kanana, Heather Brookes, and participants of the 2nd African Urban Youth Languages Conference at Nairobi (2015) for their many stimulating remarks and inspiring discussions.

References

Abdullah, I., & Muana, P. (1998). The revolutionary United Front of Sierra Leone. In C. Clapham (Ed.), *African guerillas* (pp. 172–194). Oxford: James Currey.

Agha, A. (2005). Voice, footing, enregisterment. *Journal of Linguistic Anthropology, 15*, 38–59.

Barrett, L. (2016 [1998]). *Fela Kuti: Chronicle of a life foretold.* Retrieved from www.wilderutopia.com/performance/sound/fela-kuti-revolutionary-insurrectionist-talismanic-afrobeat-pioneer/

Bauman, R., & Briggs, C. (1990). Poetics and performance as critical perspectives on language and social life. *Annual Review of Anthropology, 19*, 59–88.

Benjamin, W. (1968 [1940]). *Theses on the philosophy of history: Illuminations* (H. Arendt, Ed.). New York: Harcourt, Brace & World.

Chigozie, E. (2015). *100+ popular Nigerian slangs and their meanings.* Retrieved from http://buzznigeria.com/popular-nigerian-slangs-meanings/

Chow, R. (2014). *Not like a native speaker.* New York: Columbia University Press.

Deuber, D. (2005). *Nigerian pidgin in Lagos: Language contact, variation and change in an African urban setting.* London: Battlebridge.

Deumert, A. (2014). *Sociolinguistics and mobile communication.* Edinburgh: Edinburgh University Press.

Faraclas, N. (1996). *Nigerian pidgin.* London: Routledge.

Farouk, S. (2012). *Nigerian slang: The one on washing, flattery and related crimes.* Retrieved from https://moacn.wordpress.com/tag/nigerian-slang/

Fasan, R. (2015). "Wetin dey happen?": Wazobia, popular arts, and nationhood. *Journal of African Cultural Studies, 27*(1), 7–19.

Grade, P. (1892). Das Negerenglisch an der Westküste von Afrika. *Anglia XIV, 2*, 362–393.

Halliday, M. (1976). Anti-languages. *American Anthropologist, 78*(3), 570–584.

Henrici, E. (1897). Westafrikanisches Negerenglisch. *Anglia XX, 4,* 397–403.

Hollington, A., & Nassenstein, N. (Eds.). (2015). *Youth language practices in Africa and beyond.* Berlin: De Gruyter.

Kiessling, R., & Mous, M. (2004). Urban youth languages in Africa. *Anthropological Linguistics, 46*(3), 303–341.

Köler, H. (1848). *Einige Notizen über Bonny an der Küste von Guinea, seine Sprache und seine Bewohner, mit einem Glossarium.* Göttingen: Dietrische Verlagsbuchhandlung.

Kuti, F. (1977). *Sorrow, tears and blood.* Lagos: Kalakuta.

Labaran, B. (2010, October 1). Nigeria at 50: What does Naija mean? *BBC News Africa.* Retrieved from www.bbc.co.uk/news/world-africa-11447252

Lewis, M. P., Simons, G. F., & Fennig, C. D. (Eds.). (2016). *Ethnologue: Languages of the world, nineteenth edition.* Dallas, TX: SIL International. Online version: www.ethnologue.com.

Luhmann, N. (1990). Die Zukunft kann nicht beginnen: Temporalstrukturen der modernen Gesellschaft. In P. Sloterdijk (Ed.), *Vor der Jahrtausendwende: Berichte zur Lage der Zukunft* (pp. 119–150). Frankfurt: Suhrkamp.

Mark, M. (2012). Nigeria's love of pidgin dey scatter my brain yet ginger my swagger. *The Guardian.* Retrieved from www.theguardian.com/world/2012/sep/24/nigeria-pidgin-scatter-brain-swagger

Ofunne, A., & Nwokogba, O. (2007). *Naija lingo.* Retrieved from www.naijalingo.com

Stoler, A. L. (Ed.). (2013). *Imperial debris.* Durham: Duke.

Stroud, C. (2015). *Multilingualism as an utopian project.* Paper presented at Cape Town WUN Workshop October 2015 on Multilingualism and Mobility in the Northern and Southern Hemispheres.

Thurlow, C. (2005). Deconstructing adolescent communication. In A. Williams & C. Thurlow (Eds), *Talking adolescence: Perspectives on communication in the teenage years* (pp. 53–72). New York: Peter Lang.

Ubak, U. (2015). *The origin and beauty of Pidgin English in Nigeria.* Retrieved from www.konnectafrica.net/pidgin-english-nigeria/

Voegelin, S. (2010). *Listening to noise and silence.* New York: Continuum.

18
DIALECTAL VARIATION AND IDENTITY IN POST-REVOLUTIONARY LIBYAN MEDIA

The case of Dragunov (2014)

Luca D'Anna

Introduction

When Muʕammar al-Qaḏḏāfi (henceforth, Ghaddafi) was overthrown and killed in Sirt on October 20th, 2011, an entire world came to an end. The revolutionary movement started in Benghazi on February 17th, consequently known as *Ṯawrat Sabʕata ʕašara Fibrāyir*, overruled an authoritarian government that had been in power for more than 40 years (since September 1st, 1969). In that respect, Ghaddafi's rule had not been very different from the other military governments that came to power in Northern Africa and the Middle East in the wake of the decolonization process. Differently than most other authoritarian governments, however, Ghaddafi tried to build his revolutionary Libya on the basis of the so-called Third Theory, exposed in the Green Book, first published in 1975. The book, which could be found in all Libyan public places and was widely distributed abroad, was the vehicle of the utopist ideology of a stateless society, which Ghaddafi tried to build and organize around his famous *people's committees* (*liǧān šaʕbiyya*).[1]

Language, in all its facets, did not escape the impact of Ghaddafi's regime, which exerted its influence in manifold ways. In 1977, for instance, the Libyan Arab Republic arisen from the 1969 coup was renamed *al-Ǧamāhiriyya al-ʕArabiyya al-Lībiyya aš-Šaʕbiyya al-ʔištirākiyya al-ʕuḏmà*, which can be roughly translated as "Great Socialist People's Libyan Arab *Ǧamāhiriyya*". *Ǧamāhiriyya* was a neologism coined by Ghaddafi from *ǧamāhīr*, the plural form of *ǧumhūr* "mass", to designate his "Republic of the Masses". The linguistic policy of the new revolutionary government included, among other measures, a strong campaign of Arabization and a complete ban on the employment of the Latin alphabet in all public places and in road signs. Ghaddafi even forbade the teaching of any foreign language for a decade, starting from 1984.[2]

The research on the sociolinguistic situation of Libya is almost non-existent. The excellent bibliography provided by Benkato and Pereira (forthcoming), in fact, mentions only three papers on this subject (Pereira, 2007, 2010b, forthcoming). From a dialectological point of view, Philippe Marçais described the country as a relatively homogeneous area, characterized by markedly Bedouin traits that coexist, within the urban centers, with vestiges of the older sedentary varieties.[3] The traditional, although questionable in the light of more recent data, classification of Libyan dialects distinguishes between Western Libyan (Tripolitania and Fezzan), Eastern Libyan (Cyrenaica), and a transitional zone (including Miṣurata, Sebha, the Sirt region, and the Jufra area).[4] All the dialects spoken in the area belong to the Maghrebi type and feature, with the exclusion of the Judeo-Arabic once spoken in Tripoli, the following Bedouin traits:

- voiced realization of the uvular plosive /q/ (e.g., *ṭrīg* "street", *sūg* "market");
- the reduction of the ancient diphthongs /ay/ and /aw/ to [ē] and [ō] (e.g., *lēl* "night", *yōm* "day");
- plural of $C_1vC_2\bar{v}C_3C_4$ in $C_1C_2\bar{a}C_3\bar{\imath}C_4$ (e.g., *məftāḥ* "key" → *mfātīḥ*);
- suffix pronoun for the third person masculine singular – *a(h)* (e.g., *wuld-a* "his son");
- absence of long vowel reconstruction in the plural of CCv verbs (e.g., *mšū* and not *mšāw*);
- absence of any marker of indefiniteness based on the numeral *wāḥid* "one" or the noun *šayʕ* "thing".

Between the three areas, phonetic, syllabic, and lexical differences exist. The dialect of Tripoli (henceforth TA), for instance, shows a mix of Bedouin and sedentary traits. Unlike all Eastern varieties and the nomadic ones in the Fezzān, it does not preserve the interdental phonemes /θ/, /ð/, and /ðʕ/, which merged into the occlusives /t/, /d/, and /dʕ/, and it has lost gender distinction in the plural of verbs and pronouns, retained by the large majority of the other Libyan varieties.[5]

Even within this homogeneous ensemble, however, the 20th century witnessed processes of great sociolinguistic relevance, such as the progressive bedouinization of TA, caused by the progressive urbanization that started during Italian colonization (18th century) and dramatically increased in the second half of the 20th century, particularly after the oil boom.[6] Unlike in many other Arab countries, TA does not seem to have attained the status of a prestige variety within the country, partially because Benghazi had joint-capital status within the Kingdom of Libya (1951–1969), which means that most of the elites came from Eastern Libya. Speakers from different areas, thus, are invariably proud of their peculiar dialects, while the absence of a strong urban elite and the rhetoric of the regime, stressing the "Bedouin legitimacy" of the ruling class, did not play in favor of the establishment of a national koine in the last four decades.[7] In the view of historian Vandewalle, a third element in Ghaddafi's search for legitimacy focused on the social background of those who had led the revolution. Portraying the revolution as a reaction of the country's hinterland – where Ghaddafi and most RCC members came from – against its exclusion during the monarchy, the systematic recruitment and emergence of members of the country's secondary tribes provided a powerful focus for the regime. The initial appeal to the hinterlands reflected once more an aspect of Ghaddafi's populism: the fact that a new political community could be created that relied on the consultative mechanisms of a tribal system that had characterized the country before the Italian invasion.[8]

The only sociolinguistic study concerning Libya during Ghaddafi's period, with reference to speechmaking, is Mazraani (1997). The scholar analyzes two speeches delivered by Ghaddafi in 1978 and 1981, focusing on the strategies employed by the Libyan leader, including codeswitching between TA and Modern Standard Arabic (henceforward MSA). The study has some drawbacks, including the decision of the author to limit her analysis to these two varieties, while Ghaddafi often resorts to non-urban Bedouin features (interdentals, feminine plurals in verbs and pronouns etc.),[9] but it gives an idea of the variation occurring in the Colonel's speeches.

Variation and codeswitching between MSA and/or various Arabic dialects, on the other hand, have been the object of several studies in recent years. Holes (1995) shows how, in different Middle Eastern environments (Amman, Baghdad, and Bahrain), dialects associated with national or religious communities have attained the status of prestige varieties, competing with MSA at the higher end of the diglossic continuum. Other scholarly contributions have, since then, investigated the patterns of employment of the prestige varieties versus both MSA and other competing dialects. Many of these studies focused on the variable of gender, generally assuming that women are more inclined towards the employment of prestige varieties than men, mostly because of their lesser exposure to MSA and the public domains in which it is usually employed.[10] Bassiouney (2010), on the contrary, maintains that educated women employ no less MSA[11] than men and that, in most cases, their linguistic behavior can be explained in terms of indexicality. MSA is resorted to as "a symbol of authority", and "a direct relation between code choice and identity" can be envisaged in the data analyzed.[12] When speaking of indexicality, we mainly refer to Eckert (2008) and her concept of indexical fields, according to which "variables index demographic categories not directly but indirectly, through their association with qualities and stances that enter into the construction of categories".[13] In her Labovian perspective, then, indicators are simple dialectal variables that distinguish social or geographic categories without attracting notice. They are, in other words, first-order indexes. When they are noticed and linked to the social evaluation of the geographic or social membership they index, they become second-order indexes (markers). The meaning of second order indexes, however, is never fixed, but continually subject to reinterpretation and renegotiation. The difference between second and third order indexes mainly lies in the degree of metapragmatic consciousness.[14] Chapter 4 in Bassiouney (2014) applies indexicality to her Egyptian data, showing how public discourse effectively resorts to the different indexes of MSA and Egyptian Arabic to achieve its communicative goals.[15]

In times of social and political turmoil, the struggle against the unequal access to resources also includes language. "The result of this negotiation is usually a challenge to identity that manifests itself through a challenge of language practices".[16] In Libya, the absence of a universally recognized prestige variety makes these categories even more relevant, especially in the media. In a situation in which no single variety has attained an undisputed prestige status, in fact, speakers tend to stick to their native dialects. The choice of different codes, when occurring, is then strongly linked to issues of identity.

Methodology

This study will investigate the struggle for identity that took place in Libya during and immediately after the February 17th Revolution through the lens of a popular Libyan TV show, *Dragunov*. *Dragunov* (the name of a famous Russian sniper rifle) was aired in 2014 on seven Libyan channels, broadcasting from both Tripoli and Benghazi, plus a Tunisian and an Egyptian one.[17] The show consists of 15 episodes of about 40 minutes each, for a total of 594 minutes. The authors chose to exclusively employ Libyan Arabic (henceforward LA), although some of the actors were not from Libya. This fact is particularly interesting given that LA does not enjoy any international or pan-Arab prestige. Tunisian actors, thus, were explicitly requested to act in LA, which even caused surprise in the case of a famous Tunisian actress, Hana Fehri. The choice of the variety of LA employed to impersonate the different characters, as a consequence, is of particular interest, since it can be attributed to explicit authorial planning and only marginally to the native dialect of the actor.

In order to investigate how code choice reflects and interacts with the ongoing struggle of identity, the 15 episodes of the TV show (all available online) have been analyzed employing both quantitative and qualitative methods. *Dragunov* is set in Tripoli and the plot starts at the beginning of the February 17th revolution. From the first episode, the love story between Munà, daughter of one of the victims of the Abu Salim massacre,[18] and ʕumar al-Kāsiḥ, belonging to one of the most prominent families in the regime, gives the authors the opportunity to depict the escalation of the Libyan conflict until the final liberation of Tripoli.

As previously mentioned, different varieties of LA coexist in the show. Unfortunately, with the exception of Tripoli and Benghazi, complete information about the dialects spoken in other Libyan areas is lacking. Benmoftah and Pereira (forthcoming) introduce the dialect of al-Khums, and D'Anna (forthcoming) offers a preliminary account of the dialect spoken in Miṣrāta, but little is known about the other dialects of the transitional area. The state of the art concerning LA, thus, allows us to distinguish the varieties spoken in the transitional area from both TA and Eastern Libyan Arabic (henceforth ELA), but finer distinctions within the transitional area need further research. For the purpose of this study, we first selected five characters:

1. Khamīs al-Kāsiḥ (former officer in Ghaddafi's army);[19]
2. ʕabīr al-Kāsiḥ (Khamīs' daughter, director of one of the official TV channels of the regime);
3. ʕumar al-Kāsiḥ (Khamīs' youngest son, in love with Munà, considered the best sniper in the country);

4. Munà al-Fāliḥ (university student and pro-revolution activist);
5. ʕabādī al-Fāliḥ (Munà's brother, pro-revolution activist and subsequently leader of a *katība* "battalion" of *ṯuwwār* "revolutionaries").

In an attempt to understand whether any observable correlation exists between the characters' role and the variety of LA they employ, one clearly recognizable isogloss was selected and its occurrence in the speech of the five characters counted. The results were then employed to run a simple chi-square test.

Once a clear relation was established between the employment of different Libyan varieties and the role of the characters, further analyses were conducted to investigate how different identities emerge and are constructed. Our view of identity here is mainly based on Bucholtz and Hall's socio-cultural linguistic approach, which can be summarized as "the social positioning of self and other".[20] Bucholtz and Hall's analysis revolves around the five principles of *emergence*, *positioning*, *indexicality*, *relationality*, and *partialness*, most of which have been used to unfold the interactive construction of different identities in *Dragunov*.[21] The relationality principle, in particular, proved to be a powerful analytical tool in our analysis:

> Identities are intersubjectively constructed through several, often overlapping, complementary relations, including similarity/difference, genuineness/artifice and authority/delegitimacy.[22]

Conveying otherness

For our analysis, as previously said, we have selected five characters: Khamīs al-Kāsiḥ, ʕabīr al-Kāsiḥ, ʕumar al-Kāsiḥ, Munà al-Fāliḥ and ʕabādi al-Fāliḥ. Four out of five characters have clear-cut roles within the show. Khamīs and ʕabīr are spokespersons of the official ideology of the regime, wielding power over others and employing violence to ensure their position of privilege. Munà and ʕabādī, on the contrary, represent the counter-discourse of the Libyan youth that opposed Ghaddafi's regime during the February 17th Revolution. Munà is a one-dimensional positive character, while ʕabādī lets his hatred towards the regime get the better of him and eventually ends up resembling the enemy he has been fighting for his entire life. ʕumar al-Kāsiḥ represents a more nuanced character. He is Khamīs' youngest son and never disowns his legacy, yet he is not part of any institution of the regime and his love for Munà gradually leads him to express his criticism towards Ghaddafi's authoritarian government.

Our analysis aims to ascertain whether any clear correlation between the characters' roles and their language choices exists. In the selection of the isoglosses to be included in the quantitative analysis, particular attention has been paid to the actors' native dialects. Since the actors impersonating Khamīs (Hisham Rustum), ʕabīr (Hana Fehri), and Munà (Suhair bin Imara) are from Tunisia, some finer phonetic features (such as the presence of epenthetic vowels to break consonantal clusters in many Bedouin varieties, e.g., *bint* "girl" vs *binət*) had to be discarded for the purpose of quantitative analysis. A preliminary observation, however, yielded some interesting results, with particular regard to the demonstrative pronouns. The reason lies in the fact that the three areas feature three distinct sets of demonstrative pronouns whose opposition can easily be grasped by non-native speakers and then used as a *shibboleth*. The following table reports a list of the demonstrative pronouns (near deixis) in use in TA (Western Libyan), Miṣrāta (MA, transitional zone), and Benghazi (BA, Eastern Libyan):

TABLE 18.1 Demonstratives for near deixis in TA, MA, and BA.

	Tripoli Arabic	Miṣrāta Arabic	Benghazi Arabic
M. Sg.	hādā	hēdā	haḍa
F. Sg.	hādī	hēdī	haḍi
M. Pl.	hādū	hadēma	haḍowma
F. Pl.	–	hadēna	haḍeyna

The occurrence of the forms *hēdā/hēdī* in the speech of the pro-Ghaddafi characters was discussed with the director of the show, Osama Rezg, during a Skype interview I conducted. Given that two of the three actors whose characters are under analysis are not native Libyans, we asked whether precise directives had been given to them concerning the specific variety of Libyan they would have to use. The director informed us that the actors had been given audiotapes containing recordings of a central Libyan dialect (although he did not specify the town), which corresponds to the transitional zone. Unfortunately, Miṣrāta is the only town for which a description is available with regard to that area. The long vowel *ē* in the first syllable of the singular pronouns, however, clearly sets MA apart from both TA and BA and constitutes a very recognizable isogloss that even non-native speakers can easily resort to.

The occurrences of demonstratives for near deixis were thus counted in the speech of the five characters for the 15 episodes, yielding the following results:

TABLE 18.2 Near-deixis demonstratives in the speech of the five characters under analysis.

	hādā	hēdā	hādī	hēdī
ʕAbīr	1	8	0	11
Khamīs	0	8	0	3
ʕumar	9	1	3	4
Munà	5	0	4	0
ʕAbādī	9	0	1	0

The distribution of the two possible variables for each demonstrative, i.e., featuring a long *ā* or a long *ē* in the first syllable, is quite clear, with the only exception of ʕumar, which will be discussed later. Taking into consideration only ʕabīr, Khamīs, Munà, and ʕabādī (whose positions relative to the regime are clear) and reducing the four possibilities to *hādv* and *hēdv*, thus, our results can be summarized as follows:

TABLE 18.3 Distribution of the hādv and hēdv variables in pro- and anti-Ghaddafi characters

	hādv	*hēdv*
Pro-Ghaddafi (ʕabīr, Khamīs)	1	30
Anti-Ghaddafi (Munà, ʕabādī)	19	0

It is clear that the socio-political variable pro- or anti-Ghaddafi correlates with the choice of the demonstrative. A chi-square test provides further evidence, with a value of $\chi^2 = 45,82$ (in order for the null hypothesis to be proved false, a much lower value of 7,879 was required). In our context, particular attention must be paid to the fact that the object of our study is a TV show in which dialect is performed. The cases of ʕabīr and Munà are emblematic. The two actresses are Tunisian and, thus, non-native speakers of any Libyan variety. They act in LA, but feature very recognizable patterns in the selection of the two variables mentioned above and of other traits that were not the object of quantitative analysis.

ʕumar's results, on the other hand, are no less interesting. They demonstrate that the variable which correlates with the choice of the demonstrative is not "geographic origin", but rather "support" vs. "opposition" to Ghaddafi's regime. ʕumar, in fact, despite being part of the same familiar group as Khamīs and ʕabīr, displays extremely diverging results. He employs the *hādv* variable 12 times and the *hēdv* variable five times, although the actor is a TA native speaker (which means that *hēdv* is not part of his native repertoire). If we take into consideration the fact that the samples were collected from a TV show in which dialect performance was carefully planned, language attitudes and stance-taking processes that are worth investigating might be at play.

Emerging identities

As said above, ʕumar's results contradict the clear-cut pattern emerging from the other four characters. The fact that he employs *hādv* in 12 occurrences and *hēdv* in five may be due to the more complex nature of his character, torn between the loyalty to his family and the regime and his love for Munà that leads him to question this heritage. In order to obtain a clearer picture of the reasons behind the choice of the two variants, the five occurrences of the *hēdy* demonstratives have been investigated.

1. *ʕaleš sakkərət?   əl=bint   hēdī   bi=tʕaddəb=ni   wṛā=ha* (ep. 2, 17:02);
   why closed.3.F.SG DEF=girl   this.F   FUT=3.F.torture.SG=me
   after=her
   Why did she hang up? This girl will torture (and make me run) after her.

2. *nžī=k   mən   ʕyūn=i,   lākən   məzāžiyyət=ək   hēdī
   bi=tugtəl=ni* (ep. 9, 22:40);
   1.come.SG=you   from   eyes=my   but   moodiness=your   this.F
   FUT=3.F.kill.SG=me
   I'll come with all my heart, but this moodiness of yours will kill me.

3. *wa l=xulāṣa,   šən   məʕnā=hək=klām hēdā?* (ep. 10, 19:10)
   and DEF=summary   what   meaning=his   DEF=discourse   this.M
   In the end, what's the meaning of these words?

4. *wədʕ=i   u   wədʕ   ʕāylt=i. ənti   ʕārfa   nəḥna   mən,   u
   mā=nəgdər=š   nwarrəṭ   ʕāylt=i fī   mawḍūʕ zēy   hēdā* (ep. 13, 21:23);
   condition=my   and   condition   family=my   you.F
   ACT.PTCP.know.F.SG   we   who   and
   NEG=1.can.SG=NEG   1.drag.SG   family=my   in
   matter   like   this.M
   My position and my family's position. You know who we are and I can't drag my family in a matter like this.

5. *šūf, xūd=ha qāʕda   hedi   fī   ḥyāt=ək . . .* (ep. 13, 23:31);
   IMP.look.2.M.SG   IMP.take.2.M.SG=his rule this.F   in
   life=your
   Look, take this as a rule in your life.

The analysis of the contexts in which the preceding utterances occur offers some insights into the different identities that emerge and are constructed within the story. Samples 1 and 2 can be contextualized within the complex relationship between ʕumar and Munà. The two characters hold extremely different social positions, yet ʕumar's love for Munà neutralizes this imbalance in power. When he fails to understand Munà's behavior or has to face her (fake) refusal, however, he is tempted to resort to his family's social position, attempting to wield power over her through language. In Sample 3, ʕumar is facing his elder brother ʕalī, who holds a prominent position in Ghaddafi's army. Munà has just been arrested by the *ližān ṯawriyya* ("Revolutionary Committees") and, despite his disdain for the regime's system of power, he is forced to ask ʕalī for help. On this occasion, the elder brother constantly employs the *hēdv* variant and ʕumar accommodates. In Sample 4, ʕumar and Munà have finally overcome their previous misunderstandings and ʕumar has admitted his hatred for the regime. At this point,

Munà asks him why he didn't join the Revolution, triggering the response quoted above. After mentioning his family, ʕumar switches to the dialectal variety referred to above as Central Libyan, which is clear not only because of the *hēdv* variant, but also based on the first person plural pronoun *nəḥna*, clearly distinguished from TA *ḥnē*.[23] In Sample 5, finally, ʕumar is confronting ʕabādī, who will eventually kill him at the end of the TV show. ʕabādī asks him whether he has ever missed a shot in his life and why, which triggers ʕumar's answer, in a particularly tense moment within the episode.

This brief report is necessary to understand how ʕumar constructs his different and often conflicting identities through language. Despite his geographic origin, he accommodates to TA in the vast majority of his interactions and avoids positioning himself as the member of a powerful family in Ghaddafi's regime. Central Libyan, indexing family bonds and tribal affiliations, is mostly resorted to when interacting with relatives or when loyalty to one's family is brought up. As previously said, however, ʕumar's character is probably the most complex within the TV show, which reflects also on his language choices. As brilliantly put by Bucholtz and Hall (2010), "identity emerges from the specific conditions of linguistic interaction"[24] and it is often transitory rather than fixed. This is the reason why, when challenged, ʕumar takes shelter in the safe harbor of his dominant social position, constructing a different identity through the choice of specific variables, such as *hēdv*.

The indexical fields of Central Libyan, on the other hand, are also clear within the language behavior of the other two characters that employ it. This is particularly clear in the case of ʕabīr al-Kāsiḥ, the character that most uncompromisingly embodies the arrogance and arbitrary power of Ghaddafi's regime. She sticks to the *hēdv* variable throughout the show, with one notable exception:[25]

6.   *kull əlli   təšbaḥ   fī=h   tahayyuʔāt,   kull=ha mə=ṣ=ṣadma*
    all   that   2.see.M.SG   PREP=him   visions   all=her from=DEF=shock
    ən=nafsiyya   əlli   ʕəšt=ha bəʕd   mā   māt   bāt=ek fī
    DEF=psychological   that   lived.2. How is the Tetouan variety
       M.SG=her   after   that   died.3.M.SG   father=your
       in
    infiǧār   mustawdəʕ   ad=daxīra…   əlli   xallā=k həkki
    explosion   deposit DEF=munitions…   that   left.3.M.SG=you
    so
    bi=l=mənḍər hādā (ep. 14, 32:37);
    with=DEF=look   this.M
    Everything you see are visions, all from the psychological shock you suffered after your father died in the explosion of the deposit of munitions… which left you in this condition.

This utterance is part of a longer conversation that ʕabīr exchanges with her older brother in the final moments of Ghaddafi's regime, when the *ṭuwwār* have already taken Tripoli and her family, after losing everything, has to escape. Quoting Bucholtz and Hall (2010) again, "it is perhaps easiest to recognise identity as emergent in cases where speakers' language use does not conform with the social category to which they are normatively assigned".[26] From this perspective, ʕabīr's only deviation from the norm that the plot assigned her occurs when her character loses the power she used to wield with such arrogance, providing further proof of the indexical fields associated with Central Libyan.

Bedouin legitimacy

As previously said, the only variable considered for quantitative analysis was the long vowel in the demonstrative for near deixis, due to the fact that subtler phonetic traits might have been harder to reproduce for non-native speakers of Central Libyan. The three main characters belonging to the al-Kāsiḥ family, however, often display other traits that clearly diverge from TA, even though this divergence sometimes takes unexpected twists. Let us analyze, for instance, one of the most dramatic moments of the TV show, i.e., the final conversation between ʕalī al-Kāsiḥ and his father's ghost. ʕalī, tormented by his hallucinations, refuses to acknowledge the reality of the fall of Ghaddafi's regime, while the rest of his family are ready to leave Tripoli. He thus addresses his dead father, asking him to instill in his sons the sense of loyalty to the regime:

7. gūl   'l=hum   yā   bāt=i   gūl   'l=hum...   kann=ak
    IMP.say.2.M.SG   to=them.M   oh   father=my   IMP.   IMP.
        say.2.M.SG   to=them.M   how=you
    sākət?   ulād=ək   bāʕu   l=qāyəd,   gīm
    ACT.PTCP.be.silent.M.SG   sons=your   sold.3.M.PL
        DEF=leader   IMP.raise.2.M.SG
    ḥāssət   əš=šaraf   mtāʕ=ək u   ḍṛub=hum   u
    sense   DEF=honor   GEN=your   and   IMP.
        hit.2.M.SG=them.M   and
    ʕalləm=hum   inn=hum mā=ixūnū=š!   init   kəbīr
    IMP.teach.2.M.SG=them.M   that=them.M   NEG=3.
        betray.M.PL=NEG   you.M.SG   old
    əl=ʕāyla   u   init   əlli   ṛabbēt=hum   u   init
    DEF=family and   you.M.SG   who   raised.2.M.SG=them.M
       and   you.M.SG
    lāzəm   tṛabbī=hum   mən   əž=ždīd! (ep. 14, 30:54)
    ACT.PTCP.be.necessary.M.SG   2.raise.SG=them.M   from
       DEF=new

Tell them father, tell them! Why are you silent? Your sons sold the leader, recall your sense of honor and beat them and teach them not to betray! You are the oldest in the family, you are the one who raised them and you must teach them again!

The actor playing the part of ʕalī al-Kāsiḥ is Mohamed Othman, one of the most famous Libyan actors, native of Tiji (a small village south-west of Tripoli); he usually acts in TA. Here the actor strives to convey the sense of otherness already mentioned above, and does that by mixing non-TA traits actually belonging to different dialects. The vocative kinship term *yā bāt-i*, for instance, is clearly ELA, while the transitional zone, including Miṣrāta, Sirt, and Banī Walīd, has *yā bū-y*.[27] Since TA also has *yā bū-y*, however, it is probable that the actor deliberately chose to use a divergent form to mark distance. Also, *kann-ak* is a typical ELA expression, as opposed to TA *xēṛ-ek?* "what's the matter/what's wrong with you?". The pronoun *init* "you.M.SG", on the other hand, is neither TA (*ənta*)[28] nor ELA (*inta*).[29] The dialectal variety displayed here is probably nowhere to be found in Libya, yet it includes a series of non-urban and specifically non-TA traits that strongly convey the impression of a Bedouin variety from the hinterland.

The same happens with ʕabīr al-Kāsiḥ, who repeatedly employs, apart from *hēdv*, non-TA forms such as *bukra* "tomorrow", used in ELA and Fezzani Arabic (henceforth FA), while TA has *ġudwa*; and *wāžəd* "a lot", used in Miṣrāta (transitional zone) and ELA.[30] These traits were not the object of quantitative analysis, but they contribute to the creation of an indefinite Central Libyan Bedouin variety.

The linguistic dimension of the TV show was subject to some criticism on Libyan social media, especially with reference to the non-nativeness of some of the key actors (such as Hisham Rustum – Khamīs al-Kāsiḥ, Hana Fehri – ʕabīr al-Kāsiḥ, and Suhair bin Imara – Munà, who are all Tunisian). In a personal communication, the director Osama Rezg justified his choices with the non-availability of Libyan actresses for all the roles, specifying, at the same time, that all the foreign actors were constantly trained in the different varieties of LA they were supposed to speak. The attention paid by Libyans to linguistic issues is evident from the fact that, in a meeting held at the University of Tripoli, a question concerning the accuracy of the dialects portrayed was the first addressed to the director.[31] Another reason for the vagueness of the dialect spoken by the al-Kāsiḥ family probably lies in the fact that the director, in the particularly tense historical moment during which the show was filmed, did not want to brand any town with the mark of "Ghaddafism". When ʕumar and Munà first meet, thus, they do not disclose their respective native towns. They are just "not from Tripoli", but Munà is from a nearby town, which is also clear from her (non-native) TA.

8. Munà: *lahžt=ək*   *mūš*   *ṭrābəlsi...*
           dialect=your   NEG   Tripolinian
           Your dialect is not Tripolinian...

ʕumar: *bi=ḍ=ḍabṭ.*

           with=DEF=precision
           Exactly.

Munà   *zbəṭṭ=ək mən   wēn,   bi=ž=žōda!*

           recognized.1.SG=you   from   where   with=DEF=goodness
           I got you (i.e., where you are from), nice to meet you!

ʕumar: *bī=k   ažwəd,   u   ənti?*

           with=you   better   and   you.F
           Nice to meet you too, where are you from?

Munà: *mən   mədīna   gərība   ʕala   ṭrābləs...*

           from   town   near.F   from   Tripoli
           From a town near Tripoli.

ʕumar: *āh   tamām,   zbəṭṭ=ək ...* (ep. 1, 18:46)

           ah   perfect   recognized.1.SG=you
           Ah perfect, I got you!

The target, thus, is not any particular town nor dialect, but the elite of the regime, mostly coming from the Bedouin tribes of the hinterland and forming that Bedouin legitimacy upon which Ghaddafi built his revolutionary Libya. ʕumar, in fact, does not reveal his native town, but he openly admits his tribal legacy when discussing the latest events with one of his dearest friends:

9. *mūš ʕāṛəf   yā   ṣagər,   mūš   ʕāṛəf   əl=ḥagg   mʕā*

    NEG   ACT.PTCP.know.M.SG   oh   ṣagəṛ   NEG   ACT.
    PTCP.know.M.SG   DEF=right   with
    škūn.   fī=l=axīr   ənta   ʕāṛəf   wadʕ=i   u   wadʕ
    whoin=DEF=last   you.M   ACT.PTCP.know.M.SG   condition=my
    and   condition
    ʕāylt=i,   əl=gəddāfi   hāda   mən   qabīlət=na (ep. 4, 14:37);
    family=my   DEF=Ghaddafi   this.M   from   tribe=our
    I don't know, Ṣagəṛ, I don't know who's right. In the end, you know my position and my family's position, this Ghaddafi belongs to our tribe.

The dialect performed in *Dragunov*, thus, offers a counter-discourse to the Bedouin rhetoric of Ghaddafi's regime. Further evidence, in this sense, is provided by the songs performed on the TV show, in particular *yā blād-i* "Oh country of mine" (with a probable reference to the reinstated national anthem of Libya, also titled *yā blād-i*) and *naḥna naḥna lībiyyīn* "We are Libyans". The first song was written by Libyan musician Fuad Gritli specifically for the show. It closes Episode 13, when the *ṭuwwār* are entering Tripoli and all the main characters are portrayed in a final moment of unreal calm. The second song, written and performed by Samir al-Kurdi, appears twice, in Episodes 3 and 4, always in connection with ʕalāʔ al-Kāsiḥ, the youngest and most violent brother in the family. A partial version of the lyrics, with a simple free translation, is provided below.

> *yā blādi* "Oh country of mine"
> *snīn ʕayšīn*
> *əyyām mlyāna dmūʕ*
> *wēn māšīn?*
> *fī galb-ī*
> *ism-ək ənti maḥfūr*
> *yā blād-ī*
> *gūli l-kull əlli yanwā l-ək šarr*
> *mahmā kān fī bḥar wallā fī barr*
> *əḥnē žāyyīn*
> *yā blād-ī*
> *žāyyīn-ək žāybīn əl-ḥurriyya*
> *žāyyīn-ək žāybīn əl-mustaqbəl*
> *žāy bi-nəbnī-k b-īdē-yya*
> *lā li-ḍ-ḍuləm li-ṭ-ṭuġyān*
> *lā li-ž-žahəl nibbū-yyām əzmān*
> *yā blād-ī*
> *lībyā*
> Years we've been living
> Days full of tears
> Where are we going?
> In my heart
> Your name is carved
> Oh country of mine
> Tell everybody who wishes bad on you
> By land and sea
> We are coming
> Oh country of mine
> We are coming and bringing you freedom
> We are coming and bringing you future
> I'm coming to build you with my hands
> No to oppression and despotism
> No to ignorance, we want the good old days
> Oh country of mine
> Libya
> *nəḥna nəḥna lībiyyīn* "We are Libyans"
> *naḥna naḥna lībiyyīn*
> *naḥna tārīx u fursān*

naḥna mā-na xawwānīn
b-užūd-ək lībyā āmān
lānn-ək mən n-nās əl-haynīn
kēf əlli ġālī yənhān
l-lībī əl-ḥurr yirədd ed-dēyn
l-lībī əl-ḥurr əl-yōwm yibān
naḥna mā-na mərtaddīn
naḥna žnūd-ək fi-l-məydān
naḥna mā kēyf l-āxrīn
yā malək mlūk əz-zmān
naḥna ʕāyla hāḏā bū-na
naḥna ʕāyla u l-qāyəd bū-na
kəll əl-kawn əfdā l-uʕyūn-a
We are Libyans
We are history and cavaliers
We are not traitors
With your presence Libya is safe
Since you are a humble person
How is it possible to despise a dear one?
Today the free Libyan pays his debt
Today the free Libyan appears
We are not apostates
We are your soldiers on the field
We are not like the others
Oh king of the kings of time!
We are a family and this is our father
We are a family and the Leader is our father
All the universe can be sacrificed for him

The two songs are highly representative of the struggle portrayed by the TV show. While the first one conveys, sometimes in an idealized fashion, the ambitions of the *ṯuwwār*, the second expresses the traditional rhetoric of Ghaddafi's regime, infused with paternalistic tones (e.g., *naḥna ʕāyla hāḏā bū-na*) and references to the Bedouin heritage of Libya (e.g., *naḥna tārīx u fursān*). It comes as no surprise, thus, that the language employed reflects this struggle. Quoting Eckert (2008), in fact, "style is not a surface manifestation, but originates in content".[32] Although both songs are undoubtedly performed in LA, Fuad Gritli sings the first one in his native TA, as evident from the lack of interdentals (e.g., *ḍuləm*), the systematic absence of short vowels in open unstressed syllables (e.g., *snīn, mlyāna, dmūʕ*), and, morphologically, the first person plural pronoun *əḥnē*. The second song, on the contrary, features the first person plural pronoun *naḥna*, preserves the interdentals (e.g., *hāḏā*) and also displays an exclusively prefixal negation *mā-na* "we are not" (as opposed to the more common circumfixal *mā-nā-š*), all of which indicate a non-urban, Bedouin variety. Again, the absence of a detailed linguistic atlas of the Libyan dialects does not allow us to ascertain whether this variety can be identified with the dialect of a specific town or if, as already seen with the speech of Ṣalī al-Kāsiḥ, it just represents "Bedouin" Libyan Arabic.

It is clear, however, that *Dragunov* aims at undermining the Bedouin legitimacy that constituted one of the pillars of Ghaddafi's rhetoric, a point that will be further discussed in our conclusions.

Other languages

During the revolutions that swept the Arab world in 2011, language was both a weapon and a battlefield. In Egypt, for instance, the government media claimed that the protesters in Tahrir Square were not Egyptians, backing this claim by citing their alleged use of English and lack of proficiency in Arabic. On the other side, the protesters laid claims to the authoritative indexes of MSA in multiple ways, thus presenting themselves as the "real Egyptians".[33] The present study has, so far, focused on the construction of multiple identities through the manipulation of different Libyan dialects. The role of other languages (especially English) and MSA, however, also deserves some attention.

The employment of English in the TV show is restricted, with few exceptions, to a single character, Luževn. Daughter of a minister of the regime, she conspires throughout the entire show against Munà and her love for Ṣumar, denouncing her to the secret police for subversive propaganda, but opportunistically shifts to the other side a few hours before the fall of Tripoli. In the final episode, which describes events taking place a few months after the Revolution, her father is the leader of a new party and she turns into a political activist. The director of the show, during the Skype interview mentioned above, explained that he tried to depict the typical highborn Arab, who studied abroad and uses English to mark her alleged superiority. This results in unusual episodes of code-switching:

10. *gūd morning yā aḥla fādər fī d=dənyā!* (9, 12:44)

    good morning oh sweetest father in DEF=world
    Good morning, sweetest father in the world!

11.
12. *dīr šwēyya šōpping* (9, 12:58)

    1.do.SG a.little shopping
    I'll do a little shopping.

This unusual, probably unrealistic language choice can be read in the light of the harsh debate regarding the "Libyanness" of the two sides, just like in the Egyptian case. In Egypt, the poet Hishām Al-Jukh expresses this struggle with the verse, addressed to Egypt, *lā tatrukī-him yuxbirū-ki bi-ʔanna-nī/aṣbaḥtu šayʔan tāfihan muwaǧǧahā* "do not let them tell you that I have become something trivial and controlled by foreigners".[34] In a public speech contained in the last episode of *Dragunov*, in a similar way, Munà addresses Lužeyn and the likes of her in pure MSA as ʕumalāʔ yanʕatūna-nā bi-l-ʕumalāʔ "foreign agents who depict us as foreign agents" (ep. 15, 24:46).

Munà's speech is the only instance in which MSA is employed to support the revolutionary discourse. MSA features both positive and negative indexes. It is the language of the Qurʔān and of the Classical Arabic culture, which grants it divine and authoritative indexes, and also the only unifying factor for Arabs all around the world.[35] Its authoritative indexes, however, have often been exploited by representatives of authoritarian regimes to legitimate their power, and may thus backfire. During 2011, for instance, Ben Ali (who usually delivered his speeches in MSA) resorted to Tunisian Arabic, with the now famous expression *fhamt-kum* "I understood you", in a desperate attempt to regain the sympathy of his people. Mubarak, on the contrary, rigorously clung to MSA to show his authority and avoid appearing weak, despite the fact that he had usually employed Egyptian dialect in his previous speeches.[36] In *Dragunov*, similarly, the only characters who employ MSA are Khamīs al-Kāsiḥ, his son ʕalī, and Rabīʕ. Khamīs and ʕalī mostly use it to discuss military matters, while Rabīʕ, a minor character nicknamed *šeyx aṭ-ṭuġyān* "shaykh of the dictatorship", resorts to a very high-flown register of MSA to deliver a sermon in which he firmly condemns the revolutionaries and encourages the listeners to support the regime. During the 14 episodes in which the struggle against Ghaddafi goes on, thus, MSA is mostly referred to in its negative authoritative indexes. After the fall of the Regime, symbolically, the same authoritative indexes are taken back and put at the service of the revolutionary discourse.

Conclusions

The complex relationship between identity and dialect performance in *Dragunov* is rooted in the recent history of Libya. The show aims at giving a faithful picture of the struggle that took place in the country during the last months preceding the fall of Ghaddafi's regime. In doing so, it inevitably has to face some of the ideological constructions through which the regime sought to establish its legitimacy. The discourse of Bedouin legitimacy described by Vandewalle (2012), in particular, plays a major role. It shaped the official rhetoric of the regime for a long period and probably had a certain influence on the language dynamics of the country. The dialect of Tripoli is a case in point: after the oil boom, the migration of great masses of unskilled workers from the hinterland towards the capital resulted in a marked process of bedouinization of its dialect, while in other countries (such as Egypt) the newcomers adjusted to the more prestigious dialect of the capital.

Dragunov offers, from this point of view, a counter-discourse to the official rhetoric of the regime. The performance of the different Libyan dialects found in the show, in fact, follows schemes that are "ethical" more than geographical in nature. The al-Kāsiḥ family, whose native town is never revealed but whose tribal affiliation is clearly stated, speak a variety of LA that we have defined, following the director's lead, as Central Libyan. It probably does not exist as a discrete variety in the dialectal geography of Libya, i.e., it includes traits belonging to different varieties, stretching from Miṣrāta to Benghazi. All these non-urban, Bedouin traits, however, clearly set it apart from TA. ʕumar al-Kāsiḥ, the only member of the family who is not involved in the crimes of the regime, represents the only exception to this rule, once again proving that the reasons behind the choice are not entirely geographic. ʕumar is torn between two conflicting worlds, and so is his language.

TA is the most widely employed variety outside the al-Kāsiḥ family. It would be tempting to set up a simple binary conflict between urban and "Bedouin" Libya, yet the situation is undoubtedly more complex. Speakers of TA in the show encompass positive characters, such as Munà, controversial ones, such as her brother ʕabādī, but also negative ones, such as the many opportunistic characters who switched sides a few hours before the final fall of the regime and then claimed for themselves an active part in the new Libya. Other languages play a minor role in the show, but an echo of the harsh debate regarding the "nativeness" of the opposing factions is present in the frequent episodes of English-Arabic code-switching of Lužeyn.

The authors, thus, played with the dialectal geography of Libya to define a new Libyan identity in which the Bedouin legitimacy, with its core values, is reversed. At the same time, given the particularly tense political situation in the country, they did not choose a clearly recognizable Libyan Bedouin dialect to characterize the al-Kāsiḥ family, opting for a more neutral hybrid variety.

These conclusions can only be provisional. The show, in fact, narrates a delicate phase in the history of Libya, in which new identities were painfully emerging out of the ruins of Ghaddafi's regime, in a slow process that will probably need several years to be fully completed.

Acknowledgments

I wish to express my sincere gratitude to Osama Rezg for patiently answering my questions, and to Adam Benkato and Valentina Serreli for reading the manuscript of this paper and providing comments and suggestions. I am also grateful to the University of Mississippi for supporting me with their generous College of Liberal Arts Summer Research Grant.

Notes

1 On Ghaddafi's Third Theory and the concept of stateless society, see Vandewalle, 2012, pp. 96–122.
2 Pereira, 2008, p. 57.
3 Ph. Marçais, 1977, p. IX.
4 Owens, 1983, pp. 110–111. See also Pereira, 2008, p. 53.
5 Pereira, 2008, pp. 53–56.
6 Pereira, 2007, pp. 81–83.
7 Pereira, 2007, pp. 91–93. Mazraani maintains that Tripoli Arabic attained the status of a non-standard standard, but my personal observation leads me to agree with Pereira. Mazraani, 1997, pp. 144–145.

8 Vandewalle, 2012, pp. 86–87.
9 Mazraani often recognizes the presence of Bedouin traits in the two speeches, yet she somehow fails to account for them in her analysis of Ghaddafi's rhetoric style. See, for instance, Mazraani, 1997, pp. 155–157.
10 An exhaustive review of these studies is provided by Bassiouney, 2010, pp. 97–98. In the same paper, moreover, Bassiouney presents data that partially contradict these assumptions.
11 Bassiouney, 2010, p. 107.
12 Bassiouney, 2010, p. 119.
13 Eckert, 2008,p. 455.
14 Eckert, 2008, p. 464.
15 Bassiouney, 2014, pp. 149–239.
16 Bassiouney, 2014,p. 358.
17 Osama Rezg, personal communication.
18 Abū Salīm is a prison in Tripoli where, according to Human Rights Watch, 1,270 people, mostly political prisoners, were slaughtered in 1996. The arrest of Fatḥī Tirbil, a lawyer who represented the families of some of the victims, is considered among the causes that sparked the anti-Ghaddafi protests in Benghazi on January 15th 2010.
19 Khamīs is actually a ghost in the TV show, but he constantly appears and talks to his eldest son, ʕAlī al-Kāsəḥ.
20 Bucholtz & Hall, 2010, p. 18.
21 Bucholtz & Hall, 2010, p. 27.
22 Bucholtz & Hall, 2010, p. 24.
23 Pereira, 2010, p. 239.
24 Bucholtz & Hall, 2010, p. 19.
25 The occurrences of *hādv* are actually two, but the other one occurs within an utterance in MSA and has not been considered for the purpose of our analysis.
26 Bucholtz & Hall, 2010, p. 20.
27 al-Seghayar, 2006, p. 37.
28 Pereira, 2010, p. 240.
29 Owens, 1984, p. 91.
30 Pereira, 2008, p. 56.
31 The full meeting is accessible at www.youtube.com/watch?v=jNUPBkyvxXc (accessed July 22nd, 2016).
32 Eckert, 2008, p. 456.
33 Bassiouney, 2014, p. 308–325.
34 Bassiouney, 2014, p. 322.
35 Bassiouney, 2014, p. 127.
36 Bassiouney, 2014, p. 5–6.

References

Albirini, A. (2015). *Modern Arabic sociolinguistics: Diglossia, variation, codeswitching, attitudes and identity*. London/New York: Routledge.

al-Seghayar, M. (2006). Patterns of lexical variation in vocative kinship terms in Libyan Arabic. In S. Mejri (Ed.), *L'arabe dialectal: enquêtes, descriptions, interpretations (Actes d'AIDA 6). Travaux offerts au Professeur Taïeb Baccouche* (pp. 27–45). Tunis: Cahiers du C.E.R.E.S.

Bassiouney, R. (2009). *Arabic sociolinguistics: Topics in diglossia, gender, identity, and politics*. Washington, DC: Georgetown University Press.

Bassiouney, R. (2010). Identity and code-choice in the speech of educated women and men in Egypt: evidence from talk shows. In R. Bassiouney (Ed.), *Arabic and the media: Linguistic analyses and applications* (pp. 97–123). Leiden/Boston: Brill.

Bassiouney, R. (2014). *Language and identity in modern Egypt*. Edinburgh: Edinburgh University Press.
Benkato, A. (2014). The Arabic dialect of Benghazi, Libya: Historical and comparative notes. *Zeitschrift für Arabische Linguistik, 59*, 57–103.
Benkato, A., & Pereira, C. (2016). An annotated bibliography of Arabic and Berber in Libya. *Libyan Studies,* 47, 149–165.
Benmoftah, N., & Pereira, C. (2017). Preliminary remarks on the Arabic spoken in Al-Khums (Libya). In V. Ritt-Benmimoun (Ed.), *Tunisian and Libyan Arabic dialects: Common trends, recent developments, diachronic aspects* (pp. 301–326). Zaragoza: IEIOP.
Bucholtz, M., & Hall, K. (2010). Locating identity in language. In D. Watt & C. Llamas (Eds.), *Language and identities* (pp. 18–29). Edinburgh: Edinburgh University Press.
D'Anna, L. (forthcoming). Two texts in the Arabic dialect of Miṣrāta, with preliminary notes and observations. *Mediterranean Language Review*.
Eckert, P. (2008). Variation and the indexical field. *Journal of Sociolinguistics, 12*(4), 453–476.
Holes, C. (1995). Community, dialect and urbanization in the Arabic-speaking Middles East. *Bulletin of the School of Oriental and African Studies, 58*, 270–287.
Marçais, P. (1977). *Esquisse grammaticale de l'Arabe maghrebin*. Paris: Maisonneuve.
Mazraani, N. (1997). *Aspects of language variation in Arabic political speech-making*. Surrey: Curzon Press.
Owens, J. (1983). Libyan Arabic dialects. *Orbis, 32*(1–2), 97–117.
Owens, J. (1984). *A short reference grammar of Eastern Libyan Arabic*. Wiesbaden: Harrassowitz.
Pereira, C. (2007). Urbanization and dialect change: The Arabic dialect of Tripoli (Libya). In C. Miller, E. Al-Wer, D. Caubet, & J. C. E. Watson (Eds.), *Arabic in the City: Issues in dialect contact and language variation* (pp. 77–97). New York: Routledge.
Pereira, C. (2008). Libya. In K. Versteegh (Ed.), *Encyclopedia of Arabic language and linguistics*, Vol. III (pp. 52–58). Leiden /Boston: Brill.
Pereira, C. (2010). *Le parler arabe de Tripoli (Libye)*. Zaragoza: Istituto de Estudios Islámicos y del Oriente Próximo.
Pereira, C. (2010b). Les mots de la sexualité dans l'arabe de Tripoli (Libye): désémantisation, grammaticalisation et innovations linguistiques. *L'Année du Maghreb, VI,* 123–145.
Pereira, C. et al. (forthcoming). La construction socio-langagière du genre: jeunes hommes libyens, jeunes femmes marocaines et rapport à la masculinité. In M. Gasquet-Cyrus, C. Pereira, C. Trimaille, & K. Ziamari (Eds.), *D'une rive de la Méditerranée à l'autre: approche comparée des parlers jeunes en milieu urbain (Maroc – Libye – Espagne – France)*. Grenoble: ELLUG.
Suleiman, Y. (2002). *The Arabic language and national identity: A study in ideology*. Washington, DC: Georgetown University Press.
Suleiman, Y. (2013). *Arabic in the fray: Language ideology and cultural politics*. Oxford: Oxford University Press.
Vandewalle, D. (2012). *A history of modern Libya*. Cambridge: Cambridge University Press.

19
THE EFFECT OF TV AND INTERNAL VS. EXTERNAL CONTACT ON VARIATION IN SYRIAN RURAL CHILD LANGUAGE

Rania Habib

Introduction

This study examines the influence of TV and internal/local and external/urban contact on the use of the variable (q) in the speech of 50 children ages 6–18 from the village of Oyoun Al-Wadi in Syria. In other words, the study examines the impact of these factors on the spread of the urban realization of the variable (q), i.e., the glottal stop [ʔ] in place of the rural realization, the uvular voiceless stop [q].

The influence of TV is measured by the number of hours spent watching TV programs/serials in urban Syrian Arabic (mainly Damascene Arabic (DA)) or other Arabic varieties (mainly Standard Arabic (SA)). The effect of external contact is measured by the amount of time spent in contact with urban family members and friends by visiting them in cities or being visited by them in the village (cf. Stuart-Smith, Pryce, Timmins, & Gunter, 2013, p. 519). The effect of internal contact is measured by the amount of time spent in contact with local friends who use [ʔ] predominantly.

Many support the view that linguistic diffusion is the result of contact, interaction, and density of communication and that the media does not play a role in the spreading of linguistic features (Gunter, 2014; Labov, 2001; Tagliamonte, 2014; Trudgill, 2014). Some studies examined the influence of TV on language variation and change, indicating that TV is not influential in the spreading of linguistic changes (e.g., Saladino, 1990). However, some studies have found some TV influence (Kubuzono, 2007; Muhr, 2003; Naro & Scherre, 1996) or indicated that media can be influential in spreading linguistic innovations (e.g., Buchstaller, 2008). For example, Stuart-Smith et al. (2013) found that TV can have an influence if one engages emotionally and psychologically with a certain show or program. In other words, the influence is not a causal relationship; it is limited to facilitating/accelerating the spread of an innovation.

In previous studies (Habib, 2011; 2016a; 2017) on the use of the variable (q) by the same speakers of the current study, gender and age emerged as statistically significant. Boys use the rural form more than girls in the same way that men in the village use it more than women. In addition, preadolescent boys (starting at age 9) increase their use of the rural form and continue increasing their use of this form with age, indicating that boys initially, like girls, use the [ʔ] sound almost categorically, i.e., adopting [q] later in life. Gender differences were attributed to the different social meanings of [q] and [ʔ] (Habib, 2011; 2016a; 2016b; 2017); [q] is associated with localness and masculinity, and [ʔ] is associated with urbanity and femininity. The current study will reveal that TV and external contact have no significant effect and that those who have lower internal contact with local friends who use [ʔ] predominantly show higher use of the rural [q], which in turn indirectly implies higher contact with peers and people who use [q] predominantly.

Objectives

The purpose of this study is twofold: (1) to examine the influence of the less commonly examined social factors, TV and internal and external contact, on the use of the variable (q) in the village of Oyoun Al-Wadi in Syria, and (2) to introduce a new way to measure the strength and effect of contact or social networks.

Oyoun Al-Wadi: an overview

There are a number of reasons why the community of Oyoun Al-Wadi is subject to constant contact with urban linguistic features and people. First, Oyoun Al-Wadi occupies a central location with respect to three major urban centers, Hims, Hama, and Tartous, all of which are within an hour's drive of the village. Administratively, it is under the Hims Governorate. Hence, most governmental and administrative dealings and paperwork are done in the city of Hims. In addition, students seeking college degrees must attend universities in one of these three urban centers or other major urban centers such as Damascus, Aleppo, or Latakia. Furthermore, Oyoun Al-Wadi is located in a mountainous touristic area, which attracts many tourists from urban centers all over Syria. In line with these facts, the community has undergone a great shift in population due to exogenous marriages and major internal migrations to urban centers (Habib, 2014). Exogenous marriages led to a highly heterogeneous community, as most mothers are not local to the village, leading to increased contact with people from outside the village. Furthermore, internal migration, increased education, and ease of commuting between urban centers and rural areas along with the rise of infrastructure development in the village for touristic purposes also led to increased contact with urban features.

Besides contact and interaction with urban people and features, watching TV is a major daily activity in every home in the village and in most areas in Syria. With the advent of satellite TV, which was introduced illegally to the Syrian population in the early-mid-1990s, people, both adults and children, started spending hours watching TV every day, particularly Syrian drama serials. During the fasting season of the month of Ramadan, people spend even longer hours watching all the newly and specially produced drama and comedy serials for broadcasting during this holy month. One can observe that people are eager to watch during this month the largest possible number of TV serials and as long as it is possible. Even outside this special month, people show attachment to certain TV serials shown at certain times and are unwilling to miss an episode. They will go to the extreme of either canceling a visit to a friend's home or asking visitors or the people one is visiting to stay quiet during a TV serial, so they will not miss a scene or a word of the episode. This applies to both short (30 episodes or less) and long (100 episodes or more) TV serials, although in the case of the latter, one does not really miss much due to redundancies and overlapping scenes.

TV: an overview

It is worth noting that Syrian drama or comedy serials resemble something in between American soap operas (e.g., *The Bold and the Beautiful*) and season series (e.g., *Law and Order*, *Scandal*). They are not as long as soap operas and have a single unbroken story throughout the serial. Most of them do not have follow up seasons (e.g., *Ma Malakat Aymanukum* 'What Your Right Hand Possesses') like American series. Very few successful serials have had some follow up seasons, following the same storylines of the same characters (e.g., *Bab l-Hara* 'The Neighborhood's Gate'). Those can be considered series in nature as sequels of them were created in following years. The current average length of a Syrian serial is about 30 episodes. In the old days and before the growth in the production of Syrian serials in the 1990s and later, they were about 13–15 episodes long. In the past and up to the early 1990s, Egyptian serials were the most popular in the Arab world due to the long tradition of the Egyptian film industry. However, with the surge of Syrian serials in the 1990s and up to our present day, and despite the negative impact of the current civil war on actors and production, Syrian serials have gained more popularity in Syria and in other Arab countries. This is usually ascribed to the quality of the actors and the storylines of the Syrian serials. More recently, starting in 2007 (Buccianti, 2010), Turkish soap operas have been introduced to Syrian and other Arab TVs. All Turkish soap operas are dubbed by Syrian actors into DA, and most of them are in the range of 100–200 episodes. Prior to the introduction of Turkish soap operas, Latin telenovelas, particularly Mexican ones, were very popular on TV for about ten years, particularly in the 1990s (Buccianti, 2010), and they were mainly dubbed by Lebanese production companies into SA and sometimes into Lebanese Arabic. The initially lucrative dubbing of Mexican soap operas stopped when it was not cost-effective anymore. Thus, the wave of dubbing Mexican soap operas has been replaced by a wave of dubbing Turkish soap operas by the Saudi media empire MBC (Middle East Broadcasting Center) besides Syrian drama serials. Young and old people's attachment to the various TV serials can be observed in their detailed narration of events of each episode and their heated, long discussions about them. The strong attachment to certain Turkish soap operas and Syrian serials, and their social effects on people's lives, drew the attention of the Arab media and newspapers as well as religious figures (Buccianti, 2010).

Contact: an overview

Regarding contact, the following question arises: where does Oyoun Al-Wadi fall in terms of the type of social networks that exist in it? The strength of social networks according to Milroy (1980) relies on the following constructs:

- Density: the number of people with whom one has relationships.
- Multiplexity: the number of relationships one has with a single individual, e.g., a co-worker and a neighbor at the same time.
- Centrality: the closeness of one individual to all other individuals in the community.

What is understood within the social network framework (Milroy, 1980) is the following:

- Dense and tight social networks are found in small, stable communities with few external contacts and high internal cohesion.
- Loose social networks are found in large, unstable communities with many external contacts and low internal cohesion.

Oyoun Al-Wadi is somewhere in between these two types of communities. It has dense, multiplex, tight, and strong social networks as it is a small community of a constantly residing population of approximately 772, according to the 2004 Syrian Central Bureau of Statistics Census (http://cbssyr.sy/new%20web%20site/General_census/census_2004/NH/TAB04-12-2004.htm, retrieved August 3, 2016). This number is much higher in the summer, as many internal and external migrants return to the village during these months. When we include internal and external migrants, the population will increase to between 2,000 and 3,000 (Mitri, 2012). Most people are genealogically related and know each other well. They all descend from the same ancestor, Sabiq Ma'louf, who came from present-day Lebanon and settled in Oyoun Al-Wadi. They also join together and help each other in most village events, including weddings, funerals, parties, cultural activities, etc. (Habib, 2013). Based on this description of Oyoun Al-Wadi, one would not expect the present widespread use of the urban feature [ʔ] in keeping with Evans's (2004, p. 162) study of Appalachian migrants in Ypsilanti, Michigan, in which he found that the higher the Appalachian integration score, the lower their adoption of the raising of [æ] of the Northern Cities shift (NCS). That is, "a tight Appalachian social network in Ypsilanti serves as an inhibitor to adopting features of the NCS." However, Oyoun Al-Wadi also resembles large communities in having many external and loose contacts due to the multiple reasons mentioned earlier, which complicates placing it in one type of social network or the other. As a dense and tight community, one would not expect diffusion of innovations from urban centers. However, the data show widespread use of the urban form [ʔ], a change led and advanced by females in the village (Habib, 2011; 2016a; 2016b; 2017). To merely place it among loose networks, one would be neglecting the high cohesion, density, and tightness that exist among its members. It is possible to describe this community as being transitional, i.e., somewhere in the middle between a dense and a loose social network. For this reason, Oyoun Al-Wadi is undergoing linguistic urbanization demonstrated in the spread of [ʔ], but simultaneously this urbanization is counteracted by the boys' reversion to the rural form [q] (Habib, 2011; 2016a; 2016b; 2017).

The situation of Oyoun Al-Wadi does not adhere completely to Milroy and Milroy's (1985, p. 375) hypothesis that "Linguistic change is slow to the extent that the relevant populations are well established and bound by strong ties, whereas it is rapid to the extent that weak ties exist in populations." In light of this hypothesis, both slow and rapid changes are applicable to this community, as both strong and weak ties exist. The weak ties allow for the widespread use of the urban feature [ʔ], especially among females in the village who come from various backgrounds. However, this spread is limited among males in the village and is reversed by boys in the village, which could be considered evidence of the strong ties that exist among males in the village. That is, the ties among males hold steady and seem stronger than the ties among females in the village. The linguistic situation in the village accord with Milroy and Milroy's (1985, p. 359) suggestion "the closer the individual's ties to a local community network, the more likely he is to approximate to vernacular norms." In other words, "close-knit networks maintain linguistic norms of a non-standard" but "the LOOSENING of such a network structure will be associated with linguistic change." In Milroy and Milroy (1985), women are associated with the raising of /ɛ/ while men are associated with the backing of /a/. However, the backing of /a/ is a social network marker for women, who use it at higher rates than men. Similarly, the raising of /ɛ/ becomes a social network marker for men, who use it at higher rates than women. From Labov's (1980) point of view, the diffusion of change is accomplished by members who have many ties/contacts and close-knit relations within and without the community. This view could be responsible for the widespread use of [ʔ] in the village by female community members who have multiple contacts outside the village in addition to their contacts in the village. However, the tight social networks among males in the village is counteracting this spread, making [q] a social network marker for males in the village.

This study tries to implement a different way of measuring the strength of contact from Milroy's (1980) model in which the degree of social network integration score is measured by adding the scores of density and multiplexity, each of which were measured on a scale of 0–5, where 0 indicates lowest and 5 highest. Milroy's (1980) model has been adopted by many studies with slight modifications such as focusing on the origin of the friends (e.g., Evans, 2004). Other approaches have been more general and less quantitative and focused on the number of contacts a speaker makes within a period of time (Gal, 1979; Gumperz, 1982). In this study, contact does not only focus on whom one knows, the number and origin of people one knows, and the number of relations one has with each individual, but also on the amount of time spent with these people. In other words, the strength of contact is not only based on density and multiplexity, but also on the time spent in contact with certain individuals. Since Oyoun Al-Wadi is a small, dense, and multiplex community, most individuals enjoy such dense and multiplex relationships. The difference lies in the amount of time one spends communicating with individuals who use more urban or rural sounds. Therefore, time is considered when assigning an index score on a scale of 0–4 to measure the strength of internal contact and external contact in the quantitative analysis.

Methods

Participants

The naturally occurring speech of 50 children ages 6–18 constitute the data set (see Habib, 2011; 2014; 2016a; 2017 for more details about the data collection). There are equal numbers (25) of boys and girls in the data. Four age groups were identified: 6–8, 9–11, 12–14, and 15–18 (Habib, 2014). Each age group contains equal numbers of participants and equal numbers of boys and girls. To obtain information about the participants' TV habits and internal and external contact frequency, questions such as the following were asked during the unstructured interviews: How long/how many hours do you watch TV every day? What do you like to watch? Who are your best friends in the village? How many hours/how much time do you spend with them? Do you have family members, relatives, and/or friends who live outside the village? Where? How often do you see them and how much time do you spend with them? Do you visit them in the city and for how long? Do they visit you in the village and for how long? Not all speakers responded clearly to all of these questions. Participants were also asked about the speech characteristics of their parents, relatives, friends, and classmates, especially those whom they are in constant contact with locally or externally, unless the researcher, who is an in-group member, personally knew these people.

Thus, like most studies on the influence of media and TV on language change, this study is based on the participants' reports of their TV habits and their extent of internal and external contacts, which could be considered a limitation. However, it is not feasible to observe a large number of speakers on a daily basis over a long period of time to document their TV habits or their patterns of internal and external contact, hence the reliance on their personal reports.

Quantitative analyses

A mixed effects model using SPSS 23 is employed with speakers as the random effect and TV, internal contact, and external contact as the fixed effects. The reason this model is chosen is that it is expected that speakers have not only linguistic differences but also differences in their TV habits and their internal and external contact behaviors, which may influence their linguistic behavior.

The time spent watching TV and internal and external contacts are measured individually on scales of 0–4. The digits 0–4 indicate, respectively: none, very low, low, high, and very high.

Each value is calibrated with a certain number of days for internal and external contact or a certain number of hours for TV viewing (e.g., each TV serial is one hour long per day. Thus, watching one serial a day equals five hours a week; watching two serials a day equals ten hours a week; and so on). Detailed information about the scales used is given below.

The 0–4 scale for the amount of time spent watching TV as well as the type of programs watched is applied as follows:

(1) watching no TV is assigned 0, i.e., none;
(2) watching only cartoons, songs, or foreign films is assigned 1, i.e., very low;
(3) watching one extra Turkish or Syrian serial is assigned 2, i.e., low;
(4) watching two extra Turkish or Syrian serials is assigned 3, i.e., high;
(5) watching three or more Turkish or Syrian serials is assigned 4, i.e., very high.

The reasons for the above classifications are as follows. On the one hand, cartoons are mostly dubbed in SA rather than the dialect; songs can be in various Arabic dialects; foreign films are also usually broadcast with subtitles in SA, and hence the subtitles are read by the viewers, not heard. On the other hand, Syrian and Turkish serials (which are dubbed in DA) are expected to have the highest effect on the speaker's dialect as DA contains the urban feature under investigation and people love watching TV serials more than anything else. In addition, in reference to the spoken language, DA is considered the standard variety in Syria (Albirini, 2016, p. 38; Bassiouney, 2009, p. 196; Ibrahim, 1986, pp. 120–121; Mitchell, 1986, p. 15), and thus, it is expected to be more influential than SA, the written language, on viewers' speech. Nonetheless, it was difficult to set a scale number for TV influence for a number of reasons.

First, children in the youngest age group seemed to have no sense of time. For example, one 9-year-old boy said that he watched TV for six minutes, then he mentioned many programs and serials that he watched, which would require two to four hours a day. Second, some people only mentioned the name of the TV stations they watched. In this case, one can guess what is viewed on them. For example, the TV station 'Syria Drama' only shows Syrian serials, whereas 'MBC Action' only shows foreign action movies. Third, some mentioned what they like to watch daily on TV without specifying the number of hours they spend watching TV or the number of Syrian or Turkish serials they watch. I tried to factor in all of these reasons when choosing a scale number.

Likewise, a scale of 0–4 is used to identify the strength of internal contact with friends, classmates, and/or relatives within the village limits who use the [ʔ] sound predominantly. This scale is applied as follows:

(6) If there is only contact with [q] and limited contact with [ʔ], 0 is assigned, i.e., none;
(7) If three persons the speaker is continuously in contact with use [q] with some contact with [ʔ], 1 is assigned, i.e., very low;
(8) If two persons the speaker is continuously in contact with use [q], 2 is assigned, i.e., low;
(9) If one person the speaker is continuously in contact with uses [q], 3 is assigned, i.e., high;
(10) If the speaker is rarely in contact with any person who uses [q], 4 is assigned, i.e., very high.

Similarly, a scale of 0–4 is utilized for the amount of external contact with friends, family members, and relatives from outside the village. The time spent visiting relatives/friends or being visited by relatives/friends is added and measured on this scale as follows:

(11) no visitors from or visits to urban centers is assigned 0, i.e., none;
(12) visits from or to urban centers for ten days or less per year is assigned 1, i.e., very low;
(13) visits from or to urban centers for 11–20 days per year is assigned 2, i.e., low;
(14) visits from or to urban centers for 21–30 days per year is assigned 3, i.e., high;
(15) visits from or to urban centers for more than one month is assigned 4, i.e., very high.

Data

Table 19.1 provides the general distribution of the variants [q] and [ʔ] in the speech of all 50 children and in the speech of boys and girls. The table shows that in general children use the urban form more than the rural form (58% more). However, a glance at the boys' and girls' usages of the urban form shows that girls use the urban form almost categorically and much more than boys (31% more). This gendered linguistic difference emerged as statistically significant in Habib (2011; 2016a; 2017). There was also a significant interaction between the boys' age and their use of the urban form (Habib, 2017). That is, the younger the boys, the more the use of the urban form (Table 19.2). In other words, as boys grow older, their use of the urban form [ʔ] decreases. Hence, the use of [ʔ] ranges from 100% in 6-year-old boys to 0–3% in 18-year-old boys (Table 19.3). This is a major decrease in the use of [ʔ] with age. On the other hand, girls maintain a pretty sturdy usage of the urban form with age, i.e., categorical or almost categorical (Tables 19.1, 19.2, and 19.3).

Results of the mixed effects model

In the mixed effects model, the random effect, speaker, emerged as statistically significant ($p = 0.000$; *variance* $= 4.8$), indicating that inter-speaker variation exists

TABLE 19.1 General distribution of [q] and [ʔ] in the speech of the 50 children and boys and girls.

	N of [ʔ]	% of [ʔ]	N of [q] and [ʔ]
Boys	1344	61	2206
Girls	2690	92	2916
Total	4034	79	5122

TABLE 19.2 Gender and age group differences in the use of [q] and [ʔ].

Age Group	Boys' N of [ʔ]	% of [ʔ]	Boys' N of [q] and [ʔ]	Girls' N of [ʔ]	% of [ʔ]	Girls' N of [q] and [ʔ]
6–8	394	97	405	606	94	647
9–11	504	62	811	543	94	578
12–14	166	34	492	694	90	770
15–18	280	56	498	847	92	921
Total	1344	61	2206	2690	92	2916

TABLE 19.3 Social and linguistic distribution of [q] and [ʔ] in the speech of individual participants.

#	Name	Age	Gender	N of [ʔ]	% of [ʔ]	N of [q] and [ʔ]
1	'Adan	6	M	38	100	38
2	Max	6	M	49	100	49
3	Shama	6	F	136	100	136
4	Sandy	6	F	191	99.5	192
5	Jerjes	7	M	69	96	72
6	Rico	7	M	42	98	43
7	Halab	7	F	52	87	60
8	Jessy	8	F	103	97	106
9	Talia	8	F	73	80	91
10	Neomi	8	F	51	82	62
11	Eli	8	M	100	95	105
12	'Anis	8	M	96	98	98
13	Dani	9	M	46	94	49
14	Ward	9	M	125	96	130
15	Rula	9	F	72	91	79
16	Lina	9	F	77	100	77
17	Jorgos	9	M	8	11	70
18	Mary	10	F	177	96	184
19	Margaret	10	F	79	86	92
20	Jabour	10	M	93	73	129
21	Rami	11	M	123	52	236
22	Lu'ai	11	M	3	3	87
23	Jano	11	M	106	96	110

The effect of TV on variation 349

#	Name	Age	Gender	N of [?]	% of [?]	N of [q] and [?]
24	Jenny	11	F	88	93	95
25	Rasha	10	F	50	98	51
26	Fu'ad	12	M	0	0	102
27	Naji	13	M	107	98	109
28	Salina	13	F	117	97	121
29	Rouda	13	F	89	100	89
30	Rachel	13	F	83	81	102
31	Randa	13	F	114	99	115
32	Roma	13	F	213	99	215
33	Imad	13	M	8	10	80
34	Roger	14	M	1	3	38
35	Husam	14	M	34	79	43
36	Rada	14	F	76	88	86
37	Wardi	14	F	2	5	42
38	Maher	14	M	16	13	120
39	Ola	15	F	159	99	160
40	Salam	15	F	166	75	220
41	Peter	15	M	10	18	57
42	Andy	16	M	42	72	58
43	Nariman	16	F	167	95	176
44	Rimona	16	F	54	86	63
45	Miller	16	M	36	55	65
46	'Atif	17	M	82	99	83
47	Naseem	17	M	106	92	115
48	Kamal	18	M	4	3	120
49	Hala	17	F	152	99	153
50	Ghada	17	F	149	100	149
	Total			4034	78	5122

regarding the amount of time spent watching TV or in internal or external contact with friends and relatives who use [?] predominantly. These individual differences may explain any variation within the influence of each of the independent fixed factors.

Among fixed effects, only internal contact emerged as statistically significant (Figure 19.2). Those with no (0) or very low (1) internal contact with friends who use [?] predominantly use the rural [q] more than those who have more internal contact with those who use [?] predominantly (Figure 19.2 & Figure 19.3). The odds they would use [?] are 1% and 0%, respectively, of what is used by the highest internal contact group (4) (Table 19.5). The odds that those with low (2) and high (3) internal contact would use [?] are about 25% and 40%, respectively, of what is used by the highest internal contact group (4). That is, these two groups use [?] 24–25% and 39–40%, respectively, more than those with no (0) or very low (1) internal contact. This implies that those with no or very low internal contact with

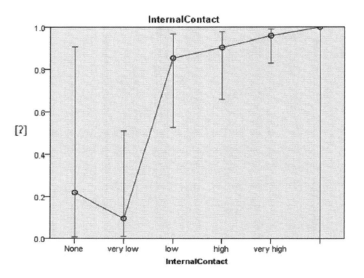

FIGURE 19.1 Main effects of the fixed effects TV, internal and external contacts. Fixed Effects Target: [?] / (q)

Source	F	df1	df2	Sig.
Corrected Model ▼	2.590	13	36	.012
TV	0.190	4	36	.942
ExternalContact	1.229	4	36	.316
InternalContact	4.475	5	36	.003

Probability distribution: Binomial
Link function: Logit

FIGURE 19.2 The effect of internal contact with friends and relatives who use [?] predominantly on the use of [q] vs. [?].

Model Term	Coefficient ▼	Std.Error	t	Sig.	95% Confidence Interval	
					Lower	Upper
Intercept	4.150	1.010	4.109	.000	2.102	6.199
TV=0	-1.676	2.557	-0.656	.516	-6.861	3.509
TV=1	-0.549	1.194	-0.460	.649	-2.971	1.873
TV=2	-0.299	0.904	-0.331	.742	-2.132	1.533
TV=3	-0.507	1.001	-0.506	.616	-2.537	1.523
TV=4	0[a]					
ExternalContact=	-0.231	1.188	-0.195	.847	-2.640	2.178
ExternalContact=1	-0.788	1.120	-0.704	.486	-3.059	1.482
ExternalContact=2	-1.753	1.127	-1.555	.129	-4.039	0.533
ExternalContact=3	0.902	1.173	0.769	.447	-1.478	3.281
ExternalContact=4	0[a]					
InternalContact=	7.996	28.655	0.279	.782	-50.119	66.110
InternalContact=0	-4.433	1.867	-2.374	.023	-8.220	-0.646
InternalContact=1	-5.415	1.312	-4.126	.000	-8.076	-2.753
InternalContact=2	-1.407	0.982	-1.432	.161	-3.399	0.585
InternalContact=3	-0.922	0.980	-0.941	.353	-2.910	1.066
InternalContact=4	0[a]					

Probability distribution: Binomial
Link function: Logit

[a] This coefficient is set to zero because it is redundant.

FIGURE 19.3 Coefficients indicating the significant categories within each fixed factor. Fixed coefficients target: [?] / (q)

[?] are most likely in contact with more people/peers who use [q] predominantly, which leads them to higher use of [q] than the other three categories: low, high, and very high.

Despite the long hours many participants spend watching TV, and contrary to some previous work about the influence of media and TV on language variation and change (Carvalho, 2004; Stuart-Smith et al., 2013; Sayers, 2014), TV did not emerge as statistically insignificant, supporting the view that TV has limited influence on language change (e.g., Gunter, 2014; Labov, 2001; Saladino, 1990 Tagliamonte, 2014; Trudgill, 2014). Likewise, external contact did not emerge as statistically insignificant. These results are surprising, as one expects more exposure to urban TV serials and external urban speakers to lead to higher use of the non-local form [ʔ].

Discussion and conclusion

These findings indicate that inter-speaker variation in the use of rural and urban forms is more related to the strength of internal contact, and is neither related to external contact nor to the frequency of watching urban TV serials. Although urban TV serials could be counteracted by cartoons and other programs that are broadcasted in SA, no evidence of the use of SA is observed. The lack of effect of external contact and TV indicates that one's immediate surroundings and peers (Labov, 2001, p. 228) are more influential in his/her use of a variant than TV and contact with people from outside the village.

The fact that external contact and TV are irrelevant in the variable use of (q) and that only internal contact is relevant fosters the idea of closeness and tightness within the community, particularly within the gendered subsections of the community, despite the extensive external contacts that the community has (cf. Milroy, 1980). In other words, the current findings reinforce previous findings that the use of the urban and rural variants is highly related to gender and age and to the social interpretations/meanings of variants, and how they situate the speaker in his/her environment as rural or urbane, and/or as masculine or feminine (Habib, 2011; 2016b). Put differently, the speakers' linguistic behavior is not related to or derived from any ideological stance regarding the prestige or powerfulness of the dominant dialect used on TV, which is DA in this study (cf. Kristiansen, 2014). Rather, the driving force behind linguistic change in this community is gendered social ideology that is enacted linguistically, leading to gendered linguistic split (Habib, 2011, 2016b). Consequently, children adopt and use the sound ([q] or [ʔ]) that appeals to them and allows them to project themselves in a specific gendered and spatial identity, demonstrating their competence in the associated social meanings and ability to manipulate their speech accordingly.

The findings of this study make it a great addition to previous studies on the influence of media, in our case TV, on language change. They align with the findings of the majority of media studies on Western languages, particularly mainstream studies on US and UK English which found no relationship between media and language change, and attributed change to contact and face-to-face interaction with stronger reference to external contact (e.g., Labov, 2001; Saladino, 1990). However, studies on German German (GG) vs. Austrian German (AG), Danish, and Portuguese espouse a different view in which contact is not necessarily the main contributor to language change. For instance, Kristiansen (2014) indicated that media and language policies have driven the Danes to abandon their traditional local dialects in favor of Copenhagen speech, developing a very strong spoken standard. In other words, broadcast media influences language ideology, and language ideology leads to linguistic change. Similarly, Muhr (2003, p. 103) indicated the influence of GG on AG in the form of contact through TV programs broadcasted via satellite, linking this influence to the amount of time spent watching TV, especially by children. He pointed out that the emergence of the modal particle *mal* and other GG lexical items in AG is due to this media exposure in addition to other factors:

> The relative powerlessness of a small language culture in permanent contact with a powerful one, the prestige of new media and their associated language usages which frequently symbolise modernity and worldliness, and lack of linguistic pride, such that the native variety is considered outmoded and provincial.

This means that powerful or prestigious dialects or languages can be influential via the media. However, in this study, this effect is absent. Although DA is considered the prestigious dialect in Syria (Albirini, 2016, p. 38; Bassiouney, 2009, p. 196; Ibrahim, 1986, pp. 120–121; Mitchell, 1986, p. 15) no influence is observed via TV drama serials or programs. This study also shows different results from Stuart-Smith et al. (2013) in that despite the participants' profound engagement with the TV serials they are watching, the linguistic influence of TV is negligible. This does not preclude the fact that some speakers may imitate some characters to create fun out of the situation, not for the sake of adopting a new feature or lexical item.

In conclusion, this study has shown that only internal contact can influence linguistic use or choice of a variant in this community, whereas TV and external contact did not emerge as statistically insignificant. This finding and previous findings in Habib (2011; 2016b) support the premise of this volume which is elegantly stated by Bassiouney (p. 1 of this volume), 'the use of dialects is not just a product of social and demographic factors, but can also be an intentional performance of identity.' It is clear that children in this study care about their surroundings and what people they closely know think about their speech, particularly peers. They also know that they should fit well linguistically within their community and in accordance with the gender appropriateness norms (Habib, 2016b), relying on their agency and competence in the social meanings of the two variants [q] and [ʔ]. Thus, they intentionally and with great capability perform and enact this metalinguistic knowledge through the use of the appropriate linguistic variant to construct their gender and spatial identities. Consequently, inter-speaker variation is observed between girls and boys, corresponding respectively to feminine/urbane and masculine/rural identities. Although the choice of a code in this study is not related to external contact or TV exposure, further research is required to better understand the effect of Arabic TV broadcasting and contact on linguistic change in the Arab world.

References

Albirini, A. (2016). *Modern Arabic sociolinguistics: Diglossia, variation, codeswitching*. London/NewYork: Routledge.

Bassiouney, R. (2009). *Arabic sociolinguistics: Topics in diglossia, gender, identity, and politics*. Edinburgh: Edinburgh University Press.

Buccianti, A. (2010). Dubbed Turkish soap operas conquering the Arab world: Socia liberation or cultural alienation? *Arab Media and Society*, *10*. Retrieved from www.arabmediasociety.com/?article=735

Buchstaller, I. (2008). The localization of global linguistic variants. *English World-Wide*, *29*, 15–44.

Carvalho, A. M. (2004). I speak like the guys on TV: Palatalization and the urbanization of Uruguayan Portuguese. *Language Variation and Change*, *16*(2), 127–151.

Evans, B. (2004). The role of social network in the acquisition of local dialect norms by Appalachian migrants in Ypsilanti, Michigan. *Language Variation and Change*, *16*, 153–167.

Gal, S. (1979). *Language and shift: Social determinants of linguistic change in bilingual Austria*. New York: Academic.

Gumperz, J. J. (1982). Social network and sanguage shift. In J. J. Gumperz (Ed.), *Discourse strategies* (pp. 38–58). Cambridge: Cambridge University Press.

Gunter, B.. (2014). Discovering theoretical models to explain mediated influences on language. *Journal of Sociolinguistics*, *18*(2), 262–271.

Habib, R. (2011). Meaningful variation and bidirectional change in rural child and adolescent language. *University of Pennsylvania Working Papers in Linguistics*, *17*(2), 81–90.

Habib, R. (2013). How to uncover social variables. In C. Mallinson, B. Childs & G. Van Herk (Eds.), *Data collection in sociolinguistics: Methods and applications* (pp. 29–32). London/New York: Routledge.

Habib, R. (2014). Vowel variation and reverse acquisition in rural Syrian child and adolescent language. *Language Variation and Change*, *26*(1), 45–75.

Habib, R. (2016a). Bidirectional linguistic change in rural child and adolescent language in Syria. *Dialectologia*, *16*, 117–141.

Habib, R. (2016b). Identity, ideology, and attitude in Syrian rural child and adolescent speech. *Linguistic Variation*, *16*(1), 34–67.

Habib, R. (2017). Parents and their children's variable language: Is it acquisition or more? *Journal of Child Language* 44(3), 628–649. doi:10.1017/S0305000916000155

Ibrahim, M. H. (1986). Standard and prestige language: A problem in Arabic sociolinguistics. *Anthropological Linguistics*, *28*(1), 115–126.

Kristiansen, T. (2014). Knowing the driving force in language change: Density or subjectivity *Journal of Sociolinguistics*, *18*(2), 233–241

Kubuzono, H. (2007). Tonal change in language contact: Evidence from Kagoshima Japanese In T. Riad & C. Gussenhoven (Eds.), *Tones and tunes: [Volume 1] Typological studies in word and sentence prosody* (pp. 323–352). Berlin: Mouton de Gruyter.

Labov, W. (1980). *Locating language in time and space*. NewYork: Academic Press.

Labov, W. (2001). *Principles of linguistic change, Volume. 2: Social factors*. Oxford, UK: Blackwell.

Milroy, J., & Milroy, L. (1985). Linguistic change, social network and speaker innovation. *Journal of Linguistics*, *21*, 339–384.

Milroy, L. (1980). *Language and social networks*. Oxford: Blackwell.

Mitchell, T. F. (1986). What is educated spoken Arabic? *International Journal of the Sociology of Language*, *61*, 7–32.

Mitri, K. (2012, April 27). *Oyoun Al-Wadi. . . Springs that implant bestowal in people.* Retrieved from www.esyria.sy/ehoms/index.php?p=stories&category=places&filename=201204271950011

Muhr, R. (2003). Language change via satellite: The influence of German television broadcasting on Austrian German. *Journal of Historical Pragmatics, 4,* 103–127.

Naro, A., & Scherre, M. M. P. (1996). Contact with media and linguistic variation. In J. Arnold, R. Blake, & B. Davidson (Eds.), *Sociolinguistic variation: Data, theory, and analysis (Selected papers from NWAV 23)* (pp. 223–228). Stanford, CA: CSLI Publications.

Saladino, R. (1990). Language shift in standard Italian and dialect: A case study. *Language Variation and Change, 2,* 57–70.

Sayers, D. (2014). The mediated innovation model: A framework for researching media influence in language change. *Journal of Sociolinguistics, 18*(2), 185–212.

Stuart-Smith, J., Pryce, G., Timmins, C, & Gunter, B. (2013). Television can also be a factor in language change: Evidence from an urban dialect. *Language, 89*(3), 501–536.

Tagliamonte, S. (2014). Situating media influence in sociolinguistic context. *Journal of Sociolinguistics, 18*(2), 223–232.

Trudgill, P. (2014). Diffusion, drift, and the irrelevance of media influence. *Journal of Sociolinguistics, 18*(2), 214–222.

INDEX

Page numbers in italics indicate figures and page numbers in bold indicate tables.

Abd-el-Jawad, H. 25
Abdullah, I. 310
Abruzzese 36
Abū Salīm massacre 324, 338n18
accents 4, 22–23, 30n7, 136, 277–281
accommodation 192–197, 253
achievement focusing 248
acrolects 71–72
Adelung, J. 213
adstrates 74–75, 79
affect 250–253
African American English (AAE) 18–20, 23–24, 27, 41
Afrobeat 309–310
afrocolombians 148–149
Afro-European *métis* society 180–181
AG (Austrian German) 352–353
age 341, **348–349**
agency 2–3, 9, 287, 291, 353
Agha, A. 246, 290
Aitken, A. 42
Aït Mous, F. 101, 105
ajami 188
Ajdir Speech (Mohammed VI) 103–105
Akhbar Al yom 117
Al-Abnoudi, A. 299
Al-Andalus 197
Albanian 36
Alexander, J.: *Butcher Boys* 306–307
Algeria 99
alien languages 73

alignment 154, 250–253, 260
Al-Jukh, H. 287, 290–300, 335–336
al-Khums dialect 324
al-Kurdi, S. 333
Allali, R.: "Who are we?" 111; Zakaria Boualem 114
allūka 198
Aluku 147–148
Amazigh 99–108
American Dialect Society 24
American English 128, 254
American nationalism 167
American pop culture 27
Amīr al-shuʿarā' ('Prince of Poets') competition 294–297
amusement 303–320
Ancient Egyptian 183
Andalusi 197
Andean Highlands Quichua 150
Andean Spanish (AS) 150–154
Anderson, B. 268
Andersson, L. 29
Androutsopoulos, J. 9
anéantissement des patois 89
anthropological-cultural approach 229
anti-ness 305, 310
Appalachian dialect 36
Appalachian migrants 343
Arabic 10, 105–106, 187–188, 193, 196–197; Baggara 75, **75**; Benghazi Arabic (BA) 326, **326**; Cairene 43,

237; Cairene Standard Arabic (CSA) 286–294, **293**, 297–300; Classical 100–103, 188, 201; Damascene Arabic (DA) 342, 346, 352–353; Darija 7, 99–124; Eastern Libyan Arabic (ELA) 324, 331; Egyptian 228–240, 288, 323; Fezzani Arabic (FA) 331; Juba 71–85, **75**; Judaeo- 193; Judeo- 200, 322; Khartoum 75–78; Lebanese 342; Libyan Arabic (LA) 324–327, 334–337; Modern Standard Arabic (MSA) 107–108, 323, 335–336; Moroccan **54**, 99–124, 192–209, 193; North African 100; Sa'idi Colloquial Arabic (SCA) 286, 289–294, **293**, 297–300; Standard Arabic (SA) 286–291, **293**, 294–300, 342, 346, 352; Sudanese 72–82; Syrian 340; Tunisian **54**, 336; Vehicular **75**
Arab identity 297–298
Árabi Júba 71–85
Arabisation 107, 193, 228–229, 233, 321
Arab-Islamism 102
Arab-Muslims 201
Arabo-Bassist ideology 102
Arab Spring 99, 105
Arrows Method *(pijltjes-methode)* 39
AS (Andean Spanish) 150–154
Athenian dialect 20
Attitudes to English Usage (Mittins) 128–129
AT&T Labs 44
attractiveness 20–23, 43
audience 9, 248–249
Auer, P. 152
ausbauization 86
Ausbau languages 86, 94–95
Ausbausprache 92–93
Austin, J. 245
Austrian German (AG) 352–353
authenticity 8, 182, 226–227, 238–239, 260, 265, 282
automatism 232–233
Aymara language 150
Ayouch, N. 110, 117, 121n24

BA (Benghazi Arabic) 326, **326**
Babou, C. 188
backwardness 234–236
bad language use 134, 137
Baggara Arabic 75, **75**
Bailey, B. 162, 173
Baker, W. 40–41
Bamba, A. 187–188
Bamberg, M. 164
Bangla **54**
banter 253, 256, 278

Banter Boys (character types) 275, *276*, 278–282
Bari language 74, 78
Barrett, R. 162
Barth, F. 161
basilects 71–72, 183
Bassiouney, R. 3–4, 10, 49, 233, 237, 303, 323, 353
Bathily, P. 185
Bauman, R. 2–3, 211, 268, 271, 287, 291, 317–318
Bauman, Z. 211
BBC: 'What does Naija mean?' 315
BBC Scotland 274
Beal, J. 271
Bean, J. 267, 270
Beaussier, M. 100
Bednarek, M. 266
Bedouin dialects 193, 288–291, 322, 323, 326, 330–337
bedouinization 322, 336–337
Bedouins 228–229
Beijing dialect 36–37
Belghouate, M. 119
Bell, A. 248
belletristic literature 87, 90
Belmokhtar, R. 117
Ben Ali, Z. 336
Bencheikh, S. 118
Benchemsi, A. 112–113; *"Wa derrej a khouya!"* 100
Benghazi Arabic (BA) 326, **326**
Benjamin, W. 316; 'Theses of the Philosophy of History' 307
Benkato, A. 321–322
Benkirane, A. 116
Benmoftah, N. 324
Benson, E. 39
Benwell, B. 299
Berber 99–108, 192, 196–197, 204–206, 229, 239
Berlin, Germany 217–218
Bernstein, B. 28, 30–31n9
Berwick 267
Beswick, J. 40
Beyoud 111, *112*
bidialectalism 23–26
Bilingual Education Act 161
bilingualism 8, 26, 166, 170, 229
Billings, A. 22
bivalency 50, 54
Black Englishes 308; *see also* African American English (AAE)
Block, D. 131
Blok, D. 39

Index **359**

Blommaert, J. 89–90, 215, 291
Boberg, C. 42
borrowing 74–75, 90, 95
Bosnia 35
Boukous, A. 104
Boum, A. 101
Bourdieu, P. 145, 169, 212–215, 252
Bourhis, R. 27
Bowie, D. 40–41
boys, language use of 55–65, **56**, *61*, 341, 344–347, **348–349**, 352
Bozal 308
Braber, N. 9–10
Bradac, J. 22
Bragg, M. 21, 25
Bratchpiece, N. *275*
Breyer, T. 288
Briggs, C. 317–318
British English 267; nonstandard 125–139
British Standard English 7
Brown, I. 276
Brown v. Board of Education 160
Bucholtz, M. 154, 162, 292, 325, 329–330
Burman 35
Burns, R. 279–280
Bush, G. 169–170
Businengetongo 147
Butcher Boys (Alexander) 306–307
BuzzNigeria (website) 312, *312–313*

Cabildos urbanos 149
cacophonia 313, 318
Cairene Arabic 43, 237
Cairene Standard Arabic (CSA) 286–294, **293**, 297–300
Calabrese, F. 39–40
Caleño Spanish (CS) 150–155
Cali, Colombia 8, 148–155
Cameron, D. 130, 238, 300
Canadian/United States border 42
Cantonese language 36, 40
Carr, J. 21
cartoons 346, 352
Casablanca Darija 113
Casablanca dialect 43
Caubet, D. 7
Caxton, W. 213
Central Libyan dialect 326–331, 337
Chafiq, M. 104
Chambers, I. 266
Chambers, J. 37, 42–43
Chao, Y. 17–18
"Charte Nationale d'Education et de Formation" (Commission Spéciale Education Formation [COSEF]) 102–103
Cheikh, S. 114
Chewin' the Fat (television show) 266–285
Chimborazo, Ecuador *149*, 150
Chimborazo Quichua (CHQ) 150
Chinese dialects 17–18, 35, 40
Chinese language 214
Chiswick, B. 38
Chow, R. 315
chracterological figures 246, 249
Christian, D. 24
civil religion 88
Classical Arabic 100–103, 188, 201
Clivio, G. 86
CNLCM ("Conseil national des langues et de la culture marocaine") 107
Cockney 21
code choice 324
codemixing 145
codes 3–4, 8–9
codes/varieties 3, 8
codeswitching 50–52, 90, 144–146, 161–163, 167–169, 216, 270, 323, 335–337
cognates 38
Cohen, A. 113
coherence 210–214, 217
Colin, G. 99–100
Cologne dialect 36
Colombian Administrative Department for Statistics 149
Colombian Spanish 150
Colomentality (Kuti) 309–310
colonialism 183, 188, 304–306, 309
colonial languages 73
comedy serials 342
Commission Spéciale Education Formation (COSEF): "Charte Nationale d'Education et de Formation" 102–103
commodification 227, 308
common Glaswegian 273–274, 281–282
Commonwealth 304
communication-based borders 43–44
communicative focusing 248
competence 21–22, 43, 353
comptoirs 180
"Conseil national des langues et de la culture marocaine" (CNLCM) 107
"Conseil supérieur de l'éducation, de la formation et de la recherche scientifique" 117
conservatism 196, 234–238
constitutionalisation 105–106

contact 6–10, 40, 180–181, 195, 226–231; internal *vs.* external 340–355, *350*; varieties in 143–159
contact dialects 179–180
conventionalisation 119
cool 222–223
Copenhagen speech 353
Cornips, L. 42
corpus planning 90, 94
COSEF (Commission Spéciale Education Formation): "Charte Nationale d'Education et de Formation" 102–103
Cotter, C. 9
Coupland, N. 2–5, 247–249, 255, 265, 270–271, 276, 282–283, 287, 290–291, 300
covert prestige 21
creative writing 118
creole-lexifier contacts 71–72
creoles 24, 71–75, 78, 83n1, 147–148, 180, 183–184, 216, 308
Cretan dialect 20
Croatia 35, 41
Croatian dialects 43
cross-dialect communication 17
crossing 8, 161–163, 170–174, 214–218, 221–222; defined 64, 170
Crossing – Language and Ethnicity among Adolescents (Rampton) 215–217
Crystal, D. 132–133
CSA (Cairene Standard Arabic) 286–294, **293**, 297–300
CS (Caleño Spanish) 150–155
CSI New York (television show) 114
cultural deprivation 19
Curzan, A. 127, 132, 137
Cyrillic script 41

Daan, J. 39
Dakar, Senegal 179–189
Damascene Arabic (DA) 342, 346, 352–353
Danish 352–353
D'Anna, L. 10, 324
Darija 7, 99–124
"*Darija langue nationale*" 108, *109*
decolonization 321
decreolization 71–72
deep Wolof 181
deficit and difference theories 27–28
De Fina, A. 6, 164
Degree-of-Difference method 39
demonstratives **326**, 326–327
Denham, K. 41
De Rooij, V. 42

Descemet, L. 180–181
descriptivism 125–131, 134
desires, social class and 252
destandardization 219
Deuber, D.: *Nigerian Pidgin in Lagos* 314
deviant language use 210–214
Diagne, A. 188
dialect boom 221
dialect borders 6, 35–48
dialect complex 214
dialect continua 35, 40, 71–72, 183–184
dialect death 6–7
dialect dilemma 23–24
dialect guise 214, 218–222
dialectization 91–95
dialectologists, biases of 42–43
dialects: aesthetic quality of 20–21; contact 179–180; defined 4, 36, 44, 287–288; in Egypt 287–291; fake 220; identities and 6, 17–34, 321–339; in Italy 51–67; language and 36–37, 86–98; linguistic characteristics of 36–37; local 5–6, 245–264; modernity and 212; in Morocco 102, 106; Naija 303–320; performance of 8–10, 49–67, 247–249; phonological features of 9; Piedmontese as 89–91; standard and nonstandard 17–34; stigmatised 6–10
dialect variation 2–3, 8–10, 143–159, 321–339
dialogicality 292–294
Dictionary of Modern English Usage (Fowler) 127
digital communication 44
diglossia 23, 71, 90–91, 95
Dinka people 80
Diop, C. 183, 189
Di Paolo, M. 40–41
disalignment 154, 253, 260
display 3, 162, 265
dispositions 212
diverse communities, dialect performances in 49–67
Dominican Americans 162, 173
double-voicing 167
Dozy, R. 100
Dragojevic, M. 22–23
Dragunov (television show) 321–339
drama serials 342–343
dual language education 161
dubbing 113–115, 342–343, 346
Du Bois, J. 154, 250, 292
Duden, K. 213
Dunbar, K. 274

Dunk, T. 253
Dutch dialects 40
Dyer, J. 42

Eastern Libyan Arabic (ELA) 324, 331
Eastern Maroon Creole 147
Ebner, C. 7
Eckert, P. 2, 50, 246, 252–253, 290, 323, 334
economic borders 40
Ecuadorian Kichwas 149
education: dual language 161; intelligibility and 18; levels of 43, 236–237; standard language use and 132–134, 137
Edwards, J. 6, 10, 21–22, 26–28
Egypt 8–10, 43, 100, 335; poetry in 286–302; Siwa Oasis in 226–242; television serials in 342
Egyptian Arabic 228–240, 288, 323
Egyptian Revolution 294–297
ELA (Eastern Libyan Arabic) 324, 331
el-Gara, Egypt 228
Ellis, S. 21, 25
emic perspectives 221–223
England 42; geographical borders in 39–40; linguistic transgressions in 210–225; presentations of self in 8
English Fens 39–40
English language 99, 237, 335–337; African American English (AAE) 18–20, 23–24, 27, 41; American 128, 254; Black 308; British 7, 125–139, 267; Naija and 304, 307–317; proper 18, 23, 310; Standard 125–137; Stylized Indian 216; Texan 36; in the United Kingdom 352; in the United States 128, 160, 165–167, 352; Welsh 276; West African 308–310; White 23, 27, 252–253; World 307–308
"English Only" policies 167
enregisterment 9, 246–249, 253, 271
epistemic stances 250, 299
ethnic borders 41
ethnic dialects 217
ethnic identities 8, 41–42, 160–178
ethnicity 88, 161
ethnographic approaches 49–67, 245
Ethnologue 36, 91
etic perspectives 221–223
European Charter for Regional or Minority Languages 36
evaluation research 43
Evans, B. 343
Ewe language 308
exogenous marriages 341
external/urban contact 340–355

Facebook 119, 135
FA (Fezzani Arabic) 331
FA (Foreign-Anglo) accent group 22–23, 30n7
Faidherbe, L.: *Vocabulaire* 181–182
fake dialect 220
Falck, O. 40
falling question intonation (FQI) 246–247, 251–254, *255*
Faraclas, N. 309
Farouk, S. 312
Fasan, R. 310
Fasold, R. 43, 246–247, 254
February 17th Revolution (Libya) 321, 324–325
February 20 movement (Morocco) 105, 115–116
Fehri, H. 324
Feliu, L. 101
fellahin 288
femininity 246, 253
Ferguson's paradigm 71
Fezzani Arabic (FA) 331
fiction 94
first-order indexicality 226–227, 231–233, 240, 246, 323
Fishman, J. 92–95
Fish, S. 131
Flash Infos (Flash News) 185
Flores, N. de la 22
focusing 248
Fogarty, M.: *Grammar Girl: Quick and Dirty Tips* 127
folk attitudes 125–139, 235
folk linguistics 229
folklorisation 91–93, 101
Fordham, S. 27, 30–31n9
Foreign-Anglo (FA) accent group 22–23, 30n7
Foreign-Other (FO) accent group 22–23
form focusing 248
Fought, C. 161
Fowler, H.: *A Dictionary of Modern English Usage* 127
Fox, S. 40–41
FQI (falling question intonation) 246–247, 251–254, *255*
francophone bourgeois identity 186
Franco-Provençal language 87
French Acadians 28
French Canadians 26
French dialect borders 38
French Guiana 8, 147–148, 155
Frenchization 93–94

French language 8, 86–89, 95, 99–101, 107, 179–191
French-Nigerian IFRA project 314
French Revolution 89, 92
Friulian 97n13
Fuller, J. 41
fundamentalists 110

Gaelic 41
Gal, S. 202, 290
Galicia 40
Garrett, P. 22
gender: language use and 55–65, **56**, *61*, 323, **348–349**, 352–353; Pittsburghese and 245–247, 253; rural child language and **348–349**, 352–353; social class and 21
Geordie dialect 36
Georgakopoulou, A. 164
German dialects 40
German German (GG) 352–353
Germany 8, 210–225
Ghaddafi, M. 321–337; Green Book 321
'Ghandi' (Shawqī) 296
Ghomara Berber 192, 196–197, 204–206
Ghomara, Morocco 8, 192–209
Gibson, A. 248
Giles, H. 20–22, 25–27
Gill, M. 4, 292
girls, language use of 55, **56**, *61*, 61–65, 341, 344–347, **348–349**, 352
Glasgow phrases 272
glass ceiling 135–137
Glaswegian identities 265–285
globalisation 72, 227–229, 234
glottonyms 80–81
Godley, A. 24
Goeman, T. 43
Goffman, E. 217–219; *The Presentation of Self in Everyday Life* 210
Gooskens, C. 38
Gorée, Senegal 180–181
goud.ma (website) 119
Grade, P. 308
Grammar Girl: Quick and Dirty Tips (Fogarty) 127
Great Britain: dialects in 20–21; digital communication and 44; geographical borders in 39–40; nonstandard British English in 125–139
Greek dialects 20
Green Book (Ghaddafi) 321
Greg and Donny (video series) 254–259
Grégoire, A. 89, 92
Grey, L. 137

Gritli, F. 332–334
group solidarity 26–27, 234–238
Guardian, The 312–313
Guèye, A. 185–186

Habib, R. 10, 353
habitus 212–213, 247, 252
HACA (High Authority for Audiovisual Communication) 115
hādv and hēdv variables 327, **327**
Hagan, A. 266–269
Hairston, M. 137
Halliday, M. 29, 305
Hall, K. 144, 154, 292, 325, 329–330
Hamburger, L. 40–41
Harabich (blogger) 119
Hassani 106
Hassan II 101–102
Hazen, K. 2
Heblich, S. 40
Hedberg, N. 254
Heeringa, W. 38
Heffer, S.: *Strictly English* 127
Heinrich, P. 8
Heller, M. 5, 290–291
Hemphill, G. 274
Henrici, E. 308–309, 314
Hentschel, G. 95
Herderian ideology 167
heritage 227, 239
heterogeneity 143–159
heterogeneous corpora 145–146
Heuser, P. 137
Hewitt, R. 162
hexis of class 252–253
High Authority for Audiovisual Communication (HACA) 115
High Life, The (television show) 276
high performance 245–251, 270
high prose 87
Hizbut Tarqiyya 188
Hoba Hoba Spirit (music group) 117
Hodson, J. 266, 271
Hokkaido 36
Holes, C. 323
homesick dialect 220
homogenization, of language 87–90
Hopper, R. 22
Hudson, R. 129
HuffPost Maroc 107
Hughes, A. 128
Human Rights Watch 338n18
humour 247–251, 265–285

IBM Research 44
iconisation 202
identity: Arab 297–298; bilingual 166; coherence/incoherence and 210–214; construction of 8–10; defined 2–3; dialects and 6, 17–34, 321–339; diverse communities and 49–67; Egyptian poetry and 286–302; ethnic 8, 41–42, 160–178; Glaswegian and Scottish 265–285; group 26–27; Libyan 321–339; linguistic 130–136, 148–155; local 199–201, 267; Moroccan 99–124; national 71–85; as performed 4, 161–162, 183–188, 237–240, 265–285, 291–294; in Siwa Oasis, Egypt 226–242; usage debate and 125–139
Idlewild (video) 255–258, *256–257*; transcript of 260–263
ifinagh 104
Ilson, R. 127
imagined community 268
Imbabura, Ecuador *149*, 150
Imbabura Quichwa (IQ) 150
immigration 52–54
imperative forms 298
imperialism 306–307, 310
"incident" 173
incoherence 210–214, 221–222
indexicalities 8–10, 50–51, 59–60, 82, 130, 221, 249, 271; orders of 226–227, 231–240, 246, 286, 323, 336
indicators 226–227
indigenous languages 73–74, 78–82
indigenous populations 148–149
inequality 213, 221–222
in-groups 126, 134, 277
Institute for German Language 217
Institut Royal de la Culture Amazighe (IRCAM) 102–107
integrity 21–22
intelligibility 17–18, 26, 51, 82, 104
internal/local contact 340–355
internal migration 341
internetworldstats (website) **119**
intersectionality 246, 253
intertextuality 296
interviews 163–164
Intha 35
intonation patterns 36–37
intra-varietal change 144
investment 250–253
IQ (Imbabura Quichwa) 150
IRCAM (Institut Royal de la Culture Amazighe) 102–107
Iriomote 212

Irvine, J. 179, 202
Islam 187–188, 298
isoglosses 37–38, 42, 87, 96n2, 325
Italian Institute for National Statistics (ISTAT) 51–52
Italianization 89–91
Italian language 36, 51–67, 86–87, 90–95, 96n8
Ito, R. 267

Jacobin model 104, 111
Jaffe, A. 10, 238, 274, 294, 298
Japan 8, 210–225
Jaspers, J. 42
Jaydane, D. 117
Jbala 194, 204
Jebli dialects 196, 202–204, 207
Jews 193
Johnson, K. 38
Johnstone, B. 3, 7, 10, 227, 237, 247–249, 252–253, 267, 270–271, 282–283, 290
Joos, M. 30n8
Jørgensen, J. 145
Juba Arabic 71–85, **75**
Judaeo-Arabic 193
Judeo-Arabic 200, 322

Kabyle 104
Kansai dialects 223n3
Karlgren, B. 17
Kashubian 38
Kautzsch, A. 24
Kazimirski, A. de B. 100
Kelly-Holmes, H. 227
Kelvinside Glaswegian 273–274, 281–282
Khartoum Arabic 75–78
Kichwas 8, 148–155
Kiernan, G. 274
Kiesling, S. 9, 154, 246, 292
Kiessling, R. 305
Kiezdeutsch 214, 217–218, 221–222, 223n2
King, K. 164
Ki-Nubi creole 83n1
Kissau, S. 21
Kiswahili 81
Kleverland dialect continua 40
Kloss, H. 94–95
koineization 86, 147
koinés 87–93, 322
Köler, H. 307–308, 314
Kordofan 75
Kratochvil, P. 17
Kreutzer, M. 255–256, 259

Krio 180
Kristiansen, T. 352–353
Ksikes, D. 112
Kuehnelt-Leddihn, E. von 88
Kuti, F.: *Colomentality* 309–310

L1s 53, 180
Labovian sociolinguistics 303, 323
Labov, W. 18–20, 24–25, 49, 226, 245, 251–252, 266, 344
"L'Académie Mohammed VI pour la langue arabe" 107
Lacoste, V. 3, 288, 291
LA (Libyan Arabic) 324–327, 334–337
Lameli, A. 40
language: attitudes towards 79–81, 197–207; categorization of 73–74; defined 4; deviant use of 210–214; dialect and 36–37, 86–98; diversity of 89, 93–95, 303; endangerment of 238; gender and 55–65, **56**, *61*, 323, **348–349**, 352–353; identity and 226–242, 266–268; indigenous 73–74, 78–82; names of 72, 99–102; as performed 265–285; policies for 6–7, 73–74, 165–167, 309; role of 88; transmission of 91–93; uniformity of 87–91; varieties between 35
language activism 91–92
language-dialect distinctiveness 18
language planning 91, 94, 309
language-rights advocacy 238
language shift 8, 150, 169
language variation 8–10, 49–67
languaging 145
langue unique approach 104–106
Laponce, J. 88–89, 93
Laroui, A. 118
late capitalism 310
late modernity 215, 223–223, 223n1
Latin 51, 127–128
Latino Threat Narrative 169–170
Lebanese Arabic 342
Lebanon 37
legitimacy 103–105, 108, 212–215, 223, 288
legitimation paradox 101
Léglise, I. 8, 145
Leimgruber, J. 288
Le Journal Hebdomadaire 111, *112*
Lenz, K. 276
Leonard, S. 128
les années de plomb 109
levelling 147, 192–207
Levenshtein distances 38
lexicons 37–38

lexifier languages 71–78
Libya 10, 43, 321–339
Libyan Arabic (LA) 324–327, 334–337
Ligurian language 87
Linguistic Atlas of France 35
linguistic borders 37–38, 71–85
linguistic brokers 180–181
linguistic choices 2–3, 267, 283
linguistic identities 130–136, 148–155
linguistic push-pull 24
linguistic resources 143–159, 290–291
linguistic transgressions 210–225
linguistic variation 143–159, 195–197
Lippi-Green, R. 4, 28
Liqa' ("Encouter") (television show) 116
l-lahajat 102
l'Maghribiya 100, 112–113
loanwords 74, 79, 82, 182, 189, 217
Lobeck, A. 41
local dialects 5–6, 245–264
local identity 199–201, 267
localness 226–229, 238, 283
Lombard language 87
London dialect 213
lookism 173–174
Lowth, R. 213
LQI 256–261
ludic language use 222
luġa/lúġa 73–74, 77–81
Luhmann, N. 307, 316
Luther, M. 213
Lyautey, L-H. 30n3
Lyiscott, J. 162

MA (Miṣrāta) 326, **326**, 331
Mackintosh, C. 279
Maghraoui, H. 115
Maghrebi dialects 322
Maher, J. 42
Mahmoud, U. 72, 75
Makhzen 118
Ma'louf, S. 343
Manfredi, S. 7
map-drawing technique 39
marabout 187
Marçais, P. 322
marginalization 304–306
marked language 212
marked speech *60–61*
markers 226–227
marketization 239
Marley, B. 310
Marlow, M. 25
marocanité 119
Maroc Hebdo International 110

Maroons 8, 147–148, 155
masculinity 246, 253, 259
matched-guise approach 22, 30n6
Mazraani, N. 323
MBC (Middle East Broadcasting Center) 342, 346
McConnell-Ginet, S. 246, 253
Mc Laughlin, F. 8, 180
mdini 195–201, 206–207
meaning focusing 248
media 8–10, 321–339
mediation/mediatisation 9
Meillet, A. 30n3
mesolects 71–72
metadiscourses 314, 318
metalinguistic discourse 6–8, 181–183, 290
metalinguistic representations 76–79, 82–83
metapragmatics 210–211, 226–227, 256, 323
métis society 180–181
metro-ethnicity 42
metropolitan French 184–186, 189
Meulen, M. van der 6
Mexican Americans 26
mexicano 167–171; *see also* New Mexican Spanish
Mexican *telenovelas* 114, 342
middle class accents 136
middle classes 269
middle class stances 246, 249, 252–253
Middle East Broadcasting Center (MBC) 342, 346
Middle Egyptian dialects 288
Middlesborough 267
Midland dialect 254
migration 41–42, 50–52, 193–194
Miller, C. 72, 107, 113, 117, 289, 300
Miller, P. 38
Milroy, J. 127–128, 288, 344
Milroy, L. 6, 127–128, 288, 343–344
Minho River 40
Minnesotan dialect 36
minority-group reaction 25
minority languages 8, 95; modernity and 212–214; preservation of 92
Miṣrāta (MA) 326, **326**, 331
mission civilisatrice 183
MIT Senseable City Lab 44
Mittins, W.: *Attitudes to English Usage* 128–129
mixed effects model 345–352
mixing 54, 147
Mobile Younger Suburban Females (MYSFs) 43

mobility 5–6, 42–43, 50, 197, 227–228
modernity 188–189, 211–219, 222
Modern Standard Arabic (MSA) 107–108, 323, 335–336
Mohammed VI: Ajdir Speech 103–105
Moll, A. 3, 291
monolingualism 6–7, 89–90, 143–144, 229, 232
Montgomery, C. 39
moral panic 130–132, 137
Moroccan Arabic **54**, 192–209; *see also* Darija
Moroccanisation 119
Moroccan Jews 193
Moroccanness 99–124
Morocco 7–8, 43, 101
morphosyntax 75–77, 82, 289
mother languages 101–102
Mother (song; Pink Floyd) 249
Mouatassim, M. 105
Moufida (television channel) 110
Mouride identity 187–189
Mous, M. 305
"Mouvement de liberté et démocratie maintenant" 115
Movida Madrileña 99
MSA (Modern Standard Arabic) 107–108, 323, 335–336
Muana, P. 310
Mubarak, H. 294–295, 336
Muhr, R. 353
Müller, C. 269
multiethnicity 218
multilingualism 8, 88–90, 143–159, 226–227
mundane performance 248
Muridiyya 187–188
Muslim identity 187–189
Myers-Scotton, C. 162
MYSFs (Mobile Younger Suburban Females) 43

Naciri-Azzouz, A. 8, 195
Naija (9ja) 10, 303–320
Naija Languej Akedemi 314–315
Naija lingo (website) 310–312, *311*
Nairaland.com (website) 312–315, *316*
named languages 72, 99–102
Nardini, G. 282
narratives 163–164
Nash, W. 126
Nassenstein, N. 307
national borders, dialects and 35–36
National Council of the Moroccan Languages and Culture 106

National Curriculum for English 129
national identity 71–85
nationalism 167
National Language Research Committee 214
National Movement 102
nation-states 6–7, 72, 87–90, 95
nativism 188–189
Nayda 99, 107, 120n1
NCS (Northern Cities shift) 343
Ndyuka 147–148
near-deixis 326, **326**
Neds (character types) *275*, 275–282, **278**
negative construction 278
Nenge(e) 147–148
neoliberalism 306
neologisms 94
neo-urban vernaculars 193
Nerbonne, J. 38
Netherlands 42–43
neutral speech *60*
New Mexican Spanish 8, 160–178
New Mexico and Colorado Spanish Survey (NMCOSS) 160–164, **163**
Ngom, F. 188–189
Nichane 111–113, 119
Nidiaye, K. 185
Nigeria 10, 303–320
Nigerian Pidgin 309–316; *see also* Naija (9ja)
Nigerian Pidgin in Lagos (Deuber) 314
Nilep, C. 144
Nile TV 295
Nilotic languages 74
njaxas 182
NMCOSS (New Mexico and Colorado Spanish Survey) 160–164, **163**
non-compliance 125, 135
Non-mobile, Older, Rural Males (NORMs) 42–43
non-narrative prose 94
Nonstandard American (NSA) accent group 22–23, 30n7
nonstandard British English 125–139
nonstandard dialect 17–34
normal Glaswegian 273
North African Arabic 100
Northern Cities shift (NCS) 343
Northwestern Morocco 192–209
novels 90–91
"Nuestro Himno" controversy 169–170

"Oath of the Saint George's Company" 86
O'Brien, C. 187
Occitan language 87

Ochs, E. 154, 292, 296
O'Donnell Christoffersen, K. 8
Ogbu, J. 23–24
Okwoche, P. 315
olof bu xóot 181
olof piir 181–184, 187
opposition 253
oppressors, voice of 165–167
order 211
organic laws 106–107
Orwell, G. 21
Osenova, P. 38
other/otherness 8, 221, 325–327
Othman, M. 331
Oussar wa Houloul (television show) 111
out-groups 126, 134–136
Oyoun Al-Wadi, Syria 10, 340–355

Palaung 35
Palermo 52–54
Palestinian city dialects 37
Pamaka 147–148
pan-Arabic ideology 107
Panjabi 216
pan-Maroon identity 147, 155
paradigm types **75**
parlers nouveaux urbans 193
parody 249
passing 8, 30, 64, 161–163, 170–174, 214–216
"Pathways to Success" conference (Zakoura Foundation) 117
patrimonialisation 239
Pauwels, A. 21
Pearce, S. 39
perceived borders 38–39
Pereira, C. 321–324
performance: defined 3; of dialect 8–10, 49–67, 247–249; Egyptian poetry and 286–302; high 245–251, 270; of identity 4, 161–162, 183–188, 237–240, 265–285, 291–294; of language 265–285; narratives and interviews as 163–164; of Pittsburghese 245–264; Scottish television comedy and 265–285; staged 248–249
performer focusing 248
peripheries 227, 234, 239–240
Petyt, K. 17
phenotypes 172–174
Philibert, E. 86
Phillipson, R. 89
phonology 9, 74–75, 82, 180, 184, 286–292, 299–300

phono-opportunities 255
pidgincreole 72–82
pidgins 72, 308–316
Piedmontese 7, 86–98
Pietikäinen, S. 227
pijltjes-methode (Arrows Method) 39
Pink Floyd: *Mother* (song) 249
pitch tracks *255*
Pittsburghese 9, 227, 245–264
PJD party 115
Pledge of Allegiance 167–170, 175n1
Plug-in (dubbing firm) 114
plurilingual corpora 145
poetry 286–302
Polish 38
politeness 253
political borders 35, 40
polylects 183
populism 116, 323
Portugal 40
Portuguese 352
positioning 164–166, 292
postcolonialism 180, 303–304
(post-)creole continua 71–72
Pouessel, S. 104
Pountain, D. 222–223
power 223
practice-oriented studies 50–51
Pratiques langagières 145
prescriptivism 125–134, 137, 213
Presentation of Self in Everyday Life, The (Goffman) 210
preservation, of languages 92, 238–239
Preston, D. 39, 267
Priestly, J. 213
primitivism 308–309
'Prince of Poets' *(Amīr al-shu'arā')* competition 294–297
pronunciation 42, 213
proper English 18, 23, 310
proscriptions 128–130
prose 87, 90, 93–94
public schools 160
public television 110–111
Puerto Ricans 28
pure Wolof 181–182, 187

Qadiriyya Sufi order 187
Queen, R. 271
Quichua language 150–155

Rabat-Casablanca axis 193, 196
racism 222–223
Radio Wazobia 312–313
Rakhaing 35

Rampton, B. 64, 162–164, 287, 290;
  Crossing – Language and Ethnicity among Adolescents 215–217
Ratti, C. 44
recontextualisation 296–298
reflexivity 7–8, 290, 303–304
register 3, 265–266
relational focusing 248
relationality principle 325
religious borders 40–41
religious identities 186
repertoire 213–215, 286–302, **293**
repertoire expansion 26
repertoire focusing 248
Rezg, O. 326, 331
Robert, S. 179
Robins, D. 222–223
Romance family 36
Roman script 41
ruination 303–320
rural child language 340–355, **348–349**
rural dialects 20–21, 36–37, 43–44, 288–291
Russian 35
rután 74–80, 83n1
ruṭāna 73–74
Ryan, E. 25
Ryukyus 211–212

Saharan model 187
Sa'idi Colloquial Arabic (SCA) 286, 289–294, **293**, 297–300
Saint-Louis du Sénégal 180–182, 189
Salminen, T. 91
Sánchez Moreano, S. 8
Santa Ana, O. 167
Sardinian 97n13
SA (Standard American) accent group 22–23, 30n7
SA (Standard Arabic) 286–291, **293**, 294–300, 342, 346, 352
Sayer, A. 131
SCA (Sa'idi Colloquial Arabic) 286, 289–294, **293**, 297–300
Schilling-Estes, N. 3, 7, 265–266, 291
Schools Council for Curriculum and Education 128
Schuchardt, H. 308
Scottish/English border 40–42
Scottish television comedy 265–285
Scottish Vowel Length Rule 268
scripts 41, 104
second-order indexicality 227, 233–237, 240, 286, 323
sedentary dialects 193

sedentary traits 322
self-conceptualisation 267–268
self-criticism 25
self, presentations of 8, 210–225
semiotic associations 226, 234
Senegal 8, 179–191
Senegalese French 184–185, 189
Senegalese Islam 187–188
Senghor, L. 183, 189
Senhaja Berber 192, 196–197, 204
SEN TV 185
Serbia 35, 41
Serreli, V. 8
shared identities 270
Shawqī, A.: 'Ghandi' 296
Shin, N. 8
Sicilian 49–65, *55*
Siegel, J. 24
signares 180
Silsal iddamm (soap opera) 290
Silverstein, M. 210, 226–227, 287–288
Šimičić, L. 43
situation focusing 248
Siwans 228–240
Siwa & Tangier project 239
Siwi language 8, 226–242
slang 306
Smakman, D. 6
Smith, A. 88
Smitherman, G. 24
soap operas 342–343
social actors 210
social belonging 130
social class 10, 21, 245–254, 259–260, 269
social connotations borders 42–43
social constructivist approach 226
social meaning 3, 8, 226–227, 233, 237, 282–283
social media **119**, 310–314
social networks 343–345
social prestige 192, 195–201, 206–207
social relationships 233–234
social status 22–23, 43, 233–234
social value 8, 192–209
societal treatment approach 229
sociolinguistics 2, 49–51, 130, 188–189, 303, 323
Sokrate, M. 119
solidarity 22–23, 26–27, 234–237
sophisticates 184–187
South Africa 41
South African National Gallery 306–307
South America 35
South Slavic dialect continua 35
South Sudan 7, 71–85

Spanish language 8, 35, 99, 148–155, 169–170; *see also* New Mexican Spanish
speech patterns 22
SPSS 23 345–346
Sranan Tongo 147–148
staged performance 248–249
stances 8–9, 148–155, 245–264, 291–294, **293**, 299
stance triangles 250–251
Standard American (SA) accent group 22–23, 30n7
Standard Arabic (SA) 286–291, **293**, 294–300, 342, 346, 352
Standard Croatian 43
standard dialects 18–19
Standard English 125–137
Standard German 218, 223n2
standardisation 22, 103–104, 125, 128–130, 213–214, 218–221
Standard Italian 51–52
Standard Japanese 37, 214, 218–221
standard language 6–7, 125, 132–137, 315
Standard Mandarin Chinese 37
Star Spangled Banner 169–170
Star Trek 127
stereotypes 9, 20–25, 29–30, 162, 219–220, 226–227, 268–271, 277–279, 282–283
stigmatised dialects 6–10
Stokoe, E. 299
Stoler, A. 306–307
Storch, A. 10
storyworlds 164–175
street language 116
Strictly English (Heffer) 127
Stroud, C. 304
Stuart-Smith, J. 9, 269, 340, 353
student movements 101
style and styling 2, 49–51, 265, 290
Stylized Indian English 216
stylized language 9–10, 270–271, 281–282
sub-cultures 305
sub-standard language 18–19
substrates 74–75, 79
subtractive bidialectalism 23
Sudanese Arabic 72–82
Südekum, J. 40
Sufi movement 187–189
Sujoldžić, A, 43
sunu olof 182
Suriname 8, 147–148
Sylla, F. 185
syntax 38
Syria 10, 340–355
Syrian Arabic 340

Syrian Central Bureau of Statistics Census 343
Syrian television serials 342–343, 346

taboo words 162, 278
Tabouret-Keller, A. 267
Tahrir Square 288, 294–297, 335
Tamazight 103
Tamil **54**
Tarifit 196–197, 205
TA (Tripoli dialect) 43, 322–326, **326**, 329–331, 334–337
Tavoyan 35
technological advances, education and 132–134
telenovelas 114, 342
television: accent groups of characters 22–23; Darija 113–115; effects of 340–355; influence of 10; Scottish 265–285
Telquel 100, 108, *109*, 111–113, 118
Tetouan, Morocco 8, 192–209
Texan English 36
Text Encoding Initiative (TEI) 145
Thailand 35
'Theses of the Philosophy of History' (Benjamin) 307
third-order indexicality 237–240
Third Theory 321
Thomas, G. 131
Thornborrow, J. 267
Thurlow, C. 317
Tijaniyya 187–189
Tirbil, F. 338n18
ToBI notational system 254
Tokyo 212, 220
Tokyo dialect 37, 214
toponyms 80–81
Tosco, M. 7, 90–94
Touba, Senegal 187–188
tourism 101, 194, 197, 239–240
translanguaging 65
Travis, C. 160
Treaty of Guadalupe Hidalgo 160
Tripoli dialect (TA) 43, 322–326, **326**, 329–331, 334–337
Trudgill, P. 6, 18–21, 29, 37, 42–43
Tunisian Arabic **54**, 336
Turin, Italy 86–89
Turkish soap operas 342–343
Turkish television serials 346
Txt-speak 133

Ubak, U. 316
Ubbi tey, jàng tey (television show) 185

Umgangssprache 218, 223n2
UNESCO Atlas of the World's Languages in Danger 91
uniformity, of language 87–91
United States: class by stance in 252–253; digital communication in 44; English language in 128, 160, 165–167, 352; geographical borders in 39–40; New Mexican Spanish in 8, 160–178
unmarked language 210, 214–215, 220
Upper Egyptian dialects 288–290
urban child language 347, 352
urban dialects 20–21, 36–37, 43–44, 196, 288–291
urbanisation 90, 180, 193, 202–204, 322, 344
Urban Scots dialect writing 269
urban Wolof 181–184, 189
usage debate 125–139
usage guides 127
utterances 55–63, 219–221, 250–251, 292

Vaillant, P. 145
Valls, E. 38
Vandewalle, D. 322–323, 336
variation 7–8, 195–197; dialect 2–3, 8–10, 143–159, 321–339; ethnographic approaches to 49–67; in heterogeneous corpora 145–146; as multidimensional 2; in multilingual settings 143–144
variationism 1–2, 49–51, 186, 265
Vehicular Arabic **75**
vendido/vendu phenomenon 24–26
verbal paradigms 76–78
vernaculars 23, 51, 99, 271
Verschueren, J. 89–90
Versteegh, K. 75
Vicente, Á. 8, 195
videos 245–264
Villa, D. 160
visible minority groups 26–27
vitality 22
Vocabulaire (Faidherbe) 181–182
vocabulary 277–281
Voegelin, S. 318
vulgarity 116

"*Wa derrej a khouya!*" (Benchemsi) 100
Wales 276
WALF-TV 189
Walser language 87
Wardhaugh, R. 41
Watt, D. 42
Wazif, M. 101
Wazobia FM 313–315

we-code 216
Weijnen, A. 39
Weinreich, M. 18, 30n3
Welsh English 276
West African English 308–310
Western Syria 37
West Indians 27
'What does Naija mean?' (BBC) 315
White English 23, 27, 252–253
"Who are we?" (Allali) 111
Wiese, H. 217
Wikipedias 93
Wolfram, W. 24
Wolof language 8, 179–191
Woolard, K. 50
working-class culture 256, 260
working-class dialects 21, 43, 245–249
working-class identity 269
working-class stances 252–253
World Englishes 307–308

Xu, D. 17–18

yabiladi.com (website) 104
Yacine, K. 99
Yingmei, J. 30n2
Yinzers 245–264
Yonaguni Island 211–212
Youssoufi, A. 102
youth 157–170, 303–320
YouTube 245–264
Ypsilanti, Michigan 343
Yugoslavia 41

Zakaria Boualem (Allali) 114
Zakoura Foundation 110; "The Pathways to Success" conference 117
Zelinsky, W. 161
Zenata group 196–197
Zentella, A. 170
Zéphir, F. 24